Retraining Cognition

Retraining Cognition

Techniques and Applications

⌁ SECOND EDITION ⌁

Rick Parenté
Douglas Herrmann

pro·ed
An International Publisher

8700 Shoal Creek Boulevard
Austin, Texas 78757-6897
800/897-3202   Fax 800/397-7633
www.proedinc.com

© 2003 by PRO-ED, Inc.
8700 Shoal Creek Boulevard
Austin, Texas 78757-6897
800/897-3202   FAX 800/397-7633
www.proedinc.com

Library of Congress Cataloging-in-Publication Data

Parenté, Rick.
    Retraining cognition : techniques and applications / Rick Parenté,
Douglas Herrmann.—
2nd ed.
      p. cm.
    Includes bibliographical references and index.
    ISBN 0-89079-905-9
    1. Brain damage—Patients—Rehabilitation.   2. Cerebrovascular
disease—Patients—Rehabilitation.   3. Cognition disorders—
Patients—Rehabilitation.   I. Herrmann, Douglas J.   II. Title.

    RC387.5.P364   2002
    616.8′043—dc21

                           2002068052

This book is designed in Goudy and Stone Sans.

Printed in the United States of America

1 2 3 4 5 6 7 8 9 10 07 06 05 04 03

Contents

Preface

The first edition of *Retraining Cognition: Techniques and Applications* was designed to integrate the existing theory of cognitive psychology with various published applications of cognitive rehabilitation. We have maintained this focus in this second edition, which contains a number of new and revised features. We have added several chapters and updated the others with new information. The content of the first edition was obtained from an integration of relevant literature in the fields of cognitive remediation, cognitive psychology, and neuropsychology. However, during the brief interval between the first and second editions, there has been a great deal of published research that has either validated or disconfirmed much of the conventional wisdom in the field. This second edition, therefore, presents techniques that have stood the test of time, are confirmed by a research database, and have proven especially effective in clinical experience.

About a third of the chapters in the second edition are new. These chapters underscore important changes in emphasis in the field that have occurred over the past 10 years. The first chapter, which is new to the second edition, presents the history of cognitive rehabilitation therapy from World War I through the present time. Chapter 11, Retraining Working Memory, is also new to the second edition. It presents the limited research on processing in working memory plus therapy procedures for retraining this vital memory store. Personality change is a common problem after brain injury. Chapter 21, Psychotherapy, which is also new to the second edition, encapsulates the development of psychotherapy techniques for treating persons with traumatic brain injury. Chapter 25 summarizes literature that has evaluated the effectiveness of cognitive rehabilitation procedures. The appendixes are complemented by the addition of the Problem–Solutions and Treatment Planner, which provides practical suggestions that therapists can use to generate treatment options quickly.

Many of the chapters in the second edition were also part of the first, but have been updated or consolidated. For example, Chapters 2 through 7 provide background knowledge necessary for therapists to give effective therapy. Chapter 2 develops a model of cognitive rehabilitation that the authors use to direct the therapy suggestions in the latter chapters. Chapter 3 summarizes recent research on neuropsychology and cognitive psychology as it pertains to cognitive rehabilitation therapy. Chapter 4 summarizes the recent literature on attention, a process that is commonly impaired after brain injury. Chapter 5 explores the physiological and cognitive processes that underlie recovery after brain injury. Chapter 6 is a discussion of the principles of transfer and generalization as they apply to treatment of cognitive deficits. Chapter 7 is a description of assessment procedures that can be used to guide the therapist when evaluating the effectiveness of treatment.

Chapters 8 through 13 update the research on retraining different cognitive processes. This section begins with a discussion of iconic memory, a brief duration memory system that is often damaged after brain injury. Specific techniques whose efficacy has been replicated in the literature are also presented. Chapter 9 builds upon the earlier discussion of attention theory (Chapter 4) and describes various procedures for retraining the attention process.

A person's ability to rehearse is, perhaps, the first process that requires therapy after brain injury. Chapter 10 describes the process of maintenance rehearsal and provides specific activities that can be used to retrain it. Chapter 12 presents training techniques for teaching memory strategies that enhance processing of materials in working memory. Chapter 13 completes the discussion by revisiting the concept of rehearsal as it interacts with these memory strategies. The procedures in this section can be used to immediately enhance a person's ability to form durable memories.

Chapters 14 through 19 are a discussion of retraining issues for higher cognitive skills. These chapters present training procedures for improving the core elements of what we call thinking. Retraining concept learning, problem solving, and decision making are topics that have not been addressed previously in the literature on brain injury. Indeed, most of the techniques presented in these chapters have not been discussed in any other source.

The next group of chapters presents indirect methods for improving cognition. Chapter 20 describes the optimal state of physical fitness for enhancing cognition. Chapter 22 builds on this information with a discussion of nutrients and drugs that may enhance cognition. Because lack of motivation is a common problem after brain injury, Chapter 23 describes an incentive-based model of cognitive rehabilitation therapy that therapists can use to motivate persons to apply their newly learned thinking skills. Chapter 24 provides a virtual library of external aids that patients can use to obviate memory and cognitive problems.

The second edition will be of enormous value to anyone who provides treatment to persons with brain injuries, strokes, developmental delays, and learning disabilities. These populations share similar problems with memory, attention, and cognitive processing. We address all of these problems in the second edition of *Retraining Cognition* and we invite therapists to use these suggestions to plan treatment.

Acknowledgments

I dedicate this book to the memory of my father, whose life was an example of the principles discussed herein. I also want to thank my wife, Janet Anderson-Parenté, for her endless support and for her collaboration over the years on many of the research projects discussed in these chapters. Many thanks to Paul Mazmanian at the Medical College of Virginia for his efforts to create a forum for others and myself to disseminate our ideas to a wider audience. Special thanks to Mary Stapleton for her support, research collaboration, and continued development of our thinking skills group at the Workforce Technology Center. I would also like to thank the Division of Rehabilitation Services in Maryland for their continued support of my research over the years.

There are many others whose ideas and input have affected the development of this book. Thanks to Jeff Kreutzer and Yahuda Ben-Yishay, whose research and theories have shaped the field of cognitive rehabilitation. I also want to thank Henry Ellis and Reed Hunt, from whom I learned the principles of cognitive psychology. Thanks to Craig Johnson, Herb Petrie, Michael Figler, and John Webster at Towson University for all of our discussions of neuropsychology, motivation, ethology, and cognition. Thanks to Maria Fracasso, chairman of the Department of Psychology at Towson University, for providing that most precious of commodities, the time I required to complete this book. I also want to thank Heidi Rubin, Sydney Dansiger, and other members of the Society for Cognitive Rehabilitation for their efforts to develop this field and to provide standards for practice. Special thanks to Anju Vaidia at the DuPont Children's Hospital for all of our discussions of pediatric cognitive rehabilitation. I also want to thank Gary and Robin Klein for their insights concerning the contributions of psychiatry and occupational therapy to brain injury rehabilitation. Finally, I would like to thank my co-author, Doug Herrmann, for contributing his vast knowledge of cognitive psychology to the development of this book.

—*Rick Parenté*

I dedicate this book to the memory of my mother, Ruth I. Herrmann, who encouraged my education and professional development every step of the way. I also thank my wife, Donna Herrmann, for her endless support on this book and research projects cited in these chapters. In addition, I thank Zachary Herrmann and Mandy and Washington Gordon for their support while I worked on this book. Many thanks to Paul Steve Deutsch and Barbara Schwartz at the VA Hospital in Washington, D.C. for enabling me to better appreciate the issues covered here. Special thanks to Miriam and Ivan Bendiksen for providing the first definitive test of the multimodal model.

There are many others who have affected this book. I want to thank Lawry Gulick, John McLaughlin, and Dick Atkinson for teaching me the fundamentals of experimental psychology. I thank also Michael Gruneberg, Veanne Anderson, Carol Yoder, and June Sprock for helping me appreciate certain cognitive and clinical aspects of retraining cognition. I also am grateful to

Scott Adams, Michael Sarapata, and Rebecca Torres for their ideas about issues covered here. Finally, I especially thank Rick Parenté for the opportunity to collaborate with him and to learn from him. He is the person who has taught me more than anyone else about the field of cognitive rehabilitation.

—Douglas Herrmann

Chapter 1

⚹

History and Systems of Cognitive Rehabilitation

Cognitive rehabilitation is a complex collection of techniques that is designed to enhance perception, attention, comprehension, learning, remembering, problem solving, reasoning, and so forth (Callahan, 2001; Cavanaugh, Kramer, Sinnott, Camp, & Markley, 1985; Evans & Over, 1996; Patten, 1990) in individuals who are impaired in these areas. For example, people who have suffered a brain injury typically lose rapid mental processing and other abilities. People with learning disabilities may not have developed these cognitive abilities in their formative years. Cognitive rehabilitation therapy (CRT) is the art and science of restoring these mental processes and teaching compensatory strategies.

The past two decades have witnessed a virtual explosion of interest in the development of CRT techniques and applications (Boake, 1991; Butler & Namerow, 1988; Godfrey & Knight, 1987; Gross & Shutz, 1986; Harrell, Parenté, Bellingrath, & Lisicia, 1992; Hayden, 1986; Herrmann, 1994; Hertel, 1994; Jacob, 1995; Parenté & Stapleton, 1993). This book summarizes many of these techniques as well as their theoretical underpinnings in cognitive psychology, neuropsychology, and speech–language therapy (Ben-Yishay & Diller, 1981; Guenther,

1998; Hunt & Ellis, 1998; Matlin, 1998; Miller, 1980, 1984; Payne & Wenger, 1998).

History

Most of the early history of CRT has been published in rather obscure sources. However, Boake (1991) and Parenté and Stapleton (1993) have published summaries of this history. The purpose of this chapter is not to reproduce these excellent summaries. Indeed, the reader is referred to either work for a more complete historical perspective. Our goal is simply to encapsulate the literature on CRT methods from World War I through World War II. We then discuss the more recent trends, issues, and controversies that have occurred since World War II. We end with a summary of what we have learned so far from this brief but rapidly evolving history of mental restoration.

The history of CRT dates back to World War I (Boake, 1991). World War II stimulated further development of these methods of rehabilitation to meet the needs of soldiers who returned from fighting with brain injuries. Indeed, many of the cognitive rehabilitation techniques and strategies that are currently used today are the same as those that were practiced in the 1920s after World War I. For example, teaching persons with brain injury functional skills that have direct transfer to the real world has been consistently emphasized since World War I.

Although it is not possible to date the first attempts at CRT, the first documented records began to appear during and after World War I. The German government, for example, created "schools for soldiers" (Boake, 1991) to serve the needs of returning war veterans. These were actually rehabilitation hospitals for injured soldiers. Assessment included tests of psychological skill and performance similar to those used today by psychologists. Programs also included the measurement of concrete skills with tests similar to work samples that are used in many rehabilitation and training facilities today. The Germans also pursued long-term follow-up of patients. Unlike many of today's programs, however, these early attempts at CRT did not emphasize attention and concentration or memory strategy training.

Boake's (1991) review described CRT as it developed in the former Soviet Union after World Wars I and II. Alexander Luria (1963, 1973, 1979) provided the first comprehensive writing on this topic in Russia. His work focused on the rehabilitation of soldiers in a neurosurgical unit in the Ural Mountains region of Russia. Many of the CRT techniques used today are offshoots of the techniques he developed. His model of rehabilitation included assessment of the individual's neurocognitive functioning, analysis of various adaptive mechanisms, and spared skills the person could use to help obviate the deficits. Luria's model of rehabilitation was designed to strengthen a patient's spared skills and to teach the patient new compensatory skills.

Boake (1991) also described the early development of CRT in Great Britain after World War II. Two of the best examples of British brain-injury rehabilitation centers were located in Oxford and Edinburgh. Zang-

will (1945, 1947) was perhaps the first person to contrast what came to be known as the *substitution* and *direct retraining* methods of CRT. The substitution approach emphasized teaching skills the person with brain injury could use in place of damaged skills. The direct retraining method involved various forms of mental exercises that were designed to strengthen a patient's mind. Zangwill generally discounted the usefulness of the direct retraining approach. Like many therapists today, Zangwill concluded that direct retraining methods had limited potential for transfer to the real world. Another of Zangwill's major contributions to CRT was to provide the first systematic evaluations of aphasia treatment.

At the same time that CRT was developing in Europe, the United States was also interested in brain injury rehabilitation, which Franz (1923) described as a form of "nervous and mental reeducation." This description developed from psychiatric influences that were growing in the United States at the time. This phrase was similar to the title of an established psychiatric journal, the *Journal of Nervous and Mental Disease,* which is still published today. Franz's unrealized dream was to organize one of the first rehabilitation research institutes in the United States that would include the study of aphasia and neuroscience.

Clearly, World Wars I and II led to considerable development of all kinds of rehabilitation techniques, including CRT. Boake (1991) pointed out that brain-injury rehabilitation centers in the United States after World War II were similar to those of today. Many of these centers created interdisciplinary teams to work with patients who were brain injured, who were often treated separately from other patients. There were also rehabilitation programs that were specifically developed for patients who had survived brain injuries. Although there were many distinct influences, much of the early development of CRT techniques in the United States was spearheaded by psychologists and speech–language pathologists (Wepman, 1951).

During the 1970s and l980s the field of CRT experienced enormous change, stimulated by advances in cognitive psychology, which grew rapidly in the 1960s (Barsalou, 1992; Eysenck, 1993; Lynch, 1987; Matlin, 1998; Mills, Nesbeda, Katz, & Alexander, 1982; Newell, 1990; Patten, 1990; Prigatano, 1987; Seron & Deloche, 1989). At the same time, members of the CRT field were intensely interested in the theories of certain distinguished figures such as Alexander Luria (1973, 1979) who advanced a number of important ideas about neurocognition and the treatment of cognitive impairments. Subsequently, several researchers investigated the effects of a variety of new rehabilitation techniques on cognitive impairment (Ben-Yishay & Diller, 1981; Gianutsos, 1991; Gianutsos & Grynbaum, 1982; Miller, 1980, 1984). New publications such as the *Journal of Head Trauma Rehabilitation* and *NeuroRehabilitation* documented advances in the field. These publications fueled a zeal for research and development that has been spurred on by an expanding patient population and a growing need for CRT.

The latter part of the 20th century included the publication of several influential CRT techniques, applications, and model programs (Gianutsos, 1991; Glisky & Schacter, 1989; Gordon & Hibbard, 1991; Herrmann & Palmisano, 1992; Herrmann, Raybeck, & Gutman, 1993; Herrmann, Rea, & Andrzejewski, 1988; Herrmann & Searleman, 1990, 1992; Parenté & Anderson-Parenté, 1991; Prigatano & Fordyce, 1987; Seron & Deloche, 1989; Sohlberg & Mateer, 1987, 1989; Wehman et al., 1989; Wood & Fussey, 1990). A brief summary of these techniques and applications follows.

Systems of Cognitive Rehabilitation

We have identified several distinct areas of CRT. These are presented in Table 1.1.

Stimulation therapy is perhaps the oldest method of CRT. Harrell et al. (1992) referred to this type of treatment as direct retraining. It is based on the assumption that cognitive functions will improve by stimulating the cognitive system. The therapy usually includes paper-and-pencil exercises or computer training that stimulates one or more mental skills. Presumably, by using these skills, a person's cognition will improve and the improvement will transfer to his or her activities of daily living. We do not discuss stimulation training in detail in this book because there is little research evidence to support its efficacy. The reader is referred to Craine and Gudeman (1981) for a comprehensive summary of various techniques.

Process training is similar to stimulation training, but process training focuses on specific areas of cognition. For example, Bracy's (1986) process approach to CRT emphasizes assessment and treatment of specific cognitive defects, such as poor visual scanning or visual neglect. Parenté, Anderson-Parenté, and Shaw (1989) and McClur, Browning, Vantrease, and Bittle (1994) discussed techniques for training processing in iconic

TABLE 1.1

Types of Cognitive Rehabilitation Therapy

Stimulation Therapy
Process Training
Attention–Concentration Training
Strategy Training
Nutrient and Drug Treatment
Prosthetic–Orthotic Devices
Domain-Specific Training
Indirect Training

memory. These techniques are discussed in detail in Chapter 8. In general, process training methods are all designed to improve specific aspects of cognition and there is some evidence that improving these cognitive skills can facilitate performance on other cognitive tasks.

Attention–concentration training is designed to improve a person's ability to focus attention, to maintain vigilance, to resist distraction, and to perform mental manipulations quickly and efficiently. It is one of the most widely researched areas of CRT and the research has produced commercially available training programs with proven efficacy (Sohlberg & Mateer, 1987, 1989). We discuss the theory and techniques for retraining attention and concentration in Chapters 4 and 9. This is an especially important area of CRT because attention and concentration precede many of the other types of higher cognitive training that we discuss in Chapters 11 through 18.

The *strategy training* method of CRT involves teaching a person mental sets that are applicable in a variety of contexts. For example, a therapist may teach a person with traumatic brain injury to use a certain strategy for solving problems, mnemonics to remember important information, or social strategies for carrying on conversations (Richardson, 1992). These methods are discussed in Chapters 11 through 19.

Nutrient and drug treatment operates on the premise that various substances can affect cognition by correcting chemical imbalance. For example, memory deficits secondary to long-term alcohol abuse can often be arrested with thiamine treatments (Elovic, 2000). This type of CRT is relatively new although the results are promising. We summarize most of the available research on cognitive-enhancing nutrients and drugs in Chapter 22.

Prosthetic–Orthotic Devices. External aids are sometimes referred to as prosthetic–orthotic devices. Their purpose is to obviate a cognitive problem rather than to retrain a defective process. Using an external aid is often the most efficient and expedient way to treat certain cognitive deficits. For example, training a person with a poor memory to use a tape recorder can improve his or her functional memory immediately but it may not have any effect on the underlying physiological cause of the deficit. Although the prosthetic devices do not rectify a person's memory deficit, the devices are especially effective and efficacious methods of treatment. We therefore discuss them in detail in Chapter 24.

Domain-specific training techniques emphasize training a person with simulated life experiences or within a specific functional domain. For example, Schacter and Glisky (1986) described the use of computer simulation to train a person to perform data entry. The theory that underlies domain-specific transfer is discussed in Chapter 6.

Indirect training is based on the idea that although CRT methods like those previously discussed may be the most direct ways to improve cognitive problems, other indirect methods may also be effective (Herrmann & Parenté, 1994; Yesavage, Rose, & Spiegel, 1982). For example, teaching a person to adhere to better sleeping and eating habits can improve cognitive function. Training a person to use a variety of external aids can result in a productive and satisfying daily routine (Herrmann & Petro, 1991; Naugle, Prevy, Naugle, & Delaney, 1988). Even the teaching of certain social skills can give some people more control over their everyday living situations so that they can make better use of their reduced cognitive functioning (Best, 1992; McEvoy, 1992).

Our approach to CRT assumes that therapy is most effective when it is focused on all relevant subsystems in a manner that improves cognitive performance (Bracy, 1986). The relevant subsystems include all those assumed to be important in cognition (e.g., attention, perception, comprehension, learning, remembering, communication, problem solving, and creative thinking) as well as other aspects of a person's life that affect cognition such as emotions, nutrition, health, stress, and social functioning (Herrmann, Weingartner, Searleman, & McEvoy, 1992). These passive manipulations can include planning a person's diet, physical fitness programs, organization of living space, and so forth.

Issues in the Development of CRT

There are several important issues that have come to a head in recent years that continue to shape CRT. Perhaps the oldest of these issues concerns who should direct treatment. This controversy began around the year 1900 between orthopedic surgeons and educational specialists, each of whom worked with patients who had brain injuries, and this issue persists today. For example, most insurance companies will fund medical interventions after brain injury but will not fund CRT.

Perhaps the most important issue concerns efficacy. Does CRT actually produce measurable and significant improvement in cognitive functioning above what would occur simply with the passage of time? Several authors addressed this issue (Carney et al., 1999; Cicerone et al., 2000; Silver, 1992) and the conclusions are mixed. Chapter 25 is devoted to an in-depth discussion of this issue. Generally, the data do not support the conclusion that CRT alone produces measurable and consistent gains. However, it is safe to say that comprehensive rehabilitation programs, in which CRT plays a role, do produce significant gains in cognition and overall functioning. It is also safe to say that before managed care companies will reimburse therapists for their efforts, therapists will have to demonstrate that their treatments result in an unequivocal gain in mental functioning. This may be difficult for several reasons. First, the

ethical considerations that arise from providing treatment to one group of patients while withholding it from another prohibit the application of most conventional research designs. Second, therapists do not have the time to do research on top of their already busy treatment schedules. Finally, the managed care corporations that have taken over the health care field do not provide funding for these types of systematic research projects.

A second issue in the development of CRT is the lack of integration or application of theory and practice. Although most of the theoretical literature on CRT provides a wealth of abstract verbiage, it has not produced many practical treatment suggestions. In addition, many therapists practicing CRT are ignorant of the vast amounts of information from other areas like cognitive psychology that could be used to direct treatment-oriented research efforts. Along with neurologists and psychiatrists, cognitive rehabilitation therapists and theorists have identified many of the subsystems of cognition and many of the variables that can affect cognitive functioning. However, most research has been directed toward mapping the cognitive system in relation to structure of the brain. Unfortunately, relatively little research has focused on treatments that improve cognition after brain injury, and there have been few attempts to summarize research findings in ways that are useful to CRT practitioners. In one notable exception, Hertel (1994) integrated a large body of research that concerned the effects of depression on memory and the implications of this research for CRT. Cicerone et al. (2000) also summarized a number of research articles and abstracted several guidelines for providing interventions after brain injury. The authors are aware of literally thousands of books and journal articles that summarize a wealth of information on cognition and human information processing. This huge database awaits exploration and integration by CRT practitioners into their field of applied research.

Another issue shaping the field is the widening set of techniques that encompass CRT. Therapists and patients alike often misconstrue CRT as structured mental exercise. There is, however, a broader canvas. For example, the development of "passive interventions" is designed to improve cognitive functioning. In general, passive interventions include arranging a person's environment, schedule, or other aspects of his or her lifestyle to make it easier for the person to function at work or home. One example is teaching a person to use an external aid, such as a tape recorder, to improve his or her memory, punctuality, and ability to retrieve necessary information quickly and efficiently. The use of nutrients and drugs for intervention is also a passive form of treatment (Kolakowsky, 1997), as are social and behavioral changes that improve a person's thinking and memory. For example, training a person's family to provide the person with reminders can eliminate many misinterpretations and missed appointments (Best, 1992; McEvoy, 1992). In general, the modern view of CRT is that it is most effective when it combines a person's internal and external systems.

Another issue in CRT is the broadening number of applications for this type of therapy. The best-known CRT targets are individuals who have suffered closed head injury or penetrating-missile brain injury. Indeed, it is fair to say that the field was developed first to help these victims. However, CRT methods are also being used to treat other disorders such as attention deficit disorder, dementia, and schizophrenia. Potentially, CRT could help the elderly cope with the cognitive challenges of self-care and self-sufficiency, such as the ability to keep appointments and to recognize others and remember their names. Some CRT methods simplify troublesome cognitive problems that would otherwise induce confusion and anxiety in an individual. In some cases, CRT methods can enable a mildly impaired client to learn an employable skill.

In addition to the rehabilitation of cognitive impairments, CRT methods may be especially useful to students with learning disablities. This population includes persons with brain injuries who may eventually return to school but have difficulty with certain courses, and students who have learning disabilities but have never had a brain injury. CRT techniques may also benefit students in early enrichment programs such as Head Start. Clearly the potential for broadening applications of CRT exists, but the field is simply too new for the research effort to provide much guidance. In essence, cognitive rehabilitation is a field of enormous challenge and promise.

A final issue is the lack of generally accepted procedures for therapist certification. Progress has been made; the Society for Cognitive Rehabilitation has created a certification procedure that has been recognized by the American Congress of Rehabilitation Medicine. The therapist's credentials must include a degree that is recognized by the therapist's professional discipline—in most cases, at least a master's degree. The therapist must also demonstrate more than 2,000 hours of supervised clinical experience and at least 100 hours of one-on-one experience providing CRT. In addition, applicants for certification must produce a videotaped therapy session and written report that is evaluated by a panel of certified members of the Society for Cognitive Rehabilitation. This certification is a major step toward creation of a standard of practice for those who treat persons with brain injury.

Conclusions

What can CRT currently provide persons with brain injury? Clearly, this population is treated far more successfully today than was possible with previous generations of clients (Grafman, 1984). Moreover, it is probably safe to say that CRT methods can arrest cognitive decline and even reverse it. For individuals who have experienced a substantial cognitive loss, cognitive rehabilitation can improve their quality of life and reduce the incidence of everyday problems.

CRT is also more widely available to patients than it was in previous years. Until just a few years ago, CRT was available only in private hospitals and centers for medical research. Until the 1990s, the topic was not addressed in textbooks (e.g., Dikengil, Lowry, & Delgado, 1993; Gruneberg, 1992; Harrell et al., 1992; Wilson, 1987) or made the object of professional conferences (Herrmann, Weingartner, Searleman, & McEvoy, 1992; Poon, Rubin, & Wilson, 1988). In recent years, various hospitals around the country have established CRT as part of their treatment offerings. There is now a professional organization, the Society for Cognitive Rehabilitation, which has established certification requirements for CRT professionals.

What does this text provide practitioners and persons with head injury? This text gives the therapist basic theoretical background that has been generally lacking in the CRT literature. To do this, we have surveyed the vast quantities of related literature in cognition and neuroscience and present summaries of this literature in a manner that the average practitioner can use. Admittedly, in many cases our summaries are speculative. We certainly do not claim to provide the level of detail that is currently available in many of the excellent books that deal with more specific aspects of brain injury rehabilitation. Our attempt to summarize the literature is based on the assumption that the field must have a theoretical grounding and that existing theory is the best place to start. Our hope is that our theoretical discussion will generate many more applied research questions than it answers. Our primary goal is to provide the CRT practitioner with techniques he or she can actually use with clients. Unlike most books on CRT, which are basically summaries of published articles, we try to apply the research we summarize by providing practical therapy strategies. In most cases, these are methods that have worked successfully for us over the years and, wherever possible, we document the efficacy of the technique with published or original research. Our hope is that therapists will use these techniques with their clients and document their efficacy. We also hope that researchers will use these therapies as a starting point for research and development of better techniques.

Finally, this book assumes that rehabilitation of impaired cognitive performance requires consideration of all modes of psychological functioning. This assumption contrasts with prior approaches, which relied primarily, if not exclusively, on improving cognition through direct retraining methods. Although we provide a thorough grounding in active retraining methods, the book also provides a thorough discussion of passive methods that can be equally effective. We believe that the combination of these approaches leads to the greatest and most rapid improvement in a person's functioning.

References

Barsalou, L. W. (1992). *Cognitive psychology: An overview for cognitive scientists*. Hillsdale, NJ: Erlbaum.

Ben-Yishay, Y., & Diller, L. (1981). Cognitive deficits. In M. Rosenthal (Ed.), *Rehabilitation of the head injured adult* (pp. 208–210). Philadelphia: Davis.

Best, D. (1992). The role of social interaction in memory improvement. In D. Herrmann, H. Weingartner, A. Searleman, & C. McEvoy (Eds.), *Memory improvement: Im-*plications for memory theory (pp. 122–149). New York: Springer-Verlag.

Boake, C. (1991). History of cognitive rehabilitation following head injury. In J. S. Kreutzer & P. H. Wehman (Eds.), *Cognitive rehabilitation for persons with traumatic brain injury* (pp. 1–12). Baltimore: Brookes.

Bracy, O. L. (1986). Cognitive rehabilitation: A process approach. *Cognitive Rehabilitation, 4*, 10–47.

Butler, R. W., & Namerow, N. S. (1988). Cognitive retraining in brain-injury rehabilitation: A critical review. *Journal of Neurologic Rehabilitation, 2,* 97–101.

Callahan, C. D. (2001). The Traumatic Brain Injury Act Amendments of 2000. *Journal of Head Trauma Rehabilitation, 16 (2),* 210–213.

Carney, N., Randall, M., Chesnut, M. D., Maynard, H., Mann, C. N., Patterson, P., & Helfand, M. D. (1999). Effect of cognitive rehabilitation on outcomes for persons with traumatic brain injury: A systematic review. *Journal of Head Trauma Rehabilitation, 14*(3), 277–307.

Cavanaugh, J. C., Kramer, D. A., Sinnott, J. D., Camp, C. J., & Markley, R. P. (1985). On missing links and such: Interfaces between cognitive research and everyday problem solving. *Human Development, 28,* 146–168.

Cicerone, K. D., Dahlberg, C., Kalmar, K., Langenbahn, D. M., Malec, J. F., Bergquist, T. F., Felicetti, T., Gaicino, J. T., Harley, P., Harrington, D. E., Herzon, J., Kneipp, S., Laatsch, L., & Morse, P. A. (2000). Evidence-based cognitive rehabilitation: Recommendations for clinical practice. *Archives of Physical Medicine and Rehabilitation, 81,* 1596–1615.

Craine, J. F., & Gudeman, H. E. (1981). *The rehabilitation of brain functions.* Springfield, IL: Thomas.

Dikengil, A., Lowry, M., & Delgado, P. (1993). An interdisciplinary group treatment for the severely brain-injured patient: Participation by four disciplines. *Cognitive Rehabilitation, 11,* 20–22.

Elovic, E. (2000). Use of provigil for underarousal following TBI. *Journal of Head Trauma Rehabilitation, 15*(4) 1068–1071.

Evans, J. St. B. T., & Over, D. E. (1996). *Rationality and reasoning.* East Sussex, United Kingdom: Psychology Press.

Eysenck, M. W. (1993). *Principles of cognitive psychology.* Hillsdale, NJ: Erlbaum.

Franz, S. I. (1923). *Nervous and mental re-education.* New York: Macmillan.

Gianutsos, R. (1991). Cognitive rehabilitation: A neuropsychological specialty comes of age. *Brain Injury, 5,* 353–368.

Gianutsos, R., & Grynbaum, B. B. (1982). Helping brain-injured people contend with hidden cognitive deficits. *International Rehabilitation Medicine, 5,* 37–40.

Glisky, E. L., & Schacter, D. L. (1989). Models and methods of memory rehabilitation. In F. Boller & J. Grafman (Eds.), *Handbook of neuropsychology* (pp. 313–328). Amsterdam: Elsevier.

Godfrey, H. P., & Knight, R. G. (1987). Interventions for amnesics: A review. *British Journal of Clinical Psychology, 26,* 83–91.

Gordon, W. A., & Hibbard, M. R. (1991). The theory and practice of cognitive remediation. In J. S. Kreutzer & P. H. Wehman (Eds.), *Cognitive rehabilitation for persons with traumatic brain injury* (pp. 12–22). Baltimore: Brookes.

Grafman, J. (1984). Memory assessment and remediation in brain-injured patients: From theory to practice. In B. A. Edelstein & E. T. Coutour (Eds.), *Behavioral assessment and rehabilitation of the traumatically brain-damaged* (pp. 102–117). New York: Plenum Press.

Gross, Y., & Shutz, L. E. (1986). Intervention models in neuropsychology. In B. P. Uzzell & Y. Gross (Eds.), *Clinical neuropsychology of intervention.* Boston: Martinus Nijhoff.

Gruneberg, M. M. (1992). The practical application of memory aids: Knowing how, knowing when, and knowing when not. In M. M. Gruneberg & P. Morris (Eds.), *Aspects of memory* (pp. 168–195). London: Routledge.

Guenther, R. K. (1998). *Human cognition.* Upper Saddle River, NJ: Prentice Hall.

Harrell, M., Parenté, R., Bellingrath, E. G., & Lisicia, K. A. (1992). *Cognitive rehabilitation of memory: A practical guide.* Rockville, MD: Aspen.

Hayden, M. E. (1986). Rehabilitation of cognitive and behavioral dysfunction in head injury. *Advances in Psychosomatic Medicine, 16,* 194–229.

Herrmann, D. (1994). The multi-modal approach to cognitive rehabilitation. *NeuroRehabilitation, 4*(3), 133–142.

Herrmann, D., & Parenté, R. (1994). The multi-modal approach to cognitive rehabilitation. *NeuroRehabilitation, 4* (3), 133–142.

Herrmann, D., & Petro, S. (1991). Commercial memory aids. *Applied Cognitive Psychology, 4,* 439–450.

Herrmann, D., & Searleman, A. (1990). The new multimodal approach to memory improvement. In G. H. Bower (Ed.), *Advances in learning and motivation* (pp. 147–206). New York: Academic Press.

Herrmann, D., & Searleman, A. (1992). Memory improvement and memory theory in historical perspective. In D. Herrmann, H. Weingartner, A. Searleman, & C. McEvoy (Eds.), *Memory improvement: Implications for memory theory* (pp. 8–20). New York: Springer-Verlag.

Herrmann, D., Weingartner, H., Searleman, A., & McEvoy, C. (Eds.). (1992). *Memory improvement: Implications for theory.* New York: Springer-Verlag.

Herrmann, D. J., & Palmisano, M. (1992). The facilitation of memory. In M. Gruneberg & P. Morris (Eds.), *Aspects of memory* (2nd ed., pp. 147–167). Chichester, United Kingdom: Wiley.

Herrmann, D. J., Raybeck, D., & Gutman, D. (1993). *Improving student memory.* Toronto, Ontario, Canada: Hogrefe & Huber.

Herrmann, D. J., Rea, A., & Andrzejewski, S. (1988). The need for a new approach to memory training. In M. M. Gruneberg, P. E. Morris, & R. N. Sykes (Eds.), *Practical aspects of memory* (Vol. 2, pp. 415–420). Chichester, United Kingdom: Wiley.

Hertel, P. (1994). Depressive deficits in memory: Implications for memory improvement following traumatic brain injury. *NeuroRehabilitation, 4*(3), 143–150.

Hunt, R. R., & Ellis, H. C. (1998). *Fundamentals of cognitive psychology.* New York: McGraw-Hill.

Jacob, L. L. (1995). Toward diagnosis and rehabilitation in cognitive control. In D. Herrmann, C. McEvoy, C. Hertzog, P. Hertel, & M. Johnson (Eds.), *Basic and applied memory research: Theory in context.* Hillsdale, NJ: Erlbaum.

Kolakowsky, S. A. (1997). Improving cognition through the use of nutrients, drugs, and other cognitive enhancing substances. *Cognitive Technology, 2,* 44–54.

Luria, A. R. (1963). *Restoration of function after brain injury*. New York: Macmillan.

Luria, A. R. (1973). *Higher cortical functions in man* (2nd ed.). New York: Basic Books.

Luria, A. R. (1979). *The making of mind: A personal account of Soviet psychology*. Cambridge, MA: Harvard University Press.

Lynch, W. (1987). Neuropsychological rehabilitation: Description of an established program. In B. Caplan (Ed.), *Rehabilitation psychology desk reference* (pp. 299–322). Rockville, MD: Aspen.

Matlin, M. W. (1998). *Cognition* (4th ed.). Orlando, FL: Harcourt Brace.

McClur, J. T., Browning, R. T., Vantrease, C. M., & Bittle, S. T. (1994). The iconic memory skills of brain injury survivors and non-brain injured controls after visual scanning training. *NeuroRehabilitation, 4*(3), 151–156.

McEvoy, C. L. (1992). Memory improvement in context: Implications for the development of memory improvement theory. In D. Herrmann, H. Weingartner, A. Searleman, & C. McEvoy (Eds.), *Memory improvement: Implications for memory theory* (pp. 210–230). New York: Springer-Verlag.

Miller, E. (1980). Psychological intervention in the management and rehabilitation of neuropsychological impairments. *Behavioral Research and Therapy, 18*, 527–535.

Miller, E. (1984). *Recovery and management of neuropsychological impairments*. Chichester, United Kingdom: Wiley.

Mills, V. M., Nesbeda, T., Katz, D. L., & Alexander, M. P. (1982). Outcomes for traumatically brain-injured patients following post-acute rehabilitation programmes. *Brain Injury, 6*, 219–228.

Naugle, R., Prevy, M., Naugle, C., & Delaney, R. (1988). The new digital watch as a compensatory device for memory dysfunction. *Cognitive Rehabilitation, 6*, 22–23.

Newell, A. (1990). *Unified theories of cognition*. Cambridge, MA: Harvard University Press.

Parenté, R., & Anderson-Parenté, J. (1991). *Retraining memory: Techniques and applications*. Houston, TX: CSY.

Parenté, R., Anderson-Parenté, J. K., & Shaw, B. (1989). Retraining the mind's eye. *Journal of Head Trauma Rehabilitation, 4*, 53–62.

Parenté, R., & Stapleton, M. (1993). An empowerment model of memory training. *Applied Cognitive Psychology, 7*, 585–602.

Patten, B. M. (1990). The history of memory arts. *Neurology, 40*, 346–352.

Payne, D. G., & Wenger, M. J. (1998). *Cognitive psychology*. New York: Houghton Mifflin.

Poon, L. W., Rubin, D. C., & Wilson, B. A. (Eds.). (1988). *Everyday cognition in adulthood and late life* (Fifth Talland Conference). New York: Cambridge University Press.

Prigatano, G., & Fordyce, D. (1987). Neuropsychological rehabilitation program: Presbyterian Hospital, Oklahoma City, Oklahoma. In B. Caplan (Ed.), *Rehabilitation psychology desk reference* (pp. 281–298). Rockville, MD: Aspen.

Prigatano, G. P. (1987). Recovery and cognitive retraining after craniocerebral trauma. *Journal of Learning Disabilities, 20*, 603–613.

Richardson, J. T. E. (1992). Imagery, mnemonics, and memory remediation. *Neurology, 42*, 283–286.

Schacter, D., & Glisky, E. (1986). Memory remediation, restoration, alleviation, and the acquisition of domain specific knowledge. In B. Uzzell & Y. Gross (Eds.), *Clinical neuropsychology of intervention* (pp. 257–282). Boston: Martinus Nijhoff.

Seron, X., & Deloche, G. (Eds.). (1989). *Cognitive approaches to neuropsychological rehabilitation*. Hillsdale, NJ: Erlbaum.

Silver, A. J. (1992). Nutritional aspects of memory dysfunction. In J. Morely, R. M. Coe, R. Strong, & G. T. Grossberg (Eds.), *Memory functions in aging and aging-related disorders*. New York: Springer.

Sohlberg, M., & Mateer, C. (1987). Effectiveness of an attention training program. *Journal of Clinical Experimental Neuropsychology, 9*, 117–130.

Sohlberg, M., & Mateer, C. (1989). *Introduction to cognitive rehabilitation*. New York: Guilford Press.

Wehman, P., Kreutzer, J., Sale, P., West, M., Morton, M., & Diambra, J. (1989). Cognitive impairment and remediation: Implications for employment following traumatic brain injury. *Journal of Head Trauma Rehabilitation, 4*, 66–75.

Wepman, J. M. (1951). *Recovery from aphasia*. New York: Ronald Press.

Wilson, B. (1987). *Rehabilitation of memory*. New York: Guilford Press.

Wood, R. L., & Fussey, L. (1990). *Cognitive rehabilitation in perspective*. London: Taylor & Francis.

Yesavage, J. A., Rose, T. L., & Spiegel, D. (1982). Relaxation training and memory improvement in elderly normals: Correlations of anxiety rating and recall improvement. *Experimental Aging Research, 8*, 198.

Zangwill, O. L. (1945). A review of psychological work at the brain injuries unit, Edinburgh, 1941–1945. *British Medical Journal, 2*(6), 248–250.

Zangwill, O. L. (1947). Apsychological aspects of rehabilitation in cases of brain injury. *British Journal of Psychology, 37*, 60–69.

Chapter 2

A Model of Cognitive Rehabilitation

This chapter introduces a model of cognition that provides a theoretical backdrop for an eclectic approach to cognitive rehabilitation. This approach is rooted in the theoretical assumption that cognition and the rehabilitation of cognitive functions are influenced by many different factors including a person's physiological state, perceptual skills, emotional status, motivation, and social skills. Changing these factors can improve the person's cognitive functioning as much as any learned compensatory strategies. A combination of environmental changes and cognitive rehabilitation produces the greatest improvement in a person's cognitive functioning (Ben-Yishay & Diller, 1981; Gianutsos, 1980). Moreover, this multimodal model provides a blueprint for a holistic approach to cognitive rehabilitation that is grounded in basic and clinical research (Herrmann, Plude, Yoder, & Mullin, 1999; McEvoy & Moon, 1988; Poon, 1980; Zachs & Hasher, 1992; see also Bracy, 1986; Johnson, 1983; Schacter, 1984).

Specific Assumptions of the Model

The multimodal model assumes that three classes of variables affect the psychological system (Parenté & Herrmann, 1996). The efficiency of cognitive processing depends on the quality of the interaction among the three modes. The active modes involve conscious thought processes. For example, any cognitive strategy a person could learn implies active mental processing. The passive modes include variables that are generally external to the mind but still exert considerable influence on thinking and memory skill, such as a person's physical condition and emotional state or the use of cognitive-enhancing nutrients and drugs. Support modes include the contribution of a person's social network, environment, and prosthetic devices. These external modes obviate memory and cognitive problems by taking over these functions for the individual.

The active, passive, and support modes affect the availability of information to a person, a person's ability to allocate responses, and a person's ability to attend and concentrate effectively (Herrmann & Parenté, 1994). Traditionally, CRT practitioners manipulate only the active mode. Our goal in this book is to get the therapist to work with all three types of modes because we believe that the passive and support modes can affect a person's cognition as much as, and perhaps more than, active mental effort. Descriptions of the multimodal processes are listed in Table 2.1

TABLE 2.1
Processes and Examples of a Multimodal Model of Cognitive Functions

Active Modes

Mental Manipulation	Use of optimal thought processes such as mnemonics, mental imagery, and other encoding strategies
Mental Sets	Cognitive sets that can be applied in situations that require thinking and processing, understanding novel information, reasoning, and learning new concepts

Passive Modes
Physiological

Physical State	Health; illness; pain; exercise; nutrition; sleep; temperature; time of day
Chemical State	Use of common substances like tobacco, coffee, caffeine; medicines like antidepressants, antibiotics, antihistamines, tranquilizers; substances like alcohol, cocaine, marijuana; also includes passive intake of environmental toxins
Health	Disease; brain tumors; anemia; low blood pressure; epilepsy; depression; chronic fatigue

Psychological

Emotional State	Anxiety about tasks, situations, memory aptitude; annoyances like chronic pain and discomfort, hassles, noise; persistent states of arousal; recent trauma; mood swings, depression, repression; stress
Attitudinal State	Extreme religious beliefs; incongruence between present and past life; stereotypes like age, culture, gender
Motivation and Incentives	Distractibility; incentive value of treatment and perceived relevance; goals; pattern of success experiences

Support Modes

Prosthetic Devices	Use of tape recorders, calculators, and so forth to compensate for poor memory and thinking skills
Social Environment	Social cover-up skills; collaborative recall with another person; social reminders; conversational ploys; social pressure; social feedback and coaching; social tolerance for deficits
Physical Environment	Environmental cues that remind, such as external aids; computer-assisted reminding

Active Modes

The active modes affect the content of memories and thoughts. Training in these modes includes techniques for encoding, retrieving information, and performing mental manipulations of ideas and images either to register memories or to perform some higher cognitive skill. Any active mode affects the content of the information in the cognitive system, such as a person's perceptions, thoughts, images, and memories (Grafman, 1989). The active modes also work by training a person to concentrate, maintain focus, and use strategies to encode new information efficiently. There are basically two types of active processes: mental manipulations and mental sets.

Mental manipulations are thought processes that foster encoding or the cuing of retrieval. Training a person to use mental manipulation includes teaching techniques such as how to use mnemonics, create mental images, and so forth. Mental manipulations are what most therapists think of as cognitive strategies (Bellezza, 1981, 1982; Ben-Yishay & Diller, 1981; Gianutsos, 1991; Higbee, 1988; Parenté & Anderson-Parenté, 1983; Parenté & Anderson-Parenté, 1991; Parenté & DiCesare, 1991; West, 1985). Mental manipulations are thought processes that create memories. They encode information for transfer to long-term memory and affect the pattern of attributes that become long-term memories. The effect of mental manipulations varies across individuals with different learning styles. Most people with good memories and thinking skills have well developed mental manipulation skills. This means that they actively and unconsciously manipulate novel information to make it more memorable.

A survey of mental manipulation techniques is presented in Chapters 8 through 18. A person who learns mental manipulation skills can focus his or her attention on the organization of the material or can use a certain strategy to process different types of information. The quality of a thought or idea formed using mental manipulation techniques depends on several factors, some under volitional control and others that operate automatically without awareness (Searleman & Herrmann, 1994). The therapist's goal is to train a person to use different strategies that encode information efficiently without conscious effort.

Mental sets are various ways of approaching a task. Training a person to use mental sets ensures that he or she will consider all necessary information before making a crucial decision or trying to solve an important problem. Mental set techniques include the cognitive strategies for problem solving, decision making, concept learning, and so forth. These are discussed in Chapters 11 and 14 through 18.

Passive Modes

Whereas the active modes directly affect the content of mental representation, the passive modes do not directly affect what is learned or remembered. Instead, the passive modes affect a person's disposition, inclination, or readiness to attempt a cognitive task. The passive modes may also make it easier for a person to process information. Three of the passive modes are physiological states that determine a person's physical readiness for memory and cognitive tasks; these modes are (1) the person's physical state, (2) his or her chemical toxicity resulting from prescription and nonprescription medicines and other mind-altering substances, and (3) his or her health.

The other three passive modes pertain to a person's readiness for cognitive processing, including (1) attitude, (2) emotions, and (3) incentive and motivation. These modes determine a person's priorities in therapy. For example, a person who is emotionally upset or who does not see any relevance to a training task will not give full effort in any therapy activity.

The way the six passive modes affect a person can change from hour to hour or day to day, and in some cases, from minute to minute. For example, long periods of strenuous exercise could reduce anyone's physiological readiness for ongoing mental activity. Medications alter a person's biochemistry and also can quickly alter physiological readiness for mental activity.

Physiological Passive Modes

A person's *physical state* includes factors of daily living such as fatigue, nutrition, sleep, rest, exercise, and so forth. Many therapy clients have had dysfunctional sleep and nutrition habits before their injuries; they must unlearn these habits and substitute others that are specifically designed to enhance their recovery. In general, a balanced diet with daily multiple vitamins can dramatically change a client's physical state if the person previously had poor eating habits. A consistent sleep regime and a light exercise program should also accompany changes in diet.

A person's *chemical state* refers to his or her neurochemistry or other physiological states that can be altered by certain substances, such as inhalants, medicines, drugs, and so forth. In situations where a client has a prior history of drug abuse, we recommend regular urine testing to ensure that the client has not returned to drug use. Common substances can impair cognitive processing; for example, tobacco smoking; drinking excessive amounts of coffee; tranquilizers; sedating antidepressants; and antibiotics may also lessen memory performance (Herrmann & Palmisano, 1992). Intake of such substances should be monitored.

A person's *health considerations* include the degree to which he or she is free of physical or emotional disease or any other debilitating condition or malady. These problems can cause a client pain, which, in turn, limits his or her cognitive processing. Anemia, brain tumors, dementia, depression, heart failure, low blood pressure, some forms of epilepsy, and syphilis are examples of health problems that interfere with a person's ability to concentrate and perform cognitive functions. Even routine disruptions of health, such as the common cold, impair cognition.

In short, a person's physiological condition affects his or her thinking and memory. Only in recent years has science begun to identify the chemistry of cognition (Squire, 1985). Substance use issues are discussed in detail in Chapter 20.

Psychological Passive Modes

A person's *attitudinal state* includes his or her emotional disposition to process different kinds of information or to interact with different people. For example, a therapy client's attraction to certain types of people or repulsion to political or social ideas and so forth can affect his or her memory and thinking skill. As a result the client's progress can improve markedly with a simple change in the therapeutic environment. For example, many clients prefer to work with a therapist of the same gender. Some prefer to work with therapists who are close to their age. Often, simply discussing the treatment and providing a choice of therapist can greatly enhance a client's progress.

A person's thinking and memory have long been known to be affected by his or her attitude regarding which cognitive tasks they do or do not like to perform (Gruneberg, 1992). A person is likely to perform better when his or her attitude toward a task is positive.

A person's *emotional state* is his or her feelings of varied intensity, quality, and value. A client's depression, elation, or apathy can significantly change the outcome of treatment. Generally, high anxiety and depression (Hertel, 1992) interfere with thinking and memory. Stress, a major factor in mood, has been associated with impaired memory for everyday information (Fisher & Reason, 1986). In therapy, these states can be modified through discussion and experience. We discuss these issues in Chapter 20.

A person's *incentive and motivation* determine his or her tendency to act in specific ways to achieve particular goals. A therapy client's motivation depends on the current incentives. An incentive-based model of cognitive rehabilitation along with specific recommendations for creating incentives is presented in Chapter 23. Generally, cognition will improve markedly in situations where there are clear incentives (McEvoy, 1992; Parenté & Anderson-Parenté, 1991). Moreover, if a client can be made to feel in control of goals and rewards that are associated with efficient thinking, then he or she becomes empowered to acquire the knowledge and methods that will produce better thinking and memory (Parenté & Stapleton, 1993).

Support Modes

Support modes do not directly control the nature of thought. Instead, these modes create ongoing conditions that guide the mental strategies, use prosthetic devices that obviate cognitive deficits, use the physical environment as a memory or cognitive aid, and structure social interactions to compensate for poor thinking and memory. The support modes position the person to benefit from the environment, his or her social situation, and various available devices. In essence, the therapist tries to get the world to work for the client rather than against him or her.

Prosthetic devices are electronic and nonelectronic devices that help a person to overcome nagging problems by replacing some damaged aspect of memory or thinking. For example, training a client to use a dictation tape recorder can improve memory functioning. Although it does not improve the client's memory per se, it does eliminate many of the common problems associated with loss of memory. We provide a detailed description of a variety of prosthetic devices in Chapter 24.

Using the *physical environment* as a support mode refers to manipulating the environment to foster encoding or the cuing of retrieval. The use of the physical environment to affect memory and thinking skills can be quite deliberate. Objects may be positioned purposely to call attention to high-priority information (Cohen, 1989; Davies & Thompson, 1988). When objects are arranged to enhance their availability, the physical environment becomes an external aid. We discuss environmental manipulation in detail at the end of Chapter 13.

The *social environment* mode refers to the use of a client's social network to improve his or her memory or cognitive state. For example, arranging for a family member to call a client each day of the week with a reminder of that day's activities can greatly reduce the frustration that most family members feel when the client misses an appointment. Sharing the responsibility among family members is usually not difficult to arrange.

The Multimodal Model in Perspective

Figure 2.1 presents a summary of the multimodal model described above (Herrmann &

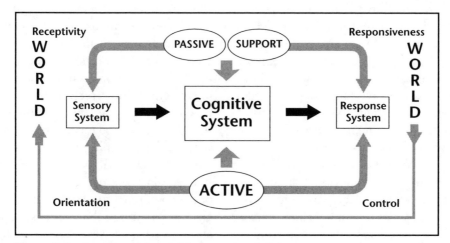

Figure 2.1. A multimodal model for cognitive rehabilitation.

Parenté, 1994; Herrmann & Plude, 1996; Herrmann & Searleman, 1992; Mullin, Herrmann, & Searleman, 1993; Parenté & Herrmann, 1996). The active, passive, and support modes together determine what a person ultimately perceives, learns, retains, remembers, and reasons. The bottom arrows in the figure connect the active processes with the sensory, response, and cognitive systems. These arrows represent the assumption that active processes operate directly on all three systems. Until recently, these bottom arrows represented what most therapists would describe as cognitive rehabilitation.

The arrows that connect the passive and support processes to the sensory, cognitive, and response systems represent the assumption that these processes also affect the three systems directly. Because the connecting arrows are of similar thickness, we assume that passive and support modes can have comparable impact on the person's overall cognitive functioning. The model also assumes that the passive support, and active modes have comparable effects on the cognitive system.

The black arrows in the center of the figure that connect the sensory system, the cognitive system, and the response system illustrate the flow of information through the system. In general, the model indicates that active, passive, and support processes operate directly on the (a) sensory input that provides raw information to the cognitive system, (b) cognitive operations performed on the sensory input, and (c) the ability to express and to communicate what one knows.

In looking again at the arrows that connect the active, passive, and support modes to the cognitive system, the large arrows in the upper part of the figure connect the passive and support processes with the sensory, response, and cognitive systems. The left arrow represents the assumption that passive and support processes affect sensitivity or receptivity to the sensory input. For example, if a person is ill, depressed, or if hearing or

vision is impaired, then he or she may miss pieces of information or fail to perceive some event entirely. A person who has no family support system to signal social transgressions may remain oblivious to his or her offenses. The middle arrow shows the influence of passive and support processes on the cognitive system and the cognitive operations performed on the input from the sensory store. For example, if a person is depressed or apathetic, then he or she may not process the contents of an important phone call as readily as if he or she were in an alert and attentive and otherwise healthy state. Without a family support system, the client may have difficulty implementing newly learned strategies in the home. The right arrow represents the assumption that the passive and support processes affect a person's responsiveness and current ability to express what one knows. For example, if a person is taking strong medications, is fatigued, or is emotionally distraught, then he or she may not be able to pronounce words easily or clearly. Computer support software may be necessary to enhance a client's speech volume or clarity.

The large arrows in the lower part of the figure connect the active processes with the sensory, response, and cognitive systems. The left arrow shows how active processes orient a person to perceive something in the environment. For example, visual scanning training may teach a client how to orient effectively to certain aspects of his or her environment by using effective eye movements. Iconic memory training can teach a client how to process more information between eye movements. These techniques are presented in Chapter 8. The middle arrow indicates that the active modes can alter cognitive processing. For example, training a person to use any of the rehearsal or memory strategies outlined in Chapters 10, 11, and 12 facilitates his or her cognitive processing. Any of the strategies for solving problems, making decisions, and so forth that we describe in Chapters 14 and 16 alter a person's ability to process facts and other information efficiently. The right arrow represents the assumption that people can control the nature of their responses, and they can choose how to express what they actually know. For example, the ANGER and CALM mnemonics that we present in Chapter 11 provide ways for clients to control their agitation and to alter their responses in potentially volatile situations.

This is a cybernetic model because it assumes that a person can make a response that changes cues in the environment. The cues, in turn, direct and alter subsequent processing. In essence, the line at the bottom of the figure, running from "World" adjacent to the response system to "World" adjacent to the sensory system illustrates the learning component of the model. A person's perceptions and cognitions control his or her eventual response. This response eventually alters the way the person views the world. For example, this loop operates when a person sets an alarm that signals an appointment. The person, thereafter, learns to use the signaling device for future appointments.

The passive and support modes probably affect memory and thinking via a person's attentional processes (Mullin, Herrmann, & Searleman, 1993). Both modes affect a person's readiness to pay attention or how much processing capacity a person has at any given moment. The active modes determine a person's ability to allocate attention, that is, the quality of the attention the person gives an object when there are other objects competing for attention.

Empirical Support for the Multimodal Approach

Three kinds of evidence support the multimodal model: (a) basic research, (b) clinical research, and (c) clinical experience. Each kind of evidence is discussed in detail.

Basic Research

There are numerous mental manipulations that enhance learning, remembering, and thinking in populations of people with head injuries and of people who are "normal" (Buschke, 1987; Herrmann, Weingartner, Searleman, & McEvoy, 1992; McEvoy, 1992; Parenté & Anderson-Parenté, 1991; Parenté, Anderson-Parenté, & Shaw, 1989; Patten, 1990; Twum, 1994). Most of these are discussed in Chapters 8 through 18. For example, learning may be enhanced by increasing intervals between successive rehearsals, relating information to a person's personal characteristics or goals, weaving information to be learned into a story, and so forth. Similarly, a person's name may come to mind when the client recites the letters of the alphabet.

There is also substantial evidence that the passive and support modes facilitate thinking and memory. Intons-Peterson and Newsome (1992) point out that a person may manipulate the physical environment (e.g., position or mark objects, write notes) to enhance acquisition, retrieval, or reasoning. Prosthetic devices have long been used to facilitate memory and thought in a variety of settings (Herrmann, Plude, Yoder, & Mullin, 1999), including machines that provide rote learning of basic skills like typing or academic skills like reading and math. Cognitive visual aids such as signs or cuing cards have long been used to remind a person of danger or to describe complex actions, such as operating a microwave. Cognitive robots execute cognitive tasks for a person like turning light switches or appliances on or off automatically. A sympathetic family member may provide reminders to the client. Friends often provide honest feedback about the client's social behavior. A person may also take drugs to improve his or her memory (Perna, Bordini, & Newman, 2001). Cognitive prosthetics are devices that take over some memory or cognitive skill. For example, a person can learn to use a personal digital assistant (PDA; e.g., Palm Pilot) as a prosthetic memory aid. Cognitive error correctors fix mistakes; for example, key finders that beep when a person whistles can be used to find misplaced keys. All of these devices illustrate that people can manipulate the physical environment to improve their memory and thinking, which supports the model's assumption of the feedback loop shown in Figure 2.1.

There is also evidence to support the effect of social facilitation of memory and thinking. Best (1992) reports that people may avoid cognitive failures by interacting with others in ways that affect the rate or substance of conversation. For example, a person can learn various conversational ploys to buy time for retrieval or to better encode information. In Chapter 12 we present a method for training clients to form name and face associations that use a similar technique. A client is trained to pretend that he or she did not hear the name so the person will repeat it. These social manipulations to improve thinking and memory also provide evidence for the model's assumption of a feedback loop.

Clinical Research

We know of only two clinical investigations that examined the effects of a multimodal treatment program. Nevertheless, these investigations, because they were well designed, provide excellent examples of the effectiveness of the multimodal approach, as well as offering some unanticipated benefits. The first investigation addressed the effects of a multimodal program on the memory and cognition of some victims of paint solvent toxicity (Bendiksen & Bendiksen, 1992, 1996). Twenty workers from a paint factory in Norway participated in the study. Their performance on 11 tasks from the Rivermead Memory Battery was assessed (Wilson, 1987). Some of these tasks were targeted for memory training

during the rehabilitation program. The targeted tasks included remembering names, objects owned, appointments, a story, and to give a message. Other tasks were not targeted for training; these nontargeted tasks included orientation, questioning, and immediate and delayed memory for pictures, faces, routes, and dates. Performance of the targeted and nontargeted tasks was assessed at four times (T): T1, T2, T3, and T4. The first assessment, T1, and second assessment, T2, preceded the rehabilitation program. T2 occurred 3 months after T1.

After the second assessment, the rehabilitation program was initiated. The program lasted 9 weeks and consisted of two sessions of 2 hours each per week. Four to 7 participants attended each session. One session was devoted to memory training that was appropriate for the targeted tasks, and involved imparting one or more mental strategies suggested by Herrmann (1990). The other session was devoted to psychosocial issues resulting from the memory and cognitive impairments of the participants, and involved instruction in coping skills and group discussion of the participants' concerns about their symptoms. At the end of the 9-week rehabilitation program, a third assessment was taken (T3).

Memory was assessed one more time, 6 months later (T4). Relative to the nontargeted tasks, performance on the targeted tasks increased significantly across the study (from T1 to T4). This increase was most pronounced for the story, name, and owned objects tasks. The most remarkable aspect of this study was evident when the different kinds of participant complaints were analyzed across the four assessment times. Complaints about cognitive and emotional functioning decreased significantly after the intervention, and somatic complaints decreased only slightly. In contrast, complaints about social adjustment and economic problems decreased after the intervention.

The multimodal approach employed in this investigation resulted in a multimodal outcome. Not only did the participants' cognitive functioning improve but so did their psychosocial functioning. The participants' emotional stability increased because of the socioemotive intervention and because of the memory intervention, which demonstrated to the participants that they could improve their memory functioning, led them to worry less about memory. Alternatively, increased social and emotional control also prepared participants to benefit more from the memory training. Because both the memory training and the social–emotional training were effective and resulted in fewer concerns about cognition and emotional issues, the participants were able to allocate more attention to their activities of daily living, directing their worries to relationships with friends and financial matters.

Another clinical study of the multimodal approach was concerned with drug rehabilitation (Herrmann, Plude, Yoder, & Mullin, 1999). This study examined the relationship of the different modes to each other in an investigation of veterans who underwent drug withdrawal and treatment. Considering that in the study described above improved system status yielded improved memory and social function for paint solvent victims (Bendiksen & Bendiksen, 1992, 1996), it was expected that treatment of substance abuse victims would yield similar results.

Eighteen veterans (10 male and 8 female) participated in an in-patient drug rehabilitation program at the Indianapolis Veterans Hospital. Their memory ability, thinking ability, and the status of their passive and support modes were rated in the first and last weeks of a 6-week program. While hospitalized, the veterans received a combination of psychogenic and chemical therapy that was designed to help people recover from an addiction. As a result of treatment, the average ratings for memory and thinking improved from pretest to posttest as did all of the modal ratings, except the physical environment ratings. Similar results were reported in studies of rehabilitation of patients injured by toxic solvents (Bendiksen & Bendiksen, 1992, 1996).

There have been several investigations that have examined the effect of interventions to optimize a particular mode. Each of the active modes has been addressed in separate studies (Bracy, 1986; Gianutsos, 1980; Parenté & Anderson-Parenté, 1983). In studies of the support modes, cognitive rehabilitation has been shown to be effectively aided by external devices (Naugle, Prevy, Naugle, & Delaney, 1988), and the importance of social interactions to rehabilitation has been increasingly recognized (Boake, 1991b). Similarly, each of the passive modes has been addressed in separate studies. For example, the role of pharmacology in cognitive rehabilitation has been assessed (Miller, 1993; Zasler, 1991). A number of studies have examined the importance of emotional rehabilitation (O'Hara, 1988). Similarly, experiments have shown the value of motivation and incentive in cognitive training (McEvoy, 1992; Parenté & Anderson-Parenté, 1991).

Clinical Experience

Finally, a great deal of support exists in the cognitive rehabilitation literature in which practitioners argue for a multimodal approach (Bracy, 1986). Five books on cognitive rehabilitation advance methods that tap into different modes, cognitive and noncognitive (Harrell, Parenté, Bellingrath, & Lisicia, 1992; McEvoy, 1992; Parenté & Anderson-Parenté 1991; Wehman & Kreutzer, 1991). Our own experience has been that the multimodal approach is useful with a wide variety of clients including victims of traumatic brain injury, stroke, dementia, chronic alcoholism, and substance abuse. The approach is also useful for caregivers and family members who may be in an especially valuable position to manipulate the social and physical environments modes. It should also be noted that the multimodal approach was previously found useful in psychotherapy (Lazarus, 1989). Because emotional difficulties often accompany neurological impairment and contribute to the level of cognitive impairment, the multimodal approach to cognitive rehabilitation may be seen to lessen the negative impact of emotional distress on cognitive functioning.

Implications of the Multimodal Model

The model presented in Figure 2.1 emphasizes the dynamic and interactive relationship between cognition and physical experience. Cognition is simply part of what we call perception and is embedded between the sensory world and our response to it. The process of cognitive rehabilitation begins by recognizing this embeddedness. This concept has several implications for treatment, diagnosis, and the education of professionals in the field.

Treatment

Cognitive rehabilitation traditionally has focused primarily on the active modes (Ben-Yishay & Diller, 1981; Boake, 1991a; Gianutsos, 1980). For example, the attention process model (Sohlberg & Mateer, 2001) trains clients to selectively attend, alternate their attention, and to sustain attention. Parenté and Anderson-Parenté (1991) described procedures to teach clients active control of his or her rehearsal processes. However, the major implication of the multimodal model is that therapy efforts are best served when a therapist uses a holistic approach. The model presented in Figure 2.1 simply provides a summary of the various areas that compose the whole.

Cognitive rehabilitation researchers and practitioners have recently begun to see the value of holistic approaches to rehabilitation. For example, the team approach where the disciplines represent different clinical specialties such as clinical psychologists, speech therapists, and social workers (Dikengil, Lowry, & Delgado, 1993; Dryovage & Seidman, 1992) emphasizes the contribution of professionals who would work specifically in one or more modalities of the model. The interdisciplinary approach has been found to be very effective and the multimodal model shows why. The interdisciplinary approach affects two or more modes and, hence, is more effective than the early cognitive approach that focused just on the active mode. This book presents techniques and applications for most of the modes that can augment any professional's knowledge regardless of his or her background or training.

Diagnostic Practices

The model implies that diagnosis should systematically assess not only neurocognitive functioning but also the current status of all other modes that affect cognition and behavior. Currently, there is no standardized assessment method that collects information about the passive and support modes. An exception is the Rivermead Memory Battery, which does provide an assessment of use of external aids in the physical environment (Wilson, 1987). To fill this void, we have provided a problem–solution checklist modal rating scale in Appendix A. Therapists can use this instrument to guide their treatment according to the multimodal model. This assessment is designed to evaluate the client's use of mental strategies, physical environment, and social environment, as well as the client's physical state, chemical state, attitudinal state, emotional state, and motivational state. Cognitive rehabilitation therapists will want a multimodal performance assessment of the survivor's active modes. Chapter 7 discusses this issue in detail and Appendix A is a working example of this type of assessment.

Planning Cognitive Rehabilitation

Probably the most obvious implication of the model concerns the nature of the treatment plan. We assert that it is no longer sufficient for a treatment plan to focus only on training a client's cognitive processes. The multimodal model shows that rehabilitation yields the quickest and most effective results when all modes are optimized. The model implies the following simple rules that will be useful to any therapist or family member.

- If a client's passive processes are in a poor state, interventions that attempt to improve active processes will have little or no effect. Alternatively, any intervention will have the greatest effect when the passive processes are brought under control or have been manipulated to work to the client's advantage. This point seems obvious but in the hectic pace of most rehabilitation services, a client's poor physical condition, mood, attitude, or motivation is often overlooked, ignored, or tolerated rather than directly addressed.

- In those situations where a client cannot be helped by training active processes, thinking and memory may still be improved by enhancing passive processes.

- Working with the support modes will likely have the most immediate effect on overall cognitive functions. These interventions may also be the easiest to implement.

Education

To our knowledge, the multimodal model is the first formal model of cognitive rehabilitation. It provides a rationale that therapists can use to explain cognitive rehabilitation to survivors, caregivers, new staff, colleagues in related health care professions, and so forth. For example, we have found Figure 2.1 especially helpful when training new staff in cognitive rehabilitation procedures. The figure streamlines the process of explaining cognitive rehabilitation and provides an aid to remembering the roles of the different modes in rehabilitation.

Discussion

This chapter described the multimodal approach to cognitive rehabilitation. The model was evaluated through findings from basic research, clinical research, and clinical experience. The basic research findings supported the general assumption that thinking and memory can be affected by noncognitive modes. Clinical research findings demonstrated that cognitive impairments could be lessened through interventions that affect one or more noncognitive modes. Clinical experience similarly supports the multimodal approach and indicates that cognitive rehabilitation has the greatest chance for success if treatment improves a client's active, passive, and support processes. Besides accounting for the effects of interventions impacting particular modes in isolation or in combination, the model also implies a new explanation of the effects of interdisciplinary cognitive rehabilitation, new diagnostic procedures, new and more comprehensive treatment plans, and a rationale to use any and all of these when educating others about cognitive rehabilitation practices.

References

Bellezza, F. S. (1981). Mnemonic devices: Classification characteristics and criteria. *Review of Educational Research, 51*, 247–275.

Bellezza, F. S. (1982). *Improve your memory skills*. Englewood Cliffs, NJ: Prentice Hall.

Ben-Yishay, Y., & Diller, L. (1981). Cognitive deficits. In M. Rosenthal (Ed.), *Rehabilitation of the head injured adult*. Philadelphia: Davis.

Bendiksen, M., & Bendiksen, I. (1996). Multi-modal memory rehabilitation for the toxic solvent injured population. In D. Herrmann, M. Johnson, C. McEvoy, C. Hertzog, & P. Hertel (Eds.), *Basic and applied memory research: New findings* (pp. 469–480). Hillsdale, NJ: Erlbaum.

Bendiksen, M., & Bendiksen, I. A. (1992). A Multidimensional intervention program for a solvent injured population. *Cognitive Rehabilitation, 10*, 20–27.

Best, D. (1992). The role of social interaction in memory improvement. In D. Herrmann, H. Weingartner, A. Searleman, & C. McEvoy (Eds.), *Memory improvement: Implications for memory theory* (pp. 122–149). New York: Springer-Verlag.

Boake, C. (1991a). History of cognitive rehabilitation following head injury. In J. S. Kreutzer & P. H. Wehman (Eds.), *Cognitive rehabilitation for persons with traumatic brain injury* (pp. 1–12). Baltimore: Brookes.

Boake, C. (1991b). Social skills training following head injury. In J. S. Kreutzer & P. H. Wehman (Eds.), *Cognitive rehabilitation for persons with traumatic brain injury* (pp. 181–190). Baltimore: Brookes.

Bracy, O. L. (1986). Cognitive rehabilitation: A process approach. *Cognitive Rehabilitation, 4*, 10–17.

Buschke, H. (1987). Criteria for the identification of memory deficits: Implications for the design of memory tests. In D. S. Gorfein & R. R. Hoffman (Eds.), *Memory and learning* (pp. 331–344). Hillsdale, NJ: Erlbaum.

Cohen, G. (1989). *Memory in the real world*. Hillsdale, NJ: Erlbaum.

Davies, G. M., & Thompson, D. M. (1988). *Memory in context: Context in memory*. Chichester, United Kingdom: Wiley.

Dikengil, A., Lowry, M., & Delgado, P. (1993). An interdisciplinary group treatment for the severely brain-injured patient: Participation by four disciplines. *Cognitive Rehabilitation, 11(3)*, 20–22.

Dryovage, J., & Seidman, K. (1992). Interdisciplinary approach to community reintegration. *Cognitive Rehabilitation, 11(2)*, 23–27.

Fisher, S., & Reason, J. T. (Eds.). (1986). *Handbook of life stress, cognition and health*. New York: Wiley.

Gianutsos, R. (1980). What is cognitive rehabilitation? *Journal of Rehabilitation, 2*, 37–40.

Gianutsos, R. (1991). Cognitive rehabilitation: A neuropsychological specialty comes of age. *Brain Injury, 5*, 353–368.

Grafman, J. (1989). Plans, actions, and mental sets: Managerial knowledge units in the frontal lobes. In E. Perecman (Ed.), *Integrating theory and practice in clinical neuropsychology* (pp. 14–29). Hillsdale, NJ: Erlbaum.

Gruneberg, M. M. (1992). The practical application of memory aids: Knowing how, knowing when, and knowing when not. In M. M. Gruneberg & P. Morris (Eds.), *Aspects of memory* (pp. 168–195). London: Routledge.

Harrell, M., Parenté, R., Bellingrath, E. G., & Lisicia, K. A. (1992). *Cognitive rehabilitation of memory: A practical guide*. Rockville, MD: Aspen.

Herrmann, D. (1990). Self-perceptions of memory performance. In W. K. Schaie, J. Rodin, & C. Schooler (Eds.), *Self-directedness and efficacy: Causes and effects throughout the life course*. Hillsdale, NJ: Erlbaum.

Herrmann, D., & Parenté, R. (1994). A multi-modal approach to cognitive rehabilitation. *NeuroRehabilitation, 4*, 133–142.

Herrmann, D., & Plude, D. (1996). Museum memory. In J. Falk & L. Dierking (Eds.), *Public institutions for personal learning: The long-term impact of museums*. Washington, DC: American Association of Museums.

Herrmann, D., Plude, D., Yoder, C., & Mullin, P. (1999). Cognitive processing and extrinsic psychological systems: A holistic model of cognition. *Zeitschrift fur Psychologie, 207*, 123–147.

Herrmann, D., & Searleman, A. (1992). Memory improvement and memory theory in historical perspective. In D. Herrmann, H. Weingartner, A. Searleman, & C. McEvoy (Eds.), *Memory improvement: Implications for memory theory* (pp. 8–20). New York: Springer-Verlag.

Herrmann, D., Weingartner, H., Searleman, A., & McEvoy, C. (Eds.). (1992). *Memory improvement: Implications for memory theory*. New York: Springer-Verlag.

Herrmann, D. J., & Palmisano, M. (1992). The facilitation of memory. In M. Gruneberg & P. Morris (Eds.), *Aspects of memory* (2nd ed., pp. 147–167). Chichester, United Kingdom: Wiley.

Hertel, P. (1992). Improving memory and mood through automatic and controlled procedures of mind. In D. Herrmann, H. Weingartner, A. Searleman, & C. McEvoy (Eds.), *Memory improvement: Implications for memory theory* (pp. 43–60). New York: Springer-Verlag.

Higbee, K. L. (1988). *Your memory* (2nd ed.). Englewood Cliffs, NJ: Prentice Hall.

Intons-Peterson, M. J., & Newsome, G. L. (1992). External memory aids: Effects and effectiveness. In D. Herrmann, H. Weingartner, A. Searleman, & C. McEvoy (Eds.), *Memory improvement: Implications for memory theory* (pp. 101–121). New York: Springer-Verlag.

Johnson, M. H. (1983). A multiple-entry, modular memory system. In G. H. Bower (Ed.), *The psychology of learning and motivation* (Vol. 17). New York: Academic Press.

Kreutzer, J. S., & Wehman, P. H. (1991). *Cognitive rehabilitation for persons with traumatic brain injury*. Baltimore: Brookes.

Lazarus, A. A. (1989). *The practice of multimodal therapy: Systematic, comprehensive, and effective psychotherapy*. Baltimore: Johns Hopkins University Press.

McEvoy, C. L. (1992). Memory improvement in context: Implications for the development of memory improvement theory. In D. Herrmann, H. Weingartner, A. Searleman, & C. McEvoy (Eds.), *Memory improvement: Implications for memory theory* (pp. 210–230). New York: Springer-Verlag.

McEvoy, C. L., & Moon, J. R. (1988). Assessment and treatment of everyday memory problems in the elderly. In M. M. Gruneberg, P. E. Morris, & R. N. Sykes (Eds.), *Practical aspects of memory: Current research and issues* (Vol. 2, pp. 155–160). Chichester, United Kingdom: Wiley.

Miller, L. (1993). Clinical, neuropsychological, and forensic aspects of chemical and electrical injuries. *Cognitive Rehabilitation, 11*, 6–19.

Mullin, P., Herrmann, D. J., & Searleman, A. (1993). Forgotten variables in memory research. *Memory, 15*, 43.

Naugle, R., Prevy, M., Naugle, C., & Delaney, R. (1988). The new digital watch as a compensatory device for memory dysfunction. *Cognitive Rehabilitation, 6*, 22–23.

O'Hara, C. (1988). Emotional adjustment following minor head injury. *Cognitive Rehabilitation, 6*, 26–33.

Parenté R., & Anderson-Parenté, J. (1983). Techniques for improving cognitive rehabilitation: Teaching organizational and encoding skills. *Cognitive Rehabilitation, 4*, 53–65.

Parenté, R., & Anderson-Parenté, J. (1991). *Retraining memory: Techniques and applications*. Houston, TX: CSY.

Parenté, R., Anderson-Parenté, J., & Shaw, B. (1989). Retraining the mind's eye. *Journal of Head Trauma Rehabilitation, 4*, 53–62.

Parenté, R., & DiCesare, A. (1991). Retraining memory: Theory, evaluation, and applications. In J. S. Kreutzer & P. H. Wehman (Eds.), *Cognitive rehabilitation for persons with traumatic brain injury* (pp. 147–162). Baltimore: Brookes.

Parenté, R., & Herrmann, D. (1996). *Retraining cognition: Techniques and applications*. Gaithersburg, MD: Aspen.

Parenté, R., & Stapleton, M. (1993). An empowerment model of memory training. *Applied Cognitive Psychology, 7*, 34–58.

Patten, B. M. (1990). The history of memory arts. *Neurology, 40*, 346–352.

Perna, R. B., Bordini, E. J., & Newman, S. A. (2001). Pharmacological treatment considerations in brain injury. *The Journal of Cognitive Rehabilitation, 19*(1), 4–9.

Poon, L. W. (1980). A systems approach for the assessment and treatment of memory problems. In J. M. Ferguson & C. B. Taylor (Eds.), *The comprehensive handbook of behavior medicine* (Vol. 1, pp. 191–212). New York: Van Norstrand Reinhold.

Schacter, D. L. (1984). Toward the multidisciplinary study of memory: Ontogeny, phylogeny, and pathology of memory systems. In L. R. Squire & N. Butters (Eds.), *Neuropsychology of memory*. New York: Guilford Press.

Searleman, A., & Herrmann, D. (1994). *Memory from a broader perspective*. New York: McGraw Hill.

Sohlberg, M., & Mateer, C. (2001). *Introduction to cognitive rehabilitation*. New York: Guilford Press.

Squire, L. (1985). *Memory and brain*. New York: Oxford University Press.

Twum, M. (1994). Maximizing generalization of cognitions and memories after traumatic brain injury. *NeuroRehabilitation, 4*(3), 157–167.

West, R. (1985). *Memory fitness over forty*. Gainesville, FL: Triad.

Wilson, B. (1987). *Rehabilitation of memory*. New York: Guilford Press.

Zachs, R. T., & Hasher, L. (1992). Memory in life, lab, and clinic: Implications for memory theory. In D. Herrmann, H. Weingartner, A. Searleman, & C. McEvoy (Eds.), *Memory improvement: Implications for memory theory* (pp. 232–248). New York: Springer-Verlag.

Zasler, N. D. (1991). Pharmacological aspects of cognitive function following traumatic brain injury. In J. S. Kreutzer & P. H. Wehman (Eds.), *Cognitive rehabilitation for persons with traumatic brain injury* (pp. 87–94). Baltimore: Brookes.

Chapter 3

ℒ

The Neuropsychology
of Thinking

To provide effective cognitive rehabilitation, the therapist must first understand the causes of cognitive failure and the effects of damage to the physiological mechanisms that control the thinking process (Banich, 1997; Benson, 1994; Cohen, 1997; Gazzaniga, 1995; Gazzaniga, Ivry, & Mangan, 1998; Giap, Jong, Ricker, Cullen, & Zafonte, 2000; McCarthy & Warrington, 1990; Rugg, 1997; Squire & Butters, 1984). Therefore, this chapter is a brief overview of the anatomical areas of the brain that affect behavior and the relationship of these areas to learning, memory, and cognition. The chapter includes a discussion of Mishkin and Appenzeller's (1987) Integrative Model of Memory as well as additional models of cognition that have been discussed in the neuropsychological literature. The chapter begins with a discussion of the physiological circuitry of memory. We also discuss the physiology of habit and memory and the causes of memory failure. Throughout the chapter, we will try to localize those areas of the brain that are responsible for higher cognitive functions such as language. We do not pretend to survey this literature in depth or even completely. However, other authors have and we therefore refer the reader to several excellent published reviews for a comprehensive treatment of specific issues (Kolb & Whishaw, 1990; Squire & Butters, 1984; Wilson, 1987).

The Physiology of Memory and Cognition

Donald Hebb (1949, 1961) was the first to posit the notion of a cell assembly. He theorized that the synapses that connected the cells in the brain eventually became interdependent through learning. He labeled this physiology the cell assembly. Cell assemblies developed from the repeated firing of adjacent cells that caused a physiological change that was shared by all the cells in the assembly. Eventually, the synapses of adjacent cells formed associations that strengthened the connection. Hebb hypothesized that memory was literally the connection that existed between cells in the larger assembly. This notion persists today. Indeed most of the artificially intelligent computer models of memory are heavily influenced by the cell assembly notion.

Hebb's model assumed that with repeated sensory stimulation, the entire neural loop would eventually form a reverberating circuit. Short-term memory resulted from the collective firing of the cells in the circuit. However, after the stimulation stopped, the circuit would continue to reverberate, which strengthened the connections among the cells in the closed loop. Long-term memory resulted from the consolidation of the cells in this closed circuit. This means that the cells eventually formed into a working assembly that was, literally, long-term memory. Consolidation occurred with ongoing stimulation of the cell assemblies, and it continued for some period of time after the stimulation ceased.

Hebb described the process of consolidation as a permanent change in the neural circuit. He assumed that memory consolidation requires approximately 15 to 60 minutes to take place (Hebb, 1949, 1961). This assumption explains the fact that brain injury usually causes amnesia for events that happened immediately before the injury. He reasoned that the injury disrupted the consolidation process and the disruptions accounted for the amnesia. However, if an event occurred more than 60 minutes before the injury, the consolidation process should have already occurred and, therefore, the memory of the event would be relatively intact. This assumption is certainly consistent with personal experience. For example, most people can recall an instance in which they could not remember where they put something after being interrupted by an important phone call. According to Hebb's theory, the phone call disrupted consolidation of the memory of where the object was placed.

Once consolidated, the neural network that represents the memory could potentially excite others (Herrmann, Ruppin, & Usher, 1993). In Chapter 12, we will discuss this mechanism again under the rubric of *spreading activation*. The notion explains many everyday phenomena such as thoughts that come to mind when a person is in the midst of a conversation. Some aspect of the conversation stimulates a neural loop that, in turn, spreads the activation to another. Memory researchers and neuroscientists have adopted this feature along with almost every aspect of Hebb's work into their theories of cognitive functioning. Indeed, some researchers have asserted that Hebb's reverberating circuit theory is a generally accepted fact of memory physiology (Goddard, 1980).

Where is Memory Located in the Brain?

According to Kolb and Whishaw (1990), memory is not located in any one portion of the brain although certain areas are primarily responsible for processing different aspects of memories. These authors' review of studies of persons who had damaged different parts of the brain indicates that memory is usually disrupted when the brain is damaged, although different types of memory may be affected depending on what part of the brain is damaged. No one area of the brain controls the entire memory process and it is therefore necessary to discuss the roles of several different areas of the brain and their control over various aspects of memory consolidation (Dudai, 1989; Squire, 1987; Squire & Butters, 1984). The gross anatomy of these brain structures is presented in Figure 3.1.

The Temporal Lobes

The temporal lobes are those areas of the brain located near the left and right temples. Milner (1970) showed that damage to the temporal lobes can have devastating effects on memory. He studied patients who had undergone surgical removal of their temporal lobes, specifically, the hippocampus. Surgeons often perform this procedure as a last resort to control a person's epileptic seizures. When studying patients who had the surgery, Milner found that the amount of the brain tissue re-

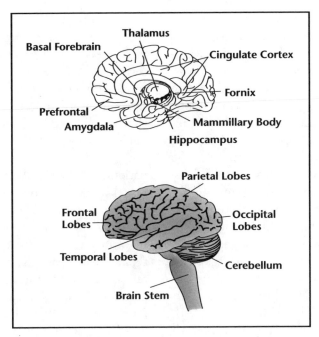

Figure 3.1. Gross anatomy of the brain. *Note.* The top portion of this figure is adapted from *Fundamentals of Human Neuropsychology* (3rd Ed., p. 534) by B. Kolb and I. Q. Whishaw, 1990, New York: Freeman. Copyright 1990 by Freeman. Reprinted with permission.

moved from a person predicted the extent of his or her memory loss.

Kolb and Whishaw (1990) summarized the work of several authors who have reported similar, although more specific, findings (Corsi, 1972; Jaccarino-Hiatt, 1978; Petrides, 1985; Petrides & Milner, 1982). For example, removal of the hippocampal region on patients' right side usually caused them impaired visual memory, but these same patients had little problem recalling verbal information. On the other hand, those patients who had their left hippocampal area removed had just the reverse problem. That is, they could recall visual images reasonably well, but had difficulty remembering verbal information (Corkin, 1965, 1968, 1979; Milner, 1965, 1966, 1968, 1970; Petrides & Milner, 1982; Smith & Milner, 1981). The collective findings suggest that the hippocampus plays a specialized role in memory formation. The left

hippocampal region is partially responsible for remembering verbal information whereas the right hippocampal region records visual information.

Several other areas of the brain contribute to memory formation, such as the mammillary bodies (Kahn & Crosby, 1972; Rizzo, 1955; Victor, Adams, & Collins, 1971), the thalamus (Lishman, 1978; Sprofkin & Sciarra, 1952; Teuber, Milner, & Vaughan, 1968), and the basal forebrain (Mishkin & Appenzeller, 1987). Each of these areas certainly contributes to memory formation in isolation; only recently has anyone described the possible interaction that exists among these brain areas for memory formation.

The Frontal Lobes

Memory deficits often occur after a person experiences damage to the frontal lobes

(Grafman, 1989). This type of injury is common during auto accidents when a person's head hits the steering wheel or the windshield. Boxers also experience frontal lobe damage after repeated blows to the head. The memory impairment that typifies frontal lobe damage is not necessarily the same as that which results from damage to other areas of the brain or from removal of areas like the hippocampus. Persons with frontal lobe damage have a difficult time with organizing, sequencing, and setting time markers that identify the past versus present (Petrides, 1985; Prisko, 1963). In addition, these individuals may not demonstrate common patterns of fatigue as they work. For example, most people fatigue after performing the same task for an extended period. The technical name for the fatigue is *proactive inhibition*. Persons with frontal lobe injury also experience proactive inhibition. When the average person shifts to another unrelated task, he or she will experience a release from proactive inhibition. This means that the person will be able to perform the new task about as well as he or she could when rested. Persons with frontal lobe damage, however, experience considerably less release from proactive inhibition. Indeed, they may experience no release at all, and their performance may continue to decline. Schacter (1987) noted that the continued decline in performance seems to be unique to frontal lobe patients. That is, persons with other types of limbic system brain injury do not show the same effect. It seems that the brain acts as an integrated circuit with different areas taking responsibility for different types of memory and, as was discussed previously, no one area is solely responsible for memory formation.

The Parietal Lobes

The parietal lobes are located on the upper sides of the brain to the top of the cortex. Damage to the rear parietal areas is known to affect memory for where things are located.

Warrington and Weiskrantz (1973) showed that damage to the juncture between the parietal and occipital areas also produced short-term memory loss, specifically, the inability to recall digit strings presented visually. This same memory failure did not occur when the person heard the digits. Damage to the parietal area near its juncture with the temporal lobe had the reverse effect. These patients could recall digit strings presented visually, but could not recall the strings when they only heard them. These findings suggest that the parietal lobes play a significant role in memory formation. The left parietal–temporal area partially controls short-term retention of verbal information, and the right parietal–occipital area controls short-term retention of nonverbal information.

This brief review of the gross anatomy of memory leads to the conclusion that different portions of the mental landscape are responsible for different aspects of memory consolidation. The hippocampus, mammillary bodies, amygdala, basal forebrain, and prefrontal cortex have all been implicated as possible sites where memories are formed. Clearly, brain injury could cause a variety of different types of amnesia depending on which area of the brain sustains the damage. There have been few attempts to map the relationships among the various mental structures and to determine the contribution of each structure to the total process that we call memory. The authors are aware of only one attempt to develop this type of integrative structure-and-function model.

An Integrative Model of Memory Consolidation

Mishkin and Appenzeller (1987) were the first to propose a model of memory consolidation that mapped the interaction of the areas of the brain discussed above. These authors acknowledged that each area contributed something unique to the total memory process. Removal of any one area, for example, the hippocampus, could produce serious memory deficits. The authors noted, however, that removal of only the hippocampus did not totally obliterate memory. Total memory loss usually required removal of the hippocampus and the amygdala. There are other areas of the brain that also affect memory consolidation. For example, the diencephalon which consists of the thalamus, the epithalamus, and the hypothalamus, also is involved in memory consolidation. Damage to this area can affect a person's ability to recognize objects. Mishkin and Appenzeller concluded that the limbic system and the diencephalon share a common circuitry. Destroying any connection in this circuit created memory loss. The entire memory circuit, however, included more than these two structures. The complete model involved the basal forebrain, amygdala and hippocampus, diencephalon, and prefrontal cortex. Each played a separate role in memory formation but the interaction among the various structures also determined memory formation.

Mishkin and Appenzeller's (1987) model includes a feedback loop with the cortex. Accordingly, information is first processed at a sensory level and it is then further processed by the amygdala and hippocampus. The diencephalon, which connects to the prefrontal cortex and the basal forebrain, then processes some of the information sequentially. Once processed by these structures, the information eventually loops back to the sensory receptors. This looping process continually updates our memories and alters our perceptions.

The amygdala and the hippocampus share an especially close relationship. Mishkin and Appenzeller (1987) found that removal of the hippocampus but not the amygdala from nonhuman primates typically produced severe visual and spatial deficits. They concluded that the function of the amygdala is to correlate different sensory memories. The amygdala also controls the release of opiates that result from a person's emotional states. The

opiate-like fibers connect the amygdala to other sensory systems. This network, therefore, controls the emotional reactions people have in different circumstances.

These authors did not specify the actual mechanism of memory consolidation. They did, however, suggest that it would likely take the form of Hebb's (1949, 1961) cell assembly. The notion of a reverberating circuit is a characterizing feature of neural models of memory like Mishkin and Appenzeller's (1987). It is also easy to see how a person's recognition of an experience might result from the activation of the looping structure described by Hebb.

Memory Versus Habit

Since around 1900, psychologists have spoken of learning as a physiological change resulting from practice. For example, Bower and Hilgard (1997) defined learning as a relatively permanent change in performance resulting from practice. The discussion of what is learned has always raised the question of whether memory and learning are two different systems. Some theorists suggest that learning occurs more during a training session, while memory occurs primarily between sessions. None of these theorists, however, felt that learning and memory could be easily separated or that they were necessarily distinct processes (Bower & Hilgard, 1997).

Mishkin, Malamut, and Bachevalier (1984) and Mishkin and Petri (1978) were perhaps the first to hypothesize an actual physiological distinction between memory and learning. These authors assumed that habits were the connections between the things people perceive and the things people do. The habit-forming process does not require a person to engage in high-level thinking; it can occur simply by repetition—the habitual actions eventually occur unconsciously. Indeed, psychologists who study animal behavior and habit learning argued for decades that it was possible to explain most behavior by simply studying people's habits. Other psychologists, however, argued that it was necessary to study higher level cognitions to understand complex human behavior (Tolman, 1932).

Mishkin and Petri (1978) theorized that habits and memories could reside in different areas of the brain. This explanation, if true, would resolve an issue that has generated enormous controversy for learning psychologists for an entire century. These authors assert that habit formation occurs in an ancient cortical structure called the *striatum*. We refer to the striatum as an ancient structure because it evolved in the brain long before the limbic system or the cortex. It is a cluster of nuclei located in the forebrain, positioned in such a way that it can both receive information from a variety of areas of the cortex and it can also send information to motor areas.

Damage to the striatum in nonhuman primates has resulted in impaired habit learning (Mishkin & Appenzeller, 1987). These authors cite research showing that infant and adult monkeys perform at about the same levels on habit-learning tasks, but adult monkeys perform substantially better on memory tests. According to the theory, because the striatum, which mediates habit formation, is fully developed in infant and adult monkeys, both groups should perform equally well when habits are tested. The difference is that adult monkeys have a fully developed limbic system and have the ability to mediate memory. This is not the case with infant monkeys, which accounts for their relatively poor performance on memory tasks.

Higher Cognitive Skills

Location of Language in the Brain

A great deal of research and controversy surrounds the localization of language functions in the brain. Kolb and Whishaw (1990) provided an elegant summary of the history of this controversy. According to their review, Gaul (1880) was the first to hypothesize a relationship between the brain and higher cognitive functions. Dax (1836) first documented several case studies that showed a decrease in language skills after damage to the left hemisphere, and Auburtin (1861) reaffirmed this assertion. About the same time, Broca (1865) demonstrated most clearly that language skills were localized in the left hemisphere and frontal lobe. These portions of the brain later became known as Broca's area, and it became recognized that damage to this area affected the motor functions of speech production. Wernicke (1875) reported that damage to the temporal–parietal cortex, which later was known as Wernicke's area, produced language disorders that were different from those reported by Broca. Wernicke reasoned that Broca's area was the locus of language production whereas Wernicke's area was the locus of language understanding.

Although several areas of the brain have been implicated as possible loci for language, there is no single area that accounts for this higher cognitive skill. Like memory, some intensive mapping of structures will probably be necessary to account for language. The conventional wisdom is that the left hemisphere, including Broca's and Wernicke's areas, are broadly responsible for language production and comprehension. However, other areas also play a role, including the association cortex and the tertiary left temporal cortex, both in the left hemisphere. The contribution of the right hemisphere and the subcortical structures to language is less clear (Kolb & Whishaw, 1990).

Disorders of Language After Brain Injury

There are a variety of language disorders that the cognitive rehabilitation therapist will encounter. *Aphasia* includes several language disorders that are apparent in the client's speech. The term also includes writing and reading disorders called *dysgraphia* and *dyslexia,* respectively. *Fluent aphasia* refers to a person's inability to produce names of objects easily, a person's poor comprehension of what he or she sees or hears, or a person's poor repetition of others' words. The word *fluent* describes a person who has no severe articulation problems. The fluent aphasias described above are usually associated with damage to Wernicke's area, and generally include the inability to comprehend words or to mentally arrange speech sounds to form coherent thoughts. *Nonfluent aphasias,* on the other hand, are usually associated with damage to Broca's area, and include labored speech, poor articulation, poor repetition, and inability to complete sentences. In general, the person can understand speech but has difficulty producing coherent speech (Goodglass & Kaplan, 1983).

The localization of language skills has not been specifically mapped in the brain. What is known suggests that the left hemisphere is responsible for processing syntax, sequences, verbal relationships, rhythm, and grammar. The left and right hemispheres share processing of physical gestures, voice inflection, word recognition, verbal meaning, concept formation, and certain aspects of visual meaning. Although the right hemisphere alone does not play a role in speech production, it does process certain aspects of language such as prosody.

Emotional Perception

Several authors have studied the brain's role in processing emotion. Again, these functions are only grossly localized in the right and left hemispheres. The right hemisphere coordinates a person's perception of others' emotional and facial expressions and a person's ability to correctly match these expressions to pictures (Dekosky, Heilman, Bowers, & Valenstein, 1980; Kolb & Taylor, 1981). The right hemisphere also controls a person's ability to judge mood in others and to interpret speech intonations (Heilman, Scholes, & Watson, 1975; Tompkins & Mateer, 1985). Damage to the left hemisphere results in problems judging propositions and humorous situations (Brownell, Powelson, & Gardner, 1983; Gardner, Ling, Flamm, & Silverman, 1975). In general, although there are certain aspects of the left and right hemispheres that control emotional responses, these areas are not as clearly defined as they are for language.

Higher Spatial Skills

Kolb and Whishaw (1990) have outlined a model of spatial representation. They postulate that the area to the rear of the parietal cortex is responsible for mentally mapping objects in a spatial coordinate system. However, this area of the brain does not identify or classify the objects. That is the function of the temporal cortex. Both areas, the parietal and temporal cortexes, receive information from the sensory cortex and send information to other areas of the brain. The frontal cortex functions to direct movement on the basis of past experience. The parietal cortex functions to direct movement within this coordinate system. The hippocampus integrates information from the temporal cortex and from the parietal cortex to associate and remember both location and identity of objects, and also stores this information in long-term memory.

Spatial disorders after brain injury are of two varieties. The first involves problems with hand–eye coordination. These disorders likely result from damaged connections between the sensory cortex and the posterior parietal cortex or between the frontal cortex and the hippocampus. The second type of spatial disorder involves difficulty with orientation in three-dimensional space. These disorders likely result from damage to the pathways between the sensory cortex and the temporal cortex and between the hippocampus and the frontal cortex (Kapur, 1988; Luria, 1959, 1963, 1973; Mayes, 1988; Talland, 1968).

The Causes of Memory and Cognitive Failure

Wilson (1987) listed a variety of causes of memory and cognitive dysfunction. We begin this section with a discussion of the factors from Wilson's list that we have also found to be common causes, and then discuss the less frequent causes. However, it is likely that a person needing CRT will have multiple problems. For example, brain injuries that result from auto accidents are frequently related to alcohol use. Therefore, many clients may have a history of alcohol and drug use. As a result, the therapist must deal not only with the effects of the injury, but also with a substance abuse problem and the physical and emotional effects of withdrawal.

Brain Trauma

Traumatic brain injury (TBI) is one of the major causes of memory and cognitive failure. Motor vehicle accidents certainly account for a large portion of the head injuries that therapists encounter. There are, however, many other causes of TBI. Penetrating wounds are common in wartime and in inner cities. Compared with motor vehicle accidents, penetrating wounds usually cause less overall trauma to the brain because there is less impact or global movement of the head (Lishman, 1978). Although it is difficult to predict the overall amount of cognitive disruption after a brain injury, the overall severity is roughly indexed by factors such as the extent of the tissue damage, secondary strokes, lack of oxygen to the brain, brain swelling, and cerebrospinal fluid buildup called edema (Miller, 1984). Penetrating

wounds can also cause infections, especially if the penetrating object has fragmented and it is impossible to remove all of the pieces.

Closed head injuries result when there is trauma to the brain without an invasive element such as a missile wound. For example, in many auto accidents, a person's head hits the steering wheel or the windshield. This can cause brain damage at the site of the impact or it can have *contrecoup effects*, meaning that damage has occured not only at the impact site but also on the opposite side (Bloomquist & Courville, 1947). Closed head injuries also create unpredictable damage to the brain because of the rapid acceleration and rotation of the brain within the skull. This causes tearing that damages tissue and disrupts vasculature.

It is difficult to predict how much a person will recover after a TBI. The extent of recovery is grossly related to any of several factors. For example, one good predictor of recovery following brain injury is the length of time a person is amnesic (Russell & Nathan, 1946; Russell & Smith, 1961). Brooks (1972, 1974) indicates that the relationship between recovery and amnesia may also vary depending on a person's age at the time of injury. Of people with TBI, about 30% to 40% of adults experience permanent memory loss, whereas only about 10% of children do (Klonoff & Paris, 1974; Lidvall, Linderoth, & Norlin, 1974; Russell, 1932; Russell & Smith, 1961). How long a person remains in a coma may also predict recovery as well as the extent of the physical damage to the brain (Evans, 1981; Miller, 1984). In general, older patients with extensive brain damage who demonstrate long-term posttraumatic amnesia are more likely to experience permanent deficits than other patients.

Cerebral–Vascular Accidents

Cerebral–vascular accidents (CVAs) are commonly known as *strokes* and typically produce memory and cognitive deficits. Strokes can result from a variety of causes such as blocked arteries, called occlusions or infarctions, or from broken arteries, which result in hemorrhage. Breakage is often caused by aneurysms, embolisms, or ischemias, which reduce blood supply to various portions of the brain, causing cell death and tissue damage. Blocked arteries usually occur in the posterior area of the brain. The condition commonly produces amnesia and can also restrict vision (Benson, Marsden, & Meadows, 1974; Bouldin, Brian, Pepin, & Barbizet, 1968; Dejong, Itabashi, & Olson, 1969; Victor et al., 1971).

Subarachnoid hemorrhages are caused by the rupture of aneurysms and cause blood to flow into the space that surrounds the brain. This type of stroke accounts for about 5% to 10% of CVAs. Aneurysms are swollen or ballooned areas in an artery that fill with blood, and usually occur where the cerebral arteries merge. If this sac of blood ruptures, the sudden loss of blood causes cell damage in the surrounding area. The breakage can result in a variety of symptoms including memory loss, confusion, impaired speech, disorientation, and so forth. How long the disorder persists is related to the extent of the damage, the amount of time before treatment, and the quality of the care received afterward.

Ischemias usually produce a global but temporary loss of memory as well as other cognitive deficits (Fisher & Adams, 1958, 1964; Hecaen & Albert, 1978; Patten, 1971; Shuttleworth & Wise, 1973), and are caused by a temporary constriction of the vasculature, usually in the posterior area of the brain. The constriction creates a sudden blockage or embolism and a resulting lack of blood in a specific area. Ischemic attacks can result from a variety of causes including severe migraine headaches, concussions, epileptic seizures, and hypoglycemia (Kolb & Whishaw, 1990). Transient ischemic attacks may not last long, but they still may cause a substantial loss of memory and may recur (Markowitsch, 1983; Mazzucchi, Moretti, Caffara, & Parma, 1980).

Substance Abuse

Alcohol and drug use often predispose one to a brain injury. Long-term use of drugs or alcohol, however, can also result in slow but measurable cognitive decline. Long-term alcohol use can lead to a thiamine deficiency that results in memory impairment. This is usually part of a larger complex of symptoms called Wernicke–Korsakoff syndrome that includes confusion, disorientation, and uncoordinated movement (Malamud & Skillicorn, 1956). Persons with this disorder typically have problems with short-term memory (Kinsbourne & Wood, 1975). They might also have difficulty recognizing familiar people, places, or things (Butters, 1979, 1984). Tasks that require complex mental switching operations, anticipation, or planning and foresight are also quite difficult for them (Benton, 1968; Corkin, 1979; Squire, 1982). They frequently undergo a noticeable personality change whereby they become docile and passive (Butters, 1979). Wernicke–Korsakoff patients do not, however, show the classic signs of dementia that include limited intellectual functions and abstract reasoning (Talland, 1965).

The *Diagnostic and Statistical Manual of Mental Disorders* (DSM–IV; American Psychiatric Association, 1994) lists a variety of substances that may cause memory and cognitive dysfunction. These problems may occur either during substance withdrawal or during intoxication or both. For example, marijuana users frequently experience memory failure while they are using the drug but the effect vanishes after about a month of withdrawal. Heavy caffeine use may result in temporary loss of cognitive efficiency during withdrawal.

The DSM–IV list includes alcohol, amphetamines, caffeine, marijuana, cocaine, hallucinogens, inhalants, nicotine, opiates, phencyclidine (PCP), and sedatives. Memory and cognitive deficits can result from long-term dependence, abuse, intoxication, or withdrawal. Substance-induced dementia, for example, includes memory impairment, aphasia, limited ability to carry out motor tasks (apraxia), inability to recognize or identify objects by touch (agnosia), and disturbed planning, organization, sequencing, and abstraction.

In our experience, long-term use of specific substances such as inhalants, PCP, alcohol, and amphetamines produces the most cognitive damage. Cognitive deficits can also result from exposure to chemicals such as lead or other toxic compounds, or can occur when a person is withdrawing from nicotine or caffeine. Certain medications such as Propranolol and Dilantin can also limit mental efficiency (Zasler, 1990).

Brain Cancer

Brain tumors will often cause specific cognitive and personality changes. The type of change and its extent depend on the location of the growth (Keschner, Bender, & Strauss, 1938; Selecki, 1964; Williams & Pennybacker, 1954). The problems are exacerbated when the tumors grow to the point where they substantially increase intercranial pressure (Brain, 1963). Whether the tumor is malignant, whether it metastasizes, and the rate of its growth have an obvious effect on cognition. Several authors have noted that tumors located in the frontal lobes produce dementia-like problems including memory loss and poor insight, planning, and organization (Hecaen & Ajuriaguerra, 1956; Sachs, 1950). Sprofkin and Sciarra (1952) noted that memory loss is most likely when the tumor is located in the brain's third ventricle.

Brain Infections

Viral encephalitis and other types of brain infections can also cause severe cognitive defects (Robbins, 1958). For example, the herpes simplex and herpes zoster viruses are known to produce memory loss when infection occurs in the temporal or frontal lobes (Lishman, 1978). Because these infections usually do not occur in the diencephalon structures, the cognitive deficits are more like those of patients who undergo surgery for removal the temporal lobes and less like those of patients with the Wernicke–Korsakoff disorder described earlier (Parkin, 1984). Brain infections can also result from invasive missile wounds, parasites, and ear infections.

Brain Surgery

Surgeries that damage the anterior portion of the hippocampus can produce severe amnesia (Milner, 1966; Penfield & Milner, 1958; Scoville & Milner, 1957). Memory loss does not seem to occur when only the amygdala is removed or damaged. The site of the surgery can have specific effects on memory. For example, removal of a person's left temporal lobe limits his or her ability to learn and remember verbal information but has relatively little effect on visual information. Processing the opposite problem occurs when the right temporal lobe is removed or damaged.

Degenerative Conditions

A variety of degenerative diseases such as Alzheimer's disease, Pick's disease, and Huntington's chorea also produce corresponding memory and cognitive impairment that worsens as a person ages (Wilson, 1987). The behavioral symptoms caused by Alzheimer's disease are similar to those of senility. The disorder occurs in approximately 10% of persons over the age of 65 (Walton, 1971). Memory impairment is usually the first symptom to appear, although the condition often progresses to include other symptoms such as disorientation and loss of ability to abstract and to generalize (Joynt & Shoulson, 1979). Pick's disease begins in the frontal lobes and results in changes in personality and behavior. As the condition progresses, the symptoms eventually become indistinguishable from those of Alzheimer's patients (Walton, 1971). Both of these conditions can produce rapid deterioration and eventual death within 2 to 5 years after diagnosis. Huntington's chorea is an inherited disease and its symptoms usually begin after age 40. The most obvious symptoms include poor control of facial muscles, uncontrolled movements, slowness of processing, and memory loss (Albert, Feldman, &Willis, 1974).

Longevity

Most people report that their memory and thinking skills decline with age. It is possible that the cell assemblies discussed previously in this chapter actually change and that the dendrites of the various brain cells establish new connections that interfere with older memories. It is also possible that young children and adults have very different memory systems. Clearly, verbal skills are poorly developed during infancy and early childhood. During these years, it is possible that memory and thinking is mediated by visual and spatial processes.

Most people have a hard time recalling their infancy although they have clearer recollections of childhood and early school years (Campbell & Spear, 1972). Their memories of the early years are usually distorted by selective attention to photographs and the recollections of parents and relatives. Persons with brain injury frequently report clear recollections of the events of their lives before the brain injury although it is difficult to evaluate the accuracy of their memories. Likewise, the elderly often have clear memories of their early life that are impossible to validate.

As people age, they probably do not lose the stored memories, but they may lose access to them. For example, many people experience a flood of memories when they return to their hometown and visit their childhood home or neighborhood. It is also likely that the priorities for memory and cognitive effort change as people mature. There are a number of explanations for what is observed to be cognitive dysfunction that may not be the result of mental deterioration.

Emotional Status

A person's emotional state also determines his or her ability to think clearly and to remember. Hunt and Ellis (1998) point out that particular emotional states are stored along with memories. It may therefore be difficult for a person to recall specific information unless his or her associated emotion is reinstated. The general phenomenon is that people who are sad show decreased learning and inability to organize and retrieve novel information. The problem is certainly consistent with Mishkin and Appenzeller's (1987) view of the function of the amygdala in memory formation. Hertel (1994) provided an excellent summary of the relationship between emotional state and cognitive functioning.

Other Causes of Cognitive Dysfunction

Some of the less common causes of cognitive dysfunction include temporal lobe epilepsy and electroconvulsive shock therapy. Epilepsy can destroy cells in the hippocampus, and is commonly a problem that accompanies brain injury. Electroconvulsive shock therapy is a procedure used for treatment of severe depression. According to Kolb and Whishaw (1990), the effects are similar to those of patients who experience seizures. The procedure involves applying an electric current to the temporal lobes, which creates a mild convulsion. Patients receive this treatment several times a week and the amount of memory loss is related to the frequency of treatment. Memory returns to near normal levels within a year after the treatments are stopped; however, there may be subtle residual memory loss for autobiographical details (Taylor, Tompkins, Demers, & Anderson, 1982).

Summary

This chapter presented a variety of information concerning the relationship between brain structure, memory, and higher cognitive skills. These relationships have been studied extensively and certain facts about the structure and function of the brain are well documented. For example, damage to the left temporal area usually results in difficulty remembering verbal information whereas damage to the right temporal region creates problems recalling visual information. Spatial information is processed in the parietal region, and the frontal area mediates memory for order, temporal sequence, and priority.

The reverberating circuit proposed by Hebb (1949, 1961) is still generally accepted as the basic physiological mechanism of memory. This model assumes that neurons fire collectively when stimulated and gradually become associated into a circuit that forms memory. When a neuron in the circuit is stimulated, its activation spreads throughout the entire circuit thus reviving the memory.

Although a number of brain structures have been identified that mediate memory and cognition, there are few integrative models that account for the complexity of thought. Mishkin and Appenzeller (1987) proposed one model of memory formation, and Kolb and Whishaw (1990) provided another model of visual–spatial processing. Mishkin and Petri (1978) also suggest that habits and memories are stored in different areas of the brain.

Several different factors account for memory and cognitive decline. Among them, closed head injury, stroke, substance abuse, brain cancer, brain surgery, degenerative diseases, and age usually produce the greatest decline. Some of the less common causes include electroconvulsive shock therapy and epilepsy.

References

Albert, M. S., Feldman, R. G., & Willis, A. L. (1974). The subcortical "dementia" of progressive supranuclear palsy. *Journal of Neurology, Neurosurgery, and Psychiatry, 37,* 121–130.

American Psychiatric Association. (1994). *Diagnostic and statistical manual of mental disorders* (4th ed.). Washington, DC: Author.

Banich, M. T. (1997). *Neuropsychology: The neural base of mental function.* New York: Houghton Mifflin.

Benson, D. F. (1994). *The neurology of thinking.* New York: Oxford University Press.

Benson, D. F., Marsden, C. D., & Meadows, J. C. (1974). The amnesic syndrome of posterior cerebral artery occlusion. *Acta Neurologica Scandinavia, 50,* 133–145.

Benton, A. L. (1968). Differential behavioral effects in frontal lobe disease. *Neuropsychologia, 6,* 53–60.

Bloomquist, E. R., & Courville, C. B. (1947). The nature and incidence of traumatic lesions of the brain: A survey of 350 cases with autopsy. *Bulletin of the Los Angeles Neurological Society, 12,* 174–183.

Bouldin, G., Brian, S., Pepin, B., & Barbizet, J. (1968). Syndrome de Korsakoff d'etiologie arteriopathique. *Revue Neurologique, 119,* 341–348.

Bower, G., & Hilgard, E. (1997). *Theories of learning.* New York: Paramount Communications.

Brain, W. R. (1963). The neurological complications of neuroplasm. *Lancet, 1,* 179–184.

Broca, P. (1865). Sur la faculté du language articulé. *Bulletins et Memoires De la Societe D'Anthropolgie de Paris, 6,* 377–393.

Brooks, D. N. (1972). Memory and brain injury. *Journal of Nervous and Mental Disease, 155,* 350–355.

Brooks, D. N. (1974). Recognition memory and brain injury. *Journal of Neurology, Neurosurgery, and Psychiatry, 37*, 794–801.

Brownell, H. H., Powelson, M. J., & Gardner, H. (1983). Surprise but not coherence: Sensitivity to verbal humor in right-hemisphere patients. *Brain and Language, 18*, 20–27.

Butters, N. (1979). Amnesic disorders. In K. M. Heilman & E. Valenstein (Eds.), *Clinical neuropsychology*. New York: Oxford University Press.

Butters, N. (1984). The clinical aspects of memory disorders: Contributions from experimental studies in amnesia. *Journal of Clinical Neuropsychology, 6*, 17–36.

Campbell, B. A., & Spear, N. E. (1972). Ontogoney of memory. *Psychological Review, 79*, 213, 236.

Cohen, N. (1997). Memory. In M. T. Banich (Ed.), *Neuropsychology: The neural base of mental function* (pp. 314–367). New York: Houghton Mifflin.

Corkin, S. (1965). Tactually-guided maze learning in man: Effects of unilateral cortical excisions and bilateral hippocampal lesions. *Neuropsychologia, 3*, 339–351.

Corkin, S. (1968). Acquisition of motor skills after bilateral medial temporal lobe excision. *Neuropsychologia, 6*, 255.

Corkin, S. (1979). Hidden-figure test performance: Lasting effects of unilateral penetrating brain injury and transient effect of bilateral cinglotomy. *Neuropsychologia, 27*, 585–605.

Corsi, P. M. (1972). *Human memory and the medial temporal region of the brain*. Unpublished doctoral dissertation, McGill University, Montreal, Quebec, Canada.

Dejong, R. N., Itabashi, H. H., & Olson, J. R. (1969). Memory loss due to hippocampal lesions: Report of a case. *Archives of Neurology, 20*, 339–348.

Dekosky, S. T., Heilman, K. H., Bowers, D., & Valenstein, E. (1980). Recognition and discrimination of emotional faces and pictures. *Brain and Language, 9*, 206–214.

Dudai, Y. (1989). *The neurobiology of memory: Concepts, findings, trends*. New York: Oxford University Press.

Evans, C. D. (Ed.). (1981). *Rehabilitation after severe brain injury*. Edinburgh, United Kingdom: Churchill Livingstone.

Fisher, C. M., & Adams, R. D. (1958). Transient global amnesia. *Transactions of the American Neurological Association, 83*, 143.

Fisher, C. M., & Adams, R. D. (1964). Transient global amnesia. *Acta Neurologica Scandinavica, 40*(Suppl. 9), 78–83.

Gardner, H., Ling, H. P., Flamm, L., & Silverman, J. (1975). Comprehension and appreciation of humorous material following brain damage. *Brain, 98*, 399–412.

Gazzaniga, M. S. (Ed.). (1995). *The cognitive neurosciences*. Cambridge, MA: MIT Press.

Gazzaniga, M. S., Ivry, R. B., & Mangan, G. R. (1998). *Cognitive neuroscience: The biology of the mind*. New York: Norton.

Giap, B. T., Jong, N. J., Ricker, J. H., Cullen, N. K., & Zafonte, R. D. (2000). The hippocampus: Anatomy, pathophysiology, and regenerative capacity. *Journal of Head Trauma Rehabilitation, 15*(3), 875–894.

Goddard, G. V. (1980). Component properties of the memory machine: Hebb revisited. In P. W. Jusczyk & R. M. Klein (Eds.), *The nature of thought: Essays in honor of D. O. Hebb*. Hillsdale, NJ: Erlbaum.

Goodglass, H., & Kaplan, E. (1983). *Assessment of aphasia and related disorders*. Philadelphia: Lea & Febiger.

Grafman, J. (1989). Plans, actions, and mental sets: Managerial knowledge units in the frontal lobes. In E. Perecman (Ed.), *Integrating theory and practice in clinical neuropsychology* (pp. 93–138). Hillsdale, NJ: Erlbaum.

Hebb, D. O. (1949). *Organization of behavior*. New York: Wiley.

Hebb, D. O. (1961). Distinctive features of learning in the higher animal. In J. F. Delafresnaye (Ed.), *Brain mechanisms and learning*. London: Blackwell.

Hecaen, H., & Ajuriaguerra, J. (1956). *Troubles mentaux au cours des tumeurs intracraniennes*. Paris: Masson.

Hecaen, H., & Albert, M. L. (1978). *Human neuropsychology*. New York: Wiley.

Heilman, K., Scholes, M. R., & Watson, R. T. (1975). Auditory affective agnosia. *Journal of Neurology, Neurosurgery, and Psychiatry, 38*, 69–72.

Herrmann, M., Ruppin, E., & Usher, M. (1993). A neural model of the dynamic activation of memory. *Biological Cybernetics, 68*, 455–463.

Hertel, P. (1994). Depressive deficits in memory: Implications for memory improvement following traumatic brain injury. *NeuroRehabilitation, 4*(3), 143–150.

Hunt, R. R., & Ellis, H. C. (1998). *Fundamentals of cognitive psychology*. New York: McGraw-Hill.

Jaccarino-Hiatt, G. (1978). *Impairment of cognitive organization in patients with temporal-lobe lesions*. Unpublished doctoral dissertation, McGill University, Montreal, Quebec, Canada.

Joynt, R. J., & Shoulson, I. (1979). Dementia. In K. M. Heilman & E. Valenstein (Eds.), *Clinical neuropsychology*. New York: Oxford University Press.

Kahn, E. A., & Crosby, E. C. (1972). Korsakoff's syndrome associated with surgical lesions involving the mamillary bodies. *Neurology, 22*, 117–125.

Kapur, N. (1988). *Memory disorders in clinical practice*. London: Butterworth.

Keschner, M., Bender, M. B., & Strauss, I. (1938). Mental symptoms associated with brain tumor: A study of 530 verified cases. *Journal of the American Medical Association, 110*, 714–718.

Kinsbourne, M., & Wood, F. (1975). Short-term memory processes and the amnesic syndrome. In M. Kinsbourne & F. Wood (Eds.), *Short-term memory*. New York: Academic Press.

Klonoff, H., & Paris, R. (1974). Immediate, short-term, and residual effects of acute head injuries in children: Neuropsychological and neurological correlates. In R. M. Reitan & L. A. Davidson (Eds.), *Clinical neuropsychology: Current status and applications*. Washington, DC: Winston.

Kolb, B., & Taylor, L. (1981). Affective behavior in patients with localized cortical excisions: Role of lesion site and side. *Science, 214*, 89–91.

Kolb, B., & Whishaw, I. Q. (1990). *Fundamentals of human neuropsychology*. New York: Freeman.

Lidvall, H. E., Linderoth, B., & Norlin, B. (1974). Causes of the postconcussional syndrome. *Acta Neurologica Scandinavia, 50*(Suppl. 56).

Lishman, W. (1978). *Organic psychiatry*. Oxford, United Kingdom: Blackwell.

Luria, A. R. (1959). Disorders of "simultaneous perception" in a case of bilateral occipito-parietal brain injury. *Brain, 82*, 437–449.

Luria, A. R. (1963). *Restoration of function after brain injury*. New York: Macmillan.

Luria, A. R. (1973). *Higher cortical functions in man*. New York: Basic Books.

Malamud, N., & Skillicorn, S. A. (1956). Relationship between the Wernicke and the Korsakoff syndrome. *Archives of Neurology and Psychiatry, 76*, 585–596.

Markowitsch, H. J. (1983). Transient global amnesia. *Neuroscience and Behavioral Review, 7*, 35–43.

Mayes, A. R. (1988). *Human organic memory disorders*. Cambridge, United Kingdom: Cambridge University Press.

Mazzucchi, A., Moretti, G., Caffara, P., & Parma, M. (1980). Neuropsychological functions in the follow-up of transient global amnesia. *Brain, 103*, 161–178.

McCarthy, R. A., & Warrington, E. K. (1990). *Cognitive neuropsychology: A clinical introduction*. San Diego, CA: Academic Press.

Miller, E. (1984). *Recovery and management of neuropsychological impairments*. New York: Wiley.

Milner, B. (1965). Visually guided maze learning in man: Effects of bilateral hippocampal, bilateral frontal, and unilateral cerebral lesions. *Society for Neuroscience Abstracts, 3*, 517.

Milner, B. (1966). Amnesia following operation on the temporal lobes. In C. W. M. Whitty & B. Zangweill (Eds.), *Amnesia*. London: Butterworth.

Milner, B. (1968). Visual recognition and recall after right temporal-lobe excision in man. *Neuropsychologia, 6*, 191–209.

Milner, B. (1970). Memory and the medial temporal regions of the brain. In K. H. Prebram & D. E. Broadbent (Eds.), *Biology of memory*. New York: Academic Press.

Mishkin, M., & Appenzeller, T. (1987). The anatomy of memory. *Scientific American, 256*(6), 80–89.

Mishkin, M., Malamut, B., & Bachevalier, J. (1984). Memories and habits: Two neuronal systems. In G. Lynch, J. L. McGaugh, & N. M. Weinberger (Eds.), *Neurobiology of learning and memory*. New York: Guilford Press.

Mishkin, M., & Petri, L. (1978). Memories and habits: Some implications for the analysis of learning and retention. In L. R. Squire & N. Butters (Eds.), *Neuropsychology of memory* (pp. 287–296). New York: Guilford Press.

Parkin, A. J. (1984). Amnestic syndrome: A lesion-specific disorder? *Cortex, 20*, 479–508.

Patten, B. M. (1971). Transient global amnesia syndrome. *Journal of the American Medical Association, 217*, 690–691.

Penfield, W., & Milner, B. (1958). Memory deficit produced by bilateral lesions in the hippocampal zone. *Archives of Neurology and Psychiatry, 79*, 475–497.

Petrides, M. (1985). Deficits on conditional associative-learning tasks after frontal- and temporal-lobe lesions in man. *Neuropsychologia, 23*, 601–614.

Petrides, M., & Milner, B. (1982). Deficits on subject-ordered tasks after frontal- and temporal-lobe lesions in man. *Neuropsychologia, 20*, 249–262.

Prisko, L. (1963). *Short-term memory for focal cerebral damage*. Unpublished doctoral dissertation, McGill University, Montreal, Quebec, Canada.

Rizzo, E. M. (1955). Sulla sindroma de Korsakoff. *Rassegna di Studi Psichiatrici, 44*, 801–816.

Robbins, C. F. (1958). The clinical and laboratory diagnosis of viral infections of the central nervous system. In W. C. Fields & R. J. Blathner (Eds.), *Viral encephalitis*. Springfield, IL: Thomas.

Russell, W. R. (1932). Cerebral involvement in brain injury. *Brain, 55*, 549–603.

Russell, W. R., & Nathan, P. W. (1946). Traumatic amnesia. *Brain, 69*, 280–301.

Russell, W. R., & Smith, A. (1961). Post traumatic amnesia in closed head injuries. *Archives of Neurology, 5*, 4–17.

Rugg, M. D. (1997). Introduction. In M. D. Rugg (Ed.), *Cognitive neuroscience* (pp. 1–10). Cambridge, MA: Massachusetts Institute of Technology Press.

Sachs, L. (1950). Meningiomas with dementia as the first and presenting feature. *Journal of Mental Science, 96*, 998–1007.

Schacter, D. L. (1987). Memory, amnesia, and frontal lobe dysfunction. *Psychobiology, 15*, 21–36.

Scoville, W. B., & Milner, B. (1957). Loss of recent memory after bilateral hippocampal lesions. *Journal of Neurology, Neurosurgery, and Psychiatry, 20*, 11–21.

Selecki, R. (1964). Cerebral midline-tumors involving the corpus callosum among mental hospital patients. *Medical Journal of Australia, 2*, 954–968.

Shuttleworth, E. C., & Wise, G. R. (1973). Transient global amnesia due to arterial embolism. *Archives of Neurology, 29*, 340–342.

Smith, M. L., & Milner, B. (1981). The role of the right hippocampus in the recall of spatial location. *Neuropsychologia, 13*, 51–58.

Sprofkin, B. E., & Sciarra, D. (1952). Korsakoff psychosis associated with cerebral tumors. *Neurology, 2*, 427–434.

Squire, L. R. (1982). Comparisons between forms of amnesia: Some deficits are unique to Korsakoff's syndrome. *Journal of Experimental Psychology: Learning, Memory, and Cognition, 8*, 560–571.

Squire, L. R. (1987). *Memory and brain*. New York: Oxford University Press.

Squire, L. R., & Butters, N. (1984). *Neuropsychology of memory* (2nd ed.). Newark, NJ: Guilford Press.

Talland, G. A. (1965). *Deranged memory*. New York: Academic Press.

Talland, G. A. (1968). *Disorders of memory*. Harmondsworth, United Kingdom: Penguin.

Taylor, J. R., Tompkins, R., Demers, R., & Anderson, D. (1982). Electroconvulsive therapy and memory dysfunction: Is there evidence for prolonged defects? *Biological Psychiatry, 17*, 1169–1193.

Teuber, H. L., Milner, B., & Vaughan, H. G. (1968). Persistent anterograde amnesia after stab wound of the basal brain. *Neuropsychologia, 6*, 267–282.

Tolman, E. C. (1932). *Purposive behavior in animals and men*. New York: Appleton-Century-Crofts.

Tompkins, C. A., & Mateer, C. A. (1985). Right hemisphere appreciation of intonational and linguistic indications of affect. *Brain and Language, 24*, 185–203.

Victor, M., Adams, R. D., & Collins, G. H. (1971). *The Wernicke–Korsakoff syndrome*. Oxford, United Kingdom: Blackwell.

Walton, J. N. (1971). *Essentials of neurology*. London: Pitman.

Warrington, E. K., & Weiskrantz, L. (1973). An analysis of short-term and long-term memory defects in man. In J. A. Deutsch (Ed.), *The physiological basis of memory*. New York: Academic Press.

Williams, M., & Pennybacker, J. (1954). Memory disturbances in third ventricle tumors. *Journal of Neurology, Neurosurgery, and Psychiatry, 17*, 173–182.

Wilson, B. (1987). *Rehabilitation of memory*. New York: Guilford Press.

Zasler, N. (1990, September). *Pharmacologic approaches to cognitive and behavior dysfunction*. Paper presented at the Conference on Cognitive Rehabilitation and Community Integration, Richmond, VA.

Chapter 4

❧

The Dynamics of
Attention and Memory

Problems with attention and memory are, perhaps, the most common deficits after brain injury (Bennett, Raymond, Malia, Bewick, & Linton, 1998; Manly, Ward, & Robinson, 2002). To provide effective rehabilitation for either of these processes, it is first necessary to understand their basic underlying mechanisms (Cowan, 1995; LaBerge, 1995; Pashler, 1998). We will therefore present a simplified overview of the various concepts and distinctions of attention and memory before discussing how to retrain these processes in Chapter 9.

Attention is a complex mental process. Attention is selective, meaning that it is a preferential process that functions to exclude certain aspects of a person's sensory field (Duncan, 1984; Parasuraman & Davies, 1984). Attention is also modulating because it involves allocation of a person's cognitive processes depending on the situation. Other aspects of attention include *signaling* and *vigilance*, meaning that attention can alert a person to important aspects of the environment and the person can choose to sustain his or her attention and to allocate processing when attention is overloaded (Kahneman & Triesman, 1984).

Models of Attention

Early- Versus Late-Selection Models

An ongoing debate in the early literature on attention was the question of where attention occurred within the broader cognitive process. Early-selection models, such as the switch and attenuator models discussed in this chapter, assumed that selective attention occurs *before* information reached long-term memory. This theory assumed that information is filtered before it is processed. Late-selection models of attention assume that all or most of the sensory information registers in long-term memory, but a person simply cannot respond to more than a fraction of the information at any one time. People with brain injury have problems that can be explained by either of these theories. These people frequently seem overwhelmed in situations where there is much information to process simultaneously. It is unclear, however, whether they are screening out most of the information or whether they are unable to organize all that they perceive.

Early-Selection Models

Perhaps the earliest models of attention came from Broadbent (1958) who proposed a *switch* model. The idea behind this model was that a person switches attention back and forth between competing sources. Various aspects of incoming information, such as the hearing of one's name, control the switching process. This process occurs quite rapidly and a person seldom notices when the switching of focus occurs. Attention failure results when the switching mechanism breaks down. For example, a person may not be able to stay focused on any individual event or conversation in a noisy room because he or she would be unable to allocate processing to one conversation to exclude another. The implication for cognitive rehabilitation is that remediation must retrain the switching process. For example, Craine and Gudeman (1981) suggested procedures such as dichotic listening as therapy for attention problems after brain injury. In this task, different messages are played into each ear simultaneously and the client is asked to repeat the facts of one message while purposely screening out the other.

Triesman (1964) postulated an *attenuation* model of attention. Her basic assumption was that attention is controlled by a filtering mechanism. Both physical and semantic cues controlled the amount of attention a person would give to any specific event. For example, when engaged in a conversation, the volume of a person's voice controls attention, but so does the quality of the message. This model explains a person's uncanny ability to switch attention when he or she detects his or her name in a conversation across the room. Triesman likened the process to a set of filters that would open in relation to the amount of attention an object or event demanded. Under this model, attention failure could be the result of any number of causes: limitations of the size of the filters, inability to open more than one filter, or the inability to inhibit the cues that control filtering. For remediation, it may therefore be necessary to train a client with attention deficits to focus on the dominant filter, eliminate distracting cues, or eliminate internal distractions that arise from thought intrusions.

Late-Selection Models

The assumption of the late-selection models of attention is that all information registers in long-term memory; however, it is difficult to process two different registrations at the same time (Deutsch & Deutsch, 1963; Norman, 1968). The implication is that attention deficit results from an inability to organize a response to seemingly overwhelming information. Accordingly, a client's ability to attend could be dramatically improved by limiting the amount of information he or she registers.

Capacity models of attention assume that the ability to attend is related to the process of allocating mental resources within a limited capacity system. Capacity refers to the amount of a person's consciousness that is taken by any given task. This theory assumes that attention is the process of allocating, prioritizing, managing, or otherwise organizing a response to incoming information so that various aspects of the task receive appropriate amounts of processing. Attention failure is presumably due to either reduced capacity or limited ability to allocate. Examples of both are quite common after brain injury. For example, people with brain injury have a reduced memory for digit spans, which measures short-term memory capacity. People with brain injury also commonly have reduced ability to perform mental control and switching operations within the limited capacity short-term memory store. One way to treat these disorders is to develop skills to become automatic so that they do not take up much capacity. Teaching encoding strategies can also help to compress information into a form that can be processed by the limited capacity system.

Selective Attention Models

Duncan (1984) summarized various types of visual attention theories that differ mainly in terms of the unit of analysis for a person's selective attention. None of these was specifically designed to explain an attention deficit after brain injury although each makes some interesting theoretical suppositions concerning the nature of attention failure. These models are described below.

Discrimination-based models assume that attention differs in terms of the number of separate discriminations a person can make in a given time frame. For example, analyzer theory assumes that people analyze simple features like lines and angles with specific mental filters (Hunt & Ellis, 1998). Difficult discriminations, such as those between the faces of identical twins, involve similar features and the interplay of similar analyzers. Perceptual difficulties arise when similar analyzers conflict with each other. Although there is no strong evidence for this type of theory, it is conceivable that people with brain injury have difficulty attending because the number and variety of analyzers they have is restricted or they are unable to control the various conflicting analyzers present for a particular task.

Space-based models liken attention to a mental spotlight or a zoom lens (Triesman & Schmidt, 1982) where information in the focus can be analyzed to the relative exclusion of everything else. The unit of analysis is therefore the span of the focal area. Accordingly, it is possible that an attention deficit after brain injury is due primarily to a restriction of this mental spotlight. Difficulties arise because a person's range of input is restricted, creating impoverished selections from the total array of information (Posner, 1973). This theory is consistent with findings reported by Parenté, Anderson-Parenté, and Shaw (1989) and by McClur, Browning, Vantrease, and Bittle (1994). These studies investigated problems with iconic memory resulting from traumatic brain injury. Iconic memory is immediate visual memory, which allows a person to store virtual snapshots of the world for a brief period. Iconic memory is the first stage of the visual memory system and if it is damaged, then other processing of information is incomplete or distorted.

Object-oriented models are some of the oldest models of attention. The unit of analysis is the number of objects that can occupy a person's perceptual field at any one time (Neisser, 1967). Neisser's model assumes that attention involves a preattentive stage where a person's focus point is divided into separate areas or separate object groupings. The division is controlled by Gestalt principles such as proximity, similarity, good continuation, closure, and so forth, which occur in parallel. Kahneman and Henik (1977) reported that these object groupings, once formed, retain their integrity. The second stage of Neisser's model involves focal attention, which occurs as a serial process across the various object groupings. This means that a person first forms perceptual groups and then allocates attention to each group in sequence. For example, a single man who enters a bar during happy hour to meet a single woman would first scan the bar looking for groups of women who seem to be without dates. Within each group is at least one potentially interesting woman to meet. The man then scans these women individually and sequentially, finally focusing on one woman to approach. This model predicts that limited attention may occur if, in the first stage, the person cannot form perceptual object groups, and in the second stage, the person performs a slow, incomplete, or inefficient serial search process. In the example, a shifting crowd, loud music, or the smell of food if he is hungry may distract the single man in the bar and keep him from perceptually grouping the women. The serial search process may be slowed because other men may approach his first or second choice, forcing him to reorganize the sequence or to reprioritize his choices. To date, there have been no applications of this model for rehabilitation although the notion of stages of attention underlies popular models of attention training like the one proposed by Sohlberg and Mateer (1987).

This discussion of attention theory is admittedly incomplete. Our purpose is to present some of the better developed models and to extract any implications from each theory for brain injury rehabilitation. Regardless of which theory is correct, there is general agreement on several points that may help a therapist understand and treat attentional problems after brain injury. Most theorists would agree that attention deficits might be due to a breakdown of basic sensory processes, which can often be rectified by simple interventions such as hearing aids, glasses, and so forth. These theories point out that there are a variety of forms of attention, such as the ability to allocate mental resources, to avoid distraction, and to mentally switch from task to task. It may therefore be necessary to work with the specific aspects of attention failure in isolation. Attentional problems usually will require restricting the amount of distraction a person encounters. For example, we have found that having a client wear earplugs while reading can greatly improve his or her attention to the reading material. Further, there is value in a hierarchical retraining regime whereby the therapist retrains simpler attentional processes such as orientation and vigilance first, followed by more complex attentional processes such as selective attention, divided attention, and the allocation of mental effort.

The Relationship Between Attention and Memory

Our discussion of attention has so far been as a separate process from memory. But it is actually difficult to separate the two processes. Without attention, there could be no memory. Without memory, it would be difficult to direct attention. Although the model presented next was designed to summarize memory processes, it is probably safe to say that the attentional processes described previously occur in parallel. This means that attention simply expands or enhances the functioning of these memory components. For example, a person usually processes advertisements received via e-mail only cursorily. If a person received a letter, however, saying that he or she had won the lottery, that person's interest and attention would greatly increase his or her memory for the details of the letter. It is, therefore, important not to think of memory and attention as separate processes. They work in tandem; attention simply amplifies the memory process.

There are a variety of well-developed models of attention and memory and excellent summaries of these models are generally available (e.g., Ellis & Hunt, 1993). Most of these were never intended for use as models of traumatic brain injury rehabilitation. Parenté and DiCesare (1991) provided a simplified memory model that could be used to understand memory deficits after brain injury. This model is presented in Figure 4.1.

Figure 4.1 is a diagram of the workings of various memory processes. The sensory memory store is thoroughly discussed in Chapter 8. In this chapter, we focus on the working memory. This is a particular portion of the cognitive system that is responsible for processing information so that it can be stored and retrieved easily. There are two aspects of the working memory that are important to rehabilitation. The first involves a person's ability to rehearse information and maintain it in memory for further processing. The second is the ability to transform the information into a form that can be easily stored and retrieved. Maintenance rehearsal is discussed in Chapter 10 and again in Chapter 13.

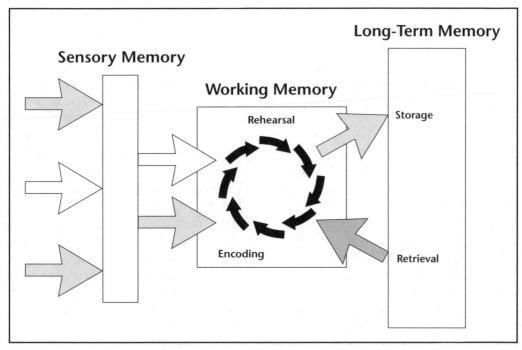

Figure 4.1. Simplified model of memory. *Note*. Adapted from "Retraining Memory: Theory, Evaluation, and Application," by R. Parenté and A. DiCesare, 1991, in *Cognitive Rehabilitation for Persons with Traumatic Brain Injury: A Functional Approach* (p. 148), by J. S. Kreutzer and P. H. Wehman (Eds.), 1991, Baltimore: Brookes. Adapted with permission.

Once information has been transformed in the cognitive system's working memory, it is stored in long-term memory. It is retrieved from long-term memory when a person needs to use it again. People with brain injury seldom have a problem storing information in long-term memory. Their usual problems include (a) the inability to generate the appropriate cues necessary for retrieval from long-term memory, (b) the inability to manipulate information in the working memory, and (c) the inability to rehearse effectively.

This model has several implications for brain injury rehabilitation. First, if the sensory system is impaired, then little information will get into the working memory. (Two chapters, Chapters 8 and 11, have been devoted to the topic of retraining the sensory and working memories.) Second, memory strategy training is only effective if a client can rehearse effectively. Without rehearsal,

the information is lost from the working memory and no strategy will help store it in long-term memory. Finally, it is crucial that therapy focus on the retrieval process. This involves teaching a client techniques for cuing and for using prosthetic devices. This topic is discussed in detail in Chapter 24.

This chapter is concerned primarily with the mechanism that creates mental transformations of information. These mental transformations are called *encodings* and their purpose is to make storage and retrieval of information quicker and more efficient. The ability to transform information in working memory is central to the process of remembering. Simply rehearsing information repeatedly ensures only that we can maintain it in the working memory. The ability to store and to retrieve information from long-term memory depends on a person's ability to transform it in working memory (Ellis, Parenté, Grah,

& Spiering, 1975; Ellis, Parenté, & Walker, 1974). Without encoding, a person is doomed to process most of life's events in a literal form, which may be quite difficult to retrieve. For example, the reader can appreciate the encoding that occurs as he or she reads the pages of this book. The reader does not remember each word, but rather the gist or meaning of each section. At first, the information registers in a literal form. However, with additional reading the meaning combines with stored experiences, and the reader can see meanings that were not initially apparent. Then the reader organizes the information into broad themes and subthemes. Only the themes are typically remembered. Theme encoding still occurs after brain injury, just at a slower pace. The goal of therapy therefore is to teach a client techniques for speeding up the encoding process. This type of training could involve any number of strategies. Some of the more common encoding strategies are discussed next.

Image codes are mental pictures that integrate information into a visual scene. For example, most people can conjure an image of their mother's face or favorite movie star. Although injury to the right side of the brain may limit a person's ability to use visual imagery, most people with brain injury can use imagery as an especially powerful memory aid. For example, in Chapter 12 we discuss how therapy clients can use imagery to recall names and faces or to remember what they read in books, magazines, and newspapers.

Verbal labels are symbols, words, or phrases that integrate meaning into a verbal unit. Most verbal labels can take on several different meanings. For example, the letter A can suggest the first letter of the alphabet. If printed in scarlet, it can suggest adultery. The word *cat* can suggest a household feline, a lion, a tiger, or an angry woman. Verbal labels are the basis for several different memory strategies including the word mnemonic

where each letter of a word signals recall of a sequence of events. Verbal labels are also especially helpful for encoding unfamiliar visual information. For example, it may be easier for a therapy client to navigate the floor plan of a building if he or she is shown that it is shaped according to a letter of the alphabet.

Motor codes are procedures learned from motor movements. Often, the only way a person can remember the procedures is to perform them. For example, it may be difficult for a guitarist to give lessons without demonstrating chord patterns on a guitar fret. Similarly, typists usually must demonstrate finger placements on a keyboard to teach others how to type. After considerable practice, motor codes may translate into verbal labels. For example, a specific fret pattern on a guitar becomes associated with an A minor or an E flat. Because people with brain injury can learn and remember motor procedures about as well as anyone else, motor codes are an especially valuable strategy for therapy. Learned combinations of motor codes may translate into employable skills. For example, a person can use motor codes to learn important phone numbers by simply typing them onto a phone's number pad 50 times. He or she might not be able to say the numbers but will be able to touch them in the appropriate sequence on a phone's number pad.

Auditory codes form memories of what a person hears. This includes conversation recollection, the nonverbal aspects of speech that are carried in voice inflections, music, warning signals, and so forth. Indeed, because much of a person's daily experience involves auditory coding of conversation, listening skills are essential for processing the aspects of spoken language that convey meaning in conversations, lectures, the media, and so forth. The LISTEN mnemonic is presented in Chapter 12; the therapist can use this technique to train effective listening skills with their clients.

Distinctions of Memory

There are different types of memory and the therapist must understand the differences between them to correctly diagnose and work with people with memory impairment. We therefore discuss some of the more common distinctions and their implications for brain injury rehabilitation.

Recognition Versus Recall

Recall is what most people think of as memory. Recall is a relatively difficult memory process that requires an active search of memory. Recognition refers to information that is right before a person's eyes; he or she has to either identify it as familiar or unfamiliar, or pick out a familiar item from several unfamiliar items. Recognition therefore involves a matching process in which a person processes an object in immediate sensory memory and transfers it automatically into the long-term store. This matching process essentially bypasses the retrieval process. People with brain injury typically do not have as much difficulty with recognition as they do with recall. They may therefore have relatively little difficulty performing jobs that require inspection of details or recognition of flawed materials or missing features.

Availability Versus Accessibility

This distinction involves the question of whether people with brain injury lose information from memory or whether they simply lose access to it. The bulk of evidence favors the latter explanation. For example, when given appropriate cues, people with brain injury can remember quite well. In general, it seems that people with brain injury lose the ability to cue themselves spontaneously. The implication for treatment is that the therapist must teach techniques for cuing. These may be internal memory strategies or the use of external prosthetic devices.

Levels of Processing Versus Cognitive Effort

Most people would agree that one has only a shallow understanding of a person after meeting him or her for the first time. After years of friendship or acquaintance, one knows him or her at a deeper level. This is because the working memory is constantly processing people, things, and events at different levels. The shallowest level of encoding involves syntactical, acoustical, or concrete features, whereas the deeper levels involve semantic encoding. The deeper the level of processing, the better the recall. However, people with brain injury do not rapidly process information at deep levels; the coding strategies outlined in Chapter 12 can help a person with brain injury process information deeply.

An alternative to the levels of processing theory is the *cognitive effort* notion (Hasher & Zacks, 1979; Tyler, Hertel, McCallum, & Ellis, 1979), which refers to the amount of the working memory that is taken by the encoding operation. This concept purports that it is not the depth of processing that determines recall but the amount of effort a person makes in processing information. Although there have been no experimental distinctions between these two concepts with people with brain injury, it is likely that a person's memories are also determined by the amount of cognitive effort he or she invests. It is perhaps safe to say that depth of processing is a manifestation of the amount of cognitive effort afforded the task. The implication for the therapist is that effortful processing is necessary for effective recollection. The therapist should therefore encourage a client to activate as many senses as possible when trying to learn. The senses are mental gates. To open them one must concentrate. Cognitive effort is the amount of the mental system taken up by a sensory experience. For example, a veteran soldier may be able to process the gist of a letter he just received from a loved one while in the midst of a battle, whereas an inexperienced soldier may be overwhelmed by the noise and confusion.

Semantic Versus Episodic Memory

Semantic memory is a person's mental storehouse of logically related information (Tulving, 1972). Examples of semantic memory include the knowledge that an airplane is a means of transportation, a dog is a canine, or that dark clouds suggest rain. Episodic memory refers to the ability to retain the novel episodes of daily life such as what clothes a person wore yesterday. Episodic memory is the logical precursor of semantic memory because it is likely that a person must store several episodes before he or she can extract meaning or knowledge from them. This distinction between semantic and episodic memory is important because people with brain injury often confuse their memory deficits. For example, people will often say they have "short-term memory loss." Actually, their short-term memories are reasonably unaffected by the injury. For example, they can remember most novel information quite well for a few seconds. The real deficit involves episodic memory formation (Baddeley, 1982; Kinsbourne & Wood, 1975). The implication is that the therapist should teach the client strategies for processing novel episodic information.

Anterograde Versus Retrograde Amnesia

Anterograde amnesia is common after a brain injury, whereas retrograde amnesia is far less common. Anterograde amnesia refers to the inability to recall new information. Retrograde amnesia is the inability to recall events that happened before the injury. For example, most people with brain injury report that they can remember their personal histories well but have difficulty remembering what someone said the previous day.

Most people with brain injury will demonstrate episodic memory loss. In some cases, the therapist may be able to build on information and skills a person had before the injury. Because the knowledge and skills a person had before the injury are spared, he or she may be able to return to gainful employment if the tasks required are routine and do not involve new learning.

Procedural Versus Declarative Memory

Procedural memories are skills or action patterns a person can learn. For example, learning how to type, how to operate a machine, or how to perform any other routine or repetitive task involves procedural learning. Squire (1982) more formally described procedural knowledge as the ability to "develop in memory a representation based on experience that changes the way an organism responds to the environment without affording access to the specific instances that led to this change" (p. 560). Declarative memory refers to the ability to learn things such as words, faces, letters, numbers, and the facts that can be deduced from this information.

A fascinating finding is that these two types of memory can exist independently of one another. People with brain injury who are taught a skill will often learn the skill but forget the study sessions (Squire, 1982, p. 560). The obvious implication is that people with brain injury can learn employable skills even if they do not remember the training.

Why People with Brain Injury Forget

There are several reasons why anyone can forget what he or she experiences. One reason is that memories may decay over time. *Decay theory* is one of the oldest models of memory and assumes that memories are like furrows that rain may create as it runs down the side of a mountain. Forgetting occurs because, eventually, the furrows are effaced by the natural actions of wind and sun (Harrell, Parenté, Bellingrath, & Liscicia, 1992). The theory predicts that the best way to remember anything is to renew the memory through rehearsal. The implication of this theory for brain injury rehabilitation is that rehearsal training is, perhaps, the most valuable of therapies because rehearsal maintains the memory trace.

Consolidation explanations of forgetting assume that when a person rehearses information, the brain undergoes structural changes that store the memory permanently. Whereas decay theory assumes that forgetting occurs because the memory trace degrades over time, consolidation theory assumes the memory is a dynamic process that occurs at both conscious and unconscious levels. Anything that interrupts the consolidation process interferes with the quality of the stored memory. The implication is that people with brain injury must ensure that consolidation is not disrupted. The therapist should advise the client that it is important to rehearse information as soon after the original experience as possible to ensure that the information is consolidated. Rehearsing the information within the first hour after the initial experience creates a vivid memory that is superior to that which would be created with several hours of rehearsal the following day. Indeed, as much as 70% of what a person perceives initially may be lost the following day without rapid rehearsal.

Interference explanations of memory failure have several variants. All of them assume that forgetting occurs because other information interferes with what a person is trying to remember. Proactive interference occurs when our memories are disrupted by a buildup of prior experience. For example, waiters become progressively less able to remember customers' names as the day goes on due to interference from all of the preceding customers.

Retroactive interference occurs when a person cannot recall something from the past because of something just learned. For example, recalling anything from the day before is easier after a good night's sleep than it is after a day of hectic wakefulness. This is because the information from the waking hours retroactively interferes with the information that preceded it. The implication is that memories are strongest when a person rehearses the information and protects the consolidation with a period of relative mental inactivity. For example, making entries into a diary before retiring at night can greatly facilitate memory of the day's activities.

The process of forgetting in clinical populations has also been summarized in the literature on amnesia. Meudell and Mayes (1982) described amnesia as a difficulty learning new information, recalling old information, and poor attention and concentration on an immediate task. In many situations, a person with amnesia may have intact reasoning and cognition skills. Wilson (1987) provided an especially cogent review of this concept.

According to Wilson (1987), one theory of amnesia assumes that people with brain injury lose the ability to allocate cognitive effort effectively. They may have problems paying attention to incoming information or cannot remain attentive for more than a few minutes. Distraction and the inability to screen out irrelevant information may also be an issue. Although the theory seems plausible on the surface, the research evidence is conflicting (Butters & Cermak, 1980; Mayes, Meudell, & Neary, 1978; Meudell & Mayes, 1982; Moscovitch, 1982; Wilson, 1987). Huppert and Piercy (1978) suggested that amnesia is caused by a failure of automatic processing of information. This refers to an inability to process information without effort, almost unconsciously (Hasher & Zacks, 1979). The theory implies that the mechanism for memory may not be damaged as much as the ability to remember without conscious effort.

Wilson (1987) also discussed two types of storage theories. The first assumes that brain injury causes more rapid decay of information. However, there is little experimental evidence for this theory (Brooks & Baddeley, 1976; Huppert & Piercy, 1978). The second type of storage theory assumes that brain injury disrupts the consolidation process. Weiskrantz and Warrington (1979) pointed out several problems with this theory. For example, people with amnesia often do well on recognition and cued recall tasks. They can also learn procedures reasonably well. These types of learning could not occur if the consolidation process was disrupted.

Wilson (1987) identified another broad class of explanation of amnesia that implicates the retrieval process. One version assumes that retrieval failure occurs because of interference from extraneous information (Warrington & Weiskrantz, 1970). For example, people with brain injury often fail to distinguish familiar from unfamiliar information (Gaffan, 1972). They also have difficulty recognizing how certain information may be associated with related information (Brooks & Baddeley, 1976). It is also difficult for them to distinguish the contexts in which different events occurred (Winocur & Kinsbourne, 1978). These results suggest that information is confused at the time of recall.

Summary and Evaluation

Despite a great deal of research effort, no clearly plausible theory of amnesia has emerged. There are, however, several findings about memory and memory failure after brain injury that are worth reiterating. The bad news is that people with brain injury have a difficult time remembering semantically related information or the gist of verbal passages or conversations. They do not store information about the time an event occurred, incidental facts about the event, or specific details. They do not recognize associations among unstructured pieces of information. They will probably not recall most novel experiences without cuing and will not retain skills without extensive overlearning.

The good news is that people with amnesia can learn procedures to high levels of proficiency even when they have no memory for the study sessions (Cohen & Corkin, 1981; Newcomb & Ratcliff, 1979; Starr & Phillips, 1970). They can recall information when appropriate cues are provided. They can learn a variety of verbal and motor skills such as line-drawing reproduction (Williams, 1953), word reproduction (Warrington & Weiskrantz, 1970), defect detection (Warrington & Weiskrantz, 1982), verbal association (Warrington & Weiskrantz, 1982), and word list recall (Twum, 1994). They also benefit from memory strategy training (Parenté, Twum, & Zoltan, 1994).

It is our opinion that brain injury limits a person's ability to automatically transform information in the working memory. Before brain injury, memory operations such as attention, rehearsal, organization, and mental transformation of new information occurred at an unconscious level (Huppert & Piercy, 1978). After brain injury, a person loses his or her ability to execute these mental operations unconsciously. Consequently, people with brain injury must learn to consciously rehearse, attend, concentrate, and manipulate information in working memory. Eventually, through conscious effort, the processes become unconscious again.

Our research and clinical experience indicates that most people with brain injury have not lost their capacity for memory and thinking. Instead, they must make extra efforts to remember while they acquire new compensatory skills. With practice, some of the acquired skills may become automatic like their native skills were prior to injury.

References

Baddeley, A. D. (1982). Amnesia: A minimal model and an interpretation. In L. Cermak (Ed.), *Human memory and amnesia*. Hillsdale, NJ: Erlbaum.

Bennett, T., Raymond, M., Malia, K., Bewick, K., & Linton, B. (1998). Rehabilitation of attention and concentration deficits following brain injury. *Journal of Cognitive Rehabilitation, 16*(2), 8–13.

Broadbent, D. E. (1958). *Perception and communication*. London: Pergamon Press.

Brooks, D. N., & Baddeley, A. D. (1976). What can amnestics learn? *Neuropsychologia, 14,* 111–122.

Butters, N., & Cermak, L. S. (1980). *Alcoholic Korsakoff's syndrome*. New York: Academic Press.

Cohen, N. J., & Corkin, S. (1981). *The amnestic patient. H. M.: Learning and retention of a cognitive skill*. Paper presented at the meeting for the Society of Neuroscience, Los Angeles.

Cowan, N. (1995). *Attention and memory: An integrated framework*. New York: Oxford University Press.

Craine, J. H., & Gudeman, H. E. (1981). *The rehabilitation of brain function*. Springfield, IL: Thomas.

Deutsch, J. A., & Deutsch, D. (1963). Attention: Some theoretical considerations. *Psychological Review, 70,* 80–90.

Duncan, J. (1984). Selective attention and the organization of visual information. *Journal of Experimental Psychology: General, 113,* 501–517.

Ellis, H. C., & Hunt, R. R. (1993). *Fundamentals of human memory and cognition*. Dubuque, IA: Brown.

Ellis, H. C., Parenté, F. J., Grah, C. R., & Spiering, K. (1975). Coding strategies, perceptual grouping, and the "variability effect" in free recall. *Memory and Cognition, 3,* 226–232.

Ellis, H. C., Parenté, F. J., & Walker, C. W. (1974). Coding, varied input versus repetition in human memory. *Journal of Experimental Psychology, 102,* 619–624.

Gaffan, D. (1972). Loss of recognition memory in rats with lesions to the fornix. *Neuropsychologia, 10,* 327–341.

Harrell, M., Parenté, R., Bellingrath, E. G., & Liscicia, K. A. (1992). *Cognitive rehabilitation of memory: A practical guide*. Gaithersburg, MD: Aspen.

Hasher, L., & Zacks, R. T. (1979). Automatic and effortful processes in memory. *Journal of Experimental Psychology, 108,* 356–388.

Hunt, R. R., & Ellis, H. C. (1998). *Fundamentals of cognitive psychology*. New York: McGraw-Hill.

Huppert, F. A., & Piercy, M. (1978). The role of trace strength in recency and frequency judgements by amnestic and control subjects. *Quarterly Journal of Experimental Psychology, 30,* 346–354.

Kahneman, D., & Henik, A. (1977). Effects of visual grouping on immediate recall and selective attention. In S. Dornic (Ed.), *Attention and performance* (Vol. 1, pp. 307–332). Hillsdale, NJ: Erlbaum.

Kahneman, D., & Triesman, A. (1984). Changing views of attention and automaticity. In R. Parasuraman & D. A. Davies (Eds.), *Varieties of attention*. New York: Academic Press.

Kinsbourne, M., & Wood, F. (1975). Short-term memory and the amnestic syndrome. In D. D. Deutsch & J. A. Deutsch (Eds.), *Short-term memory*. New York: Academic Press.

LaBerge, D. (1995). *Attentional processing: The brain's art of mindfulness*. Cambridge, MA: Harvard University Press.

Manly, T., Ward, S., & Robinson, I. (2002). The rehabilitation of attention. In P. J. Eslinger (Ed.), *Neuropsychological interventions* (pp. 105–136). New York: Guilford.

Mayes, A. R., Meudell, R. R., & Neary, D. (1978). Must amnesia be caused by either encoding or retrieval disorders? In M. M. Grudeberg, P. E. Morris, & R. N. Sykes (Eds.), *Practical aspects of memory*. London: Academic Press.

McClur, J. T., Browning, R. T., Vantrease, C. M., & Bittle, S. T. (1994). The iconic memory skills of brain injury survivors and non-brain injured controls after visual scanning training. *NeuroRehabilitation, 4*(3), 151–156.

Meudell, P. R., & Mayes, A. R. (1982). Normal and abnormal forgetting. In A. W. Ellis (Ed.), *Normality and pathology in cognition functions*. London: Academic Press.

Moscovitch, M. (1982). Multiple dissociation of function in amnesia. In L. Cermak (Ed.), *Human memory and amnesia*. Hillsdale, NJ: Erlbaum.

Neisser, U. (1967). *Cognitive psychology*. New York: Appleton-Century-Crofts.

Newcomb, F., & Ratcliff, G. (1979). Long-term consequences of cerebral lesions. In M. Ganannio (Ed.), *Handbook of behavioral neurology* (Vol. 2). New York: Plenum Press.

Norman, D. A. (1968). Toward a theory of memory and attention. *Psychological Review, 75,* 522–536.

Parasuraman, R., & Davies, D. A. (Eds.). (1984). *Varieties of attention*. New York: Academic Press.

Parenté, R., Anderson-Parenté, J. K., & Shaw, B. (1989). Retraining the mind's eye. *Journal of Head Trauma Rehabilitation, 4,* 53–62.

Parenté, R., & DiCesare, A. (1991). Retraining memory: Theory, evaluation, and applications. In J. S. Kreutzer & P. H. Wehman (Eds.), *Cognitive rehabilitation for persons with traumatic brain injury: A functional approach* (p. 148). Baltimore: Brookes.

Parenté, R., Twum, M., & Zoltan, B. (1994). Transfer and generalization of cognitive skill after traumatic brain injury. *NeuroRehabilitation, 4*(1), 25–35.

Pashler, H. E. (1998). *The psychology of attention*. Cambridge, MA: MIT Press.

Posner, M. I. (1973). *Cognition: An introduction*. Glenview, IL: Scott Foresman.

Sohlberg, M. M., & Mateer, C. A. (1987). Effectiveness of an attention-training program. *Journal of Clinical and Experimental Neuropsychology, 9*(2), 117–130.

Squire, L. R. (1982). Comparison between forms of amnesia: Some deficits are unique to Korsakoff's syndrome. *Journal of Experimental Psychology: Learning, Memory, and Cognition, 8,* 560–571.

Starr, A., & Phillips, L. (1970). Verbal and motor memory in the amnestic syndrome. *Neuropsychologia, 8,* 75–82.

Triesman, A., & Schmidt, H. (1982). Illusory conjunctions in the perception of objects. *Cognitive Psychology, 14,* 107–141.

Triesman, A. M. (1964). Selective attention in man. *British Medical Bulletin, 20,* 12–16.

Tulving, E. (1972). Episodic and semantic memory. In N. E. Tulving & W. Donaldson (Eds.), *Organization of memory.* New York: Academic Press.

Twum, M. (1994). Maximizing generalization of cognitions and memories after traumatic brain injury. *NeuroRehabilitation, 4*(3), 157–167.

Tyler, S. W., Hertel, P. T., McCallum, M. C., & Ellis, H. C. (1979). Cognitive effort and memory. *Journal of Experimental Psychology: Human Learning and Memory, 5,* 607–617.

Warrington, E. K., & Weiskrantz, L. (1970). Amnestic syndrome: Consolidation or retrieval. *Nature, 228,* 628–630.

Warrington, E. K., & Weiskrantz, L. (1982). Amnesia: A disconnection syndrome? *Neuropsychologia, 20,* 233–248.

Weiskrantz, L., & Warrington, E. K. (1979). Conditioning in amnestic patients. *Neuropsychologia, 17,* 187–194.

Williams, M. (1953). Investigations of amnestic deficits by progressive prompting. *Journal of Neurology, Neurosurgery, and Psychiatry, 16,* 14.

Wilson, B. (1987). *Rehabilitation of memory.* New York: Guilford Press.

Winocur, G., & Kinsbourne, M. (1978). Contextual cuing as an aid to Korsakoff amnestica. *Neuropsychologia, 16,* 671–682.

Chapter 5

❧

Theories and Models of Recovery

Problems with thinking and memory can result from TBI, degenerative diseases, gunshot wounds, drug overdoses, sports injuries, toxic chemical exposure, and so forth (Broek, 1999; Eslinger, 2002). In most cases, it is quite difficult to predict the course of recovery because the traumatic experience differs markedly for each person. In some cases, the problems are mild and the recovery process is quick and complete. More frequently, however, the recovery process occurs quite rapidly at first, and then the person's cognitive functions level off and eventually stabilize at a level clearly lower than before the injury (Carlesimo, 1999; Wilson, 1999). Indeed, in many cases the person's cognition never improves to its premorbid level. In most cases, though, rehabilitation can improve the person's cognitive skills to the point where he or she can function independently around the home or return to some form of self-sustaining employment.

This chapter presents an overview of the literature on recovery of cognitive skills after brain injury or as a result of degenerative processes (Kashima, Kato, Yoshimasu, & Muramatsu, 1999). This topic is central to the therapy process because most parents and family members will have questions about the therapy client's long-term outlook. Unfortunately, many therapists are simply unaware of the literature on this topic and are therefore unable to give cogent answers. The theories of recovery that do exist are rather poorly developed and vague; most do not provide statements that a therapist could use to direct treatment.

Our purpose is not to summarize these theories in detail or to build a case for or against any one of them. Several authors have made these comparisons and we refer the reader to these sources for a comprehensive review (Kolb & Whishaw, 1990; Miller, 1984; Parenté & Stapleton, 1993). Miller (1984) grouped these theories into three broad classes: brain plasticity theories, functional adaptation models, and artifact theories. He pointed out that these are broad groupings with considerable overlap. Although each class of recovery theory describes the same process, each is concerned with different aspects. None is generally accepted by most therapists, nor can any predict the recovery outcome for any individual therapy client. We have interpreted these theories loosely to extract any aspects that would dictate an optimal treatment regime or provide suggestions for treatment to enhance recovery. Our purpose in reviewing these models is to provide an overview of the basic concepts of recovery. We begin by describing various models and mechanisms of recovery, then discuss various intervention models that can be used to facilitate recovery. We end with a developmental model of recovery that summarizes our observations on the return of functioning after brain injury.

Theories of Recovery

Brain Plasticity Theories

Several authors have discussed the notion of anatomical reorganization, which is the idea that different areas of the brain reorganize as a natural consequence of injury and that the undamaged areas take over the functions of the damaged areas (Devor, 1982; Munk, 1878; Rosner, 1974). This is, perhaps, the oldest model of recovery. The model assumes that the reorganization is hierarchical, meaning that higher cortical areas can take over the functions of lower cortical areas, although the process cannot occur in reverse (Taylor, 1931).

Munk (1878) proposed a slightly different notion of brain plasticity. In his theory, the brain would reorganize only as long as it needed to do so. If one area was damaged but recovering, other areas assumed its functions until it was repaired or recovery plateaued. Then the damaged area would resume its previous activity at whatever level was possible. In some cases, the recovery was complete, but in most cases, some form of reorganization remained even after the person's functioning stabilized. Although this aspect of the reorganization model alluded to the importance of training after brain injury to facilitate the reorganization process, it did not make any clear suggestions that would direct treatment.

Functional Adaptation Models

Alexander Luria (1963) was the first to assert that recovery of cognitive function is largely a process of learning new ways to reach the same goals. Called functional adaptation, this model assumed that recovery was a compensatory process whereby a person learns new ways of doing what he or she did before. Although the brain plasticity and functional adaptation models share certain similarities, the latter requires fewer assumptions. For example, the functional adaptation model does not need to assume that brain structures reorganize or change their function. The only assumption is that humans can learn compensatory behaviors and that brain functions are flexible and can accommodate this type of new learning. According to the functional adaptation model, the degree of residual flexibility and the extent to which certain skills were spared following injury generally predict the amount of recovery. The advantage of the functional adaptation model is that it has clear implications for treatment. Treatment should emphasize teaching the person to do what he or she did before using different methods.

Artifact Theories

According to Miller (1984), artifact theories assume that damage to the brain produces irreversible effects. Moreover, the damage causes secondary and temporary disturbances in other parts of the brain. Recovery may seem to occur because the disturbances in these secondary areas resolve, producing rapid, but usually incomplete, return of function. The areas of primary loss, however, will never recover completely, resulting in permanent functional impairment. Artifact theories assume that some types of cognitive impairments are transient only because the apparent damage is due to temporary disturbance that eventually resolves.

Von Monakow (1914) discussed one type of transient phenomenon of recovery called *diaschisis*. Although the exact mechanism of diaschisis is unclear, the basic idea is that injury to the brain produces a primary damage site as well as secondary damage to collateral sites. The secondary damage results in temporary reduction of cognition, and the type of dysfunction may not resemble that which would normally be associated with the primary lesion site. The effect is as if the primary damage caused a shock wave that traversed the brain and caused damage as it passed through the tissue (Uzzell, 1986).

When the collateral areas begin to regenerate, the person experiences some recovery, though it may be incomplete. It is assumed that recovery does not result from regrowth or regeneration of receptors, the regeneration of damaged mechanisms, or the reorganization of brain functions. Instead, this theory assumes that the collateral tissues are only temporarily disabled because severe wave motion caused the damage, which disturbed the various connections between cells as the severe motion passed through the brain. Moreover, what seems to be global dysfunction may quickly resolve, leaving only minor, but relatively permanent, disorders. Unfortunately, there is little the artifact model can do to predict the extent of the diaschisis effect, and it provides even less in the way of functional suggestions to expedite recovery.

Miller (1984) provided a lucid summary of artifact, brain plasticity, and functional adaptation theories of recovery. He asserted that there are many similarities among these models, and that they are best described as interesting notions that are still in the early stages of development. Each explains certain aspects of recovery; however, none is obviously superior to another. Indeed, the major problem with these models is that most lack implications for planning treatment. Instead, they simply describe ways therapists can conceptualize cognitive dysfunction.

In summary, recovery cannot be explained by any single theory. It is safe to say, however, that in the early stages of recovery, the artifact theory is probably the most logical account. The physiological changes that occur during this period could easily account for rapid but short-lived improvement in a person's cognitive status. In the later stages of recovery, the functional adaptation model is the most applicable; therapy should emphasize compensatory training. The anatomical reorganization model is perhaps the better theory to explain recovery in developing systems, such as in young children with TBI.

Physiological Mechanisms of Recovery

Much of what we call recovery may be an artifact of some physiological process that occurs after brain injury. There are, however, several well-documented phenomena that occur with damaged tissue that are known to account for much of what we normally think of as recovery. Most involve changes in the cells or the interrelationship among cells as they regenerate. Although the theoretical mechanisms have been summarized in some detail (Kolb & Whishaw, 1990; Miller, 1984), the underlying physiological processes are neither well researched nor well understood. Consequently, we can only provide the gist of the various concepts and assert that none of the mechanisms discussed here is clearly the most viable description of physiological changes after injury to the brain. Indeed, it is likely that most, if not all, of these processes play a role in recovery.

The first type of processes involves regeneration of cells or tissue, including rerouting and sprouting. These processes re-create an interface among the damaged cells. The last four physiological processes involve improvement in the extent to which the cells can excite one another. These mechanisms include vicariation, denervation supersensitivity, silent synapses, and disinhibition. Each of these processes compensates for the lessened area of cortical synapse resulting from brain damage.

Cell Regeneration

The cell regeneration notion assumes that brain cells create new connections to the area that was previously damaged (Barrett & Gonzalez-Rothi, 2002; Giap, Jong, Ricker, Cullen, & Zafonte, 2000). Cell regeneration occurs in amphibians and in the human peripheral nervous system (Sperry, 1965). Some researchers have tried to stimulate cell regeneration in adults with brain damage. For example, Kolb and Whishaw (1990) described a substance called nerve-growth factor that physicians can inject into the damaged site to facilitate regeneration. Other researchers have used brain tissue transplants to provide a tissue bridge for the cells to reconnect a previously damaged area (Kromer, Bjorklund, & Stenevi, 1980). The transplantation of embryonic tissue may have the same effect. These techniques are still in their infancy although the initial results are promising.

Lynch, Deddwyler, and Cotman (1973) demonstrated that brain cells will *sprout* branches that take over the space left vacant by damaged tissue. Their research showed that undamaged cells send sprouts into damaged areas along with other fiber systems from adjacent portions of the cell. These cells, which are not connected with the damaged cells, grow into the vacated area. The process is quite rapid, usually occurring in the first 7 to 10 days after the injury. This new cell network promotes recovery of function in the damaged area.

Rerouting, another form of cell regeneration, involves the establishment of new connections after cells' normal pathways are disrupted. Although rerouting and sprouting provide hope that the brain can regenerate its neural connections, there is little evidence that either process occurs beyond the site of the original insult. Moreover, both types of neural activity are common only in younger, developing organisms. In addition, there is little evidence that rerouting or sprouting can compensate for the majority of degenerative events that typically follow brain injury or that occur after the onset of a degenerative disease.

Excitatory Mechanisms

Vicariation is a substitution mechanism. Some portion of the brain that was not heavily used before the injury begins to function after the injury because it must now take over the function of the damaged area. In essence, an undamaged area of the brain that is directly adjacent to the damaged area may take over the damaged area's functions. Vicariation is not strictly anatomical reorganization because the reorganization is not necessarily hierarchical. The takeover of function can occur by any number of different means.

Denervation supersensitivity refers to the idea that recovery can occur due to increased receptor sites and hypersensitivity to neurotransmitters in the brain receptor sites. In essence, more receptors become available and respond to stimulation (Ungerstedt, 1971). The notion assumes that the receptor synapses that were spared from injury become supersensitive to compensate for the reduction in the number of synapses following injury. LaVere (1975, 1980) reported that this process is especially noticeable in younger organisms and in cases where biochemical toxins, for example, cause brain lesions after destruction of the dopamine terminals of the cells (Kolb & Whishaw, 1990).

Silent synapses are connections that only begin to function after existing cells are damaged. Brain injury is assumed to activate dormant synapses or to lessen inhibition, allowing previously silent synapses to take over the functions of the damaged cells.

Most brain functions result from a complex interplay of systems that are activated and inhibited. *Disinhibition* occurs when the normal inhibitory action on one system lessens, allowing another system to function faster or with greater efficiency. For example, when anticholenestrase drugs such as physostigmine or neostigmine remove the inhibition of acetylcholine production, the brain is allowed to produce more of this neurotransmitter, which should facilitate cognition. Geschwind (1974) attributed disinhibition to the recovery of language skills. Although language is learned in and resides in both hemispheres, people typically rely on their dominant hemisphere for speech and other verbal processing. In essence, a person's dominant hemisphere inhibits his or her nondominant hemisphere. When the dominant hemisphere is damaged, the subordinate hemisphere becomes disinhibited, which leads to the recovery of language.

Intervention Models of Recovery

Many interventions designed to improve cognition after brain damage have been proposed. They include (a) surgical tissue transplants, (b) nutrient and drug treatments, (c) direct retraining, (d) environmental changes, (e) use of prosthetic devices, (f) stimulus–response conditioning, (g) process training, (h) strategy substitution, and (i) cognitive cycle. Because time and space do not permit a full discussion of these areas, the reader is referred to the appropriate references in each of the following sections.

Tissue Replacement

One of the most exciting areas of research into the recovery of function involves the physical replacement of damaged brain tissue. The sprouting and rerouting processes of regeneration discussed previously could conceivably be enhanced if a new medium replaced the damaged tissue to permit growth of the axons. Although this idea is not new (Bjorklund & Stenevi, 1985; Low et al., 1982), no one yet has proposed a well-developed or generally accepted treatment. As described by Kolb and Whishaw (1990), tissue replacement begins with the dissection of tissue from a fetal brain which contains undeveloped embryonic cells. The tissue is then treated to remove blood vessels and glia. Finally, the treated tissue is injected directly into an injured brain at the site of damage along with supplemental nerve-growth factor, which enhances the receptivity of the existing tissue. This process seems relatively immune to the body's normal rejection of foreign cellular material as long as fetal tissue is used and a supply of blood is sent rapidly to the transplanted tissue. Transplanting tissue seems to work best when it is placed directly into the damaged area. However, the transplant procedure can still be successful if the tissue is placed somewhere else because the embryonic cells can travel through the nervous system to the damaged area (Dunnett, Low, Iversen, Stenevi, & Bjorklund, 1982; Zimmer, 1981).

Nutrient and Drug Interventions

Several pharmacological interventions may improve cognition after brain injury. Many of these drugs have been used to treat memory deficits secondary to degenerative disease like Alzheimer's disease (Chase, 1984; Conners, 1984; Cooper & Herrmann, 1988; DeNoble, 1986; Dilanni, 1985; Zagler & Black, 1985). See Chapter 22 for a complete review of this topic.

Direct Retraining

Direct retraining of cognition is, perhaps, the most controversial model of neurotraining

(Parenté & Anderson-Parenté, 1991) because there is little evidence that it improves functioning more than one would expect due to passage of time alone. These techniques involve exercising a person's mind in accordance with his or her pattern of deficits. For example, if a person has difficulty with memory, then the therapist would provide mental exercises that stimulate memory. Although this type of therapy makes sense, it is not necessarily grounded in physiological or learning theory. Following the anatomical reorganization theory outlined previously, mental exercise might hasten the brain's reorganization process, but there is little empirical evidence to support this notion (Schacter & Glisky, 1986).

Cicerone et al. (2000), Bach-y-Rita (1980), and Gross and Shutz (1986) surveyed the cognitive rehabilitation literature and have provided cogent summaries of various techniques along with useful suggestions to help a therapist select appropriate techniques. Briefly, simple stimulation therapy, such as conversations, games, and physical activity, seems to help during the early stages of recovery. Also, forcing a therapy client to use a dysfunctional system can facilitate recovery. For example, if a person has limited use of his or her left arm after a stroke, then inhibiting the use of the right arm forces recovery of the left. A therapist who uses stimulation therapy should organize the exercises from simple to complex (Ben-Yishay, Piasetsky, & Rattok, 1987; Sohlberg & Mateer, 1987). The training should relate to the therapy client's real-life experiences and the therapist should provide clear incentives for good performance. Treatment should continue even after the client's progress begins to plateau.

Environmental Changes

Changing a client's environment is a passive model of treatment with the goal of making life easier for the client. The methods for or-ganizing a person's environment outlined in Chapter 14 are effective in a work setting. Certain electronic environmental control devices can take over functions for a person. For example, a device that turns lights on and off at certain times of day ensures that a person does not leave lights on for extended periods of time. Motion-sensitive switches can turn lights on and off when a person enters or leaves a room. Such devices also increase safety because the person does not need to remember things such as turning off appliances or lights.

Prosthetic Devices

Cognitive orthotics are devices that replace some memory or cognitive function with an external device (Herrmann & Petro, 1990; Parenté & Anderson-Parenté, 1991; Parenté & Stapleton, 1993). The goal is to train a person to use a device to obviate the person's need to perform the mental activity. For example, the therapist may train a person to use a small dictation tape recorder to remember conversations or complex instructions. A beeping pillbox can remind a person when it is time to take medication. Even simple devices such as checklists can remind a person of tasks he or she must complete each day. A complete list of prosthetic devices is provided in Chapter 24.

Stimulus–Response Conditioning

A basic assumption of any reinforcement theory of behavior is that behavior depends on the effect it produces. The behavior therapist's approach to rehabilitation therefore involves identifying potential rewards or punishments, then providing or withholding them to produce a desired change. Behavior therapists view complex behaviors as sequences of simple behaviors that change with appropriate rewards; conditioning occurs most rapidly when the simpler behaviors can be trained separately. Once a person has learned the smaller parts, the therapist can merge them into a complex behavior.

Process Training

Unlike the stimulus–response model, process training assumes that unobservable mental abilities are made up of microskills or subprocesses that a therapist can train separately. The therapist focuses on treating the subprocesses, which presumably strengthens the underlying global process and transfers to activities of daily living. For example, Chapter 8 presents an iconic training model that facilitates reading comprehension. The therapy client is first trained to group larger units of information in iconic memory. The client learns to efficiently scan text using more efficient eye movements. Finally, the client learns to apply these two skills to a more complex task such as reading.

Strategy Substitution

Strategy substitution is one of the oldest active rehabilitation models. Unlike direct retraining, which requires a client to perform mental push-ups, the client learns to compensate for memory and cognitive limitations by learning new organizational strategies. The therapist chooses strategies that will generalize to a variety of situations (Parenté & Stapleton, 1993). These strategies are discussed at length in Chapters 11 through 19.

Cognitive Cycle

Gross and Shutz (1986) proposed the following model, which is designed to train complex executive skills such as problem solving and decision making:

Step 1: *Self-Identification of Goals*. A person identifies exactly what he or she wants to achieve in any situation.

Step 2: *Conditional Thinking*. The person learns to generate options, ideas, or behaviors that may produce the goals identified in Step 1.

Step 3: *Planning*. The person generates a plan of action based on Step 2.

Step 4: *Reaching Goals*. The person learns that goals are obtained by following the behavioral action plan.

Step 5: *Feedback Assessment*. The person evaluates the outcome of the action plan.

Step 6: *Cognitive Cycling*. If the person does not achieve the goal, then he or she cycles though the entire process again.

Cognitive cycling requires skills such as the ability to anticipate consequences and to evaluate results of behavior. The person must also be able to initiate and self-monitor his or her behavior. Consequently, the cognitive cycle model may be appropriate only for therapy clients in later stages of recovery.

Summary and Evaluation

Most of the intervention models discussed in this chapter are appropriate for use at certain stages of recovery. Most assume that a client can learn new information and is motivated to do so. They also assume that a client will actively attempt to transfer these new skills to novel situations. When a client cannot learn rapidly, then passive intervention methods, such as nutrients and drugs, surgery, or environmental control, may be the only applicable models of rehabilitation. If a client can learn, then stimulus–response training or strategy substitution are more useful. The use of prosthetic devices may help a client who can learn but who shows limited ability to generalize his or her knowledge. If a client can learn and generalize, the therapist has several additional treatment options, including most of the techniques already mentioned. If a client can self-monitor and demonstrate some executive behavior skills, then the cognitive cycle system is worth trying.

A Developmental Model of Recovery

Parenté and Anderson-Parenté (1991) proposed a purely functional model of recovery that was designed to provide suggestions for the course of treatment at each stage of recovery. Because the major purpose of the model is to suggest different types of treatment that are appropriate at various stages of recovery, their model is not a formal theory of recovery although it does generally follow the same stages that are outlined in other treatment models (Ben-Yishay et al., 1987; Sohlberg & Mateer, 1987). It is, in essence, a description of successive therapeutic steps, with specific training at each step that will facilitate the next.

Stage 1: Arousal–Orientation

In the earliest stages of recovery, a person may not know his or her name, recognize loved ones, or know the day, month, or year. The first level of recovery focuses on the person's recapture of these basic faculties. Treatment at this level, typically in an acute care facility, usually begins shortly after a person emerges from a coma. Most of the time, the person is confused, disoriented, combative, and potentially violent. Family members are especially concerned because this is the stage where the person's behavior is least predictable. For example, it is always disquieting when a person fails to recognize family members and friends who visit or is unable to recall biographical information.

The goal at this stage is to orient the person in time and place and to person. Most people gradually relearn names, faces, and once-familiar places and events. The combativeness and verbal abusiveness subside as the person regains a sense of personal identity. Therapy that orients the person in time and place may be especially effective at this stage of recovery. Simple paired-associate training with pictures and names of family members can also be effective. Personal fact repetition tapes can also be used. Family members provide lists of personal facts about the person's life and the therapist records these facts onto an audiotape. The person then listens to the tape each day and the therapist or family quizzes the person until he or she can recall correctly the entire list of facts. The family then makes another list of facts and the process continues. Anything that reestablishes the network of personal knowledge is important at this stage. Family members can be especially useful allies because they are usually patient and can provide familiar materials, pictures, and personal information (Corregan, Arnett, Houck, & Jackson, 1985).

Stage 2: Attention and Vigilance

After the person regains a sense of personal orientation, he or she will usually begin to show increases in ability to maintain focus and vigilance on a particular task. Attention and vigilance are central to any higher level cognitive skill (Buchtel, 1987). Attention training is a multifaceted process (see Chapter 9). It assumes that the person is oriented and can maintain attention for some period of time. In the earliest stages, it may not be distinguishable from vigilance, which is simply the ability to maintain focus for increasingly longer periods. Attention training does not necessarily require a great deal of mental work. For example, the person may play computer games and the therapist may record how long he or she can maintain the activity regardless of the score the person achieves. The first measure is an index of vigilance and the second is a measure of concentration and performance. The Sohlberg and Mateer (1987) attention-process training model may be especially useful at this stage of recovery. Although these training activities may require high-level attention and concentration, they usually do not require memory. At this stage the goal is to have the person be able to maintain focus for some sustained period of time regardless of whether he or she can remember the activity.

Stage 3: Mental Control

Once a person can maintain vigilance, then improvements in concentration or performance become apparent. These improvements are not immediately obvious until the person can maintain focus long enough for the therapist to measure concentration, active processing, and mental control. There is no clear distinction between these terms; they all refer to the act of mental manipulation, transforming novel information into easily retrievable units, or otherwise performing some form of mental activity that results in a measurably correct response. This mental flexibility is essential for processing higher level information and for using strategies. It is also what most people associate with quickness of thought. Chapter 11 deals with this type of retraining.

Training at this stage typically involves providing a person with tasks that require active processing but do not necessarily involve memory. For example, a person could practice tasks that require mental manipulation such as solving anagrams or mental math problems. The latter stages of the Sohlberg and Mateer (1987) attention-process training program are suitable for use at this stage. Attention training requires some amount of mental control; however, in the authors' view, this stage

of recovery requires more concentration than attention.

Stage 4: Rehearsal

Many people report spontaneous recovery of simple strategies such as repetition. Indeed, many report that simply going over things again and again is the only method that seems to help them to remember. Usually, they reach this conclusion after having transcended the above stages. Rehearsal is the first stage of memory skill recovery, which must precede higher level memory strategy training. Rehearsal is the ability to maintain information in memory for some period of time so that the person can then apply various encoding strategies that will make the information available and accessible in the future. Memory strategies are usually useless until the person can first rehearse effectively. Moreover, the person cannot rehearse unless he or she can first attend and concentrate.

Chapters 10 and 13 discuss rehearsal training in detail. Briefly, it involves training a person to first rehearse consciously, then eventually getting the person to rehearse automatically. The therapist's goal is threefold. First, the therapist must illustrate the importance of rehearsal. Second, the person should see that his or her memory can improve dramatically simply by rehearsing. Third, the therapist must show the person how many rehearsals will be necessary. This third point is perhaps the most important aspect of this level of recovery. The extent to which the person can rehearse determines the success or failure of the stages to follow.

Stage 5:
Recovery of Episodic Memory

During this stage of recovery, a person regains the ability to remember the novel episodes of life. Success at this stage usually requires more than teaching a person to do mental push-ups or to attend to video games. It involves teaching the person to use memory strategies that he or she has not used before. This level of recovery may take years because the person may have difficulty using the strategies or may not do so spontaneously. Using memory strategies may be difficult for most people, especially those who did not use them before the injury. These strategies are more complex than stimulation therapy; they teach a person a new way of remembering.

Stage 6: Higher Order Cognition

Many people never reach this stage of recovery. It involves learning how to reason, solve problems, make decisions, set goals, and prioritize (Sternberg & Smith, 1988). Recovery of these skills requires several prerequisites such as the ability to attend and concentrate, to rehearse, and to remember. Chapters 12 through 15 present specific therapy techniques that may be useful with most people. As with any of the methods discussed in this text, the therapist must direct the training so that the person sees how it is personally relevant. For example, when teaching problem solving, the therapist should focus the technique on the person's current problems. This process is an art requiring creativity on the part of the therapist.

Stage 7: Recovery of Social Competence

The final stage of recovery involves the regaining of more subtle social skills (Broek, 1999). Retraining these skills may be especially difficult because the person may never have had good social skills. Nevertheless, this is an especially important area of recovery because it affects every aspect of the person's so-cial life. For example, training may involve helping a person recognize subtle social cues such as a conversation partner's constant checking of his or her watch. The relearning process usually requires active participation such as role playing or modeling, and it may require new learning of social cues such as body language. In our experience, this stage of recovery is seldom spontaneous or complete. It usually requires a great deal of therapy effort. Moreover, there are few discussions of training procedures that can guide the therapist (see Chapters 19 and 21).

These stages of recovery are loose descriptions of cognitive milestones after brain injury. People do not typically make rapid or consistent progress as they ascend through the various stages. Without therapy, many people may never progress past the second or third stage. Some people may never learn higher cognitive skills and those who are severely impaired do not attain a high level of social competence. Some may plateau at the third or fourth stage. The therapist must remember that the stages are progressive and, therefore, he or she will not be able to skip any stage. Many failures of treatment can be attributed to an attempt to ascend the hierarchy of recovery too rapidly.

Summary

This chapter summarizes several theories and systems of recovery after brain injury. Broad groupings of recovery theories after brain injury include brain plasticity, functional adaptation, and artifact theories. Brain plasticity models assume that the brain reorganizes itself and that the higher level areas take over the functions of the damaged areas. However, the lower areas cannot assume the functions of the higher ones. The functional adaptation model suggests that the most expedient route to recovery involves teaching the person new ways of doing things that he or she used to do.

The artifact model assumes that the damage is permanent and that recovery is the result of spared skills returning after being temporarily disabled.

Groups of physiological mechanisms of recovery include those that describe the regeneration of connections among neurons and those that describe enhanced excitatory processes among undamaged cells. The first group includes several replacement mechanisms whereby new connections are established via collateral sprouting, rerouting, or by chemicals such as nerve growth factor. Excitatory mechanisms explain recovery by the stimulation of mechanisms that are functioning at a low level or by creating new connections that previously did not function. These mechanisms include disinhibition, silent synapses, and denervation supersensitivity.

A number of intervention strategies were discussed in this chapter, including tissue transplants and drug and nutrient treatments. Various models of recovery were also discussed. These include cognitive rehabilita-

tion, which emphasizes the direct stimulation of cognitive functions. Process training is a variant of the cognitive rehabilitation model, which focuses on stimulation of specific areas of cognition that are thought to directly transfer to other areas. The prosthetic device model emphasizes use of external aids to obviate a problem with cognition. The cognitive cycle model is designed to teach a recursive reasoning process. The stimulus–response model is an application of learning and conditioning principles to effect behavioral control during recovery.

A developmental model of recovery was also presented that emphasizes return of function across a broader time span. Several stages were identified including orientation, vigilance, mental control, rehearsal, episodic memory, higher order cognition, and social competence. Different therapy procedures were described that are appropriate at each stage of recovery.

References

Bach-y-Rita, P. (Ed.). (1980). *Recovery of function: Theoretical considerations for brain injury rehabilitation*. Bern, Switzerland: Hyuber.

Barrett, A. M., & Gonzalez-Rothi, L. J. (2002). Theoretical bases for neuropsychological interventions. In P. J. Eslinger (Ed.), *Neuropsychological interventions* (pp. 16–37). New York: Guilford Press.

Ben-Yishay, Y., Piasetsky, E., & Rattok, J. (1987). A systematic method for ameliorating disorders in basic attention. In M. Meier, A. Benton, & L. Diller (Eds.), *Neuropsychological rehabilitation* (pp. 165–181). New York: Guilford Press.

Bjorklund, A., & Stenevi, U. (1985). *Neural grafting in the mammalian central nervous system* (Fernstrom Foundation Series, Vol. 5). New York: Elsevier.

Broek, M. D. van den (1999). Cognitive rehabilitation and traumatic brain injury. *Reviews in Clinical Gerontology, 9*, 257–264.

Buchtel, J. A. (1987). Attention and vigilance after head trauma. In H. S. Levin, J. Grafman, & H. M. Eisenberg (Eds.), *Neurobehavioral recovery from head injury*. New York: Oxford University Press.

Carlesimo, G. A. (1999). The rehabilitation of memory. In G. Denes & L. Pizzamiglio (Eds.), *Handbook of clinical and experimental neuropsychology* (pp. 887–897). New York: Psychology Press.

Chase, C. H. (1984). A new chemotherapeutic investigation: Piracetam effects on dyslexia. *Annals of Dyslexia, 34*, 272–278.

Cicerone, K. D., Dahlberg, C., Kalmar, K., Langenbahn, D. M., Malec, J. F., Bergquist, T. F., Felicetti, T., Gaicino, J. T., Harley, P., Harrington, D. E., Herzon, J., Kneipp, S., Laatsch, L., & Morse, P. A. (2000). Evidence-based cognitive rehabilitation: Recommendations for clinical practice. *Archives of Physical Medicine and Rehabilitation, 81*, 1596–1615.

Conners, C. (1984). Piracetam and event-related potentials in dyslexic children. *Psychopharmacology Bulletin, 20*, 667–673.

Cooper, H., & Herrmann, W. M. (1988). Psychostimulants, analeptics, nootropics: An attempt to differentiate and assess drugs designed for the treatment of impaired brain functions. *Pharmacopsychiatry, 21*, 211–217.

Corregan, J. D., Arnett, J. A., Houck, L., & Jackson, R. D. (1985). Reality orientation for brain-injured patients:

Group treatment and monitoring of recovery. *Archives of Physical Medicine and Rehabilitation, 66,* 626–630.

DeNoble, V. (1986). Vinpocetine: Nootropic effects on scopolamine-induced and hypoxia-induced retrieval deficits in step through passive avoidance response in rats. *Pharmacology, Biochemistry, and Behaviour, 24,* 1123–1128.

Devor, M. (1982). Plasticity in the adult nervous system. In L. S. Illis, E. M. Sedgwick, & H. J. Glanville (Eds.), *Rehabilitation of the neurological patient.* Oxford, United Kingdom: Blackwell.

Dilanni, M. (1985). The effects of piracetam in children with dyslexia. *Journal of Clinical Psychopharmacology, 5,* 272–278.

Dunnett, S. B., Low, W. C., Iversen, S. D., Stenevi,Y., & Bjorklund, A. (1982). Septal transplants to restore maze learning in rats with fornix–fimbria lesions. *Brain Research, 251,* 335–348.

Eslinger, R. J. (Ed.). (2002). *Neuropsychological interventions.* New York: Guilford Press.

Geschwind, N. (1974). Late changes in the nervous system: An overview. In D. G. Stein, J. J. Rosen, & N. Butters (Eds.), *Plasticity and recovery of function in the central nervous system.* New York: Academic Press.

Giap, B. T., Jong, C. N., Ricker, J. H., Cullen, N. K., & Zafonte, R. D. (2000). The hippocampus: Anatomy, pathophysiology, and regenerative capacity. *Journal of Head Trauma Rehabilitation, 15*(3), 875–896.

Gross, Y., & Shutz, L. E. (1986). Intervention models in neuropsychology. In B. P. Uzzell & Y. Gross (Eds.), *Clinical neuropsychology of intervention.* Boston: Martinus Nijhoff.

Herrmann, D. J., & Petro, S. (1990). Commercial memory aids. *Applied Cognitive Psychology, 4,* 439–450.

Kashima, H., Kato, M., Yoshimasu, H., & Muramatsu, T. (1999). Current trends in cognitive rehabilitation for memory disorders. *Keio Journal of Medicine, 48,* 79–86.

Kolb, B., & Whishaw, I. Q. (1990). *Fundamentals of human neuropsychology.* New York: Freeman.

Kromer, L. F., Bjorklund, A., & Stenevi, U. (1980). Innervation of embryonic hippocampal implants by regenerating axons of cholinergic neurons in the adult rat. *Brain Research, 210,* 153–171.

LaVere, T. E. (1975). Neural stability, sparing and behavioral recovery following brain damage. *Psychological Review, 82,* 344–358.

LaVere, T. E. (1980). Recovery of function after brain damage: A theory of the behavioral deficit. *Psychological Review, 82,* 297–308.

Low, W. C., Lewis, P. R., Bunch, T., Dunnett, S. B., Iversen, S. D., Bjorklund, A., & Stenevi, Y. (1982). Function recovery following neural transplantation of embryonic septal nuclei in adult rats with septohippocampal lesions. *Nature, 300,* 260–261.

Luria, A. (1963). *Recovery of function after brain injury.* New York: Macmillan.

Lynch, G. S., Deddwyler, S., & Cotman, C. W. (1973). Post lesion axonal growth produces permanent functional connections. *Science, 180,* 1364–1366.

Miller, E. (1984). *Recovery and management of neuropsychological impairments.* New York: Wiley.

Munk, H. (1878). Weitere Mettheilungen zur Physiologie der Grosshirnrinde. *Archives of Anatomy and Physiology, 3,* 581–592.

Parenté, R., & Anderson-Parenté, J. K. (1991). *Retraining memory: Techniques and applications.* Houston: CSY.

Parenté, R., & Stapleton, M. (1993). An empowerment model of memory training. *Applied Cognitive Psychology, 7*(7), 585–602.

Rosner, B. S. (1974). Recovery of function and localization of function in historical perspective. In D. G. Stein, J. J. Rosen, & N. Butters (Eds.), *Plasticity and recovery of function in the central nervous system.* New York: Academic Press.

Schacter, D. L., & Glisky, E. (1986). Memory remediation: Restoration, alleviation, and the acquisition of domain-specific knowledge. In B. Uzzell & Y. Gross (Eds.), *Clinical neuropsychology of intervention* (pp. 257–282). Boston: Martinus Nijhoff.

Sohlberg, M. M., & Mateer, C. A. (1987). Effectiveness of an attention training program. *Journal of Clinical and Experimental Neuropsychology, 9,* 117–130.

Sperry, R. W. (1965). Mechanisms of neural maturation. In S. S. Stevens (Ed.), *Handbook of Experimental Psychology.* New York: Wiley.

Sternberg, R. J., & Smith, E. E. (1988). *The psychology of human thought.* Cambridge, United Kingdom: Cambridge University Press.

Taylor, J. (1931). *Selected writings of John Hughlings Jackson.* London: Hodder & Stoughton.

Ungerstedt, U. (1971). Post synaptic supersensitivity after 6 hydroxy-dopamine induced degeneration of nigrostriatal dopamine system. *Acta Physiologica Scandinavia, 367* (Suppl.), 69–93.

Uzzell, B. P. (1986). Pathophysiology and behavioral recovery. In B. P. Uzzell & Y. Gross (Eds.), *Clinical neuropsychology of intervention.* Boston: Martinus Nijhoff.

von Monakow, C. (1914). *Die Lokalisation in Grosshirn und der Function durch Kortikale Herde.* Wiesbaden, Germany: Bergmann.

Wilson, B. (1999). Memory rehabilitation in brain-injured people. *Cognitive Neurorehabilitation, 6,* 333–346.

Zagler, E. L., & Black, P. M. (1985). Neuropeptides in human memory and learning processes. *Neurosurgery, 17,* 355–369.

Zimmer, J. (1981). Lesion-induced reorganization of central nervous system connections: With note on central nervous system transplants. In M. W. van Hoff & G. Mohn (Eds.), *Functional recovery from brain damage.* Amsterdam: Elsevier.

Chapter 6

✦

Transfer and Generalization
of Cognitive Skills

The ultimate goal of cognitive rehabilitation is to teach skills that generalize in novel situations (Cicerone et al., 2000; Kreutzer & Wehman, 1990; Schacter, 1996; Zoher, 1994). Despite this goal, many of the skills taught in therapy do not, in fact, generalize. This chapter presents a framework of models a therapist can use to better predict which skills will transfer and generalize, thereby making CRT as effective as possible. However, because many therapists do not understand the difference between transfer and generalization, the chapter begins with a discussion of these terms. We then discuss the history of transfer theory before presenting the models for transfer of cognitive skill.

Generalization refers to cognitive skills that are applicable to a variety of contexts (Parenté, Twum, & Zoltan, 1994; Twum, 1994). Teaching skills that generalize foster autonomy and independence (Gifford, Rusch, Martin, & White, 1985; Horner, Sprague, & Wilcox, 1986). For example, occupational therapists teach cooking and other independent living skills that will generalize to any home environment. Speech and language therapists may teach a person how to control the rate and intelligibility of his or her speech. These skills facilitate functioning and communication in different contexts. *Trans-*

fer, on the other hand, refers to the way in which specific skills can facilitate or retard new learning in a similar context (Cormier & Hagman, 1987; Ellis, 1965). Although many people with brain injury lose their ability to generalize, the skills they learn in therapy may still transfer to a similar vocational or independent living context. For example, a therapy client could learn mail-sorting skills in a training simulation that are virtually identical to those needed for his or her specific job placement.

Although the terms *generalization* and *transfer* frequently appear in publications about brain injury, with the exception of some recent work (Parenté & DiCesare, 1991; Parenté et al., 1994; Woolcock, 1990), remarkably little has appeared concerning transfer theory and its application to rehabilitation. Moreover, with the exception of the excellent work of Singley and Anderson (1987), there has been virtually no discussion of the more recent theories regarding transfer of cognitive skills, nor has there been any experimental validation of the transfer theories as they apply to brain injury rehabilitation.

Transfer and generalization theories make specific predictions about the type and amount of transfer a therapist might expect from any training program. This chapter provides the therapist with background information and a theoretical model that allows him or her to develop treatment plans that will carry over into the client's activities of daily living. First, however, it is necessary to describe the history and general principles of transfer.

A Brief History of Transfer

Ylvisaker (1993) traced the history of transfer and generalization back to the Greeks. Plato, for example, was the first to advocate a model of cognitive training that emphasized teaching abstract skills that would presumably generalize to the real world. The Sophists, however, were quick to point out that only utilitarian, concrete, and specific skills training would transfer. The Platonic model was reborn in the 20th century as a *theory of formal discipline*. This theory advocated teaching children specific subjects that were assumed to transfer to all other aspects of their academic training. These root disciplines were Latin and mathematics, two topics that were taught to provide generalizable mental skills that not only sharpened the mind, but also underlay all other disciplines.

Criticisms of the theory of formal discipline came from psychologists such as Thorndike and Woodworth (1901). These authors advocated an *identical elements theory of transfer*. Specifically, this theory stated that training in the first of two sequential tasks would carry over to the second but only to the extent that the two tasks shared identical elements: the more similar the elements, the greater the transfer. Indeed, it is unclear whether these authors even believed in the concept of generalization. Like most psychologists of their time, their goal was to describe transfer of learning within the context of a larger theory of learning that explained transfer according to the laws of association between stimuli and responses. Generalization was usually described at this time as the result of warm-up or learning-to-learn that accrued with repetition.

Bruce (1933) and Wylie (1919) put forth a similar concept of transfer. These authors stated that the amount of transfer among sequential tasks depended, in part, on the number of identical elements the training and transfer tasks shared. However, their laws also made another especially important contribution to the theory of transfer of cognitive skill. Specifically, the *Bruce/Wylie laws* stated that how the task was organized determined whether the transfer was positive or negative. That is, a necessary condition of positive transfer between any training and transfer tasks was the similarity of their organization.

Osgood (1949) summarized much of the existing research and theory as a three-dimensional space that he called the *transfer–surface*. This model of transfer provided a way to predict the amount of transfer that would likely occur in similar situations. Because Osgood's model was firmly rooted in the stimulus–response tradition of mid–20th century psychology, it defined similarity in terms of the number of identical elements and observable motor responses that two situations shared. The model did not make any assumptions about how a person may have cognitively organized the tasks. The Osgood transfer–surface is still considered an accurate summary of most motor and verbal learning transfer phenomena. It is perhaps less accurate in situations that deal with the transfer of cognitive skills.

Newell (1980) introduced the concept of the *problem space* as an explanation of the notion of transfer of learning. This idea explains transfer of learning as a mental space. Transfer results when the original mental space expands to encompass a novel situation in which that learning applies. Unlike the identical elements theory, which stressed the shared physical characteristics of sequential tasks, the problem space notion focuses on the similarity of cognitive processing demands between sequential tasks. The model makes three basic assumptions. The first is that positive transfer will occur when a person uses the same knowledge in a similar way in successive tasks (Singley & Anderson, 1987). Common elements do not ensure positive transfer. The number of elements the two tasks share is important; however, the way the person learns to organize the task is a better predictor of how much transfer or generalization will occur.

A second assumption of the problem space model is that at least two types of old learning and knowledge can influence new learning. *Declarative knowledge* is a person's existing storehouse of knowledge and facts. It provides the basis for organizing whatever common elements various tasks share. For example, in learning how to wash clothes, a person may eventually discern that certain types of fabrics require dry cleaning. *Procedural learning* refers to the acquisition of specific skills like riding a bicycle or typing. In many cases, procedural skills may apply in only one situation. For example, when preparing a therapy client for a job, it may be necessary to interview the employer to determine exactly how he or she wants the job performed. The therapist would then teach these specific skills to the client even though the unique aspects of the job may not apply in any other job the person might later acquire.

A third assumption of the problem space model is that declarative knowledge may transfer but will eventually become proceduralized. For example, it is possible to train a person with a brain injury to perform a skill such as data entry. When placed in a job, certain generic aspects of the training transfer, such as the organization of the keyboard, knowing what a disk drive is, or knowing how to use a printer. However, this declarative knowledge base eventually becomes modified to fit the specific task demands of the new job.

If the same person will later work with a keyboard that is configured differently, a different style of computer, or a different network setup, he or she will have to learn the intricacies of the new system.

Predicting Treatment Outcomes

The Bruce/Wylie laws discussed previously were perhaps the first predictive models of transfer. Osgood's (1949) transfer–surface was the first comprehensive model of transfer of stimulus–response learning. Ellis (1965) proposed a model of transfer of learning that was later modified by Parenté and Anderson-Parenté (1990), who used it to predict the amount of transfer that would likely result from various cognitive rehabilitation training procedures. Twum (1994) confirmed the predictions of this *transfer of cognitive skill* model in his study of paired-associate training. A description of his research is provided later in this chapter.

The basic concepts of the transfer model proposed by Parenté and Anderson-Parenté (1990) assumed that cognitive retraining established associations between the physical observable aspects of the training task and the unobservable cognitive organizations a person learned while performing the task. This aspect of the model was similar to the assumptions of the Bruce/Wylie laws. The transfer of cognitive skill model and the Bruce/Wylie laws assumed that in any learning task, a person learns an unobservable cognitive organization. For example, a person may group words into related categories when learning a word list. Cognitive organizations can also be procedural, such as learning a specific way of performing a motor task.

Parenté and Anderson-Parenté (1990) asserted that effective cognitive rehabilitation involves teaching a client mental sets and organizations that carry over into his or her activities of daily living. Moreover, training that generalizes involves providing the client with practice using the organizations in a wide variety of real-life situations. The Bruce/Wylie laws, the problem space theory, and the transfer of cognitive skill model assume that positive transfer occurs as long as the same training is used in the same way in two or more different situations. Singley and Anderson (1987) concurred with this principle. All of these theories predict that therapy would facilitate generalization as long as the therapist can show the client how to apply a mental organization in a variety of settings. If the client does not see how the general principle applies, then the transfer is minimal or nonexistent. For example, when training persons with brain injury to do custodial work, the therapist may teach a specific sequence of behaviors for a task, such as stripping and waxing a linoleum floor, that ensures that the job will be completed in a timely fashion. If the therapist can show a client how this organization of steps for floor stripping and waxing can be applied in a variety of work settings, then the training will generalize. If the client does not see that the method can apply from one job to the next,

then his or her efficiency will decline and additional training may be necessary. In this example, the individual task elements will vary from job to job because the context will change. However, the sequence of steps remains the same and will, possibly, generalize from job to job.

Parenté and Anderson-Parenté (1990) described several specific conditions of transfer paradigms, which are best discussed by example. The first paradigms describe the conditions of positive transfer. In these situations, the physical aspects of a person's therapy are called *task elements* (A). For example, when learning to type, the typewriter, keyboard, paper, and so forth comprise the task elements of the training context. During therapy, the person also learns to organize these elements to facilitate efficiency. For example, the therapist teaches specific ways to position fingers on the keyboard and to adjust the paper, and the intricacies of paper layout and letter design. These are *mental organizations* (B) that the client can use in any new situation that requires the same typing skills. The model assumes that the therapy will transfer as long as the *mental organizations* are maintained from task to task. Conditions for transfer are presented in Table 6.1.

TABLE 6.1
Transfer Conditions

Therapy		Real World		
Task Element	Mental Organization	Task Element	Mental Organization	Amount of Transfer
A	B	A	B	+ + + +
A	B	A′	B′	+ + +
A	B	C	B	+ +
A	B	C	D	+
A	B	A	D	− − −
A	B	A	Br	− − − −

Note. Some data are from "Vocational Memory Training," by R. Parenté and J. K. Anderson-Parenté, in *Community Integration Following Traumatic Brain Injury* (p. 158), by J. S. Kreutzer and P. H. Wehman (Eds.), 1990, Baltimore: Brookes. Copyright 1990 by Brookes. Other data are from "Retraining Memory: Theory, Evaluation, and Applications," by R. Parenté and A. DiCesare, in *Cognitive Rehabilitation for Persons with Traumatic Brain Injury: A Functional Approach* (p. 151), by J. S. Kruetzer and P. H. Wehman (Eds.), 1991, Baltimore: Brookes. Copyright 1991 by Brookes. Adapted with permission.

Conditions of Positive Transfer and Generalization

Maximum positive transfer. Situations that conform to an A-B:A-B paradigm yield positive transfer because the conditions of therapy and the real world are identical. For example, a therapy client may complete janitorial training and then begin work at the same facility where the training occurred. In this situation, the task elements (e.g., floors, walls, closets, rooms, etc.) and mental organizations (e.g., sequence of steps the therapist teaches the client to clean the building) are shared by the training and transfer tasks are identical.

Positive transfer. The A-B:A-B paradigm is seldom achieved in therapy because there is usually a distinct difference between the training a client receives in therapy and the experience he or she encounters in real life. This difference can be abbreviated by adding prime symbols next to the A and B letters. The A′ in the second row of Table 6.1 shows that the physical characteristics of therapy and life differ somewhat. Likewise, the B′ indicates that the client may learn to organize the task a certain way in training that will differ slightly from what he or she will encounter in real life. For example, if a client learns janitorial skills during an on-the-job placement, then begins work in a second placement that is similar, although not identical, to the first, then the model predicts positive transfer but less than that which occurs in the A-B:A-B paradigm.

Generalization. The A-B:C-B paradigm describes the conditions of generalization. Here, the training involves task elements (A) that are different from those the client will later encounter (C). However, the task is organized (B) in the same way. This consistent mental organization is a necessary condition for generalization. The other necessary condition is that the client must perceive the similarity between the two tasks. For example, a client may learn to sort envelopes alphabetically in one job placement, then to sort packages alphabetically in another job placement. The task elements differ (envelopes versus packages) but the envelope-sorting experience (alphabetical sorting) will generalize as long as the method used to sort both envelopes and packages is the same and the client is aware of the similarity.

These examples illustrate a general principle of effective therapy. *In any two sequential tasks, training will promote generalization to the extent that the organizations learned in the first are maintained in the second and the person is aware of the similarity.* The word *organization* means, specifically, the method or technique the person learns in the first task. This is the same principle originally proposed by Bruce and Wylie. However, simply maintaining the organization from one task to another may not produce as much specific transfer as will occur in the A-B:A-B model where both mental organization and task elements are identical. The only way a therapist can teach a generalizable skill is to vary the physical aspects of the training experience (i.e., the task elements) while, simultaneously, keeping the organization relatively constant. At the same time, the therapist must show the client how he or she can apply the same organizational technique in the various training situations.

Conditions of Negative Transfer and Generalization

Maximum negative transfer. Many therapists assume that any treatment will benefit their clients. There are, however, situations where the therapy can retard both transfer and generalization. The A-B:A-Br paradigm describes the worst of these situations because it produces massive negative transfer effects. The lowercase r next to the B shows that the task elements are reorganized within the same context. For example, a therapist may spend hours using photographs to show a client where things are located in his or her room at home. The client will eventually develop a useful mental organization of the room. However, a well-meaning family member may reorganize the room before the client returns home. The spatial environment and the objects within the room are the same. However, after returning home, the client must reorganize the room mentally. The experience is similar to one in which a person cleans and reorganizes an office space and, as a result, cannot find anything for several days.

Negative transfer. The A-B:A-D paradigm describes those situations where the task elements a client experiences in treatment (A) are similar to those he or she later encounters in the real world. However, the real-world task organization is different (B versus D). In the example above, a therapist may train the client to recall where various personal belongings are located in his or her room at home. However, unknown to the therapist, a family member may decide that the client should move into a different room upon returning home. The client may have difficulty locating items in the new room because, although the client's belongings are the same, the organizing context (B versus D) has changed.

Minimal transfer. The A-B:C-D paradigm predicts little transfer or generalization because the task elements and the mental organizations between the two tasks are dissimilar. Although there are no specific aspects of training that apply to the client's life, there may be general improvements in attention, concentration, vigilance, and immediate memory that do carry over. Consequently, therapies that conform to this transfer paradigm usually produce minimal transfer or none at all. Stimulation training and most computer-based remediation models conform to this paradigm. If the task is the same, then the client will improve. However, the improvement the client experiences during training usually does not carry over into other aspects of the client's life because computer exercises and life experiences share no common elements or organization. Many clients wonder how computer training with games and other cognitive rehabilitation computer exercises will help them to regain their faculties. This is a difficult question to answer because there is little research that documents the efficacy of computer-based or other stimulation therapies.

The transfer models we have described have several advantages. Perhaps the most important of these is that they account for both transfer and generalization phenomena. The model predicts that in any sequential situation, transfer of learning occurs when the elements and the organization are similar. Accordingly, the A-B:A-B paradigm predicts maximum positive transfer. It may not, however, produce a skill that will generalize across situations. The A-B:C-B model can produce less specific transfer but greater generalization because the client learns a generic organization that applies across situations. Again, varying the task elements during training while keeping the organization the same would produce a more durable organization that would increase the potential for generalization. This is a necessary condition for generalization. Another necessary condition is that the person see or is shown how the mental organization applies from training to the new task.

Transfer and Generalization Outcomes of CRT Methods

Parenté and Anderson-Parenté (1990) described how the above model of transfer and generalization could predict the outcome of most cognitive retraining methods. Their summary is presented below to show how certain cognitive retraining therapies can be modified to promote either generalization or positive transfer.

Stimulation Therapy

Stimulation training is one of the most popular cognitive retraining methods (Gross & Schutz, 1986; Schuell, Carroll, & Street, 1950). Therapists use both paper-and-pencil and computer-based exercises but repetitive mental exercise is the defining feature of the stimulation therapy approach. Treatments may involve an activity as simple as doing word-search puzzles or it may involve working with more sophisticated computer software chosen to match the client's pattern of deficits.

Speech and language therapists were the first to use stimulation training (Schuell et al., 1950; Taylor, 1950). Indeed, it is still the mainstay of their therapies today. According to the transfer paradigms outlined above, stimulation training conforms to the A-B: C-D model because there are no easily identifiable similarities between therapy and the real world. The model therefore predicts that therapy will produce only minimal transfer. Schacter and Glisky (1986) have made a similar assertion about this type of training. In general, there is little evidence that demonstrates either transferable effects or generalization of skills from most stimulation training efforts.

There are, however, some published findings that show how simple modifications to stimulation training procedures can produce marked improvement in functioning. For example, Parenté, Kolakowsky, Hoffman, and Blake (1998) reviewed several articles that showed how specific types of iconic memory training can improve reading skill. Similar results have been shown with visual scanning training (McClur, Browning, Vantrease,

& Bittle, 1994). Both techniques modified the typical drill-and-practice stimulation therapy routine to include materials that are similar to those the client would eventually have to process. For example, iconic training that taught the client to process intact word strings like "time to go" later facilitated performance on a reading comprehension task relative to a condition where the person received iconic training with scrambled words like "to time go." Other modifications can change the typical stimulation therapy paradigm into a training program designed to produce a transferable effect. For example, many cognitive skills computer packages provide "digit span" training. These programs present number strings and the client tries to recall them. However, rather than training the client to remember random number strings, a better goal would be to teach a mental organization that can carry over to a new situation. For example, the therapist could train the client to remember phone numbers by grouping the seven individual digits into a three-digit number followed by two two-digit numbers. The computer program could present phone numbers as individual digits (e.g., 3, 2, 4, 6, 8, 9, 5) and the client would learn to organize the digits into three groups and to recall them as 324, 68, and 95. This training would generalize to any situation where the client would have to recall a phone number because the mental organization allows him or her to encode the number string efficiently and to rehearse it rapidly. Therefore, a random computer exercise can be recast to conform to an A-B:C-B paradigm, which will produce dramatic and rapid improvement of memory for phone numbers.

Memory Strategy Training

Chapter 12 describes a variety of mnemonic memory techniques that have been found to be especially effective with people with brain injury. There is convincing research that demonstrates that mnemonic strategies can improve recall of word lists and text materials (Parenté, Anderson-Parenté, & Stapleton, 2000; Parenté & Anderson-Parenté, 1990; Wilson, 1987). In general, there is no shortage of evidence that attests to the usefulness of mnemonic strategies. However, because therapy clients may not use mnemonics unless they are relevant to their lives, it is not sufficient to simply show a client how to form mnemonics and expect that he or she will do so automatically thereafter. It is necessary for the therapist to develop the mnemonic with the client and to demonstrate how it applies in his or her everyday life.

For example, Chapter 12 provides specific types of mnemonics such as words, rhymes, or mental images that a client can use to cue recall of personal information. Regardless of the specific device, the overall strategy conforms to an A-B:C-B paradigm. Once the client learns the mnemonic, the task elements will differ but the cognitive response will remain the same. For example, if the client learns the rhyme, "I before e except after c or sounding like a as in neighbor or weigh," then he or she can use it to spell most words containing a combination of the letters i and e. In this example, the specific spelling words used in training would be the A portion of the A-B:C-B paradigm and the rhyme would be the organizing rule (B). When the client encounters a new word (C) following training, he or she can then apply the organizing rule, in this case, the rhyme. The technique follows the A-B:C-B transfer paradigm, which predicts positive transfer.

Academic Remediation

Cognitive rehabilitation sometimes includes teaching functional skills such as reading and basic math. This type of therapy is effective for several reasons. First, most clients see an immediate relevance to relearning these skills. Academic remediation is also effective because it restores declarative memories and procedural skills. The training also conforms to an A-B:C-B paradigm because the learned techniques apply in a variety of novel situations. For example, teaching a client how to carry over digits when doing column addition is a procedure that the client applies the same way any time he or she adds a column of numbers. Once the client has learned to organize the task by carrying numbers from one column to the next, then it matters little what specific numbers he or she may encounter later because the same skill applies. In this example, the training problems the therapist provides are the A components of the A-B:C-B paradigm. The client learns the skill of carrying numbers from column to column, which is the B component of the model. Following training, addition problems the client may encounter will have different digits (C) but the organizing response (B), that is, the method of column addition, remains the same. This skill will therefore produce positive transfer.

Simulation and Domain-Specific Training

Simulated work environments provide training that shortens the time it takes a therapy client to become job ready. In a simulated work environment, the client performs a specific task and continues in training until he or she reaches competitive levels of performance. If the training matches the actual work environment, then the client can begin work with minimal adjustment. This type of training is also called domain specific (Schacter & Glisky, 1986) because the domain of training closely resembles the actual task the client will eventually perform.

Domain-specific training is effective because it conforms to an A-B:A'-B' transfer paradigm. However, the training is not without drawbacks. The limited therapy focus also limits the range of generalization. The client becomes like a robot who is trained to do one task. If the task changes, the client will require retraining. This problem underlies what Parenté and Stapleton (1999) called the *return loop syndrome,* whereby clients return for additional rehabilitation once their domain-specific training becomes obsolete or the task demands of the job change.

Evaluation

Two published studies have evaluated the transfer models we have described using persons with brain injury. Parenté et al. (1994) described two experiments in which participants were asked to memorize either a series of number strings or word lists that were presented so that the training–transfer sequence of tasks conformed to one of the transfer paradigms. For example, for the A-B:A-B paradigm, participants first memorized the number string 65-42-71 in training. They then memorized the same number string in the transfer phase. For the A-B:A-D paradigm, participants first memorized 6-54-271 in training then learned 65-42-71 in the transfer phase. In each case, the numbers (A) were the same, but the way they were grouped (B) differed. For the A-B:C-B paradigm, participants first learned 50-69-18 in training and then learned 65-42-71 in the transfer phase. Here, the numbers were different, but the type of grouping was the same. For the A-B:C-D paradigm, participants learned strings in which numbers and type of grouping differed (e.g., 5-06-918 and 65-42-71).

The transfer models outlined previously predict that the A-B:A-B participants would learn the second number strings quickest, followed by the A-B:C-B group, followed by the A-B:C-D group. The transfer paradigms also predict that the A-B:A-D group would actu-

ally learn the second number string more slowly than the control group (A-B:C-D). This was precisely the result. Generally, the groups whose perceptual grouping remained the same from training to the transfer task learned the second number strings quickest.

Twum (1994) reported a part–whole learning experiment that also was designed to test the transfer models. Groups of persons with brain injury learned two word lists that differed in terms of their individual words and/or their semantic organization. For example, in the A-B:A-B condition, the participants first learned the following list: Dog-Cat-Green-Red-North-South. Participants in the A-B:A-D condition first learned Dog-Green-North-Table-Venus Man. In the A-B:C-B condition, participants first learned Lion-Tiger-Blue-Yellow-South-East. In the A-B:C-B condition, participants learned Pencil-Dime-Ring-Tree-Shoe-Lamp. Each group then learned a longer list that contained the following words: Dog-Cat-Green-Red-North-South-Table-Chair-Venus-Mars-Man-Woman.

Participants in the A-B:A-B condition learned the second list most rapidly. Those in the A-B:C-B condition learned the second list almost as rapidly. Participants in the control condition (A-B:C-D) actually outperformed those in the A-B:A-D condition. This was surprising because in the A-B:A-D condition, the words on the first list were actually one half of the words on the second list. The fact that these participants performed worse than those in the A-B:C-D condition, where the two lists of words were completely unrelated, indicates that the participants in the A-B:A-C condition were unable to transfer their organization of the first list of words when learning the second list. The performance of participants in this experiment was therefore quite predictable from the transfer models. A statistical analysis indicated that the conditions in which the semantic organization was maintained from the first list to the second list had the best performance. Specifically, these were the participants in the A-B:A-B and A-B:C-B conditions. Changing the organization (A-B:A-D condition) actually retarded the participants' ability to learn the second list.

Summary and Recommendations

Although there has been a great deal of research about transfer in psychology, there has been relatively little carryover of these findings into the cognitive rehabilitation literature. The cognitive rehabilitation literature also suffers from a general lack of experimental validation of its proposed therapies and theoretical models of treatment. The purpose of this chapter was to trace the history of transfer and generalization theories and to outline models of these phenomena that predict the outcome of various rehabilitation methods. The models can also be used to improve the outcome of most cognitive rehabilitation therapies when therapists modify their treatment accordingly. Therapists can use the following suggestions to guide treatment.

▶ Train mental sets that are useful in a variety of different situations.

Teaching clients cognitive rehabilitation strategies will generalize to the real world to the extent that the clients learn mental sets that transfer intact. Specifically, therapies that conform to an A-B:C-B model will usually generalize. For example, the problem-solving strategies in Chapter 15, the decision-making strategies in Chapter 17, and the memory strategies in Chapter 12 are all useful in a variety of situations.

▶ Train specific skills that transfer.

If the goal of therapy is to train specific transferable skills, then therapy should ideally conform to an A-B:A-B or A-B:A'-B' training paradigm. This type of training is especially useful when the goal is to expedite a client's return to work. In this type of training, however, the client will learn skills that may not generalize to other situations. For example, the therapist may visit the client's workplace and then create a simulated work environment. This will ensure that the client has the requisite skills to perform the targeted job, but the skills may be inadequate or inappropriate for other jobs.

▶ Focus on relevant tasks.

Therapies are most effective when the client perceives the relevance of the training to his or her activities of daily living. There are two types of strategies that are relevant. The first is a general rule that the survivor can use for a lifetime. For example, teaching the "I before e except after c . . ." rhyme is an organizing strategy the client can use forever to recall how to spell most words that contain the letters *ie*. Teaching the rhyme "lefty–loosey, righty–tightly" can help the client recall how to tighten and loosen a nut on a bolt. The second type of strategy is one that trains memory for a specific context. For example, teaching a client a specific way of performing a skill on the job may be useful for that particular job but not for any other.

▶ Vary the training examples.

Several authors have emphasized the importance of using a variety of training examples when trying to teach clients generalizable strategies (Glick & Holyoak, 1987; Woolcock, 1990). According to the transfer paradigms in this chapter, diversifying training examples would facilitate generalization because a wide variety of task elements would become associated to a single organizational response.

▶ Provide overlearning and verification.

It is not sufficient to simply show a client a strategy and expect that he or she will use it spontaneously. Most clients will need several practice situations with a variety of training examples before they will even remember the skill. The therapist should therefore provide overlearning sessions when teaching a strategy and then test to see if the client has learned the skill by providing new examples.

▶ Avoid reorganization.

The therapist should avoid training that will eventually force a client to learn new response sets to the same task elements. It is especially important to avoid training in which the same responses are eventually reassociated or mismatched with the same task elements. These situations produce negative transfer, frustration for the client, and failure. For example, one client was trained to perform data entry with a specific template for his keyboard that summarized various function keys. When the client returned to work, he was trained with a different organizing template, which meant that he had to reorganize his mental set of the keyboard. This created a serious negative transfer problem and he had to eventually retrain.

In general, the goal of treatment is to promote positive transfer and to reduce negative transfer. In most cases, the therapist will have far greater success if he or she plans treatment by first asking how the therapy will achieve an outcome that carries over into a client's everyday life. If the answer to this question is not forthcoming, then the treatment is probably not worth pursuing.

References

Bruce, R. W. (1933). Conditions of transfer of training. *Journal of Experimental Psychology, 16,* 343–361.

Cicerone, K. D., Dahlberg, C., Kalmar, K., Langenbahn, D. M., Malec, J. F., Bergquist, T. F., Felicetti, T., Gaicino, J. T., Harley, P., Harrington, D. E., Herzon, J., Kneipp, S., Laatsch, L., & Morse, P. A. (2000). Evidence-based cognitive rehabilitation: Recommendations for clinical practice. *Archives of Physical Medicine and Rehabilitation, 81,* 1596–1615.

Cormier, S. M., & Hagman, J. D. (1987). *Transfer of learning: Contemporary research and applications.* London: Academic Press.

Ellis, H. C. (1965). *The transfer of learning.* New York: Macmillan.

Gifford, J., Rusch, F., Martin, J., & White, D. (1985). Autonomy and adaptability: A proposed technology for maintaining work behavior. In N. Ellis & N. Bray (Eds.), *International review of research on mental retardation* (Vol. 12, pp. 285–314). New York: Academic Press.

Glick, M. L., & Holyoak, K. J. (1987). The cognitive basis of knowledge transfer. In S. M. Cormier & J. D. Hagman (Eds.), *Transfer of learning: Contemporary research and applications* (pp. 9–42). London: Academic Press.

Gross, Y., & Schutz, L. (1986). Intervention models in neuropsychology. In B. Uzzell & Y. Gross (Eds.), *Clinical neuropsychology of intervention* (pp. 22–27). Boston: Martinus Nijhoff.

Horner, R. H., Sprague, J., & Wilcox, B. (1986). Intervention models in neuropsychology. In B. Wilcox & G. T. Belamy (Eds.), *Design of high school programs for severely handicapped students* (pp. 179–204). Baltimore: Brookes.

Kreutzer, J., & Wehman, P. (Eds.). (1990). *Community integration following traumatic brain injury.* Baltimore: Brookes.

McClur, J. T., Browning, R. T., Vantrease, C. M., & Bittle, S. T. (1997). Iconic memory training with stroke patients. *Journal of Cognitive Rehabilitation, 14,* 21–27.

Newell, A. (1980). Reasoning, problem-solving, and decision processes: The problem space as a fundamental category. In R. Nikerson (Ed.), *Attention and performance VIII.* Hillsdale, NJ: Erlbaum.

Osgood, C. E. (1949). The similarity paradox in human learning: A resolution. *Psychological Review, 56,* 132–143.

Parenté, R., & Anderson-Parenté, J. K. (1990). Vocational memory training. In J. Kreutzer & P. Wehman (Eds.), *Community integration following traumatic brain injury* (pp. 157–169). Baltimore: Brookes.

Parenté, R., Anderson-Parenté, J. K., & Stapleton, M. (2000). The use of rhymes and mnemonics for teaching cognitive skills to persons with acquired brain injury. *Brain Injury Source, 5*(1), 16–19.

Parenté, R., & DiCesare, A. (1991). Retraining memory: Theory, evaluation, and applications. In J. Kreutzer & P. Wehman (Eds.), *Cognitive rehabilitation for persons with traumatic brain injury* (pp. 147–162). Baltimore: Brookes.

Parenté, R., Kolakowsky, S., Hoffman, B., & Blake, S. (1998). Retraining the mind's eye: A review of existing research. *Topics in Stroke Rehabilitation, 5*(1), 48–58.

Parenté, R., & Stapleton, M. (1999). Development of a cognitive strategies group for vocational training after traumatic brain injury. *NeuroRehabilitation, 13*, 13–20.

Parenté, R., Twum, M., & Zoltan, B. (1994). Transfer and generalization of cognitive skill after traumatic brain injury. *NeuroRehabilitation, 4*(1), 25–35.

Schacter, D., & Glisky, E. (1986). Memory remediation, restoration, alleviation, and the acquisition of domain-specific knowledge. In B. Uzzell & Y. Gross (Eds.), *Clinical neuropsychology of intervention* (pp. 357–282). Boston: Martinus Nijhoff.

Schacter, D. L. (1996). *Searching for memory: The brain, the mind, and the past.* New York: Basic Books.

Schuell, H. M., Carroll, V., & Street, B. S. (1950). Clinical treatment of aphasia. *Journal of Speech and Hearing Disorders, 20*, 43–53.

Singley, M. K., & Anderson, J. R. (1987). *The transfer of cognitive skills.* Cambridge, MA: Harvard University Press.

Taylor, M. T. (1950). Language therapy. In H. G. Burn (Ed.), *The aphasic adult: Rehabilitation and treatment* (pp. 156–200). Charlottesville, VA: Wayside Press.

Thorndike, E. L., & Woodworth, R. S. (1901). The influence of improvement in one mental function upon the efficiency of other functions. *Psychological Review, 8*, 247–261.

Twum, M. (1994). Maximizing generalization of cognitions and memories after traumatic brain injury. *NeuroRehabilitation, 4*(3), 157–167.

Wilson, B. A. (1987). *Rehabilitation of memory.* New York: Guilford Press.

Woolcock, W. (1990). Generalization strategies. In J. Kreutzer & P. Wehman (Eds.), *Vocational rehabilitation for persons with traumatic brain injury* (pp. 243–263). Gaithersburg, MD: Aspen.

Wylie, H. H. (1919). An experimental study of transfer of response in the white rat. *Behavioral Monographs, 3*, 16.

Ylvisaker, M. (1993, June). *Historical perspectives and general principles.* Paper presented at the conference "Cognitive rehabilitation: A practical approach," Edmonton, Alberta, Canada.

Zoher, A. (1994). Teaching a thinking strategy: Transfer across domains and self-learning versus class-like settings. *Applied Cognitive Psychology, 8*, 547–563.

Chapter 7

ℐ

The Intervention Assessment

Two Approaches to Assessment

Most neuropsychological assessments are based on one-shot procedures that assess various brain–behavior relationships (Spreen & Strauss, 1991). We refer to these procedures as *static* methods because they evaluate a person at a specific time. Examples include medical imaging procedures such as computerized tomography (CT) and magnetic resonance imaging (MRI), and neuropsychological assessments such as the Halstead–Reitan and Luria–Nebraska batteries (Golden, Purisch, & Hammeke, 1985; Goodglass & Kaplan, 1983; Halstead, 1947; Reitan, 1955). Static test procedures are not entirely adequate to evaluate all aspects of the multimodal system presented in Chapter 2. Therefore, we provide only a brief summary of this type of evaluation; thorough discussions are provided in a variety of other excellent texts (e.g., Lezak, 1999).

Static assessments are designed primarily to predict brain functioning from correlated performances on various tests of skills. According to the logic of these tests, if the person cannot perform the skill then its correlated brain structure must be damaged, poorly developed, or otherwise defective. However, static assessments cannot predict which types of cognitive rehabilitation therapies are likely

to be the most successful. As a result, many therapists are left feeling that neuropsychological test results do not provide the information they need to plan a treatment program. Therapists often feel that the test results only tell them what they already know about the client. In essence, these evaluations determine what is wrong with the client but provide little information on what to do about the problems.

Several factors affect the usefulness of neurocognitive tests. For example, authors (e.g., Miller, 1984) have described technological advances in computer-assisted scanning procedures for diagnosing brain lesions that may eventually obviate the need for neuropsychological evaluation, as it is known today. Therapists and family members may also question how well the neuropsychological test results actually predict everyday life functioning (Acker, 1986). Hart and Hayden (1986) indicated that neuropsychological assessment lacks "ecological validity," that is, the ability to predict real-world functioning (Wilson, 1987; Wilson, Baddeley, & Cockburn, 1988). Moreover, because learning is defined as change in performance with practice (Parenté & Anderson-Parenté, 1991), and static neurocognitive evaluations are typically administered only once, the scores do not index learning. Rehabilitation is a learning process, and therefore it makes more sense to measure learning potential—the ability to change with practice. Measurement of learning potential is one of the defining features of *dynamic* assessment (Cicerone & Tupper, 1986).

Dynamic assessments evaluate whether a person's performance can be modified. Vygotsky (1978) originally discussed this concept. His "zone of proximal development" concerned the difference between unaided performance and changes in performance that would occur with guidance and instruction. The zone of proximal development was the difference between the level of performance and functioning when a person is alone versus when he or she interacts with a skilled partner. The measure indexed a person's potential for improvement or learning; static assessments do not measure this potential. Although there have been some attempts to develop formal dynamic test procedures (Feuerstein, Klein, & Tannenbaum, 1991; Toglia, 1992a, 1992b), they are not yet widely used in clinical practice. However, dynamic assessment techniques seem to be quite useful for a therapist trying to plan a treatment program for a person with traumatic brain injury.

Despite the problems with the conventional neurocognitive evaluations mentioned above, both static and dynamic assessment have distinct advantages and should be used together whenever time and resources permit. Although the goals of dynamic assessment differ from those of standard neuropsychological evaluations, the conventional evaluations certainly provide a wealth of valuable information. For example, neuropsychological test data provide comprehensive baseline information and a way to determine which cognitive processes are likely impaired and the extent of impairment. Neuropsychological and imaging measures can also document and localize a brain injury for legal and medical purposes (Ricker, 2001). Skills-based evaluations are valuable for assessing behavioral and subtle cognitive deficits that are not readily apparent from imaging measures such as MRI and CT.

Comparing Dynamic Assessment and Static Assessment

Differences Between Dynamic and Static Assessment

The purpose of the dynamic assessment procedures presented in this chapter is to answer three basic questions about a person's functional learning skills: (1) What types of information is the person capable of learning? (2) Which types of therapy techniques and strategies are most likely to benefit the person? (3) Which types of training are most likely to transfer or to generalize to the real world? Dynamic assessment procedures are uniquely suited to answer these three questions. While static assessment is typically based on a one-shot evaluation of performance, dynamic assessment is primarily concerned with a person's learning potential, or the ability to improve with practice. Dynamic assessment also measures a person's intervention potential, or the ability to change with training. Finally, it evaluates a person's transfer potential, or the ability to apply the newly learned skills in novel situations.

A second difference between the two types of assessments is that conventional static assessments uses test scores that can compare a person's performance to that of a large body of people who have taken the test in the past (norms). Dynamic assessment uses change scores to measure how much a person improves with practice. It is possible to compare these scores with norms but it is not of primary importance. The major interest is whether a person improves performance on the task with practice, which is indexed by the change scores.

A third difference is that static assessment is geared toward localizing brain dysfunction (Buschke, 1987), whereas dynamic assessment assists with planning treatment programs by identifying the treatment interventions that will most likely lead to improvement with practice.

Learning Versus Performance-Based Assessment

As mentioned previously, the essential difference between conventional neuropsychological assessment and the dynamic techniques we have outlined is that the former assesses performance and the latter evaluates learning potential. Performance evaluations measure skill or ability at a single point in time. Static evaluations therefore yield raw scores that index the person's ability to do a certain task. Most conventional neuropsychological assessments are normed on a large number of average people. After a person takes the same test, his or her results are converted to standard scores (e.g., Z-score, T-score, IQ score), which measure the level of functioning relative to the reference group (norms). Typically a percentile rank is used for this purpose. For example, if a person's raw score falls at the 23rd percentile, it means that he or she performed better than 23% of the norming group.

Static performance measures are certainly useful for evaluating a person's current level of functioning. However, any such measurement is only a snapshot of the person and this picture is likely to change radically, especially during the early stages of recovery. Although the test results may help to pinpoint the site of a brain lesion or to document a dysfunction, the evaluator and therapist are left to wonder how well the person would have done if he or she were allowed to repeat the test several times. Static assessments leave several important questions unanswered. For example, does the person improve with repeated testings? Which skills improve most rapidly? The skills that improve most rapidly are those that will most likely respond to the therapist's rehabilitation efforts.

Hilgard and Bower (1975) define *learning* as "change in performance with practice" (pp. 13–17). The ability to improve with practice is the difference between performances on two successive tests. For example, using a scale from 1 to 10, a person may score a 5 on the first measurement of performance and a 7 on the second one. In this case, the learning score would be 2 (i.e., 7–5). Learning is the gain in performance from the first to the second assessment.

The goal of CRT is improvement with practice and intervention. We, therefore, assert that learning scores are a better method than standard scores for determining which interventions are most likely to be effective with a specific person. Some readers may be surprised by this assertion while others may think it obvious. Many therapists have never tested anything other than performance. But if the goal is to teach a person new skills, it is reasonable to suggest that a therapist must assess a person's potential to improve with practice, regardless of how he or she may perform initially. Unfortunately, however, assessment for learning potential is seldom practiced. Conventional neuropsychological assessment only measures performance and assumes that one-shot test scores are good predictors of rehabilitation potential. But performance and potential are not necessarily correlated. This point is illustrated in Figure 7.1, which shows the results of a word-learning task for two people with TBI.

Performance on the repeated administration of the test is measured by the y-axis. The x-axis records 7 repeated study and test trials. The figure shows that one person began at a considerably higher level than the other. If the evaluator had stopped testing after the first administration, then one person would seem severely impaired and the other would seem to be average.

A distinctly different pattern emerges, however, with repeated testing. The person who was initially quite impaired improved rapidly with practice. Because this person's

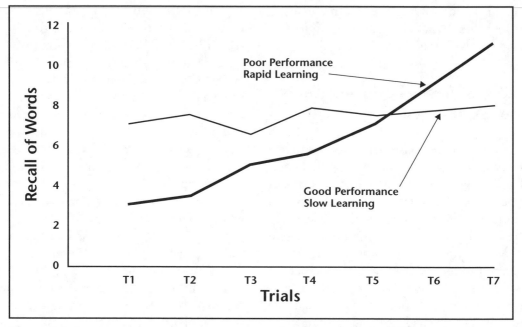

Figure 7.1. Learning versus performance comparison for two people with traumatic brain injury on a 12-item word list.

learning curve is steeper, he or she is actually learning faster than the other person. Therefore, the rapidly improving person has greater learning potential on this task.

The difference between learning and performance measures can produce quite different conclusions about a person's potential for rehabilitation. Unfortunately, the difference usually goes unnoticed because most tests are designed for a single administration. Many of these same tests, however, can be administered repeatedly and the change in performance over trials can provide a wealth of new information that can change the rehabilitation outlook. An example of this type of evaluation is presented in Figure 7.2.

Figure 7.2 shows the results of a procedure that was designed to determine which of several memory strategies would be most beneficial for one person. The therapist began with a sentence mnemonic to help the person learn a word list. Imagery instructions were provided next, followed by rehearsal training. The results indicated that simple rehearsal produced the greatest initial perfor-

mance and imagery training was less successful on Trial 1. The sentence mnemonic seemed to be the worst of the three methods initially. Each of the techniques was repeated over several trials, which led to different conclusions. With practice, imagery produced the greatest improvement. The sentence mnemonic also was helpful, and the rehearsal was least useful.

The above discussion leads to several guidelines for dynamic assessment of learning potential: First, tasks on which a person demonstrates improvement with practice identify cognitive skills that are potentially the best candidates for intervention. Repeated testing that yields no learning effects indicates skills that are not as likely to improve and that may cause frustration for the therapist and client. This rule applies regardless of the initial level of performance. Second, CRT should focus on those skills that show the greatest potential for improvement, and the therapist should avoid treatment when the results of the dynamic assessment indicate little learning potential.

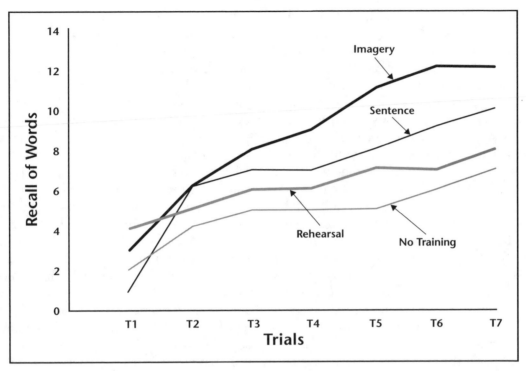

Figure 7.2. Learning potential for one person under four training conditions.

Dynamic assessment provides an answer for the question of when to begin therapy. One school of thought suggests that therapy should start soon after the injury occurs. Another school suggests that therapy should wait until the deficits stabilize. The learning model outlined above predicts that therapy will be effective as long as it is focused on skills that the client can learn. Regardless of whether the client is 6 months or 6 years postinjury, effective treatment is possible if the therapist works with skills that show improvement with practice.

Dynamic Assessment Procedures

The concept of intelligence in western European cultures is typically discussed as static and unchanging. Vygotsky (1978) was one of the first to describe intelligence as the ability to learn and to benefit from instruction.

Cicerone and Tupper (1986) also described this concept of "zone of rehabilitation potential," which is important for predicting success in a cognitive rehabilitation treatment program. This intervention potential, along with the ability to improve with practice and the ability to generalize new learning, are the critical aspects of dynamic rehabilitation assessment. The ability to improve performance with practice can be defined as *learning potential*. The ability to benefit from instruction is *intervention potential*. The ability to transfer or generalize the newly learned skills is *transfer potential*. Each of these skills must be evaluated in dynamic assessment.

Measuring Learning Potential

Parenté and Anderson-Parenté (1991) outlined a method for evaluating learning potential that can be used with a variety of static assessments. Their procedure involves repeated testing until a client reaches a criterion of average performance. The evaluator begins with any test that has published norms, which are an index of average performance. The client repeats the test until his or her performance reaches average levels or plateaus. This procedure measures how many repetitions are necessary to improve performance to average levels or to reach a point where further improvement is impossible. The therapist need not use standardized tests for this type of assessment. Any measurable behavior can be evaluated to determine if it improves with practice. For example, a client may require five repetitions of the same task before his or her performance reaches a level that would be considered average or above average. With other tasks, performance may reach average levels after one or two repetitions. Learning potential is the number of repetitions necessary to reach the average range. The average range can be taken from existing norms or from local norms that are compiled from testing willing volunteers.

In our experience, those tasks where the number of repetitions to reach the average range is less than five indicate skills with clear potential for improvement with treatment. Those requiring more than five repetitions can be treated but will probably respond slowly. Treating those that require more than 10 repetitions will probably produce frustration.

One advantage of this type of measure is that it is relatively easy to explain the results of the testing to family members. For example, most family members will understand a statement such as, "Your son may have to read a magazine article five times before he'll remember it." Another advantage is that the therapist can evaluate all or most abilities using this technique. One disadvantage is that the number of trials it takes a person to reach an average level may be misleading because the person may fall in the average range on the first testing but not improve markedly thereafter. Consequently, the technique may create a false impression of a person's learning potential in some situations.

In addition to repeated testing, another measure of learning potential is the slope of a person's learning curve for any given measure. One simple way to assess this is to rank which curves have the steepest slant on a graph. This should be apparent after the scores are plotted. A more exact method is to subtract scores on successive testings. For example, on the scale mentioned earlier (1 to 10), if a person scores a 4 on the first testing, a 6 on the second, and an 8 on the third, the evaluator would simply subtract the first score from the second (difference of 2), the second from the third (difference of 2), then average the differences ($2 + 2 = 4 \div 2 = 2$). On another performance test, the first difference may be 3 and the second 5, yielding an average difference of 4 ($3 + 5 = 8 \div 2 = 4$). The task that yields an average difference score of 4 shows the steepest learning curve and the greatest potential for new learning.

The advantage of using slope measures is that it is not necessary to compare a person's score to an average range. They are simple measures of the extent to which a person's performance improves with practice. The disadvantage is that they can be labor-intensive to compute.

Measuring Intervention Potential

The purpose of testing various interventions is to determine which are most likely to improve a person's thinking and memory. For example, the therapist might train categorization (Parenté & Anderson-Parenté, 1991) and measure performance after each instruction session. The therapist would then compare the person's performance with and without the intervention. If performance improved markedly, usually between 50% and 100% within two trials, then the therapy was effective. If there was no substantial change, then the therapist would try another treatment.

Transfer Potential

The third aspect of the intervention assessment concerns whether the person is able to carry over his or her strategies to a new situation (LaBlanc & Hayden, 2000). Therefore, after training the skill, the therapist's next step is to assess whether the training will aid learning and memory in a similar task. For example, after training a person to use a number chunking strategy to recall phone numbers, the therapist may have the person call the telephone operator and require the person to recall the phone number provided by the operator in grouped fashion (see Chapter 12 for a complete discussion of this technique). If the treatment does not produce any carry-over effects, then the therapist should provide further training or abandon it. Clearly, the choice of intervention tasks will be partially dictated by whether they have any obvious transferable quality (Twum, 1994).

It is important to distinguish between the transfer potential of a strategy and whether a therapy client uses the strategy spontaneously. A particular strategy may work well for a client but he or she may not readily implement it. On the other hand, a client may not find a particular strategy useful. In the former case, the therapist must realize that training the client to the point where the strategy is used spontaneously may take a long time. Transfer potential refers to the potential usefulness of the strategy, not to the client's willingness to use it or his or her compliance with the therapist's suggestion to use it.

The Initial Assessment Battery

As mentioned previously, we feel that *both* static and dynamic procedures of evaluation have distinct advantages and should be used whenever time and resources permit. If a comprehensive neuropsychological evaluation is available, the therapist should use it as an estimate of the client's cognitive capacity before beginning treatment. However, therapists often do not have access to neuropsychological test results or cannot get them before they begin treatment. We therefore provide several tests that any therapist can perform that will also assess a variety of basic cognitive processes (see Table 7.1 and Appendix C for more details on each test and its administration). They require no special credentials to obtain or administer, are generally available, and are relatively simple to use and to evaluate. If they reveal any outstanding deficits, however, a complete neuropsychological assessment may be necessary. Many other tests will serve the same purposes as the ones listed here, and the reader may certainly substitute those that he or she is accustomed to using.

Most of the tests in Table 7.1 were chosen because they can be administered repeatedly to evaluate the client's potential for improvement with practice or instruction. This is the dynamic aspect of the assessment battery. But for others, which measure aspects of functioning that are typically viewed as relatively static (e.g., IQ), a one-time administration should be sufficient.

Tasks that assess memory should be administered first. This is because once the initial learning sessions are finished, the therapist must provide a meaningful interpolated task to keep the client from rehearsing the learned material before the long-term retention is tested. The interpolated task should last for at least 30 minutes (preferably 1 hour or more) to ensure that the subsequent memory testing is tapping long-term retention. In practice, we use the rest of the battery as the interpolated task, but any interpolated task will work as long as it keeps the person occupied.

After the interpolated task, the therapist administers three testings for those measures

TABLE 7.1

Initial Battery for Assessing Multimodal Model of Cognition

Cognitive Ability	Test Procedure
Sensory Memory	
Iconic	Brief-duration flashes
Echonic	Continous dialogue task
Attention/Concentration	Digit span
	Visual memory span
Working/Long-Term Memory	
Rehearsal	Rehearsal card games
Verbal Memory	Buschke Selective Reminding Task
Visual Memory	Rey Figure Recall Task
	Zoo picture task
Memory Strategy	Multiple encoding task
Storage/Retrieval	Retesting on any or all of the above tests (1) for free recall, (2) for recognition, and (3) for savings
Thinking Skills	
General Intelligence	Test of Nonverbal Intelligence
	Kent IQ Test
Verbal Reasoning	Poison Foods test
Nonverbal Reasoning	Tinker Toy Test
Concept Learning	Playing Card Sequence
Cognitive Flexibility	Uses of Objects Test
Expressive Skills	Word fluency/figural fluency
	Rey Figure Copy
	Taylor Complex Shape Copy Task
	Repeating letters
	Writing sample

that index long-term memory. The first is a free recall test. That is, the client recalls all that he or she learned on the memory tasks during the first stage without any prompting. This is a gross index of transfer from short-term to long-term memory. Obviously, if the client can recall anything after an hour, then some information must have traversed short-term memory into long-term memory. However, even if there is no free recall, it does not mean that no memory transfer occurred.

After free recall, the therapist tests the client's ability to recognize the learning materials after a delay. Transfer from working memory to long-term memory has occurred if the client can recognize the materials, even if he or she cannot recall them. The problem in this case is that the information was not accessible, even though it was available. Storage occurred but the client could not retrieve the information. On the other hand, if the client can neither recognize the items nor free-recall them, then the information may not have made it into long-term memory. In this case, there may have been a problem with storage rather than retrieval.

Storage and retrieval problems are different disorders. In our experience, retrieval deficits are the more common of the two after head injury and involve the inability to spontaneously generate the retrieval cues necessary for free recall. Therapy for this type of disorder involves teaching a person retrieval strategies or providing prosthetic devices for cuing. Problems with storage are far more difficult disorders to treat.

The final measure of long-term retention is called *savings*. For this measure, an additional learning trial is given to the person after the interpolated task. If the client can relearn the original material at a level that exceeds that of his or her initial learning trial, then some amount of transfer must have occurred. The therapist readministers the same test once more during the delayed retention testing period, usually after the free recall and recognition tests. How well the person performs on this re-test is compared to his or her performance the first time the task was administered (at least 30 minutes earlier). The difference in performance between the two administrations is the index of savings.

Several conclusions can be reached using these methods for testing memory. Usually, if there is poor recognition, then there is poor recall and virtually no savings. In most situations, if the person cannot recognize, then storage is the problem. If the person can recognize but not recall, then retrieval is the problem. Likewise, if there is poor delayed recall, and there are savings, then retrieval is the problem. Perhaps the most consistent deficit is poor free recall with good recognition and savings. This is the common pattern associated with a retrieval deficit.

Observation

Although the initial assessment battery evaluates a variety of information that may not be available from other sources, it does not look at the client's everyday functioning. Family members and friends, however, do make these types of observations. Thus it may be especially useful to give the questionnaire in Appendix A to both the client and family members. This will typically provide different results. For example, as Anderson-Parenté (1994) discovered, clients can assess the concrete aspects of their behavior quite accurately, but family members are more accurate in assessing the client's ability to deal with abstractions. The combination of the two assessments can provide a useful adjunct to the performance-based testing outlined above.

Observational notes are especially useful during the test phase. For example, the therapist should note the client's optimal learning style. Does the client learn visual or verbal information most rapidly and which does he or she retain longest? How many rehearsals are necessary before the client can retain the information? What time of day is best to work with the client? How long can he or she work before fatiguing? How does the client respond to verbal reinforcement? What is the optimal distribution of practice? Answers to these questions are especially important to other therapists who might work with the client later. Lewkowics and Whitton (1995) present an excellent survey for this purpose.

Summary

This chapter presents methods for evaluating the multimodal model of cognition and also for assessing potential for success in therapy. Measures of multimodal performance are presented in Appendix C.

Conventional performance-based assessments and observational measures provide a good starting point for assessing a therapy client. However, other techniques are necessary to determine which abilities will respond most rapidly to treatment. Because rehabilitation is a learning process, it is necessary to measure not only performance at one point in time, but also the potential for improvement of performance with practice. The chapter presented dynamic assessment procedures for measuring the client's zone of rehabilitation potential. This evaluation examines three characteristics of a client's cognitive skills: the ability to improve with practice, the ability to respond to various interventions, and the ability to implement the newly learned skills into his or her daily life.

The chapter discussed several measures of learning potential. All of these index a client's ability to improve with practice. Intervention potential is based on assessment of a client's ability to benefit from various strategies the therapist may attempt. Transfer potential is a measure of how well a client can apply the newly learned skill outside of the training environment. All three measures allow the therapist to determine which interventions will have the greatest impact.

References

Acker, M. (1986). Relationship between test scores and everyday life functioning. In B. Uzzell & Y. Gross (Eds.), *The clinical neuropsychology of intervention* (pp. 85–118). Boston: Martinus Nijhoff.

Anderson-Parenté, J. K. (1994). A comparison of metacognitive ratings of persons with traumatic brain injury and their family members. *NeuroRehabilitation, 4*(3), 168–173.

Buschke, H. (1987). Criteria for the identification of memory deficits: Implications for the design of memory tests. In D. Gorfein & R. Hoffman (Eds.), *Memory and learning*. Hillsdale, NJ: Erlbaum.

Cicerone, K., & Tupper, D. E. (1986). Cognitive assessment in the neuropsychological rehabilitation of head-injured adults. In B. Uzzell & Y. Gross (Eds.), *The clinical neuropsychology of intervention* (pp. 59–84). Boston: Martinus Nijhoff.

Feuerstein, R., Klein, P. S., & Tannenbaum, A. J. (Eds.). (1991). *Mediated learning experience (MLE): Theoretical, psychosocial and learning implications*. London: Freund.

Golden, G. J., Purisch, A. D., & Hammeke, T. A. (1985). *Luria–Nebraska neuropsychological battery: Forms I and II manual*. Los Angeles: Western Psychological Services.

Goodglass, H., & Kaplan, E. (1983). *Assessment of aphasia and related disorders*. Philadelphia: Lea & Febiger.

Halstead, W. C. (1947). *Brain and intelligence*. Chicago: University of Chicago Press.

Hart, T., & Hayden, M. (1986). The ecological validity of neuropsychological assessment and remediation. In B. Uzzell & Y. Gross (Eds.), *The clinical neuropsychology of intervention* (pp. 21–50). Boston: Martinus Nijhoff.

Hilgard, E., & Bower, G. (1975). *Theories of learning*. Englewood Cliffs, NJ: Prentice Hall.

LaBlanc, J. M., & Hayden, M. E. (Eds.). (2000). Ecological validity in traumatic brain injury. *Journal of Head Trauma Rehabilitation, 15*(4), 937–1041.

Lewkowics, S., & Whitton, J. (1995). A new inventory for exploring neuropsychological change resulting from brain injury. *Cognitive Rehabilitation, 13*, 8–20.

Lezak, M. D. (1999). *Neuropsychological assessment* (2nd ed.). New York: Oxford.

Miller, E. (1984). *Recovery and management of neuropsychological deficits*. New York: Wiley.

Parenté, R., & Anderson-Parenté, J. K. (1991). *Retraining memory: Techniques and applications*. Houston, TX: CSY.

Reitan, R. M. (1955). An investigation of Halstead's measures of biological intelligence. *Archives of Neurology and Psychiatry, 73*, 28–35.

Ricker, J. H. (Ed.). (2001). Advances in neuroimaging: Applications to traumatic brain injury [Special issue]. *Journal of Head Trauma, 16*(2), 117–191.

Spreen, O., & Strauss, E. (1991). *A compendium of neuropsychological tests: Administration norms and commentary*. New York: Oxford.

Toglia, J. P. (1992a). A dynamic interactive approach to cognitive rehabilitation. In N. Katz (Ed.), *Cognitive rehabilitation: Models for intervention in occupational therapy* (pp. 104–143). Boston: Medical.

Toglia, J. P. (1992b). Generalization of treatment: A multicontext approach to cognitive perceptual impairment in adults with brain injury. *The American Journal of Occupational Therapy, 45*, 505–516.

Twum, M. (1994). Maximizing generalization of cognitions and memories after traumatic brain injury. *NeuroRehabilitation, 4*(3), 157–167.

Vygotsky, L. (1978). *Mind in society: The development of higher psychological processes*. Cambridge, MA: Harvard University Press.

Wilson, B. (1987). *Rehabilitation of memory*. New York: Guilford Press.

Wilson, B. A., Baddeley, A. D., & Cockburn, J. (1988). Trials, tribulations, and triumphs in the development of a test of everyday memory. In M. M. Gruneberg, P. E. Morris, & R. N. Sykes (Eds.), *Practical aspects of memory: Current research and issues*. Chichester, United Kingdom: Wiley.

Chapter 8

⚜

Retraining Iconic Memory

Most people can recall seeing someone whirl a glowing ember from a campfire or recall an usher's moving flashlight in a darkened theater. These lighted objects seem to trace a path in the air. The spokes on a turning bicycle wheel also appear in fluid motion as they change position in the visual field. These phenomena occur because even though a person's eyes constantly scan the environment, visual experience occurs only during the brief fixations, called *iconic memory* (IM), that punctuate the eye movements (Sperling, 1960, 1963). This type of visual experience is analogous to a movie camera in that each frame persists in IM, thereby creating the illusion of motion.

The IM is sometimes referred to as the visual sensory register (Ballesteros, 1994; Hunt & Ellis, 1998; Massaro & Loftus, 1996). (A person's other four senses also are each a sensory register.) It is also the first phase of the multimodal model of cognition described in Chapter 2. The IM's function is to hold new information for further processing by the working memory. Because the IM is the first phase of a person's visual information processing system, damage to it is especially limiting. A damaged IM will cause the working memory and all other information processing systems to be impaired. The effects of TBI on the IM are not well understood.

Although IM is only one of the five sensory registers, IM research continues to dominate the published literature in the field of sensory memory probably because the techniques for studying IM are well defined and because humans rely on visual processing more so than on other sensory processing. The IM literature, however, has focused on documenting the parameters of the IM; only a few researchers have assessed the human potential for expanding processing capacity in the visual sensory register (McClur, Browning, Vantrease, & Bittle, 1994, 1997; Parenté, Anderson-Parenté, & Shaw, 1989). These studies investigated training the IM with persons with TBI. An additional study, Hamid, Garner, and Parenté (1996), replicated and extended these findings with college student populations. These investigations of IM training showed that humans can learn to process more information in the IM. Therefore, the specific goal of this chapter is to summarize the entire body of research on IM training. Also, step-by-step training procedures that therapists can use to retrain IM are provided and the conditions under which this type of training may generalize to other skills such as reading are evaluated.

Studies of visual persistence indicate that visual perception continues for a short time after the physical stimulation of the retina ends (Haber & Hershenson, 1980; Haber &

Nathanson, 1968; Sackitt, 1976; Sperling, 1960). Iconic memory occurs during this brief period of visual perception after the object is no longer physically present. Sperling (1960) documented the physical parameters of the IM and found that it is a large-capacity information processing system that stores a perceptual snapshot of the world for only a few hundred milliseconds (DiLollo & Dixon, 1988, 1992). However, the most fascinating characteristic of IM is that it is more than just an afterimage; it persists in the brain, not in the eye.

Measuring Iconic Memory

The measurement of visual persistence is both old and new. For example, as early as 1740, Segner (described by Baddeley, 1998) used a very simple but ingenious procedure for estimating the duration of IM. He mounted a glowing coal onto the spinning wheel of a cart. He then adjusted the rate of spin for the wheel so that the coal seemed to trace a smooth circle with no gaps in the arc. He estimated a person's visual persistence by measuring the time it took to complete one revolution from the point at which the viewer no longer perceived any breaks in the arc. Segner estimated that visual persistence was approximately 100 milliseconds, which is generally consistent with estimates from modern methods.

Baddeley (1998) described a study by Hamilton (1859) who estimated how much information could be apprehended in a single glimpse. Hamilton asked participants to count the number of marbles that he threw before them. He concluded that in the milliseconds when the marbles scattered in the visual field, an average person could perceive as many as six or seven marbles accurately. He also found that if he scattered the marbles in groups of

two, three, four, or five, a person could accurately perceive the groups as well as the individual marbles.

Although there are several recently developed methods for studying IM (Loftus & Busey, 1992; Loftus, Duncan, & Gehrig, 1992; Long & O'Saben, 1989; Mewhort, Butler, Feldman-Stewart, & Tramer, 1988), most investigations have used a variant of the *partial-report procedure* (Sperling, 1960) similar to the one described next. This method was originally designed to assess the capacity of IM and recently it has been used to train IM in research studies.

In the partial-report procedure, a participant initially focused on a cross on a computer screen that indicated the exact spot where a letter matrix would flash on the screen (see Table 8.1). The matrix would appear on screen for less than 50 milliseconds. Immediately after the letter matrix disappeared from view, a signal (usually an auditory tone) cued the participant to report a certain row of letters from the array. Because the participant did not know before the tone sounded which portion of the array he or she would be asked to report, and because the flash was less than 50 milliseconds, it was impossible for the participant to scan the array with eye movement. This characteristic of the experimental design is important because it ensured that saccadic eye movements could not account for processing. Moreover, because the physical image of the matrix was no longer in view at the time the participant made the partial report, the processing must have occurred at the cortical level.

TABLE 8.1.

Classic Partial-Report Procedure

Focus Stimuli	Array			Signal
	X	B	Z	High Tone
+	K	L	Q	Medium Tone
	R	D	M	Low Tone

Using this procedure, most researchers estimated that humans could perceive 100% of a 9-letter matrix, and 75% of a 12-letter matrix. This finding was constant regardless of the participants' educational level. This same procedure was used by Parenté et al. (1989) and by McClur et al. (1994, 1997) to study the characteristics of IM in persons with TBI. Their results indicated that IM was initially reduced after brain injury. Parenté et al. (1989) found, however, that IM improved with training, approaching average levels after 6 months to 1 year postinjury. These studies of IM is persons with TBI generally showed that training with the partial-report procedure improved a person's performance to levels comparable to those obtained in participants with no injury.

Models of Iconic Memory

A review of the literature revealed a number of subtly different definitions of IM. Chow (1986) defined IM as a kind of visible persistence that allows a person to scan, peruse, or otherwise select information from the visual image. Other authors define IM as an after-effect that persists following stimulation of the retina (Haber & Nathanson, 1968; Haber & Standing, 1969; Sackitt, 1967, 1975, 1976). Coltheart (1980) described IM as a persistent form of information that has no encoded meaning or organization. All of these descriptions portray a transient memory that must be studied with specialized procedures that allow the researcher to study the IM before it fades.

Single-Stage Models

Early definitions of IM assumed that it was a single processing system with three main characteristics (Hunt & Ellis, 1998). First, information is stored in a near-photographic form with no priority assigned to the type of information that can be retrieved from the image. Second, the sensory register is a high-capacity storage system. Finally, information remains in the sensory register for only a brief period of time; the information decays rapidly and is imperceptible within 1 second. These characteristics suggest that information in the IM would be blurred if two scenes were registered in quick succession. This is precisely the reason why a movie appears as a fluid sequence of actions — the frames are presented on the screen so rapidly that the IM cannot discern the individual pictures.

Sperling (1960, 1963) also assumed that IM sustains a cortical image of the array, thereby allowing additional processing. He did not assume that meaning was processed in IM. His assumption was consistent with Orenstein and Holding (1987), who found no differences between memory for information the person attended to or did not attend to in the IM. Most researchers assumed that because the IM is virtually a photograph of the world at a specific moment in time, there was no priority of processing for any given aspect of the picture. Each definition of IM emphasized visual persistence, rapid decay, and the notion that the persistence is too brief to permit meaningful verbal encoding. This last assumption has recently been questioned, resulting in the proposal of a variety of two-stage models of IM (DiLollo & Dixon, 1988; Loftus & Busey, 1992; Long, 1985).

Two-Stage Models

Unlike the single-stage models, two-stage models assume that iconic processing involves two steps. The first stage is the processing of a literal image of information. In the second stage, a character buffer processes abstractions of the information received in the first stage. Two-stage models allow for the possible processing of meaning in the IM during the second stage. Long (1985) and Orenstein and Holding (1987) proposed similar two-stage models of IM that assumed a secondary representation of an event was produced following the initial photographic IM. A first buffer processed the basic features of the visual image and a second buffer transformed features into meaningful characters. These authors' research suggested that recognition and identification failures occur because of misperceptions in the feature (or first) buffer, whereas other types of failures result either from an inability to effectively scan the character (or second) buffer or from incorrect translations of features into characters.

Examples of these problems are readily apparent after a brain injury. For example, the misperception of letters such as *b* or *d*, letter reversals when reading, or failure to recognize an object as familiar or unfamiliar may result from a person's inability to scan the feature buffer effectively. Because the IM decays rapidly, these problems will probably increase the longer a person has to wait before associating additional information to the features that are stored in the IM (Mewhort, Butler, Feldman-Stewart, & Tramer, 1988). For example, a person may have difficulty remembering a face and corresponding name if he or she does not hear the name immediately upon seeing the face. Misperceptions in the character buffer occur in situations when a person confuses closely connected sections of text he or she may have read, or words with other words that have similar meanings, sounds, or spellings. Therefore, under the two-stage model, misperception in the IM can result from at least two sources (feature and character buffer) and can affect various activities of daily living such as reading or the identification of people who are encountered (Coltheart, 1980; Orenstein & Holding, 1987).

Training Iconic Memory and the Transfer of Iconic Memory Training

Although there is no shortage of theoretical investigations of IM (Haber & Hershenson, 1980; Neisser, 1967), there have been only a few practical applications of this research. These applications involve IM training and the effects of this training on tests of reading comprehension. The general pattern of results that has emerged from this line of research indicates that, with practice, persons with TBI were able to improve their IM to levels comparable to those of uninjured persons (McClur et al., 1994, 1997; Parenté et al., 1989).

Parenté et al. (1989) investigated using the partial-report procedure as a therapy for IM deficits in persons with TBI. Their results showed that persons with TBI improved their IM processing through practice. This finding was later replicated by McClur et al. (1994, 1997). Moreover, Parenté et al. (1989) showed that measures of reading such as word identification, reading rate, and reading comprehension improved following IM training.

McClur et al. (1994) extended the IM training procedure to include visual scanning training. They investigated the relationship between visual scanning training and IM training by first providing participants with brain injury visual scanning training and then transferring each person to an IM training task. A control group did not receive visual scanning training before IM training. Their results showed that ability to process in IM was unrelated to visual scanning.

As mentioned previously, in their recent study, McClur et al. (1997) again replicated the finding that performance on a combined IM and visual scanning task improved with practice. The findings in this study did not, however, replicate Parenté et al.'s (1989) finding that IM training improved performance on a reading comprehension task. A summary of these studies is presented in Table 8.2. The table indicates that accumulated results from Parenté et al. (1989), McClur et al. (1994), and McClur et al. (1997) show that IM is a trainable memory. However, for persons with TBI, there is less consistent evidence that the training facilitates reading comprehension in a transfer task.

In addition to persons with TBI, IM training has also been studied with college students. Hamid et al. (1996), for example, investigated training and transfer effects after IM training. This study showed that IM training improved various measures of reading, including reading comprehension. However, different types of IM training produced different effects on reading. For example, using the Sperling partial-report procedure for training improved reading rate, but not comprehension, on the transfer task. The lack of carryover of IM training to a reading comprehension task is similar to the results McClur et al. (1997) reported. When Hamid et al. (1996) used meaningful sentences rather than letter arrays during training, the training improved reading comprehension but did not affect reading rate. Although the Hamid et al. (1996) procedure was slightly different, their result was similar to that of Parenté et al. (1989). An important feature of the Hamid et al. (1996) study is that it is the first to show that meaning may be processed in IM consis-

tent with the two-stage model of IM just discussed. The finding is contrary to the previous assumptions that the iconic store is a preverbal stage of memory (DiLollo & Dixon, 1992). It also suggests that this type of IM training has its effect on the second stage of the two-stage models discussed previously.

Because reading speed and comprehension are related to visual scanning efficiency, it is reasonable to assume that if IM training is given before visual scanning training, then both procedures would interact to produce an enhanced effect on reading skills. This is because the trainee would first learn how to group words efficiently in IM, then learn how to scan the page rapidly. Scanning training would therefore be most effective if it was administered after, not before, IM training, but just before a conventional reading task. This is precisely the opposite procedure of the one used by McClur et al. (1994, 1997).

To further investigate the effects of IM training followed by scanning training, Hamid et al. (1996) replicated their first study using a variety of different IM training procedures. These authors used phrases (e.g., *the tall tree*), nonsense word strings (e.g., *tree tall the*), and random letter strings (e.g., *hte ltal eret*) as IM training items followed by computerized scanning training. A computer program flashed the word and letter strings on a monitor for approximately ⅓ second. The IM training began with simple two-word

TABLE 8.2

Summary Iconic Memory Training Research for Learning and Transfer Effects

Study	Type of Iconic Memory Training	Iconic Memory Learning Effect	Iconic Memory Transfer Effect
Parenté et al., 1989	Sperling partial-report procedure	Yes	Yes
McClur et al., 1994	Sperling partial-report procedure	Yes	NA
McClur et al., 1997	Sperling partial-report procedure	Yes	No
Hamid et al., 1996	Letter strings	Yes	Yes

Note. NA = not available.

sentences and ended with longer four-word sentences, word series, and letter strings. The IM training continued for approximately 1 hour before the scanning training began. Each participant practiced visual scanning for approximately 30 minutes before the transfer task.

During the scanning training task, another computer program presented short segments of text on a computer monitor. The text was formatted like a paragraph, but participants never saw the paragraph as a whole, only groups of words that were flashed in the same order as they would have appeared in the paragraph. The effect was to force the participant to process the short word segments iconically, as well as to move their eyes in a scanning motion across the screen.

Hamid et al. (1996) reasoned that if a person was first trained to process iconically, then taught to scan, this specific sequence of training procedures would improve reading comprehension because the two skills would produce a transferable combination. This was generally the effect. Hamid et al. (1996) found that training participants to process intact strings of words that formed grammatically correct phrases or sentences followed by visual scanning training improved reading comprehension on the *Nelson Reading Skills Test* (Hanna, Schell, & Schreiner, 1971). IM training with the same sentences where the words were rearranged to produce nonsense word strings did not improve reading comprehension and had little transferable quality.

Summary and Discussion

Why is it important to study IM and IM training? This is a complex question with a multifaceted answer. It is important to study IM because this type of memory largely determines what a person initially perceives of his or her world. Anything that limits the sensory store also affects the rest of the information processing system and the ability to encode and respond to the visual world.

The effect that TBI has on the IM has not been thoroughly studied. Parenté et al.'s (1989) and McClur et al.'s (1994, 1997) results showed that TBI can cause serious impairment of visual sensory memory, especially during the initial stages of recovery. Unfortunately, most cognitive skills training drills hand–eye coordination, teaches general memory strategies, or trains higher intellectual processes. However, the research results outlined previously suggest that during early recovery, these training strategies may have limited effect. Long-term goals of therapy will be served by focusing early treatment on sensory and attentional processes rather than on retraining higher cognitive skills.

Why is it important to study IM training? The available literature indicates that it is possible to train persons to improve processing in the sensory iconic system, and that IM training can be an effective therapy after brain injury. The results also indicate that meaning is processed in IM. Hamid et al.'s (1996) finding that meaningful items were processed more efficiently in IM than non-meaningful items has theoretical implications because most early researchers assumed that IM was a literal stage of memory. This finding supports the two-stage models of IM outlined previously.

Research studies showing that both persons with TBI and college students could improve their iconic processing with practice indicate that it is possible to improve a person's IM. These findings are especially important in light of the available literature on IM, in which there has not been much practical application of the volumes of published research on IM. Perhaps the major value of the IM literature is that it provides a good understanding of the complexities of the iconic sensory register. These studies indicate that IM is more than just a simple afterimage.

What is the best way to train the IM? Although a person's IM may eventually make a full recovery after TBI, certain types of practice can accelerate recovery. In general, short-duration exposures can be used to train a person to perceive complex visual sensory information. Any task will work as long as the duration of exposure is short enough to prohibit scanning with eye movements (approximately 50 milliseconds). This type of training, followed by visual scanning training, can improve a person's performance on reading tasks when the IM training materials are intact word strings that are similar to those the person will encounter in the later reading task. Without IM training, a person must make additional scanning eye movements to understand long word sequences. But during IM training, a person learns to process more information per eye fixation. After IM training, a person can process larger word phrases as units with a single glimpse. With extended IM training, it is conceivable that persons with TBI could learn to group clusters of words together into a single unit of meaning within their IM.

Guidelines for Iconic Memory Training

The Sperling (1960) partial-report procedure was never intended as a therapeutic activity, although it has been used as such in research studies. Although there is some evidence that it may be a useful precursor to reading training, it is better suited as a measurement task and we do not recommend that therapists use it for treatment. IM training will be most effective if the training materials are similar to those the client will encounter in everyday life. For example, when training a person's reading skills, it is necessary to use words and phrases as the IM training materials. Indeed Hamid et al. (1996) found that intact word strings provided better transfer to a reading

task than the same words or letter strings rearranged into nonsense. Given these constraints, we propose the following guidelines for IM training.

▶ 1. Use training materials that have practical value.

As mentioned previously, the Sperling partial-report procedure was never intended as a training procedure. If the goal is to retrain reading, the therapist should use intact words or word strings (e.g., Hamid et al., 1996) that the person is likely to encounter day to day. For example, a therapist could use words and phrases from warning signs or newspaper articles.

▶ 2. Determine a set of transferable target behaviors that are measurable.

A therapist could choose a commercially available computer program for measuring reading recognition or comprehension. This measurement instrument is necessary to determine if the IM training has had any effect. The therapist should define the target behaviors before the training to ensure that they are concrete and measurable. Advanced selection of target behaviors will force the therapist and client to mutually define treatment goals and success or failure.

▶ 3. Train the client to perceive progressively more information with brief-duration flashes.

Although computers are often useful for this purpose, there are other methods that may work better, especially if the therapist is providing treatment to groups. Regardless of the specific medium, in the first stage of treatment, the therapist trains the client to scan and process information that is available in brief durations. Specifically, information is presented at durations so brief that the client is forced to scan the information without using eye muscle movements. A client's habit of using eye muscles to scan may be especially difficult to break. If training reading skills, the training items should initially be no more than two words, then gradually increase to three or four words. Training may require several hundred trials at each number of words.

Computer software is ideal for this purpose, but other less technical methods can achieve the same goal. For example, Parenté et al. (1989) suggested a simple way to present information for brief durations using a standard slide projector. When training reading skill, the therapist types one-, two-, three-, or four-word phrases onto a standard sheet of white paper leaving at least a 2-inch border around each phrase. The typed words must be small enough to fit within a slide frame, about 1-inch square. The sheet of paper is then photocopied onto a transparency, which is available at any office supply store. The therapist then purchases 35 mm slide binders, which are available from most photography stores. The therapist then cuts out each of the words or phrases from the transparency with a pair of scissors and inserts each into a slide binder, thereby creating a training slide. Each transparency can create about 30 slides. The end product is a set of slides that the therapist can use to present words or phrases via the slide projector.

To create the brief-duration flashes, the therapist inserts the slides into the projector tray leaving an empty slot between each successive slide. IM training occurs when the therapist, positioning the projector on one of the empty slide slots, presses and holds the forward button on the projector which advances the tray from slide to slide without stopping. A slide is therefore flashed on the screen then removed immediately to the next blank slot in the tray. The slide flashes on the screen for about ¼ second, which creates the tachistoscopic IM training effect. The therapist flashes all of the slides in the tray, asking the client to repeat each word or phrase as he or she sees it.

IM training using the above procedure is inexpensive. Brief-duration flashes training is most effective when it follows a particular sequence. The therapist should begin with single-word flashes, followed by two-word phrases. Each of these items require at least 100 training flashes. Once the client can process these without error, then the length of the items is increased to three and eventually four words. Five-word phrases are seldom feasible.

▶ 4. Reassess the target behaviors.

Ideally, the therapist will have tested the client before treatment begins. Give the client an alternate form of the same reading test (Hanna et al., 1971) to determine if the IM training is having the desired effect. There may not be a discernible effect until the client has completed several sessions of training with the longer sequences.

▶ 5. Provide visual scanning training.

Hamid et al. (1996) found that visual scanning training is most effective when it follows IM training. Therefore IM training should be followed by intensive visual scanning training. Flashreader computer software can be used for this purpose although several other software packages are available (see McClur et al., 1997). The larger goal of combining IM training and visual scanning training is to first train the client to group more information per visual (iconic) glance, then to train the scanning skill that interacts with the IM training to enhance reading skill.

▶ 6. Reassess reading skill.

Provide a third test of reading using an alternate form of the reading test used in the earlier evaluations.

In our experience, for reading skills, the brief-duration flash procedures outlined above provided the greatest positive transfer. The procedures are also appropriate for other training goals. For example, Parenté et al. (1989) discussed using this procedure for a person to rapidly process road signs as a precursor for driver training. It may also be useful for training a person to recognize and respond rapidly to hazard signs if he or she is returning to a potentially dangerous job. Generally, the training is appropriate in any situation where the goal is to facilitate rapid and transferable processing of either visual or verbal information.

Iconic memory training may not be appropriate for everyone. The training requires long-term practice, vigilance within the training session, and frustration tolerance. Hundreds of trials may be necessary before significant practical improvement in reading or some other related skill is apparent. Clients who are disoriented, partially blind, severely depressed, have limited frustration tolerance, or those who are simply uninterested may not benefit from IM training.

The most appropriate candidates for IM training are those persons in the initial stages of recovery from TBI. This is because the rest of a person's information processing system may not respond to therapy until the IM has improved. The training is also rather easy to implement and most people can do it without a great deal of effort. Students with reading disorders are also good candidates for IM training. The step-by-step procedures outlined above are well-suited for this type of therapy. Clients who must read signs and respond rapidly will also benefit from this training. For example, using IM training with warning signs and hazard labels can decrease a person's reaction time, thereby increasing safety. Furthermore, IM training with road signs can benefit anyone who is learning to drive. In general, IM training is appropriate whenever the goal is to improve speed of processing and to decrease reaction time.

References

Baddeley, A. (1998). *Human memory*. Englewood Cliffs, NJ: Prentice Hall.

Ballesteros, S. (Ed.). (1994). *Cognitive approaches to human perception*. Hillsdale, NJ: Erlbaum.

Chow, S. L. (1986). Iconic memory, location, information, and partial report. *Journal of Experimental Psychology: Human Perception and Performance, 12*, 455–465.

Coltheart, M. (1980). Iconic memory and visible persistence. *Perception and Psychophysics, 27*, 183–188.

DiLollo, V., & Dixon, P. (1988). Two forms of persistence in visual information processing. *Journal of Experimental Psychology: Human Perception and Performance, 14*, 671–681.

DiLollo, V., & Dixon, P. (1992). Is the icon worth apples or oranges? Some fruitful thoughts on Loftus, Duncan, and Gehrig. *Journal of Experimental Psychology: Human Perception and Performance, 18*, 550–555.

Haber, R. N., & Hershenson, M. (1980). *The psychology of visual perception*. New York: Holt, Rinehart & Winston.

Haber, R. N., & Nathanson, L. S. (1968). Post-retinal storage? Some further observations on Parke's camel as seen through the eye of a needle. *Perception and Psychophysics, 3*, 349–355.

Haber, R. N., & Standing, L. G. (1969). Direct measures of short-term visual storage. *Quarterly Journal of Experimental Psychology, 21*, 43–54.

Hamid, M., Garner, R., & Parenté, R. (1996). Improving reading rate and reading comprehension with iconic memory training. *Cognitive Technology, 1*(1), 19–24.

Hamilton, W. (1859). *Lectures in metaphysics and logic* (Vol. 1). Edinburgh, Scotland: Blackwood.

Hanna, G., Schell, L. M., & Schreiner, R. (1971). *The Nelson Reading Skills Test*. Itasca, IL: Riverside.

Hunt, R. R., & Ellis, H. C. (1998). *Fundamentals of cognitive psychology*. New York: McGraw-Hill.

Loftus, G. R., & Busey, T. A. (1992). Multidimensional models and iconic decay: Reply to DiLollo and Dixon. *Journal of Experimental Psychology: Human Perception and Performance, 18*, 556–561.

Loftus, G. R., Duncan, J., & Gehrig, P. (1992). On the time course of perceptual information that results from a brief visual presentation. *Journal of Experimental Psychology: Human Perception and Performance, 18*, 530–549.

Long, G. M. (1985). The varieties of visual persistence: Comments on Yeoman and Irwin. *Perception and Psychophysics, 38*, 381–385.

Long, G. M., & O'Saben, C. L. (1989). The changing face of visual persistence. *American Journal of Psychology, 102*, 197–210.

Massaro, D. W., & Loftus, G. R. (1996). Sensory and perceptual storage: Data and theory. In E. L. Bjork &

R. A. Bjork (Eds.), Memory (pp. 68–99). San Diego, CA: Academic Press.

McClur, J. T., Browning, R. T., Vantrease, C. M., & Bittle, S. T. (1994). The iconic memory skills of brain injury survivors and non–brain injury controls after visual scanning training. NeuroRehabilitation, 4, 151–156.

McClur, J. T., Browning, R. T., Vantrease, C. M., & Bittle, S. T. (1997). Iconic memory training with stroke patients. Journal of Cognitive Rehabilitation, 14, 21–27.

Mewhort, D. J. K., Butler, B. E., Feldman-Stewart, D., & Tramer, S. (1988). "Iconic memory," location information, and the bar-probe task: A reply to Chow, L. (1986). Journal of Experimental Psychology: Human Perception and Performance, 14, 729–737.

Neisser, V. (1967). Cognitive psychology. New York: Appleton-Century-Crofts.

Orenstein, H. B., & Holding, D. H. (1987). Attentional factors in iconic memory and visible persistence. The Quarterly Journal of Experimental Psychology, 39, 149–166.

Parenté, R., Anderson-Parenté, J. A., & Shaw, B. (1989). Retraining the mind's eye. Journal of Head Trauma Rehabilitation, 4(2), 53–62.

Sackitt, B. (1967). Psychological correlates of photoreceptor activity. Vision Research, 16, 129–140.

Sackitt, B. (1975). Locus of short-term visual storage. Science, 190, 1318–1319.

Sackitt, B. (1976). Iconic memory. Psychological Review, 83, 257–276.

Sperling, G. (1960). The information available in brief visual presentations. Psychological Monographs, 74, 1–29.

Sperling, G. (1963). A model for visual memory tasks. Human Factors, 5, 19–31.

Chapter 9

❧

Retraining Attention

Disorders of attention are some of the most common and pervasive cognitive problems after brain injury. These acquired attention deficits are especially limiting because the person may no longer be able to register information in memory (Barnard & Teasdale, 1991; Cowan, 1988; Nissen & Bullemer, 1987), to solve problems, or to respond properly in social situations (Eysenck & Keane, 1990; Koriat, Ben-Zur, & Sheffer, 1988; Triesman, 1988). Even minor brain injuries can produce major attention problems. Attention deficits may go unnoticed and are frequently misdiagnosed (Gentilini, Nichelli, & Schoenhuber, 1989; Whyte, 1986). Indeed, many disorders of memory are actually disorders of attention (Plude, 1992). Although the severity of attention deficits usually lessens over time, the problems may persist for years after an injury.

There is no shortage of published research on attention in the cognitive psychology literature (Cowan, 1995; LaBerge, 1995; Pashler, 1998). The gist of this literature is that attention is a complex psychological process (Baddeley, 1981; Baddeley & Hitch, 1974; Broadbent, 1958, 1971; Cowan, 1988; Johnson & Wilson, 1980; Posner & Rothbart, 1994; Triesman, 1988); there are several different states of attention and many ways it can be impaired. As a result, the rehabilitation of attention is not a simple matter (Sohlberg & Mateer, 1988).

This chapter begins with a review of the different kinds of attention and attention deficits. We then describe various treatments that can be useful for improving attention deficits after TBI. The reader should consult Wood (1992) for an especially cogent review of this topic.

The Topology of Attention

Attention involves a focusing of mental processes on some aspect of the environment or on a concept (Johnson & Dark, 1986). Because attention involves focusing, it has a limit. This limit is called the span of attention.

Preattentive Processes

The processes that follow are precursors to attention. A person can demonstrate all of them, yet still lack attention. However, without these processes, attention cannot occur.

Arousal. Arousal refers to a person's readiness to pay attention (Posner & Rafal, 1988). Fatigue and lack of sleep render a person drowsy and unresponsive. Low levels of arousal limit a person's attentive powers (Jennings, 1986a, 1986b). However, a person can be sufficiently aroused and still fail to pay attention.

Orientation. When people hear sounds, they adjust their heads to better perceive them. This is called orientation and it functions to identify those objects, events, or ideas that may deserve attention in the near future. However, a person can be sufficiently oriented and still fail to pay attention. Orientation is typically described in three ways—in time, in place, and to person. Temporal orientation is the ability to perceive time and the passage of time. After brain injury, a person may not know the time of day or be aware of time passing. Place orientation is the recognition of familiar surroundings and the ability to navigate within them. Person orientation is the ability to recognize familiar people and to respond appropriately to them.

Alertness. Alertness describes the ability to maintain a wakeful state. When a person's eyes are open and he or she perceives sights, sounds, and other sensations, then that person is alert. But a person can be alert and still fail to pay attention.

Again, these three preattentive qualities do not ensure attention. A person with a brain injury can demonstrate all three conditions, but still have difficulty attending to the therapist's instructions.

Attentive Processes

The following are active cognitive processes that define attention. One or more of these attentional processes may be damaged after brain injury.

Routine attention. Activities of daily life such as dressing, eating, performing chores, and so forth require a person's focus. Routine attention is a person's ability to perform a simple task without exerting a great deal of mental work. Routine attention can vary in degree from paying a little attention to paying a great deal of attention. The duration of routine attention also varies, from focusing momentarily to focusing indefinitely. The duration of attention is often called *vigilance*.

Nonroutine attention. Nonroutine attention requires intense focusing on one or more objects. There are several types of nonroutine attention, which are discussed below.

Focused attention is the result of a rapid increase in focusing, caused by an unusual or important event. For example, men and women often momentarily focus attention on an especially nice-looking person of the opposite sex who enters a room. While the man or woman focuses on the distracting person, he or she may also be momentarily inattentive to the surroundings. *Vigilance* refers to the duration of focused attention. A person's vigilance is how long he or she can stay focused and concentrate.

Divided attention requires a person to focus on two things at once. For example, most people have tried to write a check, wash the dishes, or do some other simple chore while talking on the telephone. This type of divided attention often causes brief pauses in conversation.

Alternating attention refers to a person shifting focus back and forth between different aspects of the environment. For example, students often try to watch television while studying.

Concentration involves working on something mentally. For example, a student doing math problems in his or her head is using a great deal of concentration. Clearly, this activity requires the student to focus intensely, ignore distractions, and perform mental work. Concentration is similar to the concept of working memory, which is described in Chapter 11.

Discrimination involves the progressive detection of differences in a perceptual field or set of ideas. For example, most college students must detect subtle differences among answers on multiple-choice tests. To identify someone in a crowd, a person must discriminate between the subtle characteristics of different people.

Impaired Attention

After a brain injury, a person may experience problems with either routine or nonroutine attention. For both kinds of attention problems, it is important for the therapist to rule out low arousal or poor orientation before concluding a person has attention problems. For example, in Chapter 23 we discuss how monetary incentives can provide immediate improvement in attention and concentration. Therefore, providing incentives may be one way of eliminating low arousal as a contributor to what seems to be an attention deficit. Furthermore, limited sensory function also can be mistaken for attention deficits. Therefore, before a person is diagnosed with an attention deficit, he or she should receive an eye exam or a hearing evaluation.

If a person is easily distracted, even from routine attention tasks, his or her problems may include difficulty resisting distraction (poor focus), inability to pay attention to two things either at once or in alternation (poor control over shifts of focus), or difficulty remaining vigilant (fatigue or boredom). Indeed, one or more, or even all, of these disturbances may be evident after a brain injury. Perhaps the best way to evaluate the effects of distraction is to ask a person to perform a task in a noisy environment and in quiet environment, then evaluate the extent of the difference in performance.

Models of Attention

Models of attention were discussed in detail in Chapter 4. To briefly review, for a long time, attention was thought to involve a single mental switching mechanism. Researchers thought that the purpose of attention was to focus, divide, concentrate, and discriminate, as well as be vigilant or relaxed while doing so. In recent years, theorists have come to recognize that a person's ability to pay attention is seldom uniform across all of these tasks or across all situations (Eysenck & Keane, 1990). A person's attention mechanism is part of his or her biological inheritance but it is affected by experience and current environment. For example, a person may not necessarily pay attention as well at home as he or she does in the clinic because the clinic environment is contrived to produce optimal attention.

Theoretically, attention processes are governed by preconscious and conscious mechanisms (Logan, 1988; Shiffrin & Schneider, 1977; Spelke, Hirst, & Neisser, 1976). Preconscious mechanisms process perceptions without awareness and can process several things simultaneously. The conscious mechanisms voluntarily execute the attentive processes of focusing, dividing, concentrating, and discriminating. For example, even though a person is intensely absorbed in a newspaper article or television program, he or she may still be aware that someone else is in the room. The preconscious processes cause awareness of the other person's presence while the conscious mechanisms process the article or program.

Retraining Attention and Concentration

Because the topic of attention is so complicated, several different models of attention retraining have been developed. Each model has its own emphasis and is better suited for certain kinds of patients with specific disorders. Most involve a hierarchical approach in which simple attentional processes are retrained first followed by more complex processes.

Orientation Remediation Module

Ben-Yishay, Piasetsky, and Rattok (1987) developed an orientation remediation module of attention training that has proven effective for rehabilitating attention deficits after brain injury. This is one of the oldest systematic attention training programs (Ben-Yishay et al., 1980). The therapy client performs a series of tasks that are designed to gradually improve attentional processes through conditioning.

The first goal is to train the client to attend and react to visual and verbal signals. A device called an attention-reaction conditioner trains the client to respond to simple stimulations, it measures performance, and it provides feedback in a reaction-time task. An attention-reaction conditioner is any device that presents a stimulus for a measured interval and then times how long it takes a person to respond to the stimulus. It also measures the accuracy of the person's response. Computers are especially useful for this purpose because they can display different items on the monitor and measure how long it takes a person to press the space bar when he or she sees the item.

The client also learns to shift attention. For example, a device called a zero-accuracy conditioner is similar to a clock and trains the client to time his or her responses to a constantly changing stimulus source. The client holds down a button that activates a sweep hand. The sweep hand stops when the button is released. The therapist tells the client to stop the sweep hand on a randomly chosen time marking on the clock. The client then tries to position the sweep hand as close as possible to the target before stopping it, gradually decreasing errors in placement with practice.

The orientation remediation module also includes vigilance and discrimination training. A device called a visual-discrimination conditioner consists of a panel with two movable cubes and is used to train the client to maintain active vigilance. One cube contains a digital display. The other contains five colored lights. The therapist controls the display of colors, numbers, or color and number combinations. The client's task is to scan the display for predetermined combinations of colors and numbers.

This model also focuses on training a client to estimate time, an integral part of paying attention and remaining vigilant. In time-estimation training, a client learns to perceive the passage of time using a special stopwatch. The client uses the stopwatch to check his or her estimate of different time intervals.

Another of the orientation remediation module tasks addresses a client's ability to pay attention to sequencing. Using a device called a rhythm-synchrony conditioner, the client responds to a series of Morse code–like tones. Eventually he or she learns to anticipate the rhythm and responds using a telegraph key.

Ben-Yishay et al. (1987) demonstrated that persons with brain injury can improve their performance on these tasks. The training produces a lasting effect because the gains have been maintained on 6-month follow-up tests. Ben-Yishay et al. (1980, 1987) demonstrated that performance on the various tasks is significantly correlated with 19 marker variables including basic psychomotor skills, integrative functions, memory, reasoning, and interpersonal functioning.

Attention-Process Training

Sohlberg and Mateer (1986, 1988) developed a systematic method of attention-process training. This method retrains focused attention, divided attention, alternating attention, and vigilance. Attention-process training is designed to increase a person's ability to respond to different kinds of stimulation and involves detection and orientation. Clients also learn to activate and inhibit responses selectively, and to discriminate among stimuli.

Attention-process training is a graded procedure that steps a client through levels of training. Mateer and Sohlberg (1988) demonstrated that the training is effective for improving performance on standardized memory tests and also on informal measures of independent living skills.

Seven-Level Model of Attention Training

Parenté and Anderson-Parenté (1991) proposed an attention training model that covers the following processes: (a) basic arousal, (b) orientation, (c) attention with discrimination, (d) concentration, (e) distracted attention, (f) attention with immediate memory, and (g) interference resistance training.

This hierarchical model gives clients progressively more difficult information to process at each level. The client must master each level before moving to the next. In many ways, the various levels are similar to those proposed by Sohlberg and Mateer (1986) in their attention-process training model and by Ben-Yishay et al. (1987) in their orientation remediation module. Indeed, the seven-level model was designed to subsume both of these earlier attention training systems. The seven-level model was not, however, designed with specific exercises. Although examples of therapy techniques are provided at each level, the therapist is encouraged to create others that have the same characteristics. Because it is the most inclusive of all the systems, we detail its levels below and point out the similarities to the orientation remediation module and attention-process training model wherever possible.

Level I: Basic Arousal

The first stage of attention training is usually carried out in an acute care facility. It involves training the client to maintain tonic arousal for increasingly longer periods of time. For example, the therapist may have the client watch television or videos, or listen to the radio. Any activity that provides arousal can be used at this stage, and activities will vary depending on the client's interests. The measure of performance is the length of time the client can maintain the activity.

Level II: Simple Orientation to a Visual–Auditory Stimulus

The therapist's goal in Level II is to provide exercises that get the client to adjust his or her body position to correctly perceive a stimulus. The following are examples of therapy exercises; therapists are encouraged to develop similar ones:

1. The client sits blindfolded in a room on a swivel chair. The therapist walks around the room clapping his or her hands. The client swivels in the chair to orient to the clapping.

2. In a semidarkened room, the therapist turns on a flashlight. The client orients to the flashlight.

3. The therapist moves a finger from side to side in front of the client's face. The client follows the finger as it traverses the visual field.

4. Using a stereo, the therapist plays music and changes the balance control so that the music moves from side to side in a pair of headphones. The client listens on the headphones and points to the ear that is receiving the music.

5. The therapist instructs the client to orient toward the door in the therapy room

every time a person passes by in the hallway.

The measure of performance for all of these exercises is the number of times the client correctly orients. The therapist should not allow the client to go on to Level III until he or she can correctly orient consistently. For Levels III through VII, the therapist should also maintain the same length of time for each therapy session that was achieved in Level II. For example, if the client's vigilance improved to a 30-minute session in Level II, then the therapist should require this same amount of vigilance as a baseline for Levels III through VII.

Level III: Attention with Discrimination

Discrimination is more difficult than focused attention. To discriminate, the client must not only attend but produce a response. Here are some therapy suggestions for training discrimination:

1. In a dark room, the therapist asks the client to orient to a red light but not to a green one. Alternatively, the client can practice orienting in a lighted room to loud handclaps but not to soft ones.

2. The client shuts his or her eyes, then the therapist touches the client's hands with a pencil eraser or pencil point. The therapist may ask, "What do you feel, the point or the eraser?"

3. The therapist asks the client to orient to either males or females passing by the door. The client should orient only to one gender and not the other.

4. The therapist presents pictures of models cut from department store catalogs, two at a time, then asks the client to answer questions such as the following: "Which one has green eyes?" "Which one is

taller?" "Which one is blonde?" Also, the therapist asks the client to pick out pictures of family members from photos that also include strangers.

5. The therapist asks the client to sit with eyes closed and identify all the sounds he or she hears in the room, such as the air conditioner, people talking in an adjacent room, traffic sounds in the street, and so forth.

6. The therapist presents different perfumes and ask the client to identify the differences in scents while blindfolded.

7. The therapist repeats the same sentence in several different tones and after each repetition asks the client to determine the meaning of the sentence from the tone of voice.

8. The therapist presents different soft drinks and asks the client to discriminate between them. For example, the client could be asked to identify Coke, 7-Up, and lemonade while blindfolded.

None of these exercises require sustained memory, but all require sustained attention and some degree of discrimination and concentration. Many are similar to those outlined by Sohlberg and Mateer (1988) in their focused attention category. Most of the exercises are practical activities similar to those the client will encounter in everyday life. The therapist should measure (a) vigilance, that is, how long the client can do the tasks, and (b) discrimination, that is, the accuracy of performance on each task.

Level IV: Concentration and Mental Control

The Level IV exercises train mental manipulation and cognitive effort. The training materials always should be in plain view during the therapy session so that the tasks do not require a great deal of memory. The therapy suggestions for this level include the following:

1. The therapist asks the client to solve simple arithmetic problems, such as 2 + 4 − 1. The therapist should present the problems on index cards and provide several possible answers below each problem so that the problem is always in view. This eliminates the need for the client to remember the problem.

2. The therapist uses real money to present practice problems in making change mentally.

3. The therapist asks the client to solve simple riddles that are presented on cards, such as, "What do cats like to chase?"

4. The therapist presents hypothetical news events such as, "Indian and Pakistani troops are massing on the border," then asks the client to choose a likely outcome from alternatives such as (a) a battle begins, or (b) the two countries sign a peace treaty.

5. The therapist makes up simple verbal math problems such as, "Out of 20 students in a class, 8 are girls. How many are boys?"

6. The therapist presents scrambled letter strings and asks the client to unscramble the letters mentally (e.g., TCA = CAT).

7. The therapist asks the client to look at a complex or poorly worded sentence and simplify or clarify it.

The measures of performance for this level are (a) whether the client can carry on the activity for longer than 30 minutes, (b) the client's ability to respond correctly, and (c) whether the client improves with practice. The therapist can also manipulate the complexity of the problem (e.g., the number of alternative responses, whether recall rather than recognition is used).

Level V: Distracted Attention

The Level V exercises are similar to Sohlberg and Mateer's (1988) divided attention category. The reader is urged to use Sohlberg and Mateer's exercises in addition to those presented here. At this level, the client processes two sources of information, eventually learning to ignore one source while attending to the other. This training should directly mimic the real world, that is, the client should learn to screen out distractions such as music or conversations. The therapist can try the following exercises:

1. The client should solve arithmetic problems while listening to music on the radio.

2. The therapist and client play simple card games, and the therapist asks the client to estimate how much time has passed since the start of the game or since the last query.

3. The client wears headphones and listens to music while playing video games.

4. Dichotic listening procedures are also quite useful for training distracted attention. The client can wear headphones that present different messages simultaneously to each ear. He or she must repeat the information reaching one ear and ignore the information in the other.

The measures of performance in Level V are (a) the number of correct responses and (b) the amount of time the person can sustain the dual input.

Level VI: Attention with Immediate Memory

Level VI training is designed to improve attention, concentration, and short-term retention. Suggestions for therapy are as follows:

1. The client rocks back and forth to the beat of a song on the radio. The therapist

stops the music and asks the client to continue rocking to the same beat and times how long he or she can maintain the rhythm. This exercise is similar to the rhythm-synchrony conditioner training of Ben-Yishay et al. (1987), discussed earlier.

2. The therapist presents familiar sequences (e.g., 2, 4, 6, 8, and so on), then asks the client to continue the sequence (e.g., 10, 12, 14, and so on).

3. The client performs short sequences of body movements on command, such as "stand up," "sit down," "turn around," "blink your left eye." The therapist first says the entire sequence, then the client performs the movements from memory.

4. Claridge (1967) suggested a procedure that requires the client to monitor sequences of random digits and tap the top of the table each time a particular sequence occurs. The therapist creates a list of 50 to 100 three-digit numbers and recites them aloud to the client. The client is asked to tap the table every time he or she hears a certain sequence (e.g., 1-2-3), which the therapist intersperses throughout the digit series. A variation on the theme is for the client to tap his or her finger when odd numbers are presented.

5. The client traces the correct path in a maze with a finger (rather than a pencil) so that no mark is left on the maze. The therapist measures improvement in speed of performance with practice. The client must remember the maze solution to improve.

Measures of performance for this type of attention training are (a) session's length of time (vigilance), (b) number of errors (accuracy), and (c) length of time the client can sustain the activity using his or her recent memory (immediate memory).

By this stage, the therapist should begin to include an additional index of task difficulty. For example, the therapist might begin with simple exercises such as, "Continue this sequence after I stop: A, B, C," or "Stand up, sit down." Once the person has reached perfect mastery, the next series would make the tasks more difficult. For example: "A, D, G," or "Raise your right hand, raise your left hand, stand up, turn around."

Level VII: Interference Resistance Training

The Level VII exercises train the client to remember something after a second task has interfered with memory of the first. Each involves presention of a cognitive problem, followed by a second one, then a test. The following are suggestions a therapist can use:

1. Ask the client to answer simple questions such as, "Add 2 + 2 in your head. Now add 4 + 5 in your head. What was the answer to the first problem? What was the answer to the second?" The second activity interferes with the memory for the first, and the client must sustain both answers in memory long enough to answer questions about either. The therapist should gradually increase the number of activities in the sequence to match the client's level of functioning. Again, it is important to bring the client to mastery at any level before making the task more difficult.

2. The therapist reads a simple paragraph to the client. The therapist then reads another. Next, the therapist asks questions about the first, followed by questions about the second.

3. Many card games (e.g., see Chapter 10) are potentially good sources for training Level VII attention skills.

4. Using an extension phone, the therapist simulates a telephone call to the client. After a brief first conversation, the thera-

pist and client carry on a second conversation. The therapist asks the client to recall the contents of the first conversation then discuss the second.

Measures of performance include (a) correct recall of either piece of information and (b) length of time the client can sustain the activity.

Neurotherapy

Neurotherapy is a relatively new therapeutic procedure that uses either biofeedback or electroencephalograph (EEG) readings as feedback to train a person to control his or her attention. The person wears a device that monitors his or her biofeedback or EEG and provides this information to the wearer (Wallace, Wagner, Wagner, & McDeavitt, 2001). The wearer tries to manipulate the signals mentally, which presumably makes him or her aware of the underlying psychological processes. Certain patterns of EEG correlate with attention deficit disorder, such as increased theta activity and decreased beta activity, (Abarbanel, 1995; Lubar & Lubar, 1984), and other patterns describe a person who does not have attention deficit disorder. The goal of neurotherapy in treating attention deficit disorder is to teach the person to mentally create the optimal EEG pattern. Generally, the interventions try to increase beta and to decrease theta activity. Although these procedures have not been widely used with persons with brain injury, they have shown promise as a potential treatment for memory dysfunction (Fenger, 1998; Thornton, 2000). In addition, there is an increasingly large body of research that shows that neurotherapy is effective with persons who suffer from attention deficit (Boyd & Campbell, 1998; Linden, Habib, & Radovejic, 1996; Nag & Rao, 1999; O'Donnell, 1995; Rasey, Lubar, McIntyre, Zofutto, & Abbot, 1996; Thompson & Thompson, 1998; Wadhwani, Radvanski, & Carmody, 1998). It

may therefore be useful for treating similar problems with attention deficits resulting from brain injury.

Other types of neurotherapy devices are especially attractive because they convert an otherwise boring process into an engaging and interactive game. MindDrive (www .other90.com) is a biofeedback-based system that includes a variety of games. The device measures heart rate, temperature, and galvanic skin response using a finger sensor, and then uses the information to control computer games. A person wears the finger sensor and learns to play the games by learning to control these aspects of their physiology. The PlayAttention system (www.PlayAttention .com) is an EEG-based game. A person wears a helmet that monitors EEG, which, in turn, controls the game. Both systems are commercially available. Another quantitative EEG system has been used to train attention in persons with brain injury. In this system, a person's EEG controls a blinking light source that is embedded in eyeglasses the person wears (Schoenberger, Shiflett, Esty, Ochs, & Matheis, 2001). This biofeedback control of the photopic stimulation improved attention span in 12 participants who were treated over several months.

We used the MindDrive system in a pilot study to see if it improved attention span in 10 adults with brain injury. The participants played the first of the card games outlined in Chapter 10 as a baseline measure. Each participant played three of the MindDrive games, then was tested a second time with the card game. The difference in performance between the two testings was an index of the extent of improvement resulting from playing the MindDrive games. A control group played the card games twice, with the same intervening time, but did not play the MindDrive games in between testings. The results showed that those participants who played the MindDrive games improved their card game scores an average of 10 cards from the first to the second administration.

The control group improved an average of 1 card. These results suggest that this type of therapy may be a useful approach for treating attention disorders after brain injury.

Additional Suggestions

Before beginning any of these attention training exercises, the therapist should collect baseline scores that document the client's initial performance level. It is important to keep a running record of performance relative to the baseline to demonstrate improvement.

It is essential for the therapist to provide feedback on attention training results to the client, especially when the task is boring. Training attention requires using activities that interest the client, that have an obvious transferable quality, and that are relatively simple to implement. Simply exposing the client to the training situation does not ensure participation. Reinforcement and incentives are usually necessary for vigilance and concentration.

The therapist should adjust the difficulty level of the various activities by extending the duration of the task or by increasing task complexity. Furthermore, the client should never end a session making more mistakes than correct responses. This situation can only lead the client to frustration and despair.

Once the client's attention has improved, the therapist should substitute exercises that mimic real-world activities. For example, after Level III, the client should learn to associate *go* with green and *stop* with red. Better still, the therapist should incorporate real-world exercises directly into the therapy regime as a concomitant measure of improvement. In Level VII, the therapist could place certain objects, such as keys, wallet, or purse, in various parts of the room and instruct the client at the beginning of the session to remember where the objects are located. At the end of the session (which becomes an interference activity), the therapist asks the client to find the objects.

Real-life activities can give the therapist some indication that the therapy is transferring positively to the client's activities of daily living. The reader may wonder why treatment does not simply begin with real-world activities if they are so vital. If possible, we certainly would recommend beginning treatment with real-world activities. However, the contrived exercises mentioned above are usually easier to create and to quantify. Moreover, there may not be any activities of daily living that can be readily adapted for those clients who are in the earliest stages of recovery.

Summary

This chapter began by providing a brief discussion of attentional processes. Then different models of training attention were examined, including a seven-level model that includes the following stages: basic arousal, orientation, attention with discrimination, concentration and mental control, distracted attention, attention with immediate memory, and interference resistance training. A person with brain injury must pass through all of these stages before he or she will benefit from other types of memory training that are discussed in later chapters. Attention training is perhaps the most important cognitive retraining a therapist can provide because it has direct transfer to real-life activities. Without attention, higher level information processing is impossible.

References

Abarbanel, A. (1995). Gates, states, rhythms, and resonances: The scientific bases of neurofeedback training. *Journal of Neurotherapy, 1*(1), 15–38.

Baddeley, A. D. (1981). The concept of working memory: A view of its current state and probable future development. *Cognition, 10*, 17–23.

Baddeley, A. D., & Hitch, G. J. (1974). Working memory. In G. A. Bower (Ed.), *The psychology of learning and motivation* (Vol. 8, p. 475). New York: Academic Press.

Barnard, P. J., & Teasdale, J. D. (1991). Interacting cognitive subsystems: A systematic approach to cognitive-affective interaction and change. *Cognition and Emotion, 5*, 1–39.

Ben-Yishay, Y., Piasetsky, L., & Rattok, J. (1987). A systematic method for ameliorating disorders in basic attention. In M. Meier, A. Benton, & L. Diller (Eds.), *Neurological rehabilitation.* New York: Guilford Press.

Ben-Yishay, Y., Rattock, J., Ross, B., Lakin, P., Cohen, J., & Diller, L. (1980). A remedial module for the systematic amelioration of basic attentional disturbances in head-trauma patients. In Y. Ben-Yishay (Ed.), *Working approaches to remediation of cognitive deficits in brain damaged persons.* New York: New York University Medical Center.

Boyd, W. D., & Campbell, S. E. (1998). EEG biofeedback in the schools: The use of EEG biofeedback to treat ADHD in a school setting. *Journal of Neurotherapy, 2*(4), 64–70.

Broadbent, D. E. (1958). *Perception and communication.* London: Pergamon Press.

Broadbent, D. E. (1971). *Decision and stress.* New York: Academic Press.

Claridge, G. S. (1967). *Personality and arousal: A psychological study of psychiatric disorder.* Oxford, United Kingdom: Pergamon Press.

Cowan, N. (1988). Evolving conception of memory storage, selective attention, and their mutual constraints within the human information-processing system. *Psychological Bulletin, 104*, 163–191.

Cowan, N. (1995). *Attention and memory: An integrated framework.* New York: Oxford University Press.

Eysenck, M. W., & Keane, M. T. (1990). *Cognitive psychology: A student's handbook.* Hillsdale, NJ: Erlbaum.

Fenger, T. N. (1998). Visual–motor integration and its relation to EEG neurofeedback brainwave patterns: Reading, spelling, and arithmetic achievement in attention deficit disordered and learning disabled children. *Journal of Neurotherapy, 3*(1), 9–18.

Gentilini, M., Nichelli, P., & Schoenhuber, R. (1989). Assessment of attention in mild brain injury. In H. Levin, H. Elsenberg, & A. Denton (Eds.), *Mild head injury.* New York: Oxford University Press.

Jennings, J. R. (1986a). Bodily changes during attending. In M. G. H. Coles, E. Donchin, & S. W. Porges (Eds.), *Psychophysiology: Systems, processes, and applications.* New York: Guilford Press.

Jennings, J. R. (1986b). Memory, thought, and bodily response. In M. G. H. Coles, E. Donchin, & S. W. Porges (Eds.), *Psychophysiology: Systems, processes, and applications.* New York: Guilford Press.

Johnson, W., & Wilson, H. (1980). Perceptual processing of non-targets in an attention task. *Memory and Cognition, 8*, 372–377.

Johnson, W. A., & Dark, V. J. (1986). Selective attention. *Annual Review of Psychology, 37*, 43–75.

Koriat, A., Ben-Zur, H., & Sheffer, D. (1988). Telling the same story twice: Output monitoring and age. *Journal of Memory and Language, 27*, 23–39.

LaBerge, D. (1995). *Attentional processing: The brain's art of mindfulness.* Cambridge, MA: Harvard University Press.

Linden, M., Habib, T., & Radovejic, V. (1996). A controlled study of the effects of EEG biofeedback on cognition and behavior of children with attention deficit disorder and learning disabilities. *Biofeedback and Self-Regulation, 21*, 35–49.

Logan, C. D. (1988). Toward an instance theory of automatization. *Psychological Review, 95*, 492–527.

Lubar, J., & Lubar, J. (1984). Electroencephalographic biofeedback of SMR and beta for treatment of attention deficit disorders in a clinical setting. *Biofeedback and Self-Regulation, 9*, 1–23.

Mateer, C., & Sohlberg, M. (1988). A paradigm shift in memory rehabilitation. In H. Whitaker (Ed.), *Neuropsychological studies of non-focal brain injury: Dementia and closed head injury.* New York: Springer-Verlag.

Nag, S., & Rao, S. L. (1999). Remediation of attention deficits in head injury. *Neuropsychologia India, 47*, 32–39.

Nissen, M. J., & Bullemer, P. (1987). Attentional requirement of learning : Evidence from performance measures. *Cognitive Psychology, 19*, 1–32.

O'Donnell, P. H. (1995). Evaluation of the effectiveness of EEG neurofeedback training for ADHD in a clinical setting as measured by changes in TOVA scores, behavioral ratings, and WISC–R performance. *Biofeedback and Self-Regulation, 20*, 83–99.

Parenté, R., & Anderson-Parenté, J. K. (1991). *Retraining memory: Techniques and applications.* Houston, TX: CSY.

Pashler, H. E. (1998). *The psychology of attention.* Cambridge, MA: MIT Press.

Plude, D. (1992). Memory improvement and attention training. In D. Herrmann, H. Weingartner, A. Searlman, & C. McEvoy (Eds.), *Memory improvement: Implications for memory theory.* New York: Springer-Verlag.

Posner, M. I., & Rafal, R. (1988). Cognitive theories of attention and the rehabilitation of attention deficits. In M. Meier, A. Benton, & L. Diller (Eds.), *Neuropsychological rehabilitation.* New York: Guilford Press.

Posner, M. I., & Rothbart, M. K. (1994). Attentional regulation: From mechanism to culture. In P. Bertelson, P. Eelen, & G. D'Ydewalle (Eds.), *International perspectives on psychological science: Vol 1, Leading themes.* Hillsdale, NJ: Erlbaum.

Rasey, H. W., Lubar, J. E., McIntyre, A., Zofutto, A. C., & Abbot, P. L. (1996). EEG biofeedback for enhancement of attentional processing in normal college students. *Journal of Neurotherapy, 2*(3), 15–21.

Schoenberger, N. E., Shiflett, S. C., Esty, M. L., Ochs, L., & Matheis, R. (2001). Flexyx neurotherapy system in the treatment of traumatic brain injury: An initial evaluation. *Journal of Head Trauma Rehabilitation, 16*(3), 260–274.

Shiffrin, R. N. J., & Schneider, W. (1977). Controlled and automatic human information processing: II. Perceptual learning, automatic attending, and a general theory. *Psychological Review, 84,* 127–190.

Sohlberg, M. M., & Mateer, C. A. (1986). *Attention process training (APT).* Puyallup, WA: Association for Neuropsychological Research and Development.

Sohlberg, M. M., & Mateer, C. A. (1988). Effectiveness of an attention training program. *Journal of Clinical and Experimental Neuropsychology, 9,* 117–130.

Spelke, E. S., Hirst, W. C., & Neisser, U. (1976). Skills of divided attention. *Cognition, 4,* 215–230.

Thompson, L., & Thompson, M. (1998). Neurofeedback combined with training in metacognitive strategies: Effectiveness in students with ADHD. *Applied Psychophysiology and Biofeedback, 23,* 243–263.

Thornton, K. (2000). Improvement/rehabilitation of memory functioning with neurotherapy/QEEG biofeedback. *Journal of Head Trauma Rehabilitation, 15*(6), 285–296.

Triesman, A. M. (1988). Features and objects: The 14th Bartlett Memorial Lecture. *Quarterly Journal of Experimental Psychology, 40A,* 201–237.

Wadhwani, S., Radvanski, D. C., & Carmody, D. P. (1998). Neurofeedback training in a case of attention-deficit/hyperactivity disorder. *Journal of Neurotherapy, 3*(1), 47–54.

Wallace, B. E., Wagner, A. K., Wagner, E. P., & McDeavitt, J. T. (2001). A history and review of quantitative electroencephalography in traumatic brain injury. *Journal of Head Trauma Rehabilitation, 16*(2), 165–190.

Whyte, J. (Ed.). (1986). Attention and memory. *Journal of Head Trauma Rehabilitation, 1*(3), 1–85.

Wood, R. (1992). Disorders of attention: Their effect on behavior, cognition, and rehabilitation. In B. Wilson & N. Moffat (Eds.), *Clinical management of memory problems* (pp. 216–242). San Diego, CA: Singular.

Chapter 10

⚘

Maintenance Rehearsal

Rehearsal is what most persons with brain injury call repetition. Both terms imply that a person must repeat something until it solidifies in his or her mind (Atkinson & Shiffrin, 1968). The conventional wisdom is that this process creates vivid and lasting memories. Elementary school teachers, for example, often teach their students that "practice makes perfect." Indeed, most persons with brain injury report that their major method for remembering is repeating something until it sticks in memory. There is, however, much more to rehearsal than the simple maintenance of information in memory (Spelke, Hirst, & Neisser, 1976). Consequently, two chapters of this book are devoted to this important aspect of treatment. This chapter describes maintenance rehearsal and various techniques for training it. Maintenance rehearsal is the first step of rehearsal training; the client learns the value of repetition and determines the number of repetitions necessary for him or her to remember novel experiences. The second step, discussed in Chapter 12, is teaching memory strategies that the client can use in conjunction with maintenance rehearsal. Chapter 13 concerns the interaction between rehearsal skill and memory strategies.

What Is Rehearsal?

The conventional view of rehearsal defines it as the mechanism responsible for transferring information from a temporary to a permanent memory state (Atkinson & Shiffrin, 1968). For example, students learn history or chemistry facts by studying their notes repeatedly. However, rehearsal does not always create a permanent memory. Most people can recall the last time they called directory assistance and did not have a pencil to write down the phone number received. It was probably necessary for them to repeat the phone number over and over until they dialed it. They remembered the number only temporarily. Indeed, people usually have no need to store in memory many of the events they encounter each day. For example, a person seldom memorizes the phone numbers for dry cleaners, the local dump, or even a favorite pizza delivery shop. If a person meets someone casually at a party, he or she often will recall the person's name during the conversation but not the following day. These examples illustrate common situations in which people rehearse information not intending to learn it. This type of processing is *maintenance rehearsal* (Craik & Watkins, 1973; Rundus, 1977).

Instruction in maintenance rehearsal could help a person with brain injury in many situations, such as recalling the phone number of a business or remembering instructions for a simple task. In each of these situations, the goal is to maintain information in memory long enough to use it, then to forget it.

There are several ways to improve maintenance rehearsal (Herrmann, Raybeck, & Gutman, 1993; Payne, 1992; Pressley & El-Dinary, 1992). For example, a client will maintain information in working memory longer if he or she rehearses it with rhythmic repetition, such as, "Set the table, pour the wine, serve the dinner, dessert at nine." The client could also use a *cumulative rehearsal* technique in which he or she repeats the sequence, gradually adding more items to it. For example, "Set the table—set the table, pour the wine—set the table, pour the wine, serve the dinner—set the table, pour the wine, serve the dinner, dessert at nine." Either of these techniques will help maintain the information in memory until the client completes the task. In many situations, however, temporary maintenance is not the goal. More often than not, people seek to permanently store information in memory. Strategies related to this goal are called *storage rehearsal*, because the purpose is long-term storage of the information, or *elaborative rehearsal*, because permanent storage may require a client to expand or to embellish the information (Herrmann et al., 1993).

Training maintenance rehearsal is a necessary antecedent for any memory training. Maintenance rehearsal keeps information in memory so that the client can encode, elaborate, reduce, or alter the information so that it is stored in a form that can be retrieved later (Harrell, Parenté, Bellingrath, & Lisicia, 1992; Parenté & Anderson-Parenté, 1991). Without maintenance rehearsal, a person with brain injury typically cannot remember novel experiences for longer than a few seconds, dooming him or her to a lifetime of immediate perception. Without storage rehearsal, the person cannot store and retrieve information from long-term memory, limiting him or her to a lifetime of immediate memory experience. It is, therefore, essential for a person with brain injury to relearn both types of rehearsal.

Most people use rehearsal strategies subconsciously and automatically. A person with brain injury, however, often loses the ability to rehearse automatically (Baddeley, Harris, Sunderland, Watts, & Wilson, 1967). It is therefore necessary to retrain this skill consciously and actively at first. With practice, the activity eventually becomes automatic (Harrell, Parenté, Bellingrath, & Lisicia, 1992).

Rehearsal Practice

It seems obvious to say that practicing rehearsal is essential for those clients with memory deficits. Indeed, several authors report that rehearsal practice can improve memory, often dramatically and substantially after traumatic brain injury (Chase & Ericsson, 1982; Colley & Beech, 1989; Healy & Borne, 1995; Parenté, Twum, & Zoltan, 1994). Ideally, rehearsal training should mimic some real-life activity. For example, the best practice for learning how to remember names is to experience introductions as often as life provides. Unfortunately, life rarely provides enough introductions to become skilled at learning names. Therefore, clients usually receive extra practice in artificial situations. Therapy in rehearsal practice is a three-stage process. First, the therapist demonstrates that the client's current method of rehearsal is inefficient. Second, the therapist creates an activity that forces the client to rehearse. This activity demonstrates to the client that rehearsal noticeably improves his or her memory. Finally, the activity shows the client the number of rehearsals necessary to improve his or her memory in other situations.

Most people with brain injury notice immediate and substantial improvement in their memory when they rehearse effectively. When training rehearsal, the therapist should begin by training maintenance rehearsal. Specifically, the therapist must determine the number of rehearsals necessary to bring the client's memory to average levels. For typical adults, one or two repetitions are enough. But people with brain injury typically require many more. Because clients do not know how many rehearsals they need, the therapist must demonstrate that additional rehearsals will help their memory function much better, often at average levels.

Many people with brain injury may resist repeating things several times. Because they had no need to do so before the injury, they may not see any reason for doing so now. The different kinds of rehearsal and training activities in this chapter will help clients recognize their benefits and overcome reluctance. The card games discussed in this chapter can demonstrate the effects of maintenance rehearsal and illustrate how many rehearsals will be necessary to improve a client's ability to learn and retain new information. The reader should note that while these games may not have any direct transfer to the client's activities of daily living, the skill they teach does generalize (Deaton, 1991).

There are three important points the therapist must remember when teaching a transferable memory skill. First, the training must demonstrate how effective and immediately useful the technique can be for the client (Pressley & El-Dinary, 1992). Such a demonstration increases the client's confidence in his or her memory capabilities and the client's hope that he or she may eventually regain rehearsal skills. Second, the therapist should present memory skills like rehearsal in such a way that the client can see their use in everyday life activities. Finally, the therapist should demonstrate how the technique applies in various situations. The

major challenge for the therapist is getting the client to use the strategy outside of the therapy context.

Card Games for Training Rehearsal Skill

The therapist can use several card games to train maintenance rehearsal. Each game demonstrates the immediate improvement that the client will experience with maintenance rehearsal. There are three purposes to the games. The first purpose is to demonstrate the effectiveness of rehearsal for the client. The second purpose is to demonstrate how much better the client's memory can be if he or she rehearses spontaneously. The third purpose is to determine how many rehearsals are necessary to improve the client's performance to an acceptable level.

The games are easy to learn and require only a deck or two of playing cards. In addition, the card games improve attention and concentration at least as well as most cognitive rehabilitation computer software. The advantage of these games is they do not require a computer. Family and friends can play the games with the client.

The therapist should teach one card game in a therapy session. The client then plays the game between sessions. At the next session, the therapist determines whether the client demonstrates improvement. Once the client has improved at one game, the therapist presents another game. The therapist continues the training until the client has learned all the games.

All of the games have three phases. The first phase establishes a baseline that documents the client's current performance. During the second phase, the therapist forces the client to consciously rehearse, which typically results in immediate and noticeable improvement. During the third phase, the therapist asks the client to continue to play the game and encourages the use of the newly learned rehearsal strategy. At this phase, the therapist also adjusts the number of rehearsals to the point at which the client no longer makes mistakes. The goal is to determine how many rehearsals are necessary to see noticeable improvement in the client's memory. This will be obvious because the client will make fewer mistakes when forced to rehearse. Most clients will see that they can improve their memories 100% by simply rehearsing three to five times.

It is vital that the therapist keep accurate records of performance to demonstrate progress during each phase of training. It is also important to explain to the client that what he or she has lost is the ability to rehearse automatically. That is, the games teach the client that he or she must rehearse most things consciously until the process becomes automatic again. Because many clients feel that constant rehearsal is too labor intensive, the therapist should remind the client that extra rehearsal is not necessary in all situations. It is only necessary for those in which the client must remember something or someone.

Number of Rehearsals

Adjusting the number of rehearsals in the third phase is extremely important. Most people assume that they need only hear or see things once to remember them. The major purpose of these card games is to determine exactly how many times a client will have to hear new information before he or she can retain it effectively. The number of required rehearsals will vary from person to person. It is crucial for the therapist to impress on the client that he or she will have to repeat, rehearse, or perhaps rethink new information several times before it will "stick" in memory. Once clients begin rehearsing, their performance on the card games and during the day will improve noticeably.

Design of the Games

Most of the card games follow a similar design. First, the client tries the game without instruction. Then, the therapist provides instruction and demonstrates improvement. Finally, the client shows spontaneous use of the strategy in a real-world task.

Like any other memory technique, maintenance rehearsal is only useful if the client begins to use it spontaneously in everyday activities. The card games are not, necessarily, therapeutic in and of themselves. The basic purpose of the games is to train a strategy that generalizes to the real world. Moreover, several games are presented and not every person with brain injury will play all of them. Perhaps one game will be sufficient to train the strategy with a particular client. Nevertheless, several games have been provided because different clients will prefer different games.

The therapist should purchase two inexpensive decks of cards, one with red backs, and the other with blue. The decks should be identical in every other way. The games are each discussed and labeled according to the type of maintenance rehearsal process they train. Similar games were discussed by Parenté and Anderson-Parenté (1991).

Game 1: Interference Resistance

Interference refers to a situation in which a person is experiencing one event, but a second event occurs and interrupts the person's memory for the first. For example, a ringing telephone may interrupt a person's memory for what he or she was doing while cooking dinner. The person must resume cooking at a point just prior to the interruption point. Likewise, a person's memory for one conversation may diminish when someone temporarily interrupts it. In general, this card game trains the client to rehearse in situations where the second of two sequential activities interferes with memory for the first (Spelke et al., 1976).

Baseline. The therapist shows the client a card from a deck and asks him or her to say aloud the number or face and suit of the card (e.g., "five of hearts"). The therapist then places this card face down on the table in front of the client. The therapist draws a second card, the client states its number or face and suit (e.g., "jack of diamonds"), and the therapist then places the second card face down next to the first.

The client must then recall the number or face and suit of the first card. If correct, the client places the card in a pile to his or her right side. If incorrect, he or she places the card in a pile to his or her left side.

The therapist displays a third card and, once again, the client says the number and suit aloud. The therapist places the card face down next to the second card, and then the client says the number and suit of the second card. In other words, after saying the number and suit of one card, the client must recall the number and suit of the card that he or she saw immediately before.

The process continues until the deck is exhausted. The therapist always displays a card, asks the client to say its number and suit, and then places the card face down next to another that the client has previously labeled. The therapist points to the old card and asks the client to identify it. If the client incorrectly identifies the card, then the therapist places it in the "wrong" pile. If correctly identified, it goes in the "right" pile. The therapist replaces this card with one from the deck, and the client must then identify the old card.

The measure of performance is the number of cards in each pile when the deck is exhausted. This is a measure of how well the client can retain information in the short term. Clients generally miss about every third card. The therapist should either record the number of errors or simply leave the piles

on the table to show correct and incorrect responses before beginning the second phase with a new deck. When the client's performance in the rehearsal phase is compared to his or her baseline performance, the client can see that the rehearsal strategy works.

Rehearsal Phase. The therapist repeats the game, this time forcing the client to rehearse. After the client says the name and suit of the first card, the therapist places it face down (as before). This time, however, the therapist points to it again before showing a second card and asks, "Now, what did you say this first card was?" This modification forces the client to rehearse the identification of the facedown card before seeing another. If the client continues to make mistakes, then it may be necessary to ask for more than one rehearsal. ***The therapist adjusts the number of rehearsals until the client does not make any errors.*** We usually begin with five rehearsals and adjust the number upward or downward until the client eliminates all mistakes.

The game proceeds as before, with this new rehearsal feature added. That is, before the client identifies each new card, the therapist requires him or her to rehearse the old card that is still face down on the table. When forced to rehearse, clients often will not make any mistakes. Most are impressed to see the immediate improvement in their accuracy.

Again, it is critical for the therapist to adjust the number of rehearsals until the client no longer makes errors. The number of rehearsals necessary indicates the number of times the client will need to rehearse most information. Ideally, the therapist should leave the client with the knowledge that, from now on, he or she must rehearse most things at least that many times to remember effectively.

Modification. It is easy to adjust the difficulty level of this game depending on the severity of the client's brain injury. The therapist can make the game easier simply by having the person remember the color (red or black) of the card rather than the suit and number. Or, the client can recall just the number or the suit alone. The therapist can make the task more difficult by using more than two cards. Three cards is usually quite difficult for most persons with brain injury. More than three is virtually impossible. Before the therapist makes this game more difficult, however, the client must demonstrate perfect performance several times with only two cards.

Generalization. Once the client can play the game without substantial errors (typically fewer than five cards in the "wrong" pile), then the therapist can show how the technique relates to the real world. For example, the therapist can give the client sequential directions and ask the person to perform the first after performing the second. This activity requires the client to rehearse the first while performing the second. For example, the therapist can direct the client to turn the television to a certain channel. The client is then asked to switch channels. The therapist then asks the client to switch back to the first channel. This requires the client to rehearse the first channel while watching the second one. In another variation, the therapist requires the client to perform some activity, but then interrupts it with another. For example, the client is asked to boil water for a cup of tea, then is asked to go to the living room to water a plant. Then the client is asked to return to the kitchen to continue the original activity. The therapist should encourage the client to rehearse each activity as many times as was necessary to eliminate most errors in the card game. These activities are similar to those discussed in Chapter 9 for retraining the latter stages of the seven-level attention model.

Game 2: Rehearsing Multiple Sets

Rehearsing multiple sets requires a person to remember the number of occurences in several different categories. For example, elementary school teachers keep mental records of how often each student answers questions correctly or misbehaves. Most people mentally track how many times they use certain words in a conversation to avoid overusing them. Salespeople keep track mentally of how many of a particular item they have sold each day. These activities require a person to maintain multiple categories and mentally tally occurences of each category over time.

Baseline. The therapist shows the client three cards, one at a time, and places each face down after presentation. The therapist tells the client to "remember how many there are of each suit." Then the therapist asks the client to say aloud the number of cards he or she recalls from each suit (e.g., "two diamonds and one spade"). The therapist picks up the cards and evaluates whether the client's memory is correct. If the client is correct, the therapist places all the cards in the "right" pile. If any answers are incorrect, then all the cards go in the "wrong" pile. The client should play the game initially without forced rehearsals, trying to remember the cards whatever way he or she can. These two piles constitute baseline performance.

Rehearsal. In the rehearsal phase of this game, the client must use cumulative rehearsal, that is, keep a running total aloud, as the therapist presents each card. For example, when the first card is displayed, the client would say, "diamond." After the second card, the client would say, "one diamond, one spade." After the third card, the client would say, "one diamond, two spades." After having seen and rehearsed all the cards, the client repeats how many of each suit there were in the hand. If his or her recall is correct, all the cards go in the "right" pile. If the recall is incorrect, then all the cards go in the "wrong" pile.

Modification. The therapist can easily modify the game to fit the client's abilities. For example, persons who are severely impaired can be asked to count only the numbers of red cards and black cards. This makes the game considerably easier. The therapist can make the game more difficult by increasing the number of cards from three to five.

Generalization. The therapist can use real-world categories for maintenance of multiple sets. For example, the client can keep track mentally of how many television shows he or she watched between sessions that were of different genres, such as action, drama, and comedy.

Game 3: Spatial Rehearsal

Spatial rehearsal refers to memory for people or things in a three-dimensional space. This common activity of daily living involves recalling where something is located or where to find something similar. For example, if a person is shopping at a mall, he or she may not buy a piece of clothing at one store because he or she recalls seeing the same item on sale in another store. Training this skill involves a game that is similar to the popular child's game *Memory* or the television quiz show *Concentration*.

Baseline. The game begins with 16 cards, 4 from each suit (i.e., 4 clubs, 4 spades, 4 diamonds, 4 hearts). Any 4 cards from each suit will work. The therapist shuffles the 16 cards and arranges them into a square grid. The client turns over any four cards, leaving them in the same position in the grid. If the four cards have the same suit, the therapist takes them off the grid. If the cards are not all from the same suit, the therapist turns them face down again, leaving them in the same position in the grid. The client must remember the cards' suit and position in the grid.

Next, the client turns over four more cards. The therapist should restate that the goal is to turn over four of the same suit. As before, if they are all of the same suit, then all four are cleared from the grid. If not, the ther-

apist turns them back over, leaving them in the same position in the grid. This procedure continues until the client clears the entire board.

Rehearsal. The game begins again, but this time the client is required to rehearse the card positions in the facedown set after each attempt. If the client turns over four cards that are not of the same suit, he or she must immediately turn the cards face down as before. But before looking at four more cards, the therapist asks the client to rehearse the position and suit of the four cards that were just turned. Specifically, the client should point to the four cards that he or she just saw and identify each card's suit from memory. This rehearsal procedure usually results in a 100% reduction of the number of guesses necessary to clear the board. If not, then the therapist should adjust the number of required rehearsals accordingly.

Modification. Increasing or decreasing the number of cards the client must match changes the difficulty of the game. Also, the therapist can make the game less difficult by asking the client to arrange colors only (e.g., reds on the left and blacks on the right) instead of suits.

Generalization. To generalize this skill, the therapist can create a situation using the client's immediate environment. The client could learn the floor plan of his or her facility and then identify staff members with a shared attribute. For example, the client could try to pick out staff members with similar size offices. He or she could also identify therapists of the same sex, with similar hair color, or by approximate age using the floor plan. Placing Polaroid photographs of the therapists on a floor plan of the building in the approximate location of their offices is one way to apply this spatial rehearsal strategy. If the client can move around freely, then the therapist might take the client to a shopping mall to identify pairs of stores with similar items.

Game 4:
Rehearsing Changing Sets

People frequently have to identify something as familiar even though its context is changing. For example, restaurant waiters must recall orders from several tables at a time even though the people at the various tables are slowly changing as parties finish their dinners and others are seated (Ericsson & Poulson, 1988). Portions of a waiter's spatial memories are constantly changing whereas other portions are temporarily the same. These tasks require a person to maintain a set of information in memory, to modify it over time, and to maintain the new set until the next change occurs. The following game comes close to simulating this activity.

Baseline. The client sees three cards, one at a time, and names each one aloud as the therapist places them face down on the table. The therapist then shows the client other cards from the deck, one at a time, until he or she identifies one that is the same face (king, queen, jack, or ace) or number (2 through 10) as one of the three cards that is face down on the table. For example, if one of the facedown cards is a seven and the client sees another seven (any suit) while going through the deck, he or she must identify which of the facedown cards is the match. The therapist checks to see if the match is correct and, if so, puts the pair in the "right" pile. If the pair does not match, then the pair goes in the "wrong" pile. When a match is made, the therapist shows the client another card from the deck and uses it to replace the one from the set of three facedown cards that he or she just matched. As a result, the set of facedown cards will be constantly changing as the client makes matches from the deck. This process continues until the deck is exhausted. The baseline measure is the number of cards in each pile.

Rehearsal. In the rehearsal stage, the client plays the game in the same way, except rehearses the current facedown set several times before searching the deck for matches. Each time a new card is added to the facedown set, the client rehearses the entire set.

Modification. The therapist can make the game more or less difficult by adding or subtracting cards in the matching set. Persons who are severely impaired can begin with two cards and gradually increase to four. Persons who are mildly impaired can begin with four and increase to five, then six, and so forth.

Generalization. The therapist can create a cooking task that requires the client to maintain a changing list of items needed to cook a particular dish. The client looks for different items from each set. After the client finds a match, the therapist replaces it with a new item. For example, to bake a cake, the client will need a bowl, spoon, and sugar. The client rehearses bowl, spoon, and sugar, and then searches the kitchen for any of these items. When he or she finds one, the therapist introduces another to the existing set. For example, after finding the spoon, the therapist deletes this item from the list and adds flour. The client rehearses bowl, sugar, flour, then searches again and retrieves a bowl. The therapist deletes bowl and adds butter, and the client rehearses sugar, butter, flour, and so forth.

Game 5: Rehearsing Sequence

Throughout the course of a given day, people must organize and prioritize their actions. For example, when washing a car, a person automatically rehearses the sequence of steps that will get the task done quickly and efficiently. When cooking dinner, a person will arrange the ingredients and subtasks to create the meal in the shortest amount of time. The following card game trains the client to rehearse this type of sequential activity.

Baseline. The therapist shows the client five cards (one at a time). After each card is shown, the therapist places it face down on the table in a random order, until all five cards are face down. The client must then arrange the cards in numerical order from left to right, lowest to highest. The task requires the client to remember the cards so he or she can arrange them in the proper order. If the client correctly arranges the card sequence, the therapist places them in the "right" pile. If the person does not arrange all five cards correctly then the therapist places them all in the "wrong" pile. The game continues until the deck is exhausted. The baseline measure is the number of cards in each pile.

Rehearsal. In this phase, the client begins the game again, but this time he or she rehearses the identification of the facedown cards in their various positions before rearranging them from lowest to highest. Specifically, the client waits until all the cards are laid down, then rehearses the positions. The goal at this stage is to identify how many rehearsals are necessary to ensure errorless performance. The therapist should encourage at least that many rehearsals for the rest of the game. To rehearse, the client says the number (or face) of each of the facedown cards.

Modification. The therapist can make the game easier or more difficult by using fewer (e.g., two) or more (e.g., seven) facedown cards. The game is quite easy if the client arranges only red (first) then black (second) cards in that sequence.

Generalization. The therapist can train the client to rehearse sequences of everyday activities, such as those for cleaning a house or washing a car. The therapist can list the steps on the backs of index cards and ask the client to arrange the facedown index cards in the correct order, thus forcing memory for the events in the sequence.

Game 6: Logical Rehearsal

Many problem-solving tasks require a person to rehearse facts that eventually accumulate until the person solves the problem. For example, when the television breaks, a person will try several possible solutions until one or a combination solves the problem. The person accumulates those things he or she has already tried, such as, "It's plugged in—It's turned on—The cable is hooked up," and so forth. Each of these facts eliminates a possible solution until the person eventually identifies the correct one. The following card game illustrates this type of rehearsal.

Baseline. The therapist begins the game by giving the client one of the card decks. The therapist selects a single card from the other deck. The client then asks questions about the card the therapist is holding. The client does not know the identity of the card and the goal of the game is for the client to remember the answers the therapist provides. The client must correctly identify the therapist's card, then produce it from the client's deck. For example, the client might ask, "Is it a red or a black card?" The therapist would say, "Red." The client might then ask, "Is it a face card or a numbered card?" The therapist would say, "A numbered card." This questioning goes on until the client can produce the correct card.

The critical feature of this game is that the client must remember and use the information the therapist provides to search out the correct card. The client may need to sift through his or her deck after each question until the game procedures become more familiar. The therapist may later require the client to ask all of the questions first, before beginning the search. The task, therefore, forces the client to remember the answers to as many as 5 to 10 questions to select the appropriate card.

This game is quite challenging at first, and the therapist will notice that clients repeatedly ask the same questions because they have forgotten the answers. If the client correctly matches the card, then the match goes into the "right" pile. If the guess is incorrect, the therapist places the cards in the "wrong" pile. Stable baselines can be achieved after going through about one half of the deck.

Rehearsal. The therapist should instruct the client to rehearse the answers to all previous questions before asking another. The game then continues with this forced rehearsal procedure. The client will be surprised to see a 100% reduction in the number of errors after the therapist adjusts the number of necessary rehearsals.

Modification. The therapist can make the game more difficult by having the client consider two cards at the same time. That is, questioning would continue until the client has identified two cards correctly. The task requires that he or she hold the information about both cards in memory at the same time.

Generalization. The therapist can ask the client to use this technique to answer questions about everyday life. For example, the therapist could ask the client to figure out on which street a friend lives by questioning. For example, "Is it in this neighborhood?" "Is it close to us?" and so forth. The game of charades is similar to this activity.

Evaluation of Card Activities

There are several major advantages to these card activities. First, they are simple to understand and they do not require any elaborate materials. Second, clients can play the games during leisure time. After a certain point, the games do not require special supervision. The therapist can also train a family member to play the games with the client. However, the most important feature of the games is that they clearly illustrate the power of rehearsal. When shown how to rehearse, clients usually realize a 100% improvement in their performance (Payne, 1992). The noticeable increase in performance using the rehearsal strategy is sufficient to convince the client that rehearsal is something worthwhile, and that he or she should make an effort to rehearse. These games are useful because the clients learn a strategy that is easy to apply in a variety of contexts (Hasher & Zacks, 1988). Once clients begin to rehearse spontaneously, the therapist's next step is to refocus training so the newly acquired skill generalizes to activities of daily living. This is the "bottom line" of rehearsal training. Without generalization, it is questionable whether the therapy is useful.

Generalization Training Exercises

The following generalization exercises are certainly not the only ones a therapist could use. They are simply ones that we have used largely because they are convenient and do not require elaborate materials. Regardless of which exercises the therapist uses, they should mimic the real world.

Rehearsing Numbers

Read ZIP codes, telephone numbers, or Social Security numbers (Chase & Ericsson, 1982), and ask clients to say the numbers repeatedly. They may be able to recall a ZIP code without rehearsal, but phone numbers are more difficult to remember and require additional restatement before dialing. The training should show the client the number of times he or she will have to rehearse in order to recall a phone number accurately. Usually, this is the same number of rehearsals that were required to play the card games without error.

Name and Face Association

For name and face association training, the therapist makes flash cards using faces taken from magazines and names randomly assigned from the telephone directory. The therapist glues the pictures on the fronts of index cards and says the names verbally. The goal is to train clients to rehearse each name several times while viewing the associated face before going on to the next name and face combination. After showing several cards, the therapist repeats the cards and the client must recall the associated names. The measure of accuracy is simply the number of names the client correctly recalls. The therapist should adjust the number of times the names are rehearsed until the client no longer makes errors, then encourage the client to rehearse names and faces at least that many times in the future.

Following Instructions

The therapist gives the client a series of instructions, and asks him or her to restate them before carrying them out. For example, the therapist says, "Write your name, age, Social Security number, and date of birth." The client repeats the command sequence aloud before doing it. The measure of accuracy is the number of commands the client correctly carries out. Again, the goal is to determine how many rehearsals of the instructions are necessary before the client can follow the directions correctly. Once the number is established, the client should rehearse directions at least that many times.

Reading Text

The therapist asks the client to repeat from memory the gist of text he or she has just read aloud. If this is too difficult, then the client rereads it one or more times. In addition to demonstrating the effects of rehearsal, this activity teaches the client a valuable self-monitoring skill, that is, not to read further until he or she can repeat what was just read. This skill is extremely important for those who go on to formal educational training because most academic topics require sequential reading comprehension. That is, the student must understand what he or she has already read because new topics build on previously introduced ones.

Seeing Improvement

We recommend including real-life activities as measures of transfer after the client learns the card games. That is, after each training session, the therapist may assign common activities to determine whether the client is using maintenance rehearsal. As therapists teach the strategy of rehearsal while playing the games, they should also show the client that the same strategy generalizes to more practical real-life activities such as dialing a phone or taking a message.

It is helpful for therapists to chart client performance on all tasks as the therapy proceeds so that the client can see improvement. Clients should practice each of the games every day. The therapist should not allow a client to transcend one level of difficulty in any game until he or she has demonstrated complete mastery of the previous levels. Therapists may wonder why they should start with the card games instead of beginning with the real-life activities. First, the games are easy to learn, making it easy for clients to practice between therapy sessions. All the therapist and client need is a deck of cards. It is more difficult for clients to construct transfer materials such as photographs, digit strings, or text passages. Second, the games are easier to quantify. Other activities may not provide uniform difficulty. For example, text passages will vary in complexity and length.

References

Atkinson, R. C., & Shiffrin, R. M. (1968). Human memory: A proposed system and its control processes. In K. W. Spence & J. T. Spence (Eds.), *The psychology of learning and motivation* (Vol. 2, pp. 418–420). New York: Academic Press.

Baddeley, A., Harris, J., Sunderland, A., Watts, K. P., & Wilson, B. (1967). Closed head injury and memory. In H. S. Levin, J. Grafman, & H. M. Eisenberg (Eds.), *Neurobehavioral recovery from brain injury*. New York: Oxford University Press.

Chase, W. G., & Ericsson, K. A. (1982). Skill and working memory. In G. H. Bower (Ed.), *The psychology of learning and motivation* (Vol. 16). New York: Academic Press.

Colley, A. M., & Beech, J. R. (1989). *Acquisition and performance of cognitive skills*. New York: Wiley.

Craik, F. I. M., & Watkins, M. J. (1973). The role of rehearsal in short-term memory. *Journal of Verbal Learning and Verbal Behavior, 12*, 599–607.

Deaton, A. V. (1991). Rehabilitating cognitive impairments through the use of games. In J. S. Kreutzer & P. H. Wehman (Eds.), *Cognitive rehabilitation for persons with traumatic brain injury*. Baltimore: Brookes.

Ericsson, K. A., & Poulson, P. G. (1988). An analysis of the mechanisms of a memory skill. *Journal of Experimental Psychology: Learning, Memory, and Cognition, 14*, 305–316.

Harrell, M., Parenté, R., Bellingrath, E. G., & Lisicia, K. A. (1992). *Cognitive rehabilitation of memory: A practical guide*. Rockville, MD: Aspen.

Hasher, L., & Zacks, R. T. (1988). Automatic and effortful processes in memory. *Journal of Experimental Psychology: General, 108*, 356–388.

Healy, A. F., & Borne, L. E., Jr. (1995). *Learning and memory of knowledge and skills: Durability and specificity*. Thousand Oaks, CA: Sage.

Herrmann, D., Raybeck, D., & Gutman, D. (1993). *Improving student memory*. Toronto, Canada: Hogrefe & Huber.

Parenté, R., & Anderson-Parenté, J. K. (1991). *Retraining memory: Techniques and applications*. Houston, TX: CSY.

Parenté, R., Twum, M., & Zoltan, B. (1994). Transfer and generalization of cognitive skill after traumatic brain injury. *NeuroRehabilitation, 4*, 25–35.

Payne, D. (1992). Memory improvement and practice. In D. Herrmann, H. Weingartner, A. Searleman, & C. McEvoy (Eds.), *Memory improvement: Implications for memory theory*. New York: Springer-Verlag.

Pressley, M., & El-Dinary, P. M. (1992). Memory strategy instruction that promotes good information processing. In D. Herrmann, H. Weingartner, A. Searleman, & C. McEvoy (Eds.), *Memory improvement: Implications for memory theory*. New York: Springer-Verlag.

Rundus, D. (1977). Maintenance rehearsal and single level processing. *Journal of Verbal Learning and Verbal Behavior, 16*, 665–681.

Spelke, E. S., Hirst, W. C., & Neisser, U. (1976). Skills of divided attention. *Cognition, 4*, 215–230.

Chapter 11

❧

Retraining Working Memory

Most persons with traumatic brain injury complain that they have problems with short-term memory (Glisky & Glisky, 2002). Actually, their short-term memories are intact. That is, they can remember new information for very brief periods about as well as anyone else. However, they often have a problem processing information effectively in short-term memory, so the information does not readily transfer to long-term memory. Consequently, they lose access to the information and have difficulty retrieving it later. The problem is more one of limited working memory than it is a deficit of short-term memory (Crowder, 1993). Unfortunately, the concept of working memory has not been well defined within the brain injury literature (Almli & Finger, 1988). Indeed, we have found only one research article that studied working memory differences in persons with TBI (Parenté, Kolakowsky-Hayner, Krug, & Wilk, 1999). We, therefore, devote this chapter to a discussion of working memory as it applies to brain injury rehabilitation with the hope that other researchers will invest similar effort toward understanding this crucial aspect of memory. The chapter opens with a brief history of working memory, followed by a discussion of some original research that defines the working memory concept in persons with brain injury. The chapter ends with suggestions for improving clients' working memories after brain injury.

Working Memory— Past to Present

The concept of memory has changed markedly in the last 50 years. In the late 1960s, Atkinson and Shiffrin (1968) outlined an information processing model of memory, which defined short-term memory as having brief duration and limited capacity for information storage. The function of the short-term memory was to maintain information in memory so that it could be processed and transferred into long-term memory. In contrast, long-term memory was described as a repository with seemingly limitless capacity, into which the processed information from the short-term store is deposited (Cowan, 1988). Recall from short-term memory depended on rehearsal and a fixed selection process (Peterson & Peterson, 1959). That is, the more a person rehearsed information, the better he or she could store and retrieve it later. No central mechanism was responsible for directing or prioritizing the recall of information from short-term memory. This concept of short-term memory persists to the present. For example, persons with brain injury or degenerative conditions such as Alzheimer's disease frequently report limited short-term memory.

Recent research shows that this concept of short-term memory may not completely describe the workings of short-term processing (Just & Carpenter, 1992). In the early 1970s, several authors began to explore the idea that information may be processed at different levels. For example, one initially processes information at a surface level when meeting another person for the first time. At this first encounter, one might describe the other person as nice, pretty, or tall. Later, one processes the deeper structure as he or she gets to know the other person better. At that point, one might think of the other person as shallow, demure, or classy (Baddeley, 1978; Craik & Lockhart, 1972; Nelson, Walling, & McEvoy, 1979). Other studies showed that the way information is processed in short-term memory affects a person's ability to do other tasks such as complex reasoning and problem solving (Baddeley, 1966, 1992, 1998; Baddeley & Hitch, 1974). These authors were, in part, reacting to Atkinson and Shiffrin's (1968) model that did not completely describe the active processing function of short-term memory. Consequently, the concept of working memory emerged, which emphasizes active processing in the short-term store (Baddeley, Grant, Wright, & Thompson, 1975; Daneman & Carpenter, 1980; Engle, Cantor, & Carullo, 1992).

Baddeley and Hitch's (1974) model of working memory has been an exceptionally influential component of modern cognitive science. These authors suggested that working memory includes a central executive, which is responsible for the control and processing of two slave subsystems: the phonological loop and the visuospatial sketchpad. These subsystems have limited-capacity storage buffers that allow access to information for a brief period. Such information is immediately accessible and easily processed by the central executive.

Evidence of Distinct Working Memory Processes

The concept of a phonological loop was originally posited to account for evidence regarding those aspects of short-term memory that were involved with processing of speech (Baddeley & Hitch, 1974). For example, several authors have noted that similar-sounding words, such as *beach* and *reach*, are more likely to be acoustically confused (Baddeley, 1966; Conrad & Hull, 1964), which can cause memory confusions. Evidence also indicated that the phonological loop is a mechanism that is specific to speech-and-language-based phenomena (Martin, 1987). For example, Salamé and Baddeley (1982, 1986, 1989) demonstrated that lyrics, whether in a foreign or native tongue, can interfere with recall more than music without speech or white noise. This may account for the difficulties people have with processing text materials when they are simultaneously reading and listening to music with lyrics. These authors showed that forcing a person to repeat an irrelevant sound (e.g., the word *the*) while trying to recall lists of words would limit memory for the word list. This same procedure did not affect performance on the visual memory-span task. These findings indicated that memory is not a single, central buffer, but rather separate, modality-specific buffers. That is, humans process verbal and visual information differently, perhaps in parallel, but using different memory mechanisms. The phonological loop is one of the mechanisms involved in processing verbal and auditory information. Damage to the phonological loop after brain injury can limit the processing of conversation. It can also result in misperceived words or inability to remember long sentences. On the other hand, the phonological loop probably does not substantially influence the processing of visual or spatial information.

Baddeley (1986) proposed a separate system to account for this type of memory.

The visuospatial sketchpad is the analog of the phonological loop (Baddeley, Grant, Wright, & Thompson, 1975; Farah, 1988). Although there continues to be some debate as to whether this sketchpad is primarily visual or spatial (Baddeley et al., 1975; Logie, 1986; Quinn & McConnell, 1996), the bulk of the evidence indicates that the visuospatial sketchpad functions independently of the phonological loop (Kosslyn, 1980; Shephard & Feng, 1972; Shephard & Meltzer, 1971). Unfortunately, no one has clearly defined the visuospatial sketchpad aspect of the larger working memory model. In general, it is analogous to a movie camera that records continuous images of a person's world. However, the images are short lived; they begin to decay immediately. In addition, one image overlaps the next and they interfere with one another in memory. Rehearsal can sustain the image on the sketchpad, but it will not maintain the image in its original form. The process is similar to that of looking at successive frames of film on a movie camera. The picture changes slightly from frame to frame but the gist of the image stays the same. The central executive can direct processing to specific aspects of the sketchpad and a person's experience can alter his or her perceptions of the image as well. Because the right hemisphere of the brain is the likely storehouse of visual and spatial information, damage to this area will impair the overall functioning of the sketchpad.

The central executive is the administrative system that controls and integrates the phonological loop and the visuospatial sketchpad. This concept has continued to evolve largely based on Norman and Shallice's (1986) model of a supervisory attentional system (Baddeley, 1992). This component of the working memory model accounts for selective attentional processes (McLeod & Posner, 1984; Posner & Boies, 1971), planning, decision making, and the maintenance of cognitive sets (Baddeley, 1998; Gold, Carpenter, Randolph, Goldberg, & Weinberger, 1997; Lhermitte, 1983). Such mental activities serve to process and regulate the flow of information to and from the subsystems. Again, because no one has thoroughly researched this aspect of the working memory model, its workings are speculative. The executive is thought to be analogous to a supervisor of a work crew who oversees various projects and allocates efforts or materials to those aspects of a job that most require additional work. Many students notice the functioning of the central executive when taking tests. They prioritize their processing by spending most of their time on those questions that require the greatest effort. A homebuilder may spend the most time on those aspects of a blueprint that are most complex or least familiar.

Measures of Working Memory

Most measures of working memory derive from a dual-processing paradigm (Daneman & Carpenter, 1980, 1983). For example, a person has to determine whether a series of sentences he or she heard were comprehensible. This is one aspect of the dual-processing task. In the second part, the person tries to remember the last word of each sentence. The number of sentences increases until the person can no longer perform the task. Presumably, the ability to recall the last word is one index of working memory capacity whereas any measure of how well the person understands the sentence is an index of central executive functioning. Increasing the length of the sentences increases the difficulty of the task.

Parenté et al. (1999) found that a working memory measure like the example described above was significantly related to reading comprehension. Daneman and Carpenter

(1980, 1983) reported a similar finding. A study by Baddeley, Logie, Nimmo-Smith, and Brereton (1985) required participants to recall sentences and to remember some other aspect of each sentence, such as whether it made sense. All of these studies documented significant correlations between working memory and reading comprehension.

Recent research has demonstrated a relationship between working memory and the ability to acquire new information (Kylonnen & Christal, 1990; Woltz, 1988) by using standardized measures for assessing working memory. The *Wechsler Adult Intelligence Scale–Third Edition* (WAIS–III; Wechsler, 1997a) and the *Wechsler Memory Scale–Third Edition* (WMS–III; Wechsler, 1997b) both contain a Working Memory Index (WMIx; Wechsler, 1997a, 1997b, 1997c). The WAIS–III WMIx comprises the Arithmetic, Digit Span, and Letter–Number Sequencing subtests. The Letter–Numbering Sequencing subtest was specifically designed to measure working memory based on the work of Gold et al. (1997). In this subtest, a person hears a string of letters and numbers that are presented in random order. He or she must recall the numbers first, then the letters in numerical and alphabetical order, respectively. For example, after hearing "1-B-2-C-3-A," a person would rearrange the numbers and letters and recall the string as "1-2-3-A-B-C." Because the person hears the letters and numbers, it is impossible to assess the role of the visuospatial sketchpad. The working memory measure in the WMS–III addresses this issue by including the Letter–Number Sequencing subtest and the Spatial Span subtest, a visual analog of the classic digit-span task. The Spatial Span task is similar to the popular game *Simon*. The evaluator taps a series of blocks in a certain order and the person must touch the blocks in the same sequence.

Recent research with persons with learning disabilities and persons with traumatic brain injury suggests that the impact of work-

ing memory deficiencies extends beyond the storage vault for information called short-term memory (Parenté et al., 1999). Other research indicates that these populations demonstrate marked differences in working memory performance (Almli & Finger, 1988; Klingberg et al., 2000) compared to control groups.

A review of the literature indicates that there are few studies of working memory in persons with brain injury (Montgomery, 1995; Morris, 1984, 1986). One reason for this dearth of research has been the lack of definition of the concept. Although Baddeley (1986) provided in-depth discussions of working memory in his writings, there are no generally accepted definitions of working memory and there is no clear consensus about how information is processed in working memory. Furthermore, there are no generally accepted measures of working memory.

Working Memory Research with Persons Who Have Brain Damage

Many questions must be answered before the concept of working memory will be useful to brain injury therapists and researchers. First, what is working memory as it pertains to persons with brain injury? Do assessments that provide working memory scores measure something more than short-term auditory memory? Are the various indexes of working memory all measuring the same process? Second, within the population of persons with brain injury, what is the relationship between working memory, other kinds of memory, and academic skills such as reading, math, and spelling? Third, are there therapeutic procedures that can improve working memory functioning?

Parenté et al. (1999) studied 73 persons with traumatic brain injury who received neuropsychological evaluations. Participants were evaluated using a battery of tests including a standardized measure of working memory from the WAIS–III and a dual-processing task that required participants to recall the last word of sentences that they repeated (Cowan, 1988; Daneman & Carpenter, 1980). The battery of tests also included a standardized neuropsychological battery and tests of academic functioning. A licensed psychologist administered the entire battery in one 5-hour session, providing breaks every hour.

The authors looked at the resulting data in three ways. Their first concern was to define the components of working memory within the population of persons with brain injury. They used all of the scaled WAIS–III subtest scores in a regression analysis to predict the WMIx Working Memory subtest scaled score. This analysis indicated that the three subtests that measured memory span, ability to do mental arithmetic problems, and ability to perform mental manipulations accounted for approximately 90% of the variance in the WMIx score. These results showed that in persons with brain injury, the WMIx measured more than auditory attention span. It also measured the ability to do mental control operations such as complex sequencing and mental arithmetic.

Each participant, as part of his or her evaluation, was administered a dual-processing task in which he or she was asked to first recall several sentences and then recall the last word of each sentence (Daneman & Carpenter, 1980). Specifically, the test included four groups of four sentences each. After repeating the four sentences, participants were asked to recall the last word of each sentence. The number of correct last-word recalls from this dual-processing task was another measure of working memory. Cowan (1988) cites a number of working memory studies that use similar procedures. The task is not domain specific. For example, one could use arithmetic word problems and require the participant to first solve the problem mentally and then to recall the last word of the problem. One could also ask participants to evaluate whether a sentence made sense and then to recall the last word of the statement.

Parenté et al. (1999) showed a marginally significant relationship between this dual-processing measure and the WAIS–III measures. However, the only significant WAIS–III predictor was the Letter–Number Sequencing score.

The authors performed a second set of analyses to determine if working memory in persons with brain injury was related to other forms of memory. Because working memory is a form of memory, it is reasonable to assume that measures of it would correlate with other traditional measures of memory. The authors correlated the working memory measures with the Paragraph Recall and Visual Reproduction subtests' scores taken from the *Expanded Halstead–Reitan Battery* (Heaton, 1998). The Paragraph Recall subtest score was an index of the ability to recall text passages over a five-trial study–test sequence. The Visual Memory subtest score measured the ability to draw visual shapes from memory over a five-trial sequence. These tests also had delayed-recall components that indexed long-term retention of verbal and visual information. Correlational analyses indicated that the WAIS–III WMIx score correlated significantly with measures of performance in the initial learning task and with the delayed retention measure.

A third set of analyses assessed the relationship between working memory and various measures of academic performance. Previous research established a link between working memory and reading comprehension. The authors assessed whether working memory scores could predict performance on academic skills such as math competency, spelling, and reading. They also asked if working memory measures could predict these academic measures better than measures of attention and concentration.

Each analysis used the Digit Span subtest results from the WAIS–III, the WMIx from the WMS–III, and the dual-processing working memory measure to predict scores on the Reading Recognition, Reading Comprehension, Spelling, and Arithmetic subtests from the *Peabody Individual Achievement Test* (Markwardt, 1989). The results of these analyses were quite consistent. They showed significant positive relationships between the working memory measures and the academic measures. However, only the WAIS working memory and the dual-processing measures were significant predictors. The digit span scores did not predict any of the academic variables.

Because the WMIx and the dual-processing working memory scores are presumably measuring the same mental process, it is reasonable to assume that they would correlate significantly with each other. Correlational analyses indicated that the two measures were correlated but only marginally, suggesting that these different indexes of working memory measure different memory processes within the working memory concept.

Given that working memory is a unique type of memory that is distinct from that which digit-span tasks measure, then it is reasonable to ask how this type of memory can be improved after a brain injury. Parenté et al. (1999) reported the results of a small sample study that addressed this issue. The purpose was to test several persons with brain injury on two occasions and to give them tasks that trained working memory between the tests. The change in their performance from the pretest to the posttest could be compared to members of another group who were simply tested twice with no intervening training.

Ten participants who had been referred for therapy were administered the Digit Span subtest and the Letter–Number Sequencing subtest from the WAIS–III. Both of these tests were part of an initial evaluation that all therapy referral clients received. Each participant was then assigned several tasks as part of his or her memory training, designed to enhance working memory. Specifically, each participant played the card games outlined in Chapter 10 of this text that were chosen because the games required dual processing. The participants also solved mental arithmetic problems, anagrams, and serial logic tasks. The participants did these tasks for approximately 1 hour between the pretest and posttest. The Letter–Number Sequencing and Digit Span subtests were then readministered to demonstrate the effect of the treatment.

Repeated testing of a separate group of persons with brain injury provided control data on these same subtests from the WAIS–III and the WMS–III. These two tests have identical digit-span and letter–number sequencing tasks. Therefore, the difference between these two administrations of the tests given 1 hour apart provided a control comparison from participants who did not receive any intervening treatment. The length of time between administrations of these tests was approximately 1 hour. These participants matched the experimental group in characteristics such as gender, age, and type of injury.

This was not a true experimental design because the researchers did not randomly assign the participants to the various conditions before the experiment began because of ethical considerations. With the participants who received therapy, the two administrations of the tests assessed whether the mental exercises produced an effect. The use of a pretest and a posttest measure to determine efficacy of treatment is a standard procedure with all clients. The treatment addressed the nature of the deficit in working memory identified in the initial evaluation. In the control group, the two administrations of the same subtests were simply part of the normal administrations of the test batteries.

The results indicated that the performance of the therapy group and control group differed only on the letter–number sequencing measure. There were no significant differences between the groups for the digit span measure. These results showed that working memory could improve with treatment, and could change without corresponding changes in digit span.

There are several implications of these findings that may be useful to therapists who work with persons with brain injury. Working memory is not a simple storage vault for information that enters the system. While the rehearsal process maintains information in short-term memory, the information is manipulated in working memory. Measures of working memory in persons with brain injury are, therefore, more than what has been traditionally defined as auditory memory span. Whereas memory span is a measure of storage capacity in short-term memory, measures of working memory index the ability to process and to encode information in short-term memory.

Although working memory is a significant predictor of conventional measures of learning and retention, it does not correlate highly with these measures. The two measures of working memory used here were significantly but minimally correlated with measures of learning and delayed retention of paragraphs and novel visual information. This result suggests that working memory may be an early stage of information processing whereas paragraph- and shape-recall scores are measuring long-term storage and retrieval. The fact that working memory correlates at all with measures of learning also suggests it is a form of active processing.

These working memory measures were also significant predictors of academic skill. This finding replicates Daneman and Carpenter (1980). However, Parenté et al. (1999) also found that working memory tasks consistently predicted two measures of reading skill (word pronunciation and comprehension), a measure of spelling, and a measure of arithmetic skill. Working memory, therefore, determines partially how well a person

with brain injury can read, spell, and reason numerically.

How can a therapist improve a client's working memory? The approach described in the experiment just outlined was to actively stimulate the process of working memory. The researchers chose a variety of therapeutic activities that were relatively easy to implement. Some improvement occurred but it is difficult to say how long the improvement would last or which of the activities was the most useful. Nevertheless, the results suggest that the working memory is malleable. The following are suggestions that therapists should try when treating working memory deficits.

1. *Shorten the length of directions and instructions.* This will allow better allocation of processing to the stored components. In addition, ask the client to repeat directions or instructions in his or her own words to ensure messages were processed and to minimize partial processing.

2. *Provide training that simulates real-world processing.* Exercises such as calculating restaurant bills mentally require working memory skills that have obvious transfer value. On the other hand, repeating random number strings backward or solving anagrams may not have any useful carryover to everyday tasks.

3. *Avoid a fast speaking rate, especially in instructional settings.* Listening to fast speech causes rapid and incomplete processing. However, it may be possible to train a client's working memory using a tape recorder that allows the therapist to manipulate the rate of speech. For example, listening to books on tape at progressively faster speeds may be useful for training rapid processing of speech in working memory.

4. *Emphatic stress on target words or phrases in sentences will help a person to allocate processing to the most important parts of the sentence.* It may also be helpful to place the most important information at the beginnings and ends of sentences and paragraphs to capitalize on

the primacy and recency effect in working memory. (The primacy and recency effect is discussed in more detail in Chapter 12).

5. *Increase response automaticity.* This can be achieved through overlearning and extra rehearsal, which will facilitate processing in working memory by reducing the load on memory. For example, when teaching a complex task like typing to a person with working memory deficits, the therapist should spend two or three times more time than is typical for helping the client learn the various home key finger placements. Eventually the home keys will become overlearned or automatic, which allows better processing of the keys above and below the home row. Practice does not necessarily mean typing drills. Allowing the client to practice with different keyboards or to play typing games may also enhance automaticity.

6. *Use a part–whole learning strategy.* The therapist should teach the client to analyze the demands of a specific task and then break the task down into components and overlearn the smaller components. This strategy reduces the amount of information the client has to process at any one time. Eventually the client can hook these components into a larger whole.

7. *Because working memory depends on rehearsal, rehearsal training will necessarily precede working memory training.* Parenté et al. (1999) provide a summary of this issue. Practical suggestions for retraining rehearsal are provided in Chapter 10.

References

Almli, C. R., & Finger, S. (1988). Toward a definition of recovery of function. In S. Finger, T. E. LeVere, C. R. Almli, & D. G. Stein (Eds.), *Brain injury and recovery: Theoretical and controversial issues*. New York: Plenum Press.

Atkinson, R. C., & Shiffrin, R. M. (1968). Human memory: A proposed system and its control processes. In K. W. Spence & J. T. Spence (Eds.), *The psychology of learning and motivation* (Vol. 2). New York: Academic Press.

Baddeley, A. (1986). Working memory and comprehension. In D. Broadbent, J. McGaugh, M. Kosslyn, N. Mackintosh, E. Tulving, & L. Weiskrantz (Eds.), *Working memory*. Oxford, United Kingdom: Oxford University Press.

Baddeley, A. D. (1966). The influence of acoustic and semantic similarity on long-term memory for word sequences. *Quarterly Journal of Experimental Psychology, 18*, 302–309.

Baddeley, A. D. (1978). The trouble with levels: A re-examination of Craik and Lockhart's framework for memory research. *Psychological Review, 85*, 139–152.

Baddeley, A. D. (1992). Is working memory working? *Quarterly Journal of Experimental Psychology, 44*, 1–32.

Baddeley, A. D. (1998). *Human memory: Theory and practice*. Boston: Allyn & Bacon.

Baddeley, A. D., Grant, S., Wright, E., & Thompson, N. (1975). Imagery and visual working memory. In P. M. A. Rabbitt & S. Dornic (Eds.), *Attention and performance* (pp. 205–217). London: Academic Press.

Baddeley, A., & Hitch, G. (1974). Working memory. In G. Bower (Ed.), *The psychology of learning and motivation* (Vol. 8, pp. 47–90). New York: Academic Press.

Baddeley, A. D., Logie, R., Nimmo-Smith, I., & Brereton, N. (1985). Components of fluent reading. *Journal of Memory and Language, 24*, 119–131.

Conrad, R., & Hull, A. J. (1964). Information, acoustic confusion, and memory span. *British Journal of Psychology, 55*, 429–432.

Cowan, N. (1988). Evolving conceptions of memory storage, selective attention, and their mutual constraints within the human information-processing system. *Psychological Bulletin, 104*, 163–191.

Craik, F. I. M., & Lockhart, R. M. (1972). Levels of processing: A framework for memory research. *Journal of Verbal Learning and Verbal Behavior, 11*, 671–684.

Crowder, R. G. (1993). Short-term memory: Where do we stand? *Memory and Cognition, 21*, 142–145.

Daneman, M., & Carpenter, P. A. (1980). Individual differences in working memory and reading. *Journal of Verbal Learning and Verbal Behavior, 19*, 450–466.

Daneman, M., & Carpenter, P. A. (1983). Individual differences in integrating information between and within sentences. *Journal of Experimental Psychology: Learning, Memory, and Cognition, 9*, 561–584.

Engle, R., Cantor, J., & Carullo, C. (1992). Individual differences in working memory and comprehension: A test of four hypotheses. *Journal of Experimental Psychology: Learning, Memory, and Cognition, 18*, 972–992.

Farah, M. (1988). Is visual imagery really visual? Overlooked evidence from neuropsychology. *Psychological Review, 95*, 303–317.

Glisky, E. L., & Glisky, M. L. (2002). Learning and memory impairments. In P. Eslinger (Ed.), *Neuropsychological interventions* (pp. 137–162). New York: Guilford Press.

Gold, J. M., Carpenter, C., Randolph, C., Goldberg, T. E., & Weinberger, D. R. (1997). Auditory working memory and Wisconsin Card Sorting Test performance in schizophrenia. *Archives of General Psychiatry, 54*, 159–165.

Heaton, R. K. (1998). *The Expanded Halstead-Reitan Battery.*

Just, M., & Carpenter, P. (1992). A capacity theory of comprehension: Individual differences in working memory. *Psychological Review, 99*, 122–149.

Klingberg, T., Hedehus, M., Temple, E., Salz, T., Gabrieli, J. D., Moseley, M. E., & Poldrack, R. A. (2000). Microstructure of temporo-parietal white matter as a basis for reading ability: Evidence from diffusion tensor magnetic resonance imaging. *Neuron, 25*(2), 493–500.

Kosslyn, S. M. (1980). *Image and mind.* Cambridge, MA: Harvard University Press.

Kylonnen, P. C., & Christal, R. E. (1990). Reasoning ability is (little more than) working memory capacity? *Intelligence, 14*, 389–433.

Lhermitte, F. (1983). Utilization behavior and its relation to lesions of the frontal lobe. *Brain, 106*, 237–255.

Logie, R. H. (1986). Visuo-spatial processes in working memory. *Quarterly Journal of Experimental Psychology, 38*, 229–247.

Markwardt, F. C. (1989). *The Peabody Individual Achievement Test.* Circle Pines, MN: American Guidance Service.

Martin, R. (1987). Articulatory and phonological deficits in short-term memory and their relation to syntactic processing. *Brain and Language, 32*, 159–192.

McLeod, P., & Posner, M. I. (1984). Privileged loops from percept to act. In H. Bouma & D. C. Bouwhuis (Eds.), *Attention and performance* (pp. 55–66). Hove, United Kingdom: Erlbaum.

Montgomery, J. (1995). Sentence comprehension and children with specific language impairment: The role of phonological working memory. *Journal of Speech and Hearing Research, 38*, 177–189.

Morris, R. G. (1984). Dementia and the functioning of the articulatory loop system. *Cognitive Neuropsychology, 1*, 143–158.

Morris, R. G. (1986). Short-term memory in senile dementia of the Alzheimer's type. *Cognitive Neuropsychology, 3*, 77–97.

Nelson, R. L., Walling, J. R., & McEvoy, C. L. (1979). Doubts about depth. *Journal of Experimental Psychology: Human Learning and Memory, 5*, 24–44.

Norman, D. A., & Shallice, T. (1986). Attention to action: Willed and automatic control of behavior. In R. J. Davidson, G. E. Schwartz, & D. Shapiro (Eds.), *Consciousness and self-regulation: Advances in research and theory* (Vol. 4, pp. 1–18). New York: Plenum Press.

Parenté, R., Kolakowsky-Hayner, S., Krug, K., & Wilk, C., (1999). Retraining working memory after traumatic brain injury. *NeuroRehabilitation, 13*, 157–163.

Peterson, L. R., & Peterson, M. J. (1959). Short-term retention of individual verbal items. *Journal of Experimental Psychology, 58*, 193–198.

Posner, M. I., & Boies, S. J. (1971). Components of attention. *Psychological Review, 78*, 391–408.

Quinn, J. G., & McConnell, J. (1996). Irrelevant pictures in visual working memory. *Quarterly Journal of Experimental Psychology: Human Experimental Psychology, 49*, 200–215.

Salamé, P., & Baddeley, A. (1982). Disruption of short-term memory by unattended speech: Implications for the structure of working memory. *Journal of Verbal Learning and Verbal Behavior, 21*, 150–164.

Salamé, P., & Baddeley, A. D. (1986). Phonological factors in STM: Similarity and the unattended speech effect. *Bulletin of the Psychonomic Society, 24*, 263–265.

Salamé, P., & Baddeley, A. D. (1989). Effects of background music on phonological short-term memory. *Quarterly Journal of Experimental Psychology, 41*, 107–122.

Shephard, R., & Meltzer, J. (1971). Mental rotation of three-dimensional objects. *Science, 171*, 701–703.

Shephard, R. N., & Feng, C. (1972). A chronometric study of mental paper-folding. *Cognitive Psychology, 3*, 228–243.

Wechsler, D. (1997a). *Manual for the Wechsler Adult Intelligence Scale–Third Edition.* San Antonio, TX: Psychological Corp.

Wechsler, D. (1997b). *Manual for the Wechsler Memory Scale–Third Edition.* San Antonio, TX: Psychological Corp.

Wechsler, D. (1997c). *WAIS III/WMS III Technical Manual.* San Antonio, TX: Psychological Corp.

Woltz, D. J. (1988). An investigation of the role of working memory in procedural skill acquisition. *Journal of Experimental Psychology, 117*, 319–331.

Chapter 12

⚘

Retraining Memory Strategies

In Chapter 10 we discussed rehearsal strategies for maintaining information in memory. This maintenance process is essential because without it, a person cannot convert the information into a form that can he or she can retrieve easily later. Once a person can rehearse effectively, then it is possible for him or her to learn techniques for making the information more memorable. These techniques are called encoding strategies and they are the topic of this chapter. Encoding strategies do not work well unless a person can first rehearse effectively. Rehearsal has minimal effect on memory unless a person can encode. Therefore, the two strategies work in tandem to enhance memory.

This chapter presents a variety of encoding strategies that persons with brain injury can use to improve their recall of everyday information such as phone numbers and name–face associations. These techniques allow a person to store information in long-term memory in a way that ensures durable memories (Adams, 1985; Atkinson & Wickens, 1971; Baddeley, 1986; Bellezza, 1981; Bower & Winzenz, 1970), and also allow persons with brain injury to store information so that it can be retrived easily later (Humphreys, Bain, & Pike, 1989). The chapter begins with a discussion of the reasons for poor remembering, (Dansereau, 1985; Duffy, Walker, & Montague, 1972), then provides techniques for improving storage and retrieval of infor-

mation in memory. The chapter ends with a discussion of retrieval of personal information and skills.

Things That Keep a Person from Remembering

Poor Acquisition

What seems like forgetting is sometimes not a true memory problem at all. A person may appear to have forgotten something, but perhaps he or she never learned the information in the first place or did not know what to remember. For example, many therapy clients will say they understand instructions or remember directions after hearing them once. Their failure to remember the directions later may be due more to poor storage or encoding than to retrieval failure (Eysenck, 1982). The therapist can ensure information is adequately stored by asking the client to repeat information and by insisting on additional rehearsals when necessary (Crosson & Buenning, 1984; Gianutsos, 1991; Godfrey & Knight, 1988). This technique involves three stages. First, the client hears or sees the information. Second, the client repeats it in his or her own words or tries to demonstrate mastery in some way. Third, the therapist or family member verifies that the message was received correctly. This process builds on the rehearsal strategy presented in Chapter 10 because the client must repeat the information (rehearsal) but also translate the information into his or her own words (encoding) and then rehearse the translated information again. The client should implement this three-step strategy whenever he or she hears, sees, or does anything new. For example, at home, family members should (1) say the message clearly and slowly while the client is paying attention, (2) insist that the client immediately rehearse instructions or directions in his or her own words, and (3) verify that the client's translation was correct. If possible, the client should restate the message again. When a client is learning a new skill, an instructor should demonstrate the skill while the client is paying attention, then the client should perform the skill while the instructor is watching. Finally, the instructor should verify that the client is performing the skill correctly. In situations where the client does not restate the message or perform the skills correctly, then he or she will need to restate the message or to perform the skill again. The client should not leave the situation until he or she has correctly restated a message or performed the skill correctly. This three-step strategy will not eliminate all miscommunications, but it will lessen their frequency.

Poor Perception

The client may forget information because poor eyesight or hearing prevented him or her from noticing relevant cues (Cutler & Grams, 1988). Often a new set of eyeglasses or a hearing aid can cause a remarkable improvement in memory. A client's age can change his or her priorities for what is important to remember. Furthermore, medication, depression, or life changes such as menopause can create temporary changes in memory efficiency. It is therefore necessary for the therapist to rule out other factors such as hearing or vision limitations before assigning a diagnosis of amnesia. It is worthwhile to investigate these issues because often a simple physical intervention can save the therapist hours of needless and unproductive memory therapy effort.

Inability To Generate Cues

The importance of cuing as a general method of memory improvement cannot be overemphasized (Tulving, 1983). Like most people, persons with brain injury do not forget because the information did not get into long-term memory. They forget because they are no longer able to generate the cues that are necessary to retrieve the information from the long-term store. The therapist should advise the client that he or she might have to make a conscious effort to generate memory cues. After a long period of conscious effort, the cuing process will eventually occur with relative ease.

When a person generates memory cues, it is much the same process as trying to recall the name of a file stored on a computer. Without knowing the file name, the person cannot recall the file. The trick to remembering file names is to spend time consciously generating useful file names. This can be a mnemonic device such as a distinctive word or phrase or it can be a physical reminder such as a handwritten note. Regardless of the method, a minute spent creating the cue can save an hour trying to recall the information without the cue.

Persistence

It is important for both therapist and client to understand that there is no guarantee that even prolonged use of a particular retrieval strategy will produce a desired memory. Nevertheless, the use of some retrieval strategy with a client will, more often than not, yield more information than if no attempt was made to retrieve. The therapist may need to try several strategies over an extended period of time to find one that works with a particular client; this process may be tedious and frustrating for both therapist and client.

Characteristics of Good Retrieval Cues

Generally, how well a person can remember something depends on four characteristics that affect his or her ability to retrieve the information (Ellis & Hunt, 1993; Herrmann, 1990; Higbee, 1988; McDaniel & Pressley, 1987; Payne, 1992). They are the *strength* or intensity of the memory, the number of distinctive *attributes* stored with the memory, *associations* with other memories, and the person's ability to *reconstruct* from other memories. The art of training retrieval involves helping the client to attend to these four attributes when creating memory cues.

Strength

Much of what is called memory is simply a vivid first impression. Forming memories, therefore, involves creating vivid images at storage. To create a vivid impression about an event, clients should ask questions about it, elaborate or embellish it, or otherwise make it stand out from the background of life at the time. Creating a context for the event allows the client to recall a cue that leads to retrieval. By simply asking the questions "who, what, when, where, why, and how," the client can organize an event within a larger context that makes it memorable. The following rhyme can help teach this skill:

To remember in the here and now
Ask who, what, when, where, why, and how.

To remember it again
Ask who, what, where, why, how, and when.

This poem reminds the client that vivid first impressions result from answers to these initial questions about the event. Later, the same questions can cue recall of the event.

Retrieval of stored memories is usually a function of their strength. Most people have hunches, best guesses, and feelings about certain events that they cannot specifically recall. A person may not recognize a particular person, place, or thing immediately but he or she can make a choice based on a subjective feeling of familiarity that results from the strength of the memory trace. Persons with brain injury can also use their subjective feelings to make guesses about a vague memory. For example, if a client is trying to remember a person's name, the name that seems the most familiar is likely to be the correct name or at least similar to it. The therapist should therefore advise the client to attend to his or her subjective feelings of familiarity as a way of initiating the retrieval process. Even though the initial recall may not be correct, it may spur an association that, in turn, triggers correct recall.

Attributes

A client can also jog his or her memory by recalling a portion of the larger memory. If a client is trying to cue recall of a person, he or she might try to conjure a mental image of the person or to use some physical characteristic to cue recall. Sometimes a person can remember one or a few attributes of an event, place, or person, but still not be able to retrieve the entire memory. These partial cues eventually produce correct recall. For example, most people have had the experience of trying to find a particular text passage in a book. They cannot recall the content of the passage but they can remember that it was located on the top of a page about halfway through the book. These attributes then direct and limit their search for the passage. The therapist should encourage the client to use these attributes to cue recall of the complete picture. In many cases, recalling only the single aspect will lead to the larger item.

Associations

Clients can also cue recall by focusing on those things that are associated with the information in question (Thune, 1950). Recalling attributes according to the time when something happened, who was present during an introduction, where an event occurred, and so forth can provide a useful triggering association. The *who–what–when–where–how–why* method discussed above is useful for encoding and storing information in an organized format. But a client can also use the same words to trigger recall. For example, when trying to recall a name, a client could ask the following questions: With whom is the person associated? What conditions led to our introduction? When did we meet? When did I see the person last? Where did I last see the person? How did we encounter each other? These questions force the client to produce one or more associations that will lead to recalling the person.

Reconstructions

Memory reconstructions result from associations that exist among certain facts. Reconstructions lead the client to conclusions based on a rehearsal of a previous sequence of events. For example, if a client is trying to find a wallet, purse, or keys, he or she might sit down and mentally rehearse the course of the previous day's activities. What clothes was I wearing? Where was I going that day? Where did I last see my wallet? In what pocket of my jacket did I place my keys? These ques-

tions often lead to new conclusions that directs the client to the object. The client may believe that he or she last saw the wallet 2 days ago on the nightstand in the bedroom. Because he or she does not recall picking it up and moving it anywhere else, the conclusion is that it still is on the nightstand.

Other Retrieval Techniques

Following are several additional strategies that may help a client retrieve information from memory (Goldstein et al., 1988; Harrell, Parenté, Bellingrath, & Lisicia, 1992; Parenté & Anderson-Parenté, 1983; Richardson, 1992; Schacter & Glisky, 1986). Most are derived from one or more of the characteristics outlined above. All of these strategies could possibly help a person with memory problems; therapists are advised to try them all to determine whether any are especially useful for a particular client.

Alphabet Search. The therapist trains the client to search memory using the letters of the alphabet as a cue. For example, the client may ask, "I think her name began with an A? a B? a C?" and so on through Z. This technique can often cue correct recall of a name.

Free Generation of Attributes. The client free-associates, recalling anything that may be linked with the information in question. Some aspect of free generation may cue recall of the target memory. For example, when trying to recall a woman's name, the client might generate the following characteristics: red hair, blue eyes, athletic, glasses, deep voice, and so forth. Eventually one of these attributes will trigger the memory of the name of the woman in question.

Reinstate Mood. Powerful moods and emotional states that are associated with a memory can often cue recall (Blaney, 1986). The client tries to recall any dominant emotions that were present during an event. For example, most people can recall incidents in which a person became emotional and cried or laughed heartily. Storing the mood by actively paying attention to the emotional state of another person or oneself at the time of an incident helps recall because the mood becomes associated with the scenario at the time of storage.

Tip of the Tongue. When memory of a piece of information is on the tip of a client's tongue, usually the first letter of the information comes to mind before the actual memory. Therefore, the therapist should advise the client to use the first letter of the alphabet that comes to mind to cue recall of the larger memory (Burke, MacKay, Worthley, & Wade, 1991). Once this letter is on the tip of the tongue, the client can guess names that begin with that letter until the correct name comes to mind. This technique is similar to the alphabet search method previously discussed. In the alphabet technique, a person simply begins with the letter A and generates names that start with A, then continues through the alphabet until the name comes to mind. In the tip-of-the-tongue method, however, a person begins with the letter that first comes to mind and begins generating names with that letter. For example, when trying to recall the name of a new employee, a person might have the letter *T* on the tip of his or her tongue and would proceed to say, "Theresa, Tina, Tamara," and so forth. Other word-related attributes may also trigger a memory such as the sound of the name or unusual letter combinations. For example, a client might recall that a person's name begins with an unusual consonant like Z or sounded Italian.

Retracing. This technique is a form of reconstruction. It involves remembering chronologically the events that preceded or followed the one the client wants to remember. Usually, the client tries to recall the circumstances that produced the event or situation. For example, a person may enter a room

and immediately forget what he or she entered the room to retrieve. Retracing the sequence of events that preceded entering the room can cue recall of why he or she is there. The client may have been wrapping a package and needed a pair of scissors, causing him or her to enter the kitchen. Recalling the previous activity and the need to cut wrapping paper will cue recall of the reason for entering the kitchen.

Return to the Scene. Recreating the original surroundings where an event occurred can cue recall. Walking into a room, a store, a neighborhood, and so forth can cue recall of information. For example, the therapist should advise clients who return to school to study for a test in the same room in which they will eventually take the test because different aspects of the room will cue recall of the information at the time of the test.

Behaviors and Attitudes That Affect Retrieval

Effective remembering requires more than learning a variety of retrieval strategies. A client must also be able to manage these strategies according to the demands of different situations (Hannon, de la Cruz-Schnedel, Cano, Moreira, & Nasuta, 1989; Herrmann, Raybeck, & Gutman, 1992). The therapist should therefore encourage the client to adopt certain behaviors and attitudes that may facilitate recall. The following are suggestions that therapists should make to their clients regarding behavior.

Relax. In most situations, relaxation will facilitate recall. Even if the information comes to mind, hurrying can lead the client to miss important details (Yesavage, Rose, & Spiegel, 1982). The therapist should train the client to use relaxation methods such as stretching, short meditations, head and neck rotation, and so forth to produce a calm state of mind. Trying to recall information in the period just before falling asleep can also improve retrieval.

Vary the Method. If one of the retrieval strategies discussed previously does not work, then another might. The client should always make a systematic attempt at all of the retrieval techniques before giving up. With practice, the client will find that one technique works well for certain types of retrieval whereas others work better in different situations. Often, the persistence of trying different methods will eventually lead to recall (Morris, 1984).

Use Primacy and Recency. The primacy and recency effect refers to a well-documented memory phenomenon that occurs when a person tries to recall sequences of information. The person tends to remember best what happened last and first in a sequence. The center portion of the sequence will not be as memorable. Consequently, the therapist should advise the client that in situations where information is sequential, he or she is most likely to recall what happened last, followed by what happened first, followed by what happened in the middle. Recalling the first or last sections of a sequence can cue recall of the middle. For example, if the client has difficulty recalling a conversation, he or she should initially try to recall the last part of the conversation by asking, "What was the last thing we talked about?" If the client can retrieve the last part of the conversation, then the first and middle sections will likely follow.

Any new learning situation is a time-ordered sequence. The client can structure this sequence to capitalize on the primacy and recency effect to improve retrieval. When learning anything new, the client should rehearse and summarize the information at the end of the session. This will ensure that the summary is created when the sequencing is remembered best.

Distribute the Learning. In new learning situations, the client should distribute practice over several short sessions rather than one marathon session. Distributed practice produces better retrieval because multiple practice sessions provide more first and last segments of learning sessions. Because any practice interval is a sequence of learning over time and because people remember first and last segments of any sequence best, frequent learning sessions provide more opportunity to capitalize on the primacy and recency effect.

Give It a Rest. If a client feels that his or her memory is blocked, then he or she should take a break. The client may try the retrieval techniques again just before falling asleep at night. Often the client will awaken during the night having recalled the information. Other times, it may come to mind the following morning.

Monitor Accuracy. The therapist should monitor the client's correctness in remembering and provide an assessment of any consistent distortions or embellishments. The therapist should also train the client to consider these distortions when evaluating his or her own recall. If the therapist notices, for example, that the client usually overestimates characteristics such as beauty, weight, or speed, then the client can use this information to correct the client's recollections in the future.

Retrieval of Personal Information and Skills

The techniques presented previously in this chapter are useful for retrieving the novel episodes of everyday life. However, retrieval from long-term memory also involves several other types of information. For example, the personal history of a person with brain injury is usually intact, even though he or she may have islands of memory, with some personal facts inaccessible (Kertesz, 1979; Sarno,

1981). In the earliest stages of recovery, the therapy client may be disoriented and unable to recall personal information (Wepman, 1951). Because this is an especially frustrating state for the client the therapist may need to spend considerable time reinstating these memories before trying episodic retrieval strategies. Techniques to retrieve personal information and history are called *retraining* methods because they help a person to recreate an existing long-term memory. They are specifically useful for retrograde amnesias, in which a person had some previous knowledge or skill but can no longer recall it. The training methods outlined previously in this chapter are better suited for anterograde amnesias, in which a person cannot recall recently learned information. The retraining methods presented next may also be useful for elderly persons who suffer from dementia or for those persons with progressively degenerative conditions. The therapist's major contribution with these individuals may be to restore the person's ability to recall personal histories and to retrain basic social competencies.

Personal Information

A therapist can retrain personal histories by creating personal fact repetition tapes, which involves collecting a number of personal facts from the client's family members and recording them on tape. Useful facts include date of birth, children's names, phone numbers, street addresses, names of high schools or colleges attended, and so forth. The therapist records these facts on an audiotape and then requires the client to listen to the tape repeatedly each day using headphones to ensure adequate attention. Having the client repeat the information aloud as he or she hears it can also help reestablish the memories. We frequently purchase a Walkman-type tape player and give it to the client for this purpose. The therapist should also make a list of the facts on the tape and test the client's recall of each one until he or she can demonstrate perfect mastery of the information.

Instead of using an audiotape, the therapist can record each fact on a digital recorder. This device will identify each entry with a number and the client can access any fact by keying in the number of the message. The therapist can then delete facts individually as the client masters them. This method focuses the client's attention on those facts that stubbornly resist recall. Once the client can recall all the facts from the original set, the therapist can collect another set of facts from the family, repeating the process as many times as necessary. This same procedure is useful when a person is trying to learn facts for a job or for an academic course.

Family photo albums can serve the same purpose. The therapist can use the photos as flash cards, showing them to the client one at a time and asking for recall of the event, person's name, year, city, and so forth. The photo flash card technique can be combined with the tape recorder training method.

Academic Skills

Academic remediation of previously learned skills is usually a rote process. The training typically proceeds rapidly because the client is relearning old skills rather than learning new ones. The therapist must first assess the client's functional reading, math, and spelling skills, then provide commercially available academic remediation materials. The difficulty level of the materials should be about one half year below the client's assessed grade level. Computers are especially useful for this type of training. Most software stores have shelves of excellent academic remediation software and games for all grade levels. Math training should emphasize rote learning of functional skills such as multiplication, division, and, eventually, fractions and percents.

Computer programs are also useful for training other functional skills such as typing and computer literacy.

Reading training should stress comprehension, finding main ideas, and extrapolation beyond concrete facts. Spelling and vocabulary training should emphasize understanding of current word meanings. Books such as *Absolutely Essential Words* (Bromberg, Liebb, & Traiger, 1984) are useful for providing a vocabulary of words in current use. The therapist should supply lists of opposites, synonyms, and homonyms for these vocabulary words to increase the number of alternative retrieval routes to the desired words. Vocabulary memorization usually decreases the incidence of word-finding and word-substitution problems after brain injury.

It is also useful to train the clients to recognize Greek and Latin roots in words so that they can figure out the meanings of novel words from their roots. Once a client learns several roots, he or she should try to find those roots in everyday text materials such as newspapers and magazines. This activity will help the client see the word roots in common text and show the roots embedded in unfamiliar words. When the client identifies a root but cannot define the word, then he or she should try to determine its definition from the meaning of the root and the context of the sentence. For example, while practicing this technique, one client encountered the sentence, "The chronology of the event did not match the person's recollections." The client had learned that the root *chrono* referred to time and the root *ology* referred to the study of something. He reasoned from the rest of the sentence that the person's memory was somehow discordant with the time sequence of the events.

There are several other effective techniques for retraining reading skill. The client may benefit from reading text materials into a tape recorder, then playing the tape while rereading the text. This technique produces both visual and auditory rehearsals.

A similar technique involves the client taking verbal notes from text materials. Clients who return to school can dictate notes from their readings into a tape recorder rather than write them down. This process is much quicker and it forces the client to restate or translate the information while he or she reads it. Translating written text and other materials into one's own words produces an encoding that is especially easy to retrieve later on. The therapist can use the who–what–when–where–how–why method for training reading translations. At first, the client may need to read the material several times before he or she can correctly translate it. With practice, however, the client will eventually reach the point at which he or she can read a section of text once and record an accurate summary. Under no circumstances should the client be allowed go on to the next paragraph until he or she is able to summarize the current paragraph. This procedure provides a self-monitoring system for reading comprehension. It shows the client the number of rehearsals that are needed and the size of the verbal unit he or she can process, and it provides a permanent auditory record of the gist of the material that the client can review later.

Summary

This chapter presented techniques for training retrieval and self-cuing skills. Several factors that affect retrieval may cloud the diagnosis of memory impairment, including depression, changes in priorities due to age, and medication. Because these factors can create problems with retrieval that may never respond to strategy training, the therapist should deal with these problems directly. Several techniques for training retrieval of episodic information were presented. The therapist trains the client to focus on four attributes of memories: their strength, characteristic attributes, associations with other information, and reconstructions of the surrounding context. Specific techniques for cuing recall include the alphabet method, free generation, reinstating the mood, tip of the tongue, retracing, and returning to the scene of the memory. Additional factors that facilitate retrieval include the ability to relax, to vary the retrieval method, to use primacy and recency, to distribute the learning across sessions, to give the thought a rest when retrieval becomes too difficult, and to monitor accuracy for any systematic distortions.

This chapter also presented methods for retraining retrograde memories. Listening to a tape recording of personal facts followed by regular quizzing of those facts is an especially useful technique for reinstating personal histories. Photo albums also provide convenient sources for flash cards that the therapist can use in the same manner as the tape. The therapist can use the large body of computer software to retrain academic or job-related skills the client may need to return to work.

References

Adams, L. T. (1985). Improving memory: Can retrieval strategies help? *Human Learning, 4,* 281–297.

Atkinson, R. C., & Wickens, T. D. (1971). Human memory and the concept of reinforcement. In R. Glaser (Ed.), *The nature of reinforcement* (pp. 138–180). London: Academic Press.

Baddeley, A. D. (1986). *Working memory.* New York: Basic Books.

Bellezza, F. S. (1981). Mnemonic devices: Classification, characteristics, and criteria. *Review of Education Research, 51,* 247–275.

Blaney, P. H. (1986). Affect and memory: A review. *Psychological Bulletin, 99,* 229–246.

Bower, G. H., & Winzenz, D. (1970). Comparison of associative learning strategies. *Psychonomic Science, 20,* 119–120.

Bromberg, M., Liebb, J., & Traiger, A. (1984). *Absolutely essential words.* New York: Barrons.

Burke, D., MacKay, D. G., Worthley, J. S., & Wade, E. (1991). On the tip of the tongue: What causes word finding failures in young and older adults. *Journal of Memory and Language, 30,* 237–246.

Crosson, B., & Buenning, W. (1984). An individualized memory retraining program after closed-head injury: A single-case study. *Journal of Clinical Neuropsychology, 6,* 287–301.

Cutler, S. J., & Grams, A. E. (1988). Correlates of self-reported everyday memory problems. *Journal of Gerontology, 43,* 582–590.

Dansereau, D. F. (1985). Learning strategy research. In J. W. Segal, S. F. Chipman, & R. Glasser (Eds.), *Thinking and learning skills* (Vol. 1). Hillsdale, NJ: Erlbaum.

Duffy, T. M., Walker, C., & Montague, W. E. (1972). Sentence mnemonics and the role of verb-class in paired-associate learning. *Psychological Reports, 31,* 583–589.

Ellis, H. C., & Hunt, R. R. (1993). *Fundamentals of cognitive psychology* (5th ed.). Dubuque, IA: Brown.

Eysenck, M. W. (1982). *Attention and arousal: Cognition and performance.* West Berlin, Germany: Springer-Verlag.

Gianutsos, R. (1991). Cognitive rehabilitation: A neuropsychological specialty comes of age. *Brain Injury, 5,* 353–368.

Godfrey, H., & Knight, R. (1988). Memory training and behavioral rehabilitation of a severely head-injured adult. *Archives of Physical Medicine Rehabilitation, 69,* 458–460.

Goldstein, G., McCue, M., Turner, S., Spanier, E., Malec, E., & Shelly, C. (1988). An efficacy study of memory training for patients with closed-head injury. *The Clinical Neuropsychologist, 2,* 252–259.

Hannon, R., de la Cruz-Schnedel, D., Cano, T., Moreira, K., & Nasuta, R. (1989). Memory retraining with adult male alcoholics. *Archives of Clinical Neuropsychology, 4,* 227–232.

Harrell, M., Parenté, R., Bellingrath, E. G., & Lisicia, K. A. (1992). *Cognitive rehabilitation of memory: A practical guide.* Rockville, MD: Aspen.

Herrmann, D. J. (1990). *SuperMemory.* Emmaus, PA: Rodale.

Herrmann, D. J., Raybeck, D., & Gutman, D. (1992). *Improving student memory.* Toronto, Canada: Hogrefe & Huber.

Higbee, K. L. (1988). *Your memory* (2nd ed.). Englewood Cliffs, NJ: Prentice Hall.

Humphreys, M. S., Bain, J. D., & Pike, R. (1989). Different ways to cue a coherent memory system: A theory of episodic and procedural tasks. *Psychological Review, 96,* 208–233.

Kertesz, A. (1979). *Aphasia and associated disorders: Taxonomy, localization, and recovery.* New York: Grune & Stratton.

McDaniel, M. A., & Pressley, M. (1987). *Imagery and related mnemonic processes: Theories, individual differences, and applications.* New York: Springer-Verlag.

Morris, P. E. (1984). The cognitive psychology of self-reports. In J. Harris & P. Morris (Eds.), *Everyday memory, actions, and absentmindedness* (pp. 153–172). London: Academic Press.

Parenté, F. J., & Anderson-Parenté, J. K. (1983). Techniques for improving cognitive rehabilitation: Teaching organization and encoding skills. *Cognitive Rehabilitation, 1*(4), 20–22.

Payne, D. (1992). Memory improvement and practice. In D. Herrmann, H. Weingartner, A. Searleman, & C. McEvoy (Eds.), *Memory improvement: Implications for memory theory.* New York: Springer-Verlag.

Richardson, J. T. E. (1992). Imagery mnemonics and memory remediation. *Neurology, 42,* 283–286.

Sarno, M. T. (1981). Recovery and rehabilitation in aphasia. In M. T. Sarno (Ed.), *Acquired aphasia.* New York: Academic Press.

Schacter, D. L., & Glisky, E. L. (1986). Memory remediation: Restoration, alleviation, and the acquisition of domain-specific knowledge. In B. Uzzell & Y. Gross (Eds.), *Clinical neuropsychology of intervention* (pp. 257–282). New York: Martinus Nijhoff.

Thune, L. E. (1950). The effect of different types of preliminary activities on subsequent learning of paired-associate material. *Journal of Experimental Psychology, 40,* 423–438.

Tulving, E. (1983). *Elements of episodic memory.* Oxford, United Kingdom: Oxford Univesity Press.

Wepman, J. M. (1951). *Recovery from aphasia.* New York: Ronald Press.

Yesavage, J. A., Rose, T. L., & Spiegel, D. (1982). Relaxation training and memory improvement in elderly normals: Correlations of anxiety ratings and recall improvement. *Experimental Aging Research, 4,* 123–137.

Chapter 13

❦

Rehearsal Revisited

Everyone knows the old saying, "Practice makes perfect." Actually, "Perfect practice makes perfect" is closer to the mark. In therapy, generalization of learning strategies depends on how often a person practices them. Therefore, rehearsal skill is necessary not only for maintaining information in memory but, more so, for organizing novel information (Chase & Ericsson, 1982; Ericsson, 1985; Healy & Bourne, 1995; Herrmann, Weingartner, Searleman, & McEvoy, 1992; Wilson, 1987). This latter type of rehearsal allows a person to encode information for later retrieval.

The purpose of this chapter is to develop and elaborate further the concept of rehearsal of organization, specifically showing how rehearsal skill interacts with the memory strategies discussed in Chapter 12. The exercises in Chapter 12 teach a person to recognize the organization that binds together the seemingly unrelated elements of his or her experience. In our experience, the concept of rehearsing organization is an especially difficult one for most persons with brain injury to grasp. Most spend hours rehearsing separate pieces of their daily activities without giving any thought to rehearsing the organizing structure that binds the pieces into a coherent episodic memory. The therapist should therefore teach the client that recognizing and rehearsing organization is of primary importance. If the client can recall an organization, the individual elements of the larger memory will usually fall into place. Training organization and rehearsal skill may be difficult. For example, in Chapter 14, we discuss some techniques for illustrating the concept of rehearsing organization. This involves spreading a variety of objects on a table and asking a person to rehearse the types of objects he or she sees rather than the individual objects. This type of exercise is a clear and simple demonstration of the concept of rehearsing organization.

Kinds of Rehearsal

There are four basic kinds of rehearsals (Herrmann, Ruppin, & Usher, 1993). The simplest is *maintenance rehearsal*, which was discussed at length in Chapter 10. Maintenance rehearsal strengthens a memory record through simple repetition (Rundus, 1977), such as rehearsing a phone number by repeating it aloud. Although this kind of rehearsal maintains information in a person's consciousness, it may not lead to a permanent memory unless the repetition helps the person to transform the number in some way and the mental transformation makes it especially memorable.

A second kind of mental rehearsal *encodes attributes* of the information, attributes that otherwise would not be included in the memory trace (Underwood, 1969; Wickens, 1970). For example, pointing out some unique quality of a person's face may help a client recognize the person later and recall his or her name. Or, a business may choose a phone number with an easy-to-remember sequence, such as 666–7777 or 123–1234. These numbers are easy to rehearse because the sequence creates an obvious organizational rule for memory. By rehearsing the rule, a person can generate the string.

A third type of mental rehearsal improves recall of novel information by *associating* it with something familiar that is already in memory (Tulving & Madigan, 1970). For example, noticing that Mr. Girard has an especially long neck allows a person to associate him with a giraffe. The person can rehearse the image of a giraffe with Girard, which facilitates later recall of his name. This is not simple rehearsal of the name Girard repeatedly. Instead, the person focuses rehearsal on the relationship between Girard and the giraffe.

A fourth type of rehearsal is a *physical reminder* (Chase & Ericsson, 1982; Herrmann et al., 1993). Physical rehearsals create duplicates of information. For example, a person may use a tape recorder to make a physical backup of an important phone conversation. The person can rehearse the entire conversation again whenever necessary. Diaries allow individuals to rehearse the events of their lives. Physical reminders also involve other people who remind us of some event. For example, bill collectors seldom let a person forget when a debt comes due. The rehearsal techniques that follow each involve one or more of these four types of rehearsal.

Training Rehearsal

Much of what is called memory involves forming vivid first impressions. The strength or permanence of first impressions, however, depends on the extent to which a person actively rehearses after an actual event has passed. To ensure that the rehearsal process provides adequate strength (Bellezza, 1981; Higbee, 1988), the therapist should train clients to use the following techniques whenever they have a need to store information mentally.

Scene Rehearsal. Scenes are episodes of life that we encounter every day. The serial of life becomes a still picture when a person attends to a specific portion of the day and remembers it. The phrase "making a scene" refers to an unpleasant episode in which someone attracts attention with brash or audacious behavior. Accident scenes and crime scenes are usually unforgettable because of the horrible images they create. Clearly, one aspect of scene rehearsal involves the distinctiveness of the situation.

Many scenes, however, are not very distinctive. To make a scene more memorable, a person should scan it in detail, then close his or her eyes, and then ask questions about the scene (Biederman, Mezzanotte, & Rabinowitz, 1982). This creates an eidetic or photographic copy of the scene in the person's mind. When the person later tries to remember the scene, he or she should rehearse the scene by mentally conjuring pictorial answers to questions such as, "Who was there?" "What were the people wearing?" "Where were they sitting?" and so forth (Biederman et al., 1982).

Spaced Rehearsal. This technique helps a person rehearse new information over time (Landauer & Bjork, 1978). The therapist encourages a person to remember a particular event at intervals that increase in length. Each successive interval is twice as long as the preceding one. For example, a person tries to remember a conversation 1 day later, then 3 days later, and then 6 days later, and so forth.

Fact Rehearsal. In this method, a person focuses attention on specific aspects of information that he or she needs to encode. The person can ask specific questions about the information, such as, Who? What? Where? When? Whose? Why? Under what conditions? How? How much? How many? How often? These questions direct the person's attention to the critical aspects of the event and create a vivid first impression (Loisette, 1886). If the person cannot answer a question, then he or she must rehearse the information again. For example, when reading, the person should stop after each paragraph and try to answer as many of the questions about the paragraph as possible, rereading the paragraph if necessary. In some situations, fact rehearsal is similar to scene rehearsal. The two are identical when a person is rehearsing a visual scene. However, when reading books, the person may try to rehearse critical verbal facts (fact rehearsal) or try to conjure up images of what he or she is reading (scene rehearsal).

Self-Referencing. This is a method of relating the new to the old. The goal is to integrate novel experiences into a person's existing associative network through rehearsal. In so doing, the person can then access the novel information by thinking of things that relate to it (Baron, 1994). One or more of these associations will eventually lead to recall of the novel event. Self-referencing usually involves mentally categorizing the information (Greenwald & Banaji, 1989). For example, when meeting someone new, a person may ask, "How is this person like someone I already know?"

Semantic Rehearsal. This technique involves organizing verbal materials into groupings and rehearsing their similar meanings (Tulving, 1983). When learning a new word, a person also learns synonyms for the word. In addition, the person can learn other associated words, such as antonyms, homonyms, or words that belong to the same category. Associating the target word with other words essentially puts information in different places in the person's memory. Because the memory record is in two or more places, the person is much less likely to forget the word. For example, if a person is learning the word *jam*, then he or she should associate it with *grape* and *traffic*.

Loci Rehearsal. This technique is similar in some ways to scene rehearsal. Scene rehearsal can be used to remember novel events and places, whereas loci rehearsal can be used to remember location of a person's possessions in a familiar place (DiBeni & Cornoldi, 1985). The therapist teaches a person to organize items into a familiar area and then to rehearse the organization of the items within that space. For example, if a person always returns items to the same place in his or her home, then he or she can use the spatial organization of the house to help retrieve items. Most people use loci rehearsal to some extent when someone asks them where something is located in the house. They mentally search an area of the house that they are reasonably certain contains the desired object. Loci rehearsal is a valuable technique for retrieval of other types of information. When trying to recall a list of items, if a person has mentally placed the items into different areas of the house or some other familiar place, then he or she can recall the items by taking a mental walk through the house.

One benefit of all of the above rehearsal techniques is that the person tends to remember more attributes of an event than he or she would without rehearsal. This is because as the person repeats the information, his or her mental energy directs attention to the subtle attributes of the memory record that would otherwise go unnoticed. Most people experience this phenomenon if they see the same movie twice. They see things in the second viewing that they missed in the first. A person practicing rehearsal may also draw new conclusions, suppositions, and inferences about an event that were not apparent initially. In most cases, this is a beneficial by-product of the rehearsal process. When taken to extremes, however, it can be detrimental. For example, a person may witness a horrible auto accident and rehearse the gory details of the scene to the point that he or she can no longer go to sleep without dreaming about the event and waking up terrified. Forgetting can be adaptive because it allows us to not think about things that adversely affect our mental health.

Mnemonic Rehearsal Systems

Mnemonics are especially useful for improving rote recall of lists, procedures, or rules (Loisette, 1886). These memory strategies are sometimes called *acrostics*. A person forms a sentence, poem, or series of words that cues recall. For example, many people remember how to spell words with *ie* using the rhyme, "I before *e* except after *c*, or when it sounds like *a*, as in *neighbor* and *weigh*." When learning how to loosen or tighten a nut on a bolt, a person might use the poem "lefty loosey, righty tighty" to help him or her remember to loosen the nut by turning it to the left and to tighten it by turning it to the right. "My Dear Aunt Sally" is an acrostic that helps a person recall the order of operations in arithmetic, that is, Multiplication, Division, Addition, Subtraction. We usually give our clients several mnemonics, similar to those above, that will be valuable for a lifetime. Our goal, however, is to get the client to the point where he or she can generate personal mnemonics when learning new information.

First-Letter Mnemonic. This method of acrostic rehearsal involves arranging the first letter of each to-be-recalled item to form a word (Morris & Cook, 1978). For example, the NAME mnemonic cues recall of the steps needed to remember names and faces. It cues recall of Notice the person, Ask the person to repeat his or her name, Mention the name

in conversation, and Exaggerate some special feature. By remembering NAME, a person can later recall the steps needed to form lasting name–face associations.

Near-Word Abbreviation. For this technique, a person forms a small nonsense word by using the first letters of several words he or she wants to remember. This is similar to the first-letter mnemonic but uses a "near word" that can be pronounced but does not have any meaning. A near word is something like BOMS, in which each letter cues some action. BOMS reminds a person to respond appropriately when answering questions— Bottom-line the answer, Omit the details, Maintain focus, Summarize at the end.

Sentence Generation. Nonsense sentences and phrases can also aid recall (Duffy, Walker, & Montague, 1972). For example, when learning a list of things to do before leaving home, a person might rehearse, "Lights the door, iron the stove." This nonsense phrase cues the person to turn off the lights, lock the door, check that the iron is unplugged, and turn off the stove.

Suggestions for Improving Rehearsal Training

Customize the training. Mnemonic strategy training may be too abstract or require intentional demands that are beyond a person's ability. Nevertheless, a person who cannot generate personal mnemonics may be able to use others as long as they are personally relevant. In general, it makes no sense to teach rehearsal as an abstract process because a client will not typically use an abstract process spontaneously. However, with guidance, the client and therapist can generate specific acrostics mnemonics that are personally useful. Once the person sees the usefulness of a particular mnemonic, he or she is likely to buy into the general process.

Vary the context. Many people learn a mental strategy but do not use it because they fail to recognize how it applies in novel situations. It is therefore necessary for the client to rehearse not only the strategy but also its use in a wide variety of situations (Davies & Thomson, 1988). For example, when training mental imagery (Cornoldi & McDaniel, 1991; West, Yassuda, & Welch, 1997), the therapist can teach the client how to use it to improve name–face memory, to conjure images of written text and to rehearse scenes.

Review regularly. The strength of any memory, skill, or strategy increases markedly when time is scheduled to review. For example, if a client needs to recall the staff names and faces in the facility, then he or she should review the names with pictures of the staff each day. It is seldom sufficient to teach a person a strategy and assume that he or she will remember to use it without extensive review.

Rehearse real-life scenarios. A person should rehearse actual situations in which he or she might have to remember certain information before the situation actually occurs (Hardy & Ringland, 1984). For example, the therapist might direct a person to imagine recalling his or her Social Security number when filling out various job applications. These practice situations create a set and a script on which the person can rely later.

Rehearsal Management Strategies

Effective rehearsal training involves more than teaching a person to rehearse. Whether a person is trying to form a vivid first impression of a novel event or scanning an existing body of information in memory, the therapist must teach the person to manage his or her efforts in accordance with the demands of different situations (Schoenfeld, 1985).

These managerial strategies will help the person to choose which types of rehearsals will make the information most memorable (Stigsdotter-Neely & Bachman, 1993). The following suggestions for therapists will help clients manage rehearsal strategies.

Train scanning, selection, and then rehearsal. Rehearsal is most effective if the person has already selected the most important aspects of a situation. In training, the therapist presents complex arrays of information or situations and asks the person (1) to scan the entire array, (2) to select the most important aspects of the information, and (3) to rehearse only the important information.

Train a whole–part scanning strategy. Learning is most efficient when a person rehearses a big picture or global organization first, before focusing on the individual parts. In general, it is easier to fit parts into a whole than it is to create a whole from its parts. Certain questions help a person to see the whole, such as "What's the big picture?" "What are the major points I have to remember?" "What are the three major points this author is trying to make in this article?" These questions help a person reduce large amounts of information to critical facts. Training a person with brain injury to ask these questions will improve his or her retention of novel events because the person will remember the gist of the information, rather than the individual details.

Vary the rehearsal strategy. The therapist should teach a person to use more than one kind of manipulation when possible to remember the same material. Most experts believe that the use of different techniques leads to a more durable and accessible memory trace. For example, at a party, a person could first rehearse attributes of various guests such as their hair or eye color. Next, the person could rehearse social groupings of the guests.

Distribute rehearsal sessions. Ideally, a person will learn to rehearse consistently over several sessions. In general, seven 1-hour rehearsal sessions spread over 7 days create a more durable memory than one 7-hour rehearsal marathon.

Put in the time. The therapist should emphasize that whatever method a person uses, the amount he or she learns will depend on the amount of time spent practicing.

Self-testing. The therapist should train a person to repeatedly self-test during learning and to overlearn the material if it is especially important or detailed. That is, after learning 100% of new material, a person should continue to study the material and retest until mastery. The major value of self-testing is that it shows the person those aspects of the information that he or she does not know well. The person can then focus rehearsal on that information. For example, when reading text, a person should recall the gist of each paragraph and spend the most time reviewing those paragraphs that were most difficult to recall.

Rehearse when rested. Rehearsal is functionally useless if a person is not attending to the information. It is therefore important to ensure that a person is rehearsing when he or she can attend and concentrate adequately.

Summary

This chapter presented various techniques for combining rehearsal skill with various techniques of memory strategy training (Harrell, Parenté, Bellingrath, & Lisicia, 1992; Parenté & Anderson-Parenté, 1991). Rehearsal is the mechanism that allows a person to keep information in the cognitive system. Without rehearsal, people would forget most things they heard or saw in a matter of minutes (Higbee, 1988). After traumatic brain injury, some persons lose the ability to rehearse automatically (Bargh, 1992; Parenté, 1994; Twum, 1994). The goal of treatment is to train a person to rehearse consciously, so that it will become automatic. The rehearsal process is most effective if a person rehearses the organizational structure of the information rather than its component parts.

References

Bargh, J. A. (1992). The ecology of automaticity: Toward establishing the conditions needed to produce automatic processing effects. *American Journal of Psychology, 105,* 181–200.

Baron, P. (1994). *Thinking and deciding* (2nd ed.). Cambridge, United Kingdom: Cambridge University Press.

Bellezza, F. S. (1981). Mnemonic devices: Classification, characteristics, and criteria. *Review of Educational Research, 51,* 247–275.

Biederman, I., Mezzanotte, R. J., & Rabinowitz, J. (1982). Scene perception: Detecting and judging objects undergoing relational violations. *Cognitive Psychology, 14,* 143–177.

Chase, W. G., & Ericsson, K. A. (1982). Skill and working memory. In G. H. Bower (Ed.), *The Psychology of Learning and Motivation* (Vol. 16, pp. 141–190). New York: Academic Press.

Cornoldi, C., & McDaniel, M. A. (Eds.). (1991). *Imagery and cognition.* New York: Springer-Verlag.

Davies, G., & Thomson, D. M. (1988). *Memory in context: Context in memory.* Chichester, United Kingdom: Wiley.

DiBeni, R., & Cornoldi, C. (1985). Effects of the mnemonotechnique of loci in memorization of concrete words. *Acta Psychologica, 60,* 11–24.

Duffy, T. M., Walker, C., & Montague, W. E. (1972). Sentence mnemonics and the role of verb-class in paired-associate learning. *Psychological Reports, 31,* 583–589.

Ericsson, K. A. (1985). Memory skill. *Canadian Journal of Psychology, 39,* 188–231.

Greenwald, A. G., & Banaji, M. R. (1989). The self as a memory system: Powerful but ordinary. *Journal of Personality and Social Psychology, 57,* 41–54.

Hardy, L., & Ringland, A. (1984). Mental training and the inner game. *Human Learning, 3,* 143–226.

Harrell, M., Parenté, F., Bellingrath, E. G., & Lisicia, K. A. (1992). *Cognitive rehabilitation of memory: A practical guide.* Gaithersburg, MD: Aspen.

Healy, A. F., & Bourne, L. E., Jr. (1995). *Learning and memory of knowledge and skills: Durability and specificity.* Thousand Oaks, CA: Sage.

Herrmann, D., Weingartner, H., Searleman, A., & McEvoy, C. (Eds.). (1992). *Memory improvement: Implications for memory theory.* New York: Springer-Verlag.

Herrmann, M., Ruppin, E., & Usher, M. (1993). A neural model of the dynamic activation of memory. *Biological Cybernetics, 68*, 455–463.

Higbee, K. L. (1988). *Your memory* (2nd ed.). Englewood Cliffs, NJ: Prentice Hall.

Landauer, T. K., & Bjork, R. A. (1978). Optimum rehearsal patterns and name learning. In M. M. Gruenberg, P. E. Morris, & R. N. Sykes (Eds.), *Practical aspects of memory* (pp. 625–632). London: Academic Press.

Loisette, A. (1886). *Assimilative memory: Or how to attend and never forget.* New York: Funk & Wagnall.

Morris, P. E., & Cook, N. (1978). When do first letter mnemonics aid recall? *British Journal of Educational Psychology, 48*, 22–28.

Parenté, R. (1994). Effects of monetary incentives on performance after traumatic brain injury. *NeuroRehabilitation, 4*(3), 198–203.

Parenté, R., & Anderson-Parenté, J. (1991). *Retraining memory: Techniques and applications.* Houston, TX: CSY.

Rundus, D. (1977). Maintenance rehearsal and single level processing. *Journal of Verbal Learning and Verbal Behavior, 16*, 665–681.

Schoenfeld, A. H. (1985). *Mathematical problem solving.* Orlando, FL: Academic Press.

Stigsdotter-Neely, A., & Bachman, L. (1993). Maintenance of gains following multifactorial and unifactorial memory training in late adulthood. *Educational Gerontology, 19*, 105–117.

Tulving, E. (1983). *Elements of episodic memory.* Oxford, United Kingdom: Oxford University Press.

Tulving, E., & Madigan, S. A. (1970). Memory and verbal learning. *Annual Review of Psychology, 20*, 437–484.

Twum, M. (1994). Maximizing generalization of cognitions and memories after traumatic brain injury. *NeuroRehabilitation, 4*, 157–167.

Underwood, B. J. (1969). Attributes of memory. *Psychological Review, 76*, 559–573.

West, R. L., Yassuda, M. S., & Welch, D. C. (1997). Imagery training via videotape: Progress and potential for older adults. *Cognitive Technology, 2*, 16–21.

Wickens, D. D. (1970). Encoding categories of words: An empirical approach to meaning. *Psychological Review, 77*, 1–15.

Wilson, B. A. (1987). *Rehabilitation of memory.* New York: Guilford Press.

Chapter 14

❧

Retraining Organizational Skills

Persons with brain injury often seem disorganized, have difficulty keeping track of things, or seem unable to do things systematically or in a timely fashion. It may be difficult for them to prioritize several errands that they must complete in a limited period. Their explanations are often disorganized and fragmented. Retraining these organizational skills is one of the most difficult aspects of therapy. This chapter provides ways for therapists to teach organizational skills to persons with brain injury. The chapter begins with an overview and summary of the various theories of mental organization. Although these theories were not intended to explain deficits of organization that result from brain injury, the theories do have implications for rehabilitation. Schema theory is discussed in detail because it appears to be the most likely candidate for a comprehensive theory for studying organizational deficits after brain injury. Then some original research is presented that tests the basic assumptions of schema theory. The chapter ends with a discussion of rehabilitation techniques that follow from these theories along with a description of principles of environmental organization.

Mental Organization

Before a therapist can retrain organizational skill, it is first necessary to understand how mental representations of the world are created. There is considerable literature that describes the process of mental organization with college students. There is comparatively little research that describes how persons with brain injury organize information. We therefore describe briefly different theories of mental organization and extract from them any implications for brain injury rehabilitation.

Propositional Theory

Kintch and van Dijk (1978) proposed what has become a classic and widely accepted theory of mental organization. This theory is similar to another proposed by Anderson and Bower (1973). The general idea is that comprehension is the process of forming propositions, which are relationships that integrate an existing body of information. For example, Figure 14.1 illustrates a hypothetical propositional network that relates the statement, *Alice sells fresh bagels to Tony who owns a restaurant*. The network on the left illustrates an intact propositional structure. The lines that connect the words with one another indicate a relationship that binds the subject, object, and recipient portions of the network in some way. The line between *fresh* and *object* indicates that the object *bagel* and the word *fresh* are related. Likewise, *sells* is related to the subject *Alice*. Each of the propositions is part of a larger cluster depicted in the figure. The

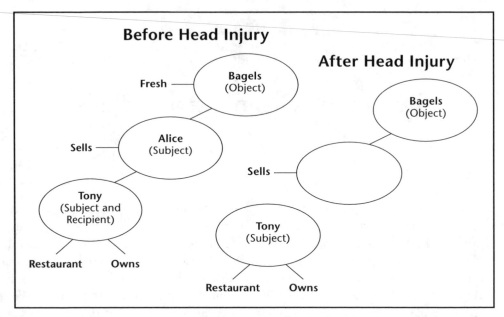

Figure 14.1. Hypothetical propositional network model before and after traumatic brain injury.

theory assumes that information is stored in memory according to a propositional structure. The structures are modified and developed by the person's past experience, goals, and values. Larger groups of propositions eventually organize around central themes.

Brain injury could affect this network in several ways. Examples of different types of damage are depicted on the right side of Figure 14.1. The damage could eliminate an entire subnetwork from the larger structure. That is, Tony could be disconnected from Alice entirely if the connection between the two were eliminated. A brain injury could also destroy associations in the network so that established relationships that existed before the injury may no longer apply. Regardless of the combination of effects, the result is an altered cognitive propositional network and a very different cognitive structure.

The implication of the propositional network model is that the therapist must focus on reconstructing the propositional structure of the network. The primary goal of therapy would be to teach the client to relate

novel information into a meaningful structure. When confronted with a novel situation, the client learns to ask, "How are these things related to one another?" This question forces the client to focus on the propositions that relate episodic information in memory. We describe a method of questioning later in the chapter that can be used for this purpose.

Associative Network Models

This type of theory assumes that knowledge is stored in a hierarchy. The first of these models (Quillian, 1968, 1969) was actually a computer program called the Teachable Language Comprehender. Quillian devised a method for storing information in a computer in such a way that the program could answer questions in a flexible fashion, similar to the way humans do. An example of his method is presented on the left side of Figure 14.2.

Quillian's model has superordinate categories with attributes attached to them. These attributes are the dots or nodes of

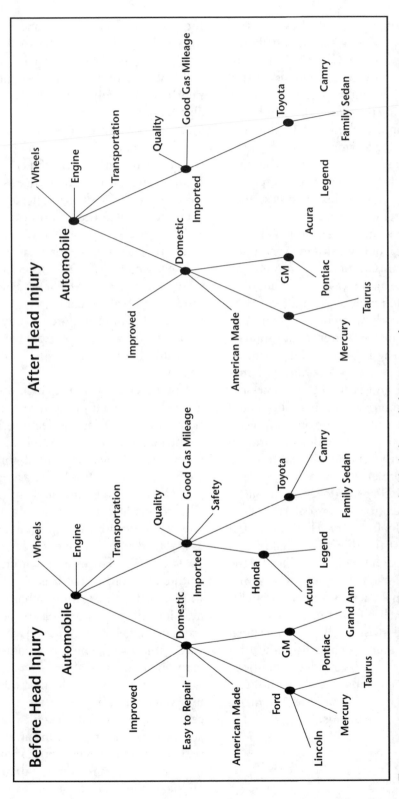

Figure 14.2. Hypothetical Teachable Language Comprehender before and after traumatic brain injury.

the hierarchy. Beneath each of these is a subordinate category with attached attributes. Individual instances were stored at the bottom of the hierarchy with their associated attributes. The computer program answers questions by tracing the query through the hierarchy. For example, when asked, "Is a Ford an automobile?" the program traces the word *Ford* to the superordinate and locates the word *automobile*, which produces a *yes* response. The process is more complex than described here, and the program can account for a variety of human performances. Quillian's model assumes that efficiency of thinking is partially related to the ability to organize information in a superordinate manner. Without the structure, retrieval from memory is limited to the capacity of the working memory (about 4 to 5 units of information after brain injury). However, when the information is organized into a superordinate and subordinate structure, then speed and accuracy of processing can be greatly improved. Brain injury could disrupt the structure by erasing one or more of the connections between nodes and from a node to an adjective that describes it. These possibilities are presented on the right side of Figure 14.2. Note that *easy to repair* and *safety* have been omitted from the associative net of the person with brain injury. The implication for therapy is that the therapist should teach organization through hierarchies. That is, the therapist should teach the client to organize information so that there is a clear hierarchical structure which allows him or her to either build or to reestablish the functional networks. For example, when listening to a conversation, the client should ask questions that force a superordinate and subordinate organization, such as "What was his major point?" "What are the details?"

Feature Set Theory

Originally proposed by Smith, Shoben, and Rips (1974), feature set theory suggested that the primary mechanism of memory is a person's ability to recognize the attribute features of his or her experience rather than the hierarchical structure. *Features* are also component parts of Quillian's (1968, 1969) Teachable Language Comprehender model. Unlike Quillian, however, these authors felt that the most important contents of memory are the attributes rather than the categories. The model assumed that knowledge is the sum of the features that describe a particular concept. In essence, there is no need for superordinate nodes in the feature set model because the attributes alone are sufficient to define the concepts. This aspect of the feature set model explains why it is difficult to describe some things concretely. For example, the word *beautiful* conjures up any number of examples of things a person believes to be beautiful, but there is no single definition for beauty.

Smith et al. (1974) distinguished between what they called *defining features* and *characteristic features*. Defining features are central to the meaning of the concept. This aspect of feature set theory accounted for Quillian's (1968, 1969) superordinate categories. Superordinates share similar defining features. Characteristic features are attributes that may be associated with the object but are not necessary to define it (Rinck, 1999; Tanaka & Taylor, 1991). For example, a characteristic feature of a Ford is that it is American made, whereas a defining feature is that it is an automobile. Things with wheels define the superordinate *automobile*. *Wheel* does not define Ford but it does define the nonautomobile superordinate *simple tool*.

The implications of this model for brain injury rehabilitation are that a client's concept of an event will depend on his or her ability to extract the defining and characteristic features of the event. For example, teaching a client to make a mental listing of the physical features of a person to whom he or she is introduced should help to make that person more memorable. The NAME device,

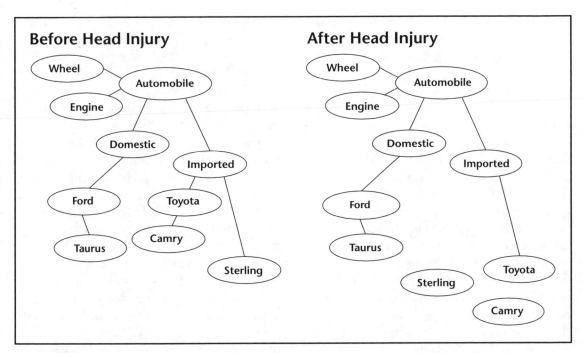

Figure 14.3. Diagram of cognitive structures according to spreading activation theory.

introduced in Chapter 13, serves this purpose when forming name–face associations.

Spreading Activation Model

The spreading activation model is a hybrid of those mentioned previously (Collins & Loftus, 1975). It is also a precursor to the modern schema theories (Mandler, 1984) that are discussed in detail later in this chapter. The model is shown in Figure 14.3. Although it is similar to the Quillian (1968, 1969) hierarchy in that it assumes that there are nodes that represent superordinate concepts, it differs in that each instance of the superordinate interconnects with other superordinates as well.

This model makes several unique assumptions. It assumes first that when a person perceives anything, the effect of the perception spreads through the entire mental network. In Figure 14.3 the length of the line that connects the various elements represents the probability that the instance or superordinate will activate another instance or superordinate. This could also have been represented by the thickness of the line connecting the various elements in the network. In Figure 14.3, for example, activating the ordinate *Ford* is more likely to activate the memory of *Taurus* than it is likely to conjure the superordinate *domestic*. The length of the line represents the strength of the association.

The term *spreading activation* refers to the assumption that any instance, ordinate, or superordinate that is stimulated will spread some amount of activation to another portion of the network. The strength of the activation will then trigger other portions of the network to fire, which will stimulate others. For example, saying *Acura* will probably trigger *imported* and may also trigger *Honda*. However, the likelihood that these are triggered depends on the strength of the original stimulus and the associations that have developed over the years. *Imported* and *Honda* will also activate other portions of the network that may conjure associations, depending on their strength. The spreading activation notion is an important part of the schema theory discussed in detail later in this chapter.

This theory has several implications for brain injury rehabilitation. The cause of cognitive dysfunction may be that the network is damaged or dysfunctional in some way. The goal of rehabilitation, therefore, is to repair the network through exercises that teach organization of semantic information (Gardiner & Hampton, 1985; Hampton, 1995; Lamberts & Shanks, 1997; Markman, 1999; Rosch, 1973; Smith, 1990). Because memory and thinking depend on the establishment of functional connections among instances and ordinates, training should include association of these characteristics. The theory also explains many of the seemingly tangential thinking processes that occur after brain injury when the activation probabilities between the instances and ordinates are damaged.

Summary and Evaluation

These models of human mental organization provide several facts that are useful for planning treatment in persons with brain injury. The common assumption of these models is that humans naturally organize information, and the way they organize determines the efficiency and accuracy of their thinking as well as the ability to retrieve information from memory (Herrmann & Chaffin, 1986). It is therefore reasonable to assume that the ability of a person with brain injury to recall semantic information depends on his or her ability to initially organize the information.

Twum and Parenté (1994) tested this hypothesis as part of a larger experiment. Persons with brain injury received lists of words that were organized semantically. The lists included the following words: *red, green, Mars, Venus, table, chair, hand, foot, north, west, dog,* *cat,* grouped by category (colors, planets, furniture, body parts, directions, animals). Before the words were given to the participants, they were mixed up so that the semantic organization was not apparent. The authors hypothesized that those persons who perceived the organization would recall more of the words. In essence, retrieval of the words for each of these persons with brain injury depended on his or her ability to perceive the organization of the list. This was precisely the result of the study. Those who recalled the words in an organized fashion usually remembered the entire list of 12 words. Those who did not perceive the organization could not recall more than half of the list even with repeated study.

After an hour of some other interpolated activity, the participants recalled as many of the words as they could remember. When they could no longer recall any more of the words, the authors prompted them by providing the categories of those words that they had not recalled. This cuing procedure generally resulted in recall of all of the words. Even cuing only one of the categories usually led to recall of words from other categories. This result suggested a spreading activation component to the participants' recall.

Elliot and Parenté (1995) followed up on this experiment to determine how to train participants to enhance their recall of the word lists. Their experiment evaluated the effects of several conditions of pretraining on the later recall of a word list. In one condition, persons with brain injury and persons with learning disabilities memorized a list of words arranged in a way that primed the participants to discover the organization of the larger list that they would memorize next. The participants in this condition first learned the following list: *yellow, blue, sun, moon, south, east.* They then learned this list: *dog, cat, table, chair, red, green, Mars, Venus, north, west.* The words on both lists were presented in a random order. The first list contained several of the categories that were also part of the second list but none of the same words. The participants in another group learned the category labels but not any of the words from the second list. These participants learned the words *animals, furniture, colors, planets, directions* before learning the larger 12-word list. In both conditions, the participants learned the second list much quicker than a group of people with similar disabilities who first learned a list of words that was totally unrelated to the second list.

Both of these experiments illustrate the importance of organization for improving thinking and memory in persons with brain injury. Teaching a person to organize information initially not only allows him or her to learn the information quickly, it also improves his or her ability to remember it long term.

Schema Theory

Schema theory is one of the oldest and most controversial concepts of how humans form mental representations of the world. Schema theory is controversial because it is difficult to verify empirically. Although the concept of a schema makes sense, it may be impossible to define a schema operationally or to verify experimentally if humans store information in memory this way. We describe this theory in greater detail than the rest because we feel that of all the theories of organization, it has the greatest potential for explaining memory and cognitive dysfunction after brain injury. Indeed, the theory has already been used to explain the mechanism that underlies amnesia (McClelland & Rummelhart, 1987). Schema theory underwent a great deal of development in the last quarter of the 20th century (Bransford & Johnson, 1972; Neisser, 1976). We begin with a limited historical perspective, then describe the more recent explanations along with a description of some initial tests of the schema model with brain-injured clients.

A Brief History of Schema Theory

Schema theory dates back to the time of Kant (1787/1987) and has been discussed most recently by McClelland and Rummelhart (1987) within the context of their parallel distributed processing model. A schema is a body of organized information that summarizes a person's experience and attitudes about any aspect of life. The theory assumes that a person has schemas for dinner, vacations, work, and so forth, and that they differ from person to person as evidenced by statements such as, "That's not my idea of a good time," or "He's a good speaker," or "She's beautiful." Each of these statements implies some inner representation that a person uses to make judgments about the world.

Schemas do not necessarily imply propositions, hierarchical structure, or categorization; some are organizations of time, space, or sequence (Mandler, 1984; Rabinowitz & Mandler, 1983). For example, most people can conjure a mental representation of the last 10 minutes, their backyard, or how to start a car. Some schemas are *scripts* that describe sequences of events that a person expects to occur in certain situations (Ericsson & Smith, 1991; Greeno, 1998; Schank & Abelson, 1977). For example, most people are aware of a certain script sequence that a waiter or waitress follows in a restaurant. Other schemas are *scenes* (Mandler, 1984; Thorndyke & Hayes-Roth, 1982) that represent a spatial organization. For example, most people have a scene schema for the furniture in their living room.

Early depictions of the schema concept were difficult for theorists to describe concretely and had little practical value. Kant (1787/1987), for example, discussed the concept of a schema in philosophical terms. Bartlett (1932) described *schemata* in relation to the recall of text materials. Piaget (1952) also used the term *schema* to explain the development of human cognition. Because of the vagueness of the term, many cognitive theorists considered the idea of a mental schema to be too diffuse to be of any practical value. More recent discussions (Bobrow & Norman, 1975; Minsky, 1975; Rummelhart, 1975; Schank & Abelson, 1977), however, use the term to describe data structures for storing information in memory. The data structures are likened to three-dimensional pictures of the outside world that describe situations, events, actions, and sequences.

Bartlett (1932) concluded that humans generally form a schema of everything they read and try to integrate new information into an existing schema of experience. This is the reason why the same event can have such different meanings to different people. Since the time of Bartlett, several basic processes of schema formation have been identified (Alba & Hasher, 1983; Eckhardt, 1990). These are especially relevant for therapists because they have direct application to brain injury rehabilitation.

The first process is *selection*. Whether or not a person will relate something new with things he or she already knows depends on whether that person allows the information to come in contact with the schema. For example, a person may not allow anyone's medical advice to alter his or her opinion unless that person is a physician. However, once the person selects certain information for processing, he or she ignores irrelevant details and incorporates certain core features into the schema. The person interprets the information by forming inferences (additional facts that could be true) and presuppositions (additional facts that must be true), which become part of the larger schema. This is the second process, *integration*.

New information may be integrated in one of three ways. It may be (a) readily assimilated into the schema, (b) tagged as similar but a little different, or (c) labeled as an ac-

ceptable variation to the general rule. Schema formation is also an actively changing process that is unique to the cultural experience of the individual. The basic implication from this overview of schema theory is that persons with brain injury must learn to focus on thematic content and try to integrate novel experiences into existing schema. The schema processes, however, may be deficient in a person with brain injury, and the therapist's challenge is to determine which ones are not functioning. For example, a person may have difficulty selecting relevant information at input. Or it may be difficult for a person to abstract the gist of the information once it reaches memory. Unfortunately, there has been little research in the brain injury field that describes these processes or what therapies are appropriate for their retraining.

Parallel Distributed Processing Model

McClelland and Rummelhart (1987) have proposed a parallel distributed processing (PDP) model of schema formation that is actually a connectionist computer program that can be used to simulate human cognition and cognitive dysfunction. The underlying logic of their model departs from other schema theories because it assumes that the brain does not store physical representations of the world per se. Rather, it creates them. The PDP model assumes that schema formation is a constructive process that occurs when something in the world stimulates or activates some portion of the schema, which, in turn, spreads the activation to the rest of the schema. The resulting memory may vary markedly depending on the extent of the original stimulation. These processes are thought to be unconscious and dependent on the person's prior learning, values, and the amount of information that is available. In essence, schemas are the mental representations that result when a person tries to interpret his or her environment.

More specifically, the PDP concept purports that the mind is composed of receptors that are sensitive to simple features. Combinations of the features create higher level organizations such as words or shapes. At this level, the PDP theory is similar to the feature set model mentioned earlier. Both models assume that features are interconnected and environmental stimuli can activate any part of this connected landscape. The activation then spreads through the network, either activating other portions or inhibiting them. The pattern of activation and inhibition develops through experience. However, depending on which aspects of the array are stimulated or inhibited, the schema that forms may vary. For example, when we see a person from afar, that person's gross features may activate the schema for a certain friend or relative. However, this same person's features may remind us of someone else as he or she gets closer.

Schema theory assumes that what is stored in memory is a set of connections that are probabilities. These connections vary from person to person and from moment to moment. After a brain injury, the connections deteriorate, rearrange, or disconnect. It therefore stands to reason that persons with brain injury would perceive the world differently because the injury alters their schemas and their methods for forming schemas. McClelland and Rummelhart's (1987) PDP model is especially useful because it is designed as a computer program that can be used to model the neural functioning of the brain. The model is unique because it assumes that humans do not form hardwired schemas to represent the novel experiences of life. Their model shows that information is processed in a probabilistic manner by a series of mental associations. Activation of an associative network spreads and potentially can trigger a variety of other schemas. The probability of conjuring a certain schema in memory increases when an experience is repeated. That is, for a given person, a certain schema is likely to arise when he or she is confronted with a certain set of events. For another person, a different schema will arise from exactly the same set of events. For example, a young child may see a woman who is standing in line at the store as *mother*, whereas a senior citizen may see the same woman as a *young lady*. The cashier may see the woman as a *customer*. Each of these schemas dictate different behavioral actions.

There have been many different uses of the PDP model for simulating human thinking and memory. One concrete example (presented in Figure 14.4) involves the program's ability to perceive common words the same way humans do.

To distinguish the words COW and SKY, the computer program perceives several different characteristics of the word at the same time. At a feature level (the bottom line in Figure 14.4), the program analyzes each angle, line, and half-line of the various letters separately. These features and their combinations determine possible letters (middle line). At the same time, the letters determine a set of possible words in memory (top line). The computer program then constructs a list of possible words that the feature and word analysis generates.

The concept of the PDP model assumes that processing occurs with all information simultaneously. For example, when a person perceives the word *cat*, he or she processes each letter at the same time. The model also assumes that the person processes the part and the whole simultaneously. The person sees each letter and the entire word in parallel, that is, at the same time. Therefore, the feedback from the word can influence our perception of any particular letter.

Figure 14.4 illustrates the idea of parallel distributed processing. All the features are

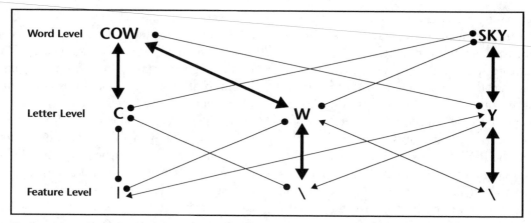

Figure 14.4. Hypothetical PDP model of word storage, activation, and inhibition in memory.

interconnected, as are the letters and the words. When any feature, letter, or word is activated (thick arrows), the activation travels through the entire model. All letters and words are activated, although differentially depending on their preset strength. There are also inhibitions (thin arrows) at each level, which limit the net excitement of a letter or a word. The words provide feedback onto the letters, which exert control on the net impact.

Excitatory connections are the lines ending in arrows, whereas inhibitory connections end in dots. At the feature level, the slanted line in the middle bottom will activate the letter W because this letter contains a slanted line. It will also inhibit the letter C because this letter does not contain a slanted line. At the letter level, the letter W will activate the word COW but it will inhibit the word SKY. At the word level, SKY will activate the letter Y but inhibit the letter C.

In the PDP model, knowledge is the connection among the units, not the units themselves. This is a major departure from other mental organization models that were discussed in the beginning of the chapter. The assumption of the PDP model is also consistent with the widely held view that the brain functions with mass action. Brain functioning is not localized to one exclusive structure such as a single neuron or a specific site.

Schema Theory Research as Applied to Brain Injury

Assuming that the model is an accurate assessment of mental organization, it is reasonable to ask what implications it has for brain injury rehabilitation. Hart and Parenté (1995) explored this question by comparing the ability of persons with and without brain injuries to process ambiguous words. The study included three groups: a control group of 17 college students, a group of 17 persons with mild brain injury, and a group of 17 persons with severe brain injury. Each participant saw the same list of words; each word was obscured with blotches over one of the letters, creating more than one possible meaning for the word. The words appeared for 1/10 second and the participants were asked to write down what word they thought they had seen.

The college students were able to correctly identify 100% of the words. Those with mild brain injuries correctly identified 71% and those with severe brain injuries correctly identified 66%. Each group's written responses to the words and the pattern of responses differed from group to group. Given the differences in the groups' responses, Hart and Parenté examined how the PDP model could explain the differences. Assuming that the PDP model is a reasonable theory of word perception, then it was reasonable to ask what modifications to the PDP computer program would be necessary for the model to simulate the pattern of correct and incorrect guesses that were obtained from each group. Because persons with traumatic brain injury are known to have difficulty inhibiting responses, changing the inhibition levels in the PDP program might allow the program to simulate the pattern of responses obtained in the study with the participants with brain injury. In addition to having difficulty with inhibition, persons with brain injury complain of slower processing. Hart and Parenté therefore predicted that the model would process at different rates depending on which type of person the program simulated.

Hart and Parenté (1995) analyzed the same words from this experiment using the McClelland and Rummelhart (1987) computer model. The program allows the user to modify several different processing characteristics. Among them are activation levels for the feature-to-letter portion of the analysis and for the letter-to-word analysis. Activation is the extent to which the feature, the letter, or the word stimulates a response and spreads to some other portion of the associative network. Inhibition levels are also controlled for these two types of analysis. Inhibition is the degree to which the features, letters, or words suppress a response throughout the network. McClelland and Rummelhart's interpretation of activation and inhibition is that the former is analogous to a person's ability to construct choices whereas the latter represents a person's ability to reject possibilities. A measure of cycling also can be modified. This is the number of times the program analyzes and reanalyzes the word it is reading before converging on a specific word from its memory. The measure is analogous to the speed of processing prior to forming an impression.

Once again, Hart and Parenté (1995) reasoned that the inhibition and cycling parameters of the computer program would be the most likely candidates for modification because they are most similar to the problems people report after brain injury. They lowered the inhibition component of the PDP model to determine if it could reproduce the pattern of word selections that resulted from each of the groups of persons with brain injury. For example, for the word *work*, the participants generated alternatives such as *word* or *worn* consistently. The computer program was modified until it produced an identical distribution of correct and incorrect alternatives as compared with the groups in the study. This procedure was carried out with all three groups. Again, the goal was to determine how to alter the model's thinking process to simulate the performance of the participants with different levels of brain injury. The results of the modifications of the computer program indicated that the biggest differences in how the program read words occurred with the cycles and inhibition modifications. Modifying the activation component caused fewer changes.

There are a variety of implications of this finding for brain injury rehabilitation. First, brain injury seems to affect a person's ability to inhibit. This is certainly consistent with literature that states that persons with brain injury are impulsive and unable to inhibit their responses. In addition, the difficulty these persons have with concentration and attention may be the result of the inability to inhibit the flood of ideas and information that comes to mind. Furthermore, persons with brain injury do not cycle as quickly or as much before settling on a schema that leads to a response. These results imply that therapists should teach their clients to inhibit responding and to process more before settling on a response. For example, it may be helpful to teach clients to mentally rehearse their statements before saying them. Many of the strategies discussed in Chapter 17 on decision making force the client to process a situation thoroughly before making a decision or acting.

From Theory to Practice

Training Organizational Skills

The various organizational theories described in this chapter suggest several techniques to help persons with brain injury organize more effectively (Mayer, 1983). Common to most of the theories is the notion that mental efficiency is the result of organization. Therefore, a goal of therapy is to train a person to extract the structure of whatever he or she experiences. A simple method for introducing this process is to force a person to recall organization rather than individual elements. This type of exercise demonstrates clearly how much faster and more accurate thinking and memory can be when the information is organized. It also illustrates the basic premise of the schema and Teachable Language Comprehender models in which elements automatically attach themselves to the organization.

Category Recall

There is a simple procedure for training category recall skill. In one variant of the exercise, the client sees a page that contains 12 to 15 words, grouped semantically, by color, by size, and by font (see Figure 14.5). Although it does not show here, some words may be printed in green, others in red, blue, or yellow.

After the client has studied the page for a minute, the therapist asks him or her to recall the categories, not the words. The client may say that some were animals, some were body parts, some were planets, and so forth. Another client may group the words according to where each was positioned on the page. The client may also group the words by color or

by font type or dark versus light. The study–test procedure continues until the client settles on a specific organization. Afterward, the therapist asks for recall of the individual words. The client then can use the organization to recall the individual elements. He or she is usually amazed to see that the words come to mind once the organization is stored. This technique shows the therapist the type of organization the client finds most useful, and it shows the client the value of organization for improving recall.

A similar exercise serves the same purpose. The therapist dumps a number of unrelated household materials on the table, such as scissors, tape, knife, fork, rubber band, paper clip, toothbrush, and comb. The therapist lets the client study these materials then removes them from view. Then the client is asked to describe the types of materials that were there, not the individual items. For example, some of the items were metal and some things were found in an office. Once the client can recall the types of materials, the therapist asks for recall of the individual items.

Both of these exercises also allow the therapist to see the dimensions the client naturally uses to organize. It is important not to force a client to use an organization method that he or she does not feel comfortable using. In the first exercise, for example, the client may use color, size of the print, or semantic organization to group the words. Any of these dimensions is acceptable. In our experience, clients in the early stages of recovery typically use concrete organization methods such as color or size, whereas higher functioning clients prefer semantic organization. In the second exercise, clients typically use a variety of methods for organizing the materials. Any of them are fine as long as retention is improved.

Self-Questioning

The organizational theories dictate that efficient processing is directly related to how well

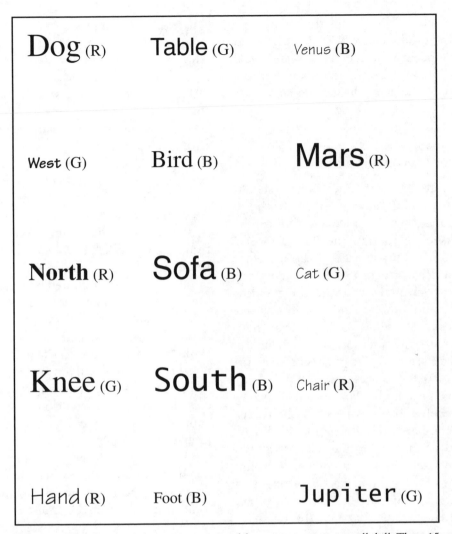

Figure 14.5. This word chart was constructed for training category recall skill. These 15 words differ in terms of font (e.g., Tekton, Times New Roman, Lucida Sans Type-writer), size (e.g., 12, 18, 24 points), and color (e.g., red, green, blue).

novel information is integrated into memory. Questions that show a client similarities between new and old information are helpful because they force the integration. Therapists should train clients to ask and answer the following questions when confronted with a novel situation:

- What is this the same as?

- To what category does this belong?

- What does this sound like? Look like? Smell like? Taste like?

- When did this occur?

- To what social group does this person belong?

Questioning requires a client to integrate the new information into the existing mental network.

A similar procedure works for reading comprehension. The therapist trains the client to extract the gist of the information by stopping after each paragraph and asking several questions: *Who* is discussed? *What* is the paragraph about? *When* did the event take place? *Where* did it occur? *Why* did it happen? *How* did it occur? This is especially effective if the client summarizes the information into a tape recorder and can rehearse the summaries later.

Adequate Processing Time

According to schema theory, therapists should train clients to inhibit any response until the situation is adequately processed. This can be accomplished by training the client to spend more time thinking about a situation before making a decision. For example, clients can be taught to mentally count to three and to say the response in their mind before speaking. Several learning situations can help clients process information better, including untimed tests, forced rehearsal techniques, rereading of text passages, and self-paced instructional materials. For example, when clients receive instructions, they should repeat them immediately. Repeating them right away will promote retention. Clients should reread information several times to ensure that they do not immediately settle on a surface-level comprehension of the material. All of these techniques teach the client to inhibit responding until he or she has fully processed the situation.

External Organization

The previous section presented methods for helping clients with mental organization. These are active rehabilitation methods that are certainly useful with most persons. There are also passive methods that are helpful and relatively easy and expedient ways to organize a client's external world. This section presents techniques for organizing a client's living space.

Attitude Adjustment

The therapist should discuss with the client several misconceptions about organization (Winston, 1989). The first misconception is that being organized means being neat. Another is that neatness is a moral issue. A third is that not being neat means the client is a bad person. Organization means only that a person's system is functional to the point at which he or she can find something when necessary. Regardless of how neat a person is, the real issue in organization is whether things are available when needed, and whether things get done on time or whether most tasks must be repeated because of a failure to anticipate obstacles. In our experience, a person may spend as much as 30% of his or her life looking for something. The goal of organization is to reduce this figure as much as possible. In mental and physical organization, the goal is to store information so that it is accessible later. The system one uses is irrelevant as long as the person can retrieve the information on demand.

Unfortunately, most people are not taught how to organize when they are children. Many people grow up with poor organizational skills that they must later unlearn and replace with more efficient habits. Similarly, most therapy clients will have to learn new organizational skills, which can be a time-consuming process. Furthermore, some clients may have problems with authority stemming from their relationships with parents and teachers, which may result in clients' resisting instruction in organizational methods because they see it as someone imposing authority over them. Other clients may rebel against instruction in organizational methods because they do not want to be controlled by some external force. For example, some people are not punctual because they do not want to be controlled by time. These issues may surface during the course of treatment and it is usually best to discuss at least the underlying motivations, knowing that the client may not readily accept nor understand the explanation. The therapist should focus on potential solutions rather than on the psychodynamics of the problem.

In many cases, it is impossible for the client to complete the whole within a limited period. The client's goal, therefore, is to complete a portion of the task and keep a record of what remains. The client should write down or record on a tape recorder what portion of the task he or she has completed. This is especially important for persons with brain injury who may have memory problems. Writing or recording which subtasks were completed keeps the client from repeating them and reminds him or her of the whole task. With these things in mind, here are some specific strategies for training clients to organize their living and work spaces.

Organizing the Environment

Organizing a client's living and work spaces involves five basic principles: *consistency*, *accessibility*, *grouping*, *separation*, and *proximity*. The best way to teach these principles is to apply them to the client's personal space. The goal is to make the client's environment work for him or her rather than against him or her (Evans, 1980). To accomplish this goal, the therapist must first evaluate the person's living and work environments and work with his or her family, employers, and so forth to arrange the space according to the following principles.

Consistency refers to the old adage, "a place for everything and everything in its place." For example, the client or a family member should place a bowl atop a pedestal table next to the front door. The client learns to always place important items like keys, wallet, and so forth into the bowl immediately upon entering the house. The minute a client spends putting these things in the bowl is usually worth an hour spent looking

for them later. This principle can be applied to other parts of the house. The goal is to get the client always to put things back in the same place or risk not being able to find them. This technique is effective because the client can use a mental image of the house as a memory aid.

Accessibility refers to keeping those things that the client uses most often physically close and keeping those that are less frequently used farther away. For example, if the client uses the same plates and cups daily and uses others only on special occasions, then the therapist places the dinnerware for daily use in a convenient cabinet in the kitchen, while the special occasion dinnerware resides on shelves that are farther away. Similarly, the client can arrange his or her desk space at work so that everyday materials such as pens and paper are kept close and special books or other materials that are infrequently used are kept on shelves farther away. A rule of thumb for accessibility is that the client should be able to stand in any room and almost touch those things that he or she uses most often.

Grouping means that items a client commonly uses together should be placed together. For example, some of the items a client should store together include cups and plates, coffee and coffee pot, and raincoats and umbrellas. Again, this technique can work quite well because the scene schema the client forms of the living space or workplace serves as a memory aid.

Separation means things should be kept in logically distinct locations, categories, or time frames. For example, a client can organize clothes in a closet in several ways. It may be helpful for one client to organize the clothes by season of the year, that is, putting all winter clothes on one side of the closet and all summer clothes on the other side. Other clients may prefer organizing by type of clothing, that is, putting all coats on one rack, pants on another, and shirts on a third. Another example of how separation is useful is in sorting mail. A client can place incoming mail into two piles based on the action required. For example, letters that require an immediate response go into one pile, while those that are interesting but that do not require immediate action go into another. The best separation method for any client becomes clear only after discussion and considerable trial and error.

Proximity means that items that are used together are kept together near the place where they are used. This principle of organization differs from accessibility only in that it refers to the convenience achieved by keeping related items close to one another. Accessibility simply means that anything that a person uses often is within reach whereas those things that a person uses less frequently are farther away. Ideally, a person should organize work and living spaces according to both principles. For example, installing a carousel hanger above a client's island stove keeps pots, pans, and utensils close to the cooking area. In an office, computer and copier supplies should be near the computer and the copier. The principle of accessibility also applies here. For example, only those pots, pans, and utensils the person uses every day should hang over the stove. Those office supplies that are used most often should be in the front of the cabinet and those that are used less frequently should be placed in the rear of the cabinet.

Although these five principles of organization may seem simple, they usually require quite a bit of time to implement. Organizing an entire house or workplace this way may take several days or weeks. The therapist should work with the client so that he or she can learn the physical schema as it is being developed. The therapist and family members can reinforce the physical schema by asking the client to shut his or her eyes and mentally walk through the house, describing where to find certain things. Once the client knows the schema, it should not be reorganized. According to the principles of transfer outlined in Chapter 6, a reorganization creates an A-B:A-Br paradigm, which would be extremely confusing, difficult to unlearn, and potentially dangerous.

Summary

This chapter described how humans organize their experiences and how brain injury may limit a person's ability to organize effectively. The chapter began with a discussion of several theories of organization and the implications of these theories for rehabilitation after brain injury. In general, humans organize new experiences unconsciously, and brain injury may destroy this automatic process. The therapist must therefore retrain the client to consciously seek organizational structure in new situations. The schema theory of mental organization was discussed in great detail because we feel it is probably the best working model of organization. An experimental test confirmed its usefulness as a model of cognitive dysfunction after brain injury. The results showed that persons may lose the ability to inhibit responding after brain injury. They may therefore perform most tasks without adequate processing, which leads to incorrect responses. The chapter closes with several suggestions for treatment based on the implications of these theories, including mental and physical organization techniques.

References

Alba, J. W., & Hasher, L. (1983). Is memory schematic? *Psychological Bulletin, 93,* 203–231.

Anderson, J., & Bower, G. (1973). *Human associative memory.* Washington, DC: Winston.

Bartlett, F. C. (1932). *Remembering: An experimental and social study.* Cambridge, United Kingdom: Cambridge University Press.

Bobrow, D. G., & Norman, D. A. (1975). Some principles of memory schemata. In D. G. Bobrow & A. Collins (Eds.), *Representation and understanding: Studies in cognitive science* (pp. 131–149). New York: Academic Press.

Bransford, J. D., & Johnson, M. K. (1972). Contextual prerequisites for understanding: Some investigations of comprehension and recall. *Journal of Verbal Learning and Verbal Behavior, 11,* 717–726.

Collins, A. M., & Loftus, E. F. (1975). A spreading activation theory of semantic processing. *Psychological Review, 82,* 407–428.

Eckhardt, B. B. (1990). *Elements of schema theory.* Unpublished paper, University of New Mexico, Albuquerque.

Elliot, A., & Parenté, R. (1995). *Organization and transfer after traumatic brain injury.* Unpublished master's thesis, Towson University, Towson, MD.

Ericsson, K. A., & Smith, J. (Eds.). (1991). *Toward a general theory of expertise.* Cambridge, United Kingdom: Cambridge University Press.

Evans, G. W. (1980). Environmental cognition. *Psychological Bulletin, 88,* 259–287.

Gardiner, J. M., & Hampton, J. A. (1985). Semantic memory and the generation of thought. *Psychology: Learning, Memory, and Cognition, 11,* 732–741.

Greeno, J. G. (1998). The situativity of knowing, learning, and research. *American Psychologist, 53,* 5–26.

Hampton, J. A. (1995). Psychological representation of concepts. In M. A. Comway (Ed.), *Cognitive models of memory.* Cambridge, MA: MIT Press.

Hart, P., & Parenté, R. (1995). First tests of a parallel distributed processing model of word perception after traumatic brain injury. *Monographs of the Human Learning, Cognition, and Information Processing Laboratories* (Vol. 1, pp. 1–10). Towson, MD: Towson State University.

Herrmann, D. J., & Chaffin, R. (1986). Comprehension of semantic relations as a function of definitions of relations. In F. Klix (Ed.), *Memoriam Herrmann Ebbinghaus: The proceedings of the Ebbinghaus Centennial Conference.* Amsterdam: Elsevier.

Kant, E. (1987). *Critique of pure reason* (2nd ed., N. Kemp Smith, Trans.). London: Macmillan. (Original work published 1787)

Kintch, W., & van Dijk, T. A. (1978). Toward a model of text comprehension and production. *Psychological Review, 85,* 363–394.

Lamberts, K., & Shanks, D. (Eds.). (1997). *Knowledge, concepts, and categories.* Cambridge, MA: MIT Press.

Mandler, J. M. (1984). *Stories, scripts, and scenes: Aspects of schema theory.* Hillsdale, NJ: Erlbaum.

Markman, A. B. (1999). *Knowledge representation.* Mahwah, NJ: Erlbaum.

Mayer, R. E. (1983). *Thinking, problem solving, cognition.* New York: Freeman.

McClelland, J. L., & Rummelhart, D. E. (1987). *Parallel distributed processing: Explorations in the microstructure of cognition: Vol. 2. Psychological and biological models.* Cambridge, MA: MIT Press.

Minsky, M. (1975). A framework for representing knowledge. In P. H. Winston (Ed.), *The psychology of computer vision* (pp. 211–277). New York: McGraw-Hill.

Neisser, U. (1976). *Cognition and reality.* San Francisco: Freeman.

Piaget, J. (1952). *The origins of intelligence in children.* New York: International University Press.

Quillian, M. R. (1968). Semantic memory. In M. Minsky (Ed.), *Semantic information processing* (pp. 216–270). Cambridge, MA: MIT Press.

Quillian, M. R. (1969). The teachable language comprehender: A simulation program and theory of language. *Communications of the Association for Computing Machinery, 12,* 459–476.

Rabinowitz, J. C., & Mandler, J. M. (1983). Organization and information retrieval. *Journal of Experimental Psychology: Learning, Memory, and Cognition, 9,* 430–439.

Rinck, M. (1999). Memory for everyday objects: Where are the digits on numerical keypads? *Applied Cognitive Psychology, 13,* 329–350.

Rosch, E. (1973). Natural categories. *Cognitive Psychology, 4,* 328–350.

Rummelhart, D. E. (1975). Notes on a schema for stories. In D. G. Bobrow & A. Collins (Eds.), *Representation and understanding* (pp. 211–236). New York: Academic Press.

Schank, R., & Abelson, R. (1977). *Scripts, plans, goals, and understanding.* Hillsdale, NJ: Erlbaum.

Smith, E. E. (1990). Categorization. In D. N. Osherson & E. E. Smith (Eds.), *Thinking: An invitation to cognitive science* (Vol. 3, pp. 33–53). Cambridge, MA: MIT Press.

Smith, E. E., Shoben, E. J., & Rips, L. J. (1974). Structure and process in semantic memory: A featural model of semantic decision. *Psychological Review, 81,* 214–241.

Tanaka, J. W., & Taylor, M. (1991). Object categories and expertise: Is the basic level in the eye of the beholder? *Cognitive Psychology*, *23*, 457–482.

Thorndyke, P. W., & Hayes-Roth, B. (1982). Differences in spatial knowledge acquired from maps and navigation. *Cognitive Psychology*, *14*, 560–589.

Twum, M., & Parenté, R. (1994). Maximizing generalization of cognitions and memories after traumatic brain injury. *NeuroRehabilitation*, *4*(3), 157–167.

Winston, S. (1989). *Getting organized*. New York: Simon & Schuster.

Chapter 15

꙳

Retraining Problem-Solving Skills

Persons with brain injury often report that problem solving is extremely difficult and frustrating. Most do not try to solve problems in a systematic or an organized fashion and many depend on others to help them solve even the simplest problems. Because problem solving is so difficult, persons with brain injury will often procrastinate with the hope that the problem will go away. Their reluctance to try to solve even easy problems on their own may frustrate others. There are, however, techniques to help persons with brain injury, or anyone else, apply a systematic and efficient method for solving daily problems (Bransford & Stein, 1984). The purpose of this chapter is to summarize much of the literature on problem solving and to make it useful for those individuals who have cognitive limitations due to brain injury.

We begin by reviewing some of the classic theories of problem solving and taking from them, wherever possible, the aspects that have implications for therapy with persons with brain injury. We then describe the characteristics of good problem solvers and discuss some common problem-solving styles. We next describe the stages of problem solving in detail, then review several methods for generating solutions to problems and discuss personal barriers to problem solving. Finally, we end with a discussion of a mnemonic that can be used to teach problem-solving skills.

Theories of Problem Solving

A problem arises whenever a person is unable to think of a means to achieve a goal. Therefore, problem-solving skill is the ability to discover the means to an end. Although there are several theories of human problem solving (Cavanaugh, Kramer, Sinnott, Camp, & Markley, 1985; Whimbey & Lockhead, 1999), this brief review focuses on three well-documented theories that have specific implications for teaching persons with brain injury. Other authors (such as Hunt & Ellis, 1998; Mayer, 1992; Schraw, Dunkle, & Bendixen, 1995; Wickelgren, 1974) provide a more comprehensive presentation of these and other theories of solving problems. Each of the following theories has several implications that may be useful for training problem-solving skills in persons with brain injury.

Stimulus–Response Model

Perhaps the earliest theory of problem solving came from the stimulus–response model of animal learning. This explanation assumed that as a person develops, he or she learns a number of problem-solving techniques through stimulus–response conditioning and uses these to solve any new problem. The person remembers the techniques that are successful and tends to use them again, but he or she may choose one to use most frequently. A person's preference for one technique over another establishes a habit family hierarchy (Hull, 1930). In essence, most people know a number of problem-solving tricks and tend to use some more frequently than others. A person organizes these tricks in a hierarchical fashion in terms of how frequently they are used. When one trick does not work, he or she tries the next. The techniques that most consistently solve problems are the ones that the person is most likely to try first in a new problem-solving situation.

The practical implication of the stimulus–response model is that persons with brain injury begin their therapy with an array of problem-solving strategies at their disposal. The theory suggests that the goals of therapy would be to organize these strategies into a workable hierarchy and to provide new strategies that will be useful in a variety of situations. These problem-solving strategies would need to be practiced so that they eventually become habitual.

Gestalt Theory of Problem Solving

The Gestalt theory of problem solving is not as well-defined as the stimulus–response model. The basic idea is that problem-solving skill depends on a person's ability to visualize the context of the problem (Kohler, 1947; Wertheimer, 1945). Good problem-solving skill is the ability to reorganize or negotiate either the context or the goal to achieve a solution. The Gestalt school emphasizes insight and creativity, which are crucial for effective problem solving. It also underscores the need for periods of long pondering before a person will achieve the insight that produces a solution. Unlike the stimulus–response theory that describes the gradual development and organiza-

tion of a problem-solving strategy, the Gestalt approach describes an all-or-none process of insight. The stimulus–response model suggests that a person will gradually realize the solution to a problem whereas the Gestalt model suggests that a person might suddenly realize the solution to a problem while brushing his or her teeth in the morning.

According to Gestalt theory, the problem-solving process involves four distinct stages. In the first stage, the person identifies the problem. This may require a great deal of thought and analysis. In the second stage, the problem and its possible solution incubate; indeed, the person might not consciously think about the problem. In the third stage, the person experiences a period of illumination whereby the solution suddenly comes to mind. In the fourth stage, the person applies the solution and evaluates whether it produced the desired result.

The information processing approach to problem solving discussed next draws heavily from the Gestalt approach. The therapist first trains the client to visualize the problem context and to spend a great deal of time thinking about it and pondering the possible solutions (Baron, 1994; Gobet & Simon, 1996). The client eventually learns that solutions seldom occur slowly over time but, more often, all at once, usually when he or she least expects them to occur. In addition, it is also necessary to train clients to use creative problem-solving strategies when the solutions are novel or unique to the specific situation. This will keep the client from using only one method that may not work for all situations.

Information-Processing Model

The information-processing approach suggests that humans create mental recipes that will produce solutions to problems. The recipes also dictate action in situations where a person may fail to solve a problem. Newell and Simon (1972) specified three necessary conditions for problem solving according to the information-processing model (Simon, 1987). The first involves feeding data to the human computer, including things like history of the problem, assumptions, constraints of the situation, and other facts the person should consider. The second step involves determining the problem space, which includes the person's global assessment of the problem and hunches about the solution. The problem space is the larger picture which includes not only the problem at hand but also any other ramifications. For example, a male client might see that a brief spat with his wife is a problem but fail to see that the pattern of altercations is leading to divorce. The third step is creating an operation or specific course of action that the person can use to carry out the solution.

This theory implies that problem-solving skills break down after a brain injury for many different reasons (Hallux, 1990). The person's set of potential solutions may also be limited or too highly structured, common after damage to the frontal lobes, which limits cognitive flexibility. It may be difficult for the person to collect facts or to analyze the available facts in a way that leads to an appropriate course of action. The person may not be able to generate new facts using if–then logic, to integrate new facts with the existing set of facts, or to abstract the big picture or bottom line. Many of the techniques and strategies discussed later in the chapter build skills that would improve these areas of human information processing.

Each of these three theories has influenced the development of the methods presented in this chapter. Although our proposed therapy approach borrows heavily from the Gestalt model, each theory has merit. Perhaps the major value of these theories is that they force therapists to think about the possible ways that people may solve problems. The next section describes the characteristics of people who are good problem solvers.

Knowing what makes a good problem solver can help therapists direct training so that clients think and behave in ways that facilitate problem solving.

Characteristics of Good Problem Solvers

Hunt and Ellis (1998) identified several personality characteristics of good problem solvers. Good problem solvers are typically *preoccupied with the problem*. They devote a great deal of mental effort to the solution and do not put the problem aside or procrastinate taking action until the situation becomes critical (Reisbeck, 1987). They feel challenged by the problem and have a sense of urgency about solving it. Consequently, finding a solution becomes a priority for them.

Good problem solvers frequently *dream solutions*. They think about the problem just before they go to sleep at night and will sometimes awaken to a solution. This unconscious processing will frequently bring the solution to mind when it is least expected, such as when showering or when brushing teeth. The fact that the solutions come to mind unexpectedly suggests an insightful process.

Good problem solvers are *set breakers*. This means that they do not get locked into one set mode of thinking; they shift from one solution to another until they find one that eventually solves the problem. It is therefore important to teach persons with brain injury that there is no single solution in most situations. Indeed, 10 different people may produce 10 different solutions to the same problem. The problem solver should therefore abandon the idea that there is a single correct solution to any problem. Although therapists should teach clients to use favored methods first, clients should also know to discard solutions that do not produce results, and try another solution. Clients should always consider the broadest possible range of solutions, never immediately rejecting a solution because it is too unconventional. Good problem solvers consider as many solutions as possible, evaluate each one, and add others to the list as they occur.

A person with brain injury is well advised to dry-run a variety of solutions before committing to any one. This procedure helps identify unexpected problems before the client wastes time, money, or effort on an unsuccessful solution. Along these lines, a therapist can create mental simulations of solutions and train clients to ask the question, "What would happen if I were to implement this solution?"

Good problem solvers *break the problem into pieces*. The problem solvers can then attack these one at a time. To train this skill, the therapist breaks down one of the client's problems, then solves the pieces to illustrate how this method results in a gradual solution of the whole.

Good problem solvers *clarify the problem through explanation*. Explaining the problem to someone else forces a person to organize it and to summarize it. The technique also involves others in listening to potential solutions and suggesting alternative solutions.

Good problem solvers *actively consider others' proposed solutions*. Therapists should encourage clients not only to explain the problem to others but also to solicit advice from others before committing to a solution. The client should determine the consensus opinion about which solutions will most likely work. In many cases, doing what most people suggest produces the fastest results.

Good problem solvers create *time for incubation*. The therapist should remind clients that when a solution evades them, they should put the problem aside and expect that at some future time, usually when they least expect it, the solution will come to mind.

The characteristics of good problem solvers suggest an insightful process whereby a person carefully considers a variety of solutions, dry-runs potential candidates, discusses the various solutions with others, then makes a decision (Bedard & Chi, 1992; Chi, Glaser, & Farr, 1988; Ericsson & Smith, 1991; Schoenfeld, 1985). The major implication of these characteristics for the therapist is that a person with brain injury may become a better problem solver simply by learning to behave like those people who are good at problem solving. The therapist should discuss these behaviors in detail with his or her clients and encourage them to change their behavior accordingly.

Stages of Problem Solving

Hunt and Ellis (1998) outlined several stages of problem solving that typically precede a solution. Polya (1957) also discussed these stages in the context of students trying to solve math problems (see also Schoenfeld, 1985).

▶ Step 1: Understanding the problem

Understanding the problem is, perhaps, the most important step in problem solving because without a clear representation of the problem, it is difficult to arrive at a clear and accurate solution. The person will have to understand not only the problem but also the costs and benefits that are associated with each potential solution. This is especially difficult in situations where the problem may be emotionally based or difficult to represent or frame.

▶ Step 2: Generating possible solutions

Generating possible solutions is similar to Polya's concept of devising a plan (Cicerone & Wood, 1987; Miller, Galanter, & Pribram, 1960; Pollens, McBratnie, & Burton, 1988). It implies that a person develops more than one plan of action and selects the one that is the most likely to succeed. Because one problem that persons with brain injury share is a fixation on a single solution, it is necessary to teach therapy clients to generate as many options as possible before committing to any one (Runco, 1990). It is also helpful to acquaint the client with the types of solutions he or she may generate that are consistently effective. One way to teach this skill is to have the client keep a problem-solving journal in which he or she describes various solutions that have been effective in the past. For example, one client had difficulty with his computer freezing up. After documenting several solutions to the problem, he realized that the best solution was to not open more than one program at a time. Eventually he realized that opening multiple programs exceeded the memory capacity of his computer.

It is worthwhile elaborating the generation stage of problem solving because it is so crucial to forming a solution. Hunt and Ellis (1998) and Greeno (1978) pointed out that most problems could be categorized as one of three types: those that require a person to see some unifying relationship, those that require a conversion solution, and those that involve rearrangement. Students often see the first type of problem on analogy tests where the purpose is to discover the relationship between four words. For example, understanding the analogy *color* is to *painter* as *car* is to *mechanic* requires seeing the unifying relationship between the words that relates them in a meaningful and predictable way. Abstracting these types of unifying relationships is often difficult for a person with brain injury. For example, the client may verbalize disgust for someone else's behavior, not realizing that he or she often behaves in a similar manner.

An example of the second type of problem, those that require conversion solutions, is a word problem that needs to be converted to a mathematical formula before it can be solved. Conversion solutions are also difficult for many persons with brain injury. For example, a client who is having difficulty with his or her marriage may not see that the real problem is that he or she is no longer working, so both partners are under stress due to a substantially lessened income.

Most people can make the necessary conversions through experience (Lave, 1988). Persons with brain injury, however, may need a great deal of coaching from family members before conversions will become apparent in real-life situations. It may take months before a client can transform problems in a way that promotes their solution. Often, the client can transform others' problems but not their own. Consequently, the first major step in problem-solving therapy may be psychosocial group training in which the client begins using mental transformation. As such, this usually involves asking the client what social problems he or she has and then trying to break the problem down into a conversion rule. For example, one client could not understand why others did not talk to her. After one group session, the other group members pointed out that she constantly interrupted and dominated the conversation. The group then converted the client's problem into a solution rule: "Speak less than half the time."

▶ Step 3: Arranging elements of the solution

Step 3 involves taking existing elements and putting them in a different order or sequence to bring about an optimal solution. A person may have everything necessary to solve the problem but needs an organization. For example, a person with brain injury may have difficulty finding things in the home. He or she can solve the problem by rearranging the home in different ways to see which way makes things more accessible. This same procedure can be applied to time management. Persons with brain injury often have difficulty arranging their days so that they avoid wasted effort and time. They can try several different schedules the night before to see which one is the most efficient.

▶ Step 4: Limiting solutions

Limiting solutions is the next stage of problem solving and occurs after a person has generated several possible solutions. In this step a person attempts to determine which solutions are most likely to succeed. The person then limits the solution set to those with the greatest chance of success.

▶ Step 5: Evaluating and following through

The final stage of problem solving is evaluating and following through with what seems like the best possible solution. This stage involves not only trying one of the solutions, but also evaluating, after the fact, whether it solved the problem. All too frequently, a person assumes that a certain action will solve a problem, only to find that it actually had little or no effect. It is therefore important to teach persons with brain injury that following through involves more than attempting a solution. It also includes evaluating whether the attempted solution produced the desired result. If it did not, then the person must cycle through the same procedures again until he or she finds a solution that works.

In our experience, training problem-solving skill in persons with brain injury is a difficult but rewarding process. Much of what the therapist does with the client involves training him or her to step back and visualize a larger picture. For example, the training may involve teaching the client to recognize that certain behavior patterns result in social rejection, certain physiological signs indicate anger, or that frequent symptoms represent a certain medical condition. Any training in problem-solving skill will usually require drill and practice using problems that are unique to the client. The overall process works best when the therapist trains the client to devote about 60% of his or her time to understanding the problem, especially with emotional or social-network problems. The other steps require the remaining 40% of the problem-solving effort. Although the other steps—generating possible solutions, limiting solutions, and evaluating and following through—are important, nothing is as crucial as understanding a problem correctly in the first place.

Formulas and Strategies for Problem Solving

The therapist should determine if the client uses a formula or a strategy method of problem solving. According to Cohen (1971), *formulas* are set procedures that will always work, but not necessarily efficiently. *Strategies* are rules that may produce a quick result, but may not solve the problem (Nisbett, 1993). There are advantages and disadvantages to each method. Formulas work well in situations where the problem has potentially few solutions or where the same problem recurs. For example, if the client knows to call one of three numbers in case of an emergency, then he or she can try all of them in sequence until one solves the problem. This method will always work, assuming the client has the time to call all three numbers. Alternatively, the strategy method would be for the client to call the number that is most likely to solve the emergency the fastest. This may result in a quicker solution, although if the call is not answered, then the client may still need to call each number to get help.

Teaching strategies is more difficult than teaching formulas, but it may be the only way a client will ever be able to solve problems. This is because many problems are too complex for formulas to solve efficiently. Consequently, the following problem-solving strategies are discussed in detail and their applications are noted for a variety of contexts. The therapist should understand that most clients have some strategy for solving problems. However, because their strategies are usually inefficient, the therapist should acquaint clients with more efficient action plans and illustrate how each plan works in the real world.

Trial-and-Error Strategy

Trial and error involves generating and testing solutions randomly until one of them successfully solves the problem. This method is inefficient because there may be a large number of possibilities and to try them all would take a long time. The number of possible solutions to a problem is a rough index of the trial-and-error method's potential for success. It is also an index of what Newell and Simon (1972) have labeled the *problem space*. In those situations where there are a large number of possible solutions, that is, where the problem space is quite large, then the trial-and-error strategy can be quite cumbersome and inefficient.

The method is especially inefficient in situations where the person has never encountered the problem in the past. In these novel contexts, the problem space and the range of possible solutions is unknown. Unfortunately, many clients attempt trial-and-error solutions even when they are obviously ineffective or when there are numerous possible solutions.

Action–Goal Strategy

Action–goal is a two-step strategy that requires breaking complex problems into various parts or subgoals. The person asks, "What do I have to do to reach the first goal?" The overall goal must first be specified, then broken down into a sequence of subgoals. The person defines what is necessary to reach each

subgoal in the sequence. A therapist might ask a client to define a long-term goal and to think about problems that could occur when trying to obtain that goal. The client may say, "I want to own my own home, have a job, and be married within 5 years." Achieving the long-term goal will require the client to achieve several subgoals. To own a home, the client must have a job. To have a job, the client must graduate from a training program. The therapist should write out the long-term goals and subgoals on paper and then describe what will be necessary to reach each of them. Clearly, the action–goal strategy is appropriate when the problem-solving situation is complex or long term.

The action–goal strategy is also appropriate for solving common problems. For example, if the television does not turn on, the client can learn to break the problem down into smaller steps, or subgoals. Asking questions such as, "Is the television getting electricity?" is a first step. This question may lead the client to check whether the television will function with other wall outlets, to check the plug, or to see if there is a blown fuse. If the television is getting electricity, the client moves to the next step: Will it work on any channel? With or without the cable hookup? Answers to these questions narrow the range of possible solutions to the problem by proceeding in a forward direction from simplest to more complex solutions. As the client answers questions at each stage, the possible cause of the problem and the range of solutions narrow.

Backward Strategy

The backward strategy is roughly the reverse of the action–goal strategy (Bransford & Stein, 1984). In this strategy, the person first assumes a goal has been met, then determines what would have been necessary to achieve it. For example, if a person's goal is to increase the number of his or her friends and acquaintances, then he or she would ask, "How does a person who has many friends behave?" Many people use backward problem solving. For example, to solve a maze, a person might start at the finish and backtrack steps to the start box. Criminal investigators always ask what must have happened for a criminal to have been able to commit a crime.

Training a person with brain injury to use the backward strategy first requires that he or she be able to define the goal or the problem clearly. For example, we recall one distraught client whose girlfriend had recently broken off their relationship, causing him to become quite depressed and isolated. The therapist first asked the man to define the problem and any acceptable solutions. After several redefinitions of the problem, the man finally realized that his girlfriend wanted to be married and to have a family. He recognized that this was impossible because he would be unable to support a family for many years to come. Once he accepted the loss of his girlfriend, he formed a new goal, which was to have friends and to meet other women. He observed that others who had reached this goal were cheerful and pleasant most of the time. They placed themselves in situations where they could meet people their own age. Using the backward strategy, he and the therapist worked out a clear strategy that would help him to eventually move beyond the loss of his girlfriend.

Contradiction Strategy

As the name implies, the contradiction strategy suggests that, to solve a problem, a person does just the opposite of what would be necessary to solve a problem. The technique works quite well when there is no obvious solution to a problem or when a person tends to deny responsibility for the role he or she played in creating the problem. In this technique, the person asks, "What could I do to make this problem worse?" By asking this question, the person often realizes that it is his or her behavior that is actually causing the problem.

For example, one of our clients was becoming increasingly reclusive, depressed, and potentially suicidal. When she was asked, "Assuming that you wanted to be very depressed and reclusive, what would you have to do to get to that point?," the client answered, "stay indoors all day, watch soap operas, get high, and eat." Others in her group began to point out that these were precisely the behaviors she exhibited. This was her first step toward realizing that her behavior was contradictory to her goal of having friends and a life. The solution to her problem was for her to behave in exactly the opposite manner.

Groups are often necessary for effective implementation of these therapy techniques. As Parenté and Stapleton (1993, 1996, 1999) pointed out, "survivors listen to survivors." That is, when a survivor hears another survivor pointing out that a certain behavior is maladaptive, the offending survivor is more likely to listen and to remember what he or she hears from other group members. These authors also underscored the need for survivors to verbalize their problems. This is because the act of verbalizing helps the survivor to organize the problem, to clarify the mental representation, and to simplify the problem space.

Explanation and Consensus Strategy

Explaining the problem and building consensus are crucial steps in the later stages of problem solving. Once possible solutions have been identified, then evaluation is necessary to determine which ones are the most likely candidates for success. Having a person explain the problem to others is perhaps the best way to ensure that he or she will organize the problem mentally because a person must organize the problem and the possible solutions to explain them clearly to others. The person should be required to explain each potential solution without using common filler phrases, such as, "you know," or vague assertions, such as, "I just feel that way!"

The therapist should insist that the person explain the problem to at least three different people who will listen and offer an opinion concerning the feasibility of any proposed solutions. The usefulness of this technique usually depends on the time frame for the solution. Minimally, the person should explain the problem to at least one person, which will help him or her clarify and organize the problem space and make it easier to evaluate the possible solutions.

The second part of this strategy, building consensus, involves mentally averaging the opinions of all persons to whom the problem has been explained. The value of consensus-based solutions is that they are correct more often than not (Parenté, Anderson-Parenté, Myers, & O'Brien, 1984). Generally, the consensus solution of a group is more accurate than a solution from any individual in the group would have been. If a person explains a problem to several people and mentally averages their responses, then using the mental average will usually result in a better and quicker solution.

Give-the-Problem-a-Rest Strategy

Most people have had the experience where the solution to a nagging problem popped into their minds when they were in the shower, brushing their teeth, or asleep. Often, the fatigue associated with a problem prohibits finding the solution. Taking a break reduces the fatigue, allowing the solution to surface. One additional trick is to think about the problem just before going to sleep. This method will sometimes facilitate dreaming the solution.

Personal Barriers to Problem Solving

Therapists typically have to retrain bad problem-solving habits that the client has used over the years. These bad habits result from at least three sources. The first involves a client's tendency to solve each new problem using the same strategy. This problem is called *set fixation*. The second concerns a client's failure to see that the elements of one problem may have different roles in another problem. This problem is called *element fixation*. The third source is the client's inability to generate novel solutions, a major problem that often predates the brain injury. This problem is called *rigid creativity*.

Set fixations occur when a person tries a certain problem-solving strategy and initially experiences some success with it (Mayer, 1983, 1992). According to stimulus–response theorists, the success rewards the strategy, which then becomes the dominant way of solving problems. The person continues to apply the same strategy, despite the possibility that another strategy may lead to a faster solution. Lack of reward may eventually cause the strategy to be replaced in the hierarchy. Until then, however, the dominant problem-solving strategy may keep the person from solving a problem. For example, one client who had sustained a frontal lobe injury had been an athlete before his injury. He had always solved his physical problems by exercising. After his injury, he persisted in physical exercise as a means of solving what was now a different kind of problem. Only after years of unemployment, social isolation, and limited cognitive gains was he convinced to try another problem-solving solution. Unfortunately, the only way to deal with set fixations is to simply let the person continue to use the dysfunctional set until he or she sees that it fails.

Element fixation refers to the tendency of a person to see the elements of a problem in only one way. The person fails to realize that one element can function in different ways, depending on the problem. As a result, the person fails to see the solution because he or she does not see the changed role of an element of the problem. For example, a client who was getting divorced blamed his wife for every negative aspect of his life since his brain injury. Because she had rejected him, he could only see her as an enemy. He could not accept that she cared for him and wanted to create a supportive friendship despite their divorce. Because of his tendency to see this element of his life myopically, he resisted all of her efforts to help. For a time he ended up homeless because he refused to accept a living arrangement she had negotiated. He quit a job that she had helped him to find. He could not solve his major problems in life because of his fixation with his wife as an enemy and his inability to accept that she could play a positive role in his rehabilitation even though they were no longer married.

Rigid creativity is more complex than set and element fixation. It refers to a person's inability to expand the problem space, to develop novel solutions, or to take risks, often stemming from personality variables that were in effect long before the brain injury. Creative persons tend to be individualistic, intuitive, self-accepting, introverted, and independent. With respect to problem solving, they are not only interested in generating solutions, but in coming up with novel and unique solutions. They purposely try to redefine problems and solve them in a novel manner. For a person who has rigid creativity, training the production of original ideas can improve problem solving. For example, the therapist can ask the client to generate alternative explanations of various situations.

We often ask our group members to generate different explanations for why a person is late, quiet, irritable, or talkative. This activity helps the client to resist the urge to converge on a single explanation for a given behavior.

The SOLVE Mnemonic

We created the SOLVE mnemonic to help persons with brain injury remember the problem-solving procedures outlined previously. These steps have been conveniently summarized by the word SOLVE which is used to provide the client with a step-by-step process that he or she can invoke in any novel problem-solving situation. The SOLVE mnemonic is also presented as a rhyme, which is easy to remember. This and other mnemonics are available on the Web site www.geocities.com/mentalarts. The rhyming SOLVE mnemonic is as follows:

Specify the problem—it must be defined

Organize your solutions—keep several options in mind

Listen to others' advice—no matter how terse

Vary your solution—ask, "What would make the matter worse?"

Evaluate your solution—read again this verse

The first step in training a client to use the SOLVE mnemonic is to have him or her memorize it to the point where he or she can repeat the steps dictated by each letter. The therapist should give the mnemonic to the client and quiz his or her recall of it during each session. Once the client learns the mnemonic, the next step is to provide the client with practice using it in real life. The client can provide an actual problem for the client and therapist to analyze using the mnemonic. This works well in a group situation where each group member can participate in the problem-solving process.

The steps of problem solving using the SOLVE mnemonic are as follows:

▶ **S**pecify the problem—it must be defined

To specify is both to define and to analyze the problem. Clients should spend at least 60% of their problem solution time specifying the problem parameters. This process involves several different aspects.

The first aspect is *identifying the data that define the parameters of the problem*. The client must determine the magnitude of the problem, its urgency, and its possible ramifications. For example, a client who must deal with an impending divorce might ask if he or she would be able to function without the support of a spouse. What would happen to the family finances? What effect would a separation have on the children?

A second aspect is *defining the problem in concrete terms*. This is usually difficult to do when the problem is an emotional one. The client must specify the problem in concrete language in order to make the solution tangible. This aspect of specification may take quite a while. Often a client will state a problem in vague terms, such as, "I'm not happy!" It may take a great deal of discussion before the client can restate the problem as, "I am not happy with the social isolation I am experiencing since my brain injury."

The third stage involves getting the client to *ask the right questions*, such as "Is this problem urgent or important? Is this really a personal problem or does it belong to someone else? What would happen if I were to do nothing?" Such questions may lead the client to realize that he or she is not responsible for the problem or its solution, providing relief from endless hours of mental preoccupation. Persons with brain injury often obsess about a problem even when there is nothing

that they can do to solve it, so the sooner they come to this realization, the better.

For example, one client reported that his major problem was that he could no longer do anything or go anywhere with his daughter. He felt that he was now an embarrassment and a burden to her and that she did not want to be seen with him in public. His daughter had recently begun college in a different state and was no longer living at home. His problem was therefore less relevant than he had imagined because it was physically impossible for him to interact with her as he once did.

▶ **O**rganize your solution—keep several options in mind

This step requires the client to write out on paper all possible options that are even remotely feasible. These options must be written in concrete terms and the list should be inclusive. During a therapy session, the therapist should write a list of possible solutions to a problem underneath its definition, preferably all on the same page. The therapist then gives this sheet to the client as a summary of the session and as an example of how the client should approach the problem-solving process in the future.

▶ **L**isten to others' advice—no matter how terse

Once the client and therapist have defined the problem and delineated the potential solutions, the next step is to discuss the solutions with others. Discussing the problem and its possible solutions with others helps the client form a clear mental representation. Other people can provide feedback about the clarity of the client's explanation, they can ask questions that point out specific areas of vagueness, and they can provide insights the client may never have considered.

They may also suggest other options that the client failed to notice.

As mentioned earlier, one of the main reasons for listening to others' advice is that the group's consensus solution will usually be superior to any other solution the client devised. Simply, if the client decides to do what the majority of people suggest, that solution will usually be correct. The client can rest assured that this strategy will be sufficient to solve most problems. Additionally, a client may often be more receptive to suggestions made by a group of persons with brain injury than to those of the therapist because the members of the group have experienced brain injuries whereas the therapist usually has not. This follows the well-established principle of social psychology that holds that people tend to trust others who are most like them.

> ▶ **V**ary your solution—ask, "What would make the matter worse?"

The therapist will have to walk the client through the contradiction strategy discussed earlier. The goal is for the client to look at the problem from as many perspectives as possible before making any firm decisions concerning a course of action. The therapist should use the opportunity to point out any clear examples of the client's set or element rigidity. Again, the therapist should write out the results of the session so the client can review them later.

> ▶ **E**valuate your solution—read again this verse

Once the client has implemented a solution, it is necessary to determine whether the chosen solution actually solved the problem. So often, clients fall into the trap of thinking that any solution they try will solve the problem. They never check to see if the solution

actually hit the mark. Without evaluating the solution, the client may not realize that the solution did not work. The evaluation process depends on a clear specification of the problem in the first place. Evaluation usually implies measures of one form or another that are used to identify changes in the problem space. The client must then monitor the measures to determine if the solution has had a desired effect.

Case Example: Jack

As a case example of how the SOLVE mnemonic works, consider Jack, a client who was facing an impending divorce.

Specify the problem—it must be defined. Jack's initial representation of the problem was, "My wife doesn't want me around anymore!" The therapist worked with Jack to redefine this problem. Questions such as, "How does your wife see you as a different person now?" and "How has your role in the family changed?" clarified the global complaint. After much discussion, Jack realized that the real issue was that his wife, Sara, was now the major provider for the family; there had been a role reversal.

The next stage involved specifying the problem in concrete terms. The therapist and Jack agreed that the real issue was that Sara was no longer a homemaker and that she could not be as attentive to Jack's needs as she once was. She was also facing work-related stresses that she had never dealt with before. Jack acknowledged that he now spent the majority of his time at home and that Sara had expected him to take on some of the home duties that she used to perform since he was there most of the day.

The conversation turned to Jack's willingness to do anything about the role-reversal problem. Jack decided that he was willing to redefine the problem and that the first step was to ask Sara whether she wanted to continue their marriage and to ask her to share her perceptions of their marital difficulties. He concluded that an attempt on his part to change roles might save the marriage.

Jack and his therapist discussed the urgency of the problem. They agreed that without immediate intervention, the marriage would end in divorce. Therefore, doing nothing could have disastrous results. Jack agreed that he and his wife shared responsibility for the problem and for the effectiveness of the proposed solution. Jack and Sara made a commitment to save their marriage through mutual change. Sara said she respected Jack, but qualified the statement by saying that her respect was partially dependent upon her perception of his willingness to change and to work within his limitations.

Organize your solution—keep several options in mind. Jack made a list of options that varied from doing nothing and letting the marriage deteriorate to making role changes upon which he and Sara could mutually agree. He considered separating and living alone, going back to work in his former job, getting a new job, or starting a home-based business. The therapist and Jack discussed the feasibility of each of these options and concluded that trying to change the marriage roles was the easiest option to implement and that he should try this first before making any other drastic lifestyle changes.

Listen to others' advice—no matter how terse. Jack had several family members whom he trusted and he agreed to discuss his options with each of them before making a final decision. One suggested formal marriage counseling. Another suggested that Jack use his free time to go back to school to prepare for a different profession. Most agreed that attempting a mutually acceptable role reversal would be the best first step. They also agreed that marriage counseling would help facilitate the role-reversal process as it progressed. There was no clear agreement about long-term vocational goals, only that the deteriorating

marriage was the problem that needed an immediate solution. Jack decided to accept the consensus opinion of his family members: to take on household duties and to seek marriage counseling.

Vary your solution—ask what would make the problem worse. Jack and his therapist discussed several ways of looking at the problem. The action–goal method suggested that they define a series of subgoals and work toward each in sequence. Several of these had already been established and accomplished. For example, the first step was to commit to solving the marital problem. The next step was to define Jack's possible alternative employment goals. A third step was to attempt one or more of the employment goals. In this way, Jack and his therapist developed a road map that clearly specified Jack's long-term goal and the subgoals necessary to reach it.

In following the backward approach, Jack first defined his long-term goal. This was quite difficult to do because he did not know what type of training or job options he wanted to pursue. There were too many possibilities and many of his options depended on the extent of his recovery. His only conclusion was that he wanted to contribute to the family income and work from home. He determined, therefore, that he would have to get additional computer training and establish a home-based computer system to accomplish this goal.

The contradiction strategy was easier for Jack to visualize. He concluded that if he were to thwart his efforts he would procrastinate any positive effort by simply doing more of what he was currently doing, which was nothing. This brought him to the conclusion that his current behavior was actually counter to all of his stated goals.

Evaluate your solution—read again this verse. Six months later, Jack and his therapist followed the *SOLVE* mnemonic again, redefining the problem and developing a new solution. Briefly, Jack began a home-based business doing bulk mailings. Jack and Sara began participating in church activities. Jack agreed to return to therapy every 6 months to repeat the problem-solving process using the *SOLVE* mnemonic.

Summary and Evaluation

This chapter presented various theories of problem solving, including the stimulus–response model, the Gestalt theory, and the information-processing approach. None of these theories was specifically intended for use in brain injury rehabilitation.

In addition, several personality characteristics of good problem solvers were presented. Generally, good problem solvers are those who are preoccupied with the problem and devote a great deal of mental effort to the solution. Problems challenge them and they feel a sense of urgency about solving them. Consequently, the solution becomes a priority for them. Good problem solvers frequently dream solutions. They frequently shift from one solution to another until they discover one that solves the problem. Considering the broadest possible range of solutions, they dry-run solutions before committing to any one. They also break down problems into pieces and clarify solutions with explanation. They listen to others' proposed solutions and will typically implement the consensus opinion. When no solution comes to mind immediately, they purposely create incubation time for the problem.

The chapter also examined the general stages of problem solving that most cognitive psychologists have investigated. These include generating possible solutions, evaluating the feasibility of each option, and following through with the most likely candidate. The methods most people use to generate solutions are either formulas or strategies. Formulas are set procedures that will always lead to a solution but that may be time consuming and cumbersome to implement. Strategies, on the other hand, are abstract shortcut methods that will produce a solution in most cases, and include the trial-and-error method, the action–goal strategy, the backward method, and the method of contradiction.

Another strategy, explanation and consensus opinion, is crucial to the problem-solving procedure. Therapists and family members should require clients to verbally explain their thinking at each stage, which forces them to clarify their understanding of the problem. Listening to other interpretations of the problem and implementing what the majority feels is the best solution will usually produce a correct solution.

Therapists should discuss several personality barriers to effective problem solving with clients, including set rigidity, element rigidity, and rigid creativity. Set rigidity is the tendency to use the same method of problem solving in all situations. Element rigidity is the tendency to see elements that are common to different problems in exactly the same way in every problem. Rigid creativity is the tendency to restrict the generation of potential options.

The chapter ended with a discussion and case example of the SOLVE mnemonic. The letters of the SOLVE mnemonic provide a framework that can be used by persons with brain injury in a variety of problem-solving contexts. The S reminds the client to *specify* and define the problem. The O is a reminder to organize the solution, generating possible solution *options* and evaluating the feasibility of each. The L is a reminder to discuss the various options with others and to *listen* to their advice. The V reminds the client to *vary* the problem-solving strategy. Finally, the E is a reminder to *evaluate* any solution option the client has implemented.

Teaching problem-solving skills is an art. It usually is most effective with higher functioning clients and it is always most successful when the therapist applies the principles outlined in this chapter to the client's personal problems. It is effective to train problem-solving skills in a group situation because the group members typically enjoy applying the process to other people's problems as well as to their own. The therapist should encourage clients to discuss their problems during therapy sessions so that their problems can serve as real-life examples of the process.

References

Baron, P. (1994). *Thinking and deciding* (2nd ed.). Cambridge, United Kingdom: Cambridge University Press.

Bedard, J., & Chi, M. (1992). Expertise. *Current Directions in Psychological Science, 1,* 135–139.

Bransford, J. D., & Stein, B. S. (1984). *The ideal problem solver.* New York: Freeman.

Cavanaugh, J. C., Kramer, D. A., Sinnott, J. D., Camp, C. J., & Markley, R. P. (1985). On missing links and such: Interfaces between cognitive research and everday problem solving. *Human Development, 28,* 146–168.

Chi, M. T. H., Glaser, R., & Farr, M. J. (Eds.). (1988). *The nature of expertise.* Hillsdale, NJ: Erlbaum.

Cicerone, K. D., & Wood, T. R. S. (1987). Planning disorder after closed head injury. *Archives of Physical Medicine Rehabilitation, 68* (February).

Cohen, J. (1971). *Thinking.* Chicago: Rand McNally.

Ericsson, K. A., & Smith, J. (Eds.). (1991). *Toward a general theory of expertise.* Cambridge, United Kingdom: Cambridge University Press.

Gobet, E., & Simon, H. A. (1996). The roles of recognition processes and look-ahead search in time-constrained expert problem solving: Evidence from grand-master-level chess. *Psychological Science, 7,* 52–55.

Greeno, J. G. (1978). A study of problem-solving. In R. Glaser (Ed.), *Advances in instructional technology* (Vol. 1). Hillsdale, NJ: Erlbaum.

Hallux, K. J. (1990). Problem solving. In D. N. Osherson & E. E. Smith (Eds.), *Thinking.* Cambridge, MA: MIT Press.

Hull, C. L. (1930). Knowledge and purpose as habit mechanisms. *Psychological Review, 57,* 511–525.

Hunt, R. R., & Ellis, H. C. (1998). *Fundamentals of cognitive psychology.* New York: McGraw-Hill.

Kohler, W. (1947). *Gestalt psychology: An introduction to the new concepts on modern psychology.* New York: Liveright.

Lave, J. (1988). *Cognition in practice.* Cambridge, United Kingdom: Cambridge University Press.

Mayer, R. E. (1983). *Thinking, problem solving, cognition.* New York: Freeman.

Mayer, R. E. (1992). *Thinking, problem solving, cognition* (2nd ed.). New York: Freeman.

Miller, G. A., Galanter, E., & Pribram, K. H. (1960). *Plans and the structure of behavior.* New York: Holt.

Newell, A., & Simon, H. (1972). *Human problem solving.* Englewood Cliffs, NJ: Prentice Hall.

Nisbett, R. E. (Ed.). (1993). *Rules for reasoning.* Hillsdale, NJ: Erlbaum.

Parenté, R., Anderson-Parenté, J. K., Myers, P., & O'Brien, T. (1984). An examination of factors contributing to delphi accuracy. *Journal of Forecasting, 3*(2), 173–182.

Parenté, R., & Stapleton, M. (1993). An empowerment model of memory training. *Applied Cognitive Psychology, 1*(7), 585–602.

Parenté, R., & Stapleton, M. (1996). Vocational evaluation, training, and job placement after traumatic brain injury: Problems and solutions. *Journal of Vocational Rehabilitation, 7,* 181–191.

Parenté, R., & Stapleton, M. (1999). Development of a cognitive strategies group for vocational training after traumatic brain injury. *NeuroRehabilitation, 13,* 13–20.

Pollens, R., McBratnie, B., & Burton, P. (1988). Beyond cognition: Executive functions in closed head injury. *Cognitive Rehabilitation, 6*(5), 26–33.

Polya, G. (1957). *How to solve it.* Garden City, NY: Doubleday Anchor.

Reisbeck, C. K. (1987). Realistic problem solving. In P. E. Morris (Ed.), *Modeling cognition.* Chichester, United Kingdom: Wiley.

Runco, M. A. (1990). *Divergent thinking.* Norwood, NJ: Ablex.

Schoenfeld, A. H. (1985). *Mathematical problem solving.* Orlando, FL: Academic Press.

Schraw, G., Dunkle, M. E., & Bendixen, L. D. (1995). Cognitive processes in well-defined and ill-defined problem solving. *Applied Cognitive Psychology, 9,* 523–538.

Simon, H. A. (1987). Information-processing theory of human problem solving. In A. M. Aitkenhead & J. M. Slack (Eds.), *Issues in cognitive modeling.* Hillsdale, NJ: Erlbaum.

Wertheimer, M. (1945). *Productive thinking.* New York: Harper & Row.

Whimbey, A., & Lockhead, J. (1999). *Problem solving and comprehension* (6th ed.). Mahwah, NJ: Erlbaum.

Wickelgren, W. A. (1974). *How to solve problems.* San Francisco: Freeman.

Chapter 16

✦

Retraining Conceptual Skills

onceptual skills are fundamental to thinking and communication. They are the skills that allow a person to understand his or her surroundings and to make sense of the events that occur within the physical and social world (Whorf, 1956). Conceptual processing occurs whenever something becomes clear to a person. Conversations frequently include statements such as, "Do you see what I mean?" or "Now I get the point." Our language is replete with phrases that imply understanding of the bigger picture; we see a mental light bulb that illuminates suddenly at the precise moment of comprehension. Conceptual skill is a centerpiece of the multimodal model of cognition that was outlined in Chapter 2. Indeed, much of what is called cognition is the process of understanding concepts, without which a person could not learn rules or test hypotheses (Bourne, 1963, 1966; Markman, 1999; Mayer, 1992; Nisbett, 1993).

Concepts, rules, and hypotheses are slightly different cognitions. A *concept* is a special combination of ideas that has a particular meaning. For example, most people can picture a police officer; this mental image may differ from their concept of a detective or private investigator. *Rules* are concepts that direct behavior because there are consequences attached to them. For example, the rules of the legal system specify that homicide will be punished by imprisonment or possibly death.

A *hypothesis* relates two or more concepts with a prediction. For example, a detective may hypothesize that a certain person committed homicide based on available evidence. Each of these cognitive skills may be impaired after a traumatic brain injury.

The goal of this chapter is to explain how concept learning occurs and to identify those things that affect the process. The chapter begins with a discussion of conceptual skills and related ideas such as rule learning and hypothesis testing. Then a method is presented for explaining new concepts to persons with brain injury. The chapter ends with a discussion of how persons with brain injury can use these methods to express themselves clearly.

The Concept of a Concept

What is a concept? It is an abstraction, a schema, an idea, a structure, or an understanding (Hampton, 1981, 1995). People form concepts almost every day, typically when someone is explaining something new. Persons with brain injury have difficulty forming concepts and rules and explaining their ideas to others. The challenge in teaching concept and rule learning to a person with brain injury is to develop a method of making concepts clear to the person and for the person to make himself or herself clear to others. To do so usually involves teaching the person other skills such as categorization and hypothesis testing.

Categories are groupings that are defined by their attributes or the rules that either distinguish them or connect them in some way (McCloskey & Glucksberg, 1978; Mervis & Rosch, 1981; Smith, 1990; Smith & Medin, 1981). Categorization is the process of seeing these commonalities. This is, perhaps, the basis of concept and rule acquisition (Bruner, Goodnow, & Austin, 1956). For example, the concept that the square and triangle have straight lines distinguishes these shapes from the circle and oval, which have curved lines.

Concepts and categories are not necessarily the same thing. Concepts are complex categories. A concept can be an idea, such as the theory of relativity, which contains several categories of thought, such as mathematics, physics, and so forth. However, in some situations, concepts and categories are the same.

There are a number of different types of categories and concepts, such as verbal and semantic, visual and perceptual, fuzzy, and basic. *Verbal and semantic* categories refer to the types of abstractions we form when using language (Lamberts & Shanks, 1997). For example, if a person sees similarities between two authors' writing styles, he or she forms a verbal category. *Visual and perceptual* categories are those that involve physical traits that can be seen or sensed in some way. For example, a person may learn "the feel" of driving different types of cars. By viewing exhibits in a museum a person can learn the categories of modern art versus classical art.

Rosch, Mervis, Gray, Johnson, and Boyers-Bream (1976) described *basic-level concepts* that are tangible, concrete, and easily learned. Basic-level concepts define a category's distinctive features and are rooted in the common language of a person's culture (Berry, 1981; Cole & Scribner, 1974). They are easy to understand and particularly useful because other people are readily familiar with the terms. For example, *dog* and *cat* are easier to understand than *canine* and *feline* or the names of particular breeds, such as *rottweiler* or *Abyssinian*. Basic-level concepts are easy for most people to visualize. For example, it is difficult for most people to imagine a *Grand Cherokee* vehicle. It is easier for them to think of a *Jeep*. This is because, although they have some idea of the attributes that define a Grand Cherokee, they are more familiar with the concept of a Jeep.

The implication of this theory for teaching a novel concept to a person with brain injury is that he or she may have difficulty understanding and abstracting concepts unless the therapist describes their features (Mervis & Rosch, 1981). The therapist should present basic-level concepts in simple, common terms using examples that are readily available in the culture. Likewise, when a person with brain injury explains a basic-level concept to another, he or she should use concrete examples that are common to the culture.

Zadah, Fu, Tanaka, and Shimura (1975) discussed the notion of *fuzzy concepts*, which are ideas with uncertain boundaries. For example, a person's concept of art is fuzzy because of the broadness of the field. Barsalou and Medin (1986) described fuzzy concepts as having *graded structure*, where the examples are not clear or can vary in their ability to define the concept. For example, the word *computer* typically conjures up the idea of a desktop model as seen in most offices. However, the fuzzy boundaries of the concept include different types of computers, including laptops, notebooks, subnotebooks, handhelds, and personal data assistants.

The preceding discussion leads to several practical conclusions that are useful for working with persons with brain injury. First, when explaining the idea of concept and rule learning, the therapist should tell the client that it is difficult to understand the idea of a concept. This is because there are many types of concepts and rules and it may be difficult to precisely define their graded or fuzzy boundaries (McCloskey & Glucksberg, 1978). Second, training concept learning involves teaching the client to focus on commonalities of his or her experience that define the concept. Third, explaining concept learning is most effective when the process is personally relevant to the client. To clarify these points, it is first necessary to briefly survey the available literature on concept learning and abstract from it what is relevant to the retraining process.

Theories of Concept Learning

Although there are several theories of concept learning, we will describe only three that seem to represent the major issues in this field. Medin (1989) described the *attribute theory*, which assumes that humans define concepts and categories by creating mental lists of features. For example, to learn a concept such as *Roman*, one person might create a list of mental attributes such as *legion*, *Rome*, and *Ben-Hur*, whereas another person might create the list *Nero*, *Caesar*, and *Pontius Pilate*. Both sets of attributes reflect common associations to ancient Rome (Smith & Medin, 1981).

The implication for training concept learning is that the therapist must teach the client to recognize and mentally list attributes that define a concept to make it clear and precise. Usually, the longer the mental list of attributes, the more precise the concept. When explaining a concept to others, the client should provide examples of the concept's attributes. Likewise, when trying to understand a concept, the client should ask for a list of concrete attributes that distinguish it from other similar concepts.

Prototype theories of concept learning assert that people learn and remember the gist or core features of a concept. The common features that people extract from different examples define the prototype. Thereafter, the prototype is stored and used to identify new examples. For example, most people have a prototype of a U.S. president, a superhero, or a college professor. Prototypes, however, vary from person to person and change with experience and age. Prototypes are similar to basic-level concepts except that prototypes can also be esoteric technical concepts that are not basic. For example, most physicists have a prototypical understanding of a nuclear reaction. The average person may have heard the phrase but cannot visualize the concept.

Modern explanations of prototype learning involve the notion of the *schema*. McClellan and Rummelhart (1986) defined a schema as connected cells in the brain that lay dormant until something activates the cell network. The more features that surround a concept in a person's memory, the greater the chance that any particular feature he or she encounters will activate the schema. For example, when a friend calls on the telephone and the person answering it does not immediately recognize the friend's voice, then a certain phrase or the friend's laugh could activate the person's schema.

The implication of prototype and schema theories for brain injury rehabilitation is that the number of relevant features a concept has determines the ease with which a person can learn it. Moreover, both theories assert that learning features and prototypes are important for concept learning. Accordingly, the best way to teach the concept of a four-wheel-drive vehicle to a person with brain injury would be to show him or her a Jeep, a Hummer, a Land Rover, a Bronco, and so forth and point out the common features. The best way for a person with brain injury to explain a concept to another is to use concrete examples similar to the ones above. This principle is discussed in more detail later in the chapter.

Exemplar theory is the reverse of the prototype theory. According to exemplar theory, examples of concepts are stored in memory. The theory assumes that a person continuously updates these concepts with new instances. This theory predicts that the ability to categorize new instances of a concept depends on the similarity of the new instances to the existing set of examples. For example, although a Hummer is probably the best example of a prototypical four-wheel-drive vehicle, until recently, only the military used it. Most civilians would not have recognized it or categorized it as a four-wheel-drive vehicle because it was not a member of their existing set of examples. Now that it is available for civilian use, most people can recognize it as a four-wheel-drive vehicle.

The implication of exemplar theory for brain injury rehabilitation is that a client's understanding of a concept depends on the therapist's ability to generate real-life examples that define it. Because the theory assumes that the client does not store prototypes, the more examples the therapist uses, the clearer the concept will be.

Rule Learning

As mentioned earlier, rule learning is similar to concept learning, but involves not only understanding a system but also associating some consequence with it. Rule learning refers to a person's sense of a system, order, or structure, and a person's ability to respond appropriately within this structure (Wason, 1960). In essence, rules are concepts with consequences. For example, most people know how to behave appropriately in restaurants because their parents have taught them how. In other social situations, however, a person may not know the rules—for example, the rules for laying out a formal dinnerware place setting. This may require additional training to ensure that the person does not do something inappropriate.

Persons with brain injury may have difficulty learning rules and understanding social concepts because they may not foresee consequences and have difficulty testing hypotheses. The therapist may therefore have to teach clients specific behaviors that are relevant in different social situations. The training may be hard to implement because of the danger that can result from inappropriate behavior. For example, a therapist cannot teach a person with brain injury that he or she is hypersensitive to drugs and alcohol by letting him or her try these substances because this practice could end in injury or arrest. Therefore, most rule learning involves paired-associate training with descriptions of situations and behaviors that the therapist labels as appropriate or inappropriate. The therapist can enhance rule learning by providing simulations and role playing to ensure that the client forms a mental image of the situations that define the rule.

Conceptual Strategies

Hypothesis testing, rule learning, concept learning, and problem solving are all interrelated skills (Bourne, 1963; Bruner, Goodnow, & Austin, 1956; Mayer, 1983). It is therefore difficult to discuss them separately. However, one difference is that hypothesis testing typically precedes the formation of a rule, concept, or solution to a problem. Hypothesis testing is a person's ability to try out several possible concepts, solutions, or rules in a systematic way to determine which is the most useful.

Now that several theories of concept learning have been presented, it is possible to discuss methods for training conceptual skills. We present these methods by ranking them according to their effectiveness with persons with brain injury. Many clients will default to using the trial-and-error method. Wherever possible, the therapist should direct the client's concept learning strategies to the *conservative focus* and *focus gambling* approaches.

Conservative focus. We have found that conservative focusing leads to the most rapid concept acquisition in persons with brain injury. It involves gradual manipulation of one aspect of a complex concept at a time until the concept clarifies. It also involves mentally ranking the various attributes of the situation and manipulating first those that are most likely to produce some result. For example, if a flashlight will not work, a person must first determine why it is broken before he or she can fix it. The person may conclude that the bulb may be defective or burned out. He or she decides to insert a new bulb. If it still does not work, the bulb has been eliminated as a potential explanation of "brokenness." The person may next suspect that the batteries are dead and replace them. The person would continue this activity until he or she discovered the reason why the flashlight did not work. If the person changed the bulb and the batteries at the same time, he or she would be manipulating two possible explanations simultaneously. We would then never know which one was the culprit.

The most important facet of the conservative focus strategy for training is that the client must learn to manipulate only one aspect of the situation at a time. Although this process may seem tedious, it typically leads to the most rapid concept learning and problem solutions. It is especially important when the concept involves some form of problem solving. Unfortunately, many persons with brain injury may not have the frustration tolerance to withstand the process. They may therefore resort to a *focus gambling* strategy.

Focus gambling. This method is similar to the conservative focusing technique, but the client tests several possible hypotheses at the same time instead of one at a time (Bruner, Goodnow, & Austin, 1956). Many persons with brain injury test hypotheses this way and they often achieve some degree of success in solving a problem. The strategy does not, however, allow the client to identify the core concept. Indeed, he or she may think that the concept or rule is clear only to find later on that some other aspect was the problem's underlying feature.

For example, one client told us that his wife complained that their marriage was deteriorating. She told him that she did not know him any longer and that they were becoming strangers. To do something about the problem, he began buying his wife gifts, spending more time at home, doing more housework, and trying to behave in a manner reminiscent of his premorbid personality. By using this tactic, the client manipulated several aspects of the situation simultaneously in an attempt to focus on the problem and to eliminate it, thereby saving the marriage. The client was gambling on the hunch that one or more of these changes would regain his wife's affections. Despite the client's efforts, the situation did not change. The client decided to add even more changes. He began writing poetry for his wife, going to movies with her, and socializing more with friends. He asked friends to describe how he used to behave and he made an effort to behave in a similar manner. The situation did improve although his wife eventually told him that his personality had changed and that his being around more often and sending her gifts had little to do with her affections for him. She appreciated most his efforts to regain his previous personality.

Perhaps the most efficient method of focus gambling is a *split-half* strategy. A person first identifies a possible set of things that make up a concept, then splits the set in half and manipulates one half at a time. In the preceding example, the client's optimal method would have been to abandon the half of the set of behaviors he changed when it did not change his wife's attitude. He would then work on the remaining set of behaviors and change these until he finally hit upon a set that made an obvious improvement in her response to him. He could eventually split this set in half, repeatedly, until he finally limited the set to those behaviors that were crucial.

Clearly, it would have been easier for the client to simply ask his wife about her dissatisfactions and adjust his behavior accordingly. However, there are many concept-learning situations where this will not work. For example, many of our clients who return to work find it difficult to approach a supervisor and ask for feedback about which aspects of their job performance will lead to a promotion. These clients may use the split-half focus gambling strategy because they feel it is the quickest method for advancement. Indeed, it may lead to a promotion, but it will not identify which specific behavior was most influential. When asked, the client may describe his or her success as, "I don't know what I did to get promoted but I can tell you what not to do." This description suggests a gradual elimination of unsuccessful behaviors until the client isolated a group of behaviors that eventually resulted in a promotion.

Scanning is another method of concept learning and involves forming global hypotheses about a concept, then modifying them in accordance with rewards and punishments. For example, one client who still drove a car after his injury continually drove slightly over the speed limit until a police officer stopped him and gave him a ticket. At that point, his concept of speeding changed along with his behavior so that he no longer exceeded the speed limit on that particular stretch of highway. However, he still sped on other highways. He learned that he could speed, but only on certain roads where speed limits were not strictly enforced. His behavior

illustrated an intricate rule structure. Clients who scan often evaluate several solutions quickly. This is rewarding because they believe they are working to solve their problem, but the scanning process is often inaccurate and incomplete.

In this method, a person continues doing something until punished. When punished, he or she may then modify the concept slightly until it eventually becomes an accurate portrayal of the world. Scanning also requires a person to have good memory because he or she must recall what rules apply in any particular setting. This is one reason why the scanning strategy does not work well for persons with brain injury.

Trial and error is one of the more common, but least efficient, hypothesis-testing procedures. Many persons with brain injury say that they "just keep trying until something works." This method produces the least rapid concept learning and least efficient means of testing hypotheses or learning rules. We usually alert the client to the fact that it is easy to fall prey to the trial-and-error method but that, in the end, it will not work as well as the conservative focus strategy.

Which of these methods works best for a particular client depends on his or her level of functioning. In our experience, persons with mild brain injury can master the conservative focus strategy, but persons with moderate to severe impairment do not possess the frustration tolerance that the conservative focus strategy requires. Many clients prefer and spontaneously use the focus gambling strategy. They are usually unaware of the split-half method but can still learn to use it. The scanning strategy is one that we never endorse or train because it usually yields slow learning and requires a good memory for complex rule structures. Unfortunately, this method is one that many clients adopt. Therefore, the therapist's goal is to acquaint the client with the pitfalls of the scanning strategy and also the trial-and-error strategy and to try to dissuade their use. The therapist should then try to teach or to substitute the conservative focus or focus gambling strategies.

Training Conceptual Skills, Rule Learning, and Hypothesis Testing

In our experience, persons with brain injury form concepts, learn rules, and test hypotheses in much the same fashion as those who have not had a brain injury. They simply do so more slowly and they are usually less able to articulate the process. We therefore define the process for them and break it down into three distinct stages: (1) identifying attributes; (2) manipulating the concept, rule, or hypothesis; and (3) eliminating inappropriate responses. For example, if the client is trying to understand the rules associated with an appropriate social greeting, it is first necessary to identify the elements of social greeting, such as handshakes, salutations, eye contact, and so forth. The client must then practice these and gain experience with how each affects the other person's behavior. The client may then focus on those elements that have the greatest discernible effect on the social exchange.

These three steps can also improve social problem solving. For example, one of our clients did not comprehend why no one understood his speech. Our first step was to identify all the things that could affect speech reception such as the rate, quality of pronunciation, clarity of word usage, and so forth. The next step was to manipulate each of these, one at a time, and notice the effect on others' comprehension (Whimbey & Lockhead, 1999). Finally, the client focused on those that seemed to improve the intelligibility of his speech.

Ellis and Hunt (1993) provided several specific suggestions for training concept ac-

quisition, including (a) generating new examples of the concept, (b) considering both positive and negative examples, (c) thinking of a variety of examples, and (d) focusing on the relevant features of the concept. We agree with this list although we suggest that therapists teach clients to do them in a specific sequence.

Like the Ellis and Hunt (1993) method, this procedure involves teaching concepts by example. The goal is to get all who are involved in the therapy process to participate in a common concept communication process.

The first step involves teaching the client to identify the concept. This happens most rapidly by using positive examples that illustrate the concept. For example, if a therapist wished to explain the concept of "the millennium woman," the best way to get the concept across would be to use photographs from present-day women's magazines. After seeing several of these, most people would have some idea of the conceptualization of the millennium woman. The therapist uses this as a means of establishing the prototype or the schema. However, the prototype would still have fuzzy boundaries because the examples contained so many variations in makeup, hairstyle, dress, height, weight, and so forth. The therapist could never know whether the client saw the concept as anything more than a fuzzy prototype. Nevertheless, this is the best way to establish the initial core concept.

At this point, it is necessary to have the client form hypotheses about the underlying concept. The therapist would ask the client to verbally state what he or she thinks defines the therapist's concept of the "millennium woman." Next, the therapist provides the client with *negative examples*. These give the client information that eliminates irrelevant details and focuses the attention on those aspects that are central to the concept. The therapist could go to women's magazines from different decades, such as the seventies, eighties, and nineties, and select pictures that illustrate women who do not conform to the concept of the millennium woman. Over the years, we have found that it is crucial to present positive examples first, followed by negative examples, not the reverse. Persons with brain injury seem to learn concepts more rapidly in this manner, presumably because the positive examples form the prototype and the negative examples subsequently refine the concept. Once again, the therapist asks the client to verbalize any hypotheses that may come to mind during this stage.

The third stage involves *sharpening* the concept by pointing out irrelevant features. For the concept of the millennium woman, hair color or height may be irrelevant. This may not be apparent when the client sees the pictures and he or she may require the therapist to point out the irrelevancy. This tends to make the features more distinctive. The therapist can enhance the distinctiveness by having the client verbalize the concept in his or her own words. Instead of presenting the positive examples first, the therapist could present the positive and negative examples simultaneously and point out the irrelevant features. This technique relieves the burden on the client's memory, whereas the first technique encourages active processing of the examples.

The final stage of concept acquisition involves *verification*. This means that the therapist must now ask the client to identify new instances of the concept. To ensure the acquisition of the millennium woman concept, the therapist would show the client new pictures and require identification of those that expressed the concept. If the client can do this, then the therapist can be satisfied that the client has acquired the concept to the point that it is functional.

Two additional procedures enhance the training of conceptual skills and rule learning. The first is verbal explanation. We typically ask clients to explain something to the rest of the group and we videotape the expla-

nation. Ideally, the topic will be something about which the other group members know nothing. We have accumulated many of these tapes and we use them to illustrate the concept of a clear presentation. After reviewing several of the tapes, we first show the group those that are especially good examples of clear explanations. We ask the group members to form hypotheses about why those presentations were so easy to understand. We next show tapes to the group in which the presentations are especially unclear. We follow these with questioning to facilitate hypothesis formation. Finally, we ask the group members to isolate those aspects of the explanations that define their concept of clarity. Verification occurs when the clients again try to explain something to the group.

We use this same procedure to train the concept of clear writing. We have collected many short writing samples from clients on a variety of topics ranging from "my biggest problems in life" to "what I'm interested in doing vocationally." We present group members with the clearest of these samples to illustrate the concept of clear written expression. After reading about 10 of these samples, we ask each group member to form hypotheses about what makes the paragraphs easy to understand. We then show the group members negative examples of writing that are illegible, tangential, extremely brief, or otherwise poorly written, and then initiate discussion about why the samples are poorly written. The next step is to identify those aspects of the paragraphs that are central to the concept of clear writing. Finally, we verify that each group member understands the concept by having each write a paragraph and share it with the group.

The concept and rule learning procedures can also be used to teach social skills. This usually involves modeling procedures and videotaping. For example, the therapist shows the client videotapes of someone asking out a potential date. The client first sees tapes that illustrate success. He or she generates hypotheses about why these approaches were successful and what things affect whether the person accepts the invitation. The client may ask, for example, how well the two people know one another or how nicely the asking party is dressed.

Next, the client sees tapes that illustrate refusals and generates hypotheses about what went wrong. For example, one tape shows a person approaching a total stranger on the street. Another illustrates a person asking for a date in a negative way: "You wouldn't want to go out with me, would you?" Another shows an unshaven and dirty man approaching a woman who refuses him because of his appearance. The client generates hypotheses about why these attempts failed. Finally, the client says what aspects of the social approach determined whether the person succeeded. In this way, clients learn the rules of engagement via social modeling.

Ellis and Hunt (1993) also outlined other crucial features that affect concept acquisition and rule learning. Those aspects of their discussion that are relevant to brain injury rehabilitation are discussed next.

Orderly arrangement. Persons with brain injury often require a great deal of structure and perceptual clarity. It is therefore necessary to define the concept or rule as concretely as possible and to arrange the concept demonstration in a logical sequence. When a therapist explains a concept to a client, it is first necessary for the therapist to explain it in words and then go through the step-by-step sequence we have outlined to limit the amount of information presented to the client at one time.

Compactness of the display. Concepts are often difficult to understand because they are too broad or expansive. In the example of the millennium woman, the therapist would ideally have all the pictures in one place on the table in front of the client. This technique minimizes the need for the client to remember previous examples that are no longer in view and to compare the various examples

quickly. It is also necessary to break the concept down into smaller pieces or to limit discussion of the concept to easily processed examples. In the previous example of the client and his wife, the wife would be well advised to stay away from explanations such as, "You're just not the same" because they present a picture that is too vague. A more compact version of the problem, such as, "You leave all the decisions to me now," is much clearer.

Consistency of concept in sequential problems. If the purpose is to teach a general rule or strategy, then it is necessary to display the rule or strategy as clearly as possible in each example. For example, if the goal is to show how to ask a person out for a date, then the elements of a successful attempt must be apparent in each example.

Saliency of the concept. The client's ability to understand a concept will depend on the clarity and concreteness of the examples used to explain it. Abstract concepts (Hampton, 1981) are obviously more difficult to explain because it is hard to find concrete examples of them. For example, it is difficult to teach the concept of truth, justice, and the American way because these terms are abstract and they have varied meanings to different people. The goal in teaching concepts is to illustrate them using concrete and familiar examples. The general rule is that the more salient the examples, the quicker the client will understand the concept. Therapists should begin by teaching a very salient concept, and then gradually introduce ones that are more abstract.

Use of color. Color helps establish a vivid first impression and adds interest to the process. For example, using color photos to explain the concept of the millennium woman will facilitate its understanding. In the writing example, using a color highlighter to mark sections of an article that best illustrate clarity of expression will facilitate concept acquisition.

Complexity and the number of relevant dimensions. The number of relevant dimensions of a concept also determines the client's ability to understand it. The implication is that for a client to learn a new concept, he or she must first identify its relevant dimensions. It is therefore necessary for the client to define these dimensions up front. This may lead to the conclusion that the concept is too difficult or fuzzy to describe.

Concept novelty. This aspect refers to a client's ability to find relevant examples. The therapist should impress upon the client that if there are no examples of this concept, then he or she might not be able to explain it. In these situations, the client should relate the novel concepts to others that are similar but not identical. For example, one of our clients was a member of the grunge music movement. None of the members of our group had ever heard of that particular movement and the client could not explain grunge philosophy or identify its specific attributes. He was able to relate certain attributes of other, more familiar groups, such as hippies or punk rockers.

The importance of feedback. This is, perhaps, the most important aspect of concept learning. The therapist must impress upon the client that feedback is a two-way street. To understand a novel concept, the client should get the other party to provide examples in the manner outlined previously. At a minimum, he or she should always ask, "Can you give me an example of what you mean?" This question will force the person who is explaining the concept to provide the positive examples that are crucial for the client's understanding. Clients should learn to say one of three things:

> "Can you give me an example of what you mean?"

> "Here is an example of what I mean. Tell me if it's clear."

> "Let me see if I can think of an example of what you're telling me. Please tell me if I get it."

These statements elicit verification of a client's understanding.

Summary

Concept learning, rule learning, and hypothesis testing are similar higher cognitive skills that involve learning by example. Explaining concepts or rules in the abstract to persons with brain injury is generally useless. The client must see examples and test hypotheses with real-world information for the concept to solidify in his or her mind. Positive examples should be presented first, followed by negative examples. This sequence will help the client establish the prototype and will facilitate the client's gradual elimination of the irrelevancies. Once the client understands a concept or rule, the therapist should focus on the critical features that define it. Finally, the therapist should verify that the client understands the concept or rule by generating concrete examples of it.

References

Barsalou, L. W., & Medin, D. L. (1986). Concepts: Static definitions or context-dependent representations? *Cahiers de Psychologie Cognitive, 6*(2), 187–202.

Berry, J. W. (1981). Cultural systems and cognitive styles. In M. R. Friedman, J. R. Das, & N. O'Connor (Eds.), *Intelligence and learning* (pp. 395–406). New York: Plenum.

Bourne, L. E. (1963). Some factors affecting strategies used in problems of concept formation. *American Journal of Psychology, 75,* 229–238.

Bourne, L. E. (1966). *Human conceptual behavior.* Boston: Allyn & Bacon.

Bruner, J. S., Goodnow, J., & Austin, G. A. (1956). *A study of thinking.* New York: Wiley.

Cole, M., & Scribner, S. (1974). *Culture and thought.* New York: Wiley.

Ellis, H. C., & Hunt, R. R. (1993). *Fundamentals of cognitive psychology.* Madison, WI: Brown & Benchmark.

Hampton, J. A. (1981). An investigation of the nature of abstract concepts. *Memory and Cognition, 9*, 149–156.

Hampton, J. A. (1995). Psychological representation of concepts. In M. A. Comway (Ed.), *Cognitive models of memory*. Cambridge, MA: MIT Press.

Lamberts, K., & Shanks, D. (Eds.). (1997). *Knowledge, concepts, and categories*. Cambridge, MA: MIT Press.

Markman, A. B. (1999). *Knowledge representation*. Mahwah, NJ: Erlbaum.

Mayer, R. E. (1983). *Thinking, problem solving, and cognition*. New York: Freeman.

Mayer, R. E. (1992). *Thinking, problem solving, cognition* (2nd ed.). New York: Freeman.

McClellan, J., & Rummelhart, N. (1986). *Parallel distributed processing: Explorations in the microstruture of cognition*. Cambridge, MA: Bradford.

McCloskey, M. E., & Glucksberg, S. (1978). Natural categories: Well-defined or fuzzy sets? *Memory and Cognition, 6*, 462–472.

Medin, D. L. (1989). Concepts and conceptual structure. *American Psychologist, 44*, 1469–1481.

Mervis, C. B., & Rosch, E. (1981). Categorization of natural objects. *Annual Review of Psychology, 32*, 89–115.

Nisbett, R. E. (Ed.). (1993). *Rules for reasoning*. Hillsdale, NJ: Erlbaum.

Rosch, E. H., Mervis, C. B., Gray, W. D., Johnson, D. M., & Boyers-Bream, P. (1976). Basic objects in natural categories. *Cognitive Psychology, 8*, 382–439.

Smith, E. E. (1990). Categorization. In D. N. Osherson & E. E. Smith (Eds.), *Thinking: An invitation to cognitive science* (Vol. 3, pp. 33–53). Cambridge, MA: MIT Press.

Smith, E. E., & Medin, D. L. (1981). *Categories and concepts*. Cambridge, MA: Harvard University Press.

Wason, P. C. (1960). On the failure to eliminate hypotheses in a conceptual task. *Quarterly Journal of Experimental Psychology, 12*, 129–140.

Whimbey, A., & Lockhead, J. (1999). *Problem solving and comprehension* (6th ed.). Mahwah, NJ: Erlbaum.

Whorf, B. L. (1956). *Language, thought, and reality*. Cambridge, MA: MIT Press.

Zadah, L. A., Fu, K. S., Tanaka, K., & Shimura, M. (1975). *Fuzzy sets and their application to cognitive and decision processes*. New York: Academic Press.

Chapter 17

⚹

Retraining
Decision Making

Decisions are problems where a person must choose among several defined options. This process may be quite difficult for a person with brain injury. He or she may have a hard time identifying the various options and determining which are best, given the existing circumstances. The underlying problem is that a person with brain injury often does not have a systematic method for making decisions. This chapter presents strategies for retraining decision-making skills. The chapter begins with a discussion of decision making and the skills that allow a person to frame a decision, to define it, and to make the best possible decision, given the available input. The techniques described in this chapter are similar to the method of cost–benefit analysis that is commonly used for making business-related decisions (Larrick, Morgan, & Nisbett, 1990; Wheelwright & Makridakis, 1980). The chapter also includes a case study showing how the decision-making training procedure would work in practice. Finally, the chapter ends with a mnemonic strategy that clients can use in most decision-making situations.

What Is a Decision?

The word *decision* implies that there is a set of two or more possible actions and that a per-son must choose among them. Decisions are a form of problem solving in which the problem is to choose from several viable options (Arkes & Hammand, 1999; Baron, 1994; Plous, 1993). Problem solving is a more general activity in which the goal is to rectify an unacceptable situation. Problem solving includes situations such as the television or the toaster not working, a person's marriage failing, and having difficulty solving math problems or writing a paper. Problem solving encompasses a number of situations that do not necessarily involve selecting among various known options. Decision making is a form of problem solving in which the goal is to determine which of several possible solutions will work best. Although problem solving often involves making decisions, they are not the same process. But they do share one major similarity: problem solving and decision making both require the central issue to be defined. That is, a major goal for a person using either skill is for him or her to ask, "What is the problem?" or "What is it that I must decide?"

For most people, issue definition is the most difficult part of making a decision (Doerner, 1987), and it is also a step that many people skip. Defining the decision is important because hasty or impulsive decisions may ignore or overlook viable options and are typically ill considered. Moreover, the person making such a decision often realizes later that the decision did not address the real issue. The art of making good decisions therefore requires a person to spend a lot of time identifying options that directly confront the issue at hand (Janis & Mann, 1977; Kahneman, Slovic, & Tversky, 1982; Reason, 1990).

In addition to defining the issue, another problem with teaching decision-making skills is that most persons with brain injury require a rather simple method that he or she can retain and implement on demand and that will usually provide a correct decision. Conventional methods of cost–benefit analysis may be too complex for most persons with brain injury to appreciate. However, the same principles of cost–benefit analysis can be reworded in ways that are easy for most therapy clients to understand and to use.

Techniques

Seven-Question Model

The seven-question technique requires a person to answer several questions about a decision before taking any action (Dawson, 1993). These questions help the person to understand the complexities of the decision and to define useful and appropriate options.

Question 1: Can I define the decision? What are the boundaries or limits of the decision? What options make sense within those limits? For example, the client may be deciding which of several movies to see. Each movie is equally attractive to the client. One limit to consider is what time he or she needs to be home after the movie. If only one of the movies ends within that time frame, then the decision is made for the client because only the one movie satisfies the constraint.

Question 2: Does the decision involve a problem or an opportunity? Often what seems to be a problem can result in substantial gain if the client views the situation as a potential opportunity. For example, many persons with brain injury believe they have only two options for income: return to work or accept Social Security disability payments. This may seem like a problem until the client discovers that both options may be possible. The client's problem becomes an opportunity when he or she realizes that a third option is to receive Social Security disability payments *and* work, perhaps part time, simultaneously.

Question 3: Is there an existing policy that dictates the decision or that otherwise overrides any decision the person may make? Depending on the situation, the client may need to investigate existing policy and make decisions in accord with it. For example, many persons with brain injury want to drive again after their injury. However, their decision to drive is often prevented by state law, which requires them to have a medical examination, to retake the written driving examination, and to get a medical clearance.

Question 4: Can the decision be classified? There are several common types of decisions, and it may be helpful to the client to figure out if his or her decision fits into one of these categories. One type of decision is the *go/no-go* decision. This type requires deciding to do something or not to do it. Usually the client has only one option and must decide whether to exercise it. For example, the client must decide whether to go to the movies. *Right/wrong* decisions involve determining the correctness of a decision. That is, there are several potential solutions available and the client must discover which one is correct (O'Hare, 1994; Reason, 1990; Strauch, 2001). For example, solving a math problem usually requires deciding to use the right systematic approach. In an *evaluation* decision, there are several potential solutions and the client must evaluate which is the best or most feasible. For example, the client may need to decide which of several movies he or she should attend. *Discovery* decisions involve identifying potential options in situations where none are known. Ideally, the therapist can use some aspect of the client's life to teach the discovery decision. The decision may involve options that were previously unimaginable for the client. For example, one of our clients had worked as an electronics assembler for 30 years before his stroke; it was the only job he had ever known. He had to examine his abilities and interests before making a decision about a new career. After intensive testing, he identified several job options that were unrelated to his previous work as an assembler. He discovered that his love of animals superceded his desire for structure and security and, after some retraining and on-the-job experience, he became a veterinarian assistant.

Question 5: Is the problem real or imagined? This question usually amounts to assessing the feasibility, necessity, or timeliness of the decision. For example, one client anguished over an unrealistic decision to apply to NASA to become an astronaut for future Mars exploration. Another obsessed about what type of car to purchase despite the fact that he did not have a license nor was he financially able to purchase a car. In each case, the problem was a nonissue and the client was wasting time.

Question 6: Does the decision involve money, people, or a combination of both? This is an issue that most people face every day. Unfortunately, there are no guidelines that work for every situation. However, it is probably safe to say that the best money decisions usually yield the best financial outcome. With people decisions, it is probably best to choose a solution that creates a win–win situation. That is, the best decision creates a situation where everyone involved either benefits from the decision, or, at a minimum, does not lose because of the decision. For example, one client opted for early retirement rather than continue in his job when the employer offered a generous package of retirement incentives. The employer felt that the client could no longer do the job and did not want to be liable for any mishap that resulted from continued employment. The client's retirement package exceeded that which he would have received if he waited until age 65. The employer was spared any potential liability that could have resulted from continued employment.

Question 7: What would happen if the person decided to do nothing? Many decisions are unnecessary because the need to make the decision would dissipate spontaneously if the client simply did nothing. For example, one client's marriage was disintegrating rapidly. He decided that if he did nothing to rectify the situation, then his wife would leave him. He also admitted that his marriage had been deteriorating for some time and that his wife had decided to leave him even before his injury. He therefore concluded that his wife would leave him, no matter what he did to save their marriage. Eventually, the couple separated and he later remarried.

These seven questions are easy for most persons with brain injury to understand and are useful in practically any decision-making situation. We train clients to begin thinking about an impending decision by asking and answering each of the seven questions. We also suggest that the client consider the decision using other tools, such as the hat method discussed next or the DECIDE mnemonic described later in the chapter. The primary goal of all of these techniques is to ensure that the client considers the decision thoroughly before committing to any course of action (Fox, 1987). The value of these methods is that they force the client through a structured process that keeps him or her from making an ill-considered choice.

The Hat Method

The hat method of decision making is an exceptionally easy-to-use and potent decision-making tool. It is a modification of a technique suggested by Bono (1990) who developed it as an offshoot of his Lateral Thinking program. This method was originally designed to use various aspects of personality to improve group decision making in the business world. This method assumes that business executives have different styles of thinking. For example, *data people*, when faced with making a decision, will collect all available information before making a choice (Frisch & Clemen, 1994; Payne, Bettman, & Johnson, 1992). The value of people with this personality is they force the group to collect all necessary information before making a final decision. However, the person may also tend to overcollect information, often to the point where the group never makes a decision because too much time is spent collecting information. Another person, an *option generator*, may spend most of his or her time defining options, but never making a decision. This type of person may be especially important because often, in the haste to make a decision, a group may neglect to define all the options. However, these people may also overdefine the options.

Another personality type is the *born skeptic*. This person will tell you everything that is wrong with each option but fails to see the value or advantage of any one. The opposite of the born skeptic is the *eternal optimist*. This person sees every option as a wonderful possibility. He or she seldom, however, sees the flaws in various options. A person with a final personality type, the *gut-level thinker*, relies on intuition to make decisions. Such individuals seldom think through their decisions because they rely more on feelings and emotion. Often, these people have a good decision-making track record although there is no easy way to account for their success.

Bono (1990) reasoned that all of these personality types could make valuable contributions to the total decision-making process as long as no one personality was allowed to dominate. He therefore developed a decision-making process that allows each personality type to make a unique contribution for equal consideration by the group. Persons using this method avoid the usual tendency to postpone decision making until the last minute and then make a hasty choice. The quality and accuracy of decisions of groups improved with this method because the group had to consider all aspects of the information before making a decision.

We have used the same technique to teach decision-making skills to persons with brain injury. The technique involves training a client to consider all aspects of a decision according to the personality styles outlined above. To create a clear picture at each stage, the therapist asks the client to imagine wearing various colored hats that bring to mind the different personality types of the decision-making process.

The therapist should purchase a number of hats of different colors; inexpensive hats work well. There must be at least a white hat, a red hat, a green hat, a blue hat, and a yellow hat. If the therapist works with clients in a group setting, then it will be necessary to have several hats of each color depending on the size of the group.

The hats are used to depict different aspects of the decision-making process. Clients wear the hats to remind them of what type of thinking is necessary at each stage. The thinking process therefore proceeds in a sequential fashion with the hat colors dictating how the client should think. The following section describes the thinking that each hat represents.

White Hat. This hat represents the process of generating information necessary to make the decision. That is, while the client is wearing the white hat, he or she can only generate information necessary to make an informed decision. Discussion of the pros or cons of the options is not allowed.

During the white hat session, the therapist should write down the information that the client generates on a flip chart or blackboard so that it is readily visible. This provides a tangible record of the information that will underlie the decision.

At the end of the session, the client and therapist should have a list of all relevant information. If the client has any confusion or uncertainty about any of the information, then further action should be postponed until the information is clear and complete.

Yellow Hat. This hat reminds the client to generate options. Generating options can only occur once all of the information relevant to the decision has been collected. The therapist should write down the options for the client and discuss each one, regardless of whether they are feasible. At the end of the session, the client should have a list of options that are candidates for further consideration.

Red Hat. This hat signals the client to shift thinking to only the negatives associated with each option. The client asks questions such as, "What could go wrong?" "Why is this a bad idea?" "How can this option create more problems than it solves?" and so forth. Only negative thinking is allowed. The therapist should write down negatives next to each of the options. The session continues until the negatives have been exhausted.

Green Hat. This hat reminds the client to think positively. It is the reverse of the red hat thinking process. The client and therapist think of only the positives associated with each possible option. The client asks questions such as, "What can I gain from this option?" "How am I better off by doing this?" and so forth. Again, the therapist writes down the positives next to each option. At the end of the session, a decision begins to take shape in the form of a structured cost–benefit analysis of each option because alongside each option is its associated costs (red hat) and benefits (green hat).

Blue Hat. This hat allows the client to put aside all logical thought and ask the question, "What is my gut-level feeling or emotional reaction to this option?" This way of thinking allows personality to influence the decision-making process but not to dominate

it; it permits emotions and intuition to play a role in decision making. However, the contribution of emotion is given equal weight with all of the other thinking modes. The therapist writes down the client's gut-level opinion of each option next to it, alongside the positives and negatives.

Once the situation has been framed in this manner, the therapist and client can make the final decision. This usually comes about after perusal of the fact sheet that was developed over several sessions. The best decision is usually obvious, but not necessarily desirable. This is, indeed, the purpose of the process. The technique shows the client that the best decisions are not always the easiest, most lucrative, or least time consuming. Clients also see that decisions are more than just gut-level responses to last-minute emotional needs to do something, regardless of how uninformed or ill considered. When decision making is structured in this manner, the client comes to realize that decisions require careful analysis and consideration. The purpose of the hat method is to provide the client with a technique that he or she can use to make practically any decision.

During the course of the decision-making process, clients may realize that the initial situation needs reframing. That is, the way the original situation was framed no longer makes sense and the process must begin anew. The process, therefore, forces the client to assess whether the decision is correct. For example, one client wanted to decide what type of new car to purchase. After going through the hat method, he concluded that all of his choices were too expensive (Beach, 1993). It was therefore necessary for the client to reframe the situation to ask whether he should purchase a new car versus a used one.

After a decision is made, the therapist sends the client off to implement it. He or she returns later to report on its success or failure. If the decision did not work out, the therapist and client go though the hat process again.

CASE STUDY: CARLOS

The following case study follows the decision-making process of Carlos, a 27-year-old man with brain injury who was trying to decide whether he should begin a training program, get a job, or apply for Social Security disability insurance (SSDI). This is a decision that many persons with brain injury face, and the methods described in this chapter have been especially effective for clients making this type of decision. In this case, Carlos and his therapist began by using the seven-question method to frame the decision then shifted to the hat method to further refine it and to establish an action plan (Cicerone & Wood, 1987; Pollens, McBratnie, & Burton, 1988). In general, we recommend that decision making be a two-stage process whereby the client structures the decision by answering the seven questions first, then goes through the hat method before making a final decision.

Seven-Question Method

Question 1: What were the boundaries of the decision? Carlos qualified for SSDI benefits and would probably get them if he applied. He would probably be able to live on the benefits alone although his standard of living would be lower than the one he currently enjoyed. Carlos would likely get bored after a time of not working and would probably lose a great deal of self-respect. There were at least three options: to work, to collect benefit payments and not work, or to do both and gradually phase out one of the sources of income.

Question 2: Did the decision present a problem or an opportunity? Carlos concluded that the decision created an opportunity because he could work and receive benefits at the same time. He also saw that the system was quite flexible, creating more options than it closed off.

Question 3: Was there an existing policy that determined the decision? After talking to a Social Security counselor, Carlos learned that there were guidelines that determined the government's decision to grant benefits. He qualified under the guidelines, however, so the decision to apply was strictly personal.

Question 4: Could the decision be categorized? Yes, it could. Carlos's decision was best categorized as an evaluation. As such, it required him to assess several options. The best course of action was for Carlos to call Social Security and get any additional information about programs that were available and determine which were the most attractive.

Question 5: Was the decision real or imagined? The answer to this question was quite clear. Carlos's decision was real because it involved his long-term source of income. Because Carlos's situation was real, but not unique, it would be useful for him to determine what other people in his situation had decided to do and to find out what factors had influenced their choices.

Question 6: If you did nothing would the situation go away? Again, the answer was quite clear. Carlos's financial situation would obviously worsen and become critical if he did nothing.

Question 7: Did the decision involve money or people or both? Carlos's decision involved both people and money because it affected his livelihood and the respect of his family.

As a result of this process, the therapist summarized the situation with Carlos. There were at least three options: (a) collect benefit payments but not work, (b) work but not collect benefit payments, and (c) do both with the gradual phasing out of one of the income sources. Carlos concluded that his problem presented an opportunity because he had the option of receiving both types of income. There was no policy that governed his choice of any option, but there were policies that limited how much money he could make from SSDI and from working. The type of decision Carlos faced was an evaluation because he had to choose among the costs and benefits of several available options. His decision, therefore, boiled down to analyzing several factors and making a judgment (Hammand, 2000) about which was best. The problem was quite real: Carlos was disabled and unemployed. His decision involved both money and people because he weighed his financial needs equally with his self-respect and his family's perceptions. If Carlos did nothing, the situation would worsen and eventually become critical. Because his problem was not unique, it would be useful for Carlos to talk to others who had made similar decisions so he could evaluate their reasoning and find out whether they felt they had made the right decision.

The Hat Method

The hat method is useful in lieu of the seven-question method or along with it. We teach both methods and encourage our clients to use the hat method after answering the seven questions. In some cases, the decision will be obvious after using either method alone. And using both methods will not work in situations where a decision is required immediately or spontaneously. However, when there is time to process the decision, both methods can work together to produce the most appropriate decision plan. As a general rule, the more time the client spends processing the decision, the better it will be.

After completing the seven-question method, Carlos and his therapist analyzed the situation using the hat method.

White Hat. After considerable research, Carlos determined that he would receive about the same amount of money from working as he would from SSDI payments. He also determined that there were programs available that allowed him to work and still receive a portion of his SSDI benefits. After working for a year or more successfully, he would lose his benefit payments entirely. He could receive SSDI payments while he was in a formal training program and SSDI would pay for coursework at community colleges and 4-year institutions.

Before researching this topic, Carlos did not realize that he had so many options and that SSDI would pay for college course work.

Yellow Hat. Carlos and his therapist listed the various options.

1. Receive SSDI payments and not work. Reassess the situation later.

2. Work and live off a paycheck without SSDI payments.

3. Receive SSDI payments and go to school, having SSDI pay for courses.

4. Work and receive a paycheck and receive SSDI payments that would be gradually reduced over a 1-year period and eventually phased out.

Red Hat. Carlos and his therapist discussed and wrote down all of the drawbacks that were involved with each option. For Option 1, the major drawback was that Carlos would eventually become bored sitting around the house all day. He enjoyed work for its mental and social stimulation. He was afraid that the longer he remained unemployed, the less motivated he would be to return to work. He was also afraid that his family would no longer respect him if he did not work.

Option 2 also contained potential negatives. Carlos determined that he had few marketable skills and that he might not make as much money working as he would collecting SSDI. He would require some amount of training before he would be able to work, which would be a time when he would have no income at all. Furthermore, he was not certain that he could hold down a full-time job. He wondered what advantage there would be to not taking some amount of money from SSDI as a backup. The therapist reminded Carlos that this was the red hat thinking stage and his last statement was not allowed because it did not deal strictly with the negative aspects of the options.

Option 3 would be difficult because Carlos had not been to school in many years. He was uncertain whether he could compete in a formal classroom environment. He did not have a high school diploma and, although he could take community college courses, he would eventually need a GED certificate to graduate from a community college. He was uncertain how long SSDI would fund his coursework, especially if he was initially unsuccessful the first few semesters. He was afraid to go to school because he had not done well in high school, and he never developed the requisite skills to succeed. He felt embarrassed about taking remedial, noncredit courses, because he was afraid that his wife and child would think he was not intelligent.

Option 4 had the same problems mentioned earlier. How much money could he make? How long could he sustain the job? What if he worked for a year and eventually lost his benefits because of his successful employment but then was fired or laid off?

Green Hat. The therapist reminded Carlos that for this stage he could only list the positive aspects of each option. Option 1 was certainly the easiest. He would simply collect a check each month, approximately the amount of his former paycheck. He could pay the rent and most of the bills. His wife's paycheck could be used for any other family needs. The couple would not need day care because Carlos could watch their child during the day. He felt that he had paid into the system and deserved the money now that he needed it.

Option 2 was attractive because Carlos had always worked hard and enjoyed his work. He wanted his child to grow up with a father who worked and supported his family. He wanted his wife's respect and for her to perceive that he was trying to make something of his life despite his injury. One of his therapists warned him that many marriages break up after one person suffers a brain injury and he worried that his might if his wife felt he was no longer making an effort.

Option 3 was attractive because Carlos had always wanted to go to school to learn a technical skill such as electronics. He thought that this would be an opportunity to finish his education and get some advanced training. He wanted his child to view him as an educated person and to not make the same educational mistakes that he had made. His wife had an associate's degree and he had always felt inferior to her because of the difference in their educational levels. Furthermore, Carlos wanted to show himself that he could still think. He could devote all of his time to studying because he had SSDI income. SSDI would also pay for the courses.

Option 4 made sense because, as Carlos put it, "Work is what I know." He felt confident that he could do his old job or something similar to it even though the doctors had warned him that it would not be feasible for him to return to work doing what he did before. If he were fired, he would still retain his SSDI payments. He would be around people and have the social stimulation he had enjoyed in the past. His wife and child would respect him because he was working again.

Blue Hat. The therapist told Carlos that it was time to feel. He should put aside all thoughts of logic and ask himself how he felt about each of the options and determine which one he felt most comfortable with. After much silence Carlos said that he felt best about Option 1. It made him feel secure to know that some money would be coming in. He also felt that he could make logical decisions about his future better after a longer period of recovery. He wanted more time to think about the situation.

Carlos's final decision was to receive the SSDI payments and not to work right away. He could live off the checks until he tired of the free time or became bored. At that time he would make the decision to either work or go to school.

The DECIDE Mnemonic

Parenté and Stapleton (1999) created a rhyming mnemonic that summarizes the decision-making process. For some persons with brain injury, this rhyme may be easier to remember and implement than the hat method and the seven-question method. The procedures it teaches are not different from those described in those two methods. The rhyme summarizes the steps into an easy-to-recall melodic sequence that may be easier to teach. This and other rhymes and mnemonics are available on the Web site www.geocities.com/mentalarts.

> **D**o not procrastinate—decide to begin
>
> **E**valuate several options—choose those that are win–win
>
> **C**reate new options when others won't do
>
> **I**nvestigate existing policies—limit what you choose
>
> **D**iscuss the decision with others—listen to their advice
>
> **E**valutate your feelings—before acting, think twice

The rhyme is easy to remember because it includes the mnemonic DECIDE and a sing-song verse. Parenté and Stapleton (1999) found that rhyming memory aids were the easiest for people to remember of several formats they tried.

Summary

Decision making is one of the core elements of cognition. It is similar in many ways to problem solving because making decisions are often attempts to solve problems. Unlike problem solving, however, the options in decision making are often known and the client's task is to make a choice among them. This chapter outlined two techniques for teaching persons with brain injury to make correct decisions: the hat method and the seven-question method. The seven-question method requires the client to answer the following questions: (a) What are the boundaries of the decision? (b) Is the situation a problem or an opportunity? (c) Is the decision covered by an existing policy? (d) Can the decision be categorized as a go/no-go choice, an identification of the correct solution, a discovery of unknown options, or an evaluation of existing options? (e) Is the problem real or imagined? (f) Does the decision involve money, people, or both? (g) What would happen if the person did nothing? Answering each of the questions allows the client to frame the decision effectively and usually leads to a correct decision.

The hat method of decision making, originally proposed by Bono (1990), was also presented. This method involves training the client to imagine wearing various colored hats, with each color suggesting a step in the decision-making process. The white hat process involves collecting all relevant information necessary to make the decision. The yellow hat involves identifying options among which the client will eventually choose. Once the options are identified, the red hat requires all of the things that could go wrong with each of the options to be listed. The green hat requires the reverse type of thinking, determining positive aspects of each option. Specifically, the client lists the benefits of each option. The blue hat requires the client to list his or her emotional feeling about each option.

Both methods of decision making have been useful with our clients. Generally, the seven-question method is more complex and works best with higher functioning clients, whereas the hat method will work with most clients and is especially useful with those who are lower functioning. Whenever possible, we suggest that the therapist use both methods and encourage clients to answer the seven questions first before beginning the hat method. This is especially valuable when the client has to make difficult or important decisions. The value of these methods is that they force the client to follow a structured thinking process before making a decision. The chapter concluded with a rhyming mnemonic, DECIDE, that summarizes much of the first two methods into a single, easy-to-remember verse.

References

Arkes, H. R., & Hammand, K. R. (Eds.). (1999). *Judgment and decision making: An interdisciplinary reader*. New York: Cambridge University Press.

Baron, J. (1994). *Thinking and deciding* (2nd ed.). Cambridge, United Kingdom: Cambridge University Press.

Beach, L. R. (1993). Broadening the definition of decision making: The role of prechoice screening of options. *Psychological Science, 4*, 215–220.

Bono, E. (1990). *The machine of mind*. New York: Penguin Books.

Cicerone, K. D., & Wood, T. R. S. (1987). Planning disorder after closed head injury. *Archives of Physical Medicine Rehabilitation, 68* (February), 127–132.

Dawson, R. (1993). *The confident decision maker*. New York: Simon & Schuster.

Doerner, D. (1987). On the difficulties that people have in dealing with complexity. In J. Rasmussen, K. Duncan, & J. Leplat (Eds.), *New technology and human errors*. London: Wiley.

Fox, J. (1987). Making decisions under the influence of knowledge. In P. E. Morris (Ed.), *Modeling cognition* (pp. 929–939). Chichester, United Kingdom: Wiley.

Frisch, D., & Clemen, R. T. (1994). Beyond expected utility: Rethinking behavioral decision research. *Psychological Bulletin, 116*, 46–54.

Hammand, K. R. (2000). *Judgements under stress*. New York: Oxford University Press.

Janis, I. L., & Mann, L. (1977). *Decision making: A psychological analysis of conflict, choice, and commitment*. New York: Free Press.

Kahneman, D., Slovic, P., & Tversky, A. (Eds.). (1982). *Judgements under uncertainty: Heuristics and biases*. New York: Cambridge University Press.

Larrick, R. P., Morgan, J. N., & Nisbett, R. E. (1990). Teaching the use of cost-benefit reasoning in everyday life. *Psychological Science, 1*, 362–370.

O'Hare, D. (1994). Cognitive failure analysis for aircraft accident investigation. *Ergonomics, 7*, 1855–1869.

Parenté, R., & Stapleton, M. (1999). Development of a cognitive strategies group for vocational training after brain injury. *NeuroRehabilitation, 13*, 13–20.

Payne, J. W., Bettman, J. R., & Johnson, E. J. (1992). Behavioral decision research: A constructive processing perspective. *Annual Review of Psychology, 43*, 87–131.

Plous, S. (1993). *The psychology of judgment and decision making*. New York: McGraw-Hill.

Pollens, R., McBratnie, B., & Burton, P. (1988). Beyond cognition: Executive functions in closed head injury. *Cognitive Rehabilitation, 6*, 26–33.

Reason, J. T. (1990). *Human error*. Cambridge, United Kingdom: Cambridge University Press.

Strauch, B. (2001). *Investigating human error in incidents and accidents*. Burlington, VT: Ashgate.

Wheelwright, S., & Makridakis, S. (1980). *Forecasting methods for management*. New York: Wiley.

Chapter 18

⚜

Retraining Reasoning
and Comprehension

Reasoning and comprehension are the core of cognition (Rips, 1990, 1998; Sternberg & Smith, 1988) and the multimodal model of cognition presented in Chapter 2. Because reasoning and comprehension have different definitions, it is important to distinguish between the concepts before retraining them is discussed.

Reasoning is the active and dynamic process of comparing, making deductions, and forming if–then relationships. Reasoning is what the human mind does to make sense of the world (Nisbett, 1993). Reasoning involves connecting, organizing, and integrating information so that a person can make inferences, generate new information, and test hypotheses. Reasoning is therefore the process that shapes a person's perceptions of the world. All individuals reason, some more quickly than others. Reasoning can be, and usually is, diminished after a brain injury. However, some individuals with brain injury are better at reasoning than others because they do not fall prey to the basic flaws in their reasoning process (Riding, 1997; Stanovich, 1999). Others do not ask the right questions to lead them to make accurate deductions (Johnson-Laird & Byrne, 1991; Rips, 1994) before they make a decision.

Comprehension is the state of a person's understanding at any given point in time. It refers to the gist or essential meaning of something that a person has experienced. For example, when a person goes to a movie, reads a book, or listens to a conversation, he or she tries to understand the theme, abstract the meaning, or get the point. Comprehension is the result of the reasoning process.

The goal of this chapter is to acquaint the reader with the logical flaws that usually underlie faulty reasoning and to demonstrate how a person with brain injury can use this knowledge to reason better. We begin by discussing the stages of understanding or how a person gradually comes to know. We then discuss the common reasoning flaws that usually cloud the reasoning process. We end the chapter with a discussion of therapy techniques that can help a person with brain injury to reason more efficiently and to think clearly.

Often, when something is difficult to understand, a person comprehends it in stages, first at a surface level, then more deeply as he or she draws inferences from the available facts. The person's understanding of the situation clarifies as he or she continues to reason with the facts. It is as if the dust in the person's mind settles and the important issues become clear. Most people use reasoning to learn skills such as division or multiplication. Eventually, though, they come to comprehend these concepts and can use them rather mechanically (Smith & Medin, 1981). Detectives and police investigators reason with the available facts of a case until, at some point, they form a working hypothesis of what must have occurred at the crime scene. At this point, the reasoning process slows and comprehension gels (Whimbey & Lockhead, 1999).

Many persons with brain injury have this same experience as they try to understand their injuries. An individual may wake up in the hospital and know nothing about the specifics of the accident. However, a relative may tell the person that the accident occurred on a specific road that was icy during a winter storm and that the front of the car was demolished. With this core knowledge, the person uses the reasoning process to elaborate and expand his or her comprehension of what has happened. After hearing those specific facts, the person may infer that he or she must have been driving home from work; the road was icy and the car possibly skidded on the ice. Because the front of the car was demolished, the collision must have been head-on or, perhaps, the car crashed into a tree.

This example illustrates the subtle differences between reasoning and comprehension. Comprehension is the current state of understanding of certain events that a person extracts from facts. Reasoning is the mental work that creates an understanding of the facts. The reasoning process is typically slowed after a brain injury and so the resulting comprehension may be ill considered or incomplete. Moreover, the person may require extensive therapy before he or she can again reason quickly and efficiently.

Reasoning and comprehension involve integration, or the combination, of relevant details into a working hypothesis that explains the available facts. The way the facts are integrated can either enhance or distort a person's comprehension of the material. For example, most people have played the party game where one person whispers a story to another who, in turn, whispers it to another, and so on, until the last person relates the story to the group. The distortion of the story is quite dramatic and usually produces a humorous version of the original. Each person in the group integrated the facts differently until the final version of the story was distorted beyond recognition. Any one person's comprehension of the story may have been quite different from that of the next person in the sequence or the person from whom he or she heard the story. This is precisely the reason why gossip can distort the truth, keeping people from making accurate judgments. On the other hand, most people know someone who seems to "get to the bottom" of an issue quickly and rapidly. Clearly, this type of person weeds out the unimportant details, which allows him or her to comprehend the basic underlying theme or idea of the issue.

Comprehension is the higher order meaning or structure that connects the other forms of information in memory. Once the details are forgotten, what is left is comprehension. It is the gist, not the syntax. Reasoning is the process of connecting, comparing, and forming structure from the syntax. Brain injury affects the reasoning process in several ways. The person loses the ability to abstract the essence, theme, gist, or main idea quickly and efficiently. The person also loses the ability to generate facts through if–then reasoning or to eliminate information that does not make sense or does not otherwise relate.

Processes of Reasoning

We begin our discussion of techniques for retraining reasoning and comprehension by defining themes and gist. We then discuss the reasoning processes of presupposition, and inference. Along the way we discuss specific techniques that can help the person with brain injury at each stage of the reasoning process.

Themes and Gist

Themes and gist are the dominant ideas that underlie most written materials and life experiences. They also form the basis of what we remember from any episode of life. Persons with brain injury often seem unable to abstract the theme or gist of movies, books, or social encounters. For example, persons with brain injury who return to school have difficulty writing papers that have an obvious or apparent theme or structure. Therefore, much of what the therapist does will revolve around teaching clients skills for extracting the gist or theme from what they read or hear or to express the gist of their ideas.

This is an important aspect of therapy because a client will most likely recall the theme or gist of an experience (Bransford & Johnson, 1973; Sulin & Dooling, 1974). In many cases, the client's ability to recall any event will depend on his or her ability to abstract a theme. Recall of the details of any of life's episodes will usually come to mind after the client recalls the gist or theme of the event. Themes are therefore central to comprehension. Their purpose is to initiate and to organize recall. They also form a lasting record of a person's experiences. A major goal of cognitive rehabilitation therapy is to teach reasoning and comprehension skills to make this record as accurate as possible. The accuracy of a person's memories is often determined by his or her ability to infer and test various presuppositions.

Presupposition

Reasoning involves a variety of processes; among them is the process of presupposition. Much of what a person sees or hears can be understood only if he or she presumes beforehand or presupposes something to be true. This process is often distorted or impaired after brain injury. The person may understand new situations only at a surface level because of an inability to generate and test presuppositions about the event. The inability to generate these presuppositions frequently distorts a person's recollection or their understanding of certain events. For example, one African American client reported that his instructor in a mechanics training program was trying to keep him from graduating and presupposed that this was occurring because his instructor was racially biased. The situation created a great deal of tension, and the topic became a focus of therapy.

The therapist listed several facts that emerged from the client's description of his interactions with the instructor. These were listed on a piece of paper so the client could review them between sessions: (a) the instructor had given the client high marks on his early performance evaluations, (b) approximately equal numbers of African American and Caucasian students had failed their examination, and (c) several other students of different racial backgrounds had received unsatisfactory ratings at this point in their training.

From these facts, the therapist and client developed lists of presuppositions: (a) the instructor wanted the client to succeed, as evidenced by high marks on the earlier performance evaluations, (b) because most of his peers were having difficulty in this portion of the training, it was likely that this was simply a difficult point in the course, and (c) because an equal number of African American and Caucasian students had failed the examination, it was unlikely that his failure was racially motivated. These and other presuppositions were sufficient to change the client's attitude about the instructor and the training. Their value was that they forced the client to compare his perception of the situation with the facts to determine which presuppositions were possible.

Using presuppositions as a therapy tool is therefore a two-step process. The therapist begins by listing a variety of possible facts about the phenomenon. The therapist and

client then begin to generate lists of suppositions that must have been true for the facts to
be true. For example, the situation just described was rectified because the therapist and
client listed several facts and discussed various presuppositions for each in relation to the
instructor's behavior.

The critical thing to remember when creating presuppositions with a client is that
they are statements about what is likely to
have preceded a certain event that has already occurred. A presupposition must have
occurred *before* the actual event and it partially explains the event in a backward manner. If the presupposition is not in accordance
with the situation, then either the client's
perception of the situation is inaccurate or
the presupposition is wrong. The therapy
proceeds until the facts of the situation and
the presuppositions agree with one another.
The presupposition that explains more of the
available facts is the one that is most likely to
be true.

Inference

Reasoning also involves forming *inferences*.
Once an event has occurred, there are usually
certain conclusions or implications that result. Inferences differ from presuppositions
because they are *logical extensions* that make
sense given the facts of the situation (Braine,
1990; Mayer, 1993; Nisbett, 1993). Presuppositions are logical precursors to the same
situation (Johnson-Laird & Byrne, 1991;
Johnson-Laird, 1993). Therefore, the therapist teaches the client to presuppose by determining what is likely to have preceded a certain situation. Similarly, the therapist teaches
the client to infer by teaching him or her to
extrapolate the logical consequences of what
is known to have already happened.

Forming inferences is also an if–then
process. Continuing the example already introduced, the therapist began forming inferences by listing the likely consequences of the

client's perceptions of the instructor. For example, given that most of the client's peers
had difficulty with this section of the training,
it was likely that they all had to meet some
stringent standard before going on to the next
level. This inference also made sense given
that the client was in a self-paced training
program and many of the clients had failed
their competency test several times but still
remained in training. The therapist then in-
ferred that failure at this stage was a natural
and common occurrence, which was necessary to ensure a standard of knowledge that
would be required to master the new material
in the next stage.

The words *presupposition* and *inference*
are difficult for most clients to understand. In
speaking with their clients, therapists may
want to call presuppositions *ideas about possible causes* and inferences *ideas about likely
results*.

Presuppositions and inferences are especially important aspects of thinking skills
training because they structure a person's understanding of any situation (Collins, 1985).
Moreover, persons with brain injury, especially those with frontal lobe injury, often get
entrenched in one mode of thinking and fail
to break that set. It is therefore important to
teach them a method of thinking that ensures
that the rooted thought is feasible or accurate. Teaching the client to list presuppositions and inferences also keeps him or her
from myopic thinking. Furthermore much of
communication involves inference and presupposition. Without these skills, the client is
doomed to form comprehensions based on
surface facts.

The ability to integrate information also
depends on a person's ability to rapidly generate inferences and presuppositions. Perhaps
the biggest value of this training is that it
forces the client to develop a picture of his or
her world that is based on a coherent and interrelated body of evidence. The client therefore learns to check his or her comprehension
of life situations by determining if it makes

sense relative to the presuppositions that preceded it and the inferences that result from it (Halpern, 1995). The process also forces the client to think about and plan for the future based on the inferences drawn from a current situation.

Therapy Techniques

Training reasoning involves teaching a broad range of skills and vocabulary (Nisbett, Fong, Lehman, & Cheng, 1987; Sternberg, 1987). First, the client must understand the importance of *facts* and *evidence*. Correct reasoning can only occur when there has been a complete and accurate listing of the facts. Furthermore, the reasoning process is beset by several common errors that the client must learn to avoid (Kahneman, Slovic, &Tversky, 1982). *Cognitive flexibility* is also essential for the client to avoid prematurely settling into an incorrect inference and presupposition. This usually happens when a client creates inferences based on incomplete evidence. *Misconceptions* may arise from incomplete evidence, *faulty inferences*, or *fixated mindsets*. Incorrect or incomplete comprehensions also result when a person mistakes evidence for proof or when he or she succumbs to *circular reasoning*. Each of these is discussed in detail.

Identifying Facts and Evidence

The first step in training reasoning is to show a client how to list facts and to evaluate evidence. Facts are the basis of reality. Like them or not, the client must use them to construct a clear picture of the world before drawing any conclusions about it. Generalization is based on the ability to cluster facts that lead to the same conclusion. Evidence is not fact. Evidence is simply a set of events that leads a person to possible conclusions. Therapy clients often mistake evidence for fact. For example, one client observed his wife eating lunch with her boss at work and took this as evidence that she and her boss were having an affair. The critical point in this stage of therapy is to teach the client to always make a clear list of the facts surrounding any situation before forming conclusions. The client can only form conclusions once the list is complete and only after he or she has spent considerable time drawing presuppositions and inferences from the facts.

Inductive and Deductive Reasoning

Once the facts have been identified then it is possible to train the client to work with them. The client can then either deduce or induce new information from the facts. Deductive reasoning usually involves forming presuppositions and inferences in a general-to-specific sequence. For example, one client asked several of his peers how long they had resided at the rehabilitation facility. From their responses he deduced that most people stayed about 6 months and that he was likely to reside there for about that long. Inductive reasoning usually involves the reverse process. Another client in the same facility wondered how long he might stay there. He knew of a person who had been a resident for 3 years. He therefore induced that his stay might last that long. In the first situation, the client learned to extract a general principle from a variety of examples. In the second, the client learned to project a possible scenario based on a specific example.

Training Identification of Common Errors in Reasoning

The following logical flaws of reasoning are presented for therapists to check their clients' reasoning in any given situation. These reasoning errors are presented as statements and examples are provided for each. The therapist should go over each reasoning error with the client and generate examples from the client's personal life.

The sequence with which we discuss these reasoning errors is based on unpublished research with 20 persons with brain injury. The group was given a list of the statements presented in this chapter, which represent common reasoning errors; each was explained in detail to the group. The group members then rated each item in terms of how often they experienced the error. We then ranked the reasoning errors with the first being the most frequently reported through the last, which was seldom reported. This ranked list shows which reasoning errors clients most often encounter.

The list of reasoning errors originally came from Ruchlis (1990) in his book *Clear Thinking*. These errors are often described as common media distortions; however, the therapist did not present them as distortions of the truth that the client could, for example, encounter while watching television. Rather, the questions were restated as "I" statements that the client could use for comparison with his or her life. This list was originally presented in the first edition of this book. The results presented here are from a replication of that original research. The results of the most recent study were virtually identical to those of the earlier study.

▶ Fixated mind-set

"I tend to see things in only one way."

The most commonly cited reasoning problem from persons with brain injury was cognitive rigidity (Mayer, 1993). Most clients reported that they became locked into one mode of thinking and that it was virtually impossible for them to see a situation from any other perspective. The therapy for this problem that has worked best over the years is to play the game "devil's advocate." The therapist presents persistent social problems and

the client must take several positions on each issue and then justify his or her position from a variety of perspectives. For example, the client tries to justify both sides of the assault weapon ban or the abortion issue. Once the therapist and client have played this game with several social issues, they try the same game with the client's personal issues.

For example, one client complained that his wife no longer seemed to be attracted to him. The therapist asked the client to pretend that he was his wife and to describe her affections for him. The therapist then asked the client to play the role of a strange woman and to describe what she found attractive about him. This stage of the game that deals with clients' personal issues can lead to a great deal of tension for many clients because it deals with emotionally charged subjects. The therapist should therefore begin the game with common social issues and only begin the second stage when the client seems strong enough emotionally to handle personal issues.

▶ Jumping to conclusions

"I form impressions of people or things without first considering all the available information."

This was also cited as a major problem after brain injury. It is similar to the fixated mind-set because, in both cases, the person creates an intransigent mind-set quickly and then generates conclusions from an incorrect comprehension of the situation.

An effective therapy for this type of thought disorder is to have the client list all the facts about a certain situation on a piece of paper until all facts are known. This will force the client to postpone forming any conclusions until all relevant information is available. Again, it is best to begin training with impersonal social issues and gradually work into more personal problems. The therapist should list the facts on paper and encourage the client to do so as he or she learns to use the technique.

▶ Mistaking evidence for proof

"I immediately interpret ambiguous situations as proof of one position or another."

One client, for example, saw his instructor having lunch with another client in the rehabilitation center. He felt that this proved that the instructor favored this client over any other.

The technique of *scenario interpretation* has proven effective for working with this problem. The therapist presents several personal scenarios and asks the client to interpret them in as many different ways as possible. For example, the therapist asks the client to interpret the following scenario: *a woman standing on a street corner late at night wearing a tight, short skirt.* The client might say, "She's a prostitute." Then he or she might say, "She's an undercover policewoman." Then the client might say, "She's a cocktail waitress waiting for a cab to take her home to her husband and five children." Short scenarios are easy to create and usually lead to a variety of interpretations. The goal is to increase the client's cognitive flexibility by providing ambiguous scenarios that show how they can be used as proof of several interpretations. This game teaches the client that even the most concrete evidence is rarely proof of any specific position.

▶ Misperception

"I seldom have a clear idea of what people tell me."

Most clients reported that they simply did not understand many communications and often leave a situation with a totally incorrect understanding of what was said or done. The problem is that the client may act on the basis of the misinterpretation and then spend hours fixing the problem, simply because he

or she did not understand the situation from the start.

The therapy for most misperception problems is to get the client, the family, and the treatment team in the habit of repeating what each other says in his or her own words (Gernsbacher, 1994; Harley, 1995). Each time the client speaks to someone, the other person should say, "Let me see if I can say this in my own words." The therapist or family member then does so and asks the client to verify that the concept has been correctly communicated. Then the procedure is reversed: When someone speaks to the client, the client should repeat the information in his or her words. This procedure will help clarify the extent and types of misperceptions the client is most prone to make. It also provides the client with additional rehearsal and restatement practice, which are essential for good memory.

▶ Selective attention

"I often see and hear only the things I want to."

Many clients reported that they would selectively screen out information or criticism that was painful, difficult to understand, or that was not in accordance with their personal values. For example, one client said that he ignored people who noticed that he had a problem pronouncing words, walking, or using his left arm. He would tell them not to help him because he chose to believe that he did not have any problems in those areas. He would, however, listen to people who noticed improvement in his cognitive and physical states. Both groups of people noticed a problem but the client only attended to those who noticed improvement.

Therapy techniques for this type of problem are best carried out in a group. The therapist asks a client to list his or her major problems. The therapist then goes around the room and asks each member of the group to say whether the client's self-perceptions are accurate. The targeted client must then re-state these criticisms in his or her own words. For example, client A said that her major problem was that she was shy and could not establish the type of friendships she desired. Client B said that she did seem shy, but her shyness was the result of low self-esteem. Client C agreed with Client B's assessment and added that client A was also quite fearful of evaluation. This interaction caused client A to reassess her problems and to eventually change her behavior.

As Parenté and Stapleton (1993, 1999) pointed out, this type of treatment works well because persons with brain injury listen to other persons with brain injury; they are far more likely to accept the opinions of others with similar problems. The therapist plays a crucial role in this situation because he or she must determine whether the client is ready to hear the other assessments. Moreover, many clients phrase their assessments in an unacceptable fashion and the therapist may need to cut short an offensive statement or reinterpret it in a way that other group members will accept. Often, the exercises must wait until the client trusts the others in the group to the point where their input would be valued rather than immediately denied and rejected.

▶ Personal mudslinging

> "I focus on the negative about myself and pay little attention to my good qualities and achievements."

Clients typically say that they are preoccupied with negative thought patterns. They focus on their failures and do not recognize their improvement over time. In addition, they are sensitive to criticism. Part of the problem stems from low self-esteem, which may have been a premorbid personality problem. Furthermore, most persons with brain injury have experienced a great deal of personal rejection and stigma over the years and have come to expect that this is the way oth-ers will automatically relate to them in the future. Some become fixated on their deficits; others deny them. Most gradually become accustomed to their growing social isolation. A few make an effort to focus on improvement and to adopt an optimistic attitude.

Therapy for this problem involves any number of interventions. One of the easiest interventions is to invite clients to a support group or psychosocial training group. Higher functioning clients will experience an immediate uplift when they realize that their deficits are less apparent than most of the other members of the group. For example, one client said that he felt immediately better about his life when he walked into a psychosocial group and introduced himself to the other members, most of whom were in wheelchairs and spoke with an obvious dysarthria. Furthermore, group members will typically make other group members feel that their problems are not unique. The therapist can capitalize on this empathy and use it to advance group treatment.

The therapist can focus the group's topic on personal mudslinging and discuss common strategies for dealing with it. Frequently cited strategies include: (a) making a list of the client's strengths and posting them on the wall, (b) making a list of positive things that happen each day, (c) posting a chart of performance on therapy tasks or in school so the client can see improvements, (d) posting goals and checking them off as the client achieves them, and (e) soliciting assessment of the client's progress from infrequently seen family and friends. These people are the most likely to see change in the client's functional status. Showing these ratings to the client provides objective evidence of recovery and identifies areas that require additional work.

The technique of *personal success review* may also help to reduce the effects of mudslinging. This method was originally developed for helping salespersons develop a positive attitude before attempting a sale (Bernstein, 1994). The same techniques work well for persons with brain injury. The therapist asks the client to think of several success experiences he or she has had over the years. For example, many clients recall standing on the stage wearing a cap and gown at their high school graduation. Some report a specific triumph during an athletic event. Others recall when they got their first high-paying job or the day they received an acceptance letter to a university or college. Most clients can, with the help of the therapist, conjure between 5 and 10 personal success experiences. The therapist then writes the client's description of each of these on index cards and instructs the client to review each card whenever he or she begins to sling personal mud. The client must close his or her eyes and imagine the various experiences and try to rekindle the feeling of success that accompanied them. Negative feelings and depression will often dissipate after reviewing all of the cards.

► Self-scare

"I can't get these fears out of my mind."

Self-scaring is similar to personal mud slinging. The client focuses on one of his or her deficit areas then begins to infer all of the problems that could result from it. For example, "What will I do when my parents die and I'm left all alone?" "I'll never be able to have children; no one would want me now and I couldn't take care of them anyway." "If an emergency situation arose, I would not be able to help myself." Clients often become preoccupied with these thoughts to the point where they dominate their thinking. In many cases, these thoughts are reasonable given the severity of their disorders. However, preoccupation with these problems is always maladaptive and unproductive.

Therapy involves first asking the client to state his or her biggest fears. Facing fears is always difficult and will often evoke an emotional response. The next step is to list several fears and to discuss strategies for dealing with

them. For example, in one case, the therapist helped the client deal with her personal emergency fear by getting her a medical warning monitor. The client could press the device and it would signal an emergency.

Clients rated the remaining reasoning flaws as less frequently problematic. Nevertheless, they should still be discussed with clients. We often watch television commercials or read newspapers with clients as a means of identifying reasoning flaws. The goal is to acquaint clients with reasoning problems they will see every day. Because clients in our survey did not rate these highly, we discuss each one only briefly.

► Taking statements out of context

"What people say and do is all that matters. I don't care what caused them to say or do it."

This refers to the problem of not considering a statement or an action in light of the situation that either precipitated it or surrounded it. For example, clients occasionally report irritation when they hear family and friends talking about them when clients are not aware of the context that led to the discussion. One therapy for overcoming this problem is to train the client to always ask others to explain the context that precipitated an action or statement. This technique also helps the client avoid acting impulsively, at least until he or she has some historical perspective.

► Circular reasoning

"I firmly believe certain things and no one can tell me they are wrong."

Many clients become overly religious after injury as a way of finding some meaningful explanation for the drastic changes in their lives. Because religion is based in faith, it is impossible to prove or to disprove its validity.

Other clients may develop other deeply rooted beliefs, also based in faith. These convictions are not necessarily wrong nor are they maladaptive or unproductive. Often, they are the only things that are helping a client adjust. Occasionally, however, clients become attracted to convictions and attitudes that create problems for the therapist. For example, clients occasionally become overzealous religious fanatics who try to convert others to their beliefs. Some may transfer their devotion to the therapist and believe that anything he or she tells them is true. Therapy for this problem involves teaching the client to ask questions that will help verify his or her convictions or personal philosophies. For example, the therapist should ask the client about the tangible ways his or her life has improved since adopting the beliefs.

▶ Externalization and scapegoating

"When things go wrong, it is usually someone else's fault."

This attitude allows clients to deny their deficits or to assume that others, not themselves, are having difficulty adjusting to their disability. Externalization often takes form in excuses, inability to accept responsibility, and interpretations of events that shift responsibility for failure onto someone or something else. For example, one client dropped a valuable piece of china and justified the situation by claiming that her sister did not dry it well. Another complained that his therapy was progressing too slowly because all of his therapists were incompetent. To deal with this problem, the client should be trained to explain events in the first person active voice ("I dropped the china") before offering any additional explanation.

▶ Faith in numbers

"Test scores and numbers usually tell the story."

This attitude reflects a belief in the ultimate truth of data and numerical analysis. Clients seldom understand that for every statistic, there is usually another that can be used to "prove" the opposite point. The therapist should acquaint the client with the fact that test scores do change, especially if they were collected during the early stages of the client's recovery. Furthermore, the client needs to know that these scores do not measure his or her potential for change. They only provide a snapshot of the performance at a single point in time. Moreover, test results are usually based on group averages whereas individual scores may not show the same picture. The individual client's recovery often differs markedly from the numerical estimations of recovery for the hypothetical average person. In addition, statistical estimates of recovery after brain injury do not factor a client's motivation into the equation.

▶ Identification

"If I really respect someone, I will usually see things their way."

Clients will occasionally model themselves after therapists, friends, relatives, or others who accept them and spend time with them. They may begin to adopt similar attitudes, behaviors, or opinions. Modeling can have positive effects if the person being imitated is a positive role model. However, some clients may model media stars, groups of unsavory friends, or others whose opinions and attitudes are maladaptive or dangerous. For example, one client began modeling "gangsta rappers" and started talking about shooting police officers. Perhaps the only way to deal with this problem is to discuss issues such as the real source of the opinion, whether the client understands the opinion, and whether the client is willing to accept responsibility for any action resulting from the opinion.

▶ Sweet deal

*"I am often convinced to buy things be-
cause they seem like such a good deal."*

Many clients are easily persuaded by advertising campaigns that describe deals of a
lifetime. Occasionally they fall prey to these
advertisements, act impulsively, and then experience financial difficulty. For example, one
client wanted to buy a computer because he
thought that playing computer games would
improve his memory. He went to a computer
store and was persuaded by a salesman to take
out a store charge card to purchase a $7,000
system. He was persuaded by the argument
that if he used the charge card, he would not
have to make any payments or pay any interest for 6 months. He did not realize that because he was living on public assistance
monies, he would not be able to pay off the
computer for 6 years. After the client went
through the embarrassing process of returning
the computer, the therapist asked him to
memorize the old adage, "If something sounds
too good to be true, it usually is."

▶ Vague emotion

*"I feel the only things in life worth going
after are fulfillment, happiness, love,
and truth."*

Clients and their families often fall prey
to this reasoning flaw. In many cases they do so
because they do not know what to expect from
the recovery process. Even though these emotional abstractions are easy to accept, they
may be difficult to achieve. For example, many
clients will describe their major goal in life as
"to be happy again." Although this is certainly
a laudable goal, it is difficult to measure. The
therapist should ask the client to explain his
or her emotions specifically using concrete,
rather than abstract, words wherever possible.

▶ Thought diversion

*"If someone else does something, why
can't I?"*

Some clients will complain that they
should be allowed to do something because
someone else or everyone else is doing it. Alternatively, they believe they should not be
sanctioned for having done something because someone else did it and was not sanctioned. For example, one client's mother ad-
monished him for leaving a candle burning in
his room. He replied, "You leave candles
burning at the dinner table all the time." The
client shifted attention away from his action
by pointing out a similar observation that
somehow justified it. The therapist pointed
out that his observation was indeed correct.
Candles should never be left unattended.
However, the instance he observed did not
justify his action.

▶ People like me

*"You can usually believe the opinions of
people who are just like you."*

Clients may occasionally adopt similar
beliefs with others of similar backgrounds or
others who have had similar life experiences.
This is different from modeling, where the
client adopts the opinions of someone else
out of respect. The people-like-me reasoning
flaw results from similarity of background
rather than from respect for another's ideas.
Occasionally, these collective opinions or attitudes can be useful. For example, one client
who was previously a member of a motorcycle
gang began to identify with the lifestyle of
friends from his old neighborhood who attended a local church. However, problems
may arise when clients adopt the lifestyle of
those whom they have outgrown. For example, one client began to identify with
those high school friends who were part of a
drug culture. Usually, clients will identify
with those individuals who accept them. If
they perceive that those people are culturally
similar to them, then a stronger or more rapid
identification process may ensue. The therapist can use the identification to the client's

advantage if the attitudes produce an improvement in functioning.

▶ Everyone's doing it

"If everyone is doing it, it must be right."

Most people fall prey to fads and people with brain injury are no exception. Occasionally though, a client's desire to be accepted leads to behavior, dress, or mannerisms that create more problems than they solve. For example, one client refused to wear shoes other than high-top tennis shoes even though his leg brace was not compatible with the shoe. The leg brace caused the shoes to wear on his ankles, causing an infection. Another client began drinking on weekends because his friends did. Clients have a difficult time explaining why they choose to adopt similar behaviors, dress, or attitudes to those who accept them as friends. The therapist should spend considerable time with each client discussing why his or her behaviors may be inappropriate or potentially dangerous. The client eventually learns to ask the basic question, "Is it right for me?"

▶ Great person

"If a famous person says something, I will usually believe it."

The media commonly show overweight ex-football players advertising a certain brand of beer, hardware, or automobiles. Characterizations of Albert Einstein are sometimes associated with "the smart choice." We will occasionally watch TV commercials with our clients to illustrate this reasoning error. The client should ask the question, "Does this person have any expertise in relation to this product or service?"

▶ Science has shown

"Scientific discoveries are always true. If a scientist says something, I will usually believe it."

Many clients tend to equate science with truth. They seldom ask whether the scientific discovery has been replicated, whether it is generally accepted, or what are the limits to the discovery. This has been especially apparent when discussing nutrients and drugs that might improve memory or thinking (Gilhooly, 1996). Most clients will listen to the available research and immediately conclude that a particular compound will improve their functioning. The best therapy is to tell the client that a single experiment does not prove or disprove anything. Scientists investigate and replicate findings until there is a consensus that evolves from the bulk of the research. A scientific discovery is never fact until the larger scientific community agrees that it is.

Summary

This chapter described the basic components of rational thought. Persons with brain injury, like most people, are prone to irrational thinking. Many have not been taught how to reason logically. It is therefore necessary to begin by distinguishing the types of reasoning and how these processes can be used to shape a person's understanding of the world. We discussed the deductive, general-to-specific, processes and their reverse, the inductive, specific-to-general, processes. We also described the presupposition and inferential reasoning methods and therapy techniques for training reasoning and comprehension. Other techniques for training reasoning include teaching the client to distinguish facts from evidence and to identify a variety of common logical flaws. A survey of common reasoning errors was given to 20 persons with brain injury who were asked to rank them in terms of how often they found that each was a problem in their lives. Those that were most frequently rated were discussed in detail and therapy techniques were provided that were appropriate for each problem.

References

Bernstein, M. (1994). *The Masters 100*. Baltimore: Human Equations Corporation.

Braine, M. D. S. (1990). The "natural logic" approach to reasoning. In W. E. Overton (Ed.), *Reasoning, necessity, and logic: Developmental perspectives* (pp. 133–157). Hillsdale, NJ: Erlbaum.

Bransford, J. D., & Johnson, M. K. (1973). Consideration of some problems of comprehension. In W. G. Chase (Ed.), *Visual information processing* (pp. 383–438). New York: American Press.

Collins, A. (1985). Teaching reasoning skills. In S. F. Chipman, J. W. Segal, & R. Glaser (Eds.), *Thinking and learning skills. Vol. 2: Research and open questions*. Hillsdale, NJ: Erlbaum.

Gernsbacher, M. A. (Ed.). (1994). *Handbook of psycholinguistics*. San Diego, CA: Academic Press.

Gilhooly, K. J. (1996). *Thinking: Directed, undirected, and creative* (3rd ed.). East Sussex, United Kingdom: Psychology Press.

Halpern, D. F. (1995). *Thought and knowledge* (3rd ed.). Hillsdale, NJ: Erlbaum.

Harley, T. A. (1995). *The psychology of language: From data to theory*. Hillsdale, NJ: Erlbaum.

Johnson-Laird, P. N. (1993). *Mental models*. Cambridge, United Kingdom: Cambridge University Press.

Johnson-Laird, P. N., & Byrne, M. J. (1991). *Deduction*. Hillsdale, NJ: Erlbaum.

Kahneman, D., Slovic, P., & Tversky, A. (Eds.). (1982). *Judgements under uncertainty: Heuristics and biases*. New York: Cambridge University Press.

Mayer, R. E. (1993). *Rules and reasoning*. Hillsdale, NJ: Erlbaum.

Nisbett, R. E. (1993). *Rules for reasoning*. Hillsdale, NJ: Erlbaum.

Nisbett, R. E., Fong, G. T., Lehman, D. R., & Cheng, P. W. (1987). Teaching reasoning. *Science, 238*, 625–631.

Parenté, R., & Stapleton, M. (1993). An empowerment model of memory training. *Applied Cognitive Psychology, 7*(7), 595–602.

Parenté, R., & Stapleton, M. (1999). Development of a cognitive strategies group for vocational training after traumatic brain injury. *NeuroRehabilitation, 13*, 13–20.

Riding, R. (1997). On the nature of cognitive style. *Educational Psychology, 17*, 2–9.

Rips, L. J. (1990). Reasoning. *Annual Review of Psychology, 41*, 321–353.

Rips, L. J. (1994). *The psychology of proof: Deductive reasoning in human thinking*. Cambridge, MA: MIT Press.

Rips, L. J. (1998). Reasoning and conversation. *Psychological Review, 105*, 411–441.

Ruchlis, H. (1990). *Clear thinking*. New York: Prometheus Books.

Smith, E. E., & Medin, D. L. (1981). *Categories and concepts*. Cambridge, MA: Harvard University Press.

Stanovich, K. E. (1999). *Who is rational? Studies of individual differences in reasoning*. Mahwah, NJ: Erlbaum.

Sternberg, R. J. (1987). *Intelligence applied: Understanding and increasing your intellectual skills*. San Diego, CA: Harcourt Brace Jovanovich.

Sternberg, R. J., & Smith, E. E. (1988). *The psychology of human thought*. Cambridge, MA: Cambridge University Press.

Sulin, R. A., & Dooling, D. J. (1974). Intrusions of a thematic idea in retention of prose. *Journal of Experimental Psychology, 103*, 255–262.

Whimbey, A., & Lockhead, J. (1999). *Problem solving and comprehension* (6th ed.). Mahwah, NJ: Erlbaum.

Chapter 19

✣

Retraining Executive Skills

The term *executive* implies a higher order supervisory capacity that directs a person's actions (Baddeley, 1998; Cicerone, 2002; Myake & Shah, 1999; Yody et al., 2000; although see Parkin, 1998). The frontal or prefrontal areas of the brain partially control a person's executive functions. Because traumatic brain injury frequently damages these areas, persons with brain injury frequently lose much or all of their executive skills and their ability to control and organize their behavior (Brown, 1978; Miller, Galanter, & Pribram, 1960; Shimamura, Janowsky, & Squire, 1991). This chapter deals with retraining the ability to self-regulate behavior in persons with brain injury. Friends, family, and the therapist will often notice that the therapy client has difficulty setting goals, prioritizing, and executing plans (Case, 1992; Duncan, 1986; Lezak, 1993; Pollens, McBratnie, & Burton, 1988). In addition, the client may not be aware of how he or she presents to others, and may have difficulty initiating and inhibiting behaviors, thinking strategically and sequentially, and evaluating progress toward goals. Good executive skills also determine a person's ability to solve problems, to act proactively in a mature and non-egocentric fashion, and to generalize newly learned skills to novel situations. These skills define a person's social competence and they are therefore especially important for getting along in the world of work (Parenté & Staple-

ton, 1999; Ylvisaker, 1995). We, therefore, have devoted an entire chapter to this most important aspect of cognitive rehabilitation.

We begin by defining executive functioning and discussing its importance in social and work situations. We next discuss how the therapist can informally evaluate self-awareness and executive functions after brain injury. We then discuss some strategies for retraining executive functions.

Several authors (Baddeley, 1986, 1990; Janowski, Shimamura, Kritchevsky, & Squire, 1989; McCarthy & Warrington, 1990; Ylvisaker, 1995) discuss the term *metacognitive functions*. This term describes thinking skills, which are similar to executive functions. Metacognition is both static and dynamic. Static metacognition refers to a person's awareness of the state of his or her cognitive processes and the appropriate procedures for improving performance or directing behavior toward a goal. Dynamic metacognition refers to a person's ability to exercise control of his or her cognition and to initiate appropriate action (Harris & Morris, 1984; Reason, 1990; Sternberg, 1985). The dynamic and static qualities of metacognition can work independently of each another. For example, a therapy client may be aware that he or she is hungry and wants a salad and pizza for dinner but not be able to plan or prepare such a dinner. This scenario reflects intact static metacognitive ability but relatively poor dynamic skill. Retraining executive skills is not only a matter of making clients aware of their deficits but, even more so, teaching them how to control their thoughts and actions (McGlynn & Schacter, 1989).

Much of a person's executive skill develops during infancy and childhood (Welsh & Pennington, 1988). This is evident in the preschool and elementary school years when parents and teachers will often see improvement in children's ability to solve problems, control attention, and regulate conversation. Executive skills continue to develop throughout adolescence and into adulthood. Retraining executive skills can be quite difficult if a client was intellectually limited, learning disabled, or emotionally delayed before the injury. Or, the injury may have exacerbated a preexisting developmental disorder. In other words, in some cases the therapist may be trying to teach skills that the client had never developed in the first place.

Assessment of Executive Functioning

Perhaps the best way to determine whether a client's executive skills were limited before the injury is to interview his or her family, friends, or coworkers concerning behavioral changes from preinjury to postinjury. Anderson-Parenté (1994) indicated that persons with brain injury and their family members can estimate different aspects of executive functioning. In her study, persons with brain injury were able to accurately evaluate the more concrete aspects of their behavior such as motor functioning. Family members could more accurately estimate the abstract aspects of the person's behavior such as social skills and abstract reasoning capacity.

Anderson-Parenté (1994) suggested that the executive skills of a person with brain injury could be assessed by asking family members to answer questions such as the following: Can the person set goals and follow through with attaining them? Can the person plan and prioritize, and organize a task, living space, and time? How well does the person self-initiate, self-inhibit, self-monitor, and self-evaluate? Can the person solve problems, make decisions, and anticipate the consequences of his or her behavior? How does the person's current level of functioning in each of these areas compare with his or her premorbid state? Has there been any noticeable improvement with therapy?

Asking the family to reflect on the client's ability to do these types of things before and after the injury can be of enormous benefit when assessing potential for improvement in executive functioning. In many cases, self-report and family observation may be the only ways to estimate the more abstract qualities of the client's behavior and to assess the client's premorbid executive capacity (Diller & Ben-Yishay, 1987; Howieson & Lezak, 1995; Lezak, 1995).

We have already discussed retraining organization, problem solving, and decision making in previous chapters. We now discuss retraining self-monitoring, goal setting, and social competence.

Self-Monitoring

Self-monitoring is a person's ability to evaluate and regulate the quality and quantity of his or her behavior. This skill can be and often is diminished after a traumatic brain injury (McGlynn & Schacter, 1989). The problem is exacerbated by the fact that self-monitoring skills are seldom taught early in life and the therapist may have to teach the skills without the client having any prior learning on which to build. Furthermore, the client may be unaware of the deficits and possibly unwilling to accept the fact that there is a problem. We describe several techniques for training the client to regulate his or her performance based on previous behavior. This list of techniques is not exhaustive; we selected the techniques that follow for discussion because they are methods that have worked in the past.

Behavioral Charting

Behavioral charting is a technique that forces a client to see changes in his or her behavior over time and to notice relationships that exist among various behaviors. The therapist and client begin by listing several aspects of life that the client wants to change. Although these should be mostly specific and measurable things such as weight or amount of time spent with the family each day, they can also include vague qualities such as perceived happiness or satisfaction with life. Ideally, the client should be able to measure all of the aspects on a 10-point scale. The therapist helps the client develop the list and shows him or her how to scale the behaviors so that each can be rated every day. For example, one client was interested in tracking his weight, the severity of daily headaches, and the number of cups of coffee he drank each day. Weight was measured on a 10-point scale that surrounded his current weight (160–170). Because the client seldom weighed less than 160 or more than 170, the scale ranged from 1 (161) through 10 (170). Number of cups of coffee was rated from 1 (a single cup) to as many as 10 cups per day. Severity of daily headaches was scaled from very low (1) through severe (10).

Each client will choose different variables because the things he or she wants to change differ from person to person. Placing all behaviors on the familiar scale of 1 to 10 is easiest for most clients to understand. The therapist may need to label certain variables at the beginning, middle, and end of the scale so the client knows what he or she is rating. This will be necessary in cases where the client wants to rate intangible variables such as de-

_____ **Coffee** (cups per day)

_____ **Anxiety** (1 = low to 10 = high)

_____ **Depression** (1 = low to 10 = high)

_____ **Headaches** (0 = none to 10 = severe)

_____ **Memory** (1 = poor to 10 = excellent)

_____ **Thinking** (1 = poor to 10 = excellent)

_____ **Energy** (1 = low to 10 = high)

_____ **Attention** (1 = low to 10 = high)

Figure 19.1. Sample behavioral rating form.

pression. Depression could be scaled from 1 (not depressed at all) to 5 (neither happy nor unhappy) to 10 (cries and is miserable every day). Selecting behaviors and defining the scales may take several sessions to complete. An example of a rating form is presented in Figure 19.1.

Once the client and therapist identify the behaviors of interest and make up the rating scale, the client then rates each variable every day or at some other mutually agreed-upon interval. The client can rate these behaviors directly on the chart or rate them on a separate form and have the therapist chart them. Either way, the result is a picture of the client's behavior across several different dimensions. The chart also provides a picture of how the different behaviors interact with one another.

The therapist and client should discuss the chart as it develops. A sample set of ratings and their corresponding chart appear in Figure 19.2. To interpret the chart, the therapist should ask several questions. First the therapist asks whether the various behaviors are at acceptable levels or whether one or more of them should be increased or decreased. For example, does the client continue to rate depression at 8 and 9, which indicates a serious problem? Which ratings are increasing or decreasing most rapidly? Which ones does the client want to decrease

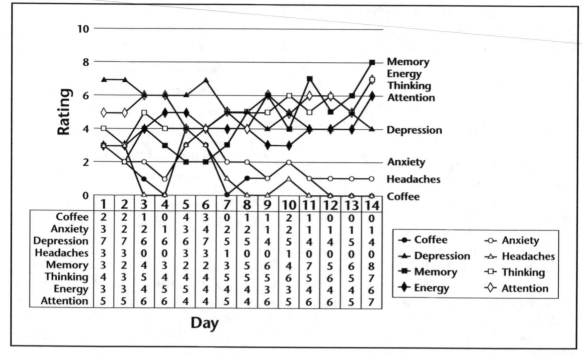

	1	2	3	4	5	6	7	8	9	10	11	12	13	14
Coffee	2	2	1	0	4	3	0	1	1	2	1	0	0	0
Anxiety	3	2	2	1	3	4	2	2	1	2	1	1	1	1
Depression	7	7	6	6	6	7	5	5	4	5	4	4	5	4
Headaches	3	3	0	0	3	3	1	0	0	1	0	0	0	0
Memory	3	2	4	3	2	2	3	5	6	4	7	5	6	8
Thinking	4	3	5	4	4	4	5	5	5	6	5	6	5	7
Energy	3	3	4	5	5	4	4	4	3	3	4	4	4	6
Attention	5	5	6	6	4	4	5	4	6	5	6	6	5	7

Figure 19.2. Sample behavioral chart.

or increase and are those behaviors going in the right direction? It is also important to look at the relationship between behaviors. Those that follow the same trend are directly related whereas those that follow opposite trends are typically inversely related. For example, the client in Figure 19.2 found that his headaches were directly related to the amount of coffee he consumed each day because the severity-of-headache rating followed the same downward trend on the chart as the cups-of-coffee rating.

The chart of behaviors shows the client that everything he or she does can potentially affect everything else. The client can learn about his or her behavior by inspecting the chart and looking for consistent trends. Clients are often surprised to see that certain behaviors they thought were related are not, and vice versa. These relationships become the focus of therapy discussions.

The client eventually learns to predict future behavior by mentally noting the behav-iors to which they are related. For example, the client in the example learned that he would usually get a headache when he drank more than three cups of coffee a day. He learned to limit his intake of coffee to de-crease the severity of his headaches.

Predicting Behavior and Its Consequences

The therapist should also train the client to predict his or her performance in most tasks and then to evaluate the accuracy of the pre-dictions. To get an idea of how well the client predicts, the therapist can ask the client to es-timate his or her performance on the various tasks of the initial evaluation. For example, we usually ask clients to predict their perfor-mance on the subtests of a neuropsychologi-cal evaluation.

We usually find that clients have a ten-dency to either overpredict or underpredict their performance. During therapy sessions, we frequently ask the client to predict how he or she will perform on tasks. Family members can also ask the client to predict performance, feelings, physical states, and so forth, and then later validate the predictions. The general goal is to get the client in the habit of predicting and evaluating as a matter of daily routine. A client may become frustrated and occasionally irritated when his or her predictions are inaccurate. The therapist and family members should tell the client that this is a necessary aspect of therapy and that his or her predictions will gradually improve.

Videotaping

Videotaping may also be an effective vehicle for training self-monitoring. The therapist videotapes the client during a session and then reviews the videotape later with the client to show how he or she performed. We find that it is most useful for training complex or abstract social skills such as communication or social interaction.

Verification

We have discussed the value of verification throughout this book. The client learns to verify whether a certain communication was correctly received by following interchanges with others with statements such as, "Let me repeat what you just said," or "Let me see if I have this correct." This gives the client the opportunity to output the information in his or her own words and to have the other person verify that the concept was correctly understood. Generally, 1 minute spent in verification is worth 1 hour later trying to fix the problems that arise from miscommunication. The procedure gradually shows the client how to self-monitor verbal exchanges and it gives the family a convenient way

of monitoring improvement in the client's comprehensions.

Goal Setting

When asked to define their goals, persons with brain injury often say something like, "I live my life day by day." This type of response reflects an inability to anticipate the future (Cicerone & Wood, 1987; Parenté, Anderson-Parenté, & Stapleton, 2001). The therapist's goal is therefore to define for the client a clear vision of the future and an action plan that he or she can use to achieve it. That is, the client learns how to set goals and prioritize.

The first step toward defining a client's goals is to ask questions that force him or her to think about the future and to define priorities. For example, the therapist can ask a question such as, "What do you want to have accomplished in 5 years?" This requires the client to define a long-term goal. The therapist and client then spend several sessions discussing priorities and manageable subgoals. The purpose of these sessions is to define a set of tangible long-term goals for the client along with a set of short-term goals that he or she can pursue en route to achieving the long-term goals. This action plan becomes the focus of the client's therapy.

It is important for the goals to be tangible, concrete, and measurable. Many clients will begin by mentioning vague goals such as, "I want to be happy and fulfilled." Although these are certainly laudable goals, they are difficult to evaluate in terms of final achievement. On the other hand, a goal such as, "I want to be self-supporting and live in my own home," is far more useful. Criteria for creating tangible goals include whether (a) the goal can be stated in concrete terms, (b) the client can set dates when the goal will be accomplished, (c) it is possible to create an action plan that will achieve the goal, and (d) the client can record progress toward the goal.

Subgoals are steps toward a long-term goal that are feasible to achieve in 1 year or less and that are necessary precursors to achieving the long-term goal. The client should post a piece of paper listing the short- and long-term goals in the home so that he or she can see them each day. The goals can be made into a poster that the client can tape to a door or a wall where it will be in plain view.

Next, the client should memorize the GOAL mnemonic presented below, which is the action plan for following through with the goals. This mnemonic details the procedure for creating goals and acting on them, and works well with the behavioral charting procedure mentioned earlier.

Go over your goals every day. The G reminds the client to spend a small amount of time rehearsing his or her goals every day, thus increasing the client's awareness.

Order your goals, short- and long-term. The therapist will help the client do this initially, breaking the goals into 5-year (long-term) and 1-year (short-term) categories.

Ask yourself several questions each day. "What did I do today to achieve my goals?" "What could I have done differently to achieve my goals?" "How close am I to achieving my goals?" "Are my goals the same or have they changed?"

Look at your goals each day. It is also useful to post the client's goals poster next to his or her behavioral chart to show how behaviors are related to goals.

As an example of goal setting, consider a client named Don whose initial goals were "to be happy and to have a fulfilling life." The therapist redefined these goals into short- and long-term components by first asking Don what he would find fulfilling and what would make him happy. Don concluded that being happy and feeling fulfilled were highly related, and that they both involved working at a stable job, having friends, and being inde-

pendent. His long-term goals were therefore to get a job and to get his own place to live. His short-term goals included getting the training necessary to get the job and to complete the training in 1 year.

Don entered a program in janitorial/custodial training that he could complete in 1 year. He and the therapist developed a self-monitoring sheet that included his weekly performance evaluations from his training plus daily self-ratings of his training. The chart also included self-ratings of headache severity, attention to detail, and other qualities he felt were necessary to succeed in the program. He posted these charts on a wall in his room at the rehabilitation center and reviewed them every day in accordance with the GOAL mnemonic.

Social Competence

Social competence is the aspect of the client's behavior that is, perhaps, the most important of any that we will discuss. It is the best predictor of whether a client will be able to maintain employment, have friendships, and feel socially accepted. It is also the most difficult skill to train, probably because it involves a vast array of interrelated behaviors, and requires the client to think in advance. Social competence is an abstract skill that includes planning, prioritizing, and anticipating the consequences of behavior, and then inhibiting behavior in accordance with the predicted consequence. Over the years, we have identified several characteristics of socially competent individuals. We review these here because they clarify our view of the type of person we are trying to create with the therapies described in this chapter.

General Traits

Socially competent individuals project a unique image. This is not a flashy image or one that is designed to draw attention, but one that is uncommon, competent, attractive, and memorable. These individuals display a sense of social control and they resist social pressure. They listen well and communicate clearly with others. They respond to social feedback and change even though they may not like what others tell them. They consider the history of a social situation before taking a stand or responding. They understand the importance of timing of responses in social encounters. They do not force themselves onto others socially, but rather initiate friendships and relationships subtly. They praise their friends' appearance and accomplishments. They learn from their errors and do not make the same mistakes twice.

Forward Thinking

Most of these personality characteristics require an abstract ability we call *forward thinking,* which is the skill of thinking in advance. We retrain forward thinking with two games. Each of these games can be carried out in a group or with individuals. Both require clients to think ahead and to consider current behavior as a precursor to something that may occur in the future.

The first game is called *What would happen if. . . ?* The therapist begins this game by asking the client to define a major problem. For example, the client might say, "I hate living at home with my family." The therapist then asks what the client wants to do about the problem. In this case, the client might respond, "I want to move out on my own." The therapist then asks, "What would happen if you did that?" The client must then respond with consequences that might arise if he or she moved out. The client would have to find a place to live, pay rent, function independently, and so forth. As the client generates each consequence, the therapist follows up with the same question, for example, "What would happen if you had to pay rent?" The

client might say, "I'd have to get a job." The therapist responds with, "What would happen if you had to get a job?" and so forth. The goal of the session is to get the client to always ask the question, "What would happen if. . . ?" before he or she takes any action. The exercise demonstrates that all behaviors have consequences and that even the simplest action can create several consequences for the client to consider before acting impulsively.

The second game is called *scenario generation.* This game begins with the therapist asking the client to describe an ideal world or life situation. The game is easiest to play after the client has gone through the goal-setting session outlined above because an ideal world is usually similar to the client's long-term goals. After the client has described his or her ideal world, the therapist asks the client to describe those behaviors that will achieve the ideal world most rapidly and completely. Again, these are usually variations on the short-term goals outlined in the above goal-setting exercises.

Next, the therapist asks the client to take the opposite position. Specifically, the client lists those behaviors that would ensure that he or she would fail to reach the ideal world. Another way of asking this question is to tell the client to list behaviors that would ensure a *worst-nightmare* scenario.

The value of this exercise is that many clients, when asked to play the reverse logic component of the game, realize that their current behaviors are more likely to lead to their worst nightmare than to produce their ideal world.

Self-Expression

Another aspect of social competence involves expressing oneself in a manner that is efficient and easy for others to understand. In the section on training conceptual skills, rule learning and hypothesis testing in Chapter 16, we mentioned that clear expression involves training the client to explain by example, using positive examples first, negative examples second, then focusing in on the relevant aspects of the concept. In addition to this procedure, we recommend another exercise that involves training the client to express a thought with progressively fewer and fewer words. The therapist begins by asking the client to state his or her biggest problem. Next, the client must restate the same problem in fewer words. The client continues this process until the problem has been stated as clearly and with as few words as possible. This exercise works well in a group setting where each group member redefines a problem in his or her own words but by using fewer words than the previous group member.

This process will often result in a redefinition and clarification of a client's biggest problems. For example, one client said that her biggest problem was that she could not go to the mall without spending all of her money on clothes, movies, or jewelry. The next person in the group redefined the problem as, "She can't control her spending." The third person restated the problem as, "poor impulse control." The client with the problem listened and agreed with each of these redefinitions. She also came to the conclusion that the gist of the problem was not that she could not resist buying clothes. It was that she could not control her impulses and that spending was simply the most obvious example of poor impulse control. The value of this exercise is that clients learn to focus on the core elements of their problems. They are also more likely to accept an analysis when it comes from other persons with brain injury rather than from the therapist. In addition, clients learn how to express their ideas in a focused manner.

Appearance

Social competence also encompasses passive characteristics of behavior such as dress and grooming. We encourage clients to dress neatly and in attire that is just slightly better than that for which the situation calls. We have found that clients who dress in this manner have improved temperaments. The more important consequence is that others relate to the client differently than they would if he or she were not so nicely dressed. This becomes apparent when the client goes out into the everyday world. Store owners, police, and passersby on the street treat the client with greater respect and take him or her more seriously.

Listening Skills

Listening skills are a critical component of social competence. The following LISTEN mnemonic helps the client remember these skills:

Look at the person to whom you are speaking. This will usually require some training to get the client to maintain eye contact. The goal is to teach the client to focus on the nonverbal aspects of language that appear in facial expressions.

Interest yourself in the conversation. Tell the client to ask questions about the statements the other person is making; to comment occasionally on the conversation; and to use social fillers such as, "Uh-huh," "I see!," or "Tell me more about that."

Speak less than half the time. This is especially important for persons with brain injury because some aspect of the conversation may trigger a schematic thought which leads to a tangential discussion.

Try not to interrupt or change the topic. This problem arises when some portion of the conversation triggers the client's memory. The client must learn to ask questions or make comments only about the topic at hand.

Evaluate what is said. Clients should be encouraged to question the content; they should not blindly accept it.

Notice body language and facial expression. The therapist can show pictures of individuals in different expressive states and train clients to recognize them. Pease (1981) is a good source for these pictures.

After the client learns the mnemonic, the therapist's next step is to engage in conversation with the client and to videotape the exchange. After about 5 minutes of conversation, the therapist stops the tape and replays it for the client. The purpose of this exercise is to have the client identify which aspects of the LISTEN mnemonic were followed or violated during the conversation.

Personal Time Management

Organization of time involves teaching the client to plan, to set priorities, and to use external aids such as a day planner and to-do lists. It also requires that the client begin to change attitudes about time and social behavior. To begin, the therapist discusses common misconceptions about time with the client, including procrastination, completion anxiety, and common principles of time management. Much of this information may be new to the client and somewhat difficult for him or her to understand.

Procrastination and completion anxiety are two different problems and many clients suffer from both. Procrastination is the problem of failing to initiate a project, whereas completion anxiety is the problem of finishing 95% of a task, but never completing the last 5%. The cause of procrastination is usually fear of committing to a task that seems overwhelming. The cause of completion anxiety is fear of evaluation, that is, the fear that

others will not approve of the final product. It is important for the therapist to discuss these two time management problems with the client and to point them out as they arise.

The following sections describe specific techniques for improving a client's ability to manage time effectively.

Protecting Peak Time. In learning to manage time effectively, a person must typically change the way he or she does things during the day. One important change is to identify peak performance times and protect them from interruption as much as possible. For example, many clients will be fresh during the morning hours and tired at the end of the day. Others will be more efficient at the end of the day or during the evening. The therapist helps clients organize their day so that important tasks are done during their peak hours. This time needs to be protected, which means that the client must ensure that he or she is not interrupted during peak hours. Many clients will have to resist the temptation of talking to friends, sitting in public areas, or making themselves available for conversation during peak time. However, most will be amazed by how many things they can accomplish when there is a clear agenda that they try to meet during peak time.

Using Bits of Time. Another behavioral change required for effective time management involves teaching the client how to use bits of time. The client could perform a productive activity during these times. For the client to use this time effectively, the therapist trains the client to keep different projects or portions of projects at arm's length at all times so that small tasks can be performed during those small time intervals that would normally be spent doing nothing. We recommend clients carry a checkbook, a digital recorder, and a cell phone at all times. Therapy should emphasize training the client to use each of these devices efficiently. It should also teach the client how long it takes to perform various tasks. For example, most phone calls take less than a minute. Writing a check and paying a bill takes fewer than 5 minutes. Listening to a to-do list on a digital recorder takes fewer than 3 minutes. Therapy involves creating simulations in which the client makes phone calls while waiting in line, pays bills while waiting for a meal in a restaurant, or listens to a list of things he or she must complete while walking in a shopping mall.

External Aids. Teaching time management skills is much easier if the therapist first gives the client an appointment calendar that is also a day planner. We recommend a planner that the client can make with software from local office supply stores. Day-Timer and Day Runner corporations sell software that allows the user to produce the inserts for each of their organizers. The therapist should create a planner with specific features. First, the pages for each day should be marked in 2-hour increments and the times listed in the margin of the page for that day. The client can then circle the time of an appointment and write a reminder next to the time.

The calendar also should have blank lined paper next to each day so the client can make notes about directions or write instructions for that day. The goal is to get the client to list all appointments for the following day on the night before. In addition to listing appointments, the client should mark the time of an appointment in the Day-Timer, and write any directions, things to bring to the appointment, or special instructions next to the appointment time.

Organizing the Day. It is important for the client to organize his or her appointments so that there is as little duplication of effort as possible. The software also allows the user to create insert pages for to-do lists. Although these may be useful for some clients, they are seldom necessary because the client can create to-do lists on the lined paper. Regardless of how the client does this, he or she should write a list of tasks to be completed that day and divide them into two groups. The first

group includes two or three tasks that must be done that day. The second group includes those tasks that would be nice to complete but are not crucial to complete that day. Furthermore, the client should check off these tasks after completing them. One advantage of writing out to-do lists is that it forces the client to structure his or her day. In addition, writing out the list the night before forces the client to anticipate all the things he or she will need to do in advance to complete the tasks the following day. Therefore, training involves not only writing out a to-do list but also listing things the client will need to do first, to find, to collect, and to have ready for the next day's activities.

Marking Time. Marking time involves several procedures. First, the client should wear a watch that beeps hourly to provide him or her with an hourly sense of time. Wearing the watch will gradually give the client a clear concept of an hour when he or she hears the watch beep at this regular interval. Another way to help a client keep mental track of time is to ask him or her to estimate how much time has passed since the last time it was mentioned. Also, asking the client to estimate how long it will likely take to finish a task is an effective way to instill a sense of future time.

Summary

This chapter summarized the concept of executive functioning, which is the ability to self-regulate thoughts that direct and organize behavior. Executive skills may be especially difficult to train after a brain injury, particularly when the client may not have developed his or her executive skills before the injury. Nevertheless, persons with brain injury can learn executive skills and the chapter presented specific techniques that have proven effective over the years.

To begin, the therapist should question family members and friends regarding the client's premorbid levels of executive skills. One of the executive skills the therapist should teach is self-monitoring. Techniques for training self-monitoring include charting behaviors, predicting consequences, and videotaping. A method for teaching the executive skill of goal setting was presented along with the GOALS mnemonic that summarized the goal-setting process. For training social competence, two games targeting the ability to think in advance were described, specifically the *What would happen if. . . ?* game and the *scenario generation game*. The importance of passive features of social competence were also discussed, including grooming and dress, listening skills, and clarity of verbal expression. The chapter ended with a discussion of techniques for training time management, including identifying peak performance times, using external aids, marking time, and planning the day's activities on the day before.

References

Anderson-Parenté, J. (1994). A comparison of metacognitive ratings of persons with traumatic brain injury and their families. *NeuroRehabiliation, 4*(3), 168–173.

Baddeley, A. D. (1986). *Working memory.* New York: Basic Books.

Baddeley, A. D. (1990). *Human memory: Theory and practice.* New York: Allyn & Bacon.

Baddeley, A. D. (1998). The central executive: A concept and some misconceptions. *Journal of the International Neuropsychology Society, 4,* 523–526.

Brown, A. L. (1978). Knowing when, where, and how to remember: A problem of metacognition. In R. Glaser (Ed.), *Advances in instructional psychology* (Vol. 1, pp. 77–165). Hillsdale, NJ: Erlbaum.

Case, R. (1992). The role of frontal lobes in the regulation of cognitive development. *Brain and Cognition, 20,* 51–73.

Cicerone, K. (2002). The enigma of executive functioning: Theoretical contributions to therapeutic interventions. In P. J. Eslinger (Ed.), *Neuropsychological interventions* (pp. 246–265). New York: Guilford Press.

Cicerone, K. D., & Wood, T. R. S. (1987). Planning disorder after closed head injury. *Archives of Physical Medicine and Rehabilitation, 68,* 127–132.

Diller, L., & Ben-Yishay, Y. (1987). Outcomes and evidence in neuropsychological rehabilitation in closed-head injury. In H. S. Levin, J. Grafman, & H. M. Eisenberg (Eds.), *Neurobehavioral recovery from head injury.* New York: Oxford University Press.

Duncan, J. (1986). Disorganization of behavior after frontal lobe damage. *Cognitive Neuropsychology, 3,* 279–297.

Harris, J. E., & Morris, P. E. (1984). *Everyday memory actions and absent-mindedness.* New York: Academic Press.

Howieson, D. B., & Lezak, M. D. (1995). Separating memory from other cognitive problems. In A. D. Baddeley, B. A. Wilson, & F. N. Watts (Eds.), *Handbook of memory disorders.* New York: Wiley.

Janowski, J. S., Shimamura, A. P., Kritchevsky, M., & Squire, L. R. (1989). Cognitive impairment following frontal lobe damage and its relevance to human amnesia. *Behavioral Neuroscience, 103,* 548–560.

Lezak, M. (1993). New contributions to the neuropsychological assessment of executive functions. *Journal of Head Trauma Rehabilitation, 8,* 24–31.

Lezak, M. D. (1995). *Neuropsychological assessment* (3rd ed.). New York: Oxford University Press.

McCarthy, R. A., & Warrington, E. K. (1990). *Cognitive neuropsychology: A clinical introduction.* San Diego, CA: Academic Press.

McGlynn, S. M., & Schacter, D. L. (1989). Unawareness of deficits in neuropsychological syndromes. *Journal of Clinical and Experimental Neuropsychology, 11,* 143–205.

Miller, G. A., Galanter, E., & Pribram, K. H. (1960). *Plans and the structure of behavior.* New York: Holt, Rinehart & Winston.

Myake, A., & Shah, P. (Eds.). (1999). *Models of working memory: Mechanisms of active maintenance and executive control.* New York: Cambridge University Press.

Parenté, R., Anderson-Parenté, J. K., & Stapleton, M. (2001). The use of rhymes and mnemonics for teaching cognitive skills to persons with acquired brain injury. *Brain Injury Source, 5*(1), 16–19.

Parenté, R., & Stapleton, M. (1999). Development of a cognitive strategies group for vocational training after traumatic brain injury. *NeuroRehabilitation, 13,* 12–30.

Parkin, A. J. (1998). The central executive does not exist. *Journal of the International Neuropsychology Society, 4,* 518–522.

Pease, A. (1981). *Signals.* Toronto, Canada: Bantam.

Pollens, R., McBratnie, B., & Burton, P. (1988). Beyond cognition: Executive functions in closed head injury. *Cognitive Rehabilitation, 6*(5), 26–33.

Reason, J. (1990). *Human error.* Cambridge, United Kingdom: Cambridge University Press.

Shimamura, A. P., Janowsky, J. S., & Squire, L. R. (1991). What is the role of frontal lobe damage in memory disorders. In H. M. Levin, H. M. Eisenberg, & A. L. Bendton (Eds.), *Frontal lobe function and dysfunction.* New York: Oxford University Press.

Sternberg, R. J. (1985). General intellectual ability. In R. J. Sternberg (Ed.), *Human abilities: An information processing approach*. New York: Freeman.

Welsh, M. C., & Pennington, B. F. (1988). Assessing frontal lobe functioning in children: Views from developmental psychology. *Developmental Neuropsychology, 4,* 199–230.

Ylvisaker, M. (1995, January). *Executive functions and communication following traumatic brain injury.* Paper presented at the annual meetings of the Society for Cognitive Rehabilitation, Albuquerque, NM.

Yody, B. B., Schaub, C., Conway, J., Peters, S., Strauss, D., & Helsinger, S. (2000). Applied behavior management and acquired brain injury: Approaches and assessment. *Journal of Head Trauma Rehabilitation, 15*(4), 1041–1060.

Chapter 20

✄

Physical and
Mental Condition

When a person feels out of sorts, it can affect his or her ability to perform everyday activities such as remembering someone's name, studying, or doing daily errands (Tariot & Weingartner, 1986). Indeed, a person's overall cognitive performance can range from good to poor as a result of his or her physical or mental condition (Davies & Thomson, 1988; Herrmann & Searleman, 1990; Mathews, Davies, Westerman, & Stammers, 2000; Risko, Alvarez, & Fairbanks, 1991). The point of this chapter is to show that a person's memory and thinking can improve markedly and rapidly when he or she exercises, gets enough sleep, and adopts a healthy diet.

Other factors also influence a person's thinking. For example, certain times of the day are better for remembering and thinking (Eysenck & Folkard, 1980); most people describe themselves as either a morning or an evening person. In addition, changes in a person's routine can interfere with his or her attention and memory. Along these lines, physical condition is probably the single most important factor that affects how a person performs incidental and intentional thinking tasks. In short, a person's physical condition largely predisposes his or her intellectual fitness.

Poor physical condition lessens thinking skill because it restricts a person's ability to pay attention and to process information in working memory. Several known physical and emotional conditions may interfere with attention and mental effort. For example, fatigue and depression affect the entire cognitive system. People who are depressed or fatigued have difficulty associating information in memory, organizing unrelated facts, or retrieving information rapidly (Blumenthal & Madden, 1988). They also report difficulty providing an appropriate response to novel information. In general, poor physical or mental constitution reduces the efficiency of the entire multimodal system.

Poor condition may impair memory processes in several ways. First, it lessens the ability of the central processor to rehearse and to attend to the contents of working memory. Because the ideas and images in working memory do not receive adequate attention, they do not produce a salient trace in working memory and the person cannot form appropriate long-term memory retrieval cues. Second, poor condition reduces physiological receptivity and readiness for processing in long-term memory (Herrmann & Searleman, 1990). A person in such condition may only attend and remember when there is a large incentive to do so (Parenté, 1994).

In some cases, a therapy client's physical deficiency may be beyond correction. Therefore, the prescriptions that follow address physical concerns most adults can correct. A heavy dose of common sense combined with a few innovative manipulations can rectify many physical and emotional problems, at least enough to improve the client's thinking skills.

Physical Fitness

Exercise helps the client maintain strength, stamina, and cardiovascular condition (Blumenthal & Madden, 1988; Crook et al., 1986; Kramer et al., 1999). It creates the potential for vigilance in most cognitive tasks. It also helps relieve the client of the "blues," lessens stress, improves sleep, and enhances digestion, all of which help cognition. Exercise reduces anxiety and tension and it is possible that reducing anxiety also improves attention and working memory. A person need not engage in strenuous exercise to improve cognition. A 30-minute walk each day is probably sufficient if the client has not been exercising previously. Any type of aerobic exercise will be beneficial as long as the person exercises for approximately ½ hour per day.

Energy Cycles

People with neurological problems are often less physically and mentally able to meet the challenges of the day. There are certain times of the day and even certain days when thinking is most lucid. For most people, the best time to perform cognitive tasks is between 11 A.M. and 4 P.M. This peak in cognitive performance probably occurs for several reasons. First, most people get more involved with their activities by midday. Second, they gradually lose their sharpness later in the day as general fatigue sets in. Third, their attentiveness varies with daily biological cycles such as body temperature, respiration rate, pulse rate,

and so forth (Wyon, Andersen, & Lundquist, 1979). Cognitive ability also tends to be at its best on Fridays and Saturdays. A peak in cognitive performance occurs on these days, probably because the anticipation of the weekend lifts a person's mood (Eysenck & Folkard, 1980; Folkard & Monk, 1978). Although the typical peak times for cognitive performance occur in the middle of the day and at the end of the week for most people, others may have different peak times. A therapist can determine a client's peak performance times simply by paying attention to when he or she is most alert and most able to think clearly.

A person's routine times for waking and sleeping also affect daily peaks for mental clarity. If a person is "a morning person," who goes to bed early and rises early, he or she will learn most efficiently earlier in the day. An "evening person" learns best in the later afternoon and at night. A person can make the best use of his or her strength by performing cognitive tasks when his or her strength reserves are at their peak. In many cases, this will be in the middle of the day and toward the end of the week. In general, if a person has control over the scheduling of an important meeting, he or she should schedule it for around 10:30 A.M., or a little earlier for a morning person, a little later for an evening person.

In addition most persons with brain injury should schedule meetings on Thursdays or Fridays. When there are anticipated disruptions of daily and weekly cycles, a therapy client and his or her family should try to minimize or at least decrease the number of cognitive tasks the client must carry out. When life does not allow the client to schedule an event at an optimal time, he or she can rely on activities that enhance alertness in general, such as getting enough sleep, exercising regularly, and maintaining a healthy diet.

Disruptions to a client's cycle can diminish his or her cognitive capacity. A client may not get regular sleep after a family dispute, when attempting new employment, or when beginning formal training. Therefore, when there is a shift in a client's cycle, the therapist and family members should allow extra recuperation time before he or she takes on major intellectual tasks.

Sleep

Proper sleep makes a person strong and alert for cognitive tasks (Blagrove & Akehurst, 2000; Idzikowski, 1984; Tilley & Statham, 1989). Getting sufficient sleep before important events such as an exam or an interview is essential for quick and accurate remembering. Most people can recall occasions when they were forced to stay awake much longer than usual. The next day they likely fumbled for words and struggled to remember answers that normally came easily. A person can ensure a good night's sleep if he or she avoids eating and drinking late in the evening, avoids thinking about personal troubles prior to bedtime, and goes to bed at approximately the same time every night.

Eating Habits

Poor nutrition places added burdens on cognition (Goodwin, Goodwin, & Garry, 1983; Kolakowsky, 1997; Silver, 1992). A balanced diet supplies the vitamin levels necessary to guard against deficiencies that produce cognitive deficits. Certain foods or a vitamin supplement must be part of a diet that supports thinking activities. Although there is considerable controversy over whether vitamin supplements enhance cognition, most researchers agree that a good diet is essential for clear thinking. Foods that experts recommend as "cognitively nutritious" include beef, pork, kidneys, liver, fish, shellfish, milk, eggs, cheese, vegetables, kelp, and onions. A recent

study reported that drinking lemonade immediately after studying facilitates later recall, apparently because sugar facilitates the transfer of information from short-term to long-term memory (Foster, Lidder, & Sunram, 1998; Gold, 1987). No matter what foods a person eats, they should be consumed in moderate amounts before a period of intense concentration (Michaud, Musse, Nicholas, & Mejean, 1991; Smith, 1988). Large amounts of food make people sleepy and unable to pay attention.

Irregular eating habits may cause a mild vitamin deficiency. If this is the case, the person should take a supplement. There is no need, however, to take large quantities of vitamins daily. One daily supplement will suffice because most of the supplement is excreted the next day anyway. A person taking a supplement should maintain a level of intake that will eventually enrich the body's naturally occurring vitamins. This will not happen overnight and it may take several months of taking a daily supplement before the appropriate levels are reached. "Cognitively nutritious" vitamins and minerals include choline, B complex vitamins (especially B_1, B_6, and B_{12}), iodine, manganese, folic acid, zinc, and L-tyrosine.

Sensory Difficulties

Poor eyesight and hearing can limit a person's thinking and memory (Cutler & Grams, 1988). Sensory difficulties slow the initial registration of information and make it harder to notice cues that facilitate remembering. Sensory difficulties also may lead others to conclude that a person has cognitive deficiencies. This erroneous conclusion stems from the assumption that cognitive failures occur only because of poor cognition or laziness. Unfortunately, when a client with a sensory deficiency explains to someone that a cognitive failure was due to a sensory deficiency, the other person may regard the client's explanation as an excuse. If the therapist suspects that a client has a sensory deficit, then a medical examination is warranted. If confirmed, the client may have to begin using a prosthetic device such as a hearing aid or prism glasses. Although these devices may impose some inconvenience for the client, the improved performance they enable more than compensates.

Illness

Major and minor illnesses may interfere with cognitive performance because discomfort diminishes attention (Herrmann, 1995). When a person's ability to pay attention is lessened, he or she does not register or remember efficiently. Similarly, he or she does not think or solve problems as readily. Even a minor illness can impair cognitive performance, and obviously, a major illness will usually result in more pronounced cognitive problems. Table 20.1 presents a list of various conditions that are known to adversely affect cognition.

Taking steps to reduce a person's discomfort and symptoms will improve cognitive performance during an illness. If the illness is chronic, there are ways the effect it has on cognition can be minimized. The therapist should check whether a client's treatment or medication is known to affect thinking and memory. Physicians and pharmaceutical companies seldom advertise these types of side effects. Occasionally the side effects are noted on the box or label or in a rapid disclaimer at the end of a television ad.

Any medicine that lowers a client's attention will also reduce how much he or she registers and remembers. If a prescription medicine has this effect, then the client or his or her caregiver should discuss the problem with a physician. Many physicians are unaware of the cognitive contraindications of prescribed and over-the-counter medications. Therefore, if a client is taking any medica-

tion, it is often worthwhile for the therapist to investigate the cognitive impact.

Several illnesses other than head injury impair cognition. As listed in Table 20.1, they include Alzheimer's disease and related diseases, Korsakoff's (alcoholic) syndrome, strokes, and low blood pressure (Khan, 1986; Mayes, 1988; Wilson, 1987). Very low blood pressure, a life-threatening condition, reduces a person's ability to register and remember because it lessens a person's ability to pay attention. Fortunately, the medicines that are used to treat low blood pressure often restore attention and alleviate the cognitive problems that accompany the condition. If a person has both a head injury and one of these cognitive illnesses, the need for specialized treatment is increased (Zasler, 1991).

Noxious Substances

Several substances impair cognitive performance (Stollery, 1988). Perhaps the best known is alcohol, sometimes called the "amnesia food." Marijuana has effects on cognition that are similar to those produced by alcohol. Indeed the pill form of marijuana, which is used in research projects, has an effect that induces a high comparable to several alcoholic drinks. People who take this pill learn a list of words more slowly than people in control groups that have taken a placebo pill (Stephens, Dahlke, & Duka, 1992). Also, when asked to recognize whether a particular digit was included in a series presented moments before, people under the influence of marijuana recognized the digit more slowly than people not under the influence. The bottom line is that cognition is most efficient when a person is sober. If a person with brain injury abused substances before the injury, it may be difficult to persuade him or her to stop usage. The therapist may need to refer the client for drug and alcohol counseling, and

TABLE 20.1
Diseases, Disorders, and Conditions of Ill Health that Impair Cognition

---

Physical Illness

Addison's disease, hyperthyroidism, AIDS (Acquired Immune Deficiency Syndrome), hypothyroidism, hypertension, anoxia, hypotension, arthritis, Korsakoff's disease, attention deficit disorder, learning disorder, brain tumor, migraine headache, cancer, cerebrovascular accident (stroke), multiple sclerosis, sensory disorders, chronic fatigue syndrome, chronic pain, loss of auditory or visual acuity, closed or penetrating head injury, heart condition, dyslexia, syphilis, encephalitis, major surgery, epilepsy, toxic exposure

Gerontological Diseases and Disorders

Age-related memory impairment (Crook, Bartus, Ferris, Whitehouse, Cohen, & Gershon, 1986), dementia (especially Alzheimer's disease), Parkinson's and Huntington's diseases, sensory disorders

Use of Controlled Substances

Alcohol, cannabis, cocaine, hallucinogens, inhalants, opiates, PCP

Minor Illness

Common cold, insomnia, influenza, headache, lack of sleep, physical fatigue

Excessive Use or Neglect of Common Substances

Excess caffeine, malnutrition, overeating, excess nicotine, hypoglycemia

Mental Illness

Manic depression, post-traumatic stress disorder, dissociative disorders, schizophrenia, dysnomia

Infectious Diseases

Boils; encephalitis; gonorrhea; pneumonia; tuberculosis; chicken pox; hepatitis; meningitis; measles; influenza; common cold; poliomyelitis; athlete's foot; ringworm; amoebic dysentery; intestinal infection; malaria; African sleeping sickness; worms in the blood, intestine, liver, or lung; flukes, tapeworms

Noninfectious Diseases

Degenerative diseases, arthritis, cardiovascular diseases, cancer, hypertension, hypotension, stroke, tumors, epilepsy, multiple sclerosis, Parkinson's disease, Pick or Addison's diseases, hormonal diseases

Congenital Diseases

Down syndrome, hemophilia, sickle-cell anemia, Huntington's disease

Immunological Diseases

Allergies, AIDS

Nutritional and Environmental Diseases

Anemia, beriberi, kwashiorkor, pellagra, scurvy, drug abuse, pollution, radiation, toxic waste

---

even require regular drug testing as a condition for further treatment.

Stimulants

It is a common belief that stimulants found in tea, coffee, soda, and tobacco make a person more attentive and, thus, better able to perform cognitive tasks. However, even common stimulants like coffee and tea can impair cognition, more so for persons who have had a brain injury. Our experience has been that low doses of stimulants may enliven a person's spirits and increase attention span. But in high doses, stimulants may also create hyperactivity that keeps a person from paying attention.

It has sometimes been assumed that nicotine facilitates memory, presumably because it may make a person alert while performing a cognitive task (Erikson et al., 1985; Peeke & Peeke, 1984; Wittenborn, 1988). However, recent research indicates very clearly that nicotine can impair memory considerably, as much as that which occurs from a few alcoholic drinks (Spilich, June, & Renner, 1992). Nonsmokers are quicker than smokers at remembering lists of digits. Moreover, nonsmokers score higher on tests of memory for a written passage, digit span, reproduction of visual patterns, and learning pairs of words. We recommend that if a person smokes, then he or she should not do so before a cognitive task. Although there are exceptions to the general rule, our review of the literature indicates that a person is usually better off not using stimulants. Stimulants may come in handy for fighting fatigue, but they may also exact a cost. Although they may improve performance on a well-learned skill, they may also retard a person's ability to learn a new skill.

Summary and Recommendations

Good physical condition is one of the necessary ingredients for good cognition. A person can avoid a performance slump caused by poor physical condition by following some common-sense guidelines:

1. *Limit discomfort due to minor illness.* Discomfort limits attention and concentration. A person should avoid studying, remembering, and engaging in important cognitive tasks when ill.

2. *Eliminate noxious or addictive substances.* These substances impair a person's ability to pay attention and can upset his or her emotional balance. The most common of these substances are caffeine (Bowen & Larson, 1993; Bowyer, Humphreys, & Revelle, 1983) and nicotine (Peeke & Peeke, 1984).

3. *Follow a well-balanced diet.* Overeating makes a person drowsy; moderate eating keeps a person more alert.

4. *Get enough sleep and adhere to consistent cycles of wakefulness and sleep.* Sufficient sleep and consistent sleep cycles are essential for effective thinking and memory.

5. *Determine energy peaks.* Figure out whether a person is a morning or an evening person and have him or her perform the most difficult tasks at that time.

6. *Stay in shape.* Physical fitness predisposes good cognition. Good physical condition also creates self-esteem.

7. *Exercise the mind.* Daily mental activity such as reading, playing cards or board games, taking courses, or doing jobs that require mental activity improve mental skill.

References

Blagrove, M., & Akehurst, L. (2000). Effect of sleep loss on confidence-accuracy relationships for reasoning and eyewitnessing memory. *Journal of Experimental Psychology: Applied, 6,* 59–73.

Blumenthal, J. A., & Madden, D. J. (1988). Effects of aerobic exercise training, age, and physical fitness on memory-search performance. *Psychology and Aging, 3,* 280–285.

Bowen, J. D., & Larson, E. B. (1993). Drug-induced cognitive impairment: Defining the problem and finding solutions. *Drugs and Aging, 3,* 349–357.

Bowyer, P. A., Humphreys, M. S., & Revelle, W. (1983). Arousal and recognition memory: The effects of impulsivity, caffeine, and time on task. *Personality and Individual Differences, 4,* 41–49.

Crook, T., Bartus, R. T., Ferris, S. H., Whitehouse, P., Cohen, G. D., & Gershon, S. (1986). Age-associated memory impairment: Proposed diagnostic criteria and measures of clinical change, Report of a National Institute of Mental Health Work Group. *Developmental Neuropsychology, 2,* 261–276.

Cutler, S. J., & Grams, A. E. (1988). Correlates of self-reported everyday memory problems. *Journal of Gerontology, 43,* 582–590.

Davies, G. M., & Thomson, D. M. (1988). *Memory in context: Context in memory.* Chichester, United Kingdom: Wiley.

Erikson, G. C., Hager, L. B., Houseworth, C., Dugan, J., Petros, T., & Beckwith, B. E., (1985). The effects of caffeine on memory for word lists. *Physiology and Behavior, 35,* 47–51.

Eysenck, M. W., & Folkard, S. (1980). Personality, time of day, and caffeine: Some theoretical and conceptual problems in Revelle et al. *Journal of Experimental Psychology: General, 109,* 32–41.

Folkard, S., & Monk, R. (1978). Time of day effects in immediate and delayed memory. In M. Gruneberg, P. E. Morris, & R. N. Sykes (Eds.), *Practical aspects of memory.* London: Academic Press.

Foster, J. K., Lidder, P. G., & Sunram, S. I. (1998). Glucose and memory: Fractionation of enhancement effects? *Psychopharmacology, 137,* 259–270.

Gold, P. E. (1987). Sweet memories. *American Scientist, 75,* 151–155.

Goodwin, J. S., Goodwin, J. M., & Garry, P. J. (1983). Association between nutritional status and cognitive functioning in a healthy elderly population. *Journal of the American Medical Association, 249,* 2917–2940.

Herrmann, D. J. (1995). *Illness and cognition.* (Report prepared for the associate director for research and methodology of the National Center for Health Statistics.) Hyattsville, MD: National Center for Health Statistics.

Herrmann, D. J., & Searleman, A. (1990). A multi-modal approach to memory improvement. In G. H. Bower (Ed.), *Advances in learning and motivation* (pp. 178–205). New York: Academic Press.

Idzikowski, C. (1984). Sleep and memory. *British Journal of Psychology, 75,* 439–449.

Khan, A. U. (1986). *Clinical disorders of memory.* New York: Plenum.

Kolakowsky, S. A. (1997). Improving cognition through the use of nutrients, drugs, and other cognitive-enhancing substances. *Cognitive Technology, 2,* 44–54.

Kramer, A. F., Hahn, S., Cohen, N. J., Banich, M. T., McAuley, E., Harrison, C. R., et al. (1999). Aging, fitness, and neurocognitive function. *Nature, 400,* 418–419.

Mathews, G., Davies, R. D., Westerman, S. J., & Stammers, R. B. (2000). *Human performance: Cognition, stress, and individual differences.* Philadelphia: Psychology Press.

Mayes, A. R. (1988). *Human organic memory disorders.* Cambridge, United Kingdom: Cambridge University Press.

Michaud, C., Musse, N., Nicholas, J. P., & Mejean, L. (1991). Effects of breakfast size on short-term memory, concen-

tration, mood, and blood glucose. *Journal of Adolescent Health, 12,* 53–57.

Parenté, R. (1994). Transfer and generalization of cognitive skill after traumatic brain injury. *NeuroRehabilitation, 4,* 25–35.

Peeke, S. C., & Peeke, H. V. (1984). Attention, memory, and cigarette smoking. *Psychopharmacology, 84,* 205–216.

Risko, V. J., Alvarez, M. C., & Fairbanks, M. M. (1991). External factors that influence study. In R. F. Flippo & D. C. Caverly (Eds.), *Teaching reading and study strategies at the college level.* Newark, DE: International Reading Association.

Silver, A. J. (1992). Nutritional aspects of memory dysfunction. In J. Morely, R. M. Coe, R. Strong, & G. T. Grossberg (Eds.), *Memory functions in aging and aging-related disorders.* New York: Springer.

Smith, A. (1988). Effects of meals on memory and attention. In M. M. Gruneberg, P. E. Morris, & R. N. Sykes (Eds.), *Practical aspects of memory: Current research and issues* (Vol. 2, pp. 477–482). New York: Wiley.

Spilich, G., June, L., & Renner, J. (1992). Cigarette smoking and cognitive performance. *British Journal of Addiction, 87,* 1313–1326.

Stephens, D. N., Dahlke, F., & Duka, T. (1992). Consequences of drug and ethanol use on cognitive function. In L. J. Thal, W. H. Moos, & E. R. Gamzu (Eds.), *Cognitive disorders: Pathophysiology and treatment.* New York: Dekker.

Stollery, B. (1988). Neurotoxic exposure and memory function. In M. M. Gruneberg, P. E. Morris, & R. N. Sykes (Eds.), *Practical aspects of memory: Current research and issues* (Vol. 2, pp. 242–247). New York: Wiley.

Tariot, P., & Weingartner, H. (1986). A psychobiological analysis of cognitive failures. *Archives of General Psychiatry, 43,* 1183–1188.

Tilley, A., & Statham, D. (1989). The effect of prior sleep on retrieval. *Acta Psychologica, 70,* 199–203.

Wilson, B. A. (1987). *The rehabilitation of memory.* New York: Guilford.

Wittenborn, J. R. (1988). Assessment of the effects of drugs on memory. *Psychopharmacology, 6,* 67–78.

Wyon, D. P., Andersen, B., & Lundquist, G. R. (1979). The effects of moderate heat stress on mental performance. *Scandinavian Journal of Work Environment and Health, 5,* 352–361.

Zasler, N. D. (1991). Pharmacological aspects of cognitive function following traumatic brain injury. In J. S. Kreutzer & P. H. Wehman (Eds.), *Cognitive rehabilitation for persons with traumatic brain injury* (pp. 87–94). Baltimore: Brookes.

Chapter 21

❧

Psychotherapy

Emotional discord affects virtually every aspect of the multimodal system. Because emotions affect attention, they can reduce a person's ability to absorb and to retain new information (Grattan & Ghahramanlou, 2002; Watts, MacLeod, & Morris, 1988; Wells & Mathews, 1994). Therefore, anything that helps to repair a person's emotional state will improve his or her concentration, memory, and ability to control and to allocate thinking and processing (Baum, Cohen, & Hall, 1993; Hertel, 1994). Medication may be necessary in situations where a person is in a great deal of emotional distress, and in some cases, the problems can be remedied with group and individual therapy. Talking therapies may be especially difficult for persons with brain injury because of their inability to abstract, to prioritize, and to anticipate the consequences of their behaviors. Moreover, there are few standardized treatment models for emotional problems that result from traumatic brain injury although numerous papers have been written that describe psychotherapy interventions after brain injury (Cicerone, 1989; Laatsch, 1996; Langer, 1992; Langer & Padrone, 1992; Lewis, 1991; Morris & Bleiberg, 1986; Prigatano & Klonoff, 1988).

We assert that many of the emotional problems that a person with brain injury may experience result from a disruption of the multimodal system. This chapter begins with a discussion of negative emotional factors that affect the system, then summarizes various approaches that have been proposed as models of psychotherapy for persons with brain injury. The chapter ends with a discussion of various therapy techniques that may improve a client's emotional state.

Negative Emotional Factors

Disorientation

A hectic and harried lifestyle can create a certain amount of disorientation and confusion (Reason, 1988), which, in turn, impairs cognition. It lowers the level of attention to a person's immediate surroundings, and it lessens his or her ability to focus attention. Alternatively, an extremely predictable and routinized lifestyle can also lower attention and ability to concentrate. Sometimes a person's efficiency lessens because he or she becomes too relaxed and adept at a task. Experience and practice with most tasks creates a skill that becomes so automatic that a person may cease to pay full attention when performing the task. As attention wanes or wanders, errors increase, possibly resulting in drastic consequences. For example, airplane accidents are sometimes caused by experienced pilots who inadvertently throw a switch in the wrong direction (Reason & MyCielska, 1983). Most people can recall times when they started to drive off in their car then realized that the safety brake was still engaged.

Environmental factors also affect a person's ability to concentrate. There are optimum levels of noise and physical comfort for performing cognitive tasks. Total silence and maximum comfort are probably not the best conditions for sustained or optimal thinking. Neither are tight-fitting clothes, uncomfortable furniture, and extremely bright lights. In general, slight discomfort will make a person more alert than will coziness. Coziness provides a feeling of safety, but it may lead a person to fall asleep. It is therefore reasonable to suggest that choosing environments and modes of dress that are not too comfortable ensures that a person will be able to maintain concentration for longer periods of time.

Stress

Stress has known adverse effects on thinking and memory. For example, nurses who work in high-stress situations, such as an intensive care ward, experience more cognitive failures than those who work on routine wards (Broadbent, Cooper, Fitzgerald, & Parks, 1982). Women scheduled to have mastectomies experience a greater number of cognitive and absent-mindedness errors than usual in the period just before surgery (Reason, 1988; Reason & Lucas, 1984). Although stress can be debilitating, most people need a minimal level of stress to function (Spielberger, Gonzales, & Fletcher, 1979). However, most persons with brain injury experience enormous stress while undergoing rehabilitation; such high levels of stress and emotional problems at home greatly slow the therapy process and can limit the extent and rate of recovery. Consequently, the therapist must take whatever steps necessary to reduce clients' stress levels, without eliminating all sources of stress. It is a balancing act for the therapist to maintain a minimal level of stress that is motivating but not overwhelming. For example, the therapist should provide constant feedback to the client and encourage improvement as compared to the last measured therapy task. Family members can let the client know that they have expectations for continued effort in treatment, and they can create tangible incentives for reaching therapy goals.

Relaxation relieves stress and decreases distractibility that interferes with cognitive performance. A person with brain injury can benefit from incorporating into his or her daily routine a variety of ways to relax, such as taking naps, reminiscing with a friend, listening to music, watching TV, and so forth. Exercise, another relaxing activity, not only reduces stress, it usually improves a person's mood. Relaxation techniques have been found to facilitate thinking and memory in the elderly (Yesavage, Rose, & Spiegel, 1982; Yesavage & Sheikh, 1988). Some published research indicates that hatha-yoga improves cognition. To the extent that these exercises help a person to relax, they can certainly provide some benefit. A person need not spend a great deal of money on exercise machines or membership in a health spa. Simple activities like stretching are just as effective.

Depression and Mood Swings

Persons with brain injury typically experience a wide range of moods that may fluctuate hourly or daily. Because moods and emotional states have such a pronounced effect on memory and cognition, it is important for the therapist to assess the extent of a client's mood swings before attempting treatment. In most cases, severe depression or wild mood swings impair memory and thinking.

Depression, whatever its intensity, impairs cognitive performance (Hertel, 1994; Williams, Watts, MacLeod, & Mathews, 1988). The slightly negative mood a person feels after someone insults him or her diminishes the ability to pay attention. Depression weakens cognitive performance because a person becomes preoccupied with unhappy thoughts, which lowers his or her attention level and reduces his or her capacity to focus attention (Hertel, 1994; Yesavage & Sheikh, 1988). Furthermore, depression can limit a person's ability to organize, which, in turn, slows absorption of novel information and the ability to retrieve stored information.

Depression weakens cognition so much that some doctors regard cognitive failure as a major indicator of clinical depression. Besides stress, most persons with brain injury experience depression periodically, if not continuously, during recovery. Thus, depression slows the cognitive rehabilitation process and it may limit the degree of recovery. Antidepressant drugs or psychotherapy can restore cognitive abilities and improve overall cognitive functioning (Watts, 1988).

Attitudes

The attitude of a person with brain injury toward his or her recovery is, perhaps, the best predictor of improvement. Part of the rehabilitation process is for clients to develop accurate self-perceptions about postinjury cognitive functioning. Maintaining a positive attitude through rehabilitation is especially difficult because the efficiency of a client's thinking skills varies from day to day and month to month due to changes in brain

physiology and the extent and intensity of rehabilitation. Also, a person with brain injury must develop a new self-concept and learn a new role within their social network. All of these factors force clients through an often unbearable attitude adjustment. Most clients have deeply rooted attitudes about cognition that stem from their memory of their ability to do certain tasks in the past. Such attitudes are not easily changed, but it is possible. Herrmann (1990) described several attitudes that affect cognitive performance. These are discussed in detail following.

A client's attitudes about the content of a cognitive task may affect his or her willingness to participate in it. Certain kinds of task content are especially difficult for some clients to register and remember. Certain kinds of problems are more difficult for some clients to solve. Each kind of task, therefore, requires a special approach so that the client's attitude about it can be altered to facilitate cognition. Problems with task content usually stem from information that is uninteresting or emotionally stressful. For example, a client may find that playing the card games discussed in Chapter 10 is boring. However, when the therapist offers a monetary incentive for participation (see Chapter 23), the client may quickly adopt a very positive attitude about the games. Incentives can be structured such that the client rarely achieves them. Nevertheless, the client will play the games with much more energy and enthusiasm than would occur without the incentive.

Another aspect of a client's attitude is his or her level of interest in rehabilitation tasks. Boring information is hard for most people to register and remember. A person will often forget something that someone said because he or she is uninterested in it. By pointing out the usefulness of the information and showing how it can help the client in some way, the therapist can override the boring aspects of the task. The person with brain injury, therefore, should learn to ask questions such as, "How is this information useful to me?" If the information has no use, then the therapist should rethink whether the task or the material is appropriate for the client. This does not mean that the therapist should only choose therapies that the client wants to do, but it does mean that the therapist should choose treatments that are relevant to the client's needs and that can be modified so that he or she wants to do them. For example, asking a client to do mental word problems may not be interesting to the client, whereas taking him or her to the mall to practice making change for purchases may be much more interesting and motivating.

Physical Causes of Emotional Problems

Inability To Process Nonverbal Communication

The deficits that occur after injury to the right hemisphere of the brain often include emotional volatility. However, persons with brain injury also have difficulty processing the nonverbal aspects of language that are carried in voice inflections, facial expressions, and body language (Borod, Koff, Perlman-Lorch, & Nicholas, 1986). These problems may exacerbate their emotional state because of frustration resulting from their inability to "read" social or interpersonal situations. Moreover, it may be difficult for them to express their emotions through facial expressions or voice inflections. Of the four avenues of communication—facial expression, body language, tone of voice, and message content—a person with brain injury may not be able to process the first three. That is, the person must depend on the content of a conversation and can no longer integrate the meaning that is carried via voice, face, or body.

Depressive and Anxiety Disorders

Depressive and anxiety disorders after brain injury often occur when the damage is to the subcortical areas and the amount of depression is related to the proximity of the injury to the frontal lobes (Starkstein, Robinson, & Price, 1987). Brain injury in the right hemisphere often produces depression although the person may not readily display outward signs of depression because this type of injury also reduces a person's ability to express emotion (House, Dennis, Warlow, Hawton, & Molyneux, 1990). Therefore, a person with brain injury may not only have difficulty perceiving nonverbal information, but also have difficulty expressing emotion by any means other than the spoken word. Because problems with speech often accompany brain injury, many persons with brain injury may be left with few means of communication.

Emotional Volatility

Rapidly fluctuating emotions are the rule rather than the exception after traumatic brain injury. Indeed, brain lesions can produce a vast array of emotional problems: aggression (Pincus, 1980), anxiety (Strauss, Risser, & Jones, 1982), flattened affect (Poeck, 1969), libido changes (Cogen, Antunes, & Correll, 1979; Taylor, 1969), and rage (Zeman & King, 1958). A previously mild-mannered person may become overly aggressive. Often, family members will say that the client is no longer the same person he or she was before the injury. These perceptions may frighten the client who may be unaware of the changes. This combination of factors may conspire to create an uncomfortable home situation. The situation often feeds upon itself and eventually results in divorce or a breakup of the family unit, loss of friends, social isolation, and increased depression.

Psychotherapy Issues in Persons with Brain Injury

Suppression, Repression, and Denial

Some memories are so threatening that a person does not allow them to surface (Erdelyi & Goldberg, 1979). Horrible memories such as the details of the client's accident are usually repressed although the emotions that are connected with these memories may surface unpredictably. Indeed, they may intrude into a client's consciousness, without warning, and cause embarrassment. For example, several of our clients cannot recall the details of their auto accidents, especially if they were somehow at fault.

Repressed memories usually cannot be remembered at will. Repression removes awareness of the information, blocking it from a person's normal means of remembering. Repressed memories are held at bay and a person does not allow them to surface. However, when some aspect of the memory breaks through the person's defenses, it usually has unpredictable emotional consequences. For example, we can recall several clients who would begin crying during a session for no apparent reason. When questioned, they said that some aspect of the session had triggered their uncontrolled crying reaction but the cause was unclear.

Suppressed memories are usually connected to moderately emotional situations. These emotions can lead a person to forget temporarily or to distort the memory of an aversive situation. In general, suppression is a common reaction to negative feelings or fear. It insulates the person against feelings of incompetence, social awkwardness, and various forms of physical pain. For example, we notice that attendance in our memory group declines sharply when the members are warned that the next session will involve either individual presentations or videotaping. When asked to explain their absences, most of the participants say that they forgot to attend that week. Many of the same clients forget dental appointments or urinalysis tests.

Unfortunately, there have been few discussions of cognitive rehabilitation therapy techniques for dealing with repression and suppression; however, we do make the following suggestions. One general approach for dealing with repression is to refocus the client so that his or her current situation is more acceptable. This is actually a form of problem solving in which the current situation is viewed not as a problem but as an opportunity for change. For example, many clients say that their accident was really a wake-up call that averted an early death due to drugs or alcohol. Refocusing a client on this aspect of the accident may help to make the current situation tolerable. Obviously, it is not always possible or appropriate to focus on the positive. However, it is important for the client to realize that something good arises out of every negative circumstance. Therefore, whenever possible, the therapist should point out any positive aspect of a negative event.

When using this technique, the therapist should bear in mind that negative feelings will remain even if the person can focus on some of the good aspects of a basically negative experience. Thus, although adopting a positive view may reduce the emotional consequences of repression, these problems may still occur with unpredictable frequency and severity.

One fascinating offshoot of this technique is that, with many persons with brain injury, repressed memories return only after the individuals come to accept the reality of their current life. This is perhaps the most valuable aspect of the therapy because it facilitates the client actually working through the cause of his or her emotional volatility. In that sense, talking about how a client's life has changed for the better can greatly accelerate his or her overall recovery. The downside to this technique is that the therapist must be ready to deal with a possible catharsis or emotional breakdown when the person with brain injury finally remembers the details of the injury. The therapist should coordinate with a psychiatrist or clinical psychologist when using this technique.

One way to deal with suppression is to keep it from causing more negative consequences. For example, one person with brain injury had a meeting with the Internal Revenue Service for an audit of his unpaid taxes since the time of the accident. He suppressed the meeting because it was going to be unpleasant. However, missing the meeting because he suppressed it led to even greater problems. By setting up backup systems to ensure that negative consequences are not worsened, the client can reduce the effects of suppression. If the client takes deliberate steps to face the negative condition, then suppression will be less likely to cause further problems. For example, this same client eventually asked a family member to take him to his next appointment in case he forgot to go on his own.

Disturbing information that is not suppressed may be distorted or simply denied. The distortion may occur either during the initial experience or later during retention. The function of distortion or denial is to make a cognition consistent with a person's self-image, goals, or fears (Greenwald, 1980, 1981). Distortions are difficult to assess because they protect a person's self-image. Some distortion in cognition is normal, but an excessive amount can lead to maladjustment. Distortion, denial, and repression protect a person from realities that may be unacceptable. It is, therefore, difficult to deal with these psychological states in a client because the therapist risks an emotional upheaval with unpredictable consequences.

The first step in therapy is to determine if the person has suppressed or repressed a memory or is in a state of denial. Again, repressed memories are difficult to handle because of their potential emotional impact. For example, we dealt with one client who described his accident as, "They told me I was driving a car." After we questioned him further, he said, "They told me everyone was killed." After several sessions, he experienced an emotional breakdown as he recalled the details of his accident. He had repressed the fact that he was driving the car, he was drunk, and he had hit a woman and her child who were crossing the street. He experienced a near-psychotic breakdown when he recalled the vivid impression of the look on the woman's and the child's faces just before the car made impact.

Repressed memories will typically come out more freely once the client comes to trust the therapist. If the client is part of a group, repression lessens when other group members share their experiences freely. Repressed memories are usually things of which the client is not proud, or that are embarrassing. For example, one client was assaulted in a park and recalled that he had attempted to fight off his attackers before being hit on the head, which caused his brain injury. He had some training in the martial arts; however, when he tried to use a well-practiced kick, he slipped and sprained his ankle. Another client recalled that just before his auto accident, he was intimately engaged with his girlfriend, which led to a temporary inattention to his driving.

Denial is also a common defense mechanism. It is, however, difficult to distinguish denial from lack of awareness. Either problem can be quite persistent. When a person is in a state of denial or is unaware of his or her problem, we often ask other group members to offer their opinions concerning that individual's state of mind. The group members' opinions are usually more accepted as compared to those offered by the therapist. The purpose is to provide the person with consistent observations from his or her peers.

Denial or lack of awareness may be persistent and lasting. For example, we have videotaped several persons with brain injury who have not performed well on various tasks. When shown the videotape, their denial or lack of awareness was so pronounced that they said, "That's not me." Once again, it is important for the therapist to realize that denial or lack of awareness is a defense mechanism that signals emotional fragility. If the problem persists, the therapist should realize that the survivor is not yet ready to deal with the issues that have been raised.

Langer (1999) posed some fundamental questions that are important for the therapist to answer when dealing with a client's denial or lack of awareness. First, the therapist should find the source or etiology of unawareness. Does it result from a physical problem (e.g., chronic pain, physical immobility), an environmental problem (e.g., living arrangement), a preexisting problem (e.g., learning disability, medical condition), or a substance abuse problem? Second, the therapist should determine the content of the client's awareness. That is, does the person with brain injury understand the nature of the injury, the details of how it occurred, and the implications of the damage? If the person is aware, then the final question for the therapist to answer concerns the level of the client's awareness. Some clients have partial or implicit awareness (Kihlstrom & Tobias, 1991; Schacter & Prigatano, 1991). The therapist should determine how much of the client's awareness is masked by depression (Folks, Freeman, Sokol, & Thurstin, 1988; Havik & Maeland, 1986). It is crucial for the therapist to answer these questions before attempting an intervention. Poor timing of an intervention can retard or even reverse a client's progress.

Anger Management

Temper control is commonly cited as a major problem after brain injury (Mateer & Williams, 1991). Therapy in such cases usually involves teaching appropriate responses to common anger-provoking situations, identifying triggers that instigate emotional reactions, and discussing the consequences of uncontrolled anger-based behaviors. Once a client can associate appropriate responses with angering situations, the therapist can begin focused treatment to ensure self-calming behavior in these situations. This is accomplished with several techniques such as watching videos on anger management, role-playing specific likely events, and discussing strategies for removing oneself from the anger-causing event or person. Parenté, Anderson-Parenté, and Stapleton (2001) developed the following rhyming mnemonic for training anger control that has been used successfully with many persons with brain injury. The ANGER sequence is discussed in this section.

Anticipate those events that trigger your rage

Never act in anger — act your age

Go through the CALM sequence — return assuaged

Evaluate the situation in retrospect

Review how you coped — reflect

The A teaches the client to attend to those aspects of his or her behavior or physiology that usually precede an angry outburst. These might include tension in the jaw muscles, clenched fists, rapid breathing, or high-pitched rapid speech. Also, the client should remember that different situations can also create stress. For example, one client reported that he was most likely to become angry when he could not figure out how to do something simple around his home, such as using the TV remote or making a long-distance phone call.

The N letter is, perhaps, the most important portion of the entire mnemonic. Most persons with brain injury have difficulty controlling their impulses. When angered, a client may have difficulty controlling the impulse to strike out at what he or she perceives to be the source of stress. The client must remember that this type of impulsive behavior usually creates more problems than it solves.

The letter G reminds the client to go through the CALM sequence. Each letter in the following CALM sequence reminds the client of a behavior that will reduce his or her anger:

Call someone you know

Allow your emotions to flow

Leave the situation—avoid the fray

Move about—get out of anger's way

This CALM sequence involves other people, preferably a trusted friend who is familiar with the client's situation and who is willing to listen in times of stress. The friend should encourage the client to let out any pent-up emotions in his or her presence. Both the client and friend should make every effort to leave the situation that is causing the stress and to walk around or move about. Removing the source of the stress along with mild physical activity will help dissipate the anger.

At this point the client returns to the E portion of the ANGER mnemonic. After the client is calm, he or she can evaluate the situation in retrospect, that is, make a rational assessment of what it was that provoked the rage. Finally, for R, the client can review any coping mechanisms that may have helped him or her control the anger. Reflection allows the client to use each angering episode as a learning experience.

Substance Abuse

Alcohol and drug abuse has been generally linked with acquired brain injury (Boyle,

Vella, & Moloney, 1991; Kreutzer, Wehman, Harris, Burns, & Young, 1991). However, therapists who work with persons with TBI often have limited knowledge of how to identify these problems or how to assess the relationship between substance abuse, emotional state, and problems with cognition.

Treatment that focuses on developing positive alternatives to drugs (Tucker, Vuchinich, & Harris, 1985; Vaillant, 1983) and feelings of satisfaction with life (Marlatt & Gordon, 1985; Polich, Armor, & Braiker, 1981) is often effective. Heinemann et al. (1995) experimentally tested two models of substance abuse treatment: the Skills-Based Substance Abuse Prevention Counseling and the Systematic Motivational Counseling models. The Skills-Based Substance Abuse Prevention Counseling model (Langley, 1995) includes four stages: evaluation, motivational enhancement, coping skills training, and generalization of skills. The therapist presents the client with information about the interaction between substance abuse and the client's individual problems. The purpose is to create awareness in the client of the fact that the substances may inhibit acquisition of personal goals. The client also learns to manage high-risk situations and learns coping strategies for use in these situations. Evaluation of this model showed that its most effective aspects were to help the client conceptualize the problem, set feasible goals, discuss the costs of substance abuse, and receive training that was personally relevant.

Systematic Motivational Counseling is based on the concept that motivation to remain substance free is crucial for successful treatment (Cox & Klinger, 1988). The goal is to shift the balance for the client so that nonchemical alternatives outweigh the incentives provided by the substances to which the person was addicted. The therapist begins by interviewing the client using a structured questionnaire (Cox, Klinger, & Blount, 1996). The therapist and the client then discuss goal setting, session-to-session goals, and long-term goals. The overall focus is to get the client to disengage from inappropriate goals and to form a new hierarchy of incentives. Evaluation of this model showed approximately 40% of persons with brain injury abstained from drug use during treatment and 20% maintained their abstinence after treatment.

Conducting Psychotherapy After Brain Injury

Langer (1999) had several suggestions for therapists working with clients who have emotional issues after brain injury. When the client has some awareness of his or her limitations, the therapist may be able to build on this structure by strengthening the client's ego mechanism. Langor also pointed out the importance of establishing a therapeutic alliance in which the client trusts the therapist's judgment and is willing to implement suggestions. This occurs most often when the therapist prioritizes the client's problems and works on those that the client feels are most important. Information that the therapist presents to the client must be measured to determine if he or she is ready to receive it, and it must be relevant in the sense that it provides information about the premorbid event, explains existing limitations, and creates hope or optimism about the future (Janis & Mann, 1977).

Assessing Potential for Successful Psychotherapy

Persons with brain injury often do not notice obvious associations between their behavior and its consequences. This may be the result of lack of awareness, posttraumatic stress, fantasies, or loss of sense of self (Horowitz, 1983). Other issues include the fact that denial, defenses, and lack of awareness serve a purpose: they protect clients from intrusive thoughts that cause stress and anxiety. Ridding clients of denial leaves them vulnerable to the issues that created it. To deal with those issues, the therapist must first determine whether a client has the intellectual resources to understand abstract descriptions of the recovery process. Moreover, if the client accepts the therapist's descriptions of his or her deficits, will the client remember the description? Will these descriptions create more problems than they solve? If the client is given potentially negative information (e.g., test results that indicate serious cognitive impairment), can he or she accept it or will he or she react violently? When provided with compensatory strategies, will the client use them? Each of these questions should be asked and answered before the therapist can provide a useful program of psychotherapy. Along these lines, Prigatano and Schacter (1991) and Simon et al. (1991) have developed excellent questionnaires that a therapist can use to assess client awareness of disability after traumatic brain injury.

Group Psychotherapy

Several authors have discussed the value of group treatment for patients with brain injury (Ben-Yishay & Diller, 1981; Deaton, 1991; Parenté & Stapleton, 1999; Prigatano et al., 1986). Relative to individual treatment, group therapy is inexpensive, which may be important to those facilities that are accountable to managed care companies. It also gives clients a chance to voice their concerns in the company of sympathetic ears, and receive advice from other members who have experienced similar difficulties in the past. Finally, the group may provide a socializing opportunity for clients.

There are, however, several disadvantages to group therapy. Many clients may not want to share their feelings publicly. The group sessions may degenerate into complaint sessions. Some group members may be too blunt with others or provide indelicate or ill-timed feedback. A client may not feel that the discussion in any given session is relevant to his or her needs. In general, though, group psychotherapy can be an effective and efficient means of treatment.

Emotional Factors That Affect Memory

So far, we have discussed the effect that emotions have on the behavior of persons with brain injury. However, the client's emotional state creates a ripple that affects many more aspects of the client's everyday life. The effect of emotions on memory has been reasonably well researched and it is possible to extrapolate from this research some general therapeutic principles. We discuss this research and the implications it has for psychotherapy for persons with brain injury in this chapter.

To some extent, a client's mood can serve as a cue for facilitating recall (Leight & Ellis, 1981). In general, it is useful to consider mood as a context that can be used to help the client retrieve information because the ability to remember may depend on returning to the state of mind in which the information was originally perceived (Bower, 1981). Several authors have proposed network theories of memory that include emotional components (Anderson & Bower, 1973; Collins & Loftus, 1975; Schneider & Shiffrin, 1977). The models assume that memories are stored as nodes in a network. The nodes are connected via association. Activating any node initiates part of a memory and the spreading activation causes complete recall. Ideas are the collections of nodes and their associations.

Bower (1981) also suggested that emotional nodes are part of a person's network of ideas. Emotional experiences are stored along with semantic and procedural information, and similar emotional experiences later evoke the associated memories. Accordingly, if a person with brain injury is depressed, then most of the information he or she learns is stored in a depressed context. Consequently, the information may come to mind only when the person becomes depressed again. It may not be accessible if the person is neutral or happy. Retrieval of information depends on a return to the state in which an event was originally experienced. If the therapist can reinstate the client's original mood, then the client may be able to retrieve information that would otherwise be unavailable. The client can learn to recall information by first asking the question, "In what mood was I when I learned this?"

The therapist may be able to teach the client to monitor his or her mood while learning novel information so that the memory of the mood can be stored along with the event and used later as a potential cue for recall. For example, one client was having difficulty remembering the details of discussions with his wife until he began to categorize the discussions by their emotional content. When asked how he felt about their conversations, he was able to recall many more of the details than he could when he did not attend to the emotional tone.

A client's emotions and moods can also affect the quality of learning. In general, learning is easier when the material fits the client's mood. For example, depressed persons will have a relatively easy time learning material presented in a negative context and a relatively difficult time with information presented in a positive light. This is probably because they pay more attention to materials that are congruent with their mood (Bower, 1981; Bower, Monteiro, & Gilligan, 1978; Plutchik, 1990).

Hertel (1994) provided an eloquent summary of the research on mood and cognition. Her review extrapolated several useful therapeutic principles for persons with brain injury from theories developed with uninjured populations. She concluded that because mood has such a dramatic effect on memory, the therapist should ask first whether treatment is even feasible and not begin cognitive rehabilitation until the client's mood has been repaired. Second, because depression limits memory most when the task requires a conscious effort, a procedure that focuses attention may be necessary to improve memory when the client is depressed, including a self-questioning procedure, an environmental manipulation, or a prosthetic device. For example, a sophisticated medication reminder may be necessary to remind a severely depressed client to take his or her medication. Third, because a client's memory may be quite good in situations that do not require a conscious or deliberate effort, the therapist should train the client to relax and not to make memory an issue. The therapist emphasizes that the client should trust his or her memory because it is probably accurate. For example, if the client is depressed and wants to call a friend but cannot immediately recall the friend's phone number, his or her first recollection of the phone number may be accurate. Becoming emotionally distraught will not improve his or her recollection.

Changing Attitudes After Brain Injury

A client's attitude toward recovery is, perhaps, the most important factor that determines the success or failure of therapy. And the client's attitudes often determine his or her underlying motivation to improve. However, attitudes are complex cognitive states that are difficult to modify. Attitudes determine a client's willingness to accept new information that might alter his or her opinions. Along these lines, psychotherapy in persons with brain injury is similar to that with anyone else. The key to changing a person's behavior is to change his or her attitudes. The key to changing their attitudes is to get them to accept new information that might conflict with their self-image (Miller, 1991). The important word is change. We often tell our therapy clients that if they want to improve their mind, all they have to do is to change it occasionally.

Most people think they can assess their performance accurately. They usually feel as confident about their ability to think and to remember as they do about other abilities such as vision or hearing. However, the truth is that most people do not have an entirely accurate view of how well they perform different cognitive tasks. When people are asked how well they perform cognitive tasks in everyday life and in the laboratory, their answers do not generally agree with objective measures of performance in either realm (Herrmann, 1990). This finding is also apparent in persons with brain injury (Anderson-Parenté, 1994). Sometimes people maintain an incorrect assessment of their skills due to lack of awareness or denial. For example, many elderly people are ignorant of their memory lapses until one or more of them create a major financial or social consequence. Sometimes people's attitudes stem from others' incorrect or biased observations about their thinking skills. For example, a blond woman may underestimate her thinking skills after hearing repeated "blond" jokes over the years. Persons with brain injury are just like other people in that their attitudes about their skills and competencies are often inaccurate. However, their problems are exacerbated by the fact that they are unable to integrate feedback in a way that allows them to make their assessments more accurate.

Anderson-Parenté (1994) studied this phenomenon in persons with brain injury and their families. She gave 40 persons with brain injury and their family members alternative forms of a learning disability questionnaire that measured cognitive attributes such as attention, memory, reasoning, and so forth. Each of the family members rated the person with brain injury on the various items and the persons with brain injury also rated themselves on the same items independently. She also tested each person with brain injury with an extensive battery of neuropsychological tests. This provided an objective measure of cognitive performance to which she correlated the subscales of the questionnaires collected from the family members and the persons with brain injury. The results indicated that persons with brain injury generally underestimated their deficits compared with the family members' ratings. The family members' ratings were more significantly correlated with a wider range of neuropsychological measures than were the ratings of the persons with brain injury.

With respect to the first finding, although the general pattern of ratings was similar for the persons with brain injury and their family members, the tendency for the persons with brain injury to underestimate their deficits was apparent across a variety of ratings. Anderson-Parenté (1994) suggested that therapists should therefore interview family members whenever possible to form a more accurate assessment of a client's skills.

Family members' ratings produced about twice as many significant correlations with the neuropsychological variables as did the persons with brain injury. This finding also suggested that family members are a valuable source of information. It is also important to note that in this study the ratings from persons with brain injury yielded more significant correlations than had been previously reported in the literature. These persons may therefore provide useful ratings on certain aspects of their skills and behaviors.

Family members' ratings of the abstract behavioral qualities such as reasoning, memory, and attention were generally correlated with the neuropsychological test scores that measured the same qualities. However, the ratings from persons with brain injury of the more concrete skills were generally correlated with the test scores that measured concrete skills. Anderson-Parenté (1994) suggested that therapists could use these findings in several ways with their clients. First, she suggested that it is important for therapists to accept a client's perceptions of his or her performance on concrete tasks such as writing or doing math. It may be necessary, however, to correct a client's attitudes about other, more abstract aspects of his or her behavior. Second, family members are a good source for estimating a client's abstract reasoning skills. Third, her research showed that clients underestimate the severity of their disorders although they may correctly assess overall patterns of strengths and weaknesses. The difference between the clients' and family members' ratings can be useful indexes of lack of awareness or denial. Therapists should get family member ratings wherever possible because the ratings provide useful information about behavior in an everyday context that the one-shot neuropsychological evaluation cannot capture.

Motivation

Great achievements involve much stress and those who triumph do so in part because they are motivated. Successful recovery from a brain injury is a great achievement. In order for clients to succeed as they hope, they must develop motivation to succeed. One way a therapist can motivate clients to perform is to pay them money to do so (Parenté, 1994). Pay a person to remember something, and he or she will recall it faster and more accurately as compared to one who is not paid or otherwise compensated. Money, however, is extrinsically rewarding and there is no guarantee that it has lasting effects. The ultimate goal of therapy is to change the client's behavior so that it is motivated by personal values or intrinsically rewarding goals. If the client cannot attain an intrinsic state of reward, then the therapist must extrinsically reward good performance. If the rewards are not apparent to the client, then the therapist must make some effort to identify them.

An important trick for developing appropriate motivation for cognitive tasks is for the therapist to point out to the client why it is important to remember the information. For example, if a client is going to attend a dull lecture or meeting that may have important consequences, he or she must make an effort to get mentally "up" for it. Some form of reward for good performance on a task will usually improve performance and memory for a learned skill. The client should learn to begin any cognitive session with questions such as, "How is this information useful to me?" and "How will this make my daily activities easier?"

Mental Condition Checklist

It is clear that a good mental condition is necessary for good cognitive performance. The following is a checklist that therapists can use to make sure that the client's lifestyle is working to his or her advantage.

1. *Maintain an optimal level of activity.* The client should avoid a hectic lifestyle and avoid getting in a rut. Too little or too much activity lessens the client's capacity to pay attention.

2. *Keep stress at a manageable level.* A little stress keeps the client alert but too much is distracting.

3. *Engage in recreational activities such as hobbies, sports, and socializing.* Activity relieves stress.

4. *Take time to relax daily, on weekends, and on annual vacations.* It will also reduce stress and renew the client's strength.

5. *Get enough rest by maintaining a regular sleep schedule.* It may help the client to take a short nap just before a period of intense cognitive effort.

6. *Exercise regularly and within limits.* The client will be less stressed and feel stronger immediately, and the feeling will remain for several hours afterward.

7. *Try innovative ways of relaxing such as yoga exercise and yoga meditation.*

8. *Talk out problems with therapists, family members, and friends.*

9. *Study in a balanced environment.* The best environment has low-level background noise, such as low-volume classical music, and does not contain overly comfortable furniture.

10. *Establish a useful attitude about tasks.* The client should learn to ask how relevant, financially lucrative, or morally right a task is before performing it.

Summary

Learning ways to manage one's emotions, attitudes, and motivation is crucial for mastering cognitive tasks. Learning and thinking are best accomplished when a client is calm, cool, and collected. The time a client spends doing calming behaviors such as stretching or resting before trying to learn something new is time well spent. The client also needs to know not to engage in complex memory or thinking tasks when emotionally upset or stressed.

Depression has dramatic negative effects on memory and thinking. If a client is depressed, then individual psychotherapy or medication may be warranted. Indeed, such measures may be necessary before the client will be able to focus well enough to benefit from cognitive rehabilitation therapy.

Mood and emotion can also have some beneficial value as memory aids. If a client experiences a strong emotion when learning something new, then he or she can attend to the emotion and use it as a cue for recalling the information later. The therapist asking how a client felt at the time of an incident is often sufficient to produce recall of the information. To use emotion as a cue, the client must flag the event with the emotion at the time when the two occur together.

References

Anderson, J., & Bower, G. (1973). *Human associative memory.* Washington, DC: Holt, Rinehart & Winston.

Anderson-Parenté, J. (1994). A comparison of metacognitive ratings of persons with traumatic brain injury and their family members. *NeuroRehabilitation, 4*(3), 168–173.

Baum, A., Cohen, L., & Hall, M. (1993). Control and intrusive memories as possible determinants of chronic stress. *Psychosomatic Medicine, 55,* 274–286.

Ben-Yishay, Y., & Diller, L. (1981). Rehabilitation of cognitive and perceptual deficits in people with traumatic brain damage. *International Journal of Rehabilitation Research, 4,* 208–210.

Borod, J., Koff, E., Perlman-Lorch, J., & Nicholas, M. (1986). The expression and perception of facial emotions in brain damaged patients. *Neuropsychologica, 24,* 169–180.

Bower, G. H. (1981). Mood and memory. *American Psychologist, 36,* 129–148.

Bower, G. H., Monteiro, K. P., & Gilligan, S. G. (1978). Emotional mood as a context for learning and recall. *Journal of Verbal Learning and Verbal Behavior, 17,* 573–578.

Boyle, M. J., Vella, L., & Moloney, E. (1991). Role of drugs and alcohol in patients with head injury. *Journal of the Royal Society of Medicine, 84,* 608–610.

Broadbent, D. E., Cooper, P. F., Fitzgerald, P., & Parks, K. R. (1982). The cognitive failures questionnaire (CFQ) and its correlates. *British Journal of Psychology, 21,* 1–16.

Cicerone, K. D. (1989). Psychotherapeutic interventions with traumatically brain-injured patients. *Rehabilitation Psychology, 34,* 105–114.

Cogen, P. H., Antunes, J. L., & Correll, J. W. (1979). Reproductive function in temporal lobe epilepsy: The effect of temporal lobe lobectomy. *Surgical Neurology, 12,* 243–246.

Collins, A. M., & Loftus, E. F. (1975). A spreading activation theory of semantic memory processing. *Psychological Review, 82,* 407–428.

Cox, W. M., & Klinger, E. (1988). A motivational model of alcohol use. *Journal of Abnormal Psychology, 97,* 168–180.

Cox, W. M., Klinger, E., & Blount, J. (1996). *Motivational structure questionnaire.* Washington, DC: National Institute on Alcohol Abuse and Alcoholism.

Deaton, A. V. (1991). Group interventions for cognitive rehabilitation: Increasing the challenges. In J. S. Kreutzer & P. H. Wehman (Eds.), *Cognitive rehabilitation for persons with traumatic brain injury: A functional approach* (pp. 201–214). Baltimore: Brookes.

Erdelyi, M. H., & Goldberg, B. (1979). Let's not sweep repression under the rug: Toward a cognitive psychology of repression. In J. F. Kihlstrom & F. J. Evans (Eds.), *Functional disorders of memory.* Hillsdale, NJ: Erlbaum.

Folks, D. G., Freeman, A. M., III, Sokol, R. S., & Thurstin, A. H. (1988). Denial: Predictor of outcome following coronary bypass surgery. *International Journal of Psychiatry in Medicine, 18,* 57–66.

Grattan, L. M., & Ghahramanlou, M. (2002). The rehabilitation of neurologically based social disturbances. In P. J. Eslinger (Ed.), *Neuropsychological interventions* (pp. 266–293). New York: Guilford Press.

Greenwald, A. G. (1980). The totalitarian ego. *American Psychologist, 35,* 603–618.

Greenwald, A. G. (1981). Self and memory. In G. H. Bower (Ed.), *The psychology of learning and motivation* (Vol. 15). New York: Academic Press.

Havik, O. E., & Maeland, J. G. (1986). Dimensions of verbal denial in myocardial infarction. *Scandinavian Journal of Psychology, 27,* 326–339.

Heinemann, A. W., Cox, M., Blount, J., Klinger, E., Miranti, S. V., Ridgely, M., et al. (1995). *Final report: Substance abuse as a barrier to employment following traumatic brain injury.* Chicago: Rehabilitation Institute of Chicago.

Herrmann, D. J. (1990). *SuperMemory.* Emmaus, PA: Rodale.

Hertel, P. (1994). Depressive deficits in memory: Implications for memory improvement following traumatic brain injury. *NeuroRehabilitation, 4,* 143–150.

Horowitz, M. J. (1983). Psychological response to serious life events. In S. Breznitz (Ed.), *The denial of stress* (pp. 129–159). New York: International Universities Press.

House, A., Dennis, M., Warlow, C., Hawton, K., & Molyneux, A. (1990). Mood disorders after stroke and their relation to lesion location. *Brain, 113,* 1113–1129.

Janis, I. L., & Mann, L. (1977). *Decision making: A psychological analysis of conflict, choice, and commitment.* New York: Free Press.

Kihlstrom, J. F., & Tobias, B. A. (1991). Anosagnosia, consciousness, and the self. In G. P. Prigatano & D. L. Schacter (Eds.), *Awareness of deficits after brain injury* (pp. 198–222). New York: Oxford University Press.

Kreutzer, J. S., Wehman, P. H., Harris, J. A., Burns, C. T., & Young, H. F. (1991). Substance use and crime patterns among persons with traumatic brain injury referred for supported employment. *Brain Injury, 5,* 177–187.

Laatsch, L. (1996). Development of a memory training program. *Cognitive Rehabilitation, 1,* 15–19.

Langer, K. G. (1992). Psychotherapy with the neuropsychologically impaired adult. *American Journal of Psychotherapy, 46,* 620–639.

Langer, K. G. (1999). Awareness and denial in psychotherapy. In K. G. Langer, L. Laatsch, & L. Lewis (Eds.), *Psychotherapeutic interventions for adults with brain injury or stroke: A clinicians treatment resource* (pp. 75–96). Madison, CT: Psychosocial Press.

Langer, K. G., & Padrone, F. J. (1992). Psychotherapeutic treatment of awareness in acute rehabilitation of traumatic brain injury. *Neuropsychological Rehabilitation, 2,* 59–70.

Langley, M. J. (1995). *Preventing alcohol-related problems after traumatic brain injury: A behavioral approach.* Chicago: Rehabilitation Institute of Chicago.

Leight, K. A., & Ellis, H. C. (1981). Emotional mood states, strategies, and state dependency in memory. *Journal of Verbal Learning and Verbal Behavior, 20,* 251–266.

Lewis, L. (1991). Role of psychological factors in disordered awareness. In G. P. Prigatano & D. L. Schacter (Eds.), *Awareness of deficit after brain injury* (pp. 223–239). New York: Oxford University Press.

Marlatt, G. A., & Gordon, J. R. (Eds.). (1985). *Relapse prevention: Maintenance strategies in the treatment of addictive behaviors.* New York: Guilford Press.

Mateer, C. A., & Williams, D. (1991). Management of psychosocial and behavior problems in cognitive rehabilitation. In J. S. Kreutzer & P. H. Wehman (Eds.), *Cognitive rehabilitation for persons with traumatic brain injury: A functional approach* (pp. 117–126). Baltimore: Brookes.

Miller, L. (1991). Psychotherapy of the brain-injured patient: Principles and practices. *Cognitive Rehabilitation, 9,* 24–30.

Morris, J., & Bleiberg, J. (1986). Neuropsychological rehabilitation and traditional psychotherapy. *International Journal of Clinical Neuropsychology, 8,* 133–135.

Parenté, R. (1994). Effects of monetary incentives on performance after traumatic brain injury. *NeuroRehabilitation, 4,* 198–203.

Parenté, R., Anderson-Parenté, J. K., & Stapleton, M. (2001). The use of rhymes and mnemonics for teaching cognitive skills to persons with acquired brain injury. *Brain Injury Source, 5*(1), 16–19.

Parenté, R., & Stapleton, M. (1999). Development of a cognitive strategies group for vocational training after traumatic brain injury. *NeuroRehabilitation, 13,* 13–20.

Pincus, J. H. (1980). Can violence be a manifestation of epilepsy? *Neurology, 30,* 304–307.

Plutchik, R. (1990). *Emotion: A psychoevolutionary synthesis.* New York: Harper & Row.

Poeck, K. (1969). Pathophysiology of emotional disorders associated with brain damage. In P. Vinken & G. W. Bruyn (Eds.), *Handbook of neurology* (pp. 343–367). New York: Elsevier.

Polich, J. M., Armor, D. J., & Braiker, H. B. (1981). *The course of alcoholism: Four years after treatment.* New York: Wiley.

Prigatano, G. P., Fordyce, D. J., Ziner, H. K., Roueche, F. R., Pepping, M., & Wood, B. C. (Eds.). (1986). *Neuropsychological rehabilitation after brain injury.* Baltimore: Johns Hopkins University Press.

Prigatano, G. P., & Klonoff, P. S. (1988). Psychotherapy and neuropsychological assessment after brain injury. *Journal of Head Trauma Rehabilitation, 3,* 45–56.

Prigatano, G. P., & Schacter, D. L. (1991). *Awareness of deficit after brain injury: Clinical and theoretical issues.* New York: Oxford University Press.

Reason, J. T. (1988). Stress and cognitive failure. In S. Fisher & J. T. Reason (Eds.), *Handbook of life stress, cognition, and health.* New York: Wiley.

Reason, J. T., & Lucas, D. (1984). Using cognitive diaries to investigate naturally occurring memory blocks. In J. Harris & P. Morris (Eds.), *Everyday memory, actions, and absentmindedness.* London: Academic Press.

Reason, J. T., & MyCielska, M. (1983). *Absentmindedness.* Englewood Cliffs, NJ: Prentice Hall.

Schacter, D. L., & Prigatano, G. P. (1991). Forms of unawareness. In G. P. Prigatano & D. L. Schacter (Eds.), *Awareness of deficit after brain injury* (pp. 258–262). New York: Oxford University Press.

Schneider, W., & Shiffrin, R. M. (1977). Controlled and automatic human information processing: Detection, search, and attention. *Psychological Review, 84,* 1–66.

Simon, D., Riley, E., Egelko, S., Kaplan, E., Newman, B., & Diller, L. (1991). *A new instrument for assessing awareness of deficits in stroke.* Poster session presented at the 99th annual convention of the American Psychological Association, San Francisco.

Spielberger, C. D., Gonzales, H. P., & Fletcher, T. (1979). Test anxiety reduction, learning strategies, and academic performance. In H. F. O'Neill & C. D. Spielberger (Eds.), *Cognitive and affective learning strategies.* New York: Academic Press.

Starkstein, S. E., Robinson, R. G., & Price, T. R. (1987). Comparsion of cortical and subcortical lesions in the production of poststroke mood disorders. *Brain, 110,* 1045–1059.

Strauss, E., Risser, A., & Jones, M. W. (1982). Fear responses in patients with epilepsy. *Neurology, 39,* 626–630.

Taylor, D. C. (1969). Aggression and epilepsy. *Journal of Psychiatric Research, 13,* 229–236.

Tucker, J. A., Vuchinich, R. E., & Harris, C. V. (1985). Determinants of substance abuse relapse. In M. Galizio & S. A. Maistro (Eds.), *Determinants of substance abuse: Biological, psychological, and environmental factors* (pp. 158–214). New York: Plenum Press.

Vaillant, G. E. (1983). *The natural history of alcoholism: Causes, patterns, and paths to recovery*. Cambridge, MA: Harvard University Press.

Watts, F. N. (1988). Memory deficit in depression. In M. M. Gruneberg, P. E. Morris, & R. N. Sykes (Eds.), *Practical aspects of memory*. Chichester, United Kingdom: Wiley.

Watts, F. N., MacLeod, A. K., & Morris, L. (1988). A remedial strategy for memory and concentration problems in depressed patients. *Cognitive Therapy and Research, 12,* 185–193.

Wells, A., & Mathews, G. (1994). *Attention and emotion: A clinical perspective*. Hillsdale, NJ: Erlbaum.

Williams, J. M. G., Watts, F. N., MacLeod, C., & Mathews, A. (1988). *Cognitive psychology and emotional disorders*. New York: Wiley.

Yesavage, J. A., Rose, T. L., & Spiegel, D. (1982). Relaxation training and memory improvement in elderly normals: Correlations of anxiety ratings and recall improvement. *Experimental Aging Research, 8,* 198.

Yesavage, J. A., & Sheikh, J. I. (1988). Nonpharmacologic treatment of age-associated memory impairment. *Comprehensive Therapy, 14,* 44–46.

Zeman, W., & King, F. A. (1958). Tumors and the septum pellicidum and adjacent structures with abnormal affective behavior: An anterior midline structure syndrome. *Journal of Nervous and Mental Disease, 127,* 490–502.

Chapter 22

*

Cognitive-Enhancing
Nutrients and Drugs

Good nutrition is essential for high-level cognitive functioning. Indeed, many people would experience a substantial improvement in thinking and memory simply by changing their diet. Although a "smart pill" would be the most expedient means for improving cognition after traumatic brain injury, attempts to develop this type of medication have met with mixed success. There are a variety of cognitive-enhancing substances that purportedly improve thinking and memory, including prescription medications, nutrients, vitamins, minerals, and herbs. The pharmaceutical drugs can be further classified into nootropics, vasodilators, and mechanism-based drugs. There is a substantial literature that has described a variety of substances for treating such things as medical ailments, psychological problems, and learning disabilities (Dean & Morgenthaler, 1990; Dean, Morgenthaler, & Fowkes, 1993; Pelton, 1989; Potter & Orfali, 1993; Whyte, 2002). Unfortunately, there is little in the way of efficacy literature that supports any of these substances. The purpose of this chapter is not to validate or to disclaim any of these substances. Our goal is to create awareness of the vast array of nutrients and drugs that may be helpful to individual persons with brain injury.

The search for drugs that improve thinking has intensified in recent years and there are now several published summaries plus a variety of popular books on the topic (Bowyer, Humphreys, & Revelle, 1983; Dean & Morgenthaler, 1990; Dean et al., 1993; Hock, 1987; Pelton, 1989). Kolakowsky and Parenté's (1997) review is probably the most comprehensive and cogent. There is also an abundance of research that concerns the underlying chemical mechanisms for these drugs (Altomare et al., 1995; Benishin, 1992; Blandizzi et al., 1995; Caccia et al., 1994; Chepkova et al., 1995; Corasaniti et al., 1995; Corona et al., 1989; Desai, Valli, Monn, & Schoepp, 1995; Du, Wu, Jiang, & Gu, 1994; Govoni, Lucchi, Battaini, & Trabucchi, 1992; Kariya, Tanaka, & Nomura, 1994; Kresyun & Rozhkovskii, 1993; Lucchi et al., 1993; Mangoni, Sioufi, & Godbillon, 1995; Mondadori, Gentsch, Hengerer, Ducret, et al., 1992; Ono et al., 1995a, 1995b, 1995c; Shul'gina & Okhotnikov, 1991; Spaldin et al., 1995; Stancheva & Alova, 1994; Stoll, Schubert, & Muller, 1992; Tsai et al., 1992; Vermeij & Edelbroek, 1994; Vernyi, Derzhiruk, & Mogilevskii, 1995; Viana, Marinho, & Sousa, 1992; Yamada et al., 1994; Zivkovic et al., 1995). O'Shanick and Zasler (1990) provided an excellent review of the literature on the use of drugs for treating behavioral problems after brain injury.

This chapter limits discussion to those drugs and nutrients whose cognitive-enhancing effects have been documented in published scientific papers. Even with this criterion, we discovered a great deal of variability in the experimental findings. There is also considerable variability between the results reported in animal versus human trials. Generally speaking, there seems to be no experimentally proven drug or nutrient effect that has been consistently documented in published studies of groups. Also, much of the research has been done with elderly populations who suffer from progressively degenerative conditions like Alzheimer's disease (Kolakowsky & Parenté, 1997). Our basic conclusion from this review is that whether to begin a drug or nutrient trial is largely an individual matter. Although there are few group comparison studies that show beneficial effects in well-controlled clinical trials, many persons with brain injury may experience improvement of their thinking skills individually with certain drug or nutritional interventions.

The therapist's role when discussing nutrients and drugs with a client is only to acquaint him or her with the variety of different substances that are available. The therapist may also provide the client's physician with materials that describe the effects of various substances on cognition and emotion (Bowen & Larson, 1993; Eysenck & Folkard, 1980; Loke, 1988) so that the client and his or her physician can make an informed decision about the usefulness of any of these substances (Goodwin, Goodwin, & Garry, 1983). Our experience is that many persons with brain injury will want to try these substances; however, we recommend their use only with proper guidance and monitoring. A danger is that many of the nutrients discussed in this chapter are available without prescription and some clients may self-medicate with unpredictable consequences. Therefore, *we strongly recommend that persons with brain injury always consult a physician before making any changes in their diet or begin using any cognitive-enhancing substances discussed in this chapter or any other books.*

We begin our discussion with a summary of various nutrients that may improve a client's thinking and memory. We then discuss some of the drugs that have been developed for the same purpose.

Nutritional Supplements

The term *nutrient* implies a substance that nourishes. Human bodies manufacture many of these substances although they are also available from nutritional supplements at health food stores. Indeed, an entire industry has grown up around the concept of *feeding the mind*. Usually, nutrients provide adjunctive treatment to a total wellness plan that includes reducing stress and exercising (Mathews, Davies, Westerman, & Stammers, 2000; Michaud, Musse, Nicholas, & Mejean, 1991; Revelle, Humphreys, Simon, & Gilliland, 1980; Silver, 1992). We discuss some of the more popular substances in alphabetical order below.

Acetyl-l-carnitine is a substance that can be purchased without a prescription. Barnes et al. (1990) showed that administering acetyl-l-carnitine to rats improved their ability to learn and remember, and, further, it protected their brains from neurotoxic exposure (Steffen et al., 1995). Acetyl-l-carnitine has also been shown to have beneficial effects in humans. For example, Santarelli et al. (1995) showed that the acetyl-l-carnitine lessened the effect of prenatal ethanol exposure. It has also been used as a treatment for peripheral neuropathies (Onofrj et al., 1995). Alzheimer's patients who took acetyl-l-carnitine showed fewer declines in repeated long-term testing on various cognitive tasks that measured attention and memory (Parnetti et al., 1990; Sano et al., 1992).

Dehydroepiandrosterone (DHEA) is a steroid hormone that has been used to treat a variety of cognitive deficits (Parenté & Herrmann, 1996). Because DHEA is found predominantly in brain tissue, some researchers have speculated that the substance protects the tissue from age-related degeneration, like Alzheimer's disease (Kolakowsky & Parenté, 1997).

Dimethlaminoethanol (DMAE) is a form of cortical stimulant and mood elevator (Hochschild, 1973; Pfeiffer, 1957). Small amounts of DMAE are produced by the body, and it is thought to increase the synthesis of the neurotransmitter acetylcholine in the brain (Ceder, 1978) by raising choline levels in the blood. However, the effect of DMAE is unlike that of stimulants. There is no reported jitteriness, only a mild stimulation that is more akin to a heightened state of awareness or alertness. Furthermore, there is no reported withdrawal or depression when it is discontinued. For these reasons, it may be useful as an alternative treatment for hyperactivity and attention deficit disorder and for treating learning and behavioral disorders (Oettinger, 1958; Pfeiffer, 1959).

Deanol is a prescription drug that is similar to DMAE and has a similar effect. It was originally marketed for treatment of learning problems and attention deficit. Murphree (1960) suggested that it increased attention and concentration, and Hochschild (1973) reported that it increases life span in rats.

Ginkgo biloba comes from a tree whose origin dates back 300 million years. Ginkgo biloba, which is distilled from the leaves of this tree, has been used in Chinese and European medicine for years; herbalists have used it to improve cerebral circulation, mental alertness, and overall brain functioning. Homeopathic physicians believe that it alters brain chemistry by accelerating glucose metabolism. It may also prevent and repair free-radical damage to the brain (Dean & Morgenthaler, 1990; Pelton, 1989), as well as increase choline uptake in the brain (Kristofikova, Benesova, & Tejkalova, 1992).

Recent studies of the efficacy of ginkgo biloba have produced mixed results. Tighilet and Lacour (1995) showed that ginkgo biloba facilitated recovery of locomotion in cats af-

ter one side of their vestibular nerve was removed. Chopin and Briley (1992) induced amnesia in rats by injecting them with scopolamine and later found that ginkgo biloba reduced the amnesia. Several authors reported increased attention and concentration after using ginkgo in studies with both rats and humans (Allard, 1986; Hindmarch, 1986). Schaffler and Reeh (1985) report improved respiration after taking ginkgo. A variety of other effects have also been reported, including improved short-term memory (Hindmarch, 1986) and lessened deterioration due to aging and degenerative disease (Allard, 1986; Warburton, 1986). It is unclear how ginkgo effects these changes although it is possible that ginkgo increases blood flow in the brain by relaxing the microcapillaries. Not only is the mechanism by which ginkgo works unclear, but positive findings have not always emerged in well-controlled studies of people who were given graded doses of ginkgo (Kunkel, 1992).

Ginseng, an oriental herb, has been used to improve circulation and mental functioning (Petkov, 1987; Quiroga & Imbriano, 1979). Ginseng improves cognition in several ways: (a) by increasing production of various neurotransmitters, (b) by stimulating the adrenal cortex, (c) by increasing the supply of blood to the brain, or (d) by increasing blood flow and general metabolism via its effect on areas of the brain such as the hypothalamus and pituitary glands. Most of the positive findings reported in the literature suggest that ginseng improves fine motor coordination and attention, and it shortens reaction time. Simon (1977) reported that ginseng improved memory and concentration in animals and in elderly humans.

Ginseng comes in a variety of forms but they all contain the same basic active ingredients: vitamins A, E, B_1, B_2, and B_{12}, along with folic acid, biotin, and ascorbic acid. Ginseng compounds may also contain minerals such as calcium, copper, cobalt, iron, magnesium, manganese, phosphorous, potassium, sulfur, and sodium. There are several varieties of ginseng although the most common are Siberian ginseng, which comes from Russia, and Panax ginseng, which comes from Asian countries such as China, South Korea, and Russia.

Phosphatidylserine is another substance that has been widely touted as a cognitive-enhancing nutrient (Crook et al., 1991; Dean et al., 1993). It reportedly maintains the solubility of fatty acids, increases glucose metabolism, and maintains the fluidity of cell membranes in the brain. It may also increase the sensitivity of neurotransmitter sites in the brain. Several studies concluded that phosphatidylserine is effective as a cognitive enhancer in healthy humans. It may also be an effective treatment for Alzheimer's disease (Crook, Petrie, Wells, & Massari, 1992; Dean et al., 1993; Heiss et al., 1994; Rupprecht, Maurer, Dierks, & Ihl, 1989).

Pyritinol, a nutrient that is similar to vitamin B_6, may improve cerebral blood flow and cerebral metabolism (Fischhof et al., 1992) and has a beneficial effect on sensorimotor functioning (Hindmarch, Coleston, & Kerr, 1991). Benesova et al. (1990) reported that pyritinol improved memory in aged rats after 3 months of continuous ingestion. Toledano and Bentura (1994) showed that after they induced mild brain lesions in rats, pyritinol enhanced cortical recovery in those rats. However, the rats with severe lesions did not benefit. This result suggests that pyritinol may be an effective treatment for mild brain injury.

Nutrient cocktails are several concentrated vitamin compounds or "brain formulas" that contain high levels of vitamins and minerals essential for cognitive functioning. These compounds purportedly treat cognitive disorders that are caused by vitamin deficiencies. For example, memory loss due to chronic alcohol use results, in part, from thiamine deficiency. Perhaps some portion of a person's cognitive deficit can be attributed to poor nutrition and this problem can be remedied with a multivitamin supplement. We have noticed a number of these vitamin compounds with brand names like Brain Pep, Brain II Formula, IQ Plus, MemorAid, Nutrimental, Memory 2000, and so forth. They are usually available in health food stores at exorbitant prices. Although the various formulas certainly contain a specific collection of nutrients that are necessary for thinking and memory, there is no documented evidence that any particular brand is superior to another. Moreover, there is little evidence that any one of them improves thinking and memory any more than a multivitamin supplement does.

Most of these compounds contain a variety of amino acids such as cystine, glutamine, methionine, phenylalanine, tyrosine, and so forth. They may also include ascorbic acid, biotin, chromium, cobalamine, folic acid, germanium, inositol, manganese, phosphatidylserine, potassium, ribonucleic acid, riboflavin, taurine, thiamine, and zinc. All of these nutrients have been shown to be essential for the brain to function normally. There is little evidence, however, that massive doses of them produce rapid or significant improvement in cognitive skill. There is some evidence that thinking skills are improved with regular use of beta-carotene, vitamin E, and ascorbic acid (Lesser, 1980). The effects are gradual and may take months to notice. This is because most of the nutrients are excreted the following day, so it may take several weeks before there is a sufficient level in the blood to produce a noticeable improvement. Much of the evidence of cognitive enhancement with megavitamin therapy is anecdotal. There are no nutrients that will produce immediate improvement of memory and cognition. Indeed, what most nutrient supplements will produce is expensive urine. However, there is the possibility that with extended use, a person may eventually notice improvement in thinking and memory so long as the vitamin supplements accompany a lifelong change in diet and exercise.

Cognitive-Enhancing Drugs

A variety of drugs have been investigated as potential "smart pills" (Dean & Morgenthaler, 1990). These are prescription substances that generally fall into four categories (Moos, Davis, & Gamzu, 1991): (a) vasodilators, (b) nootropics, (c) mechanism-based drugs, and (d) psychostimulants. Some of the drugs discussed in the following section fall into more than one category.

Aricept is the newest of the drugs that have been shown to enhance memory. Aricept increases cognitive functioning by enhancing cholinergic functioning. The idea behind aricept is to increase the concentration of acetylcholine, a neurotransmitter, and decrease the inhibition of acetylcholine production. This drug is most often used to treat patients with memory loss due to Alzheimer's disease. It has not been widely used in persons with brain injury.

Hydergine dilates the microcapillaries in the brain. Its drug action increases blood flow and oxygen to the brain, increases glucose metabolism, and protects against hypoxia. Several authors have reported significant correlations between hydergine use and elevated scores of intelligence, memory, learning, recall, and reaction time (Dean & Morgenthaler, 1990; Pelton, 1989; Potter & Orfali, 1993).

Hydergine is composed of various ergot alkaloids (Exton-Smith, 1983). It has a long history of use as a treatment for memory and cognitive deficits secondary to senile dementia (Hughes, 1976; Yoshikawa, 1983). In addition to its vasodilation properties, it may also increase the amount of certain neurotransmitters in the brain (Copeland, 1981; Enmenegger & Meier-Ruge, 1968) and increase oxygen use and circulation (Rao & Norris, 1971; Weil, 1978). Nandy and Schneider (1978) suggested that hydergine also stimulates axon and dendrite growth.

Nootropics (Poschel, 1988) are some of the most interesting of the cognitive-enhancing drugs because of their ability to affect higher cognitive functions. They have also been used to treat dyslexia (Wilsher, 1987). The word *nootropic* means "toward the mind," and comes from the Greek *noos* (mind) and *tropos* (toward) (Giurgea, 1973; Giurgea & Salama, 1977). Research on nootropics began in the 1970s in Europe and has been growing rapidly throughout the last 30 years. Nootropics enhance brain metabolism and improve cerebral circulation. These benefits improve mental energy and alertness (Dean & Morgenthaler, 1990; Gouliaev & Senning, 1994; Kashiwase & Watanabe, 1991; Pelton, 1989). Various nootropic substances have been used with humans and animals; studies with humans have typically been less successful than those with animals.

Piracetam was shown to improve learning and memory in both animal and human trials (Diamond & Browers, 1976; Giurgea, 1973; Giurgea & Salama, 1977; Mindus, 1976). It may be an effective treatment for reading disorders (Bartus, 1990; Wilsher & Taylor, 1994) or for treating other maladies such as memory failure due to alcoholism, stroke, vertigo, and sickle-cell anemia (Dean & Morgenthaler, 1990). The actual drug action is unclear although it may enhance communication between the cerebral hemispheres via the corpus collosum (Benesova & Bures, 1976) or stimulate production of the neurotransmitter adenosine triphosphate (Nickerson & Wolthuis, 1976). Taking choline may augment the effects of piracetam and the combination has been shown to improve memory and cognitive functioning in persons with senile dementia (Bartus, 1981; Ferris, 1982). One of the major advantages of this drug is that it does not cause stimulation or sedation, nor does it have any analgesic effects; it generally has minimal side effects.

The potential benefits of piracetam have not been borne out in controlled research. At best, studies have produced mixed results with animal studies producing stronger effects than human trials. Animal studies usually show improved learning and retention and motor skill after piracetam has been administered (Ennaceur, Cavoy, Costa, & Delacour, 1989; Jahkel, Oehler, & Schumacher, 1994; Mondadori, Ducret, & Borkowski, 1991; Mondadori & Etienne, 1990; Sansone & Oliverio, 1989). Other researchers have shown that piracetam can lessen the negative effects on memory of electroconvulsive shock and injections of scopolamine (Chopin & Briley, 1992; Mondadori & Etienne, 1990). Still others suggest that piracetam can protect the brain against aging (Salimov, Salimov, Shvets, & Shvets, 1995). Some studies with humans indicate that piracetam can improve psychomotor performance in patients with mild cognitive deficits (Gallai et al., 1991). Research on persons with epilepsy suggests that piracetam can improve attention and vigilance (Chaudhry, Najam, DeMahieu, Raza, & Ahmad, 1992).

Another body of research has not found that piracetam produces dramatic effects on memory, motor skill, or overall cognition (Kulkarni & Verma, 1992). Mondadori, Ducret, and Hausler (1992) reported that the beneficial effects of piracetam may be offset by elevated steroid levels or damage to the adrenal gland (Mondadori, Ducret, & Petschke, 1989). DeAngelis (1992) did not find any significant improvement in learning in mice who were given piracetam. In general, piracetam seems to exert a small cognitive-enhancing effect, but it is inconsistent. Its mechanism is unknown, and it seems less apparent in humans as compared with animals.

Aniracetam is a nootropic drug that is similar to, but more powerful and potentially more useful than, piracetam (Parnetti et al., 1991; Potter & Orfali, 1993). It has been found to improve cognitive functions in animal studies (Cumin, 1982) and it may affect a wider range of skills than piracetam (Vincent, 1985). Animal studies show that it improves spatial memory and retention (Martin et al., 1992; Mondadori et al., 1991). It has also been found to reduce learning and memory deficits that are induced with drugs like scopolamine (Bartolini, Risaliti, & Pepeu, 1992; Ventra et al., 1994). Several authors have documented its use as a treatment for various types of brain maladies (Himori & Mishima, 1994; Nabeshima et al., 1991; Wesnes, Anand, Simpson, & Christmas, 1990). There is not, however, universal agreement on the effectiveness or the treatment potential of aniracetam. For example, in one study of the effects of aniracetam for treatment of chemical-exposure-related cognitive deficits, aniracetam use resulted in improvement on only 1 of 19 neuropsychological outcome measures (Somnier et al., 1990).

Oxiracetam is another member of the generic piracetam family of drugs (Ferrero, 1984; Gallai et al., 1991). Oxiracetam also improves memory in animal studies (Mondadori, 1986) and is more potent than piracetam (Itil, 1986). Ferrero (1984) reported improvement of memory and cognitive skills with humans who took oxiracetam. Ammassari-Teule (1986) reported that the offspring of female rats given oxiracetam while pregnant were superior on tests of learning and retention to those offspring of control rats. Several studies reported positive effects on learning, memory, social recognition, and retention after treatment with oxiracetam (Ammassari-Teule, Castellano, & Sansone, 1992; Cavoy, Van-Golf-Racht, & Delacour, 1994; Fordyce, Clark, Paylor, & Wehner, 1995; Hlinak & Krejci, 1992; Mondadori et al., 1991; Sansone, Castellano, Battaglia, & Ammassari-Teule, 1990, 1991; Sansone & Oliverio, 1989). Oxiracetam protects against adverse effects of several drugs including nicotine (Sansone et al., 1991), scopolamine (Bartolini et al., 1992; DeAngelis & Furlan, 1995; Magnani et al., 1992; Pitsikas & Algeri, 1992), and haloperidol (Castellano, Battaglia, & Sansone, 1992). However, like the rest of the nootropics, the efficacy data present a mixed picture. For example, DeAngelis (1992) found that oxiracetam did not affect learning or memory. Likewise, Aldenkamp et al. (1990–1991) did not find that it improved memory with epileptic patients.

Pramiracetam is another nootropic that has been found to improve learning and memory (Potter & Orfali, 1993). Animal studies show that it can improve delayed memory and partially reduce the effect of scopolamine-induced amnesia (Ennaceur et al., 1989; Mauri et al., 1994; Mondadori et al., 1991). Murry and Fibiger (1986) reported that pramiracetam enhanced rate of learning and electrical activity in certain areas of the limbic system.

Centrophenoxine and *cerebrolysin* are not nootropic drugs, but they have been shown to have positive effects on cognition (Nagy & Floyd, 1984; Popa et al., 1994). Well-controlled clinical trials suggest that it may be an effective memory enhancer with geriatric patients (Kofler, Erhart, Erhart, & Harrer, 1990).

Psychostimulants are commonly used to improve a person's attention and concentration (Coper & Herrmann, 1988; Evans & Gualtieri, 1987). The drugs increase metabolism and temporarily speed up processing. Although these drugs have been used with some success for treating attention deficit in children and adolescents, they may be less useful for treating memory and cognitive impairments after brain injury. These drugs may increase blood pressure, which increases risk of stroke. Some clients may also have a tendency to abuse them or become dependent on them. The drugs may also inhibit sleep.

Mechanism-based drugs target specific areas of the brain or neurological processes. One type of mechanism-based drug is *cholinergic agonists* (Goldberg, Gerstman, & Mattis, 1982). These substances affect the synthesis of acetylcholine in the brain and generally produce some improvement in memory as

long as the dosage is customized for the individual. Treatments that combine a choline-rich substance such as lecithin with another substance that blocks the production of choline inhibitors in the brain (e.g., aricept) generally show the greatest effect. Other drugs such as *ondansetron* and *zatosetron* have been found to block the inhibition of acetylcholine. The drugs therefore increase the release of this neurotransmitter, thereby improving cognitive performance.

The human adrenergic system is also partially responsible for the storage and retrieval of memory. Drugs such as *epinephrine*, which affects this system, have been found to facilitate memory. *Neuropeptides* such as *vasopressin* have also been shown to improve memory (Greidanus, van Wimersma, & Wied, 1985; Zagler & Black, 1985).

Vasopressin deserves special attention because it consistently improves memory and attention. Released by the pituitary gland, the production of vasopressin is enhanced by stimulant drugs and retarded by other substances such as alcohol and marijuana. Vasopressin causes a general improvement of long-term and short-term memory, concentration, recall of novel information, and retention (DeWied, 1975; Gold, 1979; Legros, 1978). Reversal of amnesic effects with vasopressin use has also been reported (Oliveros, 1978) along with significant recovery of function after brain injury and diseases such as diabetes insipidus (Laczi, 1982).

Reducing fatty deposits in the nerve cells of the brain and central nervous system is another mechanistic approach to improving cognitive functioning. *Centrophenoxine* is one drug that has been used for this purpose (Guili, 1980; Nandy & Bourne, 1966; Nandy & Schneider, 1978; Riga & Riga, 1974), although it has not been widely used in persons with brain injury.

Several other drugs have been reportedly used for treatment of various dementia conditions after brain injury and degenerative diseases. Many of these substances have been found to be effective in human trials and worthy of mention as potential treatments for cognitive deficits.

Tacrine, also known as tetrahydroaminoacridine, has been shown to improve executive functions, memory, and motor skill, and to reverse scopolamine-induced memory loss (Abe, 1991; Benesova, Kristofikova, & Tejkalova, 1991; Chopin & Briley, 1992; Eguchi, Yuasa, Egawa, & Tobe, 1994; Mondadori et al., 1991; Ohta, Matsumoto, Shimizu, & Watanabe, 1994; Parenté & Herrmann, 1996; Riekkinen et al., 1995; Ritzmann, Kling, Melchior, & Glasky, 1993; Rupniak et al., 1990). It may also preserve acetylcholine in the brain (Potter & Orfali, 1993). Once again, though, the reports are mixed. Some studies have shown no clear cognitive-enhancing effects of tacrine while others suggest that it may be toxic if administered for long periods of time (Ahlin, Junthe, Hassan, & Nyback, 1995; Dean et al., 1993; Pepeu, 1994).

The U.S. Food and Drug Administration has approved tacrine for use with patients with Alzheimer's disease. In these patients, it has been found to significantly improve attention (Sahakian & Coull, 1993) and performance on neuropsychological measures (Alhainen, Hellkala, & Riekkinen, 1993; Nordberg et al., 1992). However, this has not been a consistent finding (Fitten & Ganzell, 1992). Tacrine also elevates liver enzymes (Ahlin et al., 1991; Ahlin et al., 1992; Davies et al., 1990) and creates nausea (Davies et al., 1990).

Physostigmine is a cholinesterase inhibitor that has been found to enhance learning, memory, and retention (Rupniak et al., 1990; Sansone et al., 1993; Mondadori et al., 1991), and to reverse both age- (Ritzmann et al., 1993) and scopolamine-induced memory deficits in laboratory rodents (Abe, 1991; Buxton et al., 1994; Rupniak et al., 1990; Yamazaki et al., 1995). Physostigmine has been shown to improve memory, communication,

and long-term verbal memory (Sano et al., 1993; Sevush, Guterman, & Villalon, 1991) in healthy participants and in elderly patients with cognitive deficits (Tritsmans, Clincke, Devenijns, Verhoosel, & Amery, 1988).

Vinpocetine is another metabolic enhancer that is thought to improve microcirculation and increase glucose and oxygen use in the brain. The drug is derived from vincamine, which is extracted from periwinkle. Vinpocetine has been shown to improve memory in a majority of patients who suffered a variety of neurological disorders (Otomo, 1985; Subhan & Hindmarch, 1985).

Summary and Evaluation

Many persons with brain injury will want to try nutrient and drug treatments to improve their thinking skills. These substances are especially attractive because of the premise that by simply taking a pill, the client may improve his or her cognitive functions overnight. It is important for the therapist to inform the client that, with the exception of hydergine, there are few drugs that are routinely prescribed for treating cognitive dysfunction. This chapter illustrated that there are a variety of potential drug and nutrient candidates for use, but physicians are usually unaware of these drugs, their proper dosage or course, and their potential side effects. It therefore comes as no surprise that most physicians are reluctant to prescribe these substances. Moreover, although many nonprescription nutrients have been found to improve cognitive functioning, their effects may take months to appear. Megadoses of nutrients will probably have little effect because the client will excrete most of the dose within days. In addition, expensive brain formulas are probably no more effective than a multivitamin.

We want to reemphasize that self-medication with drugs or nutrients is potentially dangerous. The therapist should warn the client that drugs or nutrients should only be taken under medical supervision. Although many of the drugs mentioned in this chapter are available via mail order, the client should be specifically warned against this practice.

What can a client do to improve his or her cognition using cognitive-enhancing nutrients and drugs? First, he or she can consult a nutritionist to determine an appropriate diet, perhaps with a multivitamin supplement. Second, the client should get at least 8 hours of sleep each night, avoid alcohol, nicotine, and stimulants such as coffee, tea, and soda (Erikson et al., 1985), and maintain a regular exercise program. The client should consult a physician to determine if any of the substances discussed in this chapter would be appropriate for his or her specific situation. Above all, the client should not self-medicate. Even though nutrients are sold without prescriptions, they can still produce negative side effects, especially if they interact with a prescription medication the client is taking.

References

Abe, E. (1991). Reversal effect of DM-9384 on scopolamine-induced acetylcholine depletion in certain regions of the mouse brain. *Psychopharmacology, 105*(3), 310–316.

Ahlin, A., Adem, A., Junthe, T., Ohman, G., et al. (1992). Pharmacokinetics of tetrahydroaminoacridine: Relations to clinical and biochemical effects in Alzheimer patients. *International Clinical Psychopharmacology, 7*(1), 29–36.

Ahlin, A., Junthe, T., Hassan, M., & Nyback, H. (1995). One year on tacrine (THA): clinical and biochemical effects in patients with dementia of the Alzheimer type. *International Psychogeriatrics, 7*(1), 75–83.

Ahlin, A., Nyback, H., Junthe, T., Ohman, G., et al. (1991). Tetrahydroaminoacridine in Alzheimer's dementia: Clinical and biochemical results of a double-blind crossover trial. *Human Psychopharmacology, Clinical and Experimental, 6*(2), 109–118.

Aldenkamp, A. P., Van Wieringen, A., Alpherts, W. C., Van Emde Boas, W., et al. (1990–1991). Double-blind, placebo-controlled neuropsychological and neurophysiological investigations with oxiracetam (CGP 21690E) in memory-impaired patients with epilepsy. *Neuropsychobiology, 24*(2), 90–101.

Alhainen, K., Hellkala, E. L., & Riekkinen, P. J. (1993). Psychometric discrimination of tetrahydroaminoacridine responders in Alzheimer patients. *Dementia, 4*(1), 54–58.

Allard, M. (1986). Treatment of old-age disorders with ginkgo biloba extract. *La Presse Medicale, 15*(31), 1540.

Altomare, C., Cellamare, S., Carotti, A., Casini, G., Ferappi, M., Gavuzzo, E., et al. (1995). X-ray crystal structure, partitioning behavior, and molecular modeling study of piracetam-type nootropics: Insights into the pharmacophore. *Journal of Medicinal Chemistry, 38*(1), 170–179.

Ammassari-Teule, M. (1986). Avoidance facilitation in adult mice by prenatal administration of nootropic drug Oxiracetam. *Pharmacological Research Communications, 18*(12), 1169–1178.

Ammassari-Teule, M., Castellano, C., & Sansone, M. (1992). Enhancement by oxiracetam of passive avoidance improvement induced by the presynaptic muscarinic antagonist secoverine in mice. *Behavioural Brain Research, 47*(1), 93–95.

Barnes, C. A., Markowska, A. L., Ingram, D. K., Kametani, H., Spangler, E. L., Lemken, V. J., et al. (1990). Acetyl-l-carnitine: Effects on learning and memory performance of aged rats in simple and complex mazes. *Neurobiology of Aging, 11*(5), 499–506.

Bartolini, R., Risaliti, R., & Pepeu, G. (1992). Effect of scopolamine and nootropic drugs on rewarded alteration in a T-maze. *Pharmacology, Biochemistry, and Behavior, 43*(4), 1161–1164.

Bartus, R. (1981, March). Profound effects of combining choline and piraceta on memory enhancement and cholinergic function in aged rats. *Neurobiology of Aging,* pp. 105–111.

Bartus, R. T. (1990). Drugs to treat age-related neurodegenerative problems: The final frontier of medical science? *Journal of the American Geriatric Society, 38*(6), 680–695.

Benesova, O., & Bures, J. (1976). Piracetam induced facilitation of interhemispheric transfer of visual information in rats. *Psychopharmacologia, 46*, 93–102.

Benesova, O., Kristofikova, Z., & Tejkalova, H. (1991). Experimental study of long-term administration of cholinesterase inhibitors in aging rats. *Homeostasis in Health and Disease, 33*(4), 170–172.

Benesova, O., Tejkalova, H., Kristofikova, Z., Binkova, B., et al. (1990). The evaluation of nootropic drug effects in aging rats. *Activitas Nervosa Superior, 32*(1), 53–55.

Benishin, C. G. (1992). Actions of ginsenoside Rb-sub-1 on choline uptake in central cholinergic nerve endings. *Neurochemistry International, 21*(1), 1–5.

Blandizzi, C., Natale, G., Carignani, D., Colucci, R., Lazzeri, G., & Del Tacca, M. (1995). Central administration of cholecystokinin stimulates gastric pepsinogen secretion from anesthetized rats. *Neuroscience Letters, 193*(1), 13–16.

Bowen, J. D., & Larson, E. B. (1993). Drug induced cognitive impairment. Defining the problem and finding solutions. *Drugs and Aging, 3*, 349–357.

Bowyer, P. A., Humphreys, M. S., & Revelle, W. (1983). Arousal and recognition memory: The effects of impulsivity, caffeine, and time on task. *Personality and Individual Differences, 4,* 41–49.

Buxton, A., Callan, O. A., Blatt, E. J., Wong, E. H. F., et al. (1994). Cholinergic agents and delay-dependent performance in the rat. *Pharmacology, Biochemistry, and Behavior, 49*(4), 1067–1073.

Caccia, S., Confalonieri, S., Guiso, G., Bernasconi, P., et al. (1994). Brain uptake and distribution of the potential memory enhancer CL 275,838 and its main metabolites in rats: Relationship between brain concentrations and in vitro potencies on neurotransmitter mechanisms. *Psychopharmacology, 115*(4), 502–508.

Castellano, C., Battaglia, M., & Sansone, M. (1992). Oxiracetam prevents haloperidol-induced passive avoidance impairment in mice. *Pharmacology, Biochemistry, and Behavior, 42*(4), 797–801.

Cavoy, A., Van-Golf-Racht, B., & Delacour, J. (1994). Relationships between arousal and cognition-enhancing effects of oxiracetam. *Pharmacology, Biochemistry, and Behavior, 47*(2), 283–287.

Ceder, G. (1978). Effects of 2-Dimethylaminoethanol (Deanol) on the metabolism of choline in plasma. *Journal of Neurochemistry, 30,* 1293–1296.

Chaudhry, H. R., Najam, N., DeMahieu, C., Raza, A., & Ahmad, N. (1992). Clinical use of piracetam in epileptic patients. *Current Therapeutic Research, 52*(3), 355–360.

Chepkova, A. N., Doreulee, N. V., Trofimov, S. S., Gudasheva, T. A., Ostrovskaya, R. U., & Skrebitsky, V. G. (1995). Nootropic compound L-pyroglutamyl-D-alanine-amide restores hippocampal long-term potentiation impaired by exposure to ethanol in rats. *Neuroscience Letters, 188*(3), 163–166.

Chopin, P., & Briley, M. (1992). Effects of four non-cholinergic cognitive enhancers in comparison with tacrine and galanthamine on scopolamine-induced amnesia in rats. *Psychopharmacology, 106*(1), 26–30.

Copeland, R. L. (1981). Behavioral and neurocortical effects of hydergine in rats. *Archives of International Pharmacodynamics, 252,* 113–123.

Coper, H., & Herrmann, W. M. (1988). Psychostimulants, analeptics, nootropics: An attempt to differentiate and assess drugs designed for the treatment of impaired brain functions. *Pharmacopsychiatry, 21,* 211–217.

Corasaniti, M. T., Paoletti, A. M., Palma, E., Granato, T., Navarra, M., & Nistico, G. (1995). Systemic administration of pramiracetam increases nitric oxide synthase activity in the cerebral cortex of the rat. *Functional Neurology, 10*(3), 151–155.

Corona, G. L., Cucchi, M. L., Frattini, P., Santagostino, G., et al. (1989). Clinical and biochemical responses to therapy in Alzheimer's disease and multi-infarct dementia. *European Archives of Psychiatry and Neurological Sciences, 239*(2), 79–86.

Crook, T., Petrie, W., Wells, C., & Massari, D. C. (1992). Effects of phosphatidylserine in Alzheimer's disease. *Psychopharmacology Bulletin, 28*(1), 61–66.

Crook, T., Tinklenberg, J., Yesavage, J., Petrie, W., Nunzi, M. G., & Massari, D. C. (1991). Effects of phosphatidylserine in age-associated memory impairment. *Neurology, 41*(5), 644–649.

Cumin, R. (1982). Effects of the novel compound aniracern upon impaired learning and memory in rodents. *Psychopharmacology, 78,* 104–111.

Davies, B., Andrewes, D., Stargatt, R., Ames, D., et al. (1990). Tetrahydroaminoacridine in Alzheimer's disease. *International Journal of Geriatric Psychiatry, 5*(5), 317–321.

Dean, W., & Morgenthaler, J. (1990). *Smart drugs.* Menlo Park, CA: Health and Freedom.

Dean, W., Morgenthaler, J., & Fowkes, S. W. M. (1993). *Smart drugs II.* Menlo Park, CA: Health and Freedom.

DeAngelis, L. (1992). The nootropic drugs piracetam and oxiracetam do not reduce anxiety in mice during elevated-x-maze testing. *Current Therapeutic Research, 52*(2), 230–237.

DeAngelis, L., & Furlan, C. (1995). The effects of ascorbic acid and oxiracetam on scopolamine-induced amnesia in a habituation test in aged mice. *Neurobiology of Learning and Memory, 64*(2), 119–124.

Desai, M. A., Valli, M. J., Monn, J. A., & Schoepp, D. D. (1995). 1-BCP, a memory-enhancing agent, selectively potentiates AMPA-induces (-sup-3H) norepinephrine release in rat hippocampal slices. *Neuropharmacology, 34*(2), 141–147.

De Wied, D. (1975). *Vasopressin and memory consolidation: Perspectives in brain research.* New York: Elsevier.

Diamond, S. J., & Browers, E. Y. M. (1976). Increase in the power of human memory in normal man through the use of drugs. *Psychopharmacology, 49,* 307–309.

Du, Y. C., Wu, J. H., Jiang, X. M., & Gu, Y. J. (1994). Characterization of binding sites of a memory-enhancing peptide AVP(4–8) in rat cortical synaptosomal membranes. *Peptides, 15*(7), 1273–1279.

Eguchi, J., Yuasa, T., Egawa, M., & Tobe, A. (1994). Effects of a novel compound MCI-225 on impaired learning and memory in rats. *Pharmacology, Biochemistry, and Behavior, 48*(2), 345–349.

Enmenegger, H., & Meier-Ruge, W. (1968). The actions of hydergine on the brain. *Pharmacology, 1,* 65–78.

Ennaceur, A., Cavoy, A., Costa, J. C., & Delacour, J. (1989). A new one-trial test for neurobiological studies of memory in rats: II. Effects of piracetam and pramiracetam. *Behavioural Brain Research, 33*(2), 197–207.

Erikson, G. C., Hager, L. B., Houseworth, C., Dugan, J., Petros, T., & Beckwith, B. E. (1985). The effects of caffeine on memory for word lists. *Physiology and Behavior, 35,* 47–51.

Evans, P. W., & Gualtieri, C. T. (1987). Treatment of chronic closed brain injury with psychostimulant drugs: A controlled case study and an appropriate evaluation procedure. *Journal of Nervous and Mental Disease, 175*(2), 104–110.

Exton-Smith, A. N. (1983). Clinical experience with ergot alkaloids. *Aging, 23,* 323.

Eysenck, M. W., & Folkard, S. (1980). Personality, time of day, and caffeine: Some theoretical and conceptual problems in Revelle et al. *Journal of Experimental Psychology: General, 109,* 32–41.

Ferrero, E. (1984). Controlled clinical trial of oxiracetam in the treatment of chronic cerebrovascular insufficiency in the elderly. *Current Therapeutic Research, 36,* 298–308.

Ferris, S. H. (1982). Combination of choline/piracetam in the treatment of senile dementia. *Psychopharmacology Bulletin, 18,* 94–98.

Fischhof, P. K., Saletu, B., Ruther, E., Litschauer, G., et al. (1992). Therapeutic efficacy of pyritinol in patients with senile dementia of the Alzheimer type (SDAT) and multi-infarct dementia (MID). *Neuropsychobiology, 26*(1–2), 65–70.

Fitten, L. J., & Ganzell, S. (1992). Spouses' assessments of Alzheimer patients' response to THA and lecithin. *American Journal of Psychiatry, 149*(4), 575.

Fordyce, D. E., Clark, V. J., Paylor, R., & Wehner, J. M. (1995). Enhancement of hippocampally-mediated learning and protein kinase C activity by oxiracetam in learning-impaired DBA/2 mice. *Brain Research, 672*(1–2), 170–176.

Gallai, V., Mazzotta, G., del Gatto, F., Montesi, S., et al. (1991). A clinical neurophysiological trial on nootropic drugs in patients with mental decline. *Acta Neurologica, 12*(1), 1–12.

Giurgea, C. E. (1973). The nootropic approach to the pharmacology of integrative activity in the brain. *Conditioned Reflex, 8*(2), 108–115.

Giurgea, C. E., & Salama, M. (1977). Nootropic drugs. *Progress in Neuropsychopharmacology, 1,* 235–247.

Gold, P. (1979, November). Effects of 1desamo-8-arginine vasopressin on behavior and cognition in primary affective disorders. *Lancet,* pp. 992–994.

Goldberg, I., Gerstman, L. J., & Mattis, S. (1982). Effect of cholinergic treatment on post-traumatic anterograde amnesia. *Archives of Neurology, 38,* 581.

Goodwin, J. S., Goodwin, J. M., & Garry, P. J. (1983). Association between nutritional status and cognitive functioning in a healthy elderly population. *Journal of the American Medical Association, 249,* 2917–2940.

Gouliaev, A. H., & Senning, A. (1994). Piracetam and other structurally related nootropics. *Brain Research Reviews, 19*(2), 188–222.

Govoni, S., Lucchi, L., Battaini, F., & Trabucchi, M. (1992). Protein kinase C increase in rat brain cortical membranes may be promoted by cognition enhancing drugs. *Life Sciences, 50*(16), PL125–PL128.

Greidanus, T., van Wimersma, B., & de Wied, D. (1985). Hypothalamic neuropeptides and memory. *Acta Nearochirurgica, 75,* 99–105.

Guili, D. (1980). Morphometric studies of synapses of the cerebellar glomerulus: The effect of centrophenoxine treatment in old rats. *Mechanisms of Aging and Development, 14,* 265–271.

Heiss, W. D., Kessler, J., Mielke, R., Szelies, B., et al. (1994). Long-term effects of phosphatidylserine, pyritinol, and cognitive training in Alzheimer's disease: A neuropsychological, EEG, and PET investigation. *Dementia, 5*(2), 88–98.

Himori, N., & Mishima, K. (1994). Amelioration by aniracetam of abnormalities as revealed in choice reaction performance and shuttle behavior. *Pharmacology, Biochemistry, and Behavior, 47*(2), 219–225.

Hindmarch, I. (1986). Activity of ginkgo biloba extract on short-term memory. *La Presse Medicale, 15*(31), 1592.

Hindmarch, I., Coleston, D. M., & Kerr, J. S. (1991). Psychopharmacological effects of pyritinol in normal volunteers. *Neuropsychobiology, 24*(3), 159–164.

Hlinak, Z., & Krejci, I. (1992). Prolonged social recognition in male rats treated with alaptide or oxiracetam. *Behavioural Brain Research, 3*(2), 129–131.

Hochschild, R. (1973). Effect of dimethylaminoethyl p-chlorophenoxy-acetate on the lifespan of male Swiss webster albino mice. *Experimental Gerontology, 8,* 177–183.

Hock, F. J. (1987). Drug influences on learning and memory in aged animals and humans. *Neuropsychobiology, 17,* 145–160.

Hughes, J. P. (1976). An ergot alkaloid preparation (hydergine) in the treatment of dementia: A critical review of the clinical literature. *Journal of the American Geriatrics Society, 24,* 490–497.

Itil, P. M. (1986). CNS pharmacology and clinical therapeutic effects of oxiracetam. *Clinical Neuropharmacology, 9*(Suppl. 3), 570–578.

Jahkel, M., Oehler, J., & Schumacher, H. E. (1994). Influence of nootropic and antidepressive drugs on open field and running wheel behavior in spontaneously high and low active mice. *Pharmacology, Biochemistry, and Behavior, 49*(2), 263–269.

Kariya, K., Tanaka, J., & Nomura, M. (1994). Systemic administration of CCK-8S, but not CCK-4, enhances dopamine turnover in the posterior nucleus accumbens: A microdialysis study in freely moving rats. *Brain Research, 657*(1–2), 1–6.

Kashiwase, H., & Watanabe, M. (1991). Geriatric psychiatry in Japan. *Journal of Geriatric Psychiatry, 24*(1), 47–57.

Kofler, B., Erhart, C., Erhart, P., & Harrer, G. (1990). A multidimensional approach in testing nootropic drug effects (Cerebrolysin). *Archives of Gerontology and Geriatrics, 10*(2), 129–140.

Kolakowsky, S., & Parenté, R. (1997). Nootropics, nutrients, and other cognitive enhancing substances for use in cognitive rehabilitation: A review and bibliography. *Journal of Cognitive Rehabilitation, 15*(2), 12–24.

Kresyun, V. I., & Rozhkovskii, Y. V. (1993). The features of the influence of psychotropic agents on the structural-functional state of the adrenals of intact and stressed animals. *Neuroscience and Behavioral Physiology, 23*(4), 357–360.

Kristofikova, Z., Benesova, O., & Tejkalova, H. (1992). Changes of high-affinity choline uptake in the hippocampus of old rats after long-term administration of two nootropic drugs (tacrine and ginkgo biloba extract). *Dementia, 3*(5–6), 304–307.

Kulkarni, S. K., & Verma, A. (1992). Evidence for nootropic effect of BR-16A (Mentat), a herbal psychotropic preparation in mice. *Indian Journal of Physiology and Pharmacology, 36,* 29–33.

Kunkel, H. (1992). EEG profile of three different extractions of ginkgo biloba. *Neuropsychobiology, 27*(1), 40–45.

Laczi, F. (1982). Effects of lycine vasopressin on memory in healthy individuals with diabetes insipidus patients. *Psychoneuroendocrinology, 7*(2), 185–191.

Legros, J. J. (1978, January). Influence of vasopressin on learning and memory. *Lancet,* pp. 41–42.

Lesser, M. (1980). *Nutrition and vitamin therapy.* New York: Bantam Books.

Loke, W. (1988). Effects of caffeine on mood and memory. *Physiology and Behavior, 44,* 367–372.

Lucchi, L., Pascale, A., Battaini, F., Govoni, S., et al. (1993). Cognition stimulating drugs modulate protein kinase C activity in cerebral cortex and hippocampus of adult rats. *Life Sciences, 53*(24), 1821–1832.

Magnani, M., Pozzi, O., Biagetti, R., Banfi, S., et al. (1992). Oxiracetam antagonizes the disruptive effects of scopolamine on memory in the radical maze. *Psychopharmacology, 106*(2), 175–178.

Mangoni, P., Sioufi, A., & Godbillon, J. (1995). Stereospecific high-performance liquid chromatographic determination of an S(−)-benzopyran methyl ester derivative (CGP 50 068), its (−)-carboxylic acid metabolite (CGP 55 461) and the related (+)-enantiomer (CGP 54 228) in human and dog plasma. *Journal of Chromatography, 664*(2), 393–400.

Martin, J. R., Cumin, R., Aschwanden, W., Moreau, J. L., et al. (1992). Aniracetam improves radical maze performance in rats. *Neuroreport: An International Journal for the Rapid Communication of Research in Neuroscience, 3*(1), 81–83.

Mathews, G., Davies, R. D., Westerman, S. J., & Stammers, R. B. (2000). *Human performance: Cognition, stress, and individual differences.* Philadelphia: Psychology Press.

Mauri, M., Sinforiani, E., Reverberi, F., Merlo, P., et al. (1994). Pramiracetam effects on scopolamine-induced amnesia in healthy volunteers. *Archives of Gerontology and Geriatrics, 18*(2), 133–139.

Michaud, C., Musse, N., Nicholas, J. P., & Mejean, L. (1991). Effects of breakfast-size on short-term memory, concentration, mood and blood glucose. *Journal of Adolescent Health, 12,* 53–57.

Mindus, P. (1976). Piracetam-induced improvement of mental performance: A controlled study on normally aging individuals. *Acta Psychiatrica Scandinavia, 54,* 150–160.

Mondadori, C. (1986). Effects of oxiracetam on learning and memory in animals: Comparison with piracetam. *Clinical Neuropharmacology, 9*(Suppl. 13), 527–537.

Mondadori, C., Ducret, T., & Borkowski, J. (1991). How long does memory consolidation take? New compounds can improve retention performance, even if administered up to 24 hours after the learning experience. *Brain Research, 555*(1), 107–111.

Mondadori, C., Ducret, T., & Hausler, A. (1992). Elevated corticosteroid levels block the memory-improving effects of nootropics and cholinomimetics. *Psychopharmacology, 108*(1–2), 11–15.

Mondadori, C., Ducret, T., & Petschke, F. (1989). Blockade of the nootropic action of piracetam-like nootropics by adrenalectomy. An effect of dosage? *Behavioural Brain Research, 34*(1–2), 155–158.

Mondadori, C., & Etienne, P. (1990). Nootropic effects of ACE inhibitors in mice. *Psychopharmacology, 100*(3), 301–307.

Mondadori, C., Gentsch, C., Hengerer, B., Ducret, T., et al. (1992). Pretreatment with aldosterone or corticosterone blocks the memory-enhancing effects of nimodipine, captopril, CGP 37 849, and strychnine in mice. *Psychopharmacology, 109*(4), 383–389.

Moos, W. H., Davis, R. E., & Gamzu, E. R. (1991). Pharmacological perspectives. In L. J. Thal, W. H. Moos, & E. R. Gamzu (Eds.), *Cognitive disorders: Pathophysiology and treatment* (pp. 309–328). New York: Dekker.

Murphree, H. B. (1960). The stimulant effect of 2-Dimethylamino-ethanol (deanol) in human volunteer subjects. *Clinical Pharmacology and Therapeutics, 1,* 303–310.

Murry, C. L., & Fibiger, H. C. (1986). The effect of pramiracetam (CI-879) on the acquisition of a radial arm maze task. *Psychopharmacology, 89,* 378–381.

Nabeshima, T., Ogawa, S. I., Kameyama, T., Shiotani, T., et al. (1991). Effects of DM-9384 and aniracetam on learning in normal and basal forebrain-lesioned rats. *Research Communications in Psychology, Psychiatry, and Behavior, 16*(1–2), 1–14.

Nagy, I., & Floyd, R. (1984). Electron spin resonance spectroscopic demonstration of the hydroxyl free radical scavenger properties of dimethylaminoethanol in spin trapping experiments confirming the molecular bases for the biological effects of centrophenoxine. *Archives of Gerontology and Geriatrics, 3*(4), 297–310.

Nandy, K., & Bourne, G. H. (1966). Effects of centrophenoxne on the lipofuscin pigments of the neurons of senile guinea pigs. *Nature, 210,* 313–311.

Nandy, K., & Schneider, F. (1978). Effects of dihydroergotoxine mesylate on aging neurons in vitro. *Gerontology, 24,* 6670.

Nickerson, V. J., & Wolthuis, O. L. (1976). Effect of the acquisition-enhancing drug piracetam on rat cerebral energy metabolism comparison with methamphetamine. *Biochemical Pharmacology, 25,* 2241–2244.

Nordberg, A., Lilja, A., Lundqvist, H., Hartvig, P., et al. (1992). Tacrine restores cholinergic nicotinic receptors and glucose metabolism in Alzheimer patients as visualized by positron emission tomography. *Neurobiology of Aging, 13*(6), 747–758.

Oettinger, L. (1958). The use of deanol in the treatment of disorders of behavior in children. *Journal of Pediatrics, 3,* 671–575.

Ohta, H., Matsumoto, K., Shimizu, M., & Watanabe, H. (1994). Paeoniflorin attenuates learning impairment of aged rats in operant brightness discrimination task. *Pharmacology, Biochemistry, and Behavior, 49*(1), 213–217.

Oliveros, J. C. (1978). Vasopressin in amnesia. *Lancet, 42,* 70–76.

Ono, S., Yamafuji, T., Chaki, H., Morita, H., Todo, Y., Maekawa, M., et al. (1995a). Studies on cognitive enhancing agents. I. Antiamnestic and antihypoxic activities of 2-dimethylaminoethyl ethers and related compounds. *Chemical & Pharmaceutical Bulletin, 43*(9), 1483–1487.

Ono, S., Yamafuji, T., Chaki, H., Morita, H., Todo, Y., Maekawa, M., et al. (1995b). Studies on cognitive enhancing agents. II. Antiamnestic and antihypoxic activities of 1-aryl-2-(2-aminoethoxy) ethanols. *Chemical & Pharmaceutical Bulletin, 43*(9), 1488–1491.

Ono, S., Yamafuji, T., Chaki, H., Morita, H., Todo, Y., Maekawa, M., et al. (1995c). Studies on cognitive enhancing agents. III. Antiamnestic and antihypoxic activities of a series of 1-bicycloaryl-2-(omega-aminoalkoxy) ethanols. *Chemical & Pharmaceutical Bulletin, 43*(9), 1492–1496.

Onofrj, M., Fulgente, T., Melchionda, D., Marchionni, A., Tomasello, F., Salpietro, F. M., et al. (1995). L-acetylcarnitine as a new therapeutic approach for peripheral neuropathies with pain. *International Journal of Clinical Pharmacology Research, 15*(1), 9–15.

O'Shanick, G. J., & Zasler, N. D. (1990). Neuropsychopharmacological approaches to traumatic brain injury. In J. Kreutzer & P. Wehman (Eds.), *Community integration following traumatic brain injury* (pp. 15–28). Baltimore: Brookes.

Otomo, E. (1985). Comparison of vinpocetine with ifenprodil tartrate and dihidroergotoxine mesylate treatment and results of long-term treatment with vinpocetine. *Current Therapeutic Research, 37*(5), 811–821.

Parenté, R., & Herrmann, D. (1996). *Retraining cognition: Techniques and applications.* Gaithersburg, MD: Aspen.

Parnetti, L., Bartorelli, L., Bonaiuto, S., Cucinotta, D., et al. (1991). Aniracetam (Ro 13–5057) for the treatment of senile dementia of Alzheimer type: Results of a mulitcentre clinical study. *Dementia, 2*(5), 262–267.

Parnetti, L., Gaiti, A., Mecocci, P., Gottfries, C. G., et al. (1990). Effect of acetyl-L-carnitine on serum levels of cortisol and adrenocorticotropic hormone and its clinical effect in patients with senile dementia of Alzheimer type. *Dementia, 1*(3), 159–168.

Pelton, D. (1989). *Mind food and smart pills: A sourcebook for the vitamins, herbs, and drugs that can increase intelligence, improve memory, and prevent brain aging.* New York: Doubleday.

Pepeu, G. (1994). Memory disorders: Novel treatments, clinical perspective. *Life Sciences, 55*(25–26), 2189–2194.

Petkov, V. (1987). Effects of standardized ginseng extract on learning, memory, and physical capabilities. *American Journal of Chinese Medicine, 15*(1), 19–29.

Pfeiffer, C. (1957). Stimulant effect of 2-Dimethylaminoethanol: Possible precursor to brain acetylcholine. *Science, 126*, 610–611.

Pfeiffer, C. (1959). Parasympathetic neurohormones. Possible precursors and effects on behavior. *International Review of Neurobiology, 10*, 195–224.

Pitsikas, N., & Algeri, S. (1992). Effect of oxiracetam on scopolamine-induced amnesia in the rat in a spatial learning task. *Pharmacology, Biochemistry, and Behavior, 43*(3), 949–951.

Popa, R., Schneider, G., Mihalas, P., Stefaniga, I. G., Mihalas, R., & Mateescu, R. (1994). Antagonstic-stress superiority

versus Meclofenoxate in gerontopsychiatry (Alzheimer type dementia). *Archives of Gerontology and Geriatrics, 7* (Suppl. 4), 197–206.

Poschel, B. P. H. (1988). New pharmacologic perspectives on nootropic drugs. In L. L. Iverson, S. D. Iverson, & S. H. Snyder (Eds.), *Handbook of Psycopharmacology* (Vol. 20, pp. 11–18). New York: Plenum Press.

Potter, B., & Orfali, S. (1993). *Brain boosters: Foods and drugs that make you smarter.* Berkeley, CA: Ronin.

Quiroga, F., & Imbriano, A. E. (1979). The effect of panax ginseng extract on cerebrovascular deficits. *Orientacion Medica, 28*, 86–87.

Rao, D., & Norris, J. (1971). A double blind investigation of hydergine in the treatment of cerebrovasaular insufficiency in the elderly. *Johns Hopkins Medical Journal, 130*, 317.

Revelle, W., Humphreys, M. S., Simon, L., & Gilliland, K. (1980). The interactive effect of personality, time of day, and caffeine: A test of the arousal model. *Journal of Experimental Psychology: General, 109*, 1–31.

Riekkinen, P., Jr., Kuikka, J., Soininen, H., Helkala, E. L., Hallikainen, M., & Riekkinen, P. (1995). Tetrahydroaminoacridine modulates technetium-99m labeled ethylene dicysteinate retention in Alzheimer's disease measured with single photon emission computed tomography imaging. *Neuroscience Letters, 195*(1), 53–56.

Riga, S., & Riga, D. (1974). Effects of centrophenoxine on the lipofuscin pigments of the nervous system of old rats. *Brain Research, 72*, 265–275.

Ritzmann, R., Kling, A., Melchior, C. L., & Glasky, A. J. (1993). Effect of age and strain on working memory in mice as measured by win-shift paradigm. *Pharmacology, Biochemistry, and Behavior, 44*(4), 805–807.

Rupniak, N. M., Field, M. J., Samson, N. A., Steventon, M. J., et al. (1990). Direct comparison of cognitive facilitation by physostigmine and tetrahydroaminocridine in two primate models. *Neurobiology of Aging, 11*(6), 609–613.

Rupprecht, R., Maurer, K., Dierks, T., & Ihl, R. (1989). Topographic mapping of pharmaco-EEG before and after application of phosphatidylserine. *Psychiatry Research, 29*(3), 417–418.

Sahakian, B. J., & Coull, J. T. (1993). Tetrahydrominocridine (THA) in Alzheimer's disease: An assessment of attentional and mnemonic function using CANTAB. *Acta Neurologica Scadinavica, 88*(Suppl. 149), 29–35.

Salimov, R., Salimov, N., Shvets, L., & Shvets, N. (1995). Effect of chronic piracetam on age-related changes of crossmaze exploration in mice. *Pharmacology, Biochemistry, and Behavior, 52*(3), 637–640.

Sano, M., Bell, K., Cote, L., Dooneief, G., Lawton, A., Legler, L., et al. (1992). Double-blind parallel design pilot study of acetyl levocarnitine in patients with Alzheimer's disease. *Archives of Neurology, 49*(11), 1137–1141.

Sano, M., Bell, K., Marder, K., Stricks, L., et al. (1993). Safety and efficacy of oral physostigmine in the treatment of Alzheimer disease. *Clinical Neuropharmacology, 16*(1), 61–69.

Sansone, M., Castellano, C., Battaglia, M., & Ammassari-Teule, M. (1990). Oxiracetam prevents mecamylamineinduced impairment of active, but not passive, avoidance learning in mice. *Pharmacology, Biochemistry, and Behavior, 36*(2), 389–392.

Sansone, M., Castellano, C., Battaglia, M., & Ammassari-Teule, M. (1991). Effects of oxiracetam-nicotine combinations on active and passive avoidance learning in mice. *Pharmacology, Biochemistry, and Behavior, 39*(1), 197–200.

Sansone, M., Castellano, C., Palazzesi, S., Battaglia, M., et al. (1993). Effects of oxiracetam, physostigmine, and their combination on active and passive avoidance learning in mice. *Pharmacology, Biochemistry, and Behavior, 44*(2), 451–455.

Sansone, M., & Oliverio, A. (1989). Avoidance facilitation by nootropics. *Progress in Neuro-Psychopharmacology & Biological Psychiatry, 13*(Suppl.), S89–S97.

Santarelli, M., Granato, A., Sbriccoli, A., Gobbi, G., Janiri, L., & Minciacchi, D. (1995). Alterations of the thalamo-cortical system in rats prenatally exposed to ethanol are prevented by concurrent administration of acetyl-L-carnitine. *Brain Research, 698*(1–2), 241–247.

Schaffler, K., & Reeh, P. (1985). Long-term drug administration effects of ginkgo biloba on the performance of healthy subjects exposed to hypoxia. In J. Angoli (Ed.), *Effects of ginkgo biloba extracts on organic cerebral impairment* (pp. 77–84). Amsterdam: Eurotext.

Sevush, S., Guterman, A., & Villalon, A. V. (1991). Improved verbal learning after outpatient oral physostigmine therapy in patients with dementia of the Alzheimer type. *Journal of Clinical Psychiatry, 52*(7), 300–303.

Shul'gina, G. I., & Okhotnikov, N. V. (1991). Dynamics of synchronization in the functioning of neurons of the new cortex and hippocampus during learning before and after the administration of nootropic agents and narcotics. *Neuroscience and Behavioral Physiology, 21*(5), 416–422.

Silver, A. J. (1992). Nutritional aspects of memory dysfunction. In J. Morely, R. M. Coe, R. Strong, & G. T. Grossberg (Eds.), *Memory functions in aging and aging-related disorders*. New York: Springer.

Simon, W. C. M. (1977, February). Efficiency control of a gerotherapeutic containing ginseng by means of Kraepelin's working test. *Proceedings of the International Gerontological Symposium* (pp. 199–206). Singpore, Thailand.

Somnier, F. E., Ostergaard, M. S., Boysen, G., Bruhn, P., et al. (1990). Aniracetam tested in chronic psychosyndrome after long-term exposure to organic solvents: A randomized, double-blind, placebo-controlled cross-over study with neuropsychological tests. *Psychopharmacology, 101*(1), 43–46.

Spaldin, V., Madden, S., Adams, D. A., Edwards, R. J., Davies, D. S., & Park, B. K. (1995). Determination of human hepatic cytochrome P4501A2 activity in vitro use of tacrine as an isoenzyme-specific probe. *Drug Metabolism & Disposition, 23*(9), 929–934.

Stancheva, S. L., & Alova, L. G. (1994). Biogenic monoamine uptake by rat brain synaptosomes during aging: Effects of nootropic drugs. *General Pharmacology, 25*(5), 981–987.

Steffen, V., Santiago, M., de la Cruz, C. P., Revilla, E., Machado, A., & Cano, J. (1995). Effect of intraventricular injection of 1-methyl-4-phenylpyridinium: Protection by acetyl-L-carnitine. *Human & Experimental Toxicology, 14*(11), 865–871.

Stoll, L., Schubert, T., & Muller, W. E. (1992). Age-related deficits of central muscarinic cholinergic receptor function in the mouse: Partial restoration by chronic piracetam treatment. *Neurobiology of Aging, 13*(1), 39–44.

Subhan, Z., & Hindmarch, I. (1985). Psychopharmacological effects of vinpocetine in normal healthy volunteers. *European Journal of Clinical Pharmacology, 28*, 367–371.

Tighilet, B., & Lacour, M. (1995). Pharmacological activity of the ginkgo biloba extract (Egb 761) on equilibrium function recovery in the unilateral vestibular neuroectomized cat. *Journal of Vestibular Research Equilibrium and Orientation, 5*(3), 187–200.

Toledano, A., & Bentura, M. L. (1994). Pyritinol facilitates the recovery of cortical cholinergic deficits caused by nucleus basalis lesions. *Journal of Neural Transmission—Parkinson's Disease & Dementia Section, 7*(3), 195–209.

Tritsmans, L., Clincke, G., Devenijns, F., Verhoosel, G., & Amery, W. K. (1988). Memory study with sabeluzole in a population with a mean age of 85 years: A pilot experiment. *Current Therapeutic Research, 44*(6), 966–974.

Tsai, M., Su, J. L., Chen, M. L., Fan, S. Z., et al. (1992). The effect of 3,3-di-pyridyl-methyl-1-phenyl-2-indolinone on the nerve terminal currents of mouse skeletal muscles. *Neuropharmacology, 31*(9), 943–947.

Ventra, C., Grimaldi, M., Meucci, O., Scorziello, A., et al. (1994). Aniracetam improves behavioural responses and facilitates signal transduction in the rat brain. *Journal of Psychopharmacology, 8*(2), 109–117.

Vermeij, T. A., & Edelbroek, P. M. (1994). High-performance liquid chromatographic and megabore gas-liquid chromatographic determination of levetiracetam (ucb L059) in human serum after solid-phase extraction. *Journal of Chromatography B: Biomedical Applications, 662*(1), 134–139.

Vernyi, I., Derzhiruk, L. P., & Mogilevskii, A. (1995). Izmenenie pokazatelei funktsional'noi aktivnosti neironov pod deistviem piratsetama kak vozmozhnaia osnova relizatsii effektov nootropov. [Changes in the indices of neuronal functional activity under the action of piracetam as a possible basis for realizing the effects of nootropic agents.] *Zhurnal Vysshei Nervnoi Deiatelnosti I. P. Pavlova, 45*(4), 791–801.

Viana, G. S., Marinho, M. M., & Sousa, F. C. (1992). Effect of piracetam administration on -sup-3H-N-methylscopolamine binding in cerebral cortex of young and old rats. *Life Sciences, 50*(13), 971–977.

Vincent, G. (1985). The effects of aniracetam (RO-13-5057) on the enhancement or protection of memory. *Annals of the New York Academy of Sciences, 244*, 489–491.

Warburton, D. M. (1986). Clinical psychopharmacology of ginkgo biloba extract. *La Presse Medicate, 15*(31), 1595.

Weil, C. (1978). Pharmacology and clinical pharmacology of hydergine. In C. Weil (Ed.), *Handbook of experimental pharmacology*. New York: Springer-Verlag.

Wesnes, K. A., Anand, R., Simpson, P. M., & Christmas, L. (1990). The use of a scopolamine model to study the potential nootropic effects of aniracetam and piracetam in healthy volunteers. *Journal of Psychopharmacology, 4*(4), 219–232.

Whyte, J. (2002). Pharmacological treatment of cognitive impairments. In P. Eslinger (Ed.), *Neuropsychological interventions* (pp. 59–79). New York: Guilford Press.

Wilsher, C. R. (1987). Piracetam and dyslexia: Effects on reading tests. *Journal of Clinical Pharmacology, 7*(4), 230–237.

Wilsher, C. R., & Taylor, E. A. (1994). Piracetam in developmental reading disorders: A review. *European Child and Adolescent Psychiatry, 3*(2), 59–71.

Yamada, K., Nakayama, S., Shiotani, T., Hasegawa, T., et al. (1994). Possible involvement of the activation of voltage-sensitive calcium channels in the ameliorating effects of nefiracetam on scopolamine-induced impairment of performance in a passive avoidance task. *Journal of Pharmacology and Experimental Therapeutics, 270*(3), 881–892.

Yamazaki, M., Matsuoka, N., Maeda, N., Kuratani, K., Ohkubo, Y., & Yamoguchi, I. (1995). FR121196, a potential anti-

dementia drug, ameliorates the impaired memory of rat in the Morris water maze. *Journal of Pharmacology and Experimental Therapeutics, 272*(1), 256–263.

Yoshikawa, M. (1983). A dose-response study with dihydeoergctoxine mesylate in cerebrovascular disturbances. *Journal of the American Geriatrics Society, 31*(1), 1–7.

Zagler, E. L., & Black, P. M. (1985). Neuropeptides in human memory and learning processes. *Neurosurgery, 17*, 355–369.

Zivkovic, I., Thompson, D. M., Bertolino, M., Uzunov, D., et al. (1995). 7-Chloro-3-methyl-3-4-dihydro-2H-1,2,4 benzothiadiazine S,S-dioxide (IDRA 21): A benzothiadiazine derivative that enhances cognition by attenuating DL-a-amino-2,3-dihydro-5-methyl-3-oxo-4-isoxazole-propanoic acid (AMPA) receptor desensitization. *Journal of Pharmacology and Experimental Therapeutics, 272*(1), 300–309.

Chapter 23

❦

Incentives and
Cognitive Rehabilitation

etting the client to comply with treatment goals and to use strategies spontaneously is perhaps one of the most difficult aspects of cognitive rehabilitation. Damage to one or more areas of the brain may destroy critical brain structures that mediate or control a client's motivation to comply with therapy (Arkes, 1991). Many therapists notice that a client makes marked improvement when he or she can see a tangible goal, and many therapists come to believe that success or failure in therapy reduces to the client's motivation. Unfortunately, there has been a general dearth of research that has determined what motivates persons with brain injury in therapy and the extent to which incentives facilitate cognitive rehabilitation (Ellis, Ottaway, Varner, Becker, & Moore, 1997; Fowles, 1988; Humphreys & Revelle, 1984; Parenté, 1994).

The purpose of this chapter is to provide practical suggestions that therapists can use to improve their treatment effectiveness and compliance. The chapter begins with a brief historical overview of the concept of incentives and a discussion of reward, punishment, and motivation as they apply to rehabilitation. Next, an incentive-based model of cognitive rehabilitation is presented and evaluated. The model assumes that thinking and memory will improve immediately and dramatically as long as there is a relevant incentive to perform. The results of several experiments that test this assumption and expand on it are discussed. The results of these experiments indicated that poor recall after a brain injury can be substantially improved with an appropriate incentive. The implications of this on the model for rehabilitation treatment planning are presented in detail along with specific suggestions that therapists can implement.

What Is Incentive?

The fact that humans will work for what they perceive to be valuable is nothing new. However, during the mid-1940s, Clark Hull (1943), an American psychologist, formally theorized that human behavior and cognitive skill could be systematically manipulated with incentives. He described a theory of incentive-based learning in his book *Principles of Behavior* and he integrated the concept into his larger theory of behavior. Students of this behavioral theory, such as Logan (1960, 1968), were quick to refine and elaborate the incentive portion of Hull's theory. The incentive notion was not systematically applied within the brain injury field until the latter part of the 20th century (Parenté, 1994).

271

According to the early incentive theorists, the things that a person knows how to do are called *habits*. Those things that have value to a person are called *incentive-motivators*. Incentive theorists assume that the combination of incentives, such as money, and physiological drives, such as hunger or thirst, are responsible for energizing habits into actions. Basically, people learn habits over the years because of physiological needs, such as eating, drinking, and having a comfortable place to live. There is, however, another learning process that occurs in addition to habit learning. This is called *incentive learning*, which is the understanding that all behavior has consequences. These two types of learning usually occur together. For example, most people are motivated for advancement in their job because they foresee a higher salary and increased prestige. However, incentive and habit learning can function independently. For example, although many people are aware of the monetary incentives associated with certain professions, they never become doctors, lawyers, or business executives.

The early theorists documented several principles of incentive-based learning. First, performance was faster and more accurate when the reward was larger rather than smaller. These theorists also noticed that the size of the reward was not the only factor that controlled behavior. Other things such as the quality of the reward or how much time intervened between the behavior and the reward also contributed to behavior. For example, most people will work harder and longer when the reward is an expensive dinner at a four-star restaurant versus getting a hamburger and french fries at a fast-food restaurant. People might also be inclined to postpone the work if the anticipated dinner is to occur at a distant and unspecified time in the future.

The early theorists also noticed that the incentive value of a reward depended on the type of reward a person was accustomed to receiving. Working for a reward initially resulted in less performance when a person was shifted from a large reward to smaller ones. Conversely, after receiving a small reward, performance improved markedly when the size or quality of the reward increased. For example, it may be difficult for a person to give full effort in a job that pays $20,000 a year after being laid off from a job that paid $40,000 a year. Likewise, many employees make a dramatic increase in work performance when they move from a low-paying position to one that provides a marked increase in salary.

Clark Hull and his students were not the only psychologists to discuss the concept of incentive. Mowrer (1956, 1960), for example, considered the topic from a slightly different perspective. He believed that learning resulted from an association of behavior with one of four emotional states. A person might associate a certain behavior with a pleasurable state. The person could also associate the same behavior with something unpleasant or noxious. These two ideas are obvious and are something that most people experience every day. Mowrer also discussed two other ideas that are less obvious but no less important. A person could also associate a behavior with the removal of something pleasant. For example, a client may realize that certain behaviors result in the removal of the warm and nurturing tone from the therapist's voice. Morwrer also described the association of a behavior with the removal of something that is noxious. For example, a client may perceive lunch in the cafeteria in the middle of a stressful day as rewarding.

According to Mowrer, when a person's behavior resulted in a reward, some aspect of the situation came to elicit *hope*. When behaviors resulted in an unpleasant outcome, the situation became associated with *avoidance*. Individuals learned *disappointment* when their behavior resulted in the removal of something they cherish. They learned *relief* when some event signaled the removal of something unpleasant.

Mowrer's model (1956, 1960) of behavior assumed that incentive was the anticipation of a positive, pleasurable, or rewarding state. Although his description of the process differed from Hull's (1943), both models assumed that humans use the feedback from their gains and losses to modify their behavior. In Mowrer's system the feedback from a person's interaction with the environment and with other people determined their state of hope, disappointment, relief, or avoidance.

Other theorists such as Skinner (1969) and Ferster and Skinner (1957) developed the notion of schedules of reward and discussed how schedules could be used to explain the incentive notion. Briefly, these theorists noted that the quality and amount of a person's behavior could be predicted by the pattern and quality of the rewards he or she received. The notion of incentive learning was actually quite similar to how Skinner described the concept of reward in his model of behavior. Logan (1968) produced the most comprehensive incentive theory, which later became part of Hull's learning theory outlined above. Both Logan and Skinner asserted that incentive-motivators such as the delay and the quality of reward affected behavior along with drives such as hunger or other physiological needs.

The importance of these early theorists is that they identified two basic types of learning. Habit learning was the creation of behavioral blueprints, while incentive learning was the knowledge of possible gains that certain behaviors were likely to produce. Both types of learning were necessary for behavior to take place. Many cognitive rehabilitation therapists teach their clients skills to the point at which they can demonstrate satisfactory proficiency during a session. However, if the clients do not use the skill in everyday life and receive rewards as a result, then they will probably not use the skill spontaneously.

The similarities among the theories discussed have clear implications for rehabilitation after brain injury. Perhaps the most important commonality is the assumption that there are at least two types of learning, habit learning and incentive learning. Although habit and incentive learning coexist, they can also occur independently. Both are necessary for a learned behavior to occur spontaneously. Habits are the action plans that gradually develop through experience with the world. However, people also learn the incentive value of the various action plans, that is, they realize that a specific behavior always has a consequence. Without habit learning, there would be no action plans to follow. Without incentive learning, there would be no way to direct behavior.

This incentive learning process is typically disrupted after traumatic brain injury. That is, persons with TBI either have difficulty learning incentives or they cannot retain the incentive relationships that they do learn. It is therefore reasonable to suggest that persons with brain injury may be able to learn habits but may not be able to implement them because they cannot effectively pair the incentive relationship to the habit.

Incentive Versus Motivation

There is no clear distinction between incentive and motivation. The two words describe different psychological states that are similar to a push-and-pull mechanism. As applied to the field of brain injury rehabilitation, the distinction implies that the therapist can use at least two methods to change a client's behavior. Unfortunately, most therapists feel that they can only push or prod a client into adopting a more efficient or more socially appropriate behavior. Often the therapist unwittingly assumes the role of police officer or parent. However, the therapist can foster a far more productive therapy environment by creating attractive incentives for performance (Atkinson & Wickens, 1971). This is the carrot-on-a-stick approach. In our experience, the most effective therapists spend a great deal of time creating incentives for good performance and for compliance with treatment goals (Parenté, 1994). We have found that pushing a client to perform is less useful. This is, figuratively, the gun-to-the-head approach, in which the client performs because he or she feels that some negative consequence will occur otherwise. Clients typically work hardest in therapy when there is a carrot-on-a-stick pulling them in any given direction. When pushed or prodded, they may dig in their heels and resist treatment.

Rewards and Punishments

It should be clear to the reader that the terms incentive and motivation are intimately related to the idea of reward and punishment. It is tempting to think of incentives as rewards and punishments as motivators. This is not the case, however, and it is important for the therapist to realize the differences between these terms and the implications these differences have for working with persons with traumatic brain injury. *Rewards are used to increase a desired behavior. Punishments are designed to decrease an unwanted behavior* (Wolpe, 1973). For example, a therapist may reward a client for using a memory strategy spontaneously whereas the same client may be punished in some way when he or she behaves in an obnoxious manner. In our experience, rewards are effective for modifying clients' behaviors. Punishments generally are not effective for this purpose.

Rewards and punishments can also be positive and negative. *Positive* refers to the application or giving of something whereas *negative* refers to taking something away. A positive reward is therefore something a client receives that increases the likelihood that he or she will respond the same way in the future (Kleinsmith & Kaplan, 1963). For example, giving a client verbal praise after each correct response in a therapy session is a positive reward. Positive rewards are typically effective and, in most cases, easy to use. A negative reward occurs when a therapist gets a client to increase a behavior by removing something unpleasant. This type of reward does not work well in most situations because the therapist would first have to put the client into a noxious state in order to remove it later.

Positive punishments can occur when the therapist would like to reduce one or more of a client's behaviors. The therapist can modify the client's behavior by doing something he or she does not like each time the behavior occurs. We do not recommend using positive punishments because they usually lead to aggressive behavior and can have unpredictable consequences. Negative punishment means the therapist takes something away from a client each time an undesirable behavior occurs. For example, if the client smokes, then his or her smoking break could be eliminated. Negative punishments can produce hostility and aggression and should be used sparingly, only when the therapist feels that the punishment will not produce a response that is more undesirable than the one he or she was trying to eliminate in the first place.

An Incentive-Based Model of Cognitive Rehabilitation

Therapists often begin treatment with the assumption that the client's thinking and memory processes are damaged. Parenté and Anderson-Parenté (1991) refer to this assumption as the *broken brain* model of cognitive rehabilitation. The treatment goals are therefore to teach the client compensatory strategies that get around the problem, to strengthen the damaged process via stimulation therapy, or to train the client to use some compensatory device that obviates the problem. Unfortunately, many therapists will not give much thought to the incentive value of their treatment. Their primary goal is to teach clients new cognitive skills and they assume that clients will use these skills when the need arises (Levy, 1977; Levy & Loftus, 1984). However, it is often the case that clients learn the skills but never actually apply them spontaneously. Parenté (1994) outlined an incentive-based model of cognitive rehabilitation that predicts this phenomenon. We discuss this model along with its implications for treatment intervention.

The incentive-based model of cognitive rehabilitation is consistent with the theories of learning previously discussed. It is, however, most closely aligned with Logan's (1960, 1968) concept of incentive-motivation. As applied to brain injury rehabilitation, the model has two basic assumptions. First, there are at least two types of learning that go on in cognitive rehabilitation, strategy learning and incentive learning. Strategies are memory techniques or cognitive skills that the client learns in order to perform some type of task. Ideally, the therapist teaches the client strategies that will presumably carry over into the client's activities of daily living. However, the client also learns the incentive value of the new behaviors, that is, he or she realizes that use of the strategies produces a reward or attains some desired state of affairs. These two types of learning coexist in most situations, although they can also occur independently. Second, both types of learning must occur before the client will spontaneously use the learned strategies. Incentive learning occurs through real-world experience. Without incentive learning, the client may learn compensatory strategies but will not necessarily use them.

The incentive-based model of cognitive rehabilitation differs from the broken brain model because it assumes that the cognitive system is still basically intact and can function quite well under certain conditions. The broken brain assumption denies the client's ability to think and remember effectively under most conditions and the goal is to compensate for its malfunction. The incentive model assumes that cognitive deficits can be dramatically improved with incentive learning. Accordingly, the primary goal of therapy is to create an environment where there is an appropriate incentive, one that is sufficient to ensure adequate levels of cognitive performance and where the client can associate newly learned strategies with rewards.

It may be difficult for many therapists to lessen their reliance on the broken brain model. Clearly brain injury produces tissue damage, which certainly affects a client's thinking skills. Most clients reportedly had adequate thinking skills before their injury and there is a clear decrease in these skills after the injury. It therefore seems obvious that the damage to the brain following the injury has affected the client's ability to think and to remember. We do not entirely reject this assumption. We do, however, question its value as an effective model of brain injury rehabilitation. It is necessary to consider other factors that may affect the recovery process and determine the course of treatment.

The multimodal model discussed in Chapter 2 identified several factors that could produce cognitive deficits. Diet, drug use, and premorbid educational level are just a few of these factors. The depression and elation that often accompany rapid mood swings have known effects on thinking. They both restrict a person's ability to organize information because the mood swings keep him or her from attending and processing (Hertel, 1994). Moreover, in many cases, the client cannot think and remember effectively because there is no clear or obvious reason to do so. The lack of incentive learning in most therapy situations leads many clients to question the value of the treatment because they do not see its relevance.

Evaluation

The incentive-based model of cognitive rehabilitation assumes that the memory and cognitive deficits that accompany brain injury can be ameliorated with appropriate incentive learning. Therapists can teach clients strategies that will improve their performance in certain situations; however, clients will usually not use them unless they also learn the incentive relationship that will elicit the strategy spontaneously. Teaching strategies creates the potential for behavior. Teaching incentives shows the client how to initiate the behavior spontaneously.

Tests of the Incentive-Based Model

Parenté (1994) provided preliminary tests of the incentive-based model in a series of experiments. These experiments have continued and the results have remained unchanged and stable. In each experiment, the model predicted that persons with brain injury could remember quite well so long as there was a reason to do so. It was therefore reasonable to assume that manipulations of incentive could produce rapid and dramatic improvements in thinking skills. This prediction stood in sharp contrast to the broken brain model, which predicted that thinking skill would improve slowly as a person gradually learns effective compensatory strategies.

Three experiments were conducted that addressed this issue. The overall conclusion is that cognitive skills can improve immediately and dramatically after brain injury, often to average levels, when the therapist creates a relevant incentive to activate a client's performance. An abbreviated discussion of these experiments follows. The reader is referred to Parenté (1994) for an in-depth treatment of these results.

Initially, 24 persons with brain injury participated in these experiments. Since the time these results were first reported, we have involved more than 100 participants in similar experiments with the same result. The complete results for 40 of the participants are presented. Each of these participants was receiving cognitive rehabilitation therapy after a traumatic brain injury. The participants' ages varied from 17 to 64. Their IQs generally fell in the low average range (mean = 89) and tests of memory indicated a general decline (mean MQ = 80). Each participant was considered mild to moderately impaired according to criteria adopted by Maryland's Division of Rehabilitation Services.

Although the therapeutic goal of each of these experiments was to show the participant that his or her attention and memory could change markedly with appropriate incentives and environmental changes (Davies & Jones, 1975), the treatment also provided experimental evidence in favor of the incentive-based model of cognitive rehabilitation outlined above.

In the first experiment, participants played the first card game that is discussed in Chapter 10. As described in that chapter, the number of correctly and incorrectly identified cards was used as a measure of performance. There were 20 participants in this experiment and each repeated this card game four times, each time under a different incentive condition. The first game was a baseline condition in which no incentive was provided. In the second game, the therapist provided a $100 incentive. No incentive was provided in the third game, and the fourth game again had a $100 incentive. The incentive was an actual $100 bill placed in front of the participant so that he or she could see it while playing the game. The therapist told the participant in the second and fourth conditions that getting the $100 was contingent on perfect performance.

Again, the therapeutic purpose of the experiment was to demonstrate for the participant that his or her thinking processes could improve rapidly when there was a reason to perform. The entire experiment occurred over a period of less than an hour and it would have been unreasonable to conclude that improvement was due to some long-term organic change.

Twenty additional persons with traumatic brain injury were asked to play the game once. These participants played the game with no incentive and their group performance served as a basis for comparison.

The original 20 participants who played the game four times performed initially about as well as one would expect from a sample of persons with brain injury. With no incentive, their performance in the first and third conditions was within the range of the 20 participants who had done the experiment once with no incentive. Generally, they scored about two-thirds correct responses and one-third incorrect responses. However, when a $100 bill was placed in front of them, their performance increased immediately to the point where it fell in the lower end of the range expected of college students with no brain injury. Removal of the incentive had the effect of lowering performance to a level within the range of the participants who had done the task once. Reinstating the incentive had the effect of increasing performance to the lower end of the college student range.

The results of the first experiment showed that a monetary incentive was sufficient to improve performance in a card game task that measured attention and immediate memory. In the second experiment, we replicated this result but used a different task in order to extend the generalizability of the incentive effect. Ten persons with brain injury were tested, five with a digit-span task and five with a letter-span task. The digit-span group was asked to recall random number strings that were presented on a computer screen. The strings increased by one digit with each presentation and the test continued until the participant could no longer recall the string on three successive attempts. The participant's digit span was the largest digit string he or she could recall during the session. The letter-span participants received a similar test although they recalled consonants rather than digits. The participant's letter span was the longest string of consonants he or she could recall during the session.

The experimental design was identical to the one used in the first experiment. There was no incentive in the first and third conditions and a $100 incentive in the second and fourth conditions. The participants were told that they would receive the $100 incentive if they correctly recalled a nine-digit or nine-letter string correctly on two successive trials. We measured digit and letter spans for 20 college students and 20 persons with brain injury for comparison purposes.

The results of this experiment were quite similar to those of the first. There was significant improvement of performance when the incentive was provided. Although these participants performed at a level comparable to most other persons with brain injury when there was no incentive, their performance improved to levels comparable to college students when an incentive was provided.

The first two experiments indicated that monetary incentives were sufficient to improve performance on tests of attention and immediate memory. The third experiment examined the effect of incentive on other, subtler aspects of memory. Specifically, the third experiment assessed the effect of incentive on information storage, the transfer of information between immediate and long-term memory, and long-term retention.

The third experiment evaluated the effects of monetary incentive on performance in a word-learning experiment that used the

Buschke Selective Reminding Procedure (Buschke, 1973). We chose the Buschke procedure because it measures several different memory processes simultaneously. These include short-term memory, specifically a person's dependence on short-term memory; long-term storage, which is the ability to transfer information from short- to long-term memory; long-term retrieval, which is the ability to retrieve information from long-term memory; consistent long-term retrieval, which is the ability to repeatedly retrieve information from long-term memory; and organization, which is the ability to recognize and use the built-in semantic organization of the word list.

Ten persons with brain injury participated in this experiment. We read a 12-item list of common nouns, which could be organized into six semantic categories. The words used were *dog, cat, table, chair, red, green, north, west, Mars, Venus, gun, knife*. The words were read in a random order on the first trial. The participant then recalled as many of the words as he or she could remember in any desired order. When the participant could not recall any more of the words, the therapist repeated only those words that the participant had been unable to recall. The participant attempted to recall the entire list again and when his or her recall failed, the therapist restated those words that were not recalled on that trial. This type of learning procedure is called *selective reminding* because the therapist reminded the participant of only those items he or she failed to recall on a given trial. The procedure continued until the participant could recall all 12 words on two successive trials. This was the baseline condition in which no incentive was provided.

In the incentive condition, the same participants learned a second list: *paper, pen, hand, foot, moon, sun, wall, floor, day, night, yellow, blue*. The participants were offered $100 for two perfect consecutive recalls of the word list within six trials. Five of the participants learned the first list, then the second

list, and five learned the lists in the reverse order. This procedure was necessary to protect the results from bias due to the possibility that one list may have been easier to learn than the other.

The results of this experiment were also consistent with those of the first two experiments. Incentive affected most of the measures of memory. The largest difference occurred with the long-term storage, consistent long-term retrieval, and organization measures. The results were less striking for the overall recall measure, long-term retrieval, and the short-term retrieval measures. Incentive improved the participants' ability to restore information in long-term memory and to perceive the built-in semantic organization. Because this effect occurred within minutes, it could not have been the result of a gradual improvement of cognitive functions.

From Theory to Practice

The broken brain model assumes that cognitive dysfunction after brain injury is due to a damaged neural mechanism. We have not abandoned that model; however, we now believe that the mechanisms of memory and cognition may not be as damaged as was once thought. Our thesis is that the person with brain injury has lost the ability to automatically associate the appropriate incentive motivators and habits, which are both necessary and sufficient conditions for the initiation of effortful processing. Although the therapist can certainly teach a client habits and strategies, creating incentives is perhaps the only way to ensure compliance with treatment goals, attention and concentration during treatment sessions, and spontaneous use of strategies (see also Eysenck & Eysenck, 1980).

The incentive-based model of cognitive rehabilitation provides clear directions for treatments that are quite different from those derived from the broken brain model. Accordingly, therapy interventions should focus on identifying incentives that are uniquely relevant to the client, specifically, those the client will work to achieve. Without these incentives, therapy efforts will be overly time consuming and produce only marginal improvement.

Monetary incentives are not the only effective rewards (Dolan & Norto, 1977). Therapy clients also value social praise, companionship, interesting games, and stimulation (Maslow, 1970). Computer software for cognitive rehabilitation may be useful when it engages a client's interest. But once the novelty of the program wears off, the computer may sit unused. On the other hand, many clients will play computer games for a much longer period of time because they find them interesting and engaging, even though the games may be of questionable therapeutic value. We have found that computer software for cognitive rehabilitation usually produces gains only in attention and concentration and it is unclear if these same gains also would have occurred by having the client play the more interesting computer games. There are currently a great many computer games that are not only challenging but that also require logic, foresight, and reasoning. Moreover, as games become more sophisticated, their incentive value will likely increase markedly.

Current Needs and Interests

Therapists are well advised to carefully monitor a client's needs and interests to determine what types of activities he or she finds interesting. For example, one client was a merchant marine before his brain injury. We tried to get him to play the children's game *Memory*, which is a takeoff of the TV game show *Concentration*. Briefly, several pairs of pictures are placed face down in an array on the table and the player must turn over two cards at a time and remember the location of the pair. The merchant marine client, who loved auto racing, found the game boring and childish until we replaced the original cards with two decks of playing cards. Each card deck had racing cars on the flip side of the card. Using these stimuli, the client played for hours at a time. Indeed, this same technique was never useful with any other client, and it shows how a simple manipulation of an often-used memory-training game can produce a level of incentive that greatly facilitates compliance.

Premorbid Interests

The therapist should interview a client's family and friends to assess his or her premorbid interests and try to construct therapy materials that capitalize on these interests. For example, one client was interested in motorcycles. We determined that he had severe reading problems. His reading comprehension training therefore used motorcycle magazines. He was also asked to disassemble and reassemble a motorcycle engine, which required reading an entire engine repair manual.

Social Relationships

A client's relationships with family, friends, and other persons with brain injury can have a powerful incentive value. The incentive is especially strong when the client becomes romantically involved or finds an accepting friend. The incentive may involve a sexual aspect, but, more often, it is based on acceptance, companionship, and a sense of inclusion within a social network. We have noticed that many clients will make a special effort in treatment simply because they want to be accepted by their family or friends. For this reason, we encourage social relationships and remind the client that respect from others will largely depend on the client's effort.

Positive Reinforcement System

We encourage family members to establish a positive reinforcement system in the home. The family should chart the client's progress toward goals and highlight the rewards for certain goals. Rewards can be anything, such as dinner at the client's favorite restaurant. One family promised their son a Caribbean cruise if he obtained a certain GPA in college after he returned from his convalescence. The importance of these goals and rewards is that they yield a sense of accomplishment.

Direct Payment

If the client agrees, the family can allocate payment of Social Security and disability benefits on an allowance basis. These monies are then paid to the client contingent on a certain level of performance. The client's "job" then becomes his or her therapy. This type of situation must be purely voluntary, however, with the client agreeing to it beforehand.

Another form of direct payment involves building a monetary incentive system directly into computer games and software for cognitive rehabilitation. That is, the reward occurs when the client achieves a certain level of performance on the task. For example, we modified many computer-training exercises so that a random number and letter code would appear on the screen once the client reached a certain level of performance. The code remained on the screen for about 10 seconds and the client had to memorize the code and report it to the therapist in order to receive a monetary reward. The codes were relatively easy to remember for the lower levels of performance. For example, a code such as X5ZP7 yielded a $10 reward when the client achieved 70% performance on a reading comprehension program. Remembering larger strings such as L4B4ZX earned $20 once the client achieved 80% performance on the same task. In each case, the client had to remember the code long enough, without writing it down, to report it correctly to the therapist who would give the reward.

Addictions

Any legal addiction, such as cigarettes, caffeine, and so forth, can have powerful incentive value. Although the therapist should not encourage smoking, clearly many clients do smoke and most will continue to do so despite counseling and other pressures to get them to stop. Many clients drink excessive amounts of coffee or soda, which creates a caffeine addiction. Allowing the client to continue is in no one's best interest, but the therapist can derive some good from the addiction by using the cigarettes or coffee as an incentive and a reward. If the client agrees to participate, the therapist can make smoking or caffeine consumption contingent on performance in therapy. When used in this manner, the client will probably reduce his or her overall cigarette or caffeine consumption in the long term. The reward is not increased as the task becomes more difficult and so the use of these substances may actually decrease as the client improves.

Continuous Availability of Incentives

The therapist should encourage the client to play the games at home. Often it is necessary to enlist a family member to play the games with the client during the week between therapy sessions. One way to ensure that the client practices the games is to offer a reward if he or she can demonstrate perfect performance on the task during any therapy session. In our experience, before we made the incentive continuously available, the clients would not practice the games on their own. After the incentive was made available, most participants reported practicing the card game every day. The fact that most participants were willing to perform on their own for the chance to earn a reward later is, perhaps, the most efficient aspect of the incentive-based model.

Believability of Incentives

The value of the incentive will depend on the client's belief that he or she will eventually receive it. Disbelief can occur for several reasons. Some clients find that certain rewards are not adequate to engage their interest. For example, one client who was financially independent did not see much value in a $10 reward. Social stimulation was a better incentive for him. Other clients may not believe that the therapist will actually give them the reward once they achieve the specified performance level. Some do not believe that they can perform well enough to achieve the incentive. Usually, though, clients will give the task a try once they see another client try and succeed.

Feasibility of Incentive

It may seem to the reader that arranging social incentives or giving monetary rewards is either too difficult or too expensive to be practical. Social activity can be fun and novel and the therapist can usually arrange with the family to provide this type of incentive. With respect to monetary rewards, we have found that most clients never quite reach the required performance criteria to achieve the reward, but they still make the effort. The monetary rewards are therefore quite efficient. For example, only two participants ever received the $100 dollar reward offered in the experiments reported earlier. Moreover, many clients will work quite hard for a far smaller reward. In general, the use of incentives will usually turn out to be an exceptionally inexpensive treatment compliance technique.

Summary

This chapter presented practical suggestions that a therapist can use to improve compliance with treatment. The chapter began with a discussion of concepts such as motivation, incentive, reward, and punishment. Although there is no clear distinction between incentive and motivation, it may be useful to think of motivators as proverbial "guns to the head." Motivation stimulates performance by threatening some negative consequence. Incentives are the proverbial "carrots on the stick." Incentives increase performance by promising reward. The chapter also distinguishes various forms of reward and punishment. Positive rewards increase a desired behavior by giving the person something he or she wants after the desired behavior occurs. Mothers often reward washing hands before dinner with a good meal. Negative rewards increase a certain behavior by reducing some noxious state each time the behavior occurs. A client who is bored sitting around the home may perform at a certain level in a therapy exercise for the reward of an activity that allows him or her to escape bordom. Positive punishments decrease an undesireable behavior by causing something the person dislikes to occur each time the undesirable behavior occurs. A therapist could end the session early each time the client made an inappropriate gesture or comment. Negative punishments decrease behavior by removing something the person wants each time the behavior occurs. The therapist could disallow a cigarette break each time the person displayed an inappropriate behavior. Other models of incentive by Mowrer (1956, 1960) and Skinner (1969) were also discussed.

The chapter also presented an incentive-based model of cognitive rehabilitation. According to this model there are at least two types of learning, habit learning and incentive learning. Habit learning is the potential to perform a specific physical or mental skill whereas incentive learning is the knowledge of potential gain when the skill is performed. Both types of learning are necessary for behavior to occur. Most CRT therapists teach clients new habits to the point where the client can perform the habits unassisted. However, if the client is not rewarded for using the skill day to day, then he or she will not use the skill with any regularity and may not learn to generalize the skill in a novel situation. The results of several experiments that tested this model were discussed. These data indicate the basic assumption of the model, which is that memory and cognition can improve dramatically as long as there is an appropriate incentive to perform.

References

Arkes, H. R. (1991). Costs and benefits of judgment errors: Implications for debiasing. *Psychological Bulletin, 110*, 486–498.

Atkinson R. C., & Wickens, T. D. (1971). Human memory and the concept of reinforcement. In R. Glaser (Ed.), *The nature of reinforcement* (pp. 118–138). London: Academic Press.

Buschke, H. (1973). Selective reminding for analyses of memory and learning. *Journal of Verbal Learning and Verbal Behavior, 12*(5), 543–549.

Davies, D. R., & Jones, D. M. (1975). The effects of noise and incentives upon attention in short-term memory. *British Journal of Psychology, 66*, 61–68.

Dolan, M., & Norto, J. (1977). A programmed training technique that uses reinforcement to facilitate acquisition and retention in brain-damaged patients. *Journal of Clinical Psychology, 33*, 496–501.

Ellis, H., Ottaway, S., Varner, L., Becker, A., & Moore, B. (1997). Emotion, motivation, and text comprehension: The detection of contradictions in passages. *Journal of Experimental Psychology: General, 126*, 131–146.

Eysenck, M. W., & Eysenck, M. C. (1980). Effects of monetary incentives on rehearsal and on cued recall. *Bulletin of the Psychonomics Society, 15*, 245–247.

Ferster, C. S., & Skinner, B. F. (1957). *Schedules of reinforcement.* New York: Appleton-Century-Crofts.

Fowles, D. C. (1988). Psychophysiology and pathology: A motivational approach. *Psychophysiology, 25*, 373–391.

Hertel, P. (1994). Depressive deficits in memory: Implications for memory improvement following traumatic brain injury. *NeuroRehabilitation, 4*(3), 143–150.

Hull, C. (1943). *Principles of behavior.* New York: Macmillian.

Humphreys, M. S., & Revelle, W. (1984). Personality, motivation, and performance: A theory of the relationship of individual differences and information processing. *Psychological Review, 91*, 153–184.

Kleinsmith, L. J., & Kaplan, S. (1963). Paired associate learning as a function of arousal and interpolated interval. *Journal of Experimental Psychology, 66*, 190–196.

Levy, R. L. (1977). Relationship of overt commitment to task compliance in behavior therapy. *Journal of Behavior Therapy and Experimental Psychology, 8*, 25–29.

Levy, R. L., & Loftus, G. R. (1984). Compliance and memory. In J. E. Harris & P. E. Morris (Eds.), *Everyday memory, actions, and absentmindedness.* London: Academic Press.

Logan, F. A. (1960). *Incentive: How the conditions of reinforcement affect the performance of rats.* New Haven, CT: Yale University Press.

Logan, F. A. (1968). Incentive theory and changes in reward. In J. Spence & G. Bower (Eds.), *The psychology of learning and motivation* (Vol. 2, pp. 1–30). New York: Academic Press.

Maslow, A. H. (1970). *Motivation and personality* (2nd ed.). New York: Harper & Row.

Mowrer, O. H. (1956). Two factor learning theory reconsidered, with special reference to secondary reinforcement and the concept of habit. *Psychological Review, 63*, 114–128.

Mowrer, O. H. (1960). *Learning theory and behavior.* New York: Wiley.

Parenté, R. (1994). Effects of monetary incentives on performance after traumatic brain injury. *NeuroRehabilitation, 4*, 198–203.

Parenté, R., & Anderson-Parenté, J. (1991). *Retraining memory: Techniques and applications.* Houston, TX: CSY.

Skinner, B. F. (1969). *Science and human behavior.* New York: Macmillan.

Wolpe, J. (1973). *The practice of behavior therapy* (2nd ed.). New York: Pergamon Press.

Chapter 24

✻

External Aids to Cognition

Many cognitive problems after brain injury can be solved by training the person to use a device that obviates the problem. These aids enhance or replace poorly functioning cognitive skills (Baddeley, 1982, 1992). The purpose of using external aids is to obviate the memory problem rather than to teach new memory strategies. Intons-Peterson and Fournier (1986) found that people generally prefer to use external memory aids like tape recorders over internal aids such as mnemonic strategies. Other authors have pointed out that external aids are the primary way people cope with memory problems (Graumann, 1985; Harris, 1992; Hertel, 1988; Intons-Peterson & Fournier, 1986; Jackson, Bogers, & Kersholt, 1988; Kapur, 1995). These authors have also found that external aids are an especially effective way to improve certain aspects of memory after traumatic brain injury. The goal of this chapter is to acquaint therapists with the wide range of cognitive aids available today and with the considerations that may dictate which devices they recommend to their clients.

Historical Perspective

In the past two decades, several discussions of prosthetic aids have appeared in the literature on memory retraining. These authors discussed the value of prosthetic devices as therapy aids (Herrmann, 1996; Parenté & Herrmann, 1996). Park, Smith, and Cavanaugh (1986) and Kirsch, Levine, Fallon-Krueger, and Juros (1989) were the first to use the term *cognitive orthosis*. These authors referred to cognitive orthotic devices as guidance systems that would help a person with brain injury to perform a well-defined task. Henry, Friedman, Szekeres, and Stemmler (1989) discussed computer hardware devices that were designed to assist cognitively impaired persons with different tasks. Parenté and Anderson-Parenté (1991) discussed the use of artificially intelligent expert system shells (computer programs) to perform routine but complex cognitive tasks. Chute and Bliss (1994) and Chute, Conn, Dipasquale, and Hoag (1988) described *Prosthesisware*, which was software specifically designed for people who were cognitively impaired. Likewise, Egert (1988) discussed the importance of software for prosthetic applications that was specifically designed for use with persons with brain injury. Cole, Dehdashti, and Petti (1994) described a model of computer and human interaction that they had used to develop a prosthetic computer system that was specifically designed for persons who were cognitively impaired. Cole et al.'s computer-based cognitive prosthetic model emphasized ongoing assessment of a person's abilities and disabilities so that computer hardware and software could fit his or her special needs.

The use of phone and mail reminding systems has also been discussed in the prosthetics literature. Levy and Loftus (1984) reviewed the medical literature on the effects of phone and mail reminders on compliance with appointments. Reminders increase compliance by 10% to 20% over that for people not given reminders (Leirer, Morrow, Pariante, & Sheikh, 1991; Leirer, Morrow, Tanke, & Pariante, 1991; Leirer, Tanke, & Morrow, 1994). Because reminding services often involve social interaction over a telephone, it is unclear how much the service aids memory and how much it increases a person's motivation to keep appointments that he or she already remembers. More recently, Hersh and Treadgold (1994) discussed the use of a telephone paging system with an alphanumeric display that could be used to remind persons with brain injury about their appointments. Wilson, Evans, Emslie, and Malinek (1997) tested this device with a sample of persons with brain injury and found that it did increase the number of appointments they kept.

The use of cognitive prosthetics is not without its critics. Plato (circa 3 B.C.) suggested that the use of external memory aids would lead people to avoid developing their natural memories (Loisette, 1896). Many math teachers have claimed that use of pocket calculators has degenerated math education. There is, however, little evidence for this assertion. Alternatively, the reverse may be true in certain contexts. For example, Hertel (1988) found that the most productive research scholars (the ones who publish the most on a topic) tended to maintain the most extensive external memory files in their offices.

Hersh and Treadgold (1994) pointed out that many cognitive prosthetics might be too difficult for many persons with brain injury to use. To use such devices, these persons must have a certain degree of sophistication with electronic devices and the ability to maintain the device and to protect it from harm. However, making the devices less complex may also make them less useful. What the devices gain in terms of ease of use, they may lose in terms of versatility. Although nonelectronic devices such as notebooks, journals, and so forth are perhaps the most readily accepted prosthetic devices, they are also bulky and limited in use. Moreover, even those persons with brain injury who can learn to use these devices will often forget them or simply not use them.

Kinds of Cognitive Aids

Herrmann and Petro (1990) developed a rough taxonomy of external cognitive aids that is presented in Table 24.1 (see also Intons-Peterson, 1993).

Table 24.1 indicates that there are several kinds of external cognitive aids. Many of the devices discussed in this chapter have overlapping functions and are therefore difficult to classify into only one of the categories of the taxonomy in Table 24.1. Nevertheless, there are specific devices that define each category. *Behavioral prosthetics* are changes in behavior that are specifically designed to remind a person to do something. For example, a person may tie a string on his or her finger or put a rubber band around his or her wrist as a reminder. *Cognitive prosthetics* refer to a general class of devices that take over some memory process. For example, a digital recorder can serve as a person's prosthetic memory, facilitating conversation (Bourgeois, 1990, 1993) and other functions. Many business executives use hand-held electronic organizers, such as Palm Pilots, to store and retrieve large amounts of personal information. A *cognitive robot* carries out a repetitive task for an individual. For example, a calculator will perform routine algorithms such as division and multiplication that otherwise must be done mentally. Some automatic coffeemakers will pre-

TABLE 24.1
Types of External Cognitive Aids

Type of Aid	Description
Behavioral prosthetic	a behavior that reminds
Cognitive prosthetic (orthotic)	obviates memory and cognitive problems
Cognitive robot	carries out a routine cognitive task for a person
Cognitive corrector	finds and corrects errors
Cognitive assessor	evaluates a person's cognitive capability
Cognitive trainer	provides stimulation therapy, instruction, and performance feedback
Cognitive archive	maintains or supplements knowledge
Cognitive art	visual memory and other wall hanging summaries
Cognitive superstitious possession	e.g., "my lucky test-taking pencil"

of past experience so that a person does not have to store and retain this information internally in his or her memory. For example, computerized encyclopedias hold a vast amount of information that supplements a person's memory. These sources also provide a simplified retrieval system. Photo albums and personal video libraries document a person's experiences for later review. *Cognitive art* refers to visual displays that facilitate cognitive processing. For example, a chart with nutritional information can provide a person with information to plan his or her food intake across a day. A floor plan can help orient a person in a hospital setting. Finally, *cognitive superstitious possessions*, such as a "lucky test-taking pencil," help give a person confidence when performing cognitive tasks.

The rest of this chapter provides several examples of each kind of aid and describes how they may be used to assist a person with brain injury.

pare coffee at a designated time without the user having to remember to turn on the coffeemaker. A *cognitive corrector* will remember something forgotten or figure out something overlooked or ignored. For example, a spell-checker or a grammar–punctuation–style-checker on a computer will detect words that have been incorrectly spelled or incorrect grammar. *Cognitive assessors* evaluate a person's memory capability. For example, some persons may monitor their cognitive skills in terms of their scores on various hand-held electronic games. *Cognitive trainers* present a person with the opportunity to learn new skills and to practice them. For example, computer-assisted rehabilitation software packages provide specific stimulation training exercises. Academic remediation software provides a wealth of self-paced learning exercises. *Cognitive archives* maintain knowledge and records

Behavioral Memory Aids

Many people perform some novel behavior that helps them to remember. Others enlist friends or relatives to provide the necessary reminders. Table 24.2 presents examples of various behaviors that persons with brain injury say have helped them to remember. This list is not exhaustive, but it does provide examples of techniques persons with brain injury actually use. Because most of these behaviors are self-explanatory, we will not discuss them further.

These behaviors are simple methods for recalling things a person has to do during the day. Often, these behaviors are all a person needs do to remember individual events, objects, or activities. More sophisticated methods are necessary when the task becomes more complex. Many persons are unaware of these behaviors. Others do not use them even though they are aware of them. In many

TABLE 24.2
Examples of Behavioral Memory Aids

Ask someone to remind

Put something in a special place

Wear colored rubber band on wrist

Write note on hand

Switch wallet pocket, watch hand, or ring finger

Wear unusual clothing

Maintain a diary

Put everything back where it belongs

Put something to be taken in an unusual or a conspicuous place

Use an automatic bill payment system with the bank

Place mementos and souvenirs on display

TABLE 24.3
Examples of Nonelectronic Prosthetics

Checklists
Colored key jackets
Medication organizers
Notepads and Post-it notes
Possession organizers
Possession tags
Photo albums and collages
Appointment calendars and diaries
Lists and signs
Large wall calendar
Cue cards posted in critical places
Whistling teapot

cases, the person will use the technique if the therapist trains him or her to use it and the technique solves the person's problem.

Cognitive Prosthetics

Nonelectronic Devices

Nonelectronic aids are relatively simple to implement and are generally available. Most are simple devices that can be purchased at an office supply store. Table 24.3 lists various devices that we have found especially useful over the years. We detail the use of some of these devices below.

Color Coding. Color coding is an especially effective and simple technique for organizing information. For example, color-coded stackable trays, available at most office supply stores, are useful for organizing mail. Color-coding information with a highlighter in books can be used to index important text and prioritize the importance of the information. Colored Post-it notes can cue important reminders. Red, orange, and yellow could indicate various degrees of urgency, whereas

blue and green could suggest importance but not urgency.

Checklists. A person with brain injury may leave home either forgetting to do something before leaving or forgetting to bring something with him or her. For example, the person may forget to turn off an appliance such as the stove or iron. Not only is this dangerous but the fear of catastrophe often leads to obsessive behavior. Sometimes persons with brain injury return home two or three times after leaving to lock a door or to turn off an appliance.

This problem can be solved by creating notepads with a printed list of things a person must do before leaving the house. The therapist can train a person to go through the complete checklist before leaving home. The family can post more than one copy of the checklist for each day so that the person can tear off the list and take it along as a reminder that the various activities were completed. The following is an example of such a checklist:

☐ Turn off stove, TV, and lights

☐ Lock all of the doors

☐ Turn off the faucets

☐ Check to see if I am completely dressed

The person may then stick the checked-off list on his or her dashboard, wallet, purse, or other place where it is clearly visible. The person learns to keep the most recently checked-off list in plain view so that he or she remembers completing the activities.

Checklists are useful for managing a daily routine and in any situation where a person must repeat a routine activity. The checklist ensures consistency, completeness, and accuracy of the procedure. For example, when a person with brain injury returns to work, checklists ensure that job functions are completed correctly. They also can be used to remind a person to take medication. Finally, checklists serve as a record of the behaviors that a person has and has not completed. Regular use of a checklist provides sufficient rehearsal so that the person eventually will no longer need it. A checklist, therefore, gradually trains a person to perform a complex task.

Colored Key Jackets. Persons with brain injury can become especially frustrated trying to discriminate among their keys. This difficulty can be avoided by coding the keys with colored jackets that can be purchased at most lock-and-key stores. Once the keys are marked with different colors, the therapist can begin paired-associate training for key–color associations. This type of training usually progresses quickly; using the keys each day reinforces the training.

Medication Organizers. Persons with brain injury, stroke patients, and the elderly sometimes forget to take their medication. Family members may write reminder notes or lay out the full daily number of pills in a dish each morning, then check the number left at each medication time to ensure timely compliance with the medication regimen. Others make use of devices that remind them to take their medication. The simplest reminder is a small box with several compartments that is about the size of a person's hand. These boxes may be labeled for the days of the week or for the time of day. The more elaborate boxes have lights that the therapist can program to blink when it is time for a person to take a specific medication.

Park and Kidder (1996) reviewed the literature on methods for improving medication compliance. They noted that taking medication is primarily time-based; however, some medication is event-based because it is taken only after symptoms arise. For medication that is time-based, the use of timing devices such as alarm clocks, pill cap alarms, and reminding services help because memory for time for a person with brain injury is generally poor. Users of both time- and event-based medication benefit from pill organizers because they make it visually apparent when a pill was not taken. Those pill organizers that provide an auditory cue are preferable because they also signal a measured passage of time. The therapist can teach a person to attend to a need when the device signals, such as when medication is due (Folkard, 1979; Folkard & Monk, 1980). If medication is due at 10 A.M. and again at 2 P.M., the person will eventually learn to associate the auditory warning with midmorning and midafternoon. Eventually, this cue may obviate the need for an auditory reminder.

Notepads and Post-it Notes. Blank notepads are very useful for listing things that need to be done. They are also useful for storing temporary records of phone numbers, addresses, and names. The therapist should train clients to carry notepads and to write down information rather than attempting to remember it. Stick-on notepads come in a variety of sizes; the smaller variety is recommended so that important messages can be affixed to car dashboards, appointment calendars, refrigerators, doors, and other places where the client is likely to notice them during the day.

The value of Post-it notes cannot be overemphasized. These notes, with their sticky backs, can be put anywhere a person will later encounter them. The ability to immediately create portable labels, signs, or directions with these notes, to color-code the messages for importance, and to place the notes anywhere, makes it more likely that a person will see the note and perform the desired act.

Possession Organizers. Possession organizers collect and organize a person's possessions in different settings. Organizers are helpful on a desk, in a closet, or in utensil drawers. For example, fishing tackle boxes can be used to organize a variety of objects, not just fishing gear. Desk organizers sort pencils, pens, scissors, tape, and so forth. Closet organizers hold ties, belts, or shoes. File boxes are well-suited for personal and financial records. Stackable trays are useful for sorting papers on a desk. If possible, organizational devices should be color-coded to ensure easy visual scanning from a distance.

Organizers only work when a person uses them. Perhaps the major portion of the therapy will involve teaching the client to put items back in the organizer. We often tell our clients that "a minute spent using the organizer will save hours searching for the item later."

Possession Tags. To avoid persons with brain injury misplacing their possessions, family members should mark them in a conspicuous manner, such as with brightly colored labels. Bright-colored embroidery or Day-Glo tags are especially noticeable. Embroidering names on clothes, writing names on important possessions, and putting identification tags in wallets can greatly reduce the anxiety that occurs when people lose a possession or an article of clothing.

Photo Albums and Collages. Everyone likes photos but a photo album can be especially helpful to a person who cannot recall the past or make a connection between the present and past. Specially prepared collections of photos provide a visual record of names and faces of family and friends. Periodic photos taken after the injury can help a therapy client regain a sense of the present. Photo collages are a collection of photos pasted to a large piece of cardboard and displayed in a conspicuous place. Photo collages are especially useful for clients in the early stages of recovery. For example, when a collage is placed in a hospital room, the therapist can train the client to recognize his or her relatives and friends.

Appointment Calendars and Diaries. We include appointment calenders and diaries in one group because, ideally, they can be one book. Many therapists recommend that clients keep a memory book or other daily record of events and information they need. The act of keeping a daily record facilitates cognition in three ways. First, it relieves a person's memory of having to retain all of the details of the day. Second, it fosters a better memory for events, because the act of making a record prompts additional review of what happened during the day. Third, at a later time, the personal notes in a record will enhance understanding of life events. Combining a written record with a visual image, such as a photo or videotape of an event, can be especially useful for creating lasting memories.

We recommend that therapists train clients to use an appointment calendar that can also serve as a diary. The calendar should have two sheets of paper for each day. One sheet should be printed with 2-hour time intervals so a client can use it for appointments by circling the time and writing the appointment description next to the time. The second sheet of paper should contain only blank lines. This is used to write down directions, instructions, phone messages, and so forth next to the corresponding day. We recommend that the client reserve approximately half of the blank page to make a diary entry at the end of the day. He or she should review the day's activities in the evening and try to summarize its events. This activity greatly improves the client's memory for the events in the long term.

These diary–appointment calendars are easy to construct. The companies Day-Timer and Day Runner sell software that can format a variety of calendar types. Once created, the calendar inserts can be three-hole-punched and inserted into an inexpensive binder. At the end of the year, the client can store contents of the binder on a shelf for a permanent and complete record of the daily events of that year.

The remaining items in Table 24.3 require little explanation. However, some examples of their use may be helpful. For shopping lists, many therapists recommend that clients use mnemonic devices for remembering the items on the list. We have found, however, that most persons with brain injury would prefer a written list that they can take with them to the store. A large wall-hanging calendar is best placed in full view so the client cannot avoid seeing it every day. Family members should write important messages in the appropriate boxes on the calendar so the client can review this information as a matter of course every time he or she passes by it. Cue cards can remind the client of a sequence of actions necessary to operate a device or of things to do in an emergency situation. For example, most microwave ovens require three steps for operation. A cue card created to remind the client of these steps can be taped immediately adjacent to the microwave. In most cases, the cue card will be sufficient to remind the client of the steps necessary to operate the machine. Cue cards for emergency phone numbers are best placed next to the telephones in the home. Other devices can be used to cue a client to perform some action. For example, a whistling teapot reminds the client that water is boiling.

Simple Electronic Devices

Calculators. Persons with dyscalculia should learn to carry a small calculator. Inexpensive calculators (less than $5) are generally available and they can fit easily into a wallet or purse. Ideally, the calculator should have a long-life battery or be solar powered. Elaborate calculators are not necessary; the four basic functions (addition, subtraction, multiplication, and division) are sufficient. Most clients will never need functions such as percentage, square root, and so forth. In general, the therapist should purchase the simplest calculator, not the most elaborate. Training should emphasize using the calculator in common situations. For example, a therapist may create simulations where the client adds up restaurant check totals, estimates the total grocery bill in a store, or computes the correct change from a purchase.

Electronic Checkbooks. Financial transactions and banking may be very difficult for persons with traumatic brain injury. Several companies produce electronic checkbooks that combine calculator and checkbook-balancing features. The Radio Shack checkbook calculator (approximately $12) is especially useful because it is simple to operate and keeps an accurate record of a checking account. It also keeps track of two charge accounts at the same time. The user enters the amount of a deposit, payment, charge, or check with a single keystroke. The device keeps an accurate account balance as well as a grand total across all accounts. It also has a permanent memory feature that keeps the information active between uses.

Personal Data Storage Devices. There are many personal data storage systems available for purchase. These devices are useful for storing a variety of information, including phone numbers, Social Security number, address, blood type, and so forth. Rolodex, Texas Instruments, Casio, and Radio Shack all make inexpensive electronic storage devices that cost less than $20. These may be especially useful in emergency situations where rapid retrieval of names, dates, addresses, and phone numbers may be necessary. Many electronic devices have built-in autodialing features. For example, the Casio Telememo watch not only stores telephone numbers, it also can dial a selected number. When the desired telephone number appears on the device's screen, the user can press a button to make the call. The Electronic Rolodex also has this feature. These devices make it easy for a person with brain injury to make calls quickly and accurately. They are similar to the dialing telephones discussed later, but they store many more phone numbers as well as addresses and other personal information.

Dialing Telephones. Dialing telephones provide for single-button dialing. They allow the user to store several phone numbers that can later be dialed automatically by pressing a single button that corresponds to a person's name. These phones can help a person with brain injury cope with an emergency situation. The therapist should program the phone with emergency numbers such as the person's physician and neighbor; the person should also practice dialing 911. Each emergency number should be written on a chart that is placed on the wall above the phone. For example, 911 may be listed first, with the physician second, and the neighbor third. To call any of these numbers in an emergency, the client needs only to pick up the receiver and push the button for speed dial and then the number 1, 2, or 3. The phone then dials the number quickly and accurately.

Voice-activated telephones store 100 or more phone numbers and respond to voice commands. The client merely needs to say, "Call the fire department," and the phone dials the number. This type of phone is ideal for clients with severe motor coordination problems.

Speaker Phones. Speaker phones allow clients to use the telephone without holding it in their hand. These devices have sensitive microphones installed so the user can speak in a normal voice and the phone will respond. These phones are ideal for paraplegics and others who cannot lift the receiver conveniently to their ear.

Digital Recorders. Cassette or dictation recorders can serve the same purpose as a notepad. Indeed, audio recorders are far better than notepads because a person can speak much more rapidly than he or she can write. Audio recorders also pick up the nuances of conversation and other forms of discourse that are carried in voice inflections. Digital recorders, unlike tape recorders, number-mark messages so that the user does not have to blindly rewind the tape to retrieve the message. These features make digital recorders especially useful prosthetic memory aids. However, many persons with brain injury do not readily accept the recorders, preferring instead to write down new information. They may find it embarrassing to talk into a machine, especially in public places or in front of friends. Despite these objections, the advantages of using a digital recorder far outweigh the disadvantages.

Digital recorders do not replace handwritten notes in all situations. For example, recorders may be less useful than notes for remembering prospective events over several days, because the recorder may not have enough memory to store all the messages (Brandimonte, Einstein, & McDaniel, 1996; Cockburn, 1996; Flannery, Butterbaugh, Rice, & Rice, 1997). Clients may also inadvertently record over older messages with newer ones. The therapist should therefore train clients to back up important information stored on the recorder by writing down important messages (Camp, Foss, Stevens, & O'Hanlon, 1996).

Digital recorders are especially useful for making to-do lists. We recommend that clients make lists of things to do the next day on the night before. During the day, the client deletes each message as it is completed. Messages left on the recorder at the end of the day are the ones that remain to be completed.

Telememo Watches. Persons with brain injury often forget phone numbers and appointments. In recent years, several telememo wristwatches have been developed by companies such as Seiko, Casio, and others. These wristwatches typically can store up to 50 phone numbers, names, dates, and times of appointments along with brief reminder messages. The watches store the phone numbers alphabetically by first or last name. The user can search the list forward or backward, ensuring quick and accurate retrieval. Initially, the therapist or a family member should program appointments and alarms and also enter telephone numbers. After the client learns to use the watch, then he or she can learn to enter appointments and phone numbers. Although these watches have been criticized as difficult for persons with head injury to use (Naugle, Prevey, Naugle, & Delaney, 1988), we have found that most clients can learn to use the watches and many come to depend on them.

Casio makes one notable variation on this theme. It is called the Autodialer. This watch not only stores phone numbers and messages, it also dials the phone numbers that are stored in the watch. The user simply accesses any of the phone numbers, then holds the telephone receiver over the watch. He or she than presses a button that is located on the side of the watch and it makes an audible tone sequence that dials the telephone.

Timex and Microsoft have coproduced the Data-Link watch. Microsoft produced specialized software that runs on any PC-compatible computer. The user loads the software onto his or her computer and enters personal information and appointments onto the computer. The watch holds other important dates such as birthdays and anniversaries along with other reminders. Once the information is stored in the watch, the user simply holds the watch in front of the computer monitor and the data is transferred into the watch via the monitor. The software creates a pattern on the screen similar to a bar code and the watch receives this information through a special sensor on the face. The watch is inexpensive, comes in a variety of styles, and holds an exceptionally large amount of information. Moreover, it consistently reminds the wearer of important dates. The watch is waterproof and the wearer never has to remove it.

An additional advantage of telememo watches is that they can be set to beep on the hour. These beeps provide the wearer with a consistent reminder of the temporal flow of the day. The beeps can remind the wearer to review the remaining schedule for the day, thereby increasing the likelihood that he or she will comply with the planned activities presented by the watch. The watch can also be set to signal that medications need to be taken.

One drawback to these watches is that none of the models are specifically made for women. Many women are reluctant to wear watches that are large, unattractive, and appear to be designed specifically for men.

Interval Timers. Electrical or mechanical timers are valuable for monitoring tasks around the home or office. For example, a simple egg timer can cue a person to take dinner out of the oven. A timer that is built into many wristwatches can signal when it is time to finish a task. Many timers can be programmed to signal at the same times each day. In this way, they can serve as useful medication reminders. Other timers can turn lights on and off at specific times of day to reduce energy costs.

Reminding Systems. Day-Timer sells an appointment reminder device that can be affixed to a paper appointment calendar (Herrmann, 1996). This device attaches to the calendar with Velcro and is easily programmed with on–off switches that are set at half-hour intervals. The client sets the times for a reminder and the device begins to beep at that time. The client then reviews what is in his or her calendar for that time (Herrmann, Brubaker, Yoder, Sheets, & Tio, 1999; Herrmann, Yoder, Wells, & Raybeck, 1996).

Neuropage. Hersh and Treadgold (1994) presented a Neuropage system, which is specifically designed for use as a reminding system for persons with brain injury. This is a paging system that a facility can use to remind several clients of their appointments. Each client wears a pager with a message screen. Several clients' schedules are programmed into a computer system that pages the clients and reminds them of various appointments at the appropriate times. Hersh and Treadgold (1994) reported that this system virtually eliminated missed appointments with several persons with brain injury (see also Wilson et al., 1997).

Orthotic Robots

Orthotic, or cognitive, robots perform some repetitive task accurately, consistently, and completely. There are several types of robots, including computer software that performs complex but routine cognitive activities and electronic machines that perform a limited cognitive skill. Using these devices or software, persons with brain injury can usually perform job-related skills at competitive speed.

Cycling Timers

Cycling timers allow the user to program household lights and appliances to turn on and off at preset times. Many devices typically control up to eight lamps and appliances, although it is possible to obtain cycling timers that control more devices. These are usually available at appliance or electrical stores.

Motion-Sensitive Detectors

Motion detectors plug into any electrical outlet in the house and automatically turn lights on and off when motion or the lack thereof is sensed. The devices ensure that the lights are turned off when the room is not in use.

Spelling Machines

Spelling devices are ideal for those who work in jobs that involve a lot of written communication requiring high-level verbal skills. The user types in a phonetic spelling of a word and the device returns the correct spelling. The user does not even need to enter the entire word.

A speller/thesaurus finds a word's correct spelling and a synonym. Synonym generatation allows the therapist to provide paired-associate and word identification practice. A client can use the device to practice word retrieval by recalling a word and then its synonyms before checking the accuracy of his or her recall by pushing the retrieval button. The device provides the client with immediate reinforcement or correction. Some spellers/thesauri also have built-in electronic dictionaries. Most new models have all three functions: speller, thesaurus, and dictionary. These devices are generally available at office supply stores. We specifically recommend the Seiko SII model, which sells for approximately $40.

Cognitive Orthotic Devices

Personal Data Assistants (PDAs)

Palm Computing and other companies have created a variety of hand-held devices that may be useful with higher functioning clients. These devices, called personal digital assistants (PDAs), store phone numbers, appointments, addresses, and virtually any type of information that a person wants to store. The Palm series can run thousands of software packages that the user can download from the Internet. For example, the Bug Me program (www.bugme.com) allows the user to write notes on the screen of the PDA. The person can erase the notes easily or leave them stored in the PDA. A vast array of programs are available from Web sites such as www.palmgear.com. The Palm platform has the greatest amount of software available and a wide selection of devices in different price ranges.

Other companies have produced similar devices with a different operating system (Kapur, 1995; Kim, Burke, Dowds, Boone, & Park, 2000; Kim, Burke, Dowds, & George, 1999). The Windows CE system is similar to the desktop computer Windows operating system and it may be more familiar to many clients. These systems are usually more expensive than the Palm PDA and there is less software available. Nevertheless, they present an attractive alternative, which may appeal to certain clients.

Expert System Shells

Expert system shells are artificially intelligent computer programs that are designed to solve problems the way an expert would. This type of software was originally developed to solve problems for business and industry. For example, if a company has to hire an expert each time it needs to solve a technical problem, and these experts charge several thousands of dollars per visit, then the company may purchase such computer programs to eliminate the need for experts. Employees consult the expert system whenever answers are needed to some technical problem. The advice provided by expert systems is about as accurate as that of human experts.

Expert systems have also been used in traumatic brain injury rehabilitation (Parenté & Anderson-Parenté, 1991). For example, a client may be unable to recall the details of complex procedures or make appropriate decisions at his or her place of employment. If the client has a personal computer, the therapist could program an expert system to follow complex procedures and then the therapist could train the client to operate the program. An example of this type of application is provided in the case studies later in the chapter.

Computer-Based Orthotic Systems

Cole et al. (1994) described a computer system that takes over many reminding functions. A laptop computer that is hooked into a central terminal can remind a client of a variety of daily tasks as well as serve as a message center (Baguley & Landsdale, 2000; Chute & Bliss, 1994; Schreiber, Lutz, Schweizer, Kalveram, & Lutz, 1998). The client can call into the central terminal via a modem for specific advice. Chute et al. (1988) created a commercially available computer system that performs a variety of functions such as writing checks, logging appointments, and keeping track of phone messages. Both of these systems were developed specifically for use with persons with traumatic brain injury.

Cognitive Correctors

Grammar Checkers

Several computer packages, such as Microsoft Word and Corel Word Perfect, have built-in grammar checkers that advise the user on how to revise sentences to improve their clarity. These programs check documents for thousands of rules of grammar and mark each mistake. Grammatik, often bundled with Word and Word Perfect, is especially good for checking grammatical content and sentence structure and for assessing the style of an entire document. These software packages are ideal for clients who have trouble with the rules of grammar. Along with a word processor and spell-checker, these programs are sufficient to improve a client's academic performance in college or high school courses. Regular use also trains correct writing style.

Effective use of these grammar software packages, however, requires that a client have some insight into his or her difficulties with language. Typically, this software provides general advice about defects in wording, the use of complex sentences, and so forth. Whether the user chooses to correct the problems identified is still up to him or her. Use of the software, therefore, requires not only that the client learn to use it, but also learn to fix incorrect grammar. Nevertheless, grammar software packages make a good adjunct to therapy when the goal is to retrain language composition skills.

Car Finders

Everyone has had the experience of forgetting where they parked their car in the large parking lot of a shopping mall. This problem is worse when one is searching for his or her car at night. For a person with head injury, this situation can be frustrating and even dangerous.

An electronic solution to this problem is a device that blinks a car's lights and honks its horn when activated by a device affixed to the user's keychain. The device activates a receiver that has been situated under the hood of the car and connected to its battery. When activated, the lights and horn turn on, signaling the car's location in the parking lot. Almost all auto security systems have this feature and one can be installed for less than $200.

Key Finders

Another persistent problem for persons with brain injury is the misplacement of common objects such as keys. Fortunately, the solution is simple. There are a variety of devices that can be attached to keychains and other objects that make an audible alarm when they receive a certain signal. For some devices, the signal is the sound made by clapping one's hands. Whistling triggers another device. Each of these devices quickly leads the user to the misplaced object. A disadvantage of the whistle and other sound-activated devices is that they may often be set off by inadvertent noises that were not produced by the finder, such as children's voices, dishwasher noises, or other high-pitched sounds. Although such false alarms can be annoying, they also can provide random reminders of the location of the article. The hand-clap devices are not as susceptible to false alarms because there are fewer noises that sound like four equally spaced hand claps. Persons with brain injury, however, may have trouble learning to clap their hands in that particular rhythm, especially if they have motor impairment.

If the client has a cell phone, then one solution for the problem of misplaced keys is to attach a pager to the client's keychain. When the client misplaces the keys, he or she can dial the pager number and listen for its beep. This solution has the added advantage of allowing others to get in touch with the client quickly. Many paging companies will provide the service and pager for less than $60 per year.

Smart Irons

For clients with memory impairments, ironing can be as much of a hazard as it is a necessity. If the iron is put face down and the user gets distracted and leaves, there is a real danger of fire. Some irons now come with a safety shutoff switch that is activated when the iron remains flat and motionless for 30 seconds. These are sold by most department stores.

Cognitive Trainers

Cognitive trainers improve memory and cognition through use. These devices provide clients with instruction and practice in functional cognitive tasks. For example, we have mentioned spelling machines with features such as a thesaurus and dictionary. Many of these machines also contain preprogrammed word games like hangman that the user can play. Many other devices and software provide more elaborate cognitive training.

Teaching machines have been around since at least the 1930s (Benjamin, 1988). Today, computer stores have shelves stocked with self-instructional programs on many topics, including learning how to use computers. Modern multimedia variants of the teaching machines can be used to teach skills a person is trying to learn. Today any personal computer can be used as a teaching machine.

Cognitive Archives

Cognitive archives store knowledge and facts. Because persons with head injury often experience loss of knowledge or at least reduced accessibility to their knowledge, it is helpful for them to collect objects and devices that maintain knowledge and records. Ideally, a client would keep these sources in one room or in proximity to where certain tasks are performed. These knowledge sources may include encyclopedias, dictionaries, thesauri, books on hobbies and games, consumer guides, almanacs, maps, and, especially, computer CD-ROM databases such as dictionaries.

A short-term knowledge source consists of collections of recent notes or phone messages. Memo pads, shopping pads, memo stickers, and other notes are essential for a person with brain injury (Sandler & Harris, 1991; Sohlberg, White, Evans, & Mateer, 1992). Repositories of these notes serve as a kind of external memory for recent episodic information. Every record represents information that needs to be retained, filed, or immediately accessible. Memory sources also include notes from meetings, readings, and lectures.

Cognitive Art

Cognitive art includes objects and devices that present visual displays that either guide a client's use of memory or solve a problem through a logical sequence. Although it is perhaps the oldest external memory aid, the use of art in this way is not well known today. However, in the 14th, 15th, and 16th centuries, artists drew or painted the floor plans of houses, cathedrals, amphitheaters, and other buildings so that people could locate and memorize spatial information (Tufte, 1997). Complex flowcharts are useful for showing a decision-making process or different types of organizations. Airplane magazines typically show the layout of the major airports they serve to orient passengers before arrival. Posted floor plans of a client's home or hospital can provide a valuable reference. Training the client to use pictures such as floor plans, airport terminal layouts, and decision-making schematics is especially valuable.

Parenté, Anderson-Parenté, and Stapleton (2001) combined art with poetic verse to teach social skills to persons with brain injury (see www.geocities.com/mentalarts). The authors tested which poem was the most memorable. The results of their research indicated that mnemonics that were set to verse and that had an accompanying visual image were most memorable. The authors suggested several techniques that could be used to teach social skills and memory strategies. For example, cognitive art could be presented as a screen saver on personal computers. The screen saver would appear when the client was not using the computer for an extended period of time. The constant repetition of the screen saver image would eventually help transfer it into the client's long-term memory. These same images could be embossed onto cups and other objects that the client would see every day.

Cognitive Superstitious Possessions

For many people there are objects that they believe help their thinking. There are various explanations for why people might superstitiously come to believe that an object has some magical influence over cognition. Usually, people justify their belief on the grounds that the object led them to perform well in the past. For example, some students use a certain pen when taking examinations because they did especially well when they used it in the past. It has yet to be established whether so-called lucky objects actually do affect cognitive performance. Nevertheless, if a client believes that some talisman improves cognition, the therapist should encourage its use.

Evaluation

Parenté and Elliott (1994) studied the use of external memory aids in 20 persons with brain injury. They were asked to rate the usefulness of various prosthetic devices that could be used for improving memory and thinking skills. The participants rated slides of the devices on a scale of 0 (*not useful at all*) to 10 (*very useful for people with disabilities like mine*). The participants also indicated whether they had actually used the devices. Finally, they were asked to indicate whether they knew the device existed and where they could purchase it.

The participants' ratings were evaluated in three ways. The authors first tabulated the average rating of usefulness for the various devices. These results are presented in Figure 24.1. Those items that were rated with an average of less than 2 are not included in Figure 24.1. The number of participants who reported using these same devices is presented in Figure 24.2. Finally, Figure 24.3 presents the number of participants who were aware that the device existed, plotted as a function of the same devices.

The authors concluded that persons with brain injury perceive a variety of devices to be potentially useful for themselves and for others with similar disabilities. Appointment calendars, microrecorders, answering machines, hanging calendars, beeping watches, calculators, and checklists were rated highly for perceived usefulness, frequency of use, and availability. "Low-tech" items were generally preferred over "high-tech" items. Participants were generally unaware of many of the more complex electronic devices. Finally, less than half of the sample reported using any device to improve their thinking skills.

Case Studies

The following cases illustrate how the various prosthetic devices outlined in this chapter were used to facilitate a return to work for three persons with traumatic brain injury. These case examples show the value and potential of cognitive orthotic devices. The persons in the cases were able to return to work by using them, something they could not do otherwise. Training time for the clients to learn to use the computer software was always less than that necessary for return to work after conventional therapy. Advances in computer software and hardware have made this type of vocational reentry cost-effective and feasible. It has also greatly expanded the range of potential applications.

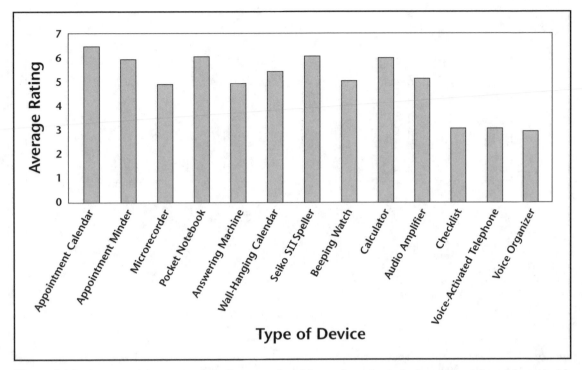

Figure 24.1. Participants' average rating of perceived usefulness of prosthetic devices. *Note.* Adapted from *Usefulness and use of prosthetic devices after head injury*, by R. Parenté and A. Elliott, August 1994, poster session presented at the Practical Aspects of Memory Conference, College Park, MD.

 JANE

Jane was a nurse in an intensive care unit before her automobile accident. After several months of cognitive skills training she tried to return to work but found that it was still too difficult for her. She forgot to give patients their medications and could not recall the various services she had to perform on her rounds in the emergency room. She was frequently late for work because she misplaced her keys. She also worked in a dangerous section of Baltimore and had to leave the hospital late at night. She would spend 30 minutes or more searching for her car in a multilevel parking garage.

We were able to reduce most of what Jane did in the intensive care unit to a checklist. It took approximately 1 month to refine the checklist to the point where it was convenient to use. The checklist was sufficient to allow Jane to return to work in the intensive care unit and to work effectively. In fact, other nurses on her unit adopted Jane's checklist once they realized how it eliminated needless repetition.

Jane still had difficulty, however, remembering physicians' instructions. The physicians were annoyed with her memory deficit and she was embarrassed to ask for understanding. We constructed a wooden clipboard for Jane so she could carry her patient checklists conveniently. Under the clipboard was a slot for her to keep her dictation recorder. It was out of sight and easily activated when physicians gave her instructions; she used the cassette recorder to tape the instructions. Jane became proficient with the devices after 5 hours of training. She also purchased several sounding devices and a car finder. She no longer misplaced her keys and other important items. She was also able to find her car in the parking garage with minimal effort. It cost less than $200 to solve all of these problems.

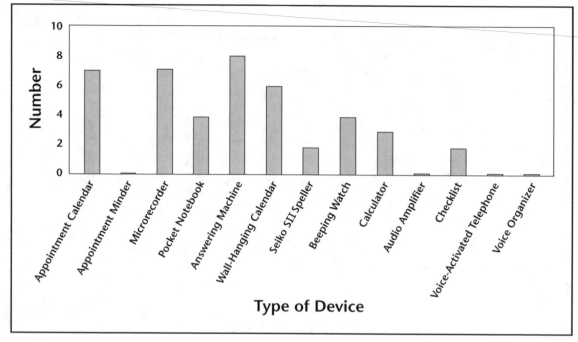

Figure 24.2. Numbers of participants reporting use of prosthetic devices. *Note.* Adapted from *Usefulness and use of prosthetic devices after head injury,* by R. Parenté and A. Elliott, August 1994, poster session presented at the Practical Aspects of Memory Conference, College Park, MD.

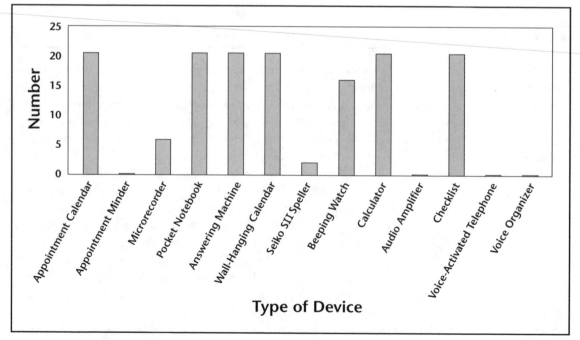

Figure 24.3 Number of participants aware that the prosthetic devices existed. *Note.* Adapted from *Usefulness and use of prosthetic devices after head injury,* by R. Parenté and A. Elliott, August 1994, poster session presented at the Practical Aspects of Memory Conference, College Park, MD.

LOIS

Lois was a stroke victim who had been employed as a dispatcher for a trucking firm. She had worked for the firm for 25 years and her skills were highly valued by the company. Her job included remembering several delivery schedules and price rates that she would convey to customers. In essence, Lois acted as a consultant, informing customers of the least expensive and fastest way to ship their freight.

After her stroke, Lois could not mentally retrieve the schedules and pricing information she needed to provide rapid and accurate estimates for customers. Although the company valued her skills, it placed her on temporary disability. Fortunately, however, her job could be reduced to a set of decision making rules. Her situation was ideal for an expert system application.

After examining Lois's job, we constructed 100 rules and input them into an expert system shell program. The entire operation took approximately 15 hours. The program posed questions that Lois would ask customers. It also provided the correct pricing, time, and the least-to-most expensive shipping method for customers, given their specific needs. Lois talked to customers over the phone and asked the sequence of questions the computer presented on the screen. She answered the program's queries, then gave customers the advice the expert system displayed at the end of the dialogue.

The software was developed and the company agreed to purchase a laptop computer that Lois could take to and from work each day. Lois took the computer to work each morning, set it up on her desk next to the phone, and used it continuously throughout the day. Her accuracy and speed improved to acceptable levels and she returned to full-time employment within 1 year after her stroke. It took approximately 2 months to study the job, develop the software, and train Lois to use it.

 TED

Ted's memory impairment resulted from an automobile accident. After a 5-month coma and 1 year of therapy, he tried, unsuccessfully, to return to his previous job as a schoolteacher. He then tried several other jobs but was fired from them because he could not manage complex tasks accurately or in a timely fashion. He was eventually hired by a workshop for persons with mental retardation. Ted's job was to count the various pieces the workers produced throughout the day. He could do the job but it was stressful and his work was prone to errors.

We wrote a computer program that would accept Ted's various data and tabulate them for him. He took his work home at night and used the computer to perform his calculations. The program printed out all of the necessary information so he could simply turn in the printout the next day. He could save, update, and correct data, and regenerate previous days' work summaries. The program took approximately 15 hours to prepare and debug. Ted learned to use it in less than 1 hour.

Summary and Recommendations

Advantages of External Cognitive Aids

This chapter presented numerous suggestions for external cognitive aids and devices. The major advantage of prosthetic cognitive aids is that they allow persons with brain injury to function independently (Bendiksen & Bendiksen, 1996). They also reduce obsessive behavior associated with poor memory that interferes with interpersonal relations (Meacham, 1988). Although prosthetic devices do not make a person's internal cognitive functions more efficient, they clearly help him or her deal with day-to-day problems and increase independence. They add life structure, improve time sense, and reduce risk of injury or embarrassment resulting from forgetting appointments.

Sometimes prosthetic devices can improve a client's internal cognitive function. For example, the use of scheduling devices and medicine reminders sometimes allows a client to learn a medication regimen or other routine. However, external cognitive aids certainly do not replace or obviate a good program of cognitive rehabilitation therapy. Nevertheless, they are invaluable adjuncts to a total memory retraining program. Perhaps their biggest advantage is that they solve immediate problems and bolster the client's spirits by demonstrating that immediate and effective interventions are possible.

Limitations of External Cognitive Aids

There are several disadvantages to many external cognitive devices. For example, many are expensive and some require extensive training time. Some clients may resist using them because they fear becoming dependent on them. Some devices create as many problems as they solve. For example, several clients have told us that beeping key chains often begin beeping randomly, making it necessary for the clients to take them out and turn them off. Alarm watches have been criticized for being too difficult for persons with head injury to use easily (Naugle et al., 1988; Wilson, 1987). Watches that beep on the hour often keep clients awake during the night.

It is commonly believed that active reminders are better than passive reminders (Harris, 1980), but there is no clear idea about the optimal number of active remindings that a person can handle in a day. If buzzers are going off frequently, then the client may eventually view them as an annoyance and turn them off without doing whatever the buzzer was reminding him or her to do.

Complex devices are intimidating and clients may resist using them because they make them feel helpless or frustrated. The client may forget how to use the device between sessions. As a first step, therapists should put information into the device for the client and then demonstrate the mechanics of retrieving information from the device. Once the client can use the device, then the therapist can train him or her to use any additional features it may have.

It has been suggested that use of external aids might reduce the cognitive skills that are being aided because the aid relieves the user of experience needed to develop such skills (Estes, 1980; Herrmann & Chaffin, 1988). For example, using a calculator exclusively to do math computations means that the client does not have to do math problems with paper and pencil. Indeed, many persons with brain injury fear that their mental skills may never improve if they become dependent on these devices. The only way to convince them that the devices will not hurt these skills is to point out that their use is only temporary. The prosthetic aid is simply a stopgap measure that the client will use while while he or she is learning other memory strategies. Often a little experience with the devices will convince the client of their worth.

Considerations

There are several considerations a therapist must make before recommending that a client buy an external aid. In general, the goal is to create a cognition-friendly environment for the client. The extent to which the environment aids cognition depends largely on the client's perception that the device will solve more problems than it creates. For example, an orderly and predictable desk is "memory friendly," because it provides an easy view of cues that facilitate the tasks at hand (Hertel, 1988; Malone, 1983). Cognition-friendly devices are usually automatic, attractive, and easy to operate. For example, many cars today come with several buzzers to remind the driver to perform chores such as buckling safety belts or turning off headlights. Some modern cars will not start unless the driver has his or her foot on the brake pedal and the car is in park. Coffeemakers with a timer allow a person to add water and coffee to the machine so that it will brew a pot of coffee at a predetermined time.

Persons with brain injury use different internal memory strategies and external aids depending on the task. Intons-Peterson and Fournier (1986) found that preferences for the use of external aids differed with the kind of memory task (see also Intons-Peterson & Newsome, 1992). External aids were preferred for remembering intentions to do things and internal aids were preferred for learning new information. Prosthetic aids may therefore be used most effectively in situations where they serve as reminders of intentions.

Finally, external aids will not be uniformly useful with all people. For example, there are clear differences defined by client age in the kinds of external aids preferred (Cavanaugh, Grady, & Perlmutter, 1983; Jackson et al., 1988; Maylor, 1990; Schumann-Hengsteler, Scheffler, & Trotscher, 1993). However, these preferences appear to have more to do with the life stage rather than any decline in memory ability with age (Harris, 1980; Lipman, Caplan, Schooler, & Lee, 1995; Petro, Herrmann, Burrows, & Moore, 1991). Of course, such differences can also be influenced by the fact that older people are generally less familiar or comfortable with technology and less likely to use it (Rybash, Hoyer, & Roodin, 1986).

Prosthetic devices can also be used for teaching internal mental strategies. For example, the Memory Works CD-ROMs (www .memoryzine.com) are excellent prosthetic aids for teaching memory strategies (Plude & Schwartz, 1996).

Where To Find External Aids

Several mail order companies sell various cognitive aids. The Sharper Image, Markline, Sporting Edge, Exeters, DAK Inc., Damark International, Selectronics, Skymall, and Maxi-Aids are some of our most frequented mail order sources. Because these companies change their listings frequently, we recommend that therapists call 800-555-1212 (800-number information) and ask for the most recent listing of any of the above companies. Perhaps the best single source for prosthetic aids is Virginia Assistive Technology Services. Therapists can access this service via modem and search several databases with virtually thousands of devices. Counselors are also available to help the therapist find specific aids in the database. This service will help the therapist find the latest CD-ROMs that have ABLE-DATA and CoNet assistive technology databases so the therapist can do his or her own searches.

References

Baddeley, A. D. (1982). *Your memory: A user's guide*. Harmondsworth, United Kingdom: Penguin.

Baddeley, A. D. (1992). Memory theory and memory therapy. In B. A. Wilson & N. Moffit (Eds.), *Clinical management of memory problems* (2nd ed., pp. 1–31). San Diego, CA: Singular.

Baguley, T., & Landsdale, M. (2000). Memory theory and the cognitive technology of spatial methods in information retrieval systems. *Cognitive Technology, 5*, 4–19.

Bendiksen, M., & Bendiksen, I. (1996). Multi-modal memory rehabilitation for the toxic solvent injured population. In D. Herrmann, M. Johnson, C. McEvoy, C. Hertzog, & P. Hertel (Eds.), *Basic and applied memory research: Practical applications* (pp. 469–480). Mahwah, NJ: Erlbaum.

Benjamin, L. (1988). The history of teaching machines. *American Psychologist, 43*, 713–720.

Bourgeois, M. (1990). Enhancing conversation skills in patients with Alzheimer's disease using a prosthetic memory aid. *Journal of Applied Behavior Analysis, 23*, 29–42.

Bourgeois, M. (1993). Effects of memory aids on the dyadic conversations of individuals with dementia. *Journal of Applied Behavior Analysis, 26*, 77–87.

Brandimonte, M. A., Einstein, G., & McDaniel, M. (Eds.). (1996). *Prospective memory: Theory and applications*. Hillsdale, NJ: Erlbaum.

Camp, C. J., Foss, J. W., Stevens, A. B., & O'Hanlon, A. M. (1996). Improving prospective memory task performance in persons with Alzheimer's disease. In M. Brandimonte, G. Einstein, & M. McDaniel (Eds.), *Prospective memory: Theory and applications*. Hillsdale, NJ: Erlbaum.

Cavanaugh, J. C., Grady, J. G., & Perlmutter, M. (1983). Forgetting and use of memory aids in 20- to 70-year-olds' everyday life. *International Journal of Aging and Human Development, 17*, 113–122.

Chute, D., Conn, G., Dipasquale, M., & Hoag, M. (1988). ProsthesisWare: A new class of software supporting activities of daily living. *Neuropsychology, 2*, 41–57.

Chute, D. L., & Bliss, M. E. (1994). ProsthesisWare: Concepts and caveats for microcomputer-based aids to everyday living [Special issue: Technology and environmental issues for the elderly]. *Experimental Aging Research, 20*, 229–238.

Cockburn, J. (1996). Assessment and treatment of prospective memory deficits. In M. Brandimonte, G. Einstein, & M. McDaniel (Eds.), *Prospective memory: Theory and applications*. Hillsdale, NJ: Erlbaum.

Cole, E., Dehdashti, P., & Petti, L. (1994). Design and outcomes of computer-based cognitive prosthetics for brain injury: A field study of three subjects. *NeuroRehabilitation, 4*, 174–186.

Egert, R. (1988). Human computer interface issues in rehabilitation medicine. *Archives of Physical Medicine and Rehabilitation, 69*, 778.

Estes, W. K. (1980). Is human memory obsolete? *American Scientist, 68*, 62–68.

Flannery, M. A., Butterbaugh, G. J., Rice, D. A., & Rice, J. C. (1997). Reminding technology for prospective memory disability: A case study. *Pediatric Rehabilitation, 1*, 239–244.

Folkard, S. (1979). Time of day and level of processing. *Memory and Cognition, 7*, 247–252.

Folkard, S., & Monk, T. H. (1980). Circadian rhythms in human memory. *British Journal of Psychology, 71*, 295–307.

Graumann, C. F. (1985). Memorabilia, mementos, memoranda: Towards an ecology of memory. In F. Klex (Ed.), *In memoriam Hermann Ebbinghaus* (pp. 63–69). Amsterdam: North Holland.

Harris, J. E. (1980). Memory aids people use: Two interview studies. *Cognition, 8*, 31–38.

Harris, J. E. (1992). Methods of improving memory. In B. A. Wilson & N. Moffit (Eds.), *Clinical management of memory problems* (pp. 56–82). San Diego, CA: Singular.

Henry, K., Friedman, M., Szekeres, S., & Stemmler, D. (1989). Clinical evaluation of a prototype portable electronic memory aid. *Proceedings of the RESNA 12th annual conference* (pp. 254–255). Washington, DC: RESNA Press.

Herrmann, D. (1996). Improving Prospective Memory. In M. Brandimonte, G. Einstein, & M. McDaniel (Eds.), *Prospective memory: Theory and applications*. Hillsdale, NJ: Erlbaum.

Herrmann, D., Brubaker, B., Yoder, C., Sheets, V., & Tio, A. (1999). Devices that remind. In F. Durso (Ed.), *Handbook of applied cognitive psychology*. Mahwah, NJ: Erlbaum.

Herrmann, D., & Chaffin, R. (1988). *Memory in historical perspectives: The literature on memory before Ebbinghaus*. New York: Springer-Verlag.

Herrmann, D., Yoder, C., Wells, J., & Raybeck, D. (1996). Portable electronic scheduling and reminding devices. *Cognitive Technology, 1*, 36–44.

Herrmann, D. J., & Petro, S. (1990). Commercial memory aids. *Applied Cognitive Psychology, 3*, 23–45.

Hersh, N., & Treadgold, L. (1994). Neuropage: The rehabilitation of memory dysfunction by prosthetic memory and cueing. *NeuroRehabilitation, 4*, 187–197.

Hertel, P. T. (1988). Monitoring external memory. In M. Gruneberg, P. E. Morris, & R. N. Sykes (Eds.), *Practical aspects of memory*. London: Academic Press.

Intons-Peterson, M. J. (1993). External memory aids and their relation to memory. In C. Izawa (Ed.), *Cognitive psychology applied* (pp. 142–166). Mahwah, NJ: Erlbaum.

Intons-Peterson, M. J., & Fournier, J. (1986). External and internal memory aids: When and how often do we use them? *Journal of Experimental Psychology: General, 115*, 267–280.

Jackson, J., Bogers, H., & Kerstholt, J. (1988). Do memory aids aid the elderly in their day to day remembering? In M. Gruneberg, P. Morris, & R. Sykes (Eds.), *Practical aspects of memory: Current research and issues* (pp. 137–142). New York: Wiley.

Kapur, N. (1995). Memory aids in the rehabilitation of memory disordered patients. In A. D. Baddeley, B. A. Wilson, & F. N. Watts (Eds.), *Handbook of memory disorders* (pp. 533–556). New York: Wiley.

Kim, H. J., Burke, D. T., Dowds, M. M., Jr., Boone, K. A., & Park, G. J. (2000). Electronic aids for outpatient brain injury: Follow-up findings. *Brain Injury, 14,* 187–196.

Kim, H. J., Burke, D. T., Dowds, M. M., Jr., & George, J. (1999). Utility of a microcomputer as an external aid for memory-impaired head injury patient during in-patient rehabilitation. *Brain Injury, 13,* 147–150.

Kirsch, N. L., Levine, J. P., Fallon-Krueger, M., & Juros, L. A. (1989). Microcomputer as an orthotic device for patients with cognitive defects. *Journal of Head Trauma Rehabilitation, 2*(4), 77–85.

Leirer, V. O., Morrow, D. G., Pariante, G. M., & Sheikh, J. I. (1991). Elder's nonadherence: Its assessment and computer assisted instruction for medication recall training. *Journal of the American Gerontological Society, 36,* 877–884.

Leirer, V. O., Morrow, D. G., Tanke, E. D., & Pariante, G. M. (1991). Elder's nonadherence: Its assessment and medication reminding by voice mail. *The Gerontologist, 31,* 514–520.

Leirer, V. O., Tanke, E. D., & Morrow, D. G. (1994). Time of day and naturalistic prospective memory. *Experimental Aging Research, 20,* 127–134.

Levy, R., & Loftus, G. (1984). Compliance and memory. In J. Harris & P. Morris (Eds.), *Everyday memory, actions, and absentmindedness* (pp. 93–112). London: Academic Press.

Lipman, P. D., Caplan, L. J., Schooler, C., & Lee, J. (1995). Inside and outside the mind: The effects of age, organization, and access to external sources on retrieval of life events. *Applied Cognitive Psychology, 9,* 289–306.

Loisette, A. (1896). *Assimilative memory.* New York: Funk & Wagnalls.

Malone, T. W. (1983). How do people organize their desks: Implications for designing office automation systems. *ACM Transactions on Office Automation Systems, 1,* 99–112.

Maylor, E. (1990). Age and prospective memory. *Quarterly Journal of Experimental Psychology, 42,* 471–493.

Meacham, J. A. (1988). Interpersonal relations and prospective remembering. In M. M. Gruneberg, P. E. Morris, & R. N. Sykes (Eds.), *Practical aspects of memory: Current research and issues* (Vol. 4, pp. 371–376). Chichester, United Kingdom: Wiley.

Naugle, R., Prevey, M., Naugle, C., & Delaney, R. (1988). New digital watch as a compensatory device for memory dysfunction. *Cognitive Rehabilitation, 6,* 22–23.

Parenté, R., & Anderson-Parenté, J. K. (1991). *Retraining memory.* Houston, TX: CSY.

Parenté, R., Anderson-Parenté, J., & Stapleton, M. (2001). The use of rhymes and mnemonics for teaching cognitive skills to persons with acquired brain injury. *Brain Injury Source, 5*(1) 16–19.

Parenté, R., & Elliott, A. (1994, August). *Usefulness and use of prosthetic devices after head injury.* Poster session presented at the Practical Aspects of Memory Conference, College Park, MD.

Parenté, R., & Herrmann, D. (1996). *Retraining cognition.* Gaithersburg, MD: Aspen.

Park, D., Smith, A., & Cavanaugh, J. (1986). Metamemories of memory researchers. *Memory & Cognition, 18,* 321–327.

Park, D. C., & Kidder, D. P. (1996). Prospective memory and medication adherence. In M. Brandimonte, G. Einstein, & M. McDaniel (Eds.), *Prospective memory: Theory and applications.* Hillsdale, NJ: Erlbaum.

Petro, S., Herrmann, D., Burrows, D., & Moore, C. (1991). Usefulness of commercial memory aids as a function of age. *International Journal of Aging and Human Development, 33,* 295–309.

Plude, D. J., & Schwartz, L. K. (1996). The promise of compact disc-interactive technology for memory training with the elderly. In D. Herrmann, C. McEvoy, C. Hertzog, P. Hertel, & M. Johnson (Eds.), *Basic and applied memory: New findings on the practical aspects of memory* (pp. 333–342). Englewood Cliffs, NJ: Erlbaum.

Rybash, J., Hoyer, W., & Roodin, P. (1986). *Adult cognition and aging.* New York: Pergamon.

Sandler, A. B., & Harris, J. L. (1991). Use of external aids with a head injured patient. *The American Journal of Occupational Therapy, 46,* 163–166.

Schreiber, M., Lutz, K., Schweizer, A., Kalveram, K. T., & Lutz, J. (1998). Development and evaluation of an interactive computer-based training as a rehabilitation tool for dementia. *Psychologische Beitraege, 40,* 85–102.

Schumann-Hengsteler, R., Scheffler, S., & Trotscher, B. (1993). Memory aids in the everyday lives of young and old adults. *Zeitschrift fur Gerontologie, 26,* 89–96.

Sohlberg, M. M., White, O., Evans, E., & Mateer, C. (1992). An investigation of the effects of prospective memory training. *Brain Injury, 6,* 139–154.

Tufte, E. R. (1997). *Visual explanations: Images and quantities, evidence and narrative.* Cheshire, CT: Graphics Press.

Wilson, B. A. (1987). *Rehabilitation of memory.* New York: Guilford Press.

Wilson, B. A., Evans, J. J., Emslie, H., & Malinek, V. (1997). Evaluation of neuropage: A new memory age. *Journal of Neurosurgical Psychiatry, 63,* 113–115.

Chapter 25

✻

Effectiveness of
Cognitive Rehabilitation

Rehabilitation after brain injury often involves an array of services that includes speech–language therapy, psychotherapy, occupational therapy, and cognitive rehabilitation therapy (CRT). And, because insurance providers closely scrutinize the cost-effectiveness of rehabilitation programs, these companies may question which of these therapies meets the complex needs of this population within the companies' cost constraints. It is, therefore, necessary to evaluate brain injury rehabilitation programs in general, and CRT interventions in particular, to ensure that persons with brain injury receive treatment that provides the best possible chance for a successful reintegration into the community (Prigatano, 1997; Prigatano & Fordyce, 1987; Prigatano, Glisky, & Klonoff, 1995; Wilson, 1999). Because this is such an important question in the era of managed care, we devote an entire chapter to a survey of the literature on efficacy of brain injury rehabilitation.

Our survey of the literature revealed two types of efficacy investigations. One type concerned evaluations of comprehensive brain injury rehabilitation programs that included CRT as part of a larger continuum of care. Although most of these studies did not involve controlled clinical trials (Carney et al., 2000; Cicerone et al., 2000), most reported signifi-

cant gains in the cognitive status, independent living skills, and employment of the person with brain injury. The second type of efficacy investigation we conducted concerned evaluation of CRT as a stand-alone treatment. There are relatively few well-controlled studies of CRT; however, those we reviewed generally indicated positive outcomes with a variety of treatments.

Research Models for the Study of Efficacy

Carney et al. (2000) and Cicerone et al. (2000) recently defined different types of efficacy studies in the field of cognitive rehabilitation. These authors labeled studies that involved well-controlled clinical trials as *Class I*. Controlled clinical trials are experimental designs that include (a) the random assignment of participants to conditions, (b) measurable and clearly defined treatments, and (c) the appropriate control conditions that eliminate possible alternative interpretations of the outcome (Isaac & Michaels, 1996). The authors described studies that did not contain these features as *Class II* or *Class III*, depending on the level of lack of control outlined above. Carney et al.

(2000) maintained that Class I studies provide the best proof of efficacy, but their review found only a small percentage of published efficacy studies that met Class I standards. Moreover, the authors criticized most of these studies on a variety of methodological grounds; they pointed out that few, if any, had been replicated. Although Carney et al. (2000) portray Class I studies as a "gold standard" of efficacy research, there are several difficulties with this type of research. Research findings from these studies have not been easily translated into procedures that can be applied in a clinical setting (Zachs & Hasher, 1992). It may be unethical to withhold treatment from a control group of participants while administering the same treatment to an experimental group. Class I studies are also difficult to carry out in acute care or hospital settings because most clinicians are not trained researchers, nor do they have the time to do research. Finally, this type of research is expensive and managed care companies have not, historically, provided incentives or funding for Class I CRT studies. It, therefore, comes as no surprise that the vast majority of evaluations of CRT efficacy have been of the variety that Carney et al. (2000) labeled as Class II or Class III.

Class II and III designs, also known as quasi-experimental designs (Isaac & Michaels, 1996), are far more common than Class I designs in the brain injury literature. These studies lack a certain degree of experimental control that is characteristic of Class I designs. Although Class II and III designs are common in the CRT efficacy literature, their use is not without problems. The definitions of rehabilitation success vary substantially from study to study. Some studies are concerned with global outcome measures such as increased independence of self-care and mobility (Heinemann et al., 1998). Others measure outcome in terms of living situation (e.g., home vs. residential treatment facility) or the number of supervision hours required daily by the person with brain injury (Cope, Cole, Hall, & Barkans, 1991). Still others (Ben-Yishay, Silver, Piasetsky, & Rattok, 1975; Johnston & Lewis, 1991) investigated the ability of the person with brain injury to resume educational, employment, or community reintegration.

With this background in mind, we begin our review of efficacy with an evaluation of whether rehabilitation that includes CRT improves functional outcome after traumatic brain injury (Ben-Yishay & Diller, 1993; Butler & Namerow, 1988; Volpe & McDowell, 1990) and whether it produces lasting gains. We then discuss the question of whether the length and intensity of treatment in a comprehensive rehabilitation program improves outcome. These are the two most important efficacy issues. Next, we discuss whether postacute treatment programs improve outcome (Mackay, Bernstein, Chapman, Morgan, & Milazzo, 1992). Finally, we address the question of whether CRT per se produces significant gains in cognitive status.

Efficacy of Brain Injury Rehabilitation Programs

Does brain injury rehabilitation improve outcome? The bulk of research evidence indicates that comprehensive rehabilitation programs produce significant gains in several outcome measures. Mackay et al. (1992) concluded that a comprehensive rehabilitation program that was initiated in an acute care setting as soon as possible after brain injury produced significant improvement in rehabilitation outcome. This study focused primarily on treatment in an acute care setting. Another study analyzed the outcomes of a multidisciplinary program of services (Semlyen, Summers, & Barnes, 1998). Unfortunately, this study did not assess the effect of specific therapies that were provided at each level of care.

The study by Mackay et al. (1992) was, perhaps, closest to Carney et al.'s (2000) definition of a Class I study in our review. Mackay et al. (1992) evaluated 17 patients from an acute care hospital where they had received therapy in a formalized brain injury rehabilitation program (TBI-F). All of these patients began treatment on initial admission. The authors then evaluated 21 patients from 10 different acute care hospitals without formalized brain injury programs (TBI-NF). All of the patients in the TBI-F group received physical therapy, occupational therapy, and speech therapy. The patients in the TBI-NF group did not receive speech therapy, and only a few of the patients received any of the other therapy services. In general, the major difference between these groups is that the patients in the TBI-F group received a variety of therapy services whereas the TBI-NF group received relatively few therapy services. The TBI-F group showed significant decreases in length of stay, significantly more discharges to home versus another facility, and significant improvement on the Ranchos Los Amigos scale as compared with the TBI-NF group.

Aronow (1987) found similar positive results with TBI patients who received comprehensive in-patient rehabilitation therapies such as physical therapy, occupational therapy, speech therapy, psychotherapy, and social work services. The author gathered patient and treatment characteristics from clinical abstracts and medical records. This study used length of posttraumatic amnesia to assess injury severity and to classify two groups of patients in terms of level of severity. The severely impaired group received a variety of rehabilitation services. A follow-up measurement scale with 13 outcome variables (e.g., vocational status, living arrangements, number of inpatient and outpatient treatments, number of cognitive and physical symptoms) and a seven-point cost-outcome measure was administered over the phone. Although the group that received comprehensive services had longer posttraumatic amnesia and more severe injuries, it had

significantly better outcomes and achieved the same level of cost containment as the less severely injured control group.

Heinemann et al. (1998) investigated the benefits of a comprehensive inpatient brain injury rehabilitation program. These authors followed 66 patients who were discharged from the Rehabilitation Institute of Chicago. They found that patients who received inpatient brain injury rehabilitation improved on measurements of activities of daily living and mobility skills over the course of their hospitalization. The activities-of-daily-living score was based on the Barthel Index computed on initial admission and on discharge. The authors used a standardized telephone interview 3 months after discharge to assess the functional status and ongoing needs of the participants.

Patients, family members, and staff members provided answers to the interview questions. The patients showed significant gains from admission to discharge. Some decline in activities-of-daily-living status was noted from discharge to follow-up in all areas except bathing. The authors concluded that the declines were probably due to family members providing additional assistance to the patient while at home. However, the gains made in rehabilitation decreased the overall amount of assistance needed by the participants after discharge.

Semlyen et al. (1998) followed patients with brain injury who had received inpatient and outpatient services that were delivered by a team of therapists with specialized knowledge of brain injury rehabilitation. The patients' treatment included nursing care, physiotherapy, speech therapy, rehabilitation medicine, counseling, and social work. These authors compared a group of patients who received multidisciplinary treatment, both as inpatients and as outpatients, to a group of patients who received a single-discipline treatment at various other facilities. The authors measured several different functional and cognitive gains throughout rehabilitation and follow-up. They also assessed the family members' levels of distress using a general health questionnaire. Although the one-discipline treatment group, which on average also received earlier therapy intervention, showed better function initially, the multidiscipline treatment group showed greater overall and continuous functional gains throughout the 2-year study. The families of the multidiscipline treatment group also reported lower levels of distress following rehabilitation than that which was reported by the families of the single-discipline treatment group.

Does brain injury rehabilitation produce a lasting outcome? Eames, Cotterill, Kneale, Storrar, and Yeomans (1989) studied this issue and concluded that comprehensive rehabilitation after brain injury produced lasting gains on ratings of cognitive and physical status 19 to 101 months postdischarge. Parenté and Stapleton (1999) showed that group thinking-skills training after brain injury produced an 80% increase in participants who could return to work. The average return-to-work rate for participants who did not receive this treatment was 50% to 60%. Although there are few published well-controlled studies related to this issue, these relatively uncontrolled studies indicate that brain injury rehabilitation does produce lasting outcomes.

Does intensity of treatment or length of treatment enhance outcome after traumatic brain injury? Spivack, Spettell, Ellis, and Ross (1992) investigated the effects of treatment intensity and length of stay on several rehabilitation outcomes. The authors used the Rancho Scale along with three measures of functional status: physical performance, higher level cognitive skills, and cognitively mediated physical skills. The patients with a longer length of stay improved significantly in all areas as compared with a group with a shorter length of stay. In addition, those who received more intense treatment showed significantly more improvement compared with those who had received less intense treatment.

Does postacute treatment enhance outcome (Mills, Nesbeda, Katz, & Alexander, 1992)? Although the majority of the studies reviewed thus far have focused on the benefits of inpatient rehabilitation, we also evaluated a number of studies that assessed postacute programs. Inpatient treatment is often only the first step in recovery after brain injury. Most individuals who sustain a traumatic brain injury are young adults who have a long life ahead of them and want to resume productive roles in society. Due to the complex needs of this population, new treatment approaches like day programs, cognitive rehabilitation programs, vocational programs, and residential treatments have evolved. The goal of these types of programs, which are considered postacute rehabilitation, is to help the person with brain injury resume some form of preinjury employment role and functional activity (Ben-Yishay et al., 1975).

A number of studies have looked at the outcomes of various postacute rehabilitation programs. Malec, Smigielski, DePompolo, and Thompson (1993) summarized the outcomes from a comprehensive program that focused on group treatments with individual therapies as needed. The participants were measured initially on several variables, including independent living status (i.e., 24-hour supervision, less than 24-hour supervision, and no supervision) and work status (also applicable to volunteer and homemaking jobs). A goal-attainment scale measured the participants' levels of accomplishment in terms of their personal goals. The participants then received training that was designed to improve awareness of their deficits, personal organization, and discussion of personal and emotional issues (Bergman, 1998). The proportion of participants living without supervision increased from about 50% to more than 90% from admission to completion of the program. The number of participants who evolved to either transitional or competitive employment increased from less than 10% to more than 50%. The number of participants who were unemployed decreased from 76% to 31%.

There were significant improvements in the participants' living and work status from admission to discharge from the program, and, in addition, no significant declines from the period between discharge and follow-up. Although some participants received earlier intervention than others, there were no significant differences between the early and late groups with regard to amount of change during treatment. However, during follow-up, significantly more participants who began treatment at an earlier time were placed in independent work settings. The participants treated at an earlier time also reached a higher percentage of their goals. This particular postacute program was also less expensive, with equal or better results when compared to similar programs, an effect thought to be partly due to the program's strong focus on group treatment and its close ties with many community resources and services.

Mills et al. (1992) evaluated similar outcomes. Their research focused on the progress made by 42 patients with brain injuries, each of whom participated in a postacute cognitive rehabilitation program with a community re-integration focus. All participants were at least 6 months postinjury; none were employed, in school, or involved in recreational or volunteer activities. The cognitive treatment program lasted 6 hours a day, 5 days a week for at least 6 weeks. For each patient, the rehabilitation team, patient, and family developed functional goals in four areas: home, community, leisure, and vocation. The authors defined success as the percent of pre-therapy goals that were achieved and the progress made in all of the four areas mentioned above with follow-ups conducted at 6, 12, and 18 months after discharge. The number of days in treatment correlated significantly with the amount of improvement in the participants' functional measures. Number of days in treatment also correlated with the number of goals each patient achieved.

The majority of patients improved their overall status in home, community, leisure, and vocational function within 6 months after discharge from a postacute program. These participants typically maintained or improved these gains at 18 months postdischarge.

Johnston and Lewis (1991) also investigated the effectiveness of a community reentry model emphasizing CRT. These authors studied the progress of 82 persons with brain injury who received therapy in nine community reentry facilities across the country. The participants' functional level on admission was determined from program records. The authors used a rehabilitation outcome questionnaire to assess function 1 year after discharge from the postacute program. The questionnaire focused on the level of care or supervision needed by the participants and whether they were able to resume a productive role in the community. The progress made by the participants was both lasting and effective. Total level of supervision decreased while the number of participants who were involved in paid employment increased. The participants involvement in school, unpaid vocational activities, and home management tasks also increased.

A study by Cope et al. (1991) yielded similar results. These authors evaluated 173 persons with brain injury who received a coordinated system of postacute rehabilitation. The system included a continuum of neurobehavioral, residential, and day treatment, along with community and home programs offering a wide range of services. This program included activities designed to improve the participants' daily life activities and vocational goals, while decreasing substance abuse. The authors also measured outcomes in terms of level of supervised care needed. The participants generally required less supervision after completing the program compared to when they entered the program. There was also a significant decrease in need for supervision (DeVreese, Belloi, Iacono, Finelli, & Neri, 1998).

Although most studies of postacute CRT programs used different outcome measures, some researchers have focused on one general outcome such as employability following brain injury. Reemployment is important to most persons with brain injury and their families who often evaluate the validity of rehabilitation by whether the person returns to work. Dikmen et al. (1994) compared adults with brain injury to a group of adults injured in areas of the body other than the head. Length of time to reemployment was the primary outcome measure. Those with the more severe brain injuries did not return to work as rapidly as those with less severe other injuries.

Ben-Yishay et al. (1975) showed significant improvements in employability for persons with brain injury who participated in a postacute cognitive rehabilitation program. This comprehensive outpatient program included activities designed to facilitate return to work. It was composed of three distinct phases of rehabilitation. The first phase involved intensive cognitive remediation (Bergman, 1998). In addition, persons with brain injury participated in group therapy sessions to improve interpersonal communication, social skills, awareness, and acceptance of their deficits. The second phase involved individualized unpaid work experiences and establishment of appropriate support systems. The third phase involved discharge, work placement, and follow-up. The majority of the participants in this study were unemployable upon admission to the postacute CRT program. Upon discharge, however, most of the participants returned to some form of competitive employment, and they were still working 3 years after discharge.

Parenté and Stapleton (1999) studied 33 persons with brain injury who participated in a group therapy program that complemented their vocational training. These authors based their treatment methods on previous research by Parenté, Stapleton, and Wheatley (1991). After 1 year, 13 of 33 participants had completed their training and were available for employment. Of these 13 participants, 10 began and maintained employment for more than 60 days. These persons with brain injury worked independently and were self-supporting. The rest of the participants remained in training programs or took college classes.

The return-to-work status for those 10 out of 13 participants who were ready to be placed after 1 year (77%) exceeded the return-to-work rate for all other persons with brain injury in the state of Maryland who received other types of postacute treatment. The authors also compared these 10 persons with brain injury to the others in Maryland's Department of Rehabilitation Services database and found that they did not differ from this group of 10 participants on 18 demographic and treatment variables. Therefore, the results could not have been due to differences in the selection of the participants. In general, the results indicated that a group therapy approach to CRT could facilitate return to work after brain injury when used as part of a larger vocational rehabilitation training program.

The Efficacy of CRT

All of the studies already outlined concerned the efficacy of comprehensive brain injury rehabilitation programs that included CRT as one of its components. Relatively few studies concerned the efficacy of specific CRT training procedures. The following studies investigated the efficacy of CRT as a stand-alone treatment or intervention.

Various theoretical models have dictated the choice of treatment (Christensen, Caetano, & Rasmussen, 1996; Luria, 1963a, 1963b, 1980; Uzzell, 1997), although the general approach is to provide activities that exercise the mind. The exercises are often presented on a computer and are selected because they address specific deficit areas. Other models, such as Sohlberg and Mateer's (1989) attention process training, use stimulation exercises that target specific cognitive deficits with tasks that become progressively more difficult.

Another approach is to provide training that teaches the client strategies to improve thinking and memory. For example, teaching a person with brain injury to use mnemonics, imagery, or specific reading skills may be useful in certain situations (McClur, Browning, Vantrease, & Bittle, 1994; Parenté, Kolakowsky, Hoffman, & Blake, 1998; Rasmusson, Rebok, Bylsma, & Brandt, 1999; Twum & Parenté, 1994). These approaches are based on the assumption that the client will be able to compensate for a memory or attention deficit by learning another way to perform a specific cognitive task. For example, it is generally known that imagery training enhances recall and that a person with no obvious impairment can recall significantly more information using imagery (Twum & Parenté, 1994). The assumption is that after imagery training, a person with a deficient memory can recall at near average levels. Although this level of improvement may be possible in a contrived laboratory setting (Twum & Parenté, 1994), it is questionable whether a person with brain injury will use the strategy spontaneously.

Stimulation Therapy

Some studies of stimulation therapy that involve treatment versus a control condition have been published within the last 3 to 13 years. Many of these studies approached what Carney et al. (2000) described as Class I designs. For example, Ryan and Ruff (1988) evaluated a treatment group that participated in 30-minute memory training sessions six times a day, 4 days a week for 6 weeks. The training included a number of memory therapies, such as memory strategy usage, rehearsal

practice, list learning, and paired-associate training. The control group spent a comparable amount of time playing card games, board games, and video games. A battery of visual, auditory, and verbal and nonverbal memory tests were used as measures of outcomes. The participants were between 1½ to 7 years postinjury. Therefore, the results could not have been due to spontaneous recovery. Generally, there were no differences between the groups on the various outcome tasks. However, the authors then separated each group based on their baseline neuropsychological test scores. The five persons in each group with the highest overall baseline scores demonstrated significantly greater gains on the various tests. This result suggests that higher functioning persons with brain injury may benefit from CRT regardless of the type of therapy exercises that are used. Lower functioning persons may not benefit or may require more treatment before any benefit is apparent.

Fryer and Haffey (1987) investigated the benefits of multifaceted cognitive retraining for individuals with brain injuries. The treatment condition involved 30 sessions of CRT over a 10-week period. The purpose of treatment was to improve the cognitive skills needed for community reintegration. The authors measured disability and psychosocial adjustment after the training and at 1-year follow-up. The sessions focused on training attention, perceptual discrimination, information integration and retrieval, and executive functions (Mateer, 1999). The authors used a disability rating scale and a psychosocial scale as outcome measures (Rappaport, Hall, Hopkins, Belleza, & Cope, 1982).

This study revealed two subgroups of patients. The successful group achieved 90% to 100% mastery in all the training tasks. The unsuccessful group achieved approximately 70% mastery on all the tasks with substantially more variation than in the first group. The group that achieved the 90% to 100%

gains demonstrated significant improvement on the disability rating scale and psychosocial scale measures relative to the other group. This effect was evident both at program discharge and at follow-up. Success in the community was defined as requiring no more than 1 hour of supervision daily. All those in the successful group met these goals by the 1-year follow-up. These data supported the conclusion that CRT is most appropriate with a select group of persons who are capable of achieving mastery of the CRT tasks. Moreover, those patients who achieved at least 90% mastery in all areas of CRT were most likely to achieve a successful community reintegration.

Ruff et al. (1989) reported a controlled study in which 20 participants received cognitive remediation that included specific attention, memory, problem-solving, and spatial-integration training. The participants received four 50-minute sessions each day. The control group played video games and received instruction in independent living, health behavior, coping skills, and art therapy. Neuropsychological test scores were the outcomes' measures. To eliminate the possibility of spontaneous recovery, all the participants in the study were between 1 and 7 years postinjury. The results indicated that both groups improved their performance on the neuropsychological battery and that there was no significant difference between the groups on the overall test battery.

Ruff et al. (1994) used a multiple baseline designed to compare two groups of persons with brain injury who received both memory and attention training. Patients received between two and four sessions per day over 10 days of multimedia computer training. One group of patients received the attention training modules first, followed by the memory training modules. Another group received the training in the reverse order. The results indicated that both groups improved on the various computer exercises and some of the neuropsychological tests of attention and concentration.

Niemann, Ruff, and Baser (1990) evaluated the effects of attention training and memory training with persons with brain injury. These participants were 1 to 6 years postinjury. Once again, these results could not have been due to spontaneous recovery. The participants received attention and memory exercises for approximately 1 hour twice a week for 7 weeks. The participants received a battery of attention and memory tests that were administered before treatment, during treatment, and after treatment. The participants who received attention training performed significantly better on one of four tests of attention in the battery relative to the memory training group.

Chen, Thomas, Glueckauf, and Bracy (1997) reported a retrospective evaluation of a computer-mediated CRT treatment program. The authors compared 20 persons with brain injury who received CRT with 20 persons who had received other therapies but not CRT. In general there was no significant mean difference between the groups, although the group that received CRT showed improvements on more of the outcome variables as compared to the group that did not receive CRT.

Bachelor, Shores, Marasszeky, Sandanam, and Lovarini (1988) also studied the effect of adding CRT exercises to a general rehabilitation program. One group received cognitive exercises via computer whereas another group received similar paper-and-pencil exercises from an occupational therapist. The two groups did not differ significantly on a battery of neuropsychological tests, although both groups' average scores showed significant improvement.

Middleton, Lambert, and Seegar (1991) studied persons with brain injury who were more than 3 years postinjury. These participants received training to improve either their attention and memory or their logical thinking and reasoning. Therapy included CRT for 4 hours per week for 8 weeks. Both groups improved on posttherapy measures of memory, attention, and reasoning.

Neistadt (1992) studied the effects of practice on a block assembly task. A treatment group of 22 persons with brain injury practiced the task while the control group of 22 persons with brain injury practiced food preparation. Both interventions were provided three times a day in 30-minute sessions for a total of 6 weeks. The participants were also enrolled in a larger long-term treatment program. The outcomes included the same block assembly task that the treatment group had practiced, the food preparation task, and a similar block assembly test. The group that had practiced the block assembly task performed significantly better on that task relative to the control group; however, the two groups' performance on the other outcome measures was comparable. Parenté, Kolakowsky-Hayner, Krug, and Wilk (2000) showed that specific exercises designed to enhance mental control (e.g., mental arithmetic problems, anagram solutions) could enhance performance on tests of working memory relative to a group that did not do these exercises.

There have also been several case studies dealing with the issue of stimulation training. Sohlberg and Mateer (1987) treated four persons with brain injury for seven to nine sessions per week with attention, memory, and visual processing training. The training occurred in 4- to 6-week treatment blocks. All four participants improved on nontraining tasks during the attention training block. Their improvement was maintained on subsequent blocks. The participants also showed better spatial functioning during the spatial training block, and two of the participants maintained this level of performance on follow-up tests. In another study, Gray and Robertson (1989) showed that three participants improved on outcome measures that measured their response to CRT, but not on unrelated tasks. Gianutsos and Gianutsos (1979) recorded some improvement in cognitive functioning on a repetitive practiced task in a single case experimental design. Weinberg, Diller, and Gordon (1977) and Parenté, Anderson-Parenté, and Shaw (1989) showed that various types of perceptual training improved the ability to read in persons with TBI.

To summarize, the most consistent finding in these studies was that CRT improved various forms of cognitive functioning. However, the computer-based treatments used in these studies did not seem to be any more or less effective when compared to other types of treatment. Cognitive remediation may be most effective in persons with brain injury who are less impaired.

Strategy Training

A number of studies of CRT focused on strategy training. This type of training involves teaching mnemonics and imagery (Ownsworth & McFarland, 1999; Richardson, 1992; see also Tate, 1997; West & Crook, 1992; West, Yassuda, & Welch, 1997) to improve recall or some other aspect of memory or academic performance. Parenté and Anderson-Parenté (1984) showed that training persons with brain injury to organize verbal materials could improve their recall. One group of 20 participants learned perceptually grouped number strings presented according to the same grouping structure from one task to another (e.g., 21 65 43 and 87 34 29). Another group learned number strings that were perceptually dissimilar (e.g., 21 65 43 vs. 216 54 3). The perceptually similar groupings enhanced the participants' ability to recall the number strings relative to a group who learned number strings with unrelated groupings.

Parenté et al. (1989) showed that iconic memory facilitated various reading measures.

Iconic memory is a brief visual information store that fades within ⅓ second. The authors reasoned that if they could teach persons with brain injury to process more information in iconic memory, then the training would transfer to other activities like reading. Six persons with brain injury received training with an iconic memory task. These participants subsequently completed the *Nelson Reading Skills Test* (Hanna, Schell, & Schreiner, 1977) that measures word recognition and reading comprehension. Another group of six persons with brain injury practiced first with a letter–span task, followed by the *Nelson Reading Skills Test*. The treatments were then reversed followed by another administration of the *Nelson Reading Skills Test*. The results showed that all participants improved on the iconic memory practice trials. This result was later replicated by McClur et al. (1994). Twum and Parenté (1994) provided verbal labeling and visual imagery instructions immediately before visual and verbal paired-associate learning. This training significantly increased performance on verbal and visual paired-associates tests on the *Wechsler Memory Scale* (Wechsler, 1997).

Prosthetic Aids

Another area of CRT involves training persons with brain injury to use external aids. This type of therapy encompasses a broad array of devices that a person can use to obviate memory and cognitive problems, such as a tape recorder or calendar. Mills et al. (1992) trained 42 persons with brain injury to use external aids as part of a 6-week postacute rehabilitation program. For example, participants used a time planner, activity lists, and an organizer for personal belongings. These participants were able to learn to use the prosthetic devices and most continued to use them. Malec et al. (1993) also reported successful use of various external aids with 29 participants in a postacute brain injury reha-

bilitation program. At the end of the program, those persons living with no supervision had increased from 59% to 93%. At the same time, unemployment decreased from 76% to 31%. After 1 year, 21 of the participants had maintained their status.

Memory notebooks and checklists are popular prosthetic aids. Burke, Zencius, Wesolowski, and Doubleday (1991) used checklists to help three clients complete vocational tasks. The checklists reduced the amount of prompting that was necessary and they also increased the number of tasks that were completed correctly. Zencius, Wesolowski, Krankowski, and Burke (1991) used a memory notebook with four clients to facilitate memory of homework assignments and of appointments. Hersh and Treadgold (1994) developed a portable paging system, Neuropage, that could be used to cue memory in persons with brain injury. Wilson, Evans, and Malinek (1997) demonstrated that the Neuropage system produced significant improvement in memory, planning, and organization between baseline and treatment in persons with brain injury who used the device. Cole, Dehdashti, and Petti (1994) reported significant improvement in participant-determined goals using an elaborate computer system that organized and prioritized participants' daily activities. In all of these studies, the use of prosthetic devices produced significant improvement in consistency of response, timeliness, and completeness of response.

Needs and Suggestions for CRT

The research described above has been generally positive. The results from the outcome studies discussed have delineated the benefits of comprehensive intervention programs following TBI. However, the studies also suffer from a number of limitations that some authors (Carney et al., 2000) have highlighted.

We summarize these problems and provide suggestions for improving efficacy research in brain injury rehabilitation and CRT.

A Need for an Appropriate Methodology

The majority of the efficacy research cited here used quasi-experimental designs. The fact that most researchers chose this type of design suggests that it may be difficult to conduct CRT efficacy studies of the Class I variety. The value of making Class I experimental designs the gold standard for efficacy research in CRT is questionable. Because the patients' needs determine the type and level of rehabilitation services, the random assignment of participants to treatment conditions is difficult in many clinical settings. Furthermore, assigning persons with brain injury to different levels of treatment intensity or to different manipulations such as early versus late intervention may not be ethical. Most hospital or facility administrators would be reluctant to permit this type of study. Moreover, most clinicians are not trained to conduct experimental research. In general, the randomized clinical trials research model, although appropriate in some areas (e.g., drug research), is perhaps not suitable for evaluating the efficacy of brain injury rehabilitation.

Our review of this literature indicates that the controlled clinical trials research model may not be a feasible methodology for studying brain injury rehabilitation in a naturalistic clinical setting. There is, however, no published methodological discussion of research designs such as quasi-experimental designs, single-case studies, or observational research techniques that are particularly appropriate for CRT research. A thorough investigation of different research designs that clinicians could implement ethically and that would provide outcome data that is acceptable to insurance providers would greatly benefit the research effort in this field (Levine & Downey-Lamb, 2002).

A Need for Alternative Research Models

Several of the studies outlined earlier in this chapter suggest that it may be valuable to cluster large groups of patients into homogenous subgroups (e.g., successful vs. unsuccessful patients). This type of study would be useful for determining which techniques are effective with certain types of patients. Another approach would be to use a small-sample participant replication research model, in which each of several patients is followed over various randomized treatment sessions. This type of design would overcome most of the ethical concerns outlined above because the purpose of the randomized treatments would be to determine which of several therapies works best with a particular person. It may also be possible to try out various treatments during an initial evaluation. Over time, therapists could accumulate a number of participants' evaluation data and compare the treatments to see which one generally provided the best outcome (Gianutsos & Gianutsos, 1979; Weinberg et al., 1977).

A Need for Comparable Outcome Measures

The majority of programs we reviewed used a variety of rehabilitation interventions and outcome measures. The outcome measures were not directly comparable, which disrupts any meta-analytic comparison. It is unlikely that researchers and clinicians will ever agree on a single set of outcome measures for evaluating efficacy. Perhaps the only meaningful approach is to define a set of multivariate outcome scales that clinicians could use as part of a standard evaluation scheme. This would facilitate comparison of outcomes from one study to another. However, it is also important to define outcome in relation to the individual study. These standard measures could be included as parts of a larger set that would allow comparison of studies but would also allow inclusion of unique measures. Defining a set of useful behavioral measures (e.g., employment status, grades in school or training classes, independent living) would also be helpful, especially for studying the later stages of recovery. These types of measures have obvious appeal for legislators who appreciate the economic value of measuring return to productive employment and independent living. The set of appropriate outcomes may be quite large because a different set would be applicable at different stages of recovery.

A Need to Operationally Define CRT

Most of the descriptions of treatments we reviewed did not include specific discussions of the actual procedures that a therapist would use to replicate the CRT treatment. It is, therefore, unclear what types of specific treatments therapists use to improve cognition and memory. These research findings may not find their way into practical use unless the researcher operationally defines the treatment by saying precisely what was done, for how long, and with what training materials.

A Need for Funding

There has been a remarkable dearth of financial or academic investment in brain injury efficacy research. Although managed care has significantly limited payment for CRT, there has been little in the way of investment in research to develop effective therapies for treating cognitive deficits resulting from brain injury. Although federal funding for CRT has increased in recent years, it has not been able to keep pace with the number of persons who suffer from brain injuries each year. Clinical coursework emphasizes the study of neuroanatomy and brain–behavior relationships, and there is little development by academic institutions of coursework that teaches actual CRT techniques. Consequently, there are no generally accepted or standardized models for CRT.

Suggestions for CRT

Cicerone et al. (2000) provided several excellent strategies that therapists should consider when providing treatment for persons with TBI or stroke. Our review leads to similar conclusions, which are presented in Table 25.1. The left column presents several types of cognitive impairment and the right column shows corresponding types of therapy with proven efficacy along with appropriate references (Della Sala & Logie, 1997). The reader should also review the problems and solutions presented in Appendix A.

Summary

This chapter reviewed published research on the efficacy of comprehensive brain injury rehabilitation programs, specific CRT efficacy studies, and research on prosthetic devices. The general conclusion from this review is that CRT is efficacious. There are, however, several problems with the research methodologies used in these studies, which cast doubt on the validity of conclusions drawn from individual studies. Despite these problems, our review supports several suggestions for future efficacy studies of brain injury rehabilitation. First, it is important that the field agree on a set of research designs that will provide acceptable proof of efficacy and that are feasible to implement in a variety of clinical settings. This effort also requires training researchers to

TABLE 25.1

Strategies for Cognitive Rehabilitation Therapy

Deficit Area	Appropriate Therapy
Severe right hemisphere stroke or TBI	Visual–spatial rehabilitation (e.g., scanning training; see McClur et al., 1994)
Severe left hemisphere stroke or TBI	Cognitive linguistic therapies (e.g., language skills training; see Wertz et al., 1986)
Mild TBI	• Functional communication training (e.g., teaching conversational skills; see Ehrlich & Sipes, 1985) • Formal problem-solving strategies for everyday living skills (see Fox, Martella, & Marchand-Martella, 1989) • Memory strategy training (e.g., imagery, mnemonics; see Parenté & Anderson-Parenté, 1984) • Functional skills training (e.g., reading comprehension, typing, computer skills, academic remediation; see Parenté & Stapleton, 1999)
Postacute TBI and stroke	• Attention training (e.g., attention/process training; see Sohlberg & Mateer, 1987) • Prosthetic aids training • Vocational rehabilitation
Moderate to severe memory impairment	Memory notebooks, prosthetic devices
Visual–spatial deficits without neglect	Visual–spatial and organizational skills training (see Weinberg et al., 1997; Zoltan, 1996)
Executive skills deficits	Verbal self-instruction (e.g., mnemonic rhymes; see Parenté & Anderson, Parenté, & Stapleton, 2001)

implement these designs in ways that do not violate ethical standards. It is also necessary to share not only research findings, but also specific therapy skills that others can use and evaluate in various clinical settings. Research and development of specific CRT procedures and studies that define a set of functional outcome measures is an especially important part of this proposed research agenda (McPherson, Berry, & Pentlan, 1997). Educating insurance providers and governmental agencies about the potential value of CRT will encourage funding for CRT research and development. Academic training programs could contribute by developing more rehabilitation-related coursework.

References

Aronow, H. U. (1987). Rehabilitation effectiveness with severe brain injury: Translating research into policy. *Journal of Head Trauma Rehabilitation, 2*(3), 24–36.

Bachelor, J., Shores, E. A., Marasszeky, J. E., Sandanam, J., & Lovarini, M. (1988). Cognitive rehabilitation of severely closed-head individuals using computer-assisted and noncomputerized treatment techniques. *Journal of Head Trauma Rehabilitation, 3*(3), 78–85.

Ben-Yishay, Y., & Diller, L. (1993). Cognitive remediation in traumatic brain injury: Update and issues. *Archives of Physical Medicine and Rehabilitation, 74,* 204–213.

Ben-Yishay, Y., Silver, S. M., Piasetsky, E., & Rattok, J. (1975). Relationship between employability and vocational outcome after intensive holistic cognitive rehabilitation. *Journal of Head Trauma Rehabilitation, 2*(1), 35–48.

Bergman, M. M. (1998). A proposed resolution of the remediation compensation controversy in brain injury rehabilitation. *Cognitive Technology, 3,* 45–52.

Burke, W. H., Zencius, A. N., Wesolowski, M. D., & Doubleday, F. (1991). Improving executive function disorders in brain-injured clients. *Brain Injury, 5,* 241–252.

Butler, R. W., & Namerow, N. S. (1988). Cognitive retraining in brain-injury rehabilitation: A critical review. *Neurological Rehabilitation, 2*(3), 97–101.

Carney, N., Chesnut, R., Maynard, H., Mann, C., Patterson, P., & Helfand, M. (2000). Effect of cognitive rehabilitation on outcomes for persons with traumatic brain injury: A systematic review. *Journal of Head Trauma Rehabilitation, 14,* 277–307.

Chen, S. H., Thomas, J. D., Glueckauf, R. L., & Bracy, O. L. (1997). The effectiveness of computer-assisted cognitive rehabilitation for persons with traumatic brain injury. *Brain Injury, 22*(3), 197–209.

Christensen, A. L., Caetano, C., & Rasmussen, G. (1996). Psychosocial outcome after an intensive neuropsychologically oriented day program: Contributing program variables. In B. P. Uzell, & H. H. Stonnington (Eds.), *Recovery after brain injury.* Mahwah, NJ: Erlbaum.

Cicerone, K. D., Dahlberg, C., Kalmar, K., Langenbahn, D. M., Malec, J. F., Bergquist, T. F., et al. (2000). Evidence-based cognitive rehabilitation: Recommendations for clinical practice. *Archives of Physical Medicine and Rehabilitation, 81,* 1596–1616.

Cole, E., Dehdashti, P., & Petti, L. (1994). Design and outcomes of computer-based cognitive prosthetics for brain injury: A field study of three subjects. *NeuroRehabilitation, 4*(3), 174–186.

Cope, D. N., Cole, J. R., Hall, K. M., & Barkans, H. (1991). Brain injury: Analysis of outcome in a post-acute rehabilitation system. Part 1: General analysis. *Brain Injury, 5,* 111–125.

Della Sala, S., & Logie, R. H. (1997). Impairments of methodology and theory in cognitive neuropsychology: A case for rehabilitation. *Neuropsychological Rehabilitation, 7,* 367–385.

DeVreese, L. P., Belloi, L., Iacono, S., Finelli, C., & Neri, M. (1998). Memory training programs in memory complainers: Efficacy on objective and subjective memory functioning. *Archives of Gerontology and Geriatrics, 6,* 141–154.

Dikmen, S. S., Temkin, N. R., Machamer, J. E., Holubkov, A. L., Fraser, R. T., & Winn, H. R. (1994). Employment following traumatic head injuries. *Archives of Neurology, 51,* 177–186.

Eames, P., Cotterill, G., Kneale, T. A., Storrar, A. L., & Yeomans, P. (1989). Outcome of intensive rehabilitation after severe brain injury: A long-term follow-up study. *Brain Injury, 9,* 631–650.

Ehrlich, J., & Sipes, A. (1985). Group treatment of communication skills for head trauma patients. *Cognitive Rehabilitation, 3,* 32–37.

Fox, R. M., Martella, R. C., & Marchand-Martella, N. E. (1989). The acquisition, maintenance and generalization of problem-solving skills by closed head injured adults. *Behavior Therapy, 20,* 61–76.

Fryer, L. J., & Haffey, W. J. (1987). Cognitive rehabilitation and community readaptation: Outcomes from two program models. *Journal of Head Trauma Rehabilitation, 2*(3), 51–63.

Gianutsos, R., & Gianutsos, J. (1979). Rehabilitating the verbal recall of brain injured individuals by mnemonic training: An experimental demonstration using single case methodology. *Journal of Clinical Neuropsychology, 1,* 117–136.

Gray, J. M., & Robertson, I. (1989). Remediation of attentional difficulties following brain injury: Three experimental single case studies. *Brain Injury, 3*(2), 163–170.

Hanna, G., Schell, L. M., & Schreiner, R. (1977). *Nelson Reading Skills Test.* Itasca, IL: Riverside.

Heinemann, A. W., Sahgal, V., Cichowski, K., Ginsburg, K., Tuel, S. M., & Betts, H. B. (1998). Functional outcome following traumatic brain injury rehabilitation. *Journal of Neurological Rehabilitation, 4,* 27–37.

Hersh, N. A., & Treadgold, L. G. (1994). NeuroPage: The rehabilitation of memory dysfunction by prosthetic memory and cueing. *NeuroRehabilitation, 4*(3), 187–197.

Isaac, S., & Michaels, D. (1996). *Handbook in research and evaluation.* San Diego, CA: Edits.

Johnston, M. V., & Lewis, F. D. (1991). Outcomes of community re-entry programs for brain injury survivors. Part 1: Independent living and productive activities. *Brain Injury, 5*(2), 141–154.

Levine, B., & Downey-Lamb, M. M. (2002). Design and evaluation of rehabilitation experiments. In P. Eslinger (Ed.), *Neuropsychological interventions: Clinical research and practice* (pp. 80–104). New York: Guilford Press.

Luria, A. R. (1963a). *Restoration of function after brain injury.* New York: Pergamon Press.

Luria, A. R. (1963b). *The working brain.* New York: Basic Books.

Luria, A. R. (1980). *Higher cortical functions in man* (2nd ed.). New York: Basic Books.

Mackay, L. E., Bernstein, B. A., Chapman, P. E., Morgan, A. S., & Milazzo, L. S. (1992). Early intervention in severe brain injury: Long-term benefits of a formalized program. *Archives of Physical Medicine and Rehabilitation, 73,* 635–641.

Malec, J. F., Smigielski, J. S., DePompolo, R. W., & Thompson, J. M. (1993). Outcome evaluation and prediction in a comprehensive-integrated post-acute outpatient brain injury rehabilitation program. *Brain Injury, 7*(1), 15–29.

Mateer, C. A. (1999). Executive function disorders: Rehabilitation challenges and strategies. *Seminar in Clinical Neuropsychiatry, 4,* 50–59.

McClur, J. T., Browning, T. R., Vantrease, C. M., & Bittle, S. (1994). The iconic memory skills of brain injury survivors and non-brain injured controls after visual scanning training. *NeuroRehabilitation, 4*(3), 151–156.

McPherson, K., Berry, A., & Pentlan, B. (1997). Relationships between cognitive impairments and functional performance after brain injury, as measured by the Functional Assessment Measure (FIM + FAM). *Neuropsychological Rehabilitation, 7*, 241–257.

Middleton, D. K., Lambert, M. J., & Seegar, L. B. (1991). Neuropsychological rehabilitation: Microcomputer-assisted treatment of brain-injured adults. *Perceptual and Motor Skills, 72*, 527–530.

Mills, V. M., Nesbeda, T., Katz, D. I., & Alexander, M. P. (1992). Outcome for traumatically brain-injured patients following post-acute rehabilitation programs. *Brain Injury, 6*(3), 219–228.

Neistadt, M. E. (1992). Occupational therapy treatments for constructional deficits. *American Journal of Occupational Therapy, 46*, 141–148.

Niemann, H., Ruff, R. M., & Baser, C. A. (1990). Computer assisted attention retraining in head injured individuals: A controlled efficacy study of an outpatient program. *Journal of Consulting and Clinical Psychology, 58*(6), 811–818.

Ownsworth, T. L., & McFarland, K. (1999). Memory remediation in long-term acquired brain injury: Two approaches in diary training. *Brain Injury, 13*, 605–626.

Parenté, R., & Anderson-Parenté, J. K. (1984). Retraining memory: Teaching organizational and encoding skills. *Cognitive Rehabilitation, 1*(4), 20–22.

Parenté, R., Anderson-Parenté, J. K., & Shaw, B. (1989). Retraining the mind's eye. *Journal of Head Trauma Rehabilitation, 4*(2), 53–62.

Parenté, R., Anderson-Parenté, J. K., & Stapleton, M. (2001). The use of rhymes and mnemonics for teaching cognitive skills to persons with acquired brain injury. *Brain Injury Source, 5*(1), 16–19.

Parenté, R., Kolakowsky, S., Hoffman, B., & Blake, S. (1998). Retraining the mind's eye: A review of existing research. *Topics in Stroke Rehabilitation, 5*(1), 48–58.

Parenté, R., Kolakowsky-Hayner, S., Krug, K., & Wilk, C. (2002). Retraining working memory after traumatic brain injury. *NeuroRehabilitation, 13*, 157–163.

Parenté, R., & Stapleton, M. C. (1999). Development of a cognitive strategies group for vocational training after traumatic brain injury. *NeuroRehabilitation, 13*, 13–20.

Parenté, R., Stapleton, M. C., & Wheatley, C. J. (1991). Practical strategies for vocation reentry after traumatic brain injury. *Journal of Head Trauma Rehabilitation, 6*(3), 35–45.

Prigatano, G., & Fordyce, D. (1987). Neuropsychological rehabilitation program: Presbyterian Hospital, Oklahoma City, Oklahoma. In B. Caplan (Ed.), *Rehabilitation psychology desk reference* (pp. 281–298). Rockville, MD: Aspen.

Prigatano, G. P. (1997). Recovery and cognitive retraining after craniocerebral trauma. *Journal of Learning Disabilities, 20*, 603–613.

Prigatano, G. P., Glisky, E. L., & Klonoff, P. (1995). Cognitive rehabilitation after traumatic brain injury. In P. W. Corrigan & S. C. Yudofsky (Eds.), *Cognitive rehabilitation and neuropsychiatric disorders*. Washington, DC: American Psychiatric Press.

Rappaport, M., Hall, K. M., Hopkins, K., Belleza, T., & Cope, D. N. (1982). Disability rating scale for severe head trauma: Coma to community. *Archives of Physical Medicine and Rehabilitation, 63*, 118–123.

Rasmusson, D. X., Rebok, G. W., Bylsma, F. W., & Brandt, J. (1999). Effects of three types of memory training in normal elderly. *Aging, Neuropsychology, and Cognition, 6*, 56–66.

Richardson, J. T. E. (1992). Imagery mnemonics and memory remediation. *Neurology, 42*, 283–286.

Ruff, R. M., Baser, C. A., Johnston, J. W., Marshall, L. F., Klauber, S. K., Klauber, M. R., et al. (1989). Neuropsychological rehabilitation: An experimental study with head-injured individuals. *Journal of Head Trauma Rehabilitation, 4*, 20–36.

Ruff, R. M., Mahaffey, R., Engel, J., Farrow, C., Cox, D., & Karzmark, P. (1994). Efficacy study of THINKable in the attention and memory retraining of traumatically head-injured individuals. *Brain Injury, 4*(4), 339–347.

Ryan, T. V., & Ruff, R. M. (1988). The efficacy of structured memory retraining in a group comparison of head trauma individuals. *Archives of Clinical Neuropsychology, 3*, 1965.

Semlyen, J. K., Summers, S. J., & Barnes, M. P. (1998). Traumatic brain injury: Efficacy of multidisciplinary rehabilitation. *Archives of Physical Medicine and Rehabilitation, 79*, 678–683.

Sohlberg, M. M., & Mateer, C. A. (1987). Effectiveness of an attention-training program. *Journal of Clinical and Experimental Neuropsychology, 9*(2), 117–130.

Sohlberg, M. M., & Mateer, C. A. (1989). *Introduction to cognitive rehabilitation, theory, and practice*. New York: Guilford Press.

Spivack, G., Spettell, C. M., Ellis, D. W., & Ross, S. E. (1992). Effects of intensity of treatment and length of stay on rehabilitation outcomes. *Brain Injury, 6*(5), 419–434.

Tate, R. L. (1997). Beyond one-bun, two-shoe: Recent advances in the psychological rehabilitation of memory disorders after acquired brain injury. *Brain Injury, 11*, 907–918.

Twum, M., & Parenté, R. (1994). Role of imagery and verbal labeling in performance of paired associates tasks by persons with closed head injury. *Journal of Clinical and Experimental Neuropsychology, 16*(4), 630–639.

Uzzell, B. P. (1997). Neuropsychological rehabilitation models. In J. Leon-Carrion (Ed.), *Neuropsychological rehabilitation: Fundamentals, innovations, and directions* (pp. 41–46). Delray Beach, FL: GR/St. Lucie Press.

Volpe, B. T., & McDowell, F. H. (1990). The efficacy of cognitive rehabilitation in patients with traumatic brain injury. *Archives of Neurology, 47*, 220–222.

Wechsler, D. (1997). *Wechsler Memory Scale–Third Edition*. San Antonio, TX: Psychological Corp.

Weinberg, J., Diller, L., & Gordon, W. (1977). Visual scanning training effect on reading-related tasks in acquired right brain damage. *Archives of Physical Medicine and Rehabilitation, 58*, 479–486.

Wertz, R. T., Weiss, D. G., Aten, J. T. L., Brookshire, R. H., Garcia-Bunuel, L., & Holland, A. L. (1986). Comparison of clinic, home, and deferred language treatment for aphasia: A Veterans Administration cooperative study. *Archives of Neurology, 43*, 653–658.

West, R., & Crook, T. (1992). Video training of imagery for mature adults. *Applied Cognitive Psychology, 6,* 307–320.

West, R. L., Yassuda, M. S., & Welch, D. C. (1997). Imagery training via videotape: Progress and potential for older adults. *Cognitive Technology, 2,* 16–21.

Wilson, B. A. (1999). Memory rehabilitation in brain-injured people. *Cognitive Neurorehabilitation, 4,* 333–346.

Wilson, B. A., Evans, J. J., & Malinek, V. (1997). Evaluation of NeuroPage: A new memory aid. *Journal of Neurosurgical Psychiatry, 63,* 113–115.

Zachs, R. T., & Hasher, L. (1992). Memory in life, lab, and clinic: Implications for memory theory. In D. Herrmann, H. Weingartner, A. Searleman, & C. McEvoy (Eds.), *Memory improvement: Implications for memory theory.* New York: Springer-Verlag.

Zencius, A., Wesolowski, M. D., Krankowski, T., & Burke, W. H. (1991). Memory notebook training with traumatically brain-injured clients. *Brain Injury, 5,* 321–325.

Zoltan, B. (1996). *Visual perception and cognition* (3rd ed.). Thorofare, NJ: Slack.

Appendix A

✤

Problem – Solutions
Treatment Planner

The purpose of this appendix is to provide therapists and clients with solutions to common problems following brain injury. This appendix is divided into two parts: (a) a problems checklist and (b) corresponding treatment solutions. The therapist should administer the checklist to clients and their family members and focus therapy on the problem areas that are reported most often.

Part I:
Problems Checklist

More than 100 persons with traumatic brain injury were asked to write down several cognitive problems they experienced each day. These problems were then summarized and ranked according to the frequency with which they were reported. The following checklist reflects these items and their rankings. The first item on the list (Problem #1) was the most frequently mentioned problem, and the last item on the list (Problem #50) was the least frequently mentioned, but reported by at least two people.

A therapist should read the items to the client and ask him or her to determine whether they experience any of those problems approximately once a week. For those problems that do occur regularly, the therapist should check the box next to the item. The therapist should repeat the process with one of the client's family members to determine the consistencies between the ratings.

Next to each check box is the name of the functional category the item describes. The categories are defined as follows:

Executive: These items require skills in foresight, insight, anticipation, and self-monitoring.

Memory: These items involve retention of novel information.

Learning: These items describe the ability to improve with practice.

Attention: These items measure focus, concentration, and immediate processing.

Processing: These items describe problems with reasoning and manipulation of information.

Hyperactivity: These items measure the ability to sit still or to maintain vigilance.

Vigilance: These items describe problems with staying on task.

Social Skills: These items index the skills of social interaction.

Expression: These items measure the ability to decode thoughts into spoken language.

Many of the items on the checklist measure more than one of the above categories. They are labeled in terms of the primary process of the item.

Once the checklist has been completed, the therapist should turn to Part II of this appendix where solutions that correspond to each problem have been presented.

Read the items and place a check in the box for any statements that seem to apply.

Process	# Item
Executive	☐ 1. I can't get myself to do the things I know I should do.
Executive	☐ 2. I can't control my anger.
Memory	☐ 3. I can't remember names and faces.
Memory	☐ 4. I can't remember what I hear.
Memory	☐ 5. I can't remember what I read.
Executive	☐ 6. I can't seem to think ahead.
Memory	☐ 7. I can't remember long directions.
Learning	☐ 8. I can't learn things quickly.
Executive	☐ 9. I do or say many things that I later regret.
Executive	☐ 10. I'll never be a success.
Executive	☐ 11. I make poor decisions.
Executive	☐ 12. It is hard for me to work on my own.
Executive	☐ 13. I can't keep track of time.
Executive	☐ 14. It is difficult to apply what I have learned in new situations.
Attention	☐ 15. I feel restless most of the time.
Hyperactivity	☐ 16. I can't sit still for very long.
Attention	☐ 17. Everything seems to distract me.
Attention	☐ 18. It is hard for me to wait for anything or anyone.
Social Skills	☐ 19. I interrupt people in midsentence and do not let them finish speaking.
Vigilance	☐ 20. I have a hard time finishing what I am told to do.
Vigilance	☐ 21. I cannot maintain focus.
Vigilance	☐ 22. I start many projects and activities but I never seem to finish anything.
Hyperactivity	☐ 23. I am hyperactive.
Hyperactivity	☐ 24. I can't seem to work quietly.
Hyperactivity	☐ 25. I talk too much and I can't seem to stop talking.

Read the items and place a check in the box for any statements that seem to apply.

Process	#	Item
Social skills	☐ 26.	I interrupt people when they talk to me.
Social skills	☐ 27.	I don't listen.
Memory	☐ 28.	I frequently lose things that I need later.
Processing	☐ 29.	I have a hard time using public transportation.
Processing	☐ 30.	I take longer than most people to finish anything.
Executive	☐ 31.	I have a hard time working outside of a structured routine.
Social skills	☐ 32.	It is hard for me to make friends or get used to new people.
Executive	☐ 33.	I can't be on time for appointments or I forget them.
Memory	☐ 34.	It is hard for me to remember complex directions.
Learning	☐ 35.	I have to be shown how to do something before I can do it.
Learning	☐ 36.	I require many more practice sessions than other people.
Executive	☐ 37.	I cannot follow schedules.
Processing	☐ 38.	It is hard for me to understand written directions.
Processing	☐ 39.	I don't understand charts, diagrams, schematics, or maps.
Executive	☐ 40.	I need prompting and reminding.
Processing	☐ 41.	I can't follow complex directions.
Expression	☐ 42.	I say one thing but mean another.
Expression	☐ 43.	I can't say things clearly.
Processing	☐ 44.	I cannot take accurate messages.
Expression	☐ 45.	It is hard for me to write my thoughts.
Expression	☐ 46.	I do not talk clearly on the phone.
Processing	☐ 47.	I can't understand big words that people use.
Expression	☐ 48.	I have to say things over and over before anyone understands me.
Processing	☐ 49.	I misinterpret what people say in conversation.
Processing	☐ 50.	I make a lot of mistakes.

Treatment Solutions

Problem #1:
I can't get myself to do things
I know I should do.

Consult Appendix B. To the therapist: This is the most common item in this problem-solutions survey. Most clients report that they know what they should do to improve their cognitive status but that they have a hard time motivating themselves to do them. This problem is so pervasive among persons with brain injury that another entire appendix, Appendix B, has been devoted to it. Some general suggestions, however, are presented below.

Take baby steps. Ask yourself, "What is the smallest thing I can do to help myself?" Try to do that and then build on your success.

Determine that you want to succeed. Many people are not motivated because they are afraid they will succeed. They feel unworthy of success and are frightened at the prospect of getting too much of it. Often they ruin their successes before they occur because they do not feel that they deserve them.

Against whom are you rebelling? To the therapist: The most common reason cited for lack of motivation was the feeling of defiance that the client felt against another person, usually a parent or family member. These people were often deceased or had limited contact with the client, and his or her desire to defy the parent or family member was, therefore, irrational. It is important to find out why the person still has control over the client's life. Is there an unsatisfied need for acceptance?

Do you feel helpless? To the therapist: Often a parent, husband, or wife, has done everything for the client over the years and now the client cannot do anything independently. He or she may feel helpless and paralyzed by the fear of not knowing what to do and the need to defer to some authority. This problem must be discussed and aired. Teaching the client skills, no matter how trivial, that demonstrate competence is the best way for him or her to overcome feelings of helplessness. For example, the client might begin by paying one bill each month without assistance and gradually paying more. Becoming proficient at a sport or hobby can also help.

Is there a fear of evaluation or accountability? To the therapist: The client's lack of motivation may stem from a fear that "Everyone will see just how dumb I really am." The client may believe that it is better not to do something at all rather than risk being exposed as incompetent. This same feeling underlies avoidance of responsibility. The client may not accept situations where he or she is accountable. To work on this problem, the client should try practicing a skill without any fear of evaluation. Self-paced study programs and multimedia CD-ROM software that the client can use at home are good places to start. Individual sports where the goal is simply to better one's own time or performance also help.

Problem #2:
I can't control my anger.

Use the ANGER and CALM mnemonics:

Anticipate the signs of anger
Never act in anger
Go through the CALM sequence
Evaluate the situation in retrospect
Review how you coped

Call someone for help
Allow yourself to emote
Leave the situation
Move about

It may seem impossible to control anger. The first step is to recognize the signs of anger such as rising body temperature, twitching jaw muscles, or clenched fists. It is especially important to never act in anger. This leads people to do something they later regret. Try to calm down before, not after, becoming angry. Call someone you know and trust and let them know you are angry. Express your anger with that person. Remove yourself from the situation that is causing the anger. Do not sit down; move about because movement will help dissipate the anger. Once you are calm, try to evaluate what it was that made you so angry. Finally, learn from the situation by reviewing the things that helped you to cope with your anger. You may wish to write these things down in a journal because they will be valuable lessons to use the next time you get angry.

Problem #3:
I can't remember names and faces.

Use the NAME mnemonic:

Notice the person with whom you speak

Ask the person to repeat his or her name

Mention the name in conversation

Exaggerate some special feature

You can remember anyone's name and face by using a few simple rules: First, look at the person when you are being introduced to him or her. Notice any special features about his or her face, voice, or the sound of his or her name. Focus on that special feature and blow it out of proportion in your mind. Ask the person to repeat his or her name even if you heard it correctly. Pretend you didn't hear the name or purposely mispronounce it to get the person to say it over again. Use the name while you are speaking to the person.

Take pictures of people with whom you live or work. Make these into a personal album and write their names on the back of each picture. Try to memorize one name and face each day.

Sketch a face on the back of a business card. You do not have to be an artist to sketch a reasonably accurate face. It is the act of sketching the face that creates a vivid image of the person in your mind.

Problem #4:
I can't remember what I hear.

Repeat it again in your own words. When someone says something to you, try to summarize it in your own words. Repeat your summary out loud and ask the person to verify its accuracy. This is especially important at the end of a conversation so that you and the other person part with the same understanding. Repeat your summary several times to ensure that you remember it. It may help to repeat the summary into a digital recorder so that you can play it again later.

Use a digital recorder. Digital recorders are different from tape recorders. They allow a person to record several messages and to mark each with a number so that the user does not have to rewind a tape and hunt for a message. The user searches the numbers or enters the number of the message and the recorder plays it back. These recorders are especially valuable for taking short directions, instructions, or phone messages, but they have many other applications. Newer models can hold up to 8 hours of information, which is more than enough for most applications. Using a digital recorder can solve most memory problems that are based on failures to remember what was heard.

Write a summary. Memory for what you hear is best saved as a summary rather than in its original form. If you prefer to write a summary rather than use a digital recorder, then carry a small notepad with you at all times.

Mentally summarize three main points. Effective summaries can usually be created as a list of three major points. Ask, "What are the three most important things I must remember?" Next, organize the points from most to least important.

Ask the person to repeat the major points. If you're not certain of the major points in the conversation, then ask the person with whom you're speaking to say what he or she thinks are the major points.

Problem #5:
I can't remember what I read.

Dictate a summary into a digital recorder. When reading, get in the habit of summarizing what you have just read, paragraph by paragraph, into a digital recorder. As a rule, do not go on to the next paragraph until you can summarize what you read in the previous paragraph. This procedure will serve several purposes. First, it will force you to pay attention to what you are reading because you cannot summarize what you have read unless you pay attention while you read it. Second, it will also show you how many times you must reread something before you can remember it. At first you might not be able to remember the material unless you have read it at least five times. As you get better with the recorder, you will eventually be able to read the paragraph and summarize it accurately after a single reading. At that point, you will be reading much differently than you did before. Specifically, you will be reading for gist rather than syntax, meaning that you will try to remember meaning rather than unrelated facts. Third, it will provide you with a set of notes that you can later review easily by replaying the recording.

Summarize major points in margin. If, for some reason, you find it uncomfortable to use a recorder, then you should try writing summaries of what you read in the margins next to the paragraph. This does not mean that you should copy what you have just read. The purpose is to force you to translate the material into your own words. It is easier and faster to do this with a recorder, but many people prefer to write summaries and seem to remember the material better that way.

Create a learning map. A learning map is a visual depiction of material you have read. Begin by drawing a circle in the center of a piece of blank paper. Then try to write a summary of the major point of what you have read in the circle. Next, draw several smaller circles around the larger one and try to summarize the minor points in each of the smaller circles. Then connect the circles in a way that organizes the material in a logical sequence. Most lectures and book materials can be summarized on a single page. Again, it may take time to become accustomed to this method. After a while, however, you will likely prefer the learning map method to slower and less accurate handwritten notes.

Problem #6:
I can't seem to think ahead.

Ask the right questions. *Foresight* and *premonition* describe the ability to think ahead. Developing forward-thinking ability is a matter of asking questions that force you to think about the consequences of what you are about to do. However, it is equally important to ask insight questions that help you understand what is going on at present and hindsight questions that help you understand the events that might have caused something to occur. Following are some questions to ask yourself.

Thinking-ahead questions

What would happen if . . . ?

Does what I want to do or say create more problems than it solves?

Is this a problem or is it an opportunity?

How will this affect me?

Will doing this help me achieve any of my personal goals?

Insight questions

What are my options?

What control do I have in this situation?

What exactly is the problem?

Hindsight questions

What could have caused this?

How could I have done this differently?

What did I say that was wrong?

Problem #7:
I can't remember long directions.

Record them. Use a digital recorder to capture the gist of the directions or to restate them verbatim. Listen to the directions several times as you complete the task or as you do the various pieces of the job.

Say them in your own words. Remember, translating something into your own words is the glue that sticks information in memory. Say the directions in your own words. Draw a map if possible and write the directions under the map.

Break them down into pieces. Try to organize long directions into smaller pieces and link the pieces in sequence.

Problem #8:
I can't learn things quickly.

Use the LEARNING mnemonic:

Listen: You cannot learn what you do not hear.

Effort: Learning requires conscious effort.

Attention: Learning requires memory and memory requires attention.

Rehearsal: Keep information in memory so that you can process it.

Notice organization: This allows you to structure the experience.

Intention to learn: Plan a learning session so that you have everything you need.

New experiences: These train us to generalize.

Goals for completion: Write goals on a sticky note and do not take a break until you have completed everything on the note.

Problem #9:
I do or say many things that I later regret.

Memorize the following poem:

Does what I want to do or say create more problems than it solves?

This question makes me think of all that is involved.

It stems the urge; it soothes the need; it makes me stop and wait.

Now ask the right question while you hesitate.

Does what I want to do or say solve more problems than it creates?

If it does, then do it; but if it doesn't, then don't.

If you follow this simple rule, then the things you want will happen

And the things you don't want—won't.

This poem will help you control your impulses by having you ask the right questions.

People often act impulsively because they see something they want and don't stop to think whether it is going to cause problems in the long term. By simply hesitating a moment, you can often avoid doing something that will come back to haunt you later.

Make a list of impulsive things you do and look for consistencies. Frequently people find themselves saying, "I can't believe I did that again," or, "I did it again; it never fails." Make a list of these impulsive behaviors that includes when you did them, with whom you did them, and other information, such as time of day, season of the year, whether it was a full moon, and any other information that might help you look for consistencies. By noticing consistencies, you can predict times when you may be likely to do those things again.

Problem #10:
I'll never be a success.

Use the SUCCESS mnemonic:

Substitute positive for negative addictions

Understand your weaknesses

Count your blessings each day

Concentrate on the future

Establish a positive social network

Suppress your urges

Smile most of the time

If you want to be good at something, watch what the good people do and do that. Successful people are positive people. They exercise, have hobbies, and have other positive addictions. They understand their weaknesses and put themselves in situations where they use their strengths. They do not focus on the negative; rather, they count their blessings every day. They concentrate on making the future more to their liking. Their friends share the same positive values and interests. They

have learned how to control their urges and impulses. They smile most of the time because they are content with their lives.

Problem #11:
I make poor decisions.

Use the DECIDE mnemonic:

Do not hesitate—decide to begin.

Evaluate your options—choose those that are win–win.

Create new options when others won't do.

Investigate existing policies and how they affect you.

Discuss the situation with others—consider their advice.

Evaluate how you feel about each option—before acting, think twice.

Collect all information about the decision. Many decisions are difficult when you are unaware of all the information you need to make an intelligent choice. Postpone making a decision until you have all the facts.

Identify all of your options. Ask, "What do I have control over?" Choose options that you can control.

List the positives and negatives of each option. Make a two-column list on a piece of paper. In the first column, write the benefits of each option. In the second column, list the problems each option may create. The best options will be obvious from looking at the two columns. The best options will have the fewest negatives and the most positives.

Ask how you feel about each option. After you have thought logically about the options, it is time to take off your thinking cap and simply ask how you feel about each option. You should not, however, make any decision based solely on how you feel about it. Your intuition is valuable, but it should be considered along with all other information. It should not dominate the decision-making process.

Problem #12:
It is hard for me to work on my own.

Do progressively harder tasks alone. Start with an easy task and try to do it alone. Gradually make the tasks more difficult.

Work progressively longer alone. Try to add at least 1 minute to every work session. This might not seem like a lot of time and you may not notice the increase each time you work. However, after ten sessions, you will be working 10 minutes longer. This is a painless way of gradually increasing the time that you can work alone.

Work alone but have someone else look in on you frequently. Work with another person who will check on you every few minutes. Ask that person to gradually lengthen the time between checks.

Problem #13:
I can't keep track of time.

Get a chiming clock. Put a clock in your home that chimes loudly on the hour and wear a watch on your wrist that also chimes hourly. In general, set devices all around your living and working spaces to remind you of time passing.

Work in rooms with clocks. When working away from home, try to choose a room that has a clock to which you can refer.

Set a timer for completion of tasks. Use an electronic timer to monitor how much time

you can spend on a task. Try to complete the task before the timer goes off.

Ask yourself throughout the day about time passing. People are often unaware of time, especially when they are distracted or interested in something else. Asking yourself, "How much time has passed since I last checked?" will help you to think about time during the day.

Try to estimate time the natural way. For example, look at the sun and try to estimate what time it is from its position in the sky. Try to estimate the time from the amount of light during twilight or in the morning.

Problem #14:
It is difficult to apply what I have learned in new situations.

Discuss applications when learning the skill. When you learn anything new, try to determine how it applies to something you already do or may be asked to do in the near future. Ask the instructor how you can use the information in the workplace or in your everyday life. Pretend you are going to teach this skill or information to someone else. Develop examples that you could use to show another how this information is useful.

Practice applying the skill in situations that are similar to training, then gradually make them different. For example, when learning how to type, apply the skill to creating a letter on a word processor. When learning basic arithmetic, try to balance your checkbook.

Observe others applying the skill. Watch others who use the skill in various situations. For example, after studying a driver's manual, observe how people drive in situations similar to those you studied in the manual. When learning to type, observe how workers type in offices that you visit.

Problem #15:
I feel restless most of the time.

Exercise. Exercise dissipates anxiety. You do not have to work yourself into a sweat to experience the benefits of exercise. Indeed, all you need is approximately ½ hour of exercise daily. The best types of exercise are those that stretch the muscles, increase the heart rate and breathing, and that are enjoyable. Meditation, t'ai chi, yoga, and stretching are especially useful exercises.

Watch caffeine and nicotine intake. Coffee and cigarettes are addictive substances. Moreover, they speed up metabolism and make people feel jittery. In low doses caffeine and nicotine are generally harmless, but in moderate to high doses they limit memory and thinking.

Get an active job. Sometimes hyperactivity can be solved by working in a situation where you can move about freely and where there is no need to sit for long periods of time.

Antihyperactivity medication. Ritalin, Cylert, Adderall, and Conserta are medications frequently prescribed for treating attention deficit. Using prescription medication may be the most expedient approach for dealing with attention problems, but they are not a permanent solution. If a person never learns the skills of paying attention, then the medication is only a temporary solution.

Take frequent breaks. Most people with learning disabilities, attention deficits, and brain injuries have limited attention spans. Study or therapy sessions that last longer than about 1 hour are probably too long. Generally, it is better to work in several short sessions than one long session.

Problem #16:
I can't sit still for very long.

Antihyperactivity medication. Hyperactivity often accompanies attention deficit. Medication can help reduce or eliminate the hyperactivity, but it is only a temporary solution.

Pick interesting activities. People with attention deficit and hyperactivity can concentrate quite well when they are interested in the activity. One of the keys to dealing with these problems is to find activities that are interesting.

Process while moving. Sometimes moving about while doing a task can improve processing. For example, read summaries of text into a recorder then study it by taking a walk and listening to it on headphones. Taking walks and talking to another about a mutual interest will often create an enduring memory.

Sit for 1 minute longer each session. Increase the length of each therapy session by 1 minute. Eventually, you will learn to sit for an extended length of time.

Frequently switch tasks. Set up tasks so that you can work on one for a brief period of time, then work on another, then on a third, and so forth. This allows you to focus for brief periods of time. Constant switching keeps you focused on the task at hand and can satisfy your need for constant stimulation.

Problem #17:
Everything seems to distract me.

Wear earplugs when concentrating. Earplugs are an easy way to eliminate noise and to screen out sounds that may distract. These are especially useful in situations where you need to concentrate, for example, when taking a test. They are also useful when you need to study, read, or meditate.

Work in a quiet area. There is no substitute for eliminating external distractions when a person is trying to concentrate. Try to eliminate distractions such as radio music, television, others' conversations, and noise from other rooms.

Read into a tape recorder. This activity forces you to concentrate on the text and process it at a deeper level. As a rule, you should read a paragraph, then try to summarize it in a single sentence into the tape recorder. At first, this will be difficult and may require five or more readings before you can successfully summarize the material. Eventually, you will reach the point where a single reading will suffice. At that point, you will be reading very differently, specifically, for gist, rather than syntax. The process will also force you to concentrate. You can review the taped summaries using headphones while exercising or doing other activities.

Repeat instructions and directions aloud. When conversing with others, use the restatement–verify method. That is, say, "Let me say that in my own words and you tell me if I understand it correctly." As a rule, do not leave a conversation until the message has been transmitted, restated, and verified. This process may take a little longer than usual but it will also eliminate many communication errors that create problems later. Generally, a minute spent doing this will save hours fixing problems due to miscommunications.

Protect time. Try to organize your day so that there is quiet time allocated for specific tasks. This should be a block of time when there are no ringing phones, no pagers, and no interruptions. Ideally, it is time when you are refreshed, alert, and rested.

Problem #18:
It is hard for me to wait for anything or anyone.

Ask someone to hold your place in line, do something else, then return. No one wants to wait. When you must wait, the best strategy is to use the time productively. If possible, have a friend, family member, or acquaintance hold your place in line so that you can do something else while the time passes. Be certain to return before your friend reaches the front of the line.

Wait until the line lessens. When you see a long line, determine whether it would be better to return at a later time when the line is shorter. For example, when doing errands, it may be possible to rearrange the tasks so that you can return later when there is less of a wait.

Distract yourself. When you must wait, do something that takes your mind off of the idleness. For example, pay some bills while you are waiting, strike up a conversation with someone else in line, read a book, or write a letter.

Problem #19:
I interrupt people in midsentence and do not let them finish speaking.

Use the LISTEN mnemonic:

Look at the person with whom you speak; maintain eye contact.

Interest in the conversation.

Speak less than half the time.

Try not to interrupt or change the topic.

Evaluate what is said; do not blindly accept it.

Notice body language and attend to the nonverbal cues in the conversation that carry information.

Listen 60% of the time and speak 40%. Good listeners listen; they do not talk. As a rule, effective listeners spend the majority of their time listening and a minority of it speaking.

Wait at least 1 second after a person has finished speaking before you begin. Be certain a person has finished what he or she said before you speak. Interrupting or not allowing a person to finish a sentence is rude and limits communication.

Remember the following poem about listening:

> Listening is the social grace
> Of hearing the words and watching the face
> Good listeners speak less than half the time
> They evaluate the reason and the rhyme
> So open your eyes and close your mouth
> Study the face, east, west, north, and south
> Remember, listening is both a skill and a choice
> Choose not to hear the sound of your own voice.

Problem #20:
I have a hard time finishing what I am told to do.

Make a list of things to do and check them off as you complete them. Create checklists for tasks that you need to complete on a regular basis and put the date on the checklist as a reminder that you have completed the task.

Divide and conquer. Break larger tasks down and set deadlines for completion of smaller tasks. Make a list of things that must be completed and order them in terms of what parts need to be completed right away and which ones can wait. For each part of the larger task ask *"Is this important or is this urgent?"* Urgent things need immediate attention whereas im-portant ones can wait until the urgent components are completed.

Repeat instructions in your own words before you begin. Always get verification from the person giving instructions that you understand the task.

Ask others to remind you of deadlines. Enlist the aid of family members and friends.

Write instructions down or tape them. Do not begin a task unless you have a record of everything you are supposed to do to complete it.

Problem #21:
I cannot maintain focus.

Take frequent breaks. Usually a person cannot concentrate for more than about 20 minutes. Remember to work on a task for 20 minutes, then take a break, then work for 20 more minutes, then a break, and so on. This schedule results in much better retention than one solid hour of work with no breaks.

Record on audiotape or videotape and listen to it or watch it later. Hearing or seeing something a second time is like seeing the same movie twice. You notice a lot of things you missed the first time. Usually, a person will need two or three rehearsals before he or she will recall most of what happened.

Antihyperactivity medication. There are a variety of drugs that will improve a person's focus. These may help, but should only be taken with caution and with medical supervision.

Gradually increase length of session by 1 minute per session. When trying to do a task, gradually make the length of the session longer by 1 minute each time. You will not notice the increase from session to session but after five sessions, you will be able to focus for 5 minutes longer. For example, if you cannot focus for longer than 10 minutes, use this technique, and after five study sessions, you will be able to study for 15 minutes at a time.

Write down goals before you begin. Keep a pad of sticky notes with you and when you begin any task, write down on a sticky note what you plan to accomplish before you get up. Post the sticky note somewhere in plain view and meet that goal before taking a break. When you return from your break, write another sticky note.

Ask, "What do I absolutely have to accomplish before I get up?" Divide tasks into those that are crucial versus those that are important. By splitting tasks into those that need to be done immediately and those that need to be done but not immediately, you will prioritize them so that the crucial tasks get done right away.

Ask, "What is the best possible use of my time right now?" This is a question that you should ask at regular intervals throughout the day. Wear a beeping watch and set it to beep on the half hour. Ask this question every time you hear the beep to avoid wasting time.

Problem #22:
I start many projects and activities but I never seem to finish anything.

Set deadlines for completion. Write down all of the projects you need to complete and write next to each one the date by which you must complete it.

Consider fear of evaluation. Often the anxiety that you feel is the result of fear that someone will look at your work and say that it does not measure up. Ask yourself if this is what you fear and if this fear is causing you to avoid completing a project.

Do not start another project until you finish the first. Not finishing projects creates anxiety. The more projects left undone, the more anxiety people feel. The reverse is also true. The more projects finished, the less anxiety people feel. One way to reduce anxiety is to finish the things you start. Make your goal to finish things, not to start them. As a rule, do not start anything new until you finish something you have started.

Reward yourself for finishing tasks. Often we finish things and never acknowledge that they are done. Finishing is important and you deserve a reward when things get done. Buy yourself a nice dinner or take a break and go to a movie. Do something fun that marks the sense of completion that you experience when something gets done.

Problem #23:
I am hyperactive.

Ask the right question at the right time. The right question is "What should I be doing right now?" or "What is the best possible use of my time right now?"

Do not dwell on intrusive thoughts. Intrusive thoughts are things that bother us. Write them down in your journal or appointment calendar and discuss them with a therapist at an assigned time.

Wear earplugs. Use earplugs to screen out distractions at important times like when you are taking a test.

Distribute your practice. When learning new things, practice for a short time several times a day rather than for one long time a day.

Repeat what you are trying to learn. Do not assume you know something just because you have heard it, seen it, or read it. Repeat the task and see if you can recite it, draw it, or perform it. This is a good way to find out what you do not know. Practice what you do not know and then repeat the task again; practice those things that are still difficult, then repeat again. This is the quickest way to learn any new skill.

Change your diet. Eating starchy carbohydrates, sugars, and stimulants may make you feel better for a short time, but it does nothing for your cognitive processing. Eating foods high in protein, vegetables, and fruits is the best diet to improve your thinking.

Avoid stimulants. Many people are hyperactive because their diet includes high levels of stimulants such as caffeine. A person taking 500 mg of caffeine (about 5 cups of brewed coffee) can become addicted to it in a short period of time. The nicotine in cigarettes is equally addictive. Reducing caffeine intake to less than 200 mg per day and eliminating smoking can dramatically reduce problems with attention.

Create personal relevance and incentive. The value you place on something determines your ability to concentrate on it. Young men with attention deficit are able to concentrate when playing video games or when talking to an attractive young woman. Money helps us all to concentrate. Ask yourself what you find interesting and try to create a life that includes those types of activities.

Problem #24:
I can't seem to work quietly.

Work alone. Work in places where noise does not matter, such as outdoors or away from others.

Choose jobs where noise is not important. Many indoor jobs are performed in noisy environments. Investigate these jobs to determine if you would work well in those types of settings.

Ask yourself, "Why do I need to make noise?" Often, making noise is a way of drawing attention to yourself. Is this type of attention important to you? Do you require attention of this sort? Why?

Problem #25:
I talk too much and
I can't seem to stop talking.

Speak less than half the time. Adopt the rule that you should listen more than you speak. Speak 40% of the time and listen 60% of the time.

Say a sentence in your mind before you say it in words. Hesitate before you answer. Think the sentence in your mind before you actually say it aloud. If there is any question about how your statement will be received, then do not say it.

Limit statements to one sentence. If your statement takes more than one sentence, then it probably is not clear to the listener.

Use the following BOMS mnemonic for conversations:

> **B**ottom line
>
> **O**mit details
>
> **M**aintain focus
>
> **S**ummarize

Say exactly what you want to say up front, in the first sentence, in one sentence. This is the bottom line. Omit as many of the details as possible and focus on the gist of the conversation. This is all the person to whom you are speaking will remember anyway so emphasize the major point. Do not go off on tangents; remain focused on the major issue. Summarize your main points at the end. Remember the old adage: *Tell them what you are going to say; tell them; then tell them what you said.*

Problem #26:
I interrupt people when they talk to me.

Speak only when spoken to. Do not offer conversation unless invited. When someone asks you for your opinion, give it, but do not overstate it. Say it clearly, forcefully, simply, and once.

Do not speak until the other person has finished his or her sentence. Try waiting for 1 second after the other person has finished before you add to the conversation.

Do not break into conversations. Wait until you are invited to contribute before you enter a conversation.

Limit sentences to 25 words or fewer. Most people cannot repeat, word-for-word, more than 25 words. Longer sentences require a person to extract the gist of what you have said, which may lead him or her to misinterpret your statement.

Problem #27:
I don't listen.

Repeat instructions in your own words and ask for verification. Repeating directions or instructions ensures that you heard them correctly and completely. If you cannot repeat directions then you will need to hear them again. However, being able to repeat them does not necessarily mean that you understand them. You must be able to say them correctly in your own words before you can assume that you understand them. Moreover, the other person must verify that your interpretation of what he or she said is correct.

Record conversations and listen to them again. Recording conversations and then listening to them again will help you to remember them. However, many people may not want to be recorded. In these cases, summarize what was said in your own words into the recorder.

Problem #28:
I frequently lose things that I need later.

Create a file, drawer, or space for each project. Common projects like doing taxes, saving recipes, or fixing things around the home require their own files. For example, keep everything you need for your taxes in one place. As you accumulate tax information throughout the year such as receipts, canceled checks, or communications with the government, save them in a file. Save manuals for devices such as vacuum cleaners, coffeemakers, and office machines in one place so that you can refer to them later.

Work in a group and assign someone else the job of filing information. If you cannot file information effectively, then assign this job to someone else. There is usually one member of a group who is willing to do the secretarial work and who is quite good at it. Around the home, try to find a family member who is willing to do this type of work. The person becomes the designated archivist.

Keep a personal organizer. Much information can be stored electronically. Personal data assistants, such as the ones made by Palm, can be used to store tremendous amounts of personal information for easy retrieval. These devices are also easy to carry and operate. It may be helpful to find someone who is familiar with such devices and who is willing to help you to enter information into it. The more personal information you enter into the device, the more you will want to use it.

Make a fix-it file. When things break around the home and as you fix them, write down the steps that were involved in a fix-it file. When something breaks again, go to the fix-it file and review what steps you took in the past to fix it. This process can save you a great deal of time and energy.

Problem #29:
I have a hard time using public transportation.

Ride buses with someone else until you feel comfortable. Ask the person to teach you what you need to know in order to ride the bus alone. Find out things such as how to pay a fare, where the various bus routes drop off, and what other types of public transportation are available.

Do not ride the bus during dangerous times. Part of people's fear of using public transportation comes from stories on the news about a robbery or some other problem that occurred on the bus, train, or subway. Learn when it is most dangerous to use public transportation and avoid doing so during those times.

Problem #30:
I take longer than most people to finish anything.

Focus on accuracy. Finishing a task involves more than performing it quickly. There are two factors that determine the quality of a person's work: speed and accuracy. In most cases, people must first learn how to do something accurately before they can improve the speed with which they do it.

Watch what the good people do and do that. One reason why people work slowly is because they are unaware of more efficient work habits. People who do a task well can teach others their techniques. Such proven techniques can help you work faster.

Problem #31:
I have a hard time working outside of a structured routine.

Write down changes in a journal and study them. When things change, describe the changes in a journal. Then write down what you must do differently to accommodate the change.

Discuss changes with coworkers. Other people are affected by the same changes you are so ask them how they are adjusting and what they are doing differently; try to adopt their methods for adjustment.

Make checklists and to-do lists. Try to summarize changes in the form of a checklist. Use the checklist to ensure consistency until you have adjusted to the changes.

Problem #32:
It is hard for me to make friends or get used to new people.

Ask one person to lunch each week. Get to know people with whom you work by asking them to have lunch during the day. Talk to them about their life outside of work. Ask about their hobbies, their families, and what they do for fun.

Greet people each day. Make the effort to smile and say hello to people with whom you work or socialize each day. Even if you do not talk to them, be certain to smile. Carry on light conversations in a public place if you do not feel comfortable with one-on-one discussions.

Call a different family member each week. Widen your social network by beginning with your family. Calling them gives them the impression that you care for them and want to be included in their circle of friends.

Problem #33:
I can't be on time for appointments or I forget them.

Use an appointment calendar. Many people use appointment calendars to remind them to be in certain places at certain times. Such a calendar should have each day marked off in half-hour intervals. This will allow you to circle the time when you are supposed to be somewhere. The calendar should also include a piece of blank lined paper next to each day so that you can write down things that you need to bring to appointments, directions, and any other important information.

Use a telememo watch. These watches allow you to store appointments in the watch and they beep at the appropriate time. Casio makes the Datalink model, which is perhaps the best of any of this type of watch. Several other types of electronic devices can also remind a person about appointments. These are usually available at office supply stores.

Have a friend call and remind. Family and friends can also remind a person of things they must do. Family and friends can share responsibility for reminding you of your appointments.

Keep a wall-hanging calendar. A wall-hanging calendar placed strategically in the house can be quite helpful as a reminder. The calendar should be large and important appointments written in red or some other bright color.

Problem #34:
It is hard for me to remember complex directions.

Repeat directions in your own words and ask for verification. Do not leave a conversation until you have heard the directions, repeated them, and have received verification that you understood them correctly.

Make a checklist of the directions. Turn directions into a checklist or a to-do list or any other list that lets you know when you have completed the task.

Break directions into pieces. Complex directions are difficult for anyone to understand. Break them into pieces and sequence the pieces in such a way that you can complete the directions in the shortest possible time.

Problem #35:
I have to be shown how to do something before I can do it.

Have someone demonstrate. Many people need to be shown how to do something before they can do it. If this is your learning style, then ask someone for a demonstration. Do not be afraid to admit that you need a person's help.

Watch a training video. Many skills can be learned effectively by watching a training video. There are also several multimedia software programs that can be used to learn a variety of academic and computer skills. These training materials can be found at video stores or computer stores. Time spent browsing through the selection at the stores can help you make a good choice.

Get directions with pictures. If you learn best by looking at pictures rather than reading words, try to find directions that emphasize visual images rather than written text.

Problem #36:
I require many more practice sessions than other people.

Arrange for extra practice time. When possible, find out if you can practice skills on your own time. For example, when learning a computer skill, it is a good idea to have a computer in the home on which you can practice.

Record lectures and listen again. Listening repeatedly to a recording of material you want to learn is a good way to learn it. For example, listening to a recording of a class lecture can help you write accurate notes. People often gain a deeper understanding of material the second time they hear it.

Mentor someone else with lower level skills. Assess your skills and try to teach the ones you know well to someone else. As you acquire higher level skills, try to teach those too. For example, when learning how to type, once you master the home row of keys, try to teach it to someone else who cannot type. Continue the process as you learn more and more keys.

Get a job coach. A job coach can watch you while you are working and make suggestions for how to improve performance. Persons in school should find someone who will tutor them one-on-one.

Problem #37:
I cannot follow schedules.

Create consequences for not following schedules. People often ignore the conse-

quences of failing to follow schedules. Thinking about such consequences may motivate you to keep a timetable. For example, when you receive a reminder in the mail saying that you have not paid a bill, make a list of the things that will happen if you fail to pay it promptly.

Keep a schedule in plain view. Make a list of things that you must do in the order in which you must do them. If possible, put dates next to each of these items. Post this schedule in plain view and cross off items as you complete them.

Ask yourself why you resist schedules. Often, people resist schedules because they do not want to be controlled by them. This is a psychological problem that cannot be solved by checklists or other strategies. Discuss this issue with a therapist or friend.

Use electronic reminding devices. Watches made by Casio and Microsoft, in the Datalink series, can be programmed to remind you of important events. The watch will beep a reminder and display a message on its screen at the appropriate time.

Problem #38:
It is hard for me to understand written directions.

Read the directions into a tape recorder. Often people do not understand instructions because their anxiety keeps them from reading all of the words. Reading the directions into a tape recorder ensures that you read all of the words and that you process them with your ears and eyes.

Read and discuss the directions with another person. Try to get others involved in the understanding process by asking them to read the directions and discuss the meaning with you.

Read directions slowly and word by word. As you read, note the places where you stop or hesitate and read those sections over again several times. Do not go on to a new section until you understand the current one. When taking tests, read the directions several times before you begin. For multiple-choice tests, read the question several times before attempting to answer. Look for critical words like *not*.

Problem #39:
I don't understand charts, diagrams, schematics, or maps.

Translate charts into words. Try using both words and pictures to describe something. For example, when someone gives you a map, try to write out the directions with words underneath the map.

Discuss the chart with someone else. Ask a person to draw a similar diagram to the one you are having trouble understanding. Also, try to redraw the chart so that it makes sense to you.

Make your own chart. Try to translate the information into your own chart as if you had to explain it to someone else. Ask yourself how you can simplify the chart and break it down into smaller charts.

Problem #40:
I need prompting and reminding.

Use sticky notes. You should always carry a pad of sticky notes with you to write reminders to yourself. Stick them in places that will remind you of what you are supposed to do. For example, put one on the refrigerator to remind you of groceries to buy at the market. Put one on the door to remind you to bring something with you when you leave the next day.

Use colored trays. Office supply stores sell colored stackable trays that can be used for organizing mail and other things around the home. For example, using three stackable trays, you could put important mail in a red tray on top to remind you that this mail is important. A green tray in the center holds mail that is less important and a blue tray at the bottom is for mail that is of interest but not crucial.

Use computer reminding devices. Several computer programs provide automatic prompting features. Screen savers can also be easily constructed to remind you of important tasks every time you turn on the computer. Simpler reminding devices include egg timers, alarm clocks, and beeping watches.

Wear data bank watches. These watches hold a great deal of information such as phone numbers, addresses, and other information you might use daily. The advantage of these watches is that they allow you to store reminder messages and carry them on your wrist. If you choose a waterproof watch, you will never have to take it off. Timex and Casio make these types of watches.

Use electronic task reminders. Hand-held computers, such as ones made by Palm, can easily be programmed to remind you of events, dates, or other personal information.

Problem #41:
I can't follow complex directions.

Break them down into small steps. Ask yourself what part of the task you can complete right now. Then ask yourself what remains to be done, and what must be done first, second, and third.

Record them and listen to them again. Record complex directions on a digital or tape recorder. Listen to them several times and try to organize them into smaller tasks as outlined above.

Ask for written directions. Ask the person giving directions to write them down on a piece of paper for you, eliminating the need for you to write them down.

Problem #42:
I say one thing but mean another.

Practice saying a sentence in your mind before saying it aloud. By practicing what you want to say in your mind before you say it aloud, you can organize the material logically. Remember, your goal is to say something correctly, clearly, and once. Other people will respect such verbal efficiency.

Join Toastmasters. Toastmasters is a club that invites people who want to learn how to speak effectively to practice their verbal skills with a sympathetic group of members. The members assume that you are not a good speaker and that their purpose is to help you to speak more clearly. At a typical meeting you may be required give a talk on a topic about which you know next to nothing. The purpose is to help you conquer your fear of speaking and provide you with feedback from others. Find a Toastmasters group in your area and try to join it.

Use BOMS mnemonic for conversation:

Bottom line

Omit the details

Maintain focus

Summarize

Follow the old saying: *Tell them what you're going to say; tell them; then tell them what you said.*

Problem #43:
I can't say things clearly.

Ask the other person if what you said makes sense. If what you said was not clear, then restate it. Always use the person to whom you are speaking to verify that your message was received correctly.

Practice making a statement with fewer and fewer words. Say what you want to say into a tape recorder. Next, say the same thing in fewer words. Try to say the same thing again with still fewer words. Practice this activity every day. It does not matter what you are trying to say as long as you can say it with equal clarity in fewer words. For example, try reading sentences out of a magazine and try to summarize them in fewer and fewer words.

Provide examples. When explaining something to another person, say, "Let me give you an example of what I mean."

Problem #44:
I cannot take accurate messages.

Use a structured message pad. Preprinted message pads contain dedicated spaces to write pertinent information, such as *who, what, when, where,* and *how.* The spaces on the message pad should prompt you to ask the appropriate questions: From whom was the message? What did the person want? When did the person call or leave the message? Where is the person or where does the person want you to go? How should the person respond?

Restate a message in your own words before writing it. Say a message back to the person who originally said it using your own words, then ask that person to verify its accuracy. Use phrases such as "Let me see if I have this straight . . ." and "There were three things that you want me to do . . . ." Keep restating in your own words until the other person verifies that you have correctly interpreted the message.

Record the message. Use a digital recorder and dictate the message in your own words into the recorder. Remember, you can speak 11 times faster than you can write. You can always record the gist of a message in your own words, but do not record it directly from the phone without the other person's permission.

Problem #45:
It is hard for me to
write my thoughts.

Use the outliner on the computer. Most word processors have an outline feature that can give you the organization of what you have just written. There are also computer programs called *idea processors* that can formulate the structure of your thoughts.

Try to list the three major points. Structure all of your writing according to the same outline. A good one contains three components: (a) introduce the topic, (b) make three basic points, and (c) summarize the points.

Practice outlines. Take a self-study course in outlining. Also, look at other written material and try to make an outline out of it.

Use computer aids. Learn to use your computer's spell-checker and grammar–punctuation–style checker.

Submit your writing for criticism when there is no consequence. Have friends evaluate your writing or take a noncredit course in writing.

Problem #46:
I do not talk clearly on the phone.

Outline your message before placing a call. Write down the major points you want to make with a call, then write down any information you need like numbers and names. When calling a company, ask the first person who answers to refer you to someone who can help you with the type of problem you have.

Speak in short sentences. Because most people cannot remember more than 25 words at a time, try to make your sentences shorter than that.

Use a structured message pad. When answering calls, use a message pad to prompt you to ask appropriate questions, such as the following: Who called? What did he or she want? What time did the person call? What does the caller want you to do?

Problem #47:
I can't understand big
words that people use.

Learn Greek and Latin word roots. Greek and Latin word roots are the core elements of the English language. Approximately 200 of these word roots make up about 200,000 words. Learning the word roots makes it easier to figure out what other words mean. For example, any word that contains the suffix ology is a word that means "the study of something." Psychology is the study of mind and anthropology is the study of man. Buy and study a book containing common word roots. Try to mark the roots that you see in words you read in magazines and newspapers.

Take a vocabulary course. There are a number of vocabulary self-study courses that you can purchase in bookstores. Many use the word-root method while others associate words and pictures. There are also several audiotape courses to which you can listen. Much of the work in learning vocabulary is self-study and whether you learn the new words depends on how much effort you invest.

Learn one new meaning each day. Try to learn a new word each day by pasting it and its definition on the refrigerator. Use the word in conversation during the day and find examples of it.

Study synonyms and antonyms. When learning words, find other words with similar meanings and find words with opposite meanings. Minimally, identify at least one word that means the same thing as the new word and one that means the opposite.

Problem #48:
I have to say things over and over before anyone understands me.

Use BOMS mnemonic for conversation. This mnemonic was presented in the solutions for Problem #42.

Say it in your mind before speaking. Try to organize what you want to say in your mind before you say it in words.

Use concrete examples. Do not speak in abstractions. Try to illustrate your points with examples that clarify. If you are using statements like, "you know," then you can be sure that the other person does not know.

Problem #49:
I misinterpret what people say in conversation.

Study body language. Much of what people hear comes through watching body language, which refers to the changes in a person's body while he or she is speaking. There are several

popular books on this topic and it is worthwhile to study the most common features of body language. For example, what does it mean when a person keeps looking at his or her watch while talking to you? It means they need to leave or would like to terminate the conversation.

Study voice inflections. You have heard that "It is not what you say, but how you say it." Changes in a speaker's voice carry as much meaning as his or her message. Try to interpret different voice inflections with a friend by saying the same sentence several times and emphasizing a different word each time. Then discuss the different meanings the sentence can imply, depending on the tone of voice used.

Study facial expressions. How a person's face changes when he or she speaks also carries meaning. Usually if the face goes forward in a grimace, the person is conveying confusion or disgust. If the face and head go backward, then the person is surprised or shocked. There are other expressions that have meaning, such as a raised eyebrow signaling mild surprise or a furrowed brow that indicates confusion.

It is not enough to know about body language, voice inflections, and facial expressions. You must also pay attention to them in conversation. People who understand conversations are good at integrating all of this information while they are talking to another person.

Problem #50:
I make a lot of mistakes.

Make a quality-control checklist. Mistakes that occur repeatedly should be identified and included as part of a checklist. For example, if you must do certain things before you leave home, then post this list on the door through which you usually leave your home. Before you leave each morning, go through the checklist to verify that all items have been completed. If you are learning a new skill, write a list of steps and use the list to make sure you have followed them. The checklist will ensure accuracy and consistency, even if you may not be able to perform the task quickly. When you no longer need the checklist, you will be performing the task efficiently.

Work slowly and check as you go. Many mistakes occur because a person never learns to do the task correctly. When learning any new task, do it slowly and correctly. Focus on mastering the skill rather than on doing the task quickly. Remember, practice does not make perfect. Perfect practice makes perfect.

Have someone or something check your work. Use feedback from others to correct your mistakes. Use devices like spell-checkers and grammar–punctuation–style checkers on a computer to check your work.

Appendix B

≿

Self-Motivation
Treatment Planner

Part I:
Problems Checklist

The following items are a list of reasons that may underlie a client's lack of motivation. Twenty people with traumatic brain injury were asked to write several reasons why they lacked motivation to use the cognitive strategies they had learned. Those items that were mentioned more than once were summarized and the following list was developed from those items. The items on the list can be used to diagnose and initiate treatment for lack of motivation.

The reasons for poor motivation are grouped into the following categories:

Helplessness: This is the feeling that results from never learning how to do things independently.

Evaluation: This is the fear that someone will discover another's inadequacies.

Accountability: This is the fear of being placed in a position of authority.

Defiance: This is the need to stand up to someone, usually a relative or parent, and to defy him or her.

Comfort Zone: This is the inability to try new things.

Adrenaline Rush: This is the feeling of stimulation that comes about when deadlines or crises result from inaction.

Self-Esteem: This is the feeling that success is not deserved.

Effort: This is the tendency to give up when things seem too difficult.

To complete this checklist, the client simply checks the box next to any statement that describes his or her behavior. The client should check the item if it occurs at least once a week. The categories next to the items that are most frequently checked describe that client's reasons for lack of motivation. He or she can then go to the solutions presented in Part II and read suggestions for improving motivation.

Read the items and place a check in the box for any statements that describe you.

Category	Item
Helpless	☐ It is hard for me to start things or to finish them.
Helpless	☐ I prefer to let others do things for me.
Comfort Zone	☐ I don't like change.
Evaluation	☐ I'm afraid people will see how dumb I really am.
Defiance	☐ My parents always forced me to do things their way.
Comfort Zone	☐ I prefer to do things the way I've always done them.
Adrenaline	☐ I wait until the last minute to do things.
Self-Esteem	☐ I feel uncomfortable with flattery.
Effort	☐ I seldom try my hardest.
Helpless	☐ My parents always did everything for me.
Evaluation	☐ I am afraid I will fail.
Accountability	☐ I avoid responsibility.
Self-Esteem	☐ I don't deserve to succeed.
Effort	☐ If something takes too long or is too hard, I give up.
Evaluation	☐ I'd rather not try than risk failing.
Accountability	☐ I'd rather take orders than give them.
Defiance	☐ I get back at people by not doing what they tell me to do.
Comfort Zone	☐ Once I learn one way of doing something I seldom change.
Adrenaline	☐ The time I do something is when it is overdue.
Defiance	☐ I often feel as though I am rebelling against something in my past.
Adrenaline	☐ I am attracted to excitement and danger.
Accountability	☐ I feel that the world controls me.
Self-Esteem	☐ Others' happiness is more important than my own.
Effort	☐ I know what I should do but I can't seem to get myself to do it.

Part II:
Treatment Solutions

Problem: Helplessness

Description

Your parents or someone else always did everything for you. You grew up feeling as though you could not do anything and had to defer most tasks to someone else.

Solutions

Take baby steps. Any task can be broken down into smaller ones. Baby steps are the smallest part of a task that a person can complete. To overcome fear of completing the entire task, the person should ask what part of the task can he or she complete given the allotted time. This smaller job is usually less threatening. At the same time, it is usually enough to get the person started on the larger task.

Practice simulated tasks. Create a facsimile of a task and practice it without any consequences for failure.

Problem: Evaluation

Description

You are afraid to complete a task because others will judge you.

Solution

Practice tasks in private. For example, use a personal computer at home to improve academics. Choose activities and computer software that will analyze your performance and let you know what types of mistakes you are making.

Problem: Accountability

Description

You do not want to be responsible.

Solutions

Practice without consequence. Becoming competent at a task often helps a person to overcome his or her fears of accountability. Practicing a task until it is overlearned can help you overcome feelings of inadequacy and fears of accountability.

Take on a lesser role. Even though you may feel uncomfortable performing a complex job, you may feel comfortable doing part of that job. Ask yourself if there is any part of the job that you feel you can do well.

Problem: Defiance

Description

You want to rebel against someone in your past or present.

Solution

Ask yourself questions. Does the person against whom you are rebelling really care about your behavior? Who is that person? Why do you seek that person's approval?

Problem: Comfort Zone

Description

You believe the way you have always done something is the easiest way to do it.

Solution

Do the task a new way and the old way. Complete a task with a new method, but have the old method available if needed. Try one new strategy each week.

Problem: Adrenaline Rush

Description

You procrastinate because you enjoy the tension created when things are past due.

Solutions

Alleviate your need for a rush. Some psychiatric medications can control the need for stimulation.

Constructively indulge your need for a rush. Play extreme sports that provide the rush you seek.

Problem: Self-Esteem

Description

You do not feel worthy of success.

Solution

Confidence begins with competence. Develop skills to the point where you can do them well. The best way to feel good about yourself is to know that you are talented and can do a good job.

Problem: Effort

Description

You cannot seem to start or finish things; your life seems stagnant; you are living day to day.

Solutions

Exercise. Exercise at least 30 minutes each day for energy.

Take baby steps. Break tasks down into smaller parts. Make to-do lists and check off items when you complete them. Ask yourself what the smallest thing is that you can do to get the project going.

Appendix C

✤

Performance Assessment
of the Multimodal System

The following tests are designed as a screening assessment. They are not intended to replace a comprehensive neuropsychological evaluation and should not be used in that way. Their purpose is to provide the therapist with an evaluation of the multimodal system components. Should the client's performance on any of these tests suggest that there is a problem, the therapist should suggest further evaluation with a more comprehensive test battery.

These tests were selected according to several criteria. The most obvious was that the test should index the appropriate component of the multimodal system. However, many of the tests overlap, and they have been placed in logically appropriate categories. The user should consider that some tests may also index other multimodal systems.

Scoring is not always discussed in detail in this appendix because it is detailed in the original sources for the tests. Therefore, the reader is referred to the original source for a thorough discussion of scoring procedures. In some cases, the tests that we provide are unpublished, and the scoring norms are based on a database of clients whom we have tested over the years. In other cases, the purpose of the test is to provide insight into the client's mode of processing. Therefore, there may be no specific scoring procedure, only the therapist's subjective observation of how the client performed the task, what strategies he or she used, or what specific behaviors the therapist noticed.

Most of these tests are readily available, and the therapist requires no special credentials to acquire them. Many come from journal articles. They may therefore be used by therapists from a variety of disciplines.

Sensory System

Iconic Memory

Brief-Duration Iconic Flashes

Brief-duration iconic flashes can be simulated using a standard slide projector. The therapist types words on a page, with each word string separated from the next by approximately 3 inches. These words form sentences that vary in length between one and five words. The page is copied onto overhead projection transparencies using a standard copier. The individual words and sentences are cut from the plastic and placed into slide binders. The slides are then placed into a carousel projector with one blank space between the slots. The therapist begins on the blank space before the first slide. When he or she holds down the advance button on the slide projector, the carousel advances to the first slide, then immediately goes on to the following blank space. The length of time the slide is projected is approximately ⅓ second. The client recalls the slide, and the task continues throughout the entire sequence of slides.

The therapist should use approximately 40 slides, 10 for each sentence length. The sentences should be written roughly at a seventh-grade reading level.

Relative Performance: The average client with mild injury can recall roughly 80% of the three-word sentences correctly. Clients with severe impairment seldom recall more than half of the two-word sentences correctly and few, if any, of the three- or four-word sentences. Typical college students can recall approximately 75% of the four-word sentences and all of the two- and three-word sentences.

Echoic Memory

Continuous Dialogue Task

The therapist makes an audiotape of 30 random letters, 30 random numbers, and 30 random nouns. He or she reads these into a tape recorder with a 1-second interval between each. The therapist also makes three index cards, each with the word *number, letter,* or *word* printed on it. During the session, the therapist plays the tape and stops it at random intervals, then points to one of the cards. This signals the client that he or she should recall the last instance of whichever item is on the card. The client never knows whether he or she will have to recall the last letter, number, or noun until the therapist stops the tape and points to one of the cards. The task continues until the client has recalled at least 40 items.

Relative Performance: Clients with mild brain injury recall about two thirds of the items correctly. Clients with severe brain injury recall about half of the items. College students miss only one or two items.

Attention and Concentration

Digit Span

The therapist makes a list of numbers that range from two to nine digits in length, taking care not to duplicate numbers within any one string. The list should progress from the two-digit length to the nine-digit length with two strings for each length. The therapist reads the numbers at approximately 1 second per number to the client, who recalls them immediately after the last number of each string. The therapist continues until the client misses two strings of the same length in a row.

Backward digit span is the reverse of the above procedure. The therapist reads digit strings forward in the same manner as above. The client repeats the string backward. The therapist continues until the client misses two strings of equal length in a row.

Relative Performance: Clients with mild brain injury will recall strings of about five digits, plus or minus two digits. Clients with severe brain injury will recall strings of about three digits, plus or minus two digits. College students will recall strings of eight digits, plus or minus two digits.

Visual Memory Span

The therapist acquires nine blocks, approximately 1- to 2-inch squares. These are usually available at toy stores or learning resource centers. On one side of each block, the therapist writes a number from *1* to *9*. In the session, the blocks are placed in a random array, but so that the numbers face the examiner and the client cannot see the numbers at all. Then using the same number strings from the digit span task above, the therapist touches the blocks in the order dictated by each number string. The client then copies the order of touches. The task continues until the client misses two sequences of the same length in a row.

The backward version of this task is similar to the backward digit span task. The therapist touches the blocks according to the same digit series used above, and the client touches them in reverse order. The task continues until the client misses two strings of the same length in a row.

Relative Performance: Clients with severe brain injury can reproduce a sequence of about three touches, plus or minus two blocks for the forward task and the same for the backward task. Clients with mild head injury correctly reproduce five touches for the forward task, plus or minus two, and four touches for the backward task, plus or minus two. College students reproduce about seven touches for the forward task, plus or minus two, and six touches for the backward task, plus or minus two.

Working Memory and Long-Term Memory

Rehearsal

Rehearsal Card Games

These games are described in detail in Chapter 10. Their goal is to assess the client's ability to rehearse novel information and to determine the number of rehearsals necessary to improve recall. The reader is referred to this chapter for a thorough discussion of these games.

Verbal Memory

Buschke Selective Reminding Task

This task is a procedure that involves repeated measurement of the client's recall of a word list. The words are simple nouns that are read at 1-second intervals. The client recalls the words, and when he or she cannot recall any more words, the therapist repeats only those words the client failed to recall. The

client again recalls the entire list of words, and the therapist reminds the client of only those words that were omitted. This procedure continues until the client can recall the entire list of 12 words on two successive trials. Buschke (1973) has created an elaborate scoring procedure that measures several aspects of memory. The reader is referred to his article for a description of this procedure. The procedure is quite flexible and works with other types of items (Buschke & Fuld, 1974; Fuld, 1980).

Relative Performance: The average person with brain injury takes 8 to 12 study-and-test trials to learn a list of 12 unrelated nouns. The average college student learns the list in 4 to 6 trials.

The therapist can evaluate certain aspects of the client's recall without elaborate scoring procedures. For example, the therapist can look for the number of words that are consistently recalled each trial. This is an index of what Buschke called *consistent long-term retrieval*. In essence, it is an index of how much information can be readily accessed. The therapist can also look for a pattern of recall over the test sequence in which the client only recalls the words he or she was given as reminders on the previous trial and fails to recall those words he or she correctly recalled on the previous trial. This pattern reflects a tendency to depend on short-term memory. The number of trials needed to attain two perfect recalls is also of interest because it indexes learning speed. Delayed recall after a 30-minute interval is a measure of long-term retention.

Visual Memory

Rey Figure Recall Task

The Rey Figure Recall Task is an extension of the Rey Figure Copy Task. This procedure is discussed in detail by Lezak (1983, p. 400). More comprehensive norms are also provided by Kolb and Whishaw (1990, pp. 845–890).

The client copies a figure; after 30 minutes, he or she attempts to recall the shape. Data for performance on the copy and recall tasks are provided for various age groups by Kolb and Whishaw.

Zoo Picture Task

We have used this task with great success over the years to measure visual memory. The therapist shows the client an illustration of a zoo scene for 15 seconds. After the study interval, the therapist removes the picture and asks the client 5 questions about the picture. The client studies the pictures for another 15-second interval, then the therapist asks 5 more questions. The therapist then administers a third trial, exactly like the first two. Then, after a 30-minute delay, the therapist asks 10 final questions.

Relative Performance: Clients with brain injury average two to three correct answers over the three training trials and four to six on the delayed trial. College students average three to four correct answers on the three training trials and seven to nine correct on the delayed trial.

Memory Strategy

Multiple Encoding Task

This task involves presenting the client with a list of nine words. There are three words in each of three categories: names (Susan, Mary, Jane), planets (Mars, Jupiter, Saturn), and animals (shark, monkey, jackal). The therapist creates a grid of the words on the page, three words across and three words down, so that there is no obvious semantic grouping. He or she can then color one of the words in each category blue, another red, and another green. A highlighter works well for this purpose. The words in the array can be encoded in a variety of ways, by spatial position of the words on the page, by the color of the words, by the first letter of each word, or by the semantic grouping to which each word belongs. This list is presented below. The therapist can highlight each word according to the color in parentheses next to it.

Susan (Red)	Monkey (Green)	Jupiter (Blue)
Mars (Green)	Jane (Blue)	Shark (Red)
Jackal (Blue)	Saturn (Red)	Mary (Green)

The therapist presents the sheet to the client, who studies it for 30 seconds. The client then writes any remembered words on a sheet of plain white paper. The therapist instructs the client that he or she can recall the words in any fashion that makes the words easier to recall. The task is repeated over several study–test sessions until the client can recall all the words correctly. The therapist also asks the client to recall the words from memory after 30 minutes.

Relative Performance: Most typical adults can recall the entire list in 1 or 2 study–test trials. Most persons with brain injury take 3 to 5 trials. It is important to note, however, not just the number of trials the client takes to recall the sheet but the method he or she uses to recall the words. For example, if the client uses a color code, this information may be helpful when training him or her to use color groupings in the future to improve recall.

Storage and Retrieval

Retest the client on any or all of the above tests for (a) free recall, (b) recognition, and (c) savings (see Chapter 7).

Thinking

General Intelligence

Several useful tests of intelligence are described in other sources. For example, Othmer and Othmer (1989, pp. 456–457) report a simple 10-question intelligence test developed by Kent (1946). The test involves asking the client 10 factual questions and scoring his or her response on a 36-point scale.

Brown, Sherbenou, and Johnsen (1997) developed a culture-free *Test of Nonverbal Intelligence–Third Edition* (TONI–3). The test requires the client to look at a sequence of sample shapes and to find the next logical shape in the sequence. The test does not require any reading and it is easy to administer. It provides an especially good index of nonverbal intelligence.

Verbal Reasoning

Poison Foods Test

Lezak (1983) summarized Arenberg's (1968) Poison Foods Test, which is a measure of verbal reasoning. The therapist provides the client with a sheet of paper to keep track of the components of several hypothetical meals and the consequences of eating them (person lived or died). The client must listen to the sequence of foods and determine which ones, if any, are poisonous. Norms for the test are provide in Lezak (1983). The test is relatively simple to administer and provides a clear assessment of the client's verbal reasoning skill.

Relative Performance: The measure of performance is how many of the poison foods the client correctly identifies. We are not aware of any formal norms for this test.

Nonverbal Reasoning

Tinkertoy Test

Lezak (1983) described an especially elegant method for assessing nonverbal reasoning using a set of Tinkertoys. The therapist provides the client with a standard 50-piece Tinkertoy set and instructs him or her to make an object from the Tinkertoys in 5 minutes.

Relative Performance: Lezak (1983) provided a scoring schema for this test. The client's performance is evaluated for characteristics such as whether he or she made a shape, how many pieces were used, number of moving parts, whether the object moved, and so forth. The total score for all the characteristics is then computed.

Concept Learning

Playing Card Sequence

The therapist uses a deck of playing cards as a screening test for sequential concept formation skill. The test was originally developed by Talland (1965) and discussed in Lezak (1983). Using two decks of standard playing cards, the therapist arranges the cards into 16 runs of black–black–red–black–red–red sequences. The client turns the cards over one at a time and tries to predict the next card in the sequence.

Relative Performance: The measure of performance is how many cards the client turns over before he or she can correctly predict three complete runs of cards in a row. Skill level varies with age and persons with brain injury, especially those with frontal lobe damage, cannot do the task at all.

Cognitive Flexibility

Uses of Objects

Getzels and Jackson (1962) described a test of divergent thinking skills. The therapist lists five common objects (brick, pencil, paper clip, toothpick, sheet of paper) along with two sample uses for each object. For example, a brick could be used to build a house or used as a paperweight. The client is required to write as many uses for each object as possible. Persons with brain injury tend to dwell on the conventional uses of the objects. For example, the client might say, "to build a house, to build a walkway, to build a fireplace," and so forth. This illustrates difficulty with mental switching.

Relative Performance: There is no formal scoring procedure for this task, only the observation of the client's response consistency and his or her ability to break set and generate a variety of novel uses of the objects.

Expressive Skills

Word Fluency

Timed Word Fluency Test

Kolb and Whishaw (1990) described one test of word fluency that simply requires the client to write as many words as he or she can think of in 5 minutes that begin with the letter S. Next, the client writes as many four-letter words that come to mind in 4 minutes that begin with the letter C. The total number of words generated has been shown to correlate with performance on tests of temporal and frontal lobe functioning.

Relative Performance: Sixty words is the cutoff point for typical college students. Persons with learning disabilities can generate about 45 words. Left frontal lobectomy patients can generate about 35 words.

Figure Fluency

Lezak (1983) described two complex figure copy tasks that have been used for years as measures of complex praxis functions. In the

Rey Figure Copy Task, the client copies a complex shape. A scoring scheme is available for both adults and children. Delayed recall at 30 minutes provides a simple test of visual retention. The Taylor Complex Shape Copy Task (as described in Lezak, 1983) is less commonly used but equally useful for assessing perceptual motor function and visual memory.

Fine Motor Control

Repeating Letters

Luria (1966) first described letter-writing procedures that require the client to write letters of the alphabet repetitively. We propose this simple test to determine a client's ability to write rapidly. The client first writes *mn* in cursive repeatedly across a piece of plain white paper for 1 minute. He or she then writes *pq* for 1 minute. Last, the client writes *bd* for 1 minute. The total score is the average number of combinations.

Relative Performance: College students can usually write about 25 to 35 combinations for any letter dyad. Persons with brain injury typically average 15 to 20.

Written Communication

Sample Paragraph

We assess writing skill by allowing the client 5 minutes to write a short paragraph concerning his or her vocational interests. The client is instructed to write as much as possible on this theme in 5 minutes and to write the paragraph in clear English.

Relative Performance: We enter the paragraph verbatim into a word processor and score it with the grammar–punctuation–style checker. This provides an index of readability, appropriate use of adjectives and adverbs, fluency, spelling accuracy, and punctuation errors.

References

Arenberg, D. (1968). Concept problem solving in young and old adults. *Journal of Gerontology, 23,* 279–282.

Brown, L., Sherbenou, R. J., & Johnsen, S. K. (1997). *Test of Nonverbal Intelligence–Third Edition.* Austin, TX: PRO-ED.

Buschke, H. (1973). Selective reminding for analysis of memory and learning. *Journal of Verbal Learning and Verbal Behavior, 12,* 543–550.

Buschke, H., & Fuld, P. A. (1974). Evaluating storage, retention, and retrieval in disordered memory and learning. *Neurology, 11,* 1019–1025.

Fuld, P. A. (1980). Guaranteed stimulus-processing in the evaluation of memory and learning. *Cortex, 16,* 255–272.

Getzels, J. W., & Jackson, P. W. (1962). *Creativity and intelligence.* New York: Wiley.

Kent, G. H. (1946). *E-G-Y scales.* New York: Williams & Wilkins.

Kolb, B., & Whishaw, I. Q. (1990). *Fundamentals of human neuropsychology.* New York: Freeman.

Lezak, M. D. (1983). *Neuropsychological assessment* (2nd ed.). New York: Oxford University Press.

Luria, A. R. (1966). *Higher cortical functions in man* (B. Haigh, Trans.). New York: Basic Books.

Othmer, F., & Othmer, S. C. (1989). *The clinical interview using the DSMIII–R.* Washington, DC: American Psychiatric Press.

Talland, G. A. (1965). *Deranged memory.* New York: Academic Press.

Appendix D

Cognitive Rehabilitation Web Sites

American Medical Association
http://www.ama-assn.org

ABI/TBI Information Project
http://www.sasquatch.com/tbi

Alcohol and drug information/U.S. Department
of Health and Human Services
http://www.health.org

American College of Neuropsychopharmacology
http://www.acnp.org

American College of Surgeons
http://www.facs.org

American Speech-Language-Hearing Association
http://www.asha.org

Antoinette Appel, PhD Web site
http://www.tbidoc.com

Aphasia (general information, support groups,
communication)
http://www.aphasia.net

Bicycle Helmet Safety Institute
http://www.bhsi.org

Brain and mental fitness commercial site
http://www.brain.com

Brain Book Life Management System
http://www.brainbook.com

Brain Aneurysm Foundation
http://www.bafound.org

Brain Injury Association of America (also
provides links to state associations)
http://www.biausa.org

Brain Train Software
http://www.bungalowsoftware.com

Centers for Disease Control and Prevention
http://www.cdc.gov

Centre for Neuro Skills
http://www.neuroskills.com

Children's issues
http://www.kidshealth.org
http://www.kidsource.com

Coma Recovery Association
http://www.comarecovery.org

Coma recovery issues
http://www.waiting.com

Dana Alliance for Brain Initiatives
http://www.dana.org

Dr. Diane Roberts Stoler (stroke, concussion,
and brain tumor information)
http://www.health-helper.com

EEG biofeedback information
http://www.eegspectrum.com

Family Caregiver Alliance
http://www.caregiver.org

Hotline for head injury information
http://www.headinjury.com

Hydrocephalus Association
http://www.hydroassoc.org

Journal of Cognitive Rehabilitation
http://www.neuroscience.cntr.com

Journal of the American Medical Association
http://www.jama.ama-assn.org

Kessler Medical Rehabilitation Research and
Education Corporation
http://www.kmrrec.org

Massachusetts General Hospital of Neurosurgery
http://www.neurosurgery.mgh.harvard.edu

Memoryzine
http://www.memoryzine.com

MentalArts
http://www.geocities.com/mentalarts

National Aphasia Association
http://www.aphasia.org

National Council on Disability
http://www.ncd.gov

National Institute of Neurological Disorders
and Stroke
http://www.ninds.nih.gov

National Institutes of Health
http://www.nih.gov

National Library of Medicine
http://www.nlm.nih.gov

National Rehabilitation Information Center
http://www.naric.com

National Resource Center for Traumatic
Brain Injury
http://www.neuro.pmr.vcu.edu

Neuropsychology Central
http://www.neuropsychologycentral.com

NeuroScience Center
http://www.neuroscience.cntr.com

Neurotherapy
http://www.post-trauma.com

NeurXCorporation
http://www.neurx.com

Northeast Rehab Health Network
http://www.northeastrehab.com

Ohio Valley Center for Brain Injury Prevention
and Rehabilitation
http://www.ohiovalley.org

Rehabilitation Center for Traumatic Brain Injury
and Spinal Cord Injury
http://www.tbi-sci.org

Social Security Administration
http://www.ssa.gov

Surgical procedures explanations
http://www.yoursurgery.com

TBI chatroom
http://www.tbichat.org

The Perspectives Network
http://www.tbi.org

The Virtual Hospital
http://www.vh.org

University of Alabama Traumatic Brain Injury
Care System
http://www.uab.edu/tbi

University of Pittsburgh Brain Trauma
Research Center
http://www.edc.gsph.pitt.edu/headinj

Virtual Naval Hospital
http://www.vnh.org

WebMD
http://www.webmd.com

Whole Brain Atlas
http://www.med.harvard.edu/AANLIB/
home.html

World Health Organization
http://www.who.int

AUTHOR INDEX

SUBJECT INDEX

About the Authors

Dr. Rick Parenté is a professor of psychology at Towson University in Baltimore. He received a PhD in psychology from the University of New Mexico in 1975 and completed a postdoctoral research fellowship in physiology in 1981. He has done individual and group cognitive skills training with persons with traumatic brain injury and learning disabilities since 1980. He regularly teaches graduate-level coursework in neuropsychological assessment and neurotraining and is a licensed psychologist and a diplomat of the American Board of Psychological Specialties in Neuropsychology. He has written three books and more than 50 journal articles on cognitive rehabilitation.

Dr. Douglas Herrmann was trained as an engineer at the U.S. Naval Academy (BS, 1964) and as a psychologist at the University of Delaware where he obtained an MS (1970) and a PhD (1972) in experimental psychology. He conducted postdoctoral research on memory processes at Stanford University (1993). After completing his postdoctoral research, he began teaching at Hamilton College in Clinton, N.Y., where he remained until 1989. At Hamilton College he became a full professor and served as the chairperson of the Psychology Department for 4 years. While on the faculty at Hamilton, he served as a research fellow at England's Applied Cognitive Psychology Unit in Cambridge, 1982 to 1983; the University of Manchester, 1985 to 1986; and the National Institute of Mental Health, 1989 to 1990. In 1990 he became the director of the Collection Procedures Research Laboratory at the U.S. Bureau of Labor Statistics (1990–1992), after which he served as the special assistant on cognitive psychology to the associate director for research and methodology at the National Center for Health Statistics. Since 1995 he has been professor and chairperson of the Psychology Department at Indiana State University and the executive director of the Practical Memory Institute. In 2001 he was awarded the university's prize for research and creativity.

Dr. Herrmann coedited the journal *Applied Cognitive Psychology* from 1987 to 1991 and is currently the editor of the journal *Cognitive Technology*. He has written or edited 20 textbooks on a variety of issues concerning memory, including the history of memory scholarship, memory functioning in everyday life, memory improvement, cognitive rehabilitation, and survey research. In 1995 he served as the president of the Society for Applied Research on Memory and Technology. He is also the director of the Practical Memory Institute, an Internet-based business (http://www.memoryzine.com).